CRIMINAL JUSTICE 80/81

Donal E.J. MacNamara, *Editor*

John Jay College of Criminal Justice
City University of New York

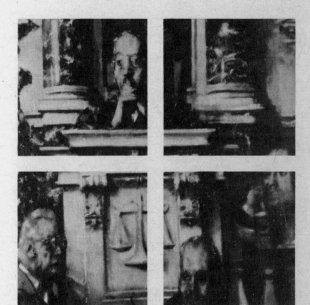

Cover painting: "The Trial" by Jack Levine. Courtesy, The Art
Institute of Chicago.

ANNUAL EDITIONS

The Dushkin Publishing Group, Inc. Sluice Dock, Guilford, Ct. 06437

Volumes in the Annual Editions Series

Abnormal Psychology
- Aging
- American Government
- American History Pre-Civil War
- American History Post-Civil War
- Anthropology
Astronomy
- Biology
- Business
Comparative Government
- Criminal Justice
Death and Dying
- Deviance
- Early Childhood Education
Earth Science
- Economics
- Educating Exceptional Children
- Education
Educational Psychology
Energy
- Environment·
Ethnic Studies

Foreign Policy
Geography
Geology
- Health
- Human Development
- Human Sexuality
- Management
- Marketing
- Marriage and Family
- Personal Growth and Adjustment
Philosophy
Political Science
- Psychology
Religion
- Social Problems
- Sociology
- Urban Society
Western Civilization
Women's Studies
World History
- World Politics

● *Indicates currently available*

Library of Congress Cataloging in Publication Data
Main entry under title:
Annual editions: Criminal Justice.
    1. Criminal justice, Administration of—United States—Addresses, essays, lectures. I. Title: Criminal Justice.
HV8138.A67   364'.973   77-640116
ISBN 0-87967-298-6

CONTENTS

1

Crime and Justice in America

2

Police

3

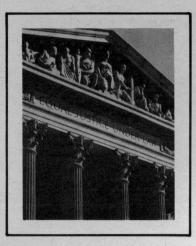

The Judicial System

4
Juvenile Justice

5
Punishment
and Corrections

Charts and Graphs

TOPIC GUIDE

This topic guide can be used to correlate each of the readings in *Criminal Justice 80/81* with one or more of the topics usually covered in criminal justice books. Each article corresponds to a given topic area according to whether it deals with the subject in a primary or secondary fashion. These correlations are intended for use as a general study guide and do not necessarily define the total coverage of any given article.

TOPIC AREA	TREATED AS A PRIMARY ISSUE IN:	TREATED AS A SECONDARY ISSUE IN:
Crimes & Criminals	2. The Criminal Ethos 3. Two Hundred Years of Social Economic Change Have Shaped Our Crime 4. UN Leader Gives Views on World-wide Crime 10. World of the Career Criminal 11. A Cold New Look at the Criminal Mind 35. How Dan White Got Away with Murder	8. A Mutual Concern 9. The Crime-Unemployment Cycle Crime Trends in English-Speaking Societies (chart) Crime Trends in Scandinavian Societies (chart) Crime Index Total (chart) Crime Clock (chart) Crimes of Violence (chart) Crimes Against Property (chart) Persons Arrested, 1978 (chart) Larceny Analysis, 1978 (chart)
The Criminal Process	1. A General View of the Criminal Justice System 27. Justice for Whom? 28. Preventive Detention 30. Judging the Judges 31. Scaring Off Witnesses 36. Where the System Breaks Down 41. Are Our Juvenile Courts Working? 43. Changing Criminal Sentences	26. Advocacy and the Criminal Trial Judge 29. Verdicts on Judges 35. How Dan White Got Away with Murder 38. People v. Juvenile Justice: The Jury Is Still Out Number of Persons Arrested That Go to Prison (chart)
Community-Based Corrections, Probation and Parole	44. Making Prisons Pay 47. Medical Model in Corrections 48. On Parole Success 49. In Search of Equity	14. Police for Hire 37. Juvenile Justice 38. People v. Juvenile Justice 41. Are Our Juvenile Courts Working? 52. A Criminal Rehabilitation Program That Works
Judges, Judicial Discretion, Sentencing	24. A Decade of Constitutional Revision 26. Advocacy and the Criminal Trial Judge 28. Preventive Detention 29. Verdicts on Judges 30. Judging the Judges 36. Where the System Breaks Down 38. People v. Juvenile Justice 43. Changing Criminal Sentences	25. Are Grand Juries Getting Out of Line? 27. Justice for Whom? 31. Scaring Off Witnesses 32. Why Suppress Valid Evidence? 35. How Dan White Got Away with Murder 37. Juvenile Justice: A Plea for Reform Number of Persons Arrested That Go to Prison (chart)
Juries: Grand and Petit	25. Are Grand Juries Getting Out of Line? 33. It's Legal Gambling 34. The Murderous Mind 35. How Dan White Got Away with Murder	24. A Decade of Constitutional Revision 32. Why Suppress Valid Evidence? 46. The Case Against Capital Punishment

TOPIC AREA	TREATED AS A PRIMARY ISSUE IN:	TREATED AS A SECONDARY ISSUE IN:
The Juvenile in the Criminal Justice System	37. Juvenile Justice 38. People vs. Juvenile Justice 39. How Fifteen-Year-Olds Get Away with Murder 40. Juvenile Inmates 41. Are Our Juvenile Courts Working? 42. Putting Johnny in Jail 45. Scared Straight	3. Two Hundred Years of Social Economic Change Have Shaped Our Crime Problem 17. Protecting Thy Father and Thy Mother 52. A Criminal Rehabilitation Program That Works Juveniles under 18 in Secure and Semi-Secure Facilities (chart)
Lawyers: Prosecution and Defense	26. Advocacy and the Criminal Trial Judge 28. Preventive Detention 29. Verdicts on Judges 31. Scaring Off Witnesses 38. People vs. Juvenile Justice	27. Justice for Whom? 35. How Dan White Got Away with Murder
Police: Problems, Procedures and Prospects	12. Police Under Fire 13. Integrated Professionalism 16. Burned-Out Cops and Their Families 18. The New Truth Machines 19. Probes, Trials and Tribulations Shake the LAPD 22. The Future of Local Law Enforcement in the United States 23. Discipline in American Policing	6. Why the Cops Can't Catch the Mob 14. Police for Hire 15. The Nun Who Became a Cop 20. Police Leaders Find FBI Mandate Is a Flawed Gem 21. Citizen Cops Juveniles under 18 in Secure and Semi-Secure Facilities (chart) Criminal History of 1,573 Persons Identified in the Killing of Law Enforcement Officers (chart) Police Employee Data (chart) Law Enforcement Officers Killed, 1969-1978 (chart) Persons Arrested, 1978 (chart)
Punishment, Jails, and Prisons	37. Juvenile Justice 40. Juvenile Inmates 41. Are Our Juvenile Courts Working? 42. Putting Johnny in Jail 45. Scared Straight 50. Co-Corrections 51. Building a Small Prison with Modern Concepts 53. On the Women's Side of the Pen	43. Changing Criminal Sentences 44. Making Prisons Pay 46. The Case Against Capital Punishment 47. Medical Model in Corrections 52. A Criminal Rehabilitation Program That Works Number of Persons Arrested That Go to Prison (chart)
Victims: Actual and Potential	8. A Mutual Concern 17. Protecting Thy Father and Thy Mother	21. Citizen Cops 31. Scaring Off Witnesses 38. People vs. Juvenile Justice Crimes of Violence (chart) Law Enforcement Officers Killed, 1969-1978 (chart)
White Collar Crime	5. Crime in the Suites 6. Why the Cops Can't Catch the Mob 7. Let's Take the Profit out of Organized Crime	

PREFACE

Until the mid-1950s the study of criminal justice, its processes, its innumerable problems, and indeed its importance to the student as a career potential were neglected by America's colleges and universities. Courses in American government concentrated on the executive and legislative branches and noted only in passing the importance of our courts, police, and prisons. Prosecutors, bail, plea-bargaining, juries, sentencing philosophies, judicial discretion, probation, and parole were seldom if ever mentioned. Courses in sociology and criminology, taken only by a fraction of university students, dealt at length with the causes of crime, went into some detail about the juvenile justice system and were rather negligent in dealing with penology and victimology. Even in these courses and the texts recommended to the students, one looked in vain for discussion of the grand jury abuse, police efficiency, corruption, the justice model for corrections, and the rights of inmates.

In the past two decades, however, criminal justice, police science, and corrections curricula have expanded—largely as the result of public awareness of the accelerating rates of serious crime. Criminal justice curricula have also grown because of the generous support made available through the federal Law Enforcement Assistance Administration. These new course offerings, and a small but growing interest in criminal justice courses among progressive secondary school educators, have created a demand for criminal justice textbooks.

The field of criminal justice is constantly changing. Standard textbooks and anthologies cannot keep pace with changes as quickly as they occur. In fact, many such texts are already out of date the day they are published. The Annual Editions series, however, maintains currency. This anthology of the latest articles, decisions, laws and statistics, revised annually, gives both instructors and students the best, as well as the most recent literature available in the criminal justice field.

We think that *Annual Editions: Criminal Justice 80/81* is one of the most useful, up-to-date books available, but we would like to know what you think. Please fill out the article rating form on the last page of this book and let us know your opinions. Any anthology can be improved. This one will be—annually.

Donal E.J. MacNamara,
Editor

Crime and Justice in America

To the uninitiated (and that includes perhaps the great majority of America's citizens), crime and justice go hand in hand. To professionals within the criminal justice system the relationship is not quite as obvious. Large numbers of serious crimes are neither observed, discovered, reported, nor recorded. Of those which, in the terminology of the *Uniform Crime Reports,* become "known to the police," scarcely one in five is "cleared by arrest." A substantially smaller number results in conviction and punishment. Last year for example, there were thirteen million serious crimes known to police, yet there were only about 100,000 new admissions to America's federal and state penitentiaries.

Some of the problems inherent in a democratic system of criminal justice administration will be discussed in this unit. These problems perhaps militate against the high level of effectiveness in combating crime that has been achieved in totalitarian states and in countries with more homogeneous populations.

The United States is a pluralistic society, deriving its culture, institutions, traditions, and problems from many sources. This is both a strength and a weakness. Homogeneous cultures and societies (those with shared backgrounds, traditions, values, mores, and taboos) experience few of the culture-conflict situations at the root of many American crime and justice problems. Comparing our crime incidence with that of Denmark, Ireland, or even Japan is as fatuous an excercise as comparing our living standards with those of Uganda, Sri Lanka, or Honduras. Our country has a high incidence of crime because of our tradition of personal freedom, our resistance to governmental controls, our diversity of cultures, our material wealth (ostentatiously displayed before our sub-culture of poverty), and partly because of our high level of tolerance for deviant behavior—indeed for aggressively hostile challenges to the rules and ukases of the dominant majority. In few countries has the outlaw (Jesse James and the Mafia) been as popularly accepted. In fewer still has the hostility to the forces of the law and social protection been as open and as virulent. When it is alleged, as it is frequently, that the institutions for criminal justice administration are skewed in favor of the criminal, our history suggests that this may well be because we want it that way.

That there are imperfections in our laws—corruption, brutality, and ineffectiveness in our law enforcement agencies, discriminatory behaviors in the processes of arrest, prosecution, trial, sentencing, correctional treatment, and even in parole decisions as they relate to various offenders—is beyond dispute. Whether in sum total such admitted imperfections make our system for administering criminal justice inferior to those of totalitarian regimes, is not at all obvious. Those who have had the opportunity to study and to experience at first hand the criminal justice systems and procedures of many countries, democratic and totalitarian, would be hard pressed indeed to denounce America's, despite its many problems, as one to be especially condemned. It has been said that while the innocent defendant is likely to get justice in most systems, it is only in America that the guilty can confidently expect equal justice. This may be a weakness; it might equally be considered a special strength.

Article 1

A general view of The Criminal Justice System

This chart seeks to present a simple yet comprehensive view of the movement of cases through the criminal justice system. Procedures in individual jurisdictions may vary from the pattern shown here. The differing weights of line indicate the relative volumes of cases disposed of at various points in the system, but this is only suggestive since no nationwide data of this sort exists.

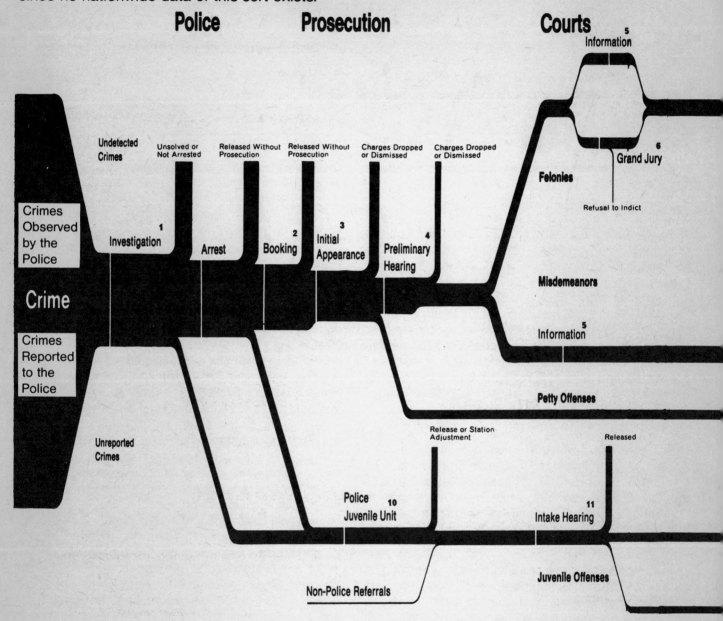

1 May continue until trial.

2 Administrative record of arrest. First step at which temporary release on bail may be available

3 Before magistrate, commissioner, or justice of peace. Formal notice of charge, advice of rights. Bail set. Summary trials for petty offenses usually conducted here without further processing.

4 Preliminary testing of evidence against defendant. Charge may be reduced. No separate preliminary hearing for misdemeanors in some systems.

5 Charge filed by prosecutor on basis of information submitted by police or citizens. Alternative to grand jury indictment; often used in felonies, almost always in misdemeanors.

6 Reviews whether Government evidence sufficient to justify trial. Some States have no grand jury system; others seldom use it.

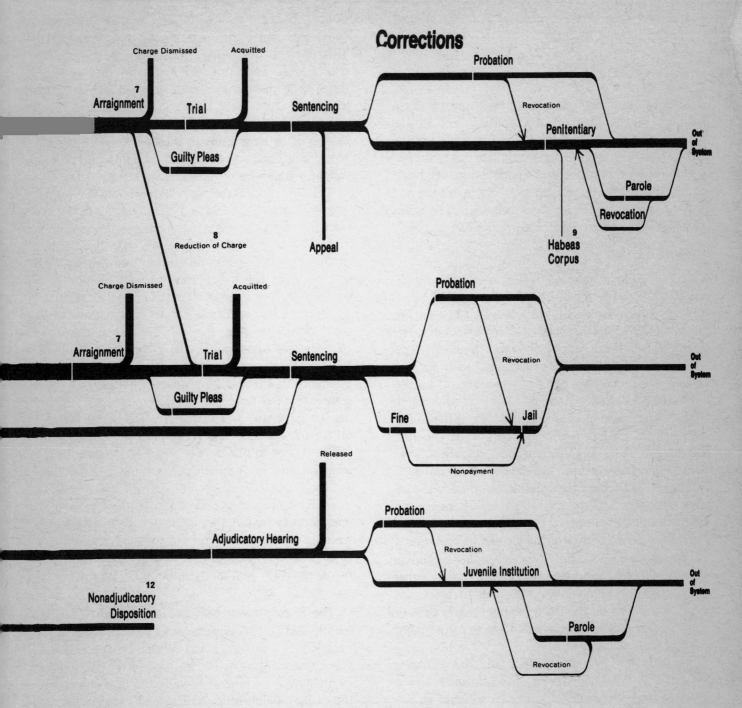

Corrections

7 Appearance for plea; defendant elects trial by judge or jury (if available); counsel for indigent usually appointed here in felonies. Often not at all in other cases.

8 Charge may be reduced at any time prior to trial in return for plea of guilty or for other reasons.

9 Challenge on constitutional grounds to legality of detention. May be sought at any point in process.

10 Police often hold informal hearings, dismiss or adjust many cases without further processing.

11 Probation officer decides desirability of further court action.

12 Welfare agency, social services, counselling, medical care, etc., for cases where adjudicatory handling not needed.

The Criminal Ethos

TED ROBERT GURR

Ted Robert Gurr is a Professor of Political Science at Northwestern University.

In the eighteen-twenties London was Europe's largest city, the commercial and political hub of the world's most prosperous society and greatest empire. It was also a dangerous, crime-ridden place. Professional robbers and receivers flourished in neighborhoods where it was worth a prosperous man's life and possessions to venture at night. Thousands of street urchins lived by petty theft during the day and slept in the noisome alleyways and courtyards. A contemporary writer summed up London's squalor and disorder when he denounced the city as "the infernal wen."

The criminal laws designed to control the rampant crime of Georgian England had a harsh bite. The death penalty was specified for more than two hundred offenses, on the widely accepted principle that severe punishment was an effective deterrent. But no centralized, professional police force existed to catch offenders. Constables, professional "thief-takers," and private citizens hailed petty offenders before magistrates who seldom were trained in law and were often venal and corrupt. The judges who heard serious cases had neither the legal discretion nor the inclination to be lenient. The defendant's hopes rested with the reluctance of many a jury to convict in capital cases, or the mercy of the Crown in commuting his death sentence to transportation to the Australian penal colonies. Such prisons as existed aimed neither to punish nor rehabilitate. Jails held debtors and those waiting to be tried or executed; the bridewells put vagrants and other petty offenders to forced labor for the profit of their officials.

Between the eighteen-twenties and the eighteen-seventies this hodgepodge was transformed into a modern system of criminal justice. A series of parliamentary acts overhauled the criminal law, penalties were prescribed in proportion to the seriousness of the offense, the death penalty was abolished for all but the most heinous crimes. London's patchwork police services of river police and Bow Street runners, constables and parish watchmen, were replaced in 1829 by the centralized Metropolitan Police. The courts were improved. Beginning in the eighteen-fifties child thieves were committed to new reformatories and kept there long enough to receive basic education and work training. Adult offenders were sentenced to long terms in the new convict prisons, where discipline was harsh and rehabilitation piously sought through hard, monotonous labor.

The zeal of London's new "bobbies" showed up at first in increased arrests and convictions. But by the eighteen-fifties common crime seemed on the decline and by the end of Queen Victoria's reign the city was thought by the English and visiting continentals alike to be one of the most orderly in all Europe. The official statistics suggest to social historians that the trend continued to the late nineteen-twenties, when the conviction rate for all indictable (serious) offenses was one-ninth of the eighteen-forties level. Police statistics on known offenses and arrests, first published in 1869, are especially convincing. Known serious offenses fell by an average of ten per cent per decade for sixty years thereafter. The arrest rate for all offenses, serious and petty ones, was down by a ratio of three to one despite a steady increase in the absolute and proportional size of the Metropolitan Police Force. Data on convictions show assault down by a ratio of five to one, total theft by four to one, robbery by more than ten to one. Burglary was the only serious offense to go against the trend, thanks to the activities of a small cadre of professional housebreakers who became increasingly successful at eluding the police.

The history of successful crime control in nineteenth- and early-twentieth-century London has many parallels. All England and Wales experienced improvements in proportion to those of the metropolis. In Sydney, Australia, at literally the opposite end of the earth, officials followed England's lead in reforming criminal justice, and indicators of convictions fell by ratios of ten to one and more. In Stockholm — a far smaller city in a very different society — high crime and the reforming impulse also coincided in

 Reprinted with permission from *The Center Magazine*, a publication of the Center for the Study of Democratic Institutions, Santa Barbara, California.

the second quarter of the nineteenth century. The results were much the same. In the century between the eighteen-forties and the nineteen-thirties the rate of convictions for crimes against persons in Stockholm declined by a ratio of about four to one and thefts by five to one. American studies identify similar trends in the annals of common crime in cities as varied as Boston, Salem, and Chicago.

We lack enough historical evidence to be certain that the century of improvement in public order was a universal Western experience. Widespread it certainly was, and it contributed to an abiding faith in the efficiency of the criminal justice policies which seemed to have produced it. But the story does not have a happy ending, because every one of the cities and countries just mentioned is today experiencing a runaway increase in rates of common crime. And the paradox is that the institutions and policies of criminal justice which have failed to stem the contemporary resurgence of disorder are essentially the same as those which helped reduce crime to its low ebb in the early decades of this century.

⌐ The common Western experience of rising crime is worth documenting, if only to help dispel the notion that America's contemporary social problems, along with her tattered virtues, are somehow unique. In London, rates of common crime started upward in the depth of the Depression.⌐ They subsided after World War II, but in the early nineteen-fifties began an inexorable increase. Indictable offenses known to police grew by 450 per cent between 1950 and 1974, with the nastiest kinds of crimes increasing most sharply; burglaries are up five hundred per cent, rape by six hundred per cent, assault by nine hundred per cent, and robbery by 1,200 per cent. London has been the bellwether for all England and Wales, whose rate of murder and assault combined grew by nine hundred per cent between 1950 and 1974, and burglary and robbery combined by five hundred per cent.

London's experience is paralleled throughout the English-speaking world—see Table 1, this page. The late nineteen-forties and early nineteen-fifties marked the low ebb of common crime in virtually every English-speaking country. Since then the trends have been consistently upward. In the United States, homicides and assaults together have increased at an average of nineteen per cent per year for a generation. Elsewhere the nineteen-fifties rates for murder and assault were lower but the increases have been swifter. The rising trends in theft have been sustained just as long, and average between eight and fourteen per cent per annum. The most serious forms

Table 1. Crime Trends in English-Speaking Societies
Known Murders and Assaults per 100,000 Population

	1950	c.1960	1970's*	Average annual increase
England and Wales	13.0	32.4	127.8	37%
London	13.0	26.2	123.5	35%
United States	58.0	91.2	225.1	12%
New South Wales	no data	15.5	21.7	4%
Canada	no data	158.2	419.1	15%
Republic of Ireland	5.9	13.7	29.6	19%

Known Thefts per 100,000 Population

	1950	c.1960	1970's*	Average annual increase
England and Wales	847	1,317	2,454	8%
London	1,056	1,942	3,624	10%
United States	1,108	1,786	4,588	13%
New South Wales	no data	604	1,467	14%
Canada	no data	1,408	3,443*	13%
Republic of Ireland	346	472	1,090	10%

*Data from 1974 except New South Wales (1970), Ireland (1971), and Canada (1973).

of property crime — robbery and burglary — have risen about twice as rapidly as total theft in all these societies. Ireland seems the most favored country in this comparison. Its relatively low volume of crime may be credited to its Gaelic culture, religious traditionalism, or simply the smallness of its cities. But these conditions have not inhibited the Irish from emulating the growing Anglo-American fondness for mayhem and theft.

🔔

Explanations abound for rising crime in these countries. Substantial social and economic inequalities exist in all of them. Everywhere the penal system is excoriated because it warehouses offenders rather than rehabilitating them. The police often are accused of corruption and a heavy-handed disregard for civil liberties. Add to this the special explanations proffered by social analysts confronted with rising crime in particular countries. Britain? Class tensions in a declining economy. The United States? An angry black underclass, its hopes stirred by promises of a

1. CRIME AND JUSTICE IN AMERICA

Great Society which never arrived. Ireland? Modernization is eroding traditional acceptance of poverty and authority. Australia? Merely beery, exuberant youths challenging unpopular police.

If there is any universal truth to these kinds of conventional liberal wisdom about the social origins of crime, the Scandinavian countries surely should be more favored than some of the English-speaking nations. They are ethnically homogenous and their social ethos is strongly egalitarian. Their cities are free of slums and their social services are among the best in the world. Economically they have prospered since the end of World War II and have had low unemployment. Their police are widely respected, justice is ordinarily even-handed and efficient. Rehabilitation is the central, overriding aim of their penal system.

Stockholm provides a historical laboratory for observing crime in Scandinavia. Unlike London, the Great Depression of the nineteen-thirties had little effect on its crime rates. During wartime, crime in neutral Stockholm rose and then subsided — until about 1950. Since then virtually every category of

offense against persons and property has skyrocketed. These are some twenty-year increases in crimes known to police: murder and attempts, six hundred per cent; assault and battery, more than three hundred per cent; rape and attempted rape, three hundred per cent; "crimes inflicting damage" (i.e., vandalism), five hundred per cent; all theft, 350 per cent; robberies alone, one thousand per cent; fraud and embezzlement, seven hundred per cent. In 1971, there was one theft reported to police for every eleven inhabitants of the city, which can be compared with 1974 figures of one per twenty Londoners, and one per eighteen New Yorkers. In fairness to Stockholmers, they are more likely to report thefts to their trusted police than are cynical New Yorkers. The point remains that Swedish welfare and criminal justice policies have not inhibited the rise of urban crime.

Stockholm represents in most severe form a criminal malaise that has affected all of Scandinavia. Some comparative data are shown in Table 2. At the national level, crimes against persons started up later and more slowly than in Stockholm or the English-speaking countries, but there is no mistaking the presence of an escalating trend. The same is true of property crime. Moreover, we find in Scandinavia a phenomenon familiar from the English-speaking countries: the most serious property offenses have increased far more steeply than common theft. In Sweden, from 1950 to 1974, known theft increased by a multiple of three while the rarer offense of robbery grew tenfold. In Finland, from 1961 to 1973, the proportional increases were: all theft, 275 per cent; robbery, 720 per cent. On the face of it the Scandinavian countries have higher rates of common crime than most of the English-speaking countries. Not too much should be made of the differences, since national crime-accounting systems vary. Trends within each country are more reliably assessed than absolute differences among them.

In the heartland of Western Europe the portrait of crime is significantly different in one major respect. There are no long-term increases in murder and assault in the continental democracies. Congratulations are premature, though, since Germany and France both began to move up in the late nineteen-sixties, too recently to certify the existence of an enduring trend. Property crime on the Continent is more of a piece with the English and Scandinavian experience. Theft rates began to rise later, sometime between 1955 and 1965, depending on the country. Since then the official statistics document steadily

Table 2. Crime Trends in Scandinavian Societies

Known Assaults and Murders per 100,000 Population

	1950	c.1960	1970's*	Average annual increase
Denmark	41.2	39.2	58.7	2%
Finland	no data	148.0	305.3	9%
Norway	no data	52.4	83.7	5%
Sweden	115.7	126.4	214.1	4%
Stockholm	90.7	266.5	403.2	16%

Known Thefts per 100,000 Population

	1950	c.1960	1970's*	Average annual increase
Denmark	1,922	2,332	5,889	9%
Finland	no data	886	2,453	15%
Norway	no data	748	1,512	9%
Sweden	1,568	2,726	4,730	9%
Stockholm	1,933	4,250	8,215	15%

*Data for 1973 except Stockholm (1971) and Norway (1972).

rising trends into the mid-nineteen-seventies — with the sole exception of Switzerland, where theft rates have held essentially steady since 1945. The generalizations about the continental countries neatly encompass Israel's experience as well.

From the Marxist-Leninist point of view, this evidence of the rising tide of disorder in Western societies is the harbinger of capitalism's long-awaited collapse. The Eastern European commentators who offer this interpretation no doubt are uncomfortably aware that their own societies are suffering a similar affliction. How serious it is neither we nor they can say, since the European Communist states have not published sufficient statistical information to determine the trends.

There is finally the case of Japan, an industrialized democratic society which has had unparalleled success in reducing crime rates — serious crime most of all — during the last two decades. Since 1955, Japan's murder and assault rates have both been halved. Simple theft has been reduced by about a quarter, known white-collar crime has been reduced to one-fifth its former levels, while the robbery rate is scarcely one-tenth of what it was in 1949-50.

This pattern of change duplicates what happened in London, Stockholm, and Sydney during their century of falling crime: as public order improved, serious offenses declined more rapidly than petty ones. And it is the reverse of what is happening in contemporary Western societies in which serious property crime has increased far faster than petty offenses.

These contrasts and images imply that a fairly high level of petty theft is endemic to prosperous societies, but that serious crime is not. Japan is a case in point. It is a capitalistic society which has had extraordinary success in reducing the incidence of murder, assault, and robbery. The improvement has been a sustained one — some twenty-five years in duration — and it has taken place in a society undergoing the rapid social and economic changes that elsewhere are assumed to be crimogenic.

In the face of nineteenth- and twentieth-century examples of successful social defense, it is reasonable to ask where contemporary Western societies have gone wrong. We can begin to clear the ground of some incorrect or partial explanations, and perhaps point out where the most general answers are to be found.

In pop sociology it has been fashionable to blame rising crime rates on intensified policing and more thorough crime-reporting systems. Contemporary examples of both can be found: there are wide fluctuations in police attention to "victimless" crimes like prostitution and drug abuse, while changes in reporting systems produce abrupt discontinuities in crime statistics. But neither explanation accounts for persistent trends up or down in the rate of common crime. If this explanation for the rising tide of theft and assault were to be taken seriously, we would have to suppose that the police forces of almost every Western society began a sustained expansion in manpower, detection, and crime reporting in the nineteen-fifties and nineteen-sixties. In none of our city or country studies is there evidence for such changes. These reforms occurred in European societies in the nineteenth century, not in the mid-twentieth century, and they coincided with falling rates of common crime, not increasing ones. Also common crimes come to police attention through reports of private citizens. If rising crime rates in Western societies were due mainly to more conscientious reporting by citizens, the increases would consist disproportionately of petty offenses. But the opposite is the case: serious offenses are increasing much more than petty ones.

The "better policing" explanation of rising rates of common crime is largely a myth. It is naive to think that crime statistics depict precisely the real incidence of crime because many victims, especially in high-crime areas, think it is useless to report their losses. But there is little doubt that the long-term trends common to postwar Western societies reflect real changes in social behavior of large magnitude. This is the social issue most in need of explanation, not the vagaries of police behavior.

The typical robber or thief in Western societies — past and present — is all too likely to be a poor, uneducated denizen of an urban slum. The liberal view has long been that common crime should therefore be reduced by social and economic improvement. The nineteenth-century experience of cities like London and Stockholm provided much sustenance for that belief. The late-twentieth-century experience has badly undercut it. Literacy and free schooling through the secondary level are universals in Western society. Supportive social services are far better now than in 1920 or 1950. The conditions of urban life, including housing quality, have improved throughout the twentieth century and especially since 1945; the United States is the only Western society whose urban environment has worsened appreciably in the last thirty years.

1. CRIME AND JUSTICE IN AMERICA

In economic terms more people live better than ever before. Inevitably some are poorer than others and some are unemployed, but a net of public support catches virtually all of them before they reach the margin of subsistence. The sophisticated liberal explanation for rising crime in prospering societies is no longer misery but resentment over one's "relative deprivation" at being left behind while almost everyone else seems to be getting richer. Theft then becomes an easy, albeit illicit, way to close the gap. And one basic reason theft in modern societies is easy is that there is so much more to steal than there was half a century ago.

These "relative deprivation" and "opportunity" explanations of rising theft are plausible but not proven, and in any case partial. They do not account for the equally sharp rise in crimes against persons. More fundamentally, they do not explain why the hypothetical victim of deprivation chooses the risks of crime over the manifold legitimate opportunities for personal advancement. The answer to this question lies less in the social environment than in people's beliefs about how they *should* respond to its variegated opportunities. In other words, it is a question of norms and morality. The rising frequency of common crime is prima-facie evidence of a widespread weakening of the basic Judeo-Christian principle that thou shall not steal or murder in the pursuit of private satisfactions.

The supposition that value change lies at the bottom of the "crime problem" is reinforced by evidence about the explosion of youth crime. In fact there are two linked explosions. One is the coming of age of the postwar baby boom, which meant that there were proportionately far more teenagers in most Western societies in the nineteen-sixties than in the nineteen-fifties. Italy, Germany, and Austria are among the few exceptions. Since youths are always more numerous among offenders, the crime rate "naturally" increased. But at the same time the number and seriousness of crimes committed by youths escalated far beyond previous levels. For example, in a recent depth-interview study by A. A. Belson, every one of a representative sample of 1,425 London boys aged thirteen to sixteen admitted to stealing. More extraordinary is that, on the average, each boy had committed eighteen different *kinds* of theft, out of a list of forty-four types. Only thirteen per cent had ever been caught by the police for stealing, mainly for the more serious kinds of offenses.

The supposition is that youth crime is high because the family, schools, and churches have failed to implant traditional values. It is problematic whether the socializing institutions really do worse than in the past because there is no direct evidence on whether they were more uniformly effective at the turn of the century, or in the nineteen-twenties and nineteen-thirties. But there is no doubt that contemporary youths have an alternative to traditional teachings. Distinctive new "post-industrial" values were articulated on university campuses during the nineteen-sixties and soon echoed by young people throughout Western society. The counter-culture's creed had many elements that were consistent with traditional values. It had other elements, encapsulated in the slogan, "Do your own thing," which are socially more corrosive and seem to have attracted wider and more enduring support than its humanitarian abstractions.

The most corrosive form of this alternative ethic is aggressive hedonism, a belief that almost any means are justified in pursuit of personal aggrandizement. It appears to be a mutation of Western materialism, stripped of its work ethic and generalized from material satisfactions to social and sexual ones. Moreover it often coexists with a sense of resentment against large, impersonal organizations — more because of their remoteness and unresponsiveness than because of tangible failures in performance. This alienation — to give it the proper sociological label — is manifest in the decline of authority of state and corporation, school and church, and in a growing defiance of their rules.

The proposition is that a distinctive syndrome of selfishness and alienation has taken root in the interstices of most Western societies. It is especially prevalent among youth, though it is not unique to them; and one of its manifestations is the rise in youthful aggression and theft that accounts for most of the rise in Western crime rates. This hypothesis is not easily tested, nor does it point toward any simple social cures, except in one ironic sense. The invisible hand of hedonism has dictated that an unprecedentedly large proportion of young people in Western societies forego having the children who would become the potential criminals and victims of the nineteen-nineties.

One thing this tentative explanation does help us understand is why the criminal law, police, courts, and prisons together cannot restrain the rising tide of crime. These institutions and their policies were effective in turn-of-the-century societies dominated by a self-confident middle class convinced that prosperity in this life and salvation in the next could be achieved through piety, honesty, and hard work. All authorities spoke with the same voice. The institutions of public order were effective because they reinforced the dominant view. They did not merely punish those who transgressed. They were missionaries to the underclass, informing them of the moral order through arrest, trial, and imprisonment.

Today, no self-confident consensus on standards of behavior is to be found in Western societies. There are many self-proclaimed authorities offering many alternatives. Bereft of a solid foundation of social support, the police, courts, and prisons drift. At worst, the police adopt a siege mentality, hostile to society and offenders alike. The courts devise expedients, such as plea bargaining, which serve administrative efficiency at the expense of both justice and public safety. And the prisons become warehouses which, like the gaols and workhouses of early-nineteenth-century England, keep the offender out of

circulation for a little while, but only inadvertently punish or rehabilitate him.

We might hope that the policies and institutions of public order in the nineteen-seventies are due for another wave of reform such as those which transformed Britain, Sweden, Australia, and the United States in the nineteenth century. But the social requisites of a coherent movement for reform are lacking. Harsh punishment violates humanitarian principles, while thoroughgoing programs of rehabilitation are very expensive. Most experts doubt that either approach works anyway. And popular protest about rising crime is muted because almost everywhere the most victimized groups are the poor and near-poor, who have less political influence than the more secure middle classes. Under these circumstances, it is scarcely surprising that politicians, experts, and officials alike are more willing to make symbolic gestures like advocating a return to capital punishment or castigating the police, than to promote expensive experiments of uncertain outcome.

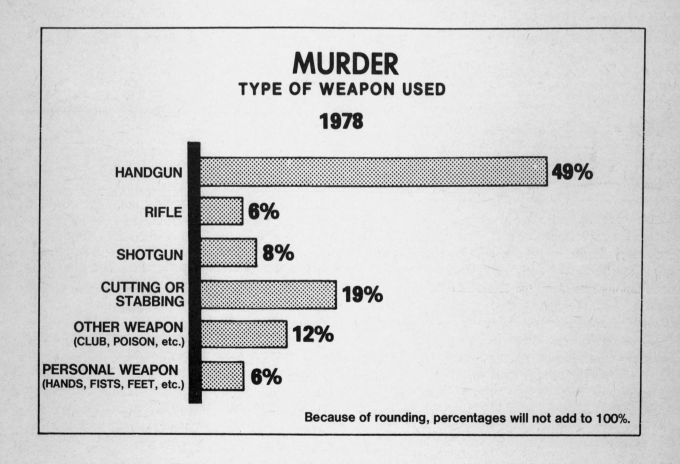

MURDER
TYPE OF WEAPON USED
1978

HANDGUN — **49%**
RIFLE — **6%**
SHOTGUN — **8%**
CUTTING OR STABBING — **19%**
OTHER WEAPON (CLUB, POISON, etc.) — **12%**
PERSONAL WEAPON (HANDS, FISTS, FEET, etc.) — **6%**

Because of rounding, percentages will not add to 100%.

Two Hundred Years of Social and Economic Change Have Shaped Our Crime Problem

Bob Eckhardt

Concern over crime in the United States is not a new phenomenon. In scanning recent history, one might characterize the two decades immediately following World War II as an era in which an interest in crime was largely the province of professionals — the police, courts, and corrections officials. Beginning in the mid-nineteen-sixties, however, the American concern over crime grew quite dramatically, often reaching a near-fever pitch. Thus, by 1968 George Gallup could report to us that Americans considered crime our most important domestic problem, and as late as June of 1975, fifteen per cent of all Americans considered crime their local community's major problem.

Solutions to crime in the United States have been put forth in such terms as "We need more police," "The courts need to be tougher," or, "The death penalty has to be reinstated." These suggestions might prove quite useful to a general discussion of the criminal justice system in America. As solutions to the problems of crime in the United States, however, I would suggest that they are cosmetic. In fact, they bear striking resemblance to the policies of the Department of Justice and the White House in the early nineteen-seventies, when we heard so much of the cry for "law and order." The strategy during those years was to attack only the symptoms of our social problems. Thus, if the black ghettos of our major cities were quiet, we had tackled our racial problems; if our students were in class instead of occupying the university president's office, we had dealt with the youth problem. Nothing could have been more misguided.

Similarly, to focus only on criminality is to ignore the more fundamental questions which should be included in any treatment of criminal justice in the United States. Rather, in dealing with criminality, it seems necessary to treat three general topics:

☐ The unchanging principles which should underlie our criminal justice system.
☐ The assumptions which seem reasonable regarding causes of human action.
☐ The changing social and economic conditions which should influence the way we examine our criminal justice system.

As a foundation upon which to build our criminal justice system, we need look no further than the Constitution, where the Preamble charges us with a responsibility to promote justice, domestic tranquillity, liberty, and the general welfare. It is these principles upon which *all* governmental action in the United States is premised.

When the framers drafted the Constitution, they were acting for a nation composed largely of farmers, craftsmen, and traders. With its frontier, abundant land, and vast resources, early America was truly a nation of farms and small hamlets. There were no cities to rival the great centers of Europe — New York in 1800 was a metropolis of seventy-nine thousand people, Washington was an uninhabitable swamp, and Chicago was only a glimmer in someone's eye. Family, social, and religious ties were strong. A man protected himself, his family, and his property. Community protection from fire and crime was left largely to a night watch; and defense was the responsibility of a state militia of volunteer citizen-soldiers.

Within this environment, a man was assumed to have almost complete control over his own destiny, and the responsibilities of government were thus considered to be few. The criminal was viewed as one who had freely and deliberately chosen his wayward path, and the community's obligation was considered to be the meting out of justice so that the offender would choose a more proper course of behavior.

It almost goes without saying that economic and social conditions have changed dramatically since this approach to criminal justice was crafted two centuries ago. What this suggests to me is a need to scrutinize and evaluate these changes so that we might obtain a better understanding of the causes and potential solutions of the problems of crime in the United States. We have, in fact, a responsibility to engage in such an exercise, for as Thomas Jefferson said, "Laws and institutions must go hand in hand with the progress of the human mind. . . . As new discoveries are made, new truths disclosed, and manners and opinions change with the change in circumstances, institutions must advance also, and keep pace with the times."

❦

You and I have grown so accustomed to change that we often forget how substantially our world has been altered. There are a number of significant changes, though, which recommend themselves to any discussion of crime in the United States. We are obviously no longer a nation of yeomen. We have undergone a revolutionary transformation from an agrarian base to mercantilism, then manufacturing, and finally to the present stage which many have called the post-industrial economy. Though agriculture today is not an insignificant industry, its relative position in the economy has declined steadily, especially since the onset of the Great Depression. Agriculture has been restructured from an individual enterprise into what is now called agribusiness: our farm population has declined, as have the number of farms, while the size of the average farm and the extent of corporate farming have increased drastically.

Similar to agriculture's changing economic status has been the continuing shift away from industry in the last three decades. From 1950 to 1975, for instance, the proportion of national income derived from manufacturing, mining, and construction has steadily fallen. In the meantime, the private service sector, by which I mean wholesale and retail trade, finance, insurance, and real estate, as well as professional, business, personal, and repair services, grew from 35.2 to 41.3 per cent of national income. A number of other economic developments should also be cited as being of possible relevance to a rethinking of our criminal justice system.

These developments become more significant to our discussion of crime if we also consider what the rise of the service economy has meant to the American labor market. Our criminal justice system was designed originally for a nation of self-sustaining farmers, shopkeepers, and traders which has long since disappeared. Today less than seven per cent of our nonagricultural work force and only half of our agricultural work force are self-employed. Over half of all American workers are now employed in the private service economy, which stands in stark contrast to the industrial economy it supplanted.

3. Two Hundred Years of Social Economic Change

Labor within the service sector is characterized by slow growth in productivity; wages and benefits significantly below those in manufacturing, mining, construction, transportation, communication, and government; low levels of unionization; large numbers of female, older, minority, and part-time employees; and lower skill and educational levels than are present in manufacturing.

Oscar Wilde may not have been too far off the mark when he asserted that "starvation, and not sin, is the parent of modern crime." A 1974 study done by the Library of Congress, for instance, found a strong correlation between prison admissions and the annual unemployment rate in the United States. That report found that "the unemployment rate can statistically describe over eighty per cent of the year-to-year variation in prison admissions at the federal level, and seventy-nine per cent at the state level."

The report did not posit *an* explanation for this phenomenon, but suggested several reasons as to why this relationship might exist: "High levels of unemployment could lead to social unrest and a lessening of support for social institutions, possibly affecting crime rates, sentencing policies, parole decisions, and other factors which in turn influence prison populations. Unemployment may also pose a stark choice in economic terms for those who are on the borderline of acceptable social action and must find alternative means of support."

Consider, for example, the case of Washington, D.C. Two years ago, when a congressional committee heard testimony on the subject of crime in Washington, they were told the alarming news that in 1973 nearly seventy per cent of those arrested for robbery were unemployed, and nearly fifty per cent of all courtroom defendants were unemployed.

Allow me, if you will, to try to bring this matter into a sharper focus. In the recent recession, those most severely affected by unemployment were teenagers, minority group members, and part-time workers. In 1975, for example, while the national unemployment rate stood at 8.5 per cent, minority group members were faced with a rate of nearly fourteen per cent; over one in ten part-time workers was without a job; and almost twenty per cent of all teenagers seeking a job were unemployed. During that year, the largest increases in reported crime were for larceny, theft, and burglary — crimes for which half of those arrested in 1975 were under eighteen years of age and over thirty per cent of whom were nonwhite.

Unfortunately, the story I have presented to you may even paint too rosy a picture of any relationship which exists between crime and a person's economic condition. This is the case for two major reasons. First, both the Federal Bureau of Investigation's crime data and the unemployment information of the Bureau of Labor Statistics underestimate the severity of the problems they describe. The F.B.I. statistics, for instance, include only offenses reported to the police; and there is a substantial body of survey research pointing to the fact that four of every ten crimes may go unreported. In the case of unemployment data we find a similar problem since these figures do not include those who have given up looking for work. An estimated one million workers fell into this category in the last quarter of 1976.

❧

The second reason why research such as that already mentioned might inadequately profile problems of crime and economic conditions is that it does not reflect the extent to which the criminal justice system punishes one for being poor.

The problem with bail is quite straightforward — the system of money bail forces the poor to go to jail because they cannot raise the bondsman's premium. A 1969 staff report to the National Commission on the Causes and Prevention of Violence summarized the ripple effect of this failure of the poor to post bail: "A defendant who cannot post bail must go to jail, lose any earning capacity at least temporarily, and possibly lose his job. In the interim, he cannot support his family, who may be forced to seek public welfare."

The problems of the indigent defendant are more extensive than bail alone. The poor usually find themselves represented by a public defender or court-appointed attorney, who is usually poorly compensated and often greatly overworked. Limited defense resources, prosecutors' tendencies to encourage grand juries to overcharge defendants, and court loads all serve as incentives for the poor to plead guilty. This dilemma can be even further exacerbated if the defendant waives his right to counsel. In addition, a defendant is often confronted by a jury whose economic and social background does not make its members peers of the accused.

Given all of these factors — and most particularly the problems surrounding the use of bail — we would anticipate that the poor would find it difficult at best to take steps to aid their own defense. The harsh realities of this expectation have been borne out by several studies conducted over the last twenty years.

The facts are most succinctly summarized by a 1972 study which concluded, "Those who stay in jail for lack of bail money are much more often convicted and, when convicted, go to prison more often and get much longer prison sentences than those who make bail."

Post-industrial poverty is not the only development to which the criminal justice system has failed to adjust. While theft in early America was simply a matter of physically expropriating another's property or possessions, today you and I are robbed indirectly to the tune of forty billion dollars annually. We are the unfortunate victims of what has come to be tagged as white-collar crime, or what the American Bar Association calls economic offenses. Sometimes

> *The connection between unemployment and crime is clear and dramatic*

it seems as if you and I wake up every morning to be shocked by some new tale of foreign bribery, consumer fraud, embezzlement, welfare fraud, kickbacks, or false advertising.

During the past generation, Americans have witnessed the increasing diversification of firms, the rise of the conglomerate, the ascension of the multinational corporation, and the expansion of their government as a producer of goods and services. Accompanying these changes has been a rapid and steady growth of white-collar employment. Half of all Americans are now employed as professional and technical workers, managers and administrators, salespersons, and clerical workers.

As these changes occurred following World War

II, our economy became ripe with opportunities for white-collar criminals. Unfortunately, the prosecution of such cases typically involves long and drawnout litigation caused by the complexity of the case, a prosecutor's use of representative counts in indictments, the extent of proof presented by the prosecutor, and the delaying tactics of the defense. Delay typically leads to the extensive use of plea bargaining in cases involving economic crimes. The use of plea bargaining in and of itself may not be an abuse of our criminal justice system. A problem exists, however, with the results of the plea bargaining process. A report just released by the American Bar Association expresses it quite clearly: "There is significant evidence that individuals convicted of economic crime offenses are not incarcerated to the same extent as individuals convicted of other offenses." I should add that this disparity even exists between nonviolent and economic crimes. The greatest threat to the American consumer in the disposition of white-collar cases is the courts' willingness to accept a plea of *nolo contendere*, which cannot be used in a civil proceeding brought by the victim of an economic crime.

Revolutionary as the economic changes mentioned have been, the growth of urban areas in the United States has proven equally dynamic. The new economic order of the nineteenth century began a population shift that still shows little sign of changing.

The 1970 census indicated that seven of every ten of us lived in a metropolitan area of one hundred thousand or more people. Even more awesome a thought is the fact that 73.5 per cent of the population lived in the 1.5 per cent of United States land area which the Census Bureau classified as urban. Thus, our urban areas averaged 2,700 people per square mile. In Chicago, on the other hand, over fifteen thousand people are packed into a typical square mile.

I can assure you that these trends are far from insignificant in our discussion of crime. As our cities mushroomed, they attracted people of increasingly diverse backgrounds. The urban landscape proved to be more than a concentration of people, however. Our cities also became the depositories for problems of health, transportation, housing, and a myriad of other social ills, including crime.

Lacking few problems, our cities found themselves without the homogeneity, stability, and physical amenities which had previously characterized smaller towns in America. Local governments responded to these conditions by providing physical improvements

and protection to their citizens. Our response today has been much the same. A report done last year by the Library of Congress, for instance, reviewed several studies done during the last two decades which point to a reduction in crime in areas of cities where improved street lighting has been installed. This is noteworthy since as much as three-fourths of all crime in our major cities may occur at night, and two-thirds of these nighttime crimes take place in dimly lighted areas. I hope that this information is of some comfort to the forty-five per cent of Americans who told the Gallup Poll in 1975 that they were afraid to walk in their neighborhoods at night.

Sad to say, our urban dwellers may have had good cause for alarm since crime rates for both violent and property crime offenses vary proportionately with the size of cities. Every year from 1965 to 1975, for example, the rate of violent crime in cities with 250,000 or more people was four to seven times greater than the rate for cities of less than ten thousand.

❧

These are what I consider to be the social trends and their implications which should prove pertinent to our discussion of crime. Even in the light of the developments I have cited, we who have the responsibility for stimulating discussion and modification of the criminal justice system have not significantly altered our approach to crime in the United States. What, then, are the obligations that we have as lawmakers?

You have a right to expect two things from those of us in Washington, your statehouse, and your city hall. Our first responsibility to you is an intellectual one. Elected officials and political candidates must abandon the emotionalism which often surrounds their thinking and speaking on crime. This implies a need to respect the intelligence of the American public and start discussing crime in its broadest dimensions. I, for one, have had my fill of candidates telling me that crime can be licked if we would only hire more judges and start televising executions from San Quentin. Instead, we must search broadly for those conditions which lead some of our fellow citizens to threaten the lives and property of others. Having focused on such causes, we must develop the necessary approaches to prevent men and women from engaging in crime or repeating their offenses.

Our second obligation is to develop public policies which are as far-reaching as I hope our thinking will be. Our actions can well be guided by a recommendation made by the staff to the National Commission on the Causes and Prevention of Violence. They told the Commission that unless "crime reduction is perceived as requiring better education, housing, health, and employment opportunities for would-be offenders, the criminal process will continue to suffer."

As a first step, we must develop a more realistic definition of criminality. This means concentrating our efforts on those activities which genuinely pose serious threats to the physical and economic well-being of our citizens. It also means reducing our present litany of illness, morals, and nuisance statutes and devising new methods of dealing with victimless crime.

Overcriminalization is the back-door approach to a problem. It can also lead to unbelievable waste. In my own city of Houston, for instance, seventy per cent of the criminal caseload in the municipal court involves victimless crime. Alternatives do exist, however. For example, a few states now deal with public drunkenness by recognizing alcoholism for what it is, a disease, and not a crime. To move in this direction will take imagination and courage. Thurman Arnold warned us forty years ago that these statutes go largely "unenforced because we want to continue our conduct, and unrepealed because we want to preserve our morals."

As lawmakers, it is also incumbent upon us to provide an environment which discourages crime. Simply put, this means emphasizing jobs and neighborhoods. And that mandates legislation which is useful at both the national and local levels. Of utmost importance here is passage of federal legislation such as the Humphrey-Hawkins full employment bill.

We cannot stop here, however. We must keep in mind that the best resource in our fight against crime is a strong and stable neighborhood. Our emphasis has to be on public works improvements, recreation, investment opportunities, and neighborhood organizations.

Federal aid for public works has become increasingly important to our cities. Traditionally, grants have been awarded on the basis of such factors as unemployment and income levels. In the future, it would behoove Congress to consider requiring neighborhood crime levels as another determinant to be used in selecting local projects for federal funding. In addition to neighborhood improvements, we must also provide open space near our major urban areas. It was this need which prompted me to introduce the Open Beaches Act back in 1969.

Several steps can be taken to improve the stability of our urban neighborhoods. The federal government must first of all guarantee that businesses in high-crime areas can obtain loans and insurance. In addition, neighborhoods can be aided by the federal government's rational use of rent subsidies, mortgage financing, and vigorous efforts against red-lining.

Strong neighborhood organizations are another source of stability in areas threatened by crime. Congress moved wisely last year when it earmarked a portion of Law Enforcement Assistance Administration funds for neighborhood anti-crime activities. More innovation is needed, however, to insure stable neighborhoods. There is a place, for instance, for such programs as the Consumer Cooperative Bank proposed in the last Congress.

Such changes in prevention must be accompanied by shifts in pre-trial, trial, punishment, and rehabilitation practices. Reforms in the grand jury system, bail procedures, and legal aid are essential to a guaranteeing of the constitutional rights of the poor defendant.

Criminals must be put on notice that they will be held responsible for their actions. Thus, the offender, not the government, might be required to make restitution to his victim in all crimes against persons and property. This will demand innovative action on the part of corrections officials to insure that criminals can take advantage of job-training, release-time, and similar programs to guarantee that the offender can make restitution and be employed following any period of incarceration.

Demanding responsibility of offenders also requires that the curtain be drawn on the double standard which exists between white-collar and other types of crime. We can no longer tolerate criminals hiding behind corporate shields. Given the nature of offenses and recidivism, we would do well to follow the suggestions of the American Bar Association and adopt stiffer fines and sentences for economic crimes. The abuses in this area have led me to sponsor such bills as the one to curb foreign bribery.

I trust that these policy recommendations will be critically examined. They are not a recipe for criminal justice reform. They were not intended to be. They are an approach to the study of crime in the United States. Not to keep in mind the economic and social changes I have sketched would be foolhardy. It would be to ignore Jefferson's profound advice and to abandon our responsibility to pursue the goals to which the Preamble of our Constitution commits us.

UN Leader Gives Views on Worldwide Crime

Gerhard O.W. Mueller has directed the United Nations' Crime Prevention and Criminal Justice Branch since 1974, during which time he served as executive secretary for the UN's Fifth Congress for the Prevention of Crime and the Treatment of Offenders.

After pursuing a brief law enforcement career with the British Military Government Water Police from 1945 to 1947, Mueller moved to the United States where he taught law at a number of institutions, including the University of Chicago, and the Yale Law School.

The holder of J.D. and LL.M. degrees, Mueller has served as consultant to a number of prestigious panels and associations such as the Senate Judiciary Committee, the Ford Foundation, the American Bar Association, and various international agencies. He has authored or co-authored 13 books related to criminal justice theory and procedure and has edited over 60 texts and monographs in the field. The recipient of numerous honors and awards, Mueller has been mentioned in *Who's Who in America.*

This interview was conducted for Law Enforcement News by Robert McCormack.

* * *

LEN: I wonder if you might tell us a little about the Crime Prevention and Criminal Justice Section of the United Nations and its function.

MUELLER: Within the U.N.'s Center of Social Development of Humanitarian Affairs, there are a number of branches that deal with various aspects of the social developments that are taking place all over the world in conjunction with economic developments. Some of these are positive future-oriented. We try to promote the lot of the handicapped, of children, of women in development, and so on. But as part of development there also are negative effects. As a society goes through economic development, it builds factories, urbanizes and makes other changes. Something negative may take place—mainly crime and the deterioration of family life.

The job of my branch is to look into these negative aspects of development and to come up with solutions to prevent these negative things from happening while a nation undergoes the developmental process. For that purpose, my branch conducts international congresses and meetings at which crime information is exchanged. We engage in research and engage in training in our institutions around the world. In addition, my staff members and expert consultants are sent to the various parts of the world, at the request of countries, to help them solve their crime problems. We take world crime census in which world crime trends and crime prevention policies are monitored. But all of this is for the purpose of helping nations to develop harmoniously, socially and economically and to avoid disruption and the cost that crime and victimization bring with it.

LEN: You have attributed at least some of the crime in society to the breakdown of the family, the schools and the community. Do you feel that in progressive, modern societies these informal means of control have deteriorated in the past year?

MUELLER: There is an eerie correlation between urbanization and all that goes with it—the breakdown of the extended family, the breakdown even of the small family, the loss of control of village and neighborhood communities and an increase in crime. It doesn't have to be that way, however. We have countries in the world which are undergoing a rapid social and economic development where there has been success in maintaining the social control of which we speak—a control not by handcuffs or squad cars or prisons, but a control by social entities such as family, community and religion. In some countries where the village community has fallen apart because of urbanization, substitutes were created. The substitutes may be political in some areas as in China or some of the socialist countries where they say that the family no longer exercises control, but they invented something else to provide social control as distinguished from law enforcement control.

LEN: That would be what? The commune?

MUELLER: Yes, it may be the commune, it may be the factory unit, it may be the neighborhood unit, or it may be the newly created family—the kibbutzim in Israel, for example. It is subject to social organisms that play the role of supporting each other. Japan is an interesting example. While in Japan the family is falling apart to some extent, the neighborhoods are still intact. As more and more neighborhoods assume social support factors, neighbors will watch you in a way, watch over you, help you and support you when you stumble. To a very large extent, the extremely low crime rates of Japan are explainable by the fact that some surrogate social forces are operative which help people from becoming involved in criminal activities.

From *Correctional Services News,* March 1978. Originally from *Law Enforcement News,* March 21, 1978. Reprinted by permission.

1. CRIME AND JUSTICE IN AMERICA

LEN: In the United States we define the criminal justice system as being the function of the police, the courts and other specific groups, but you seem to espouse an even broader picture of the system that involves other social groups. Could you give us your views on that?

MUELLER: At one time in history the Anglo-American criminal justice system was revered as the most popular because it had lay participation, popular participation, in the form of the jury. But when the jury trials gradually disappeared, with hundreds of thousands of trials or plea-bargainings taking place without a jury, this popular aspect of the American criminal justice system has been lost. But I think we have discovered popular participation in other forms, such as volunteers in probation, police auxiliaries and citizens' groups participating in crime prevention—new forms of commune in which neighborhoods organize themselves for crime prevention purposes, help delinquency-prone youngsters and participate with law enforcement agencies. There is, in other words, a new form of popular participation in America that is a far better and more effective form than the jury trial ever was.

LEN: How about organizations like the welfare system in New York City which deals specifically with problems of the poor, who apparently commit a disproportionate number of crimes in terms of their specific numbers? How about those kinds of agencies becoming a part of the criminal justice system in terms of their ability to prevent and reduce crime?

MUELLER: Even if these are agencies of crime prevention in a larger sense, I am afraid that they cannot be effective until and unless they themselves are forms of popular participation. If they are just another government bureaucracy doling out money or setting down rules and regulations, then that is not an effective means of crime prevention. But, to the extent that they become communal efforts, societal efforts of the structure—the city, the borough, the neighborhood—then they could in fact become useful crime prevention vehicles.

LEN: Are you suggesting that a decentralized version of major bureaucracy might cut crime.

MUELLER: That certainly seems to be one of the things which all the successful countries in crime prevention have in common.

LEN: Can you give us some examples of what you call "new crime?"

MUELLER: It may vary from region to region depending upon what is bothersome to a particular country. Let me give you two examples. One of the West African countries is in the process of urbanizing. A large problem of what we used to call "victimless crime" arose. Single men were drawn from the hinterland to the seashore, where they built a new city. The problems spread as soon as those men had money in their pockets. What do single men, living in shacks, do with money in their pockets? They gamble, and along with gambling starts drinking, with gambling starts fighting, and prostitutes are brought in. Little girls were brought in, 12-year-old girls. Prostitution started, venereal disease spread like wildfire, and that is the sum of crime now. That is the kind of scene where our office may be called in for advice and assistance.

Another example is one Caribbean country, where an immense problem of violence was created—stranger to stranger violence, rather than violence among friends on Friday nights after a couple of beers. It wasn't clear why, all of a sudden, there was this fantastic increase in violence. It affects the welfare of a country, it affects the economy of a country, particularly in an area that largely lives on tourism. That is a situation where the office may be called in to provide help and assistance. More and more, it is in the area of economic criminality that we are asked to help. Economic criminality, whereby a single multinational corporation can create millions or even billions of dollars of damage by criminal activities. Computer fraud is large in that area. There we may be asked to help, although there is no center for multinational corporations within the United Nations with the specific task of looking into this problem. We are charged with the task of developing a code of standards for multinational trading partners.

LEN: That really leads to the next question because one of the duties of this office, if I understand it correctly, is to measure trends in crime throughout the world. Apparently from what you just told us, certain types of crimes are just catching up with certain developing nations. Are there any identifiable trends in crime throughout the world?

MUELLER: That is a very, very broad question. We have looked at the situation country by country for all those who have reported to us, and there are 67 or 68 countries which have so far participated. It is noticeable that female criminality is increasing more rapidly than male criminality. Just look everywhere in the world. Economic criminality is also increasing in most parts of the world. One interesting trend that we see is that as a nation becomes more developed and more productive, its economic criminality increases and its criminality amongst persons decreases in proportion to each other. Overall, there is likely to be an increase of criminality, but as I said, there are some very important exceptions to it. Countries of all different kinds of ideologies and social economic systems are proof that the opposite might happen, but those are exceptions.

LEN: Does that come from the fact that in more economically advanced countries, it is easier to steal in more sophisticated ways rather than hitting someone on top of the head and taking a purse?

MUELLER: I don't think our data allow us to draw that conclusion. It might be a bit too fanciful, although there may well be a relationship with the amount of total wealth that is available. Opportunity, of course, is one of the factors: we can't steal automobiles unless there are automobiles, but that is too easy a correlation. I'm hesitant to pronounce that.

LEN: You mentioned that there is a large increase in female crime.

MUELLER: A larger increase than in male crime.

LEN: And you date that sometime around World War II when the female became a part of the work force. Could you expand on that?

MUELLER: Different countries have different trends at different times in history. Your reference to World War II is an interesting one, and Poland comes particularly to mind. With the taking of statistics, and the resumption of statistics taking in Poland in 1945 and 1946, there was a marked increase in female criminality, particularly in economic criminality. For several years this trend continued and it happens to coincide with the drawing of women into the labor force, which occurred at precisely those times. But then an interesting thing happened—it leveled off. After about eight or nine years, female criminality leveled off and went down to the pre-war level in relation to male criminality. What some of the highly industrialized countries are experiencing at this point is very similar. In those countries during the last five, six, or seven years, women were drawn in real masses into more important positions in the economic world, drawn out of the home. There are few housewives in relation to the total female population. You will find women as bank tellers, as bank presidents, as law enforcement officers, as airline pilots and whatever. And lo and behold, it turns out that as a woman is subjected to the same stresses and strains that males have traditionally been subject to, and given the same temptations and opportunities, they also tend to yield to those opportunities.

There is no reason why female bank presidents should be any more honest than male bank presidents. Apparently, we are experiencing something of that sort and it is interesting that a number of the western countries seem to be having the same experience.

LEN: Another one of your organization's mandates is to try and come up with what we call "replicable projects." In other words, you take a look at experiments that are being conducted throughout the world and determine if they have application in other places. Are there any outstanding crime prevention projects of which you are aware?

MUELLER: I could mention a couple that seem to have promise. One is the very large scale Japanese experiment with volunteers in probation and parole. For all practical purposes the individual parole officer servicing a client, a convict or an ex-con, is a private individual, just an ordinary citizen who has gone through evening classes and courses and who is being supervised by the

only professional, a parole or probation supervisor. The real day-to-day contact is done by a fellow citizen, and that seems to work like a charm. It also appears to be a lot cheaper than the system by which you use 40 trained professionals. This is a good, effective and successful form of popular participation. If it works in Japan, why can it not work somewhere else?

LEN: Why is it that a paraprofessional can be much more effective? Can you recruit more of them?

MUELLER: There are probably a number of reasons. One is the numbers game. Obviously as you know, there is one probation officer supervising 70 to 80 probationers and there's no contact—nothing takes place. In the Japanese experiment, a one-to-one relationship. But there may be other reasons why a volunteer with greater enthusiasm and undivided interest can have a greater impact on that individual. The volunteers may be less suspect vis-a-vis the probationer—that person doesn't really stand for government, state, police, or courts; he's just a citizen. So we have been trying to stimulate this kind of development in the countries that are too poor to have a one-to-one professional probation officer for each convict and this idea is catching on.

Another idea that may recommend itself is something that comes from indigenous society. Under some indigenous laws in Africa, for example, the punishment for what we would call atrocious assault or felonious assault is to nurse the victim back to health, while here in developed countries we've been desperately trying for years and years to find a victim compensation scheme that works. None has been invented that works. Here's a beauty. Why don't we try it? In lieu of sending the perpetrator to prison for a couple of years to sit there in idleness, to earn nothing, to cost the taxpayers, why not put him to work? He can restore the victim back to health, but not necessarily on a one-to-one relationship. The general idea, of course, is to utilize the energy of the perpetrator for restoration of the victim, and there are probably many other examples that would mandate that a perpetrator be responsible.

LEN: Is there any urban society that has used that last one with any kind of success?

MUELLER: Under their power to impose probation conditions, a number of judges, even in the United States have done things of that sort. We have a little file of the clippings and it's very interesting. After we publicize idea it has caught on here and there, but it does require power to impose probation conditions in urbanized today. Other than that, there has been no large experimentation, although there are different be victim compensation. In France, for example, the if a civil damage adjudication in the criminal part. The the perpetrator is found guilty of say atrocious, fendant judge is permitted to impose a court order for the rest of to pay a hundred dollars or a hundred franc his life.

19

1. CRIME AND JUSTICE IN AMERICA

LEN: Sweden has probably been one of the most progressive countries in the world in dealing with deviant individuals in society and a recent article in The New York Times stated that despite all of their progress in terms of helping individuals to correct their deviant ways, they haven't had too much success in terms of recidivism. Have you any views on that?

MUELLER: I must say I would have to look at Swedish recidivism rates. Off hand, I don't remember them. The Swedes, if I remember correctly, had a recidivism rate which was not better than the European recidivism rate as a whole. Maybe they're spending more money in crime prevention per capita than a comparable country further to the south. At the same time, they have fewer people in prison than many other countries. Finland, for example, has double the prison population of Sweden. You are driven to the conclusion that what they're doing is perhaps more humane. In other words, there are fewer prisoners languishing in prison. If you have two ways of achieving the same results, would you not rather pick the more humane way or the less humane way?

LEN: Not only that, it is probably the cheaper way in terms of what it costs to incarcerate a prisoner as compared to having a man on some sort of a work program or something like that.

MUELLER: You're quite right. On the whole it is true, although we have found that in countries with very low prison populations, the Netherlands for example, which has the lowest prison population in the world, the system spends a correspondingly larger amount on the criminal justice system in other forms. Then what you find is that there may not be less prison staff in the Netherlands than, say, in Finland, but there is more individual attention by correction officers toward the prisoners.

LEN: One of the big problems that we hear about, ~~larly~~ in the United States, is a general fear of ~~people~~ who have committed crimes to serve ~~sen~~tences or to be out on parole. Can you address ~~this~~ problem in terms of the social and economic ~~aspects~~ of crime? As a matter of fact, you talk about ~~measures~~ the feeling of anxiety among citizens in ~~cost~~ benefit analysis. How do you feel about the ~~belief~~ that people should be warehoused?

MUELLER: Well, very little real rehabilitation has ~~bui~~ endeavored, so there may have been ~~said~~ ~~pa~~rts of buildings that had a sign on them that ~~"~~rehabi~~litation~~ Center," but that doesn't mean that ~~rehabilitation~~ ~~ha~~s in fact taken place. If those systems did ~~not hav~~e ~~a noticeable~~ ~~measu~~rable effect, it should surprise no one. ~~Rehabilitation~~ ~~has~~ ~~frequently~~ as frequently been misdirected. It has ~~persons. If,~~ ~~t~~he wrong rehabilitation for the wrong ~~is at~~ ~~Alcoho~~l~~ics~~ ~~exa~~mple, the only rehabilitation in a prison ~~goes to~~ ~~rehabi~~l~~itati~~onymous once a week, then everybody ~~the day,~~ ~~includi~~ng ~~o~~n because it breaks the monotony of ~~the~~ ~~day,~~ ~~includi~~ng ~~those~~ who have no alcohol problems.

Okay, it's rehabilitation, but it's the wrong rehabilitation for the wrong people, so it cannot help. My answer would be real rehabilitation has not worked, because it really has not been undertaken. If warehousing were to help in crime control I would be all for it. We have no idea, either, that this works. In central Europe around the turn of the century, warehousing was the punishment. People were put away for fixed terms, but we have every indication that the crime rate in imperial Germany, for example, was higher than the crime rate is for the German republic today. Could we conclude therefrom that warehousing has an impact? We do know what kind of an impact warehousing does have on prisoners. They come out even more infantilized than they were to begin with, because they are told everything from morning routine to night routine. They're dependent to begin with, before they went into prison, but they're economic failures for the most part, now even softer rather than tougher once they're out, after having been warehoused. Some may have learned the tricks of the trade. All have made contact with friends and not the most desirable kind. If we look at the total picture, we are returning to imperial Germany, and all the other imperial countries who used warehousing to no good 70, 80 and 90 years ago.

LEN: Are there people who are not capable of being rehabilitated, and if they are, what do we do with them?

MUELLER: Undoubtedly, and this is why the General Assembly has approved, as one of the five major agenda items for discussion for the Sixth United Nations Congress for the Prevention of Crime and the Treatment of Offenders in Sydney, Australia, in 1980, the topic of the institutionalization of corrections and what to do with the residual prisoner. Here we're talking about the prisoner everybody fears, and no one knows what to do with. As countries are more and more successful in deinstitutionalizing corrections, they are increasingly concerned particularly with the residue of offenders. We don't know yet how to identify these people. We are very much concerned with the retrogressed types and so on, who have demonstrated to us that they are virtually unreachable by all the means of social control including control of the criminal justice system.

LEN: How about a person who has committed a very violent crime three or four times—a recidivist in that particular area?

MUELLER: Every society has a perfect right to do that. But even there I would review these cases, say at age 65 or certainly after. There is every reason to review such cases, but there will be some who will have to remain in safekeeping for the rest of their lives. But we don't quite know yet—who they are. We're probably overdoing it. We're keeping more in prison than should be there. That's why I'm asking the question: what can be done with that kind of Offender? A lot of prison wardens will tell you, "Hey, you can't take all the good guys away from me. I need some of those sofites around." With that I cannot sympathize. That's not the purpose of prisons—to put good guys into prison. It isn't worth the money then.

LEN: So you do feel they should be segregated?

MUELLER: Well, segregated in a sense. I wouldn't put non-dangerous persons in prison in the first place. But that is another question because we don't know yet.

LEN: During the recent power blackout in New York City, there was a two-day rampage of looting and burning by certain individuals in certain communities. Many of the newspapers portrayed the police as standing by and watching without too much in terms of alternatives. They couldn't arrest all of the looters because there simply weren't enough police officers. What kind of reaction did this situation get in the foreign press and among foreign police officials?

MUELLER: There was not too much surprise at this situation. There had been surprise 12 years earlier during the first blackout in New York, when virtually no crime took place. There was a standstill in crime which surprised the world tremendously. Well, weather conditions played a role there, all kinds of other things played a role. But I must say that was surprising to everybody in law enforcement.

The reaction this time was within the normal range which we have noticed elsewhere in the world. A similar particularly striking example was noted in Montreal. There, the officers were out on strike, which in effect meant that the criminal justice system was suspended and looting took place. Everybody settled their grievances in

more or less violent form. Firebombing of stores took place where people felt they had been badly treated. It is more or less a normal reaction. I don't think the police can be blamed very much for the fact that they were under-staffed and could not handle the problems. It would be dangerous for one or two officers to go into a crowd of 1,000 milling people, some of whom are armed, to stop the riots, looting and so on. The fault probably lies with management. That may be the fault of citywide management or statewide management in not providing for emergency planning which would have put adequate protection into the affected areas.

LEN: In many instances, the reason given for the looting and the burning in the second blackout was the fact that the neighborhoods had broken down and there was no form of social control. Are you saying that this is pretty much the condition in most urban areas of the world?

MUELLER: You have every reason to believe that precisely that takes precedence. One more example is of a really highly civilized country, Denmark. When the Nazis occupied Denmark in 1944 and arrested the Danish police department, the theft rate and the burglary rate increased tenfold in a cool, calm, civilized country like Denmark. Of course, it does something. It does something everywhere.

There is something to the value of having a criminal justice system, a law enforcement system. Moral values alone cannot govern a society. Strength is necessary, and that strength can come only from the criminal justice system. You take a light; you switch it off. It is no longer there and the flood gates may open.

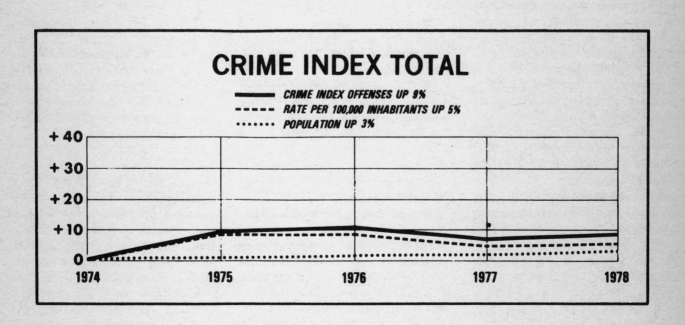

CRIME INDEX TOTAL

— CRIME INDEX OFFENSES UP 9%
----- RATE PER 100,000 INHABITANTS UP 5%
······ POPULATION UP 3%

Crime in the Suites

Will Congress Go Easy on Corporate Crooks?

Jack Newfield

I see no reason why big-shot crooks should go free while the poor ones go to jail.

—Jimmy Carter
Madison Square Garden
July 15, 1976

Why do successful politicians and sophisticated corporate executives take the risk of breaking the law?

The reason, I think, is that the American legal system is so domi-ᶜ by money, elitism, and politics that powerful people know that even if they are somehow caught and convicted, they are unlikely to go to prison. It is this absence of certainty of punishment that makes white-collar crime and political corruption such a tempting proposition.

● Joel Dolkart, a lawyer and a director of Gulf & Western, stole $2.5 million from two law firms. He got a suspended sentence.

● Yankee president and ship building executive George Steinbrenner was indicted on 14 felony counts, including coercing his own employees to lie to the FBI. His maximum legal exposure was 55 years in prison. He ended up pleading guilty to two counts and paying a $15,000 fine.

● New Jersey congressman Henry Helstoski was indicted for accepting bribes over an eight-year period from resident aliens in return for introducing bills to improve their immigration status. The case never went to trial because the courts ruled that the government could not use as evidence any of the bills the congressman sponsored. They also ruled that members of Congress have immunity from being questioned about their actions on the floor of the congress.

● Vice-president Spiro Agnew pleaded "no contest" to an indictment that charged him with accepting cash bribes in the White House. He did not go to jail for a day.

● Attorney General Richard Kleindeinst pleaded guilty to lying to a Senate committee. He got a suspended sentence.

● Congressman James Jones of Oklahoma pleaded guilty in 1976 to a misdemeanor charge of failing to report a cash contribution from Gulf Oil. Jones was fined $200. He is now the most effective and respected champion of oil interests in the House of Representatives.

● CIA director Richard Helms pleaded "no contest" to a federal indictment that accused him of lying to the Senate of the United States when he testified under oath that the CIA did not participate in the coup against Salvador Allende of Chile. Helms's punishment was a $2000 fine and one year of unsupervised probation. Afterwards Helms said he would wear his perjury conviction "like a badge of honor."

● Congressman Joshua Eilberg was indicted on conflict-of-interest charges based on his law firm receiving $500,000 in legal fees from a hospital that, with Eilberg's influence, was built with federal funds. Eilberg pleaded guilty and was fined $10,000.

● The Westinghouse Corporation pleaded guilty to paying $323,000 in bribes to a former deputy prime minister of Egypt to win a $30 million contract. The penalty was a $300,000 fine—less than the bribe.

● The Lockheed Corporation pleaded guilty to paying $2.6 million in bribes to Japanese government and business officials to facilitate the sale of 21 planes. Lockheed's penalty was a $647,000 fine, and no punishment for any individuals. The Lockheed Corporation made a substantial profit on the bribery, even though caught. Moreover, the two Lockheed officers who approved the foreign payoffs before they were made— company president Carl Kotchian and board chairman Daniel Haughton—have recently been re-hired by Lockheed's new management as "consultants."

● Sixteen major corporations, including such giants as Gulf Oil, Phillips Petroleum, American Airlines, and Diamond International, have pleaded guilty to making illegal

 "Crime in the Suites," by Jack Newfield, *The Village Voice*, October 29, 1979. Reprinted by permission.

political contributions and maintaining secret slush funds. All were let off with trivial fines, only one of which exceeded $5000, and no individuals were held accountable.

● The Ford Motor Company knew for eight years that the improper location and design of the gas tank made their Pinto models unsafe at any speed. An estimated 500 people have been killed in fiery Pinto rear-end collisions. According to internal corporate memos published last week by the *Chicago Tribune,* Ford executives knew *before* marketing the Pinto that its design was more vulnerable to fire in low-speed, rear-end crashes than other designs. One confidential memo written shortly before the Pinto went on sale recommended that an $8 part, which would have reduced fire risks, *not* be added to the car until 1976, to save the corporation $20.6 million. Another memo conceded that some safety test results were suppressed by the company.

Yet no individual corporate official has been indicted for this deadly cover-up, although a criminal case pending in Indiana does charge the corporate entity with reckless homicide.

● For 20 years the Hooker Chemical Company poured poisonous toxic wastes into Love Canal. The company knew this dumping was a severe health hazard, but did nothing to warn residents about the dangers. This year health officials ordered an evacuation and closed two schools after alarming rates of illness and disease were reported. No official of Hooker Chemical has been prosecuted under criminal law.

● Three years ago, the Allied Chemical Corporation pleaded "no contest" to civil charges that it dumped large amounts of the toxic chemical Kepone into the James River in Virginia. Hundreds, and possibly thousands of citizens were made sick. But no executive of Allied Chemical was prosecuted. It is now estimated that it will cost *$8 billion* to clean up the contamination.

The SEC has referred to the Justice Department more than 400 cases involving illegal payments by American corporations. More than one-third of *Fortune* magazine's 500 biggest corporations have admitted to making illegal or improper payments in foreign countries, totaling more than $1 billion. Ten corporations have pleaded guilty to making illegal domestic or foreign payoffs. And not one corporate official has been prosecuted individually.

I broach these examples of permissiveness toward respectable lawbreakers because the Congress will soon have a chance to do something about them.

The federal criminal code is once again up for debate and revision in both the House and the Senate. The two previous attempts at this monumental task ended in deadlock and failure. Fortunately, neither S. 1, which was introduced on January 4, 1973, or S. 1437, which was introduced in January of 1977, ever became law. S. 1437, sponsored by Edward Kennedy and the late John McClellan, passed the Senate 72 to 15 on January 30, 1978. But civil liberties advocates were tenacious enough to kill this repressive law in the House.

Now both the Senate Judiciary Committee and the House subcommitee on criminal justice have produced "rough drafts" of new omnibus criminal code recodification bills. The committees held public hearings in September, and the Senate Judiciary Committee will begin marking the bill up on November 5.

Both drafts have strengths and weaknesses. Both avoid the emotional issues of the death penalty and gun control. Both reduce the possible criminal "states of mind" from more than 60 to just four—intentional, knowing, reckless, and negligent. The Senate version now eliminates the onerous section of S. 1437 that made "failure to obey a public safety order" a crime. The American Civil Liberties Union (ACLU) had objected to this provision, pointing out that it could be used to prevent picketing, distributing leaflets, or parading. It still

contains, however, other concepts that do threaten individual rights and liberties.

But in this article I want to focus on one limited aspect of the vast and highly technical Senate and House bills—how they will affect the laws governing corporate crime, organized crime, labor racketeering, and public corruption. In this area, much to my surprise and disappointment, the House draft, the responsibility of subcommittee chairman Representative Robert Drinan, is significantly inferior to the Senate draft that is cosponsored by Judiciary Committee chairman Edward Kennedy and senior Republican Strom Thurmond.

● The Drinan bill (S. 1722) would shorten the statute of limitations from five years to two years on several white collar crimes, including labor bribery, tax misdemeanors, and many regulatory offenses. It would also transform numerous federal false-statement felonies into misdemeanors. Many white collar paper crimes are highly complex and take years to investigate adequately. The two-year limit will be a big advantage to the crooked politician or businessman.

● The Drinan bill contains lower fine levels than the Senate bill (S. 1723), and lower fines than those suggested by the Justice Department. The bill provides for maximum fines for Title 18 felonies of *$100,000* and makes no distinction between corporations and individuals. The Justice Department has recommended that maximum fines for felony convictions be set at *$1 million* for corporations and $250,000 for individuals. The recently passed Foreign Corrupt Practices Act set a maximum fine of $1 million for international corporate payoffs. Thus, under the Drinan bill, the more serious crime of bribing a United States official would be punishable by a penalty only *one-tenth* that for bribing a foreign official.

● The Drinan bill eliminates three major federal criminal statutes frequently used to prosecute politicians. It eliminates an interpretation of the Hobbs Act under which

1. CRIME AND JUSTICE IN AMERICA

Governor David Hall of Oklahoma, Mayor Hugh Addonizzio of Newark, and the chairman of the Iowa Liquor Control Commission were convicted of federal crimes. It also removes from the federal law the precise mail fraud and wire fraud provisions that led to the conviction of Maryland Governor Marvin Mandel, the state treasurer of West Virginia, and the Clerk of Cook County, Illinois.

● The Drinan bill limits the federal jurisdiction in investigating state and local corruption. This is critical because in many places the local political machine controls the local district attorneys offices and, especially in one-party areas, the guilty politicians can cover-up investigations. The interstate extortion, bribery, and graft provision of the Drinan bill only covers "a state (or local) *elected* public servant, judge, or law enforcement officer." It curbs the federal government's role in investigating nonelected party officials like Joe Margiotta and Meade Esposito, who influence elected representatives. And it limits investigations into appointed officials who decide zoning variances, franchises, concessions, casino gambling and liquor licenses, government back deposits, land acquisitions, tax assessments, paroles, and other discretionary areas of traditional graft. The Justice Department is trying to play this loophole by extending the interpretation of the Hobbs Act to clearly cover party leaders.

● The Drinan bill contains no provision for permitting the federal government to appeal sentences that are unreasonably and unjustifiably lenient in white-collar crime cases. In the Senate bill, the government is allowed to appeal if the sentence is less than the sentence prescribed in the guidelines.

● The Drinan bill eliminates from the criminal code an almost 100-year-old provision that penalizes conspiracies to defraud the federal government. Brooklyn Councilman Sam Wright was convicted under this provision of the existing law. So was Martin Sweig, an aide to House Speaker John McCormack.

● The Drinan bill eliminates the Travel Act jurisdiction over commercial bribery, and appears to reinterpret or eliminate a significant aspect of the mail-and-wire-fraud law under which several major corporate prosecutions have been brought.

● There are also two important omissions in the Drinan bill. There is no "reckless endangerment" provision, under which corporations like Ford, Hooker Chemical, Allied Chemical, and those responsible for the Three Mile Island nuclear accident might be prosecuted for "regulatory crimes."

The draft of the Kennedy bill does contain a reckless endangerment provision (Section 1617) that covers blatant environmental pollution, illegally dumping toxic chemicals, violating nuclear safety regulations, and knowingly marketing dangerous products like the Pinto. The current Senate draft says that if a person "places another person in danger of imminent death or serious bodily injury," he will be guilty of a Class D felony, punishable of up to six years in prison, "if the circumstances manifest extreme indifference to human life." This section also provides for up to three years in prison for other environmental corruption.

A separate bill in this area (H.R. 4973) has been drafted by congressmen John Conyers of Michigan and George Miller of California. Their bill would establish higher fines and minimum two-year prison terms for corporate officials who conceal information about dangerous products or working conditions. This bill was introduced on July 26, and its co-sponsors include Representatives Dellums, Eckhardt, Holtzman, Ottinger, Solarz, Downey, Weiss, and even conservative Long Island Republican Norman Lent.

The Drinan draft also lacks a consumer fraud section, which is covered by S. 1739 in the Kennedy bill. This provision would make it a federal misdemeanor to falsely advertise with intent to deceive or defraud the purchase. When Mark Green, the director of Ralph Nader's Congress

Watch, testified on September 20, he pointed out this omission:

"It is appropriate to provide for misdemeanor sanctions for the kind of deception that injures honest competitors and poisons the foundations of the market-place premised on aware consumers."

The essential case against the House draft was best summed up by Philip Heymann, the chief of the Justice Department's criminal division, when he testified before Drinan's own subcommittee on September 6. Heymann said:

"Although I do not believe that the subcommittee intends to undercut our efforts to fight white-collar crime, public corruption, organized crime, or narcotics trafficking, I believe that the current subcommittee draft would have just that effect.

"In addition, in my view, the subcommittee has thus far failed to make a number of improvements in the law that have been widely endorsed, and that would facilitate our efforts in these priority areas."

●

The apparent role being played by Father Robert Drinan is astonishing to all of us who have followed his political career. In 1978, Drinan, Elizabeth Holtzman, and Senator Howard Metzenbaum received a 98 per cent rating from Nader's Public Citizen, based on an analysis of 40 key roll call votes. Drinan was an early and trenchant critic of the Vietnam war, and he was the first member of Congress to introduce a resolution calling for the impeachment of Richard Nixon.

Drinan supported the extension of the deadline for passage of the Equal Rights Amendment. He sponsored legislation to place strict limits on searches of newspaper offices. He led the fight to abolish the House Internal Security Committee. He led the fight for effective gun control legislation. He has been a persistant critic of abuses by the CIA, and once sponsored a resolution calling for the impeachment of Richard Helms.

At first glance it appeared that Drinan's draft might represent some misguided, purist sense of civil liberties. But I can find no civil libertarian principles that would justify these particular weaker penalties and weaker laws to cope with white-collar crime.

Another possible explanation is that Drinan doesn't control his own subcommittee, and doesn't agree with this legislation that bears his sponsorship.

This theory could have an element of truth. Drinan took over the subcommittee chair in January from Representative James Mann of South Carolina, who retired. The committee has only one holdover from the last congress—Representative Sam Hall of Texas, who is a wealthy businessman of conservative views.

An insider, close to the drafting of the bill, told me:

"Don't be hard on Drinan. It's not his fault. It's just that he is not as experienced as Kennedy, and so he hasn't been able to build a coalition within his committee. Kennedy has been able to bring Thurmond and [Orin] Hatch along with him, and Drinan is stuck with a bunch of cavemen. Drinan is not probusiness. His only weakness is that he is irrationally hostile to law enforcement. On the Senate side, Thurmond and Hatch probably love the FBI as much as they love business, so Kennedy can work with them on white-collar crime issues. But I think, when the bill reaches the full judiciary committee, Drinan will be liberated from his subcommittee, and he will be fine on this issue."

If Drinan does have private doubts or disagreements, he should soon make them public and join forces with the Justice Department and Kennedy to make the code tougher on "bigshot crooks." There is no justification for him not accepting provisions endorsed by conservatives like Senator Thurmond and Representative Lent.

Interviews with staff members of the Senate and House judiciary committees, and with public interest watchdogs, suggest the most likely

Crime in the Suites

The Business Roundtable has been leading the lobbying effort to weaken the sanctions for white-collar crime in the new Federal Criminal Code. Ralph Nader's Public Citizen has compiled a study showing that 51 of the Roundtable's member corporations have admitted making illegal or improper payments. The study was based on files in the Justice Department's antitrust division, the Federal Trade Commission, and the SEC. What follows is a list of the 51 corporations, their payments, and the source of the data.

Company	Date	Amount	Nature of Payments	Source
Alcoa	1972-74	$4,000,000	foreign payments from secret fund	CiB p. 147
American Home Products	1971-75	$6,462,000	foreign political contributions	SEC
Boeing Co.	1970-75	$70,000,000	foreign commissions	CiB p. 141
Carrier Corp.	1972-75	$2,614,000	foreign commissions	SEC
Chrysler	1971-76	$2,438,000	secret funds abroad foreign payments	6/77 8K
Cities Service	1971-75	$1,049,400	foreign payments	CEP
Dresser Industries	1971-75	$24,000	payments to foreign officials	SEC
Exxon	1963-75	$56,771,000	foreign political contribs.	SEC
FMC	1973-75	$200,000	foreign payments to secure sales	CiB p. 141
Ford Motor Co.	1973-74	$60,000	payments to foreign political parties	CiB p. 144
General Tire & Rubber	1950s-75	$1,349,000	foreign and domestic political payments	SEC
B.F. Goodrich Co.	1971-75	$124,000	foreign commissions	SEC
Goodyear Tire & Rubber	1970-75	$846,000	payments to foreign officials	SEC
Gulf Oil Corp.	1960-73	$6,900,000	foreign political contribs.	CiB p. 158
Ingersoll-Rand	1971-75	$797,000	payments acknowledged but not described	CEP
Koppers Co.	1971-75	$1,500,000	foreign payments	CEP
Kraftco Corp.	1969-75	$699,500	foreign payments	SEC
	1972-76	$550	domestic campaign contributions	SEC
3M Co.	1963-72	$545,799	secret fund for domestic political campaign contribs.	SEC
	1975	$52,000	foreign payments	SEC
Reynolds Metals Co.	since 1970	N.A.	undisclosed amounts to foreign political parties	CiB, p. 147
R. J. Reynolds Ind.	1968-73	$190,000	payments to Presidential and Congressional candidates, disguised by diverting royalties	CiB p. 148
	since 1968	5,500,000	payments to foreign officials and governments, disguised on books as commissions	CiB p. 148
	1971-75	$19,000,000	foreign rebates to shippers by SeaLand, a subsidiary	CiB p. 148
Rockwell Int'l	1971-75	$676,300	foreign payments to secure sales	SEC
Standard Oil Co., of Ind.	1970-75	$1,359,400	foreign payments	SEC
Tenneco Inc.	N.A.	$865,480	foreign payments	SEC
AMAX Inc.	1972-76	$64,877	foreign payments	CEP
Armco Steel Corp.	1971-75	$18,060,000	foreign payments	CEP
Atlantic Richfield	1969-76	$262,000	foreign payments	CEP
Boise Cascade	1971-76	$340,100	foreign payments	CEP
Champion International	1971-75	$537,000	foreign payments	CEP
Clark Equipment	1971-76	$95,000	foreign payments	CEP
Coca-Cola	N.A.	$300,000	foreign payments	CEP
Dart Industries	1971-76	$126,000	foreign payments	CEP
Dow Chemical	N.A.	$2,500	foreign payments	CEP
Firestone Tire & Rubber	1970-76	$97,000	foreign payments	CEP
GAF Industries	N.A.	N.A.		CEP
General Electric	1972-75	$550,000	foreign payments	CEP

(continued on next page)

1. CRIME AND JUSTICE IN AMERICA

cause of Drinan's fine Jesuit's mind suddenly turning to mush:

The awesomely influential Business Roundtable, consisting of the chief executive officers of 192 corporations and banks, has mounted a subtle and high-class lobbying blitz on the criminal code legislation. The Roundtable avoids publicity. It has a budget of $3 million, but it does not go in for splashy advertising campaigns or direct mailings. It includes the chairmen of such corporations as Exxon, General Motors, AT&T, Coca Cola, Westinghouse, and Citibank, and through direct, private access it has become the most effective corporate lobbying instrument. Most observers believe it was the Roundtable that killed the Consumer Protection Agency, that gutted lobbying disclosure legislation, and that made sure that last year's tax bill contained plenty of what businessmen like to call "capital formation incentives."

Two full-time, professional lawyer-lobbyists on the staff of the Business Roundtable have been working on Drinan and his committee all year. They have visited each member. They have submitted thousands of pages of comments, making sophisticated legal arguments against prison terms for white-collar offenses, against a reckless-endangerment section, against a consumer fraud section, against any new laws that would hold corporate officers accountable as individuals for their actions. These submissions are dated April 6, 1978; April 28, 1978; May 22, 1978; February 27, 1979; April 17, 1979; and April 24, 1979. They are on file with the House and Senate judiciary committees.

On September 20 of this year, Irving Shapiro testified before the Senate Judiciary Committee. Shapiro is the chairman and chief

General Foods	1971-76	$162,751	foreign payments	CEP
H. J. Heinz	1971-76	N.A.	foreign payments	CEP
Hercules, Inc.	1971-75	$597,000	foreign payments	CEP
Marcor Inc. (Mobil)	1971-76	$635,517	foreign payments	CEP
Mobil Oil	1970-73	$2,000,000	foreign contributions to Italian political parties	N.A.
Monsanto	1971-76	$533,300	foreign payments	CEP
J. C. Penney	1971-75	$373,000	foreign payments	CEP
Ralston Purina	1970-76	$154,000	foreign payments	CEP
Scott Paper	1971-76	$229,000	foreign payments	CEP
Shell Oil	1969-73	$6,600,000	Royal Dutch Shell & British Petroleum to Italian pol. parties	N.A.
Stauffer Chemical	1975-76	$7,500	foreign payments	CEP
Weyerhaeuser	1971-76	$1,180,000	foreign payments	CEP
White Motor	1971-76	$1,016,000	foreign payments	CEP
Xerox Corporation	1971-75	$100,000	foreign payments	CEP
United Aircraft	1973-75	$2,040,000	sales fees to foreign government employees or officials	SEC
Westinghouse Electric	N.A.	$323,000	foreign payments	SEC

*Key: SEC-Report of the Securities and Exchange to the U.S. Senate Committee on Banking Housing and Urban Affairs, May 1976; CiB- *Corruption in Business* (New York: Facts on File, 1977); CEP- *The Invisible Hand: Questionable Corporate Payments Overseas* (New York: Council on Economic Priorities, 1976); 8K or 10K-Forms filed with SEC on dates indicated.

executive officer of E.I. DuPont Corporation. He is also the past chairman of the Business Roundtable. He read a long prepared statement that made it very clear that corporate America understood it had millions of dollars at stake in the lawyerly colloquy over the technical sentences in the 266 pages of S. 1723 and S. 1722.

Big business, in fact, has been as aggressively attentive to this year's criminal code debate as civil liberties groups have been in the past.

Mark Green's job is to monitor Congress for the Nader movement. He is also the author of several books, including *Who Runs Congress?* and is one of the most perceptive critics of corporate power. His analysis of the criminal code legislation is this:

"The Kennedy bill is preferable in terms of corporate sanctions. Drinan bent to the Business Roundtable arguments, and perhaps to the conservative composition of his subcommittee."

●

It seems obvious that something drastic ought to be done to deter America's establishment crime wave. Thirteen members of the 95th Congress have been indicted, which means the arrest rate among congressmen is higher than the arrest rate among unemployed black males under 18. The SEC says that more than 400 corporations have made illegal or improper payments. Even the *New York Times,* in an unusually indignant editorial on May 1, 1979, called for stronger sanctions against white-collar crimes and corporate misconduct.

The attempt to draft a new federal criminal code is the current vehicle for coping with society's big-shot crooks. At this early stage in the legislative process, the Drinan subcommittee, for whatever reason, has become a barrier to the goal of making justice collar blind as well as color blind.

Why the Cops Can't Catch the Mob

Nicholas Pileggi

Nicholas Pileggi is a contributing editor of New York *Magazine.*

Across the street from the Provenzano Lanza Funeral Home, on the glass-strewn sidewalk and in seedy tenements on lower Second Avenue, a group of law-enforcement officials gathered the other week to pay their respects to departed "godfather" Carmine Galante. In the tropical heat of this hazy July day, the local and federal agents focused telephoto lenses on the slow trickle of mourners who entered the undertaking emporium to visit the remains of the man whose quest for mob power ended in a barrage of gunfire in the rear garden of a small Italian restaurant in Bushwick.

Spying on mob funerals is a tradition as old as those flower-laden, grandiose affairs themselves. The difference this time was that the cops seemed like a group of alumni showing up at the wrong class reunion. These governmental voyeurs didn't know who the mourners were: a familiar face, an easily identifiable relative, but little more. And this wasn't merely because Galante's own men had presumably done the deadly deed and therefore saw no point in attending this parricidal wake. The reason was that law-enforcement officials simply don't know anymore just who the bad guys are.

Because despite the daily stream of news stories filled with lurid details of underworld conferences, notwithstanding the picturesque accounts of celebratory luncheons and authoritative-sounding speculation about the assassination, there's been one piece of information about Carmine Galante's killing that law-enforcement officials are desperately trying to keep quiet. It has nothing to do with the fact that they don't expect to convict anyone for the killing: After all, no assassin of a gangland boss has ever been jailed for such a crime.

The deep secret law-enforcement officials are trying to keep from the public and, most important, from the mob is that they no longer know what's going on.

The Galante killing has laid bare the fact that the feds—in the form of the Federal Bureau of Investigation and the Department of Justice—as well as the New York Police Department, are no longer privy to the kinds of intimate mob information that they had during the 1960s following Attorney General Robert Kennedy's decision to make fighting organized crime a priority issue.

Today, while authorities insist that they are just as involved in mob control, the truth is that they have severely cut back the kind of manpower employed in intelligence gathering, surveillance, and collating data. Where, for instance, the FBI once had five units of at least 25 men and one supervisor each matched to the city's five organized-crime families, today, though the FBI denies it, there are only 12 agents officially assigned to organized crime here. To make matters worse, almost all of their work is done at their desks at 26 Federal Plaza.

How seriously the situation has deteriorated may be illustrated this way. Recently, a well-known mob prosecutor was strolling in Little Italy. As he approached the corner of Mulberry and Hester streets, he walked passed a cluster of mob hoods, one of whom called out, "Hey, chief, how's crime?" Failing to recognize any of those gathered, the prosecutor simply gave the heckler his standard campaign smile and handshake and continued on his way to court.

Aside from the street surveillance and electronic eavesdropping currently being employed by agents for the U.S. Drug Enforcement Administration, there are virtually no federal agents keeping tabs on hoods for purely intelligence purposes. Even Carmine Galante—who the feds themselves insisted was the subject of a possible murder plot last October—was no longer the subject of surveillance at the time of his death.

"We are just not doing that kind of thing anymore. It wasn't productive enough," an Organized Crime Strike Force (OCSF) commander recently said. "Now we have intelligence groups that are collecting selective intelligence directed toward specific areas, not people."

As things now stand, our public guardians no longer have any independent intelligence on the local organized-crime chiefs, and even more significantly, they do not know anything about a whole generation of young mobsters

—many of them illegal aliens brought over from Sicily by crime bosses such as Galante—who have unquestionably begun moving in on rackets previously thought the turf of American-born hoods. For instance, there are shakedowns and takeovers of construction unions throughout the area involving foreign-born gangsters that have the feds and local police totally confused. These new hoods, the foundation of organized crime today, are also involved in everything from importing cocaine and freighters full of marijuana to murder, pizza joints, airport heists, discos, counterfeiting hit records, labor racketeering, and consumer frauds. Arthur Grubet, who headed the city's organized-crime intelligence units in the early seventies, admitted that his men "were losing track of mob operations" because more and more of the new arrivals were taking over the street operations. Many of these imported hoods began working immediately as enforcers in the Brooklyn mob, and in fact, one of the reasons why Galante was so intensely disliked by many of his American-born underlings was that he preferred foreign-born hoods to Yanks.

"They seem to be valued because they are homegrown—from the old country—and because they're disciplined," said Denis Dillon, onetime chief of Brooklyn's OCSF. "I can't tell what's going through their minds, but it seems that the old bosses don't feel that the second-generation Italians are good enough."

Despite this, despite warnings from the OCSF as far back as 1971 about this new generation, there is still no overall intelligence keeping an eye on these hoods or their inner connections. Indeed, after the Galante slaying, investigative agents tried to seek out information in numerous mob hangouts that had been closed or abandoned for years. Identifying some figures possibly involved in the Galante hit was complicated by the fact that many of the photos of hoods in law-enforcement files are 20 or 30 years out of date.

"Intelligence work and the daily surveillance of these guys may not have helped us put one of them in jail at the end of the day," Ralph Salerno, a retired Police Department organized-crime expert, recently said, "but it helped us to understand everything."

In contrast, today, law enforcement understands almost nothing.

"It's so bad that they don't even know the name of anybody in the mob under the age of 40. Look at the names they keep giving to the press. Those names have been around for 50 years. I see them using intelligence data about these guys I worked on, personally, ten and fifteen years ago." The man speaking is a former federal agent, who, like so many others involved with organized-crime prosecution, is frustrated by the current state of affairs.

"We used to follow those wise guys from morning till night. We lived with them. We listened to their wives complain. We clocked them with their girl friends. It got to be that you almost felt you knew as much about the guy you were watching as you know about yourself. I mean, after a while you knew what was going to make him mad or happy or mean.

"If another agent came up and said they heard your guy was moving into this or that and it didn't jibe with what you knew, I can't tell you how much spun rubber and wasted time that would save.

"But the most important thing we had," the former agent continued, "was that we were listening in—sometimes not so kosher—and we were watching and we had an independent basis for coming to conclusions about what was or what was not happening. Today, and don't let anyone say different, it's all informant information and they have no way of corroborating what they're being spoon-fed." Bureau-

cratic restraints have also become so depressing to many agents—who cheerfully recount how things were in times past—that the most experienced men are anxiously counting the days till their retirement.

"The way things work now," another federal agent said, "nobody really wants you to do a job because they'll have to make decisions and nobody in power wants to make decisions. They're all scared of each other and they all are worried about such *major* things as getting transferred before their kids graduate from school or losing the office with the window on the park or getting indicted because they did or didn't do something years ago that had to do with a bunch of draft-card burners.

"How the hell can we go out and make cases when we don't even have enough cars? And on top of that, we got this supersecret memo from the White House that says one car from each unit has to stay in the garage one day a week for the duration of the fuel shortage."

The New York Police Department has also run out of gas and, if possible, is in even worse shape. Where they once had scores of men concentrating on learning everything they could about each organized-crime member, today, street-level intelligence gathering has been severely curtailed.

"You know what they're doing over at Vandam Street now?" one former detective asked, referring to the location of the police intelligence unit. "They're clipping newspapers and stamping them 'Confidential.' "

While the former detective's criticism was perhaps tinged with the exaggeration of bitterness, the city's organized-crime intelligence unit has been pretty much out of business since 1973, when it was merged with the Bureau of Special Services into a unified Intelligence Division. The Bureau of Special Services (known within the department as "Bossi" and outside as "The Red Squad") originally concentrated on political surveillance, the protection of visiting dignitaries, and reporting on labor disputes.

"A little after we merged," the detective continued, "all that stuff came down about illegal political surveillance, about black-bag jobs, about opening people's mail. The criticism and lawsuits were almost all dumped on the feds, mostly the FBI, but the local police brass got so nervous that they decided to not only cut out spying on the Weathermen and Socialist Workers party, but they gave up spying on the mob as well."

An organized-crime intelligence unit that was made up of about 80 highly experienced specialists was essentially disbanded. Men who had previously spent all of their time keeping tabs on the comings and goings of key mobsters soon found themselves sitting on security details for visiting diplomats in the lobby of the Waldorf Towers or transferred to sex-crime squads or neighborhood precincts. As the extent of illicit police activities became publicized during Watergate, activities undertaken to legitimately protect the public were discarded along with those which abused the civil liberties of ordinary citizens.

In addition, budget constraints and strict enforcement of the city's labor contracts have made on-site inspection of mob facilities almost impossible. Detectives assigned to street surveillance of mob figures have always had to play loose with the time clock. The unofficial agreement with the detectives assigned to such surveillance—which might go from 6:30 A.M. to 3 A.M.—was to give the men compensating time off, but not hour-for-hour compensation.

"In those days you'd work twelve, sixteen hours on a guy," one detective said, "but the adrenaline was pumping and you didn't mind. Then, when you wanted to take a day or so off toward an early slide on your vacation or you wanted to watch your kids in the school play, you could almost always work out the time.

"Today, that is no longer possible," the detective continued, "and surveillance is just too expensive. For instance, if you're watching a guy and he leaves the house around 7:30 in the morning, you better be there at 6:30 or you might find yourself sitting on his house all day without knowing he decided to leave just five minutes before you got there. Also, where we were once able to cover one guy with four men by working overtime, today you've got to call in after your eight-hour tour and four more guys have to replace you, so you've essentially doubled the manpower need."

It has been the loss of precisely this kind of immediate, daily, street-level information that has become most evident during the current Galante investigation. The average "made man" or certified organized-crime hood spends a great deal of his time driving or being driven from one location to another, having coffee in Little Italy, a piece of fruit outside Prisco's on East 106th Street, a slice of pizza on East Tremont Avenue, picking up and passing along bits and pieces of gossip. This oral tradition, which has hoods traveling between boroughs and neighborhoods to keep in touch with their world—phones were too chancy and the media failed to provide the kind of insular detail they required—has been perfect as far as the police were concerned because it has always allowed them to recognize and chart the habits of hundreds of mobsters. Detectives who were on surveillance assignments regularly got to know if Fat Gigi was losing weight, if Johnny Lamps grew a mustache, if Big Head was driving Cheech's car, if Johnny Hooks got a "TV anchorman" haircut. None of these critical little details, of course, can be garnered from behind a desk.

In addition to inexperienced surveillance teams, a toughening of electronic-surveillance laws and their stricter interpretation by judges have also made keeping tabs on the hoods more difficult. Before the tougher laws went into effect, there were literally hundreds of legal and illegal (or "gypsy") telephone taps and bugs picking up an avalanche of invaluable raw data, mob arguments, gossip, and the like. During the bugging boom of the sixties, the police knew more about the total mob picture in New York than the hoods themselves, since the cops had access to information from all of the different crime families, while the mobsters were usually limited to information about their own particular families and interests.

Today, before a detective can install a listening device in any mob hangout, he must be able to convince a judge that he has "exhausted" all other methods of obtaining information in connection with a pending crime. He must be able to prove and swear in court that he had the mobster and the illegal activity under surveillance for some period of time as well as on a number of separate occasions. And even when judges do allow for electronic surveillance today, if information pertaining to the alleged crime is revealed on the second or third day, the wire must be closed down immediately, even if the court order allows for 30 or 60 days.

"We had a bug, one of our last really good ones," one city detective said, "in an Avenue B bar and grill, that turned up 50 convictions. During that wire we had twenty

city cops and twenty feds working the place. When we put the bug in we had to break in through the back door. That kind of stuff makes people skittish today, even though the Supreme Court now says it was okay to pick a lock or break into a place if you had a court order.

"This bar got us a counterfeit case, drugs, an attempted murder, stolen airline tickets, stolen securities, and beatings. On the very first day the first call that came in was a request for somebody to destroy garbage trucks in New Jersey. There were calls coming in from Las Vegas, Tokyo, and Italy. Somebody called with stolen securities from a Vatican bank, and the Vegas call asked a New York guy to collect $25,000 for them and keep $5,000. The ex-husband of a quite well-known singer was called in Vegas and told to go to California and beat up a guy. When he asked how serious a job was wanted, the guy in our bar said, 'Nothing serious. Just a little slap job.'" Getting such data today would be nearly impossible.

Part of the law-enforcement establishment's reluctance to amass huge dossiers on mobsters has to do with the federal Freedom of Information (FOI) Act and the fact that organized-crime lawyers have been filing FOI requests for their clients—and receiving the fruits of their queries. Some federal agents suspect that the large number of homicides involving informants may have come about as a result of mobsters' being able to deduce from their own dossiers which associates were talking to the government.

But it is not simply the courts and invasion of privacy laws which have made life easier for the New York mob; it is the dangerous and protective rivalries among the various law-enforcement branches. The city police and the FBI, for instance, have rarely cooperated with each other, a situation which tends to leave one agency in the dark about its brother agency's doings.

An example of this was brought home in the fallout from the Galante murder, when the *Daily News* headlined a story about twenty mob chieftains gathering at Bamonte's Restaurant to celebrate the fulfillment of the hit. When city police officials saw the story, they fumed. Not because it demonstrated a leak of confidential information but because they assumed the FBI had put out the story without telling them anything about it. Many cops found out about this alleged conclave from the Sunday papers.

The pretense of effective law enforcement, however, continues. Press conferences were held concerning the Galante killing by Police Department brass who never had anything to do with covering organized crime. On the afternoon of the shooting, one experienced detective had difficulty even getting into the back of the restaurant since admission seemed to be predicated upon rank rather than knowledge. "You had to have a star or an eagle to get in the back," the detective said, "and the only reason they were back there to view the body was to give them something to talk about over cocktails."

With this attitude deeply entrenched, with Galante gone and the remaining organized-crime chieftains dead, ill, or tipping precariously toward dotage, prosecutors may soon find themselves without any clearly identifiable villains. And unless they begin to figure out precisely how to work with one another in a legal manner, and how to keep tabs on a whole new generation of hoods, law-enforcement officials will shortly be able to announce the death of their last 80-year-old godfather. Thus the war on organized crime will be over—and the mobsters will have won.

Let's Take the Profit out of Organized Crime

There is a shocking contrast between huge mobster profits and token legal penalties. The law must be changed

Aaron M. Kohn

AARON M. KOHN, former managing director of the Metropolitan Crime Commission of New Orleans, is a lawyer and onetime FBI agent. He is considered by law-enforcement officials to be one of the nation's top experts on organized crime.

IN NEW YORK CITY, massage parlors—thinly disguised brothels—and porn shops can gross racketeers up to $1 million a year per establishment. Yet, when mobster James Ragonesi, with interests in 15 massage parlors, pleaded guilty in 1976 to a charge of promoting prostitution, he was sentenced to only 30 days in jail and fined $500.

• In Pennsylvania, a federal grand jury indicted five organized-crime figures in 1976 for running a massive insurance-fraud ring that had grossed more than $13 million from government agencies and private clients. Of the two defendants convicted, one got five years in jail and a $20,000 fine—a petty share of a huge profit. The other, a nephew of Philadelphia's Mafia chieftain Angelo Bruno, got six months in jail, 4½ years on probation and no fine.

• In New Orleans, former police vice-squad chief Fred Soule, a defendant in a federal racketeering-conspiracy case, admitted accepting nearly $63,000 in payoffs from illegal pinball-machine operators. In 1974 he was imprisoned for six months. But after a $5000 fine and $19,000 for income taxes were deducted, the balance of $39,000 belonged to Soule. What a way to discourage others from accepting bribes! (Had he been convicted under Louisiana state law the maximum fine for public bribery would have been $1000.)

These examples of how organized crime profits in spite of the law are hardly unique in federal, state and local courtrooms across the nation. A 1977 report to Congress by the General Accounting Office struck at the core of the problem. Covering the four-year period 1972-1975, the report analyzed sentences imposed by U.S. judges on 1226 organized-crime figures prosecuted and convicted following investigations by federal strike forces. Here are the figures: 640 (52 percent) were turned loose; only 586 (48 percent) were sentenced to prison. Of the jail terms imposed, 338 were for less than two years and 207 for less than six months. Most of those convicted would be eligible for freedom through parole after serving one third of the sentences.

Futile Fines. The appalling lack of judicial deterrents to organized crime was further emphasized in the report on economic penalties imposed. Of the convicted racketeers, 133 were set free upon paying fines of $1000 or less, one as little as $25. Only five fines exceeded $10,000. Contrast these figures with the billions of dollars leached from the national economy each year by underworld racketeers. Add to that $80 million spent annually by the federal government to investigate and prosecute racketeers.

Last year, a study was completed of sentences given defendants convicted as a result of Federal Organized Crime Strike Force activities in New Orleans over a 6½-year period. Charges ranged from labor racketeering to counterfeiting. Millions in illegal profits had been acquired by the defendants. Yet fewer than a third of those convicted received prison sentences, and those sentences averaged under two years. About half were fined, including some who went to prison, but total fines imposed were a mere seven percent of the maximum allowed by law. One convict, fined $10,000 and given five years' probation, had been running an illegal gambling operation that grossed $269,000 for the Mob in less than two weeks!

Particularly serious is the ordeal of embattled Florida, inundated by a wave of major organized-crime figures. The Florida Department of Law Enforcement reports that 17

Mafia families are operating within the state, and that the number of organized-crime figures identified there has more than doubled since 1974.

According to the department, Mob-inspired insurance frauds, land swindles, securities rackets and other conspiratorial crimes for profit cost Floridians more than $2.6 billion annually ($300 per citizen). Narcotics rings, frequently financed by illegal gambling or fraud schemes, imposed an additional $400-million burden last year through thefts by addicts, court costs and police expenses. The organized underworld has a major role in the $9-billion marijuana and cocaine traffic in south Florida.*

Yet a recent grand-jury investigation of syndicate gambling operations in Florida revealed that out of 330 indictments over an 18-month period the highest fine paid by those convicted was $1500. The longest prison sentence: three years. "Such light sentences," says Maj. Steve Bertucelli, commander of Dade County's 107-man organized-crime intelligence unit, "make our work an exercise in futility."

Vegas Junkets. In New Orleans, the files of the Metropolitan Crime Commission bulge with examples of how racketeers twist weak laws to their advantage, plea bargain and manipulate parole rules. Take the case of Walton K. Aucoin, arrested by the New Orleans police in January 1972 for illegal gambling. He pleaded guilty and was fined $500. In April that year, as a result of a court-ordered FBI wiretap, he was indicted and arrested as part of an organized-crime bookmaking ring. Two years later, awaiting trial on the federal charge, Aucoin was arrested by state authorities, charged with two counts of booking illegal wagers and fined a total of $150.

In 1976 the federal case finally came to trial, and Aucoin faced a possible maximum penalty of five years in prison, plus a $20,000 fine when he pleaded no contest. Despite Aucoin's career role in organized crime, through a plea-bargaining deal, Federal District Judge Lansing L. Mitchell fined him only $1000 and

*See "The Colombian Connection," The Reader's Digest, March '79.

released him on five years' active probation. (Investigators had established that in just one five-day period Aucoin had handled $116,000 in illegal wagers.)

Under the terms of Aucoin's probation, he was forbidden to associate with other felons and have a hand in any further illegal gambling activities. Within months, however, an official for the Flamingo Hilton Casino in Las Vegas testified that the casino was paying Aucoin at least $50,000 annually as a "junket representative." As such, Aucoin was escorting Louisiana gamblers, including convicted felons and organized-crime figures, to Las Vegas for casino weekends.

Despite the opposition of the federal probation office and the Metropolitan Crime Commission to Aucoin's continued junketing, Judge Mitchell approved Aucoin's application for a change in his probation, allowing him to continue his activities as a junketeer without interference. Nevada, however, has a prohibition against involvement of convicted gamblers in its casino operations. This February, after a three-year delay, the Nevada Gaming Control Board's investigation resulted in the denial of Aucoin's application to keep on as a junket representative.

Las Vegas continues to be a mecca for the nation's organized-crime figures. For example, in a typical two-month period, 17 major convicted racketeers, while on federal parole or probation, received permission to "vacation" there. New Orleans racketeer Frank Caracci, a probationer, was one of many convicted underworld figures who traveled to Las Vegas with official permission for annual "gin-rummy tournaments," an excellent opportunity for meetings and conferences with organized-crime figures.

Judges are not alone in routinely failing to recognize the special problems presented by organized-crime figures. The Federal Bureau of Prisons has no regulations to guide prison officials in the control of incarcerated syndicate members. It was therefore not surprising that fraud specialist James Dondich was assigned to the minimum-security facility at Lompoc, Calif. There, in a

country-club atmosphere and with few restrictions, he was actually allowed to roam the community on weekend furloughs, able to conduct business as usual.

Attack Plan. Every federal study of organized crime in the past 12 years has emphasized the critical importance of meeting the challenge of organized crime with laws and remedies likely to render its greedy conspiracies unsuccessful. Unfortunately, federal and state judges, many more familiar with corporate tax law than with the Mob, have largely ignored even the inadequate tools already at their disposal—maximum economic penalties. A dramatic example of this was found in the New Orleans study of federal sentences. In 13 cases, involving 20 organized-crime defendants found guilty of crimes for profit, the offenders' total $1.3-million "take" was punished by a token $24,000 in fines.

To overcome our dismal record in combating organized crime, we must effectively attack the Mob's source of power: money. I would suggest these steps:

▶ Federal and state judges should receive special training to enable them to recognize the *modus operandi* of organized crime and the deterrent value of stiff economic penalties, as well as imprisonment. No such education is provided now at the National Judicial College for state judges in Reno, Nev., or at the Federal Judicial Center in Washington, D.C. Curricula at these centers should be restructured to include the study of organized crime. Similar training of state and federal probation officers and prison administrators is needed.

We have a right to competent and knowledgeable judges. When citizens in Seattle, Wash., became outraged over the lenient sentences handed down by one state judge, they monitored cases passing through his court and turned the results over to the press. When the findings were made public, the judge was voted out. An informed citizenry and vigorous public opinion can generate greater judicial response to the need for realistic sentencing practices.

▶ The landmark Organized Crime Control Act passed by Congress in 1970 provides a potentially devastating weapon in the form of a provision called the Racketeer Influenced and Corrupt Organizations (RICO) section. It enables the government to seize the total assets of any organization, corporate or otherwise, that has acquired a business through illegal means, that has enabled persons to use the business in an illegal way, or that is founded on illegal profits. Since the Mob often reinvests loot in such organizations, the law can strike racketeers where it hurts most—in their treasury.

RICO has been federally invoked about 100 times, and is starting to make a significant dent in the massive economy of the Mob. But the states are perceiving the potentials of such a law too slowly, for only Florida and some half-dozen others have adopted it or variations thereof. One of the most important and useful provisions of this law allows victims of these rip-off artists to sue them for

three times the amount by which they were victimized. When enough victims become aware of this right and use it, it should prove to be one of the most damaging deterrents against top-level crooks.

▶ The maximum fine now allowed by federal law for *any* crime is $25,000 (it is usually much lower under state law). This is an inadequate penalty for big-time racketeers. The Senate Judiciary Committee will soon consider S.1437, a comprehensive redraft of the U.S. Criminal Code. Its anti-racketeering provisions would correct much of the ridiculous contrast between mobster profits and legal penalties. It would authorize federal judges to fine individual mobsters up to $500,000 and criminal corporations as much as $1 million. In addition, the proposed law empowers the imposition of penalties equal to double the gross profit of such criminal

schemes as fraud and extortion. What a blow to a racketeer and his organization—to be required to fork up $4 million after bilking a union fund, a bank or a businessman out of $2 million!

Concerned citizens and law-enforcement officers should flood their Congressmen with requests for support of the anti-racketeering provisions of S.1437. Expressions of citizen and press opinion are also needed to stimulate state legislators to enact state laws removing the profit from racketeering.

U.S. Attorney General Griffin Bell has announced the launching of an all-out counterattack against increasing organized-crime activity in illegal drugs and so-called white-collar crimes. But without laws and judicial attitudes to ensure that the profit is removed from such crimes, the attack is unlikely to make much headway.

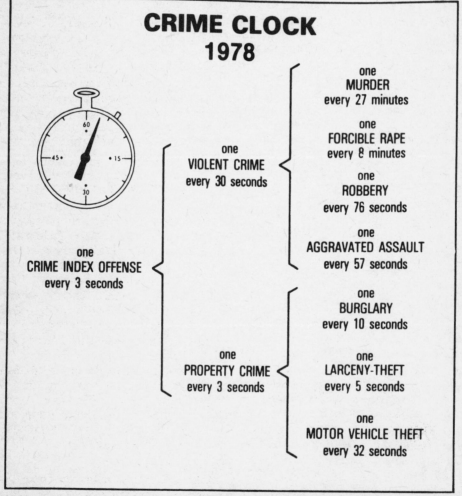

The crime clock should be viewed with care. Being the most aggregate representation of UCR data, it is designed to convey the annual reported crime experience by showing the relative frequency of occurrence of the Index Offenses. This mode of display should not be taken to imply a regularity in the commission of the Part I Offenses; rather, it represents the annual ratio of crime to fixed time intervals.

A Mutual Concern:
Older Americans
and the
Criminal Justice
System

Americans today can expect to live longer than their grandparents, thanks to advances in technology and health care. The U. S. population over the age of 65 is now estimated at 23 million. In the coming years, this age group will become a larger fraction of the population than ever because of two demographic factors—the "baby boom" that followed World War II and the declining birthrates that characterized the past two decades. By the turn of the century, we can anticipate that approximately one-quarter of the population will be at or near retirement age.

Society in general, and the criminal justice system in particular, is becoming aware of the importance of being sensitive to the needs of this growing segment of the population. More than 60 percent of the nation's elderly live in metropolitan areas, and most of these older Americans reside in the central city where victimization rates are generally higher than the national average.

Most of the recent studies and public opinion polls dealing with concerns of older people indicate that the fear of crime or the crime problem consistently ranks at or near the top of their concerns.

This concern is beneficial if it induces positive steps to reduce the chance of becoming victimized, but fear, either justified or irrational, can contribute to a sense of isolation and alienation that is detrimental to an older person's quality of life. The following information is derived from the Law Enforcement Assistance Administration's National Crime Surveys, National Prisoner Statistics programs, and other related studies.

• Persons over the age of 65 are not necessarily victimized by crime more than the rest of the population.

• Persons over the age of 65 tend to be victims of certain types of personal larceny crimes—purse-snatching, pocket-picking, consumer fraud, and con games.

• Property crimes are the most frequent crimes and they are most likely to occur when the property is unoccupied.

• Women over the age of 65 are seldom rape victims. In fact, only about 1 percent of all known rape victims are women over 50 years of age.

• Persons over the age of 65 fear crimes of violence

most—yet these are the crimes that occur least often.

• A substantial number of murders and assaults are committed by persons acquainted with, if not related to the victim.

Fear of crime among the older population often manifests itself in patterns of withdrawal from society. Low victimization rates for the elderly in some offense categories may be directly related to various precautionary measures, such as self-imposed isolation designed to minimize exposure to threatening situations on the streets. Many older people simply refuse to go out at night and forego the pleasures of theaters and social gatherings. A recent study in Maryland indicated that these restrictive lifestyles are often a direct result of the fear of crime. The facts about crime listed above reflect relevant research and indicate that the older person need not live in a world with self-imposed barriers that unnecessarily reduce the quality of life.

Interaction With the Criminal Justice System

Before considering the positive interactions between the criminal justice system and the aging, it is interesting to note that although senior citizens are seldom considered a law enforcement problem, there has been a rise in the number of senior citizens implicated in the crime of shoplifting in some locales. Analysis of data collected in one Florida city revealed that 44 percent of the shoplifting cases against persons over the age of 60 involved theft of food items valued less than $10—another indication that our society may be neglecting its senior citizens and their problems.

As their numbers grow, senior citizens have become noticibly more conscious of their interactions with the criminal justice system. Important changes are taking place within the criminal justice system in recognition of the special problems and potential contributions of this vital element in our society.

The Older Victim
Victims of crime over the age of 65 often experience greater hardships than their younger counterparts due to economic, psychological, and physical vulnerabilities. Many older people live on fixed incomes—increases in

1. CRIME AND JUSTICE IN AMERICA

the cost of living create problems, and even small losses are disastrous. Today, approximately 25 percent of the older population of the United States lives at or near the poverty level. Unexpected losses caused by burglary, purse-snatching, robbery, or confidence games can create severe trauma and economic burden for the older victim.

Psychologically, the impact of crime on an elderly victim can leave the victim with a lasting sense of invasion, threat, worry, and fear. This trauma can virtually imprison many older victims in their homes and seriously limit their opportunities for needed social contact.

The effects of aging make the older victim more susceptible to physical injury. The natural process of aging causes bones to become more brittle, loss of hearing, weakened eyesight, and reduced muscular strength and dexterity. Combined, these physical changes make the older person vulnerable to victimization and long-lasting aftereffects—generally slower to recover from physical injury than a younger counterpart.

In an effort to reduce the impact of crime on the elderly, various communities and states are now creating and implementing victim assistance programs. These programs are designed to assist the victim in finding shelter, medical care, counseling, transportation, food, and assurance. Some areas are developing victim compensation programs that provide compensation for loss of property to victims who meet minimum qualifications. Finally, several police departments have created special patrols for areas with a high concentration of older citizens.

The Older Witness

The older witness who receives a subpena to appear in court is forced to find his or her way through an often confusing and complex court system. In some areas, the older witness is faced with repeated subpenas to appear in addition to many hours in court due to court delays and continuances. Often these delays are deliberate courtroom defense tactics aimed at wearing down the older witness. Court administrators and criminal justice practitioners are beginning to realize that many older victims and witnesses do not participate in court proceedings if they are frightened, confused, or traumatized by their interactions with the criminal justice system. Victims and witnesses who are physically protected and given emotional support are more willing to press charges, present evidence, and perceive themselves as an important part of the criminal justice system and the community.

This recognition of the importance of cooperative witnesses has led many jurisdictions to institute programs to assist older witnesses through the court system. These programs often provide transportation to and from court, emotional support and reassurance, and financial support. Furthermore, they attempt to facilitate court proceedings by reducing continuances, dismissals, and unnecessary witness appearances in an effort to make the criminal justice system more responsive to all witnesses.

The Older Person as a Resource

The concept of utilizing the older person as a resource in the criminal justice system is relatively new. In the past few years, there has been a national trend toward an in-

creased use of older volunteers in many phases of the criminal justice system. This trend may be the result of simple economics since a growing number of criminal justice agencies are realizing that their agency budgets are not sufficient to maintain and improve services that are desired and demanded by the public.

The trend may also be the result of criminal justice administrators recognizing several basic points about older volunteers:

- Older people are generally supportive of the criminal justice system and are available.

- Older volunteers often have needed skills or are readily trained and they are eager to participate in improving the level and quality of services in their communities.

- Older volunteers are usually dependable and conscientious, exhibiting high workmanship standards and ethics.

- Older volunteers are experienced, bringing with them many years of practical and specialized knowledge.

- Older volunteers can perform valuable community relations services as they become personally involved in advocating the services of the agency.

Many criminal justice agencies have demonstrated that older volunteers can play important and meaningful roles in the criminal justice system. In various parts of the country, older volunteers are involved with law enforcement agencies, performing duties in the areas of crime analysis, traffic control, prisoner transport, communications, and administrative assistance. With community crime prevention programs, older volunteers are organizing block watch programs, performing security surveys, and participating in citizen patrols and escort services. Older volunteers are coordinating efforts with corrections departments to provide needed counseling for ex-offenders, both young and old. Finally, older volunteers are active in victim-witness assistance and citizen court-watching programs. The older person has been an untapped reservoir—this potential resource must be encouraged to once again become a visible, dynamic part of the criminal justice system and the community.

Suggested Readings

The following publications have been selected from the collection of the National Criminal Justice Reference Service to indicate sources of additional information about older Americans and the criminal justice system. A more extensive bibliography with descriptive abstracts may be ordered from NCJRS using the order form attached to the cover. All materials in the NCJRS collection may be borrowed from NCJRS on interlibrary loan.

BIRD, B. B. *Involvement and Use of Senior Citizens in the San Diego, California, ICAP (Integrated Criminal Apprehension Program)*. Washington: Public Administration Service, 1978. 78 p. (NCJ 47826)

BURKHARDT, J. E. and L. NORTON. *Crime and the Elderly—Their Perceptions and Their Reactions*. Rockville, Maryland, Montgomery County Police Department, 1977. 99 p. (NCJ 45224)

EDGERTON, J. *Crime Prevention Handbook for Senior Citizens*. Washington, U.S. Government Printing Office, 1977. 56 p. (NCJ 40637)

ERNST, M. and F. JODRY. *Reporting and Non-Reporting of Crime by Older Adults*. Denton, Texas, North Texas State University, 1976. 113 p. (NCJ 38138)

FLORIDA BUREAU OF CRIMINAL JUSTICE PLANNING AND ASSISTANCE. *Florida's Plan To Reduce Crime Against the Elderly, 1978* (Issued in Two Numbered Volumes). Tallahassee, Florida, 1978. 309 p. (NCJ 47457)

GOLDSMITH, J. and S. S. GOLDSMITH. *Crime and the Elderly—Challenge and Response.* Lexington, Massachusetts, D. C. Heath and Company, 1976. 184 p. (NCJ 39177)

GROSS, P. J. *Crime Prevention Programs for Senior Citizens.* Available only through NCJRS Microfiche Program, 1976. 100 p. (NCJ 37444)

GROSS, P. J. *Crime, Safety and the Senior Citizen—A Model Project on Aging—Final Report.* Washington: U. S. Department of Health, Education, and Welfare, 1977. 22 p. (NCJ 39636)

GROSSMAN, D. A. *Reducing the Impact of Crime Against the Elderly—A Survey and Appraisal of Existing and Potential Programs.* Hollywood, California, Media Five, 1977. 42 p. (NCJ 43631)

HAHN, P. H. *Crimes Against the Elderly—A Study in Victimology.* Santa Cruz, California, Davis Publishing Company, 1976. 211 p. (NCJ 40072)

MID-AMERICAN REGIONAL COUNCIL COMMISSION ON AGING. *Aid to Elderly Victims of Crime.* Available only through NCJRS Microfiche Program, 1976. 200 p. (NCJ 34905)

NEW YORK CRIME CONTROL PLANNING BOARD. *New York—Protecting the Elderly from Criminal Victimization and Providing Services to Elderly Victims of Crime—Report to the Governor, the Legislature, and to the Director of the State Office for the Aging.* New York. 90 p. (NCJ 46482)

PARKS, R. and C. UNGER. *Crimes Against the Aging—Patterns and Prevention.* Kansas City, Missouri, Midwest Research Institute, 1977. 186 p. (NCJ 40636)

RIFAI, M. A. *Older Americans' Crime Prevention Research Project—Final Report.* Portland, Oregon, Multnomah County Division of Public Safety, 1976. 356 p. (NCJ 39069)

RIFAI, M. A. *Justice and Older Americans.* Lexington, Massachusetts, D. C. Heath and Company, 1977. 218 p. (NCJ 44336)

ST. PETERSBURG POLICE DEPARTMENT. *St. Petersburg (Fl.)—Crime and the Elderly, 1974-1977.* Florida, 1978. 42 p. (NCJ 50582)

U. S. CONGRESS. *Crime and the Elderly, 1975—Hearings Before the Senate Subcommittee on Aging, August 13, 1975.* Washington: Senate Subcommittee on Aging, 1976. 213 p. (NCJ 37862)

U. S. CONGRESS. *Elderly Crime Victimization (Crime Prevention Programs)—Hearing Before the House Subcommittee on Housing and Consumer Interests, March 29, 1976.* Washington: U. S. Government Printing Office, 1976. 31 p. (NCJ 36831)

U. S. CONGRESS. *Elderly Crime Victims—Personal Accounts of Fears and Attacks—Hearings Before the House Subcommittee on Housing and Consumer Interests—September 18, 1976, in Los Angeles.* Washington: U. S. Government Printing Office, 1976. 121 p. (NCJ 40471)

U. S. CONGRESS. *Elderly Crime Victimization (Federal Law Enforcement Agencies—LEAA (Law Enforcement Assistance Administration) and FBI (Federal Bureau of Investigation)—Hearings Before the House Subcommittee.* Washington: House Subcommittee on Housing and Consumer Interests, 1976. 63 p. (NCJ 36842)

U. S. CONGRESS. *Crime Against the Elderly—Hearing Before the House Subcommittee on Federal, State and Community Services of the Select Committee on Aging.* Washington: U. S. Government Printing Office, 1977. 98 p. (NCJ 43669)

U. S. CONGRESS. *In Search of Security—A National Perspective on Elderly Crime Victimization—Report by the Select Committee on Aging—April 1977.* Washington: U. S. Government Printing Office, 1977. 89 p. (NCJ 42302)

U. S. CONGRESS. *Research into Crime Against the Elderly (Part 1)—Joint Hearings Before House Subcommittee on Domestic and International Scientific Planning, Analysis, and Consumer Interest, January 31, 1978.* Washington: House Select Committee on Aging, 1978. 87 p. (NCJ 50591)

U. S. CONGRESS. *Research into Crimes Against the Elderly (Part 2)—Joint Hearings Before the Subcommittee on Domestic and International Scientific Planning, Analysis, and Cooperation and Subcommittee on Housing and Consumer Interests, February 1, 1978.* Washington: House Select Committee on Aging, 1978. 92 p. (NCJ 50592)

U. S. CONGRESS. *Violent Crime Against the Elderly—A Briefing by the Select Committee on Aging.* Washington: U. S. Government Printing Office, 1978. 115 p.

WALSH, M., BERGER, D., and M. BRINTNALL. *Consumer Fraud and Abuse—Problems of the Elderly in the Marketplace—A Glossary of Terms and Annotated Bibliography.* Seattle, Washington, Battelle Memorial Law and Justice Study Center, 1977. 80 p. (NCJ 44305)

WEISS, J. A. *Law and the Elderly.* New York City: Practicing Law Institute, 1977. 398 p. (NCJ 51375)

Elderly

For the elderly, fear of crime is the most serious problem—more so than health, income, housing, or loneliness. Because of it, many older people virtually imprison themselves in their homes.

Many community groups are working with the elderly to dispel unreal fears about crime while teaching them how to protect themselves against real crime possibilities.

Programs in dozens of cities offer escort services—taking senior citizens on shopping trips, to banks, doctors' offices, hospitals, churches, and community programs. These services are particularly important to people whose lifelong habits unwittingly place them in danger.

For instance, "Some Chinese elders don't like to use banks or bank checks," says Augustine Chua, who heads an anti-crime program in New York City's Chinatown. "I know several who lost their life-savings because of that." Now, teenage boys escort elderly Chinese ... to the vegetable market, to doctors' offices, to hospitals. The elders travel without fear and arrive safely at their destinations, cash intact.

A minibus transport service in the rural area around Greenville, Mississippi, takes elderly people to the store and on other errands. Last year, two aging sisters starved to death in their farmhouse. "It was bad weather, they had no phone, they couldn't get help," says an official of the anti-crime program in the eight-county Delta area.

"We don't want a tragedy like that to happen again." His project—a mix of social services and crime prevention—also helps seniors repair their houses and install security locks.

After a Chillum, Maryland, woman was mugged in front of her retirement home, residents organized a crime prevention program. They arranged to have police patrol the area on motorbikes, installed a more secure door on the building and organized block watches.

In Baltimore the elderly can call the Greater Hampden Task Force on Youth to ask for help with household jobs ranging from leaf-raking to washing windows. The teenagers are from low-income families, referred by the city, and earn a minimum wage for their services. "They're good kids and they do a good job," reported one satisfied customer.

The Crime-Unemployment Cycle

Barbara Becnel

Barbara Becnel is an economist in the AFL-CIO Department of Urban Affairs.

A segment of the U.S. society lives on the edge of the economy, where legitimate opportunities practically don't exist.

This fringe of society is found, for the most part, in the nation's urban areas. They make up an army of unemployed persons—where private sector jobs are simply not available and where there are not enough public sector jobs to go around. In addition, they are young. For many, the search for economic survival leads to a life of crime. In effect, crime becomes their employment. There are few alternatives.

These young people are victims; victims of an economy that is failing to provide the most basic of needs—jobs at decent wages for all those who are able and willing to work.

Frequently, their families are experiencing severe economic hardship and are thus unable to help their offspring. Moreover, it is not unusual for the young unemployed person to be viewed by the family as an economic burden. Hence, these young people must be able to survive on their own. Unfortunately, jobs are scarce in most urban centers, and where there are jobs it is highly likely that the skills required will not match those of the inner city residents. The result is that many young people are entering adulthood without ever having had the opportunity to obtain valuable work experience and skills.

One result of long periods of joblessness has been high crime rates, particularly in the number of property crimes—robbery, burglary, larceny or auto theft—committed by youthful offenders. In addition, across the country, inner city youths are between 10 and 20 times more likely than other young people to be arrested for violent criminal offenses. Sustained unemployment breeds frustration, anger and despair. It promotes an explosive environment.

And a youth caught committing an offense is often stigmatized and further estranged from the labor market. Employability drops another notch.

Thus the link between crime and unemployment is critical. Unemployment contributes to crime; crime contributes to unemployment—the cycle is vicious.

The unemployment rate of central cities has increased precipitously in recent years, moving from 4.8 percent in 1970 to 8.9 percent in 1978. These high rates can in part be attributed to the large concentration of unemployed blacks that are housed in inner cities. Indeed, nearly 60 percent of unemployed blacks live in central cities as compared to 27 percent of unemployed whites.

Justice Department data show that the rate of arrests per 100,000 inhabitants is quite high for cities with populations over 250,000. For example, in the violent crime category the arrest rate per 100,000 was 382. In other words, for every 100,000 residents in a city with a population of over 250,000, 382 were arrested for committing violent crimes. The corresponding arrest rate for suburban areas was 137 per 100,000 inhabitants; and for rural areas 128 as of 1976, the most recent year available.

Arrest rates for property crimes were much higher, registering 1,110 per 100,000 for cities with a

"The Crime-Unemployment Cycle," by Barbara Becnel, *New York Teacher*, January 7, 1979 edition. Reprinted by permission.

population of 250,000 or more; 753 for suburban areas; and 407 for rural areas.

Thus, the unemployed, low income, unskilled urban dweller who is a potential, if not already, accused offender, must be provided meaningful economic alternatives to crime. On the whole, however, existing policy and programs have yet to provide those alternatives.

Basically, current programs can be broken down into two major categories:

●Programs that make crime more costly to the offender; and

●Programs that provide employment and training for the offender.

With few exceptions, there is very little emphasis being placed on programs designed to deter the potential offender.

Successful employment and training programs must provide not only jobs for ex-offenders, but also potential for advancement to jobs of some quality. In fact, reducing recidivism may hinge on the issue of the kind of jobs made available.

The AFL-CIO Human Resources Development Institute (HRDI) has taken note of the direct link between recidivism and the quality of jobs. HRDI—the manpower arm of the AFL-CIO—offers a wide range of employment assistance programs for ex-offenders. Further, HRDI's programs acknowledge the ex-offenders need for a decent, well paying job. One such program—Job Development and Placement—places more than a thousand ex-offenders a year in jobs. Moreover, the jobs are primarily with companies that have union collective bargaining agreements. And studies have shown that union jobs pay higher wages than comparable nonunion jobs. Moreover, union jobs offer stability and potential.

HRDI has representatives in more than 50 cities that work with employers on job development for offenders. These representatives also work with employers to revise employment practices that bar ex-offenders from being able to obtain employment. In New York state alone, ex-offenders are barred from more than 40 occupations. Such policies restrict even further the already limited employment opportunities of ex-offenders.

In addition, HRDI has established an offender job counselling program that enables HRDI representatives to work with prisoners and the courts in assessing an ex-offender's future employment plans. Ex-offenders are helped in determining their skill level and are assisted in locating training if needed.

HRDI also provides a job referral service to newly released inmates throughout the nation. Prior to an inmate's release, HRDI staff in the city where the penal institution is located contacts an HRDI representative in the city where the released inmate is returning. The HRDI staff in that city, upon the release of the prisoner, helps the former inmate obtain a job.

Additionally, HRDI serves as an innovative program developer for labor groups and companies interested in dealing with specific employment problems of ex-offenders.

HRDI has, as a result, been involved in such activities as getting unions to intercede for first time offenders in pre-trial intervention programs; helping unions to become involved in arranging for offenders to obtain jobs to work off their fines; and with HRDI's help unions and companies are becoming more and more active in providing special employment assistance for women offenders.

Alleviating the problem of training people to learn skills that are not needed is another of HRDI's priorities. In fact, HRDI staff utilizes contacts with both local unions and companies to set up in-prison and community-based training programs to offer skill training in those areas where there are currently skill shortages.

Studies of the effect of manpower programs all point to the necessity of providing the ex-offender with employment—meaningful employment—since employment appears to be the strongest tool in reducing recidivism. The Department of Labor has, as a result, developed several employment and training programs for ex-offenders designed to increase ex-offender employability and reduce recidivism.

One such program that appears to be enjoying some level of success is a demonstration project called the National Supported Work Demonstration Project. This project receives its funding from a consortium of federal agencies, as well as the Ford Foundation.

The demonstration project, which began in 1974, employs four target populations—(1) newly released ex-offenders that have been out of correctional facilities for no more than six months, (2) former drug addicts, of which approximately 77 percent have been convicted of a crime, (3) young people that have dropped out of high school, of which 45 percent have had some involvement with the criminal justice system, and (4) people that have received aid to families with dependent children for a long period of time. Note that this last target population is the only category that deals entirely with people who have had no previous contact with the criminal justice system.

Under this demonstration project, these hard-to-employ participants, in other words, potential or accused offenders, are placed in temporary jobs that maintain a controlled low-stress environment until such time as they are deemed ready to enter the regular work force.

The effectiveness of this approach is in the process of being evaluated by two research outfits—Mathematics Policy Research, Incorporated and the Institute for Research on Poverty at the University of Wisconsin. Final research results are not expected until late 1980; however, some preliminary findings are in and appear to be encouraging. Thus far, this supported work project has succeeded in decreasing the recidivism rate for ex-offenders by approximately 25 percent.

Thus solutions based on the opening up of economic opportunities are successful because they deal with the cause of crime, instead of the crime itself. The alternative to this type of approach—doing nothing—carries a cost that is far too high, a cost this nation cannot afford to bear.

In purely economic terms, the cost of maintaining a high level of unemployment, thereby limiting economic opportunity, is staggering. Dr. M. Harvey Brenner of Johns Hopkins University has gathered data on the topic, and estimates that the 1.4 percent increase in unemployment sustained from 1970-75 alone has cost the nation $210 million from the increase in imprisonment in state institutions; and $434 million resulting from the increase in homicides.

However, the human tragedy reflected by the social ills that were measured to determine monetary value is the most important cost for maintaining an economy that does not provide opportunities for all. It is the high crime rate, the increase in drug and alcohol addiction, the breaking down of the family, the frustration and the despair that are immeasurable, yet is the most serious cross to bear.

Which brings us full circle. Again, the key ingredient needed to reduce the level of crime, to rebuild the nation's urban economic base, and to restore the nation's confidence is jobs. Jobs that reduce unemployment and increase purchasing power are essential to a national environment in which crime rates are low, and in which people and communities thrive and prosper. Providing economic opportunities for all Americans is, in fact, the only answer.

Handicapped

The deaf, the blind, the frail, the crippled—these and others disadvantaged by their differences often are victims of crime simply because they are handicapped.

Yet—until recently—little was done to help these very real and potential victims until after their homes, or their property, or their persons were violated.

Such cruelty to special citizens is under attack by community anti-crime groups across the nation.

The Greater Los Angeles Council on the Deaf is trying to get teletypewriters installed in the police departments. One staff worker said, "If we can convince police that they can afford these machines and have an

obligation to have them, then deaf people will have the same access to the police that hearing people do."

The deaf person with a teletypewriter would dial a police station with reciprocal equipment and type his or her message to police. The police officer would respond by typing a return message.

"We are involved in all kinds of sensitizing activities in an attempt to get our deaf citizens involved in existing anti-crime programs," the staff worker noted. "They have to depend on their hearing neighbors."

Impaired mobility is a major problem of the handicapped. Consequently, they are often omitted from many local and neighborhood activities and services. Community workers are

identifying these isolated people, and many have included transportation services for the handicapped in their community crime prevention strategies.

"Sun-fun-run" is the name of the transportation/escort service provided by a Chicago community group whose aim is to reduce victimization of seniors and the handicapped by at least 10 percent. In addition to taking handicapped residents to and from the hospital, this group provides escort and transportation services for crime prevention, educational and social meetings, and other events.

A Roanoke, Virginia, community group recently was commended by the governor for its transportation service for handicapped residents.

WORLD OF THE CAREER CRIMINAL

The professional criminal lives in a world
with its own rules and values, and
today's rehabilitation programs won't reach him.

Frank Schmalleger

Frank Schmalleger *is associate professor of criminal justice and chairman of the department of sociology at Pembroke State University in North Carolina. He studied the deterrent effect of the death penalty in Robeson County, North Carolina, and is working on a book that stresses the need for ethical standards of professionalism in criminal justice.*

During one of my first visits to a prison, as an admittedly naïve student of criminal justice, I asked an unrepentant inmate how he could be satisfied with his life as a burglar. Why, I inquired, didn't he look for an honest, steady job? We argued this point until he became so frustrated that he threw up his hands in disgust and said, "Look, you and me, we live in different worlds."

I did not realize how true that remark was until years later. Of course the burglar was right. Most of us believe that the majority of convicts are simply people who fell on hard times and turned to crime. But over the past decade I have talked to prisoners throughout the United States—first as a student and later as a professor of criminal justice—and I have learned that most of us are wrong. Although my

conclusion is bound to be controversial, I am convinced that the habitual offender lives in a world apart from what may be called conformist society. Most convicts are professional criminals. They have been socialized into lives of crime just as the rest of us have been socialized into lives of conformity.

In our society people have a tendency to lump all criminals together, whether rapists, robbers, or murderers—except perhaps for making a sharp distinction between "white-collar" criminals and violent street thugs. A more relevant distinction, and one that criminals themselves recognize, is that crime is a *way of life* for some and the result of unfortunate circumstances and personal pathology for others.

It is important for us to take this distinction seriously because it challenges many widely held ideas about crime and criminals. If poverty and unemployment are principal sources of crime, as many sociologists suggest, then all we have to do is provide jobs and decent incomes. And yet most hardened criminals spurn conventional employment and mock those who work for a living. If people become criminals because of emotional disturbances or psychological impairment, then we should be able to set them straight through various forms of

psychotherapy. But present therapeutic programs in prisons fail more often than they succeed—for reasons I shall discuss—and the vast majority of convicted felons go back to lives of crime whenever they get out of jail.

Prison is not necessarily an unpleasant experience for the career criminal. He may even regard an occasional prison sentence as a kind of vacation and as an opportunity to cultivate new criminal associations. Once when I was visiting a Southern penitentiary, an inmate spotted a former prisoner, who had recently been convicted for another crime, being processed in the compound, and said: "Look at all those men at the fence hollering. It's like old home week. He's gonna get some good meals and he's back with his friends. He don't have to worry."

Because most of us don't know the criminal world, we often accept the notion that better prison facilities, more humane treatment, and stronger rehabilitation programs—all valid in their own right—will cure convicted felons of their criminal habits. But the career criminal sees himself as a legitimate professional, a view reinforced by his peculiar subculture. He is indeed a member of an "underworld." Perhaps it is time we recognized that there may be validity in the claim by policemen and district attorneys that most repeat offenders are criminals out of choice and not out of necessity or unhappy circumstance.

Professional criminals not only hold square society in contempt, they also have little respect for the amateur or chance criminal whose incarceration results from a twist of fate rather than from criminal dedication. At the North Carolina Correctional Center for Women, I met an inmate serving a life sentence for the murder of her lover. Until the time of the murder she had led a conventional life and had never been involved in crime. With a nervousness that betrayed her desperation she told me: "I'm not like these other women. I can't talk to them. They're the kind of people I was always afraid of. Don't you see, I'm not really a criminal."

Of course, murder is a serious crime, but it is not an activity that even habitual offenders often choose as an occupation. Personal identities are built on careers, and radical changes in self-image rarely result from isolated acts of violence. Put simply, it is one thing to be labeled "criminal" by society, but quite another to think of oneself as criminal. Just how many individuals labeled "criminal" by society have built careers on lawbreaking is difficult to determine, but recidivism statistics can shed some light on the question. Criminologists generally agree that around 70 percent of all convicted felons will be arrested again within five years of their original conviction or prison release date. Some states have habitual-offender statutes under which repeaters receive long prison terms. Yet naïve offenders who have committed a single serious crime typically receive harsher penalties than the career criminal who makes a living by preying on society. Such sentencing procedures serve the ends of punishment much better than they protect society.

Criminality is an attitude toward life that, more often than not, begins in youth, generally in the preteen or early teen years. Many of the inmates I have met have been in trouble nearly all of their lives. When interviewed, they recall that as children they craved excitement. Constantly seeking thrills, they saw most other children as weak, and they now see conforming adults in the same light. Their first real crimes, most often vandalism, stealing, and drug abuse, usually involved a small group of like-minded thrill seekers.

These early crimes tend to be committed under peer pressure and are seen as fun. Eventually the young troublemaker recognizes how profitable crime can be and begins to commit crimes more for gain than for excitement. As he becomes adult, childhood theft is replaced by armed robbery and burglary. Some offenses, such as drug use, assault, and certain sex crimes, may be committed in order to maintain an impressive reputation within criminal society rather than for profit.

Not only does crime pay financially, but the odds against being caught and punished also favor the criminal. Estimates (based on FBI statistics and independent victimization surveys) are that out of every 100 people who commit serious crimes, only one receives a prison sentence, and many of those punished are probably inexperienced first offenders. (By serious crimes I mean those classified as Part One offenses by the FBI: murder and non-negligent manslaughter, forcible rape, robbery, aggravated assault, burglary, larceny-theft, and motor vehicle theft.) The chance of being imprisoned for lesser crimes, even if the person is a habitual offender, is about one in 300. Furthermore, plea bargaining—pleading guilty to a lesser offense—results in reduced sentences in roughly 80 percent of both state and federal criminal cases.

Accompanying the need for excitement is the development of manipulative skills. Career criminals pride themselves on their ability to talk their way out of trouble and to control others. At an early age they learn how to exploit weaknesses in the criminal justice system, playing one part of the system against another. Like bargain hunters in a department store, they shop around, offering the police or prosecutor information in exchange for leniency. As their contacts with the system multiply, so do their skills.

Sometimes they are successful enough to con their way out of prosecution. In a recent case in North Carolina, a female hitch-hiker and two male companions kidnapped the occupants of a car that had stopped to pick them up. All the occupants were robbed and one was murdered. After agreeing to testify against her companions, the woman was tried on a lesser charge. Criminologist Jerome Skolnick reports a case involving two burglars caught in the act who helped the police "clear the books" by confessing to 500 additional (previously unsolved) burglaries. One of the burglars served a four-month prison sentence; the other was allowed to complete a sentence he was already serving and was released after 30 days.

No matter what the situation, career criminals see their environment in terms of chances that may or may not be worth taking. Let me cite a case in point. Not long ago a convicted thief and drug user with a history of offenses beginning in his preteens came to visit me while he was on probation. After he left I noticed that a pocket watch, which had great sentimental value, was missing. I called his probation officer, who recovered the watch. When asked why he had taken it, the probationer said simply: "I didn't think they'd miss it. They might of thought it was lost."

The special consciousness of the career criminal comes through clearly in the remarks of a 30-year-old convicted burglar. "You have to look at things in a special way to be a burglar," he told me. "You learn things. You think of how much noise you make. If you're gonna cut through a roof, you don't take a power saw. You do it by hand, and on a quiet night you saw only when traffic goes by. You look for things most people don't see—can't see. Shadows are important. So is anything you can hide behind. People can look straight at you and not see you if you're in the right place."

The criminal world attracts its members from among habitual offenders by providing a ready-made system of meaning. Criminal reality—criminals' perception of the world—is the mechanism through

Jeff Albertson—Stock Boston

Prison society is tight-knit and the camaraderie is much like that of a fraternal organization. In prison, criminal attitudes are reinforced and associations are formed that continue after an inmate is released.

which life becomes comprehensible. It tells criminals who they are, who others are, which actions are significant and what they mean. In short, it endows criminal life with purpose. The concepts of criminal reality character- ize criminal thought *itself*, while those of conformist reality provide a frame- work for theories *about* crime.

And yet it is not enough to draw a simple line between career criminals and conformists. Criminals, like the rest of us, vary greatly. Consider differ- ences in status. Criminal careers that require exposure to personal danger and refined technical skills are the most highly regarded. The armed robber receives deference from the thief. Even conformist society glorifies the bold, skillful criminal, especially when the crime is of some magnitude. The wide- spread appeal of films like *The Sting* attests to this.

But all professional criminals share

one characteristic: They live outside the law. Although the pimp, the drug dealer, the robber, and the burglar are involved in vastly different careers, which may or may not overlap, the energies of all are channeled into illegal pursuits and their livelihood usually depends on crime. They continue to enjoy the thrill of breaking the law and generally have as much trouble going straight as conformists would have stepping into lives of crime. Correc- tional programs that provide occupa- tional skills and job placement for habitual offenders are more likely to produce job-holding criminals than conformists.

Living in a world of illegitimacy creates a time frame for the criminal in which the primary locus of reality is the here and now and the not-too-distant future. Long-range goals are rarely given much thought. As one inmate told me when I asked him about his attitude

toward the future: "The present is what counts. Tomorrow is not a promise. I could get shot down with bullets the next minute." He was, of course, refer- ring to his life on the streets.

This stunted time frame helps ex- plain criminal behavior. All human action is significant only in relation to the end result. For example, a univer- sity education is meaningful to the conformist who plans to become a doctor or engineer. But because the temporal structure of the criminal world does not relate present behavior to distant goals, the significance of actions depends on immediate experi- ence. The criminal does not postpone gratification; if he wants a car, or a color television set, instead of borrow- ing or saving the necessary money, he steals it. During a philosophical discus- sion, a felon serving time in a Midwes- tern prison told me, "If you don't live in the now, you don't live anywhere."

1. CRIME AND JUSTICE IN AMERICA

The fact that many criminals leave numerous clues or break the law where they are sure to be recognized has been explained by some psychologists as an indication that many criminals want to be caught. But I think this theory is a bit of conformist thinking. As I interpret criminal thought, imperfect crimes result from the criminal's emphasis on immediate goals.

Individuals called "criminal" by the criminal justice system are not necessarily judged that way by criminals themselves. The career offender experiences little personal guilt, because criminal subcultures provide sanctions for his or her behavior. Called "rationalizations" by conformists, these sanctions structure reality in a way that favors criminal enterprise and provides the knowledge necessary for individual self-understanding. Once, while on a field trip with students to a local prison, I used the word "rationalization" in questioning the reasons a prisoner gave for his habitual crimes. "O.K.," he said. "You call that rationalizations. I know what the word means. But what you folks is doing . . . that's rationalizations. We appreciate you coming here . . . but you come because you can't stand the guilt of putting us in here."

For the conformist who has committed a crime, the consequences—discovery, formal conviction, and imprisonment—can, and usually do, have a shattering effect. But the career criminal considers these legal mechanisms irrelevant. "I don't give a damn what society says about me," an inmate in an Ohio prison told me; "I know who my friends are and I go by what they say. I don't let society tell me how to think." Asked who his friends were, he continued, "They're people just like me. Some in here, some out there. They don't buy all that propaganda society is putting out. They know what's really important."

A convicted drug dealer rationalized his activity this way: "I turn people on to the truth. That's why society is afraid of drugs . . . because they're afraid of the truth." He was certain that if enough people learned the "truth" the present social order would be replaced by enlightened leadership. Belief in his

Messianic role and in the significance of drugs was strongly supported by his fellow criminals, both on the streets and in prison. His imprisonment and the vehement denial of his "truth" by conformists only made him more certain that his interpretation was right.

As in conformist culture, generational differences flavor the ways criminals legitimate illegal activities. Property crimes probably have a longer history of sanction than do other crimes. An older criminal, socialized into criminal reality before the 1960s, defended his activities by observing: "Robbing banks, stealing cars, burglary, all that doesn't hurt anybody. Everybody's got insurance. And most of them wouldn't miss it anyway."

The radical rhetoric of the 1960s has not been lost on younger offenders, whose language reflects the reality they perceive. They never had a chance to make it in the straight world, they say, because of early deprivations, discrimination, and so on. A corollary theme among them is that most people who are victimized by crime deserve what they get, since they are the oppressors of the lower classes. Some young criminals see themselves as revolutionaries, waging war against an unjust society. Robbery, burglary, theft, and even violent crime are, in their view, simply guerrilla tactics that are made necessary by a power structure that imprisons the poor.

A prisoner in Marion, Ohio, who wore a Che Guevara outfit, explained his involvement in burglary to me as follows: "What whitey has is mine. But he won't share. So I takes it from him." Later he said, "The distribution of wealth is unequal in society. Why should we have nothing? I'm trying to fix that." When I asked him if he thought of himself as a revolutionary, he said "I *am* a revolutionary."

It has been said that prison is a sort of graduate school of crime. In American prisons inmates learn more than new criminal techniques. They acquire, through association with diverse criminal types, additional socialization into criminal reality. It is in prison that careerists from different criminal subcultures come into close contact, and it is in prison that the wellsprings of a

national criminal culture are nourished. Drug dealers, robbers, con men, pimps, who might never meet on the outside, can communicate face-to-face in prison. The result is a bond of common interests and attitudes. The occasional criminal who says he is sorry, who expresses guilt and admits "I didn't mean to do it," is despised and ridiculed by inmate society.

When the first offender steps through the prison gates, he finds support for almost any form of criminal activity. Those inmates who have had the most successful careers, generally the meanest and most ruthless, receive deference, privileges, and respect. One inmate I met had been a big-time narcotics dealer on the outside. He was reputed to have had people killed by professional hit men, and inmates feared him and would do anything for him. This man, I believe, had more influence than the warden over the lives of his fellow inmates.

Prison society, of necessity, is close-knit. The therapist who tries to inculcate inmates with the values of conformist society during the one or two hours he meets with his prison clients each week has little chance of success. The attitudes and beliefs of the career criminal, reinforced by prison society, are too ingrained to be rooted out by conventional therapeutic methods. Similarly, correctional programs that require the inmate to develop long-range job plans and to acquire the skills necessary for a steady job are generally unrealistic, for they fail to consider the career criminal's view of time.

The 30 percent or so of the inmates who do reform probably would have done so without therapy. It is likely they were occasional criminals to begin with and basically conformists at heart. The apparent, albeit limited, success of rehabilitation programs in some prisons may be nothing more than a measure of the number of occasional criminals in the inmate population. The question that needs to be asked is how many one-time offenders become irrevocably submerged in criminal reality through their prison experience?

Based on my own work in prisons, I estimate that roughly 10 percent of all inmates in the United States are conformists at heart. They are generally people who have committed serious crimes, like the murder of a spouse or lover, and who have received long prison sentences. The longer they remain in prison the more likely they are to become immersed in criminal reality. Nearly all of this group may eventually accept some aspects of the criminal's world view.

To be effective, therapeutic programs must proceed from a recognition that there are sharp differences between one-time offenders and career criminals. Individual behavior resulting from adaptation to criminal reality cannot be changed by therapies that challenge only selected aspects of criminal thought. The career criminal must simultaneously be made to abandon criminal reality and to construct a new reality that is consistent with conformist principles. In short, he must be converted.

Conversion is most likely to occur when certain basic conditions are met. First, the offender must be made consciously aware of the shortcomings of his former world view. These shortcomings may be demonstrated by pointing out internal inconsistencies or, when the person's identity is firmly anchored in criminal reality, by stimulating self-doubt. The goal of conversion therapy is to create a period of questioning and inner reflection. If therapeutic efforts at this stage are

successful, the criminal will be set adrift between conflicting realities. He will be living in a limbo of doubt. Sometimes relentless questioning is necessary. An interview using conversion therapy would go like this:

Therapist: You're not a bad person? I mean you're not evil or anything like that?

Client: No.

Therapist: You know, your mother tells her friends that she's sorry you were born. She says you'd be better off dead.

Client: Yeah.

Therapist: Your wife left you.

Client: (Shrugs)

Therapist: Your children hope you never get out of prison. They say that if you do they never want to see you. They say all you've done is cause them misery.

Client: I know.

Therapist: And you still say there's nothing wrong with you?

Client: You just don't understand.

If this approach works the client will eventually realize that he doesn't understand why he behaves as he does. If he did, he could communicate it to the therapist. Conversion therapy brings the inmate's entire way of being under attack and, if successful, engenders a crisis of identity.

Next, conformist reality is presented to the client in such a way that doubt is resolved in conformist terms. Since people tend to maintain a consistent world view, the adoption of even a few conformist premises can lead to an

increasing acceptance of conformist thought. Each time a crisis is answered in conformist terms, a new world view takes shape.

Finally, the client should be made to identify with conformist reality. In one of the most successful programs I have observed, inmates work with delinquent children. They often come to realize their own unhappiness and try desperately to save the children from a similar fate. The program may in fact do more good for the inmates than for the children.

Recognizing the existence of a special criminal reality provides a basis not only for treating individual criminals but also for understanding why career criminals behave as they do. With this understanding, we can begin to develop effective social programs designed to modify the causes of that behavior. The way to reduce crime, I believe, is to reduce the number of these professionals, and that can be accomplished only when we decide to confront the habitual offender on his own mental turf.

For further information:

Pepinsky, Harold E. *Crime and Conflict.* Academic Press, 1976.

Rogers, Joseph W. *Why Are You Not A Criminal?* Prentice-Hall, 1977.

Sellin, Thorsten. *Culture Conflict and Crime.* Kraus Reprint, 1938.

Wilson, James Q. *Thinking About Crime.* Basic Books, 1975.

Yochelson, Samuel, and Stanton E. Samenow. *The Criminal Personality.* Jason Aronson, 1976.

A COLD NEW LOOK AT THE
CRIMINAL MIND

Habitual criminals are neither mentally ill nor victims of circumstance. They have delusions and deviant thinking patterns that are present at an early age—and they deserve little sympathy—conclude two researchers in a controversial new study.

Michael S. Serrill

Michael S. Serrill, a former project specialist in criminal justice for the Ford Foundation, is now executive editor of *Corrections* magazine. Serrill has a master's degree from the Columbia Graduate School of Journalism.

SCHOLARS, PHYSICIANS, scientists, and pseudoscientists have been investigating the "criminal mind" for more than 400 years. Much of the early thinking postulated that criminals were innately evil people who could only be stopped by maiming or execution. Barely 100 years ago, the Italian criminologist Cesare Lombroso was taken very seriously when he asserted that criminality was a trait inherited from degenerate ancestors. He spent much of his professional career measuring the skulls and other anatomical parts of dead criminals in an effort to discover their typical dimensions.

More recently, legions of social scientists have devoted millions of hours and billions of dollars to more sophisticated studies. They have concluded, overwhelmingly, that criminals are victims. The sociologists say those who break the laws are victims of urbanization, family disintegration, poverty, discrimination, poor schooling, unemployment, and the pressure of peers. Psychologists and psychiatrists say criminals are victims of alcohol abuse, drug abuse, child abuse, and a variety of mental illnesses, from the all-purpose "character disorder" to psychopathy. All three professions also cite a pervasive rage of the poor against the social conditions they are forced to endure.

To suggest that individuals who commit criminal acts or adopt criminal careers are not simply responding to their environment would deny all of the insights of modern sociology and psychiatry. Yet that is just what Samuel Yochelson and Stanton Samenow do in a recently published two-volume study called *The Criminal Personality*, which has caused considerable controversy in psychiatric and correctional circles. (See box on page 47.) They argue that habitual criminals possess "thinking patterns" that distinguish them from noncriminals, and that the development of these criminal thinking patterns has little or nothing to do with either social status or mental illness.

The Yochelson and Samenow study is the result of 16 years of work with criminal patients at Saint Elizabeths Hospital in Washington, D.C. Yochelson, a respected neuropsychiatrist who died in 1976, started the Program for the Investigation of Criminal Behavior in 1961 and was joined by clinical psychologist Samenow in 1970. The two researchers studied the personalities of 240 men, spending hundreds of hours with many of them and as many as 8,000 hours with a few. The bulk of the research was done by Yochelson; after his death, Samenow put together the book from an estimated quarter of a million pages of notes compiled by his colleague. Their methodology is perhaps the most vulnerable point in the book. For Yochelson and Samenow did not conduct a formal study, with experimental and control groups. Their conclusions are simply drawn from a wealth of observation in their clinical work at Saint Elizabeths Hospital.

Perhaps the most controversial asser-

tion in *The Criminal Personality* is that there *is* a criminal personality. The authors contend that there were certain deviant thinking patterns present to an extreme degree in every one of the criminals they studied. The habitual criminal, they write, is a liar and a deceiver; he has little capacity for love, friendship, or companionship; he can commit brutal acts without a twinge of conscience and yet continue to believe that he is a "good" person. He "finds the restraints of responsible living unacceptable and even contemptible," the authors write. "The criminal disregards other people's right to live safely, but demands that others show him the utmost respect and consideration. . . . It does not bother him to injure others. . . . Untrustworthy himself, he demands that others trust him. If he happens to earn others' trust, he exploits it."

The two authors identify 52 "errors of thinking" that they claim were present in all the offenders they dealt with. They found that these thinking patterns did not, for the most part, develop in the criminals over the course of their lifetimes, but were present from a very early age (although they do not consider them innate). Some of the more prominent patterns include:

☐ *Extreme fearfulness.* The criminal mind is virtually consumed by fears, small and large, real and imagined. The offenders' lesser fears were of such things as heights, water, or closed spaces, and depended on the individual. Larger fears were characteristic of all the criminals studied. They were terrified of physical injury and death, and almost equally terrified of any event they interpreted as rejection or a "put-down." The criminal's fearfulness is "so pervasive from an early age," the researchers write, "that it almost seems independent of experience."

☐ *Extreme and persistent anger.* "The criminal is chronically angry—even as he walks down the street," Yochelson and Samenow write. "Anger is a mental state that is sometimes expressed outwardly, but more often boils within. It is most dangerous when it is not on the surface. Anger is as basic to his personality as the iris is to the eye."

☐ *Zero state.* Criminals frequently go through periods when they are convinced they are absolutely worthless and that their situation in life is hopeless, though an objective observer would not come to the same conclusion. This zero state of the criminal is not the same as depression, the authors note, because "rather than appearing flat, inert, and despairing, he is blazing with anger (often unexpressed)."

☐ *Criminal pride.* The zero state also differs from classical depression because the criminal is able to wrench himself out of it by sheer force of will and replace it with a state of mind the authors call "criminal pride." In this mental state, a person has "an extremely and inflexibly high evaluation of [him] self. It is the idea that one is better than others, even when this is clearly not the case." The assertion of criminal pride is usually discussed in terms of "manhood." To be a man, the criminal believes, is to be completely independent of all other people, of all institutions, and to be able to conquer all obstacles and challenges, especially those involving women.

☐ *Superoptimism.* The criminal, in the days or hours before the commission of a crime, convinces himself beyond a doubt that the crime will succeed and he will not be caught. When a criminal is in the state of superoptimism, he has used a mental process the authors call "cutoff" to block out completely the fears that might otherwise prevent him from committing the crime.

The wild vicissitudes of the criminal mind from the zero state to his feelings of godlike power give him a marked inclination toward suicide. Yochelson and Samenow quote one offender as saying that it is better "to be under the sod than not to be God."

While finding that unwarranted fears and delusions are characteristic of the criminal mind, the authors assert that the criminals they studied committed their crimes by deliberate choice. "They were in contact with reality. They were in control of their behavior," Samenow said in an interview, though they committed their crimes without the slightest concern for their victims, or remorse for the injury they had done.

Almost all the offenders in the study had long criminal histories. Almost all were declared not guilty by reason of insanity in federal courts and committed to Saint Elizabeths for treatment. Nonetheless, Yochelson concluded that only 3 percent were really so disturbed that they were not responsible for their actions. In most cases, the authors write, the offenders ended up in Saint Elizabeths because they were able to use their thorough knowledge of "sociologic and psychological excuses" for crime to feign mental illness. "It is when he is in personal jeopardy that a criminal calls himself whatever is necessary to excuse what he has done," the authors concluded. "The criminal does his best to convince others of his insanity. Once he accomplishes this and is committed to a mental hospital, he tries to show others that he is no longer sick. His new objective is to demonstrate a rapid recovery from an illness that he never had."

Even their severest critics do not question Yochelson and Samenow's assertion that their subjects were not mentally ill, or at least not as mentally ill as they were originally purported to be. What the critics do object to is the authors' rather casual assumption, throughout their study, that the personality traits of their patients at Saint Elizabeths apply equally well to other habitual criminals in other institutions. Samenow responds to this criticism by saying that the study is by no means definitive; he invites researchers to replicate the study among inmates of regular penal institutions.

S amenow and Yochelson started their work with the conventional view of criminals as victims of abuse and deprivation. "People viewed the criminal as somebody who really was a victim of circumstances," Samenow says. "If you could just teach him so he could find his way into the mainstream of society, that was what was necessary.

"I don't think we quarreled with much of that. But that turned out not to be the case. . . . We found with our people that they rejected the schools and their parents and the responsible forces around them before ever being rejected by them. In other words, they were more victimizers than victims."

Samenow says the study included "blacks and whites, grade-school dropouts and college graduates, people from the inner city and people from the suburbs, intact homes and broken homes. We have talked with their families, parents, sisters, brothers—in some cases at great length—as well as studying them. And in our search for why they are the way they are, there wasn't anything that stood up."

Abandoning the effort to find the causes of criminality, the researchers put all their effort into studying criminal thinking patterns and trying to find ways to change them. For the first four years, Yochelson used conventional psychiatric techniques to try to treat his clients. "He saw people in groups," said Samenow. "He put them on the couch. Free association, dreams . . . He was sincere, and he was spending hundreds of hours with people, which is more than most [therapists] are able to do in prison or hospital facilities. And he found at the end of that period that he was nowhere. He had criminals with insight, rather than without insight. They were still criminals. The techniques simply didn't work."

According to Samenow, Yochelson's subjects then added insult to injury: "After four years of working his head off, they gave a party for him, as a testimony to what a wonderful job he was doing. And they gave the party with supplies stolen from the hospital! He thought he had done so much. He hadn't done a damn thing."

A s Yochelson and Samenow learned more about the people they were working with, it became clear that the task of changing them would be huge. Samenow explains: "What you have to do is to help a person change a thinking style and a lifestyle that he has held all his life. He has to change to a way of life that he has always scorned and has regarded as 'square'—by which he means stupid.

"What's life? You go to work, you go to school, you have hassles at work, problems at school, bills to pay, family to take care of, cars that break down— all the problems of daily living. What is it? It's dull! Who wants it? And so, from very early, the oxygen of their lives, so to speak, has been to seek excitement, by doing the forbidden."

For the habitual criminal, Samenow says, crime is the ultimate excitement: "Thinking about the crime is exciting. Talking about the crime is exciting. Committing the crime is exciting. Even getting caught is exciting. Trying to figure a way to beat the rap is exciting." Steering the criminal away from his life is doubly difficult because "despite the fact that they have committed all these crimes and have injured so many people, every one of them ... believes he is a good person, that he is decent."

Yochelson's subjects were required to cooperate in therapy sessions, or else they could not get out of the hospital. Most just went through the motions; a few, however, became intensely involved in what the researchers call a "change process." Working with this group, Yochelson and Samenow developed what they believed was an effective treatment program.

The method they finally developed resembles in some ways the "reality therapy" and encounter therapies used in many prisons and community corrections programs. Samenow, however, prefers to call himself an educator and not a therapist, since he contends that the method is essentially to teach criminals, through talk and experience, about a life they have never known.

The criminal's education began when Yochelson or Samenow sat him down and told him who he was. They would make a series of statements or ask a series of questions based on what they "knew" about the criminal from the 52 characteristics. "I might say," Samenow explains, "'Isn't it true that ever since you can remember you have been a liar? Now of course you don't consider yourself a liar, because lying is a way of life for you. But isn't it true that you have lied not only when you wanted to avoid detection, or when you have wanted to get out of a jam, but you have lied just for the hell of it?'" When confronted with such questions, Samenow says, many offenders were astonished at how much the doctors seemed to know about their backgrounds and personalities.

The object of the initial interview, and subsequent group meetings that the offender attended three hours a day, five days a week, was "to hold a mirror up to the guy and try to enhance his self-disgust, rather than self-esteem." For this method to be effec-

tive, the best time to approach the criminal is "when the walls are closing in," when he has been arrested and imprisoned and feels he has failed as a criminal—when he's in the zero state.

The participants were told to take notes on their thoughts in the 24 hours before each day's meeting; the notes were thoroughly discussed, on the theory that "the criminal thought of today will be the criminal act of tomorrow." Many of them had been released from the hospital after a brief incarceration and were urged to remain in the program. If they did, they were required to abstain from alcohol and drugs, be faithful to wives and girl friends, and work at a steady job. The project was plainly "moralistic," admits Samenow, since "we teach them what they need to do to live responsibly."

And what will persuade people who are so accustomed to an exciting, irresponsible life to accept a dull, workingman's existence? "Say you have a guy who progresses from busboy to waiter," Samenow answers. "It's the first earned promotion in his life. He has the respect of the people around him. He has money he puts in the bank, that he has obtained legitimately. He has the trust of his wife or his girl friend. He doesn't have to look over his shoulder for the policeman. These are the rewards of a way of life he never knew anything about, plus his view of who he is, and his belief that he has very little choice. There is an accruing self-respect based on constructive accomplishment."

Samenow has discussed his "change process" with various groups and officials around the country, and now has the U.S. Bureau of Prisons interested in starting a pilot program at one of its institutions. He says it would not be hard to introduce on a broad scale, since "educators" to run the discussion groups can be trained easily and quickly. But he is very, very cautious when discussing the possible impact of his method. He points out that the program at Saint Elizabeths was strictly voluntary, and that the great majority of those who started it dropped out after "getting a high out of decency." Only 30 people completed the program before it ended last year, and of those, only nine have genuinely changed and are living law-abiding lives.

'I don't think this approach would reach any more than about 20 percent," he says. "Yet, think of who it is we are dealing with—people who have com-

mitted thousands of crimes, with a cost to society that is incalculable. If you really change 20 percent, you are saving society a hell of a lot. One of our people did $12 million worth of damage by the time he was 20 in fires and thefts."

While Samenow is convinced that his study refutes most conventional explanations of the causes of crime, he can shed no new light on the origins of the criminal thinking patterns. "I don't think people are born with thinking patterns," he says. "They learn thinking patterns to fulfill specific objectives." Why certain individuals develop such patterns while others from the same environment do not—a fact sometimes referred to as the "black sheep" phenomenon—remains a mystery to Samenow. He bridles, however, at the suggestion that such thinking patterns are more prevalent among certain ethnic or economic groups, insisting that his research indicates no such thing. "It is a real insult to the black community to say that because you are black and from the inner city, you are more likely to be a criminal."

He and Yochelson rejected genetic factors in criminality early in their work, and he continues to see little promise in research such as the XYY screening programs, which came to a halt two years ago in the U.S. because of a public outcry against them. Samenow thinks the causes of criminality must lie in some combination of organic, sociologic, and psychologic influences. But to try to trace and identify those influences in any offender is futile, he believes. And even if one could, he adds, the identification of the cause does not lead inevitably to the cure.

Samenow is now working on a third volume of The Criminal Personality, which will deal with the specific diagnostic and treatment problems of drug-using criminals. When he finishes that work, he hopes to test treatment methods he and Yochelson developed on juvenile offenders. Since Samenow believes the criminal's "errors of thinking" begin at a very early age, he hopes to find ways to change young offenders before they wreak havoc in society and in their own lives.

For further information, read:

Cleckley, H. M. The Mask of Sanity, C. V. Mosby, 1964, $13.95.

Eysenck, H. J. Crime and Personality, Routledge & Kegan Paul, 1977, $8.95.

Schur, E. M. Our Criminal Society, Prentice-Hall, 1969, paper, $3.25.

Szasz, Thomas. Law, Liberty and Psychiatry, Macmillan, 1963, $8.95, paper, 1968, $2.95.

'THE CRIMINAL PERSONALITY' IN PERSPECTIVE

The Criminal Personality by Yochelson and Samenow has been attacked by liberal social scientists who believe that its conclusions ignore all the evidence that criminality is rooted in poverty and mistreatment. On the other hand, the research has struck a chord among some correction officials who believe it accurately describes the people they must deal with every day.

Eric Thompson, chief psychologist at the U.S. Penitentiary at McNeil Island in Washington State, has been quoted as saying that the study is "the best I've read on the kind of work I do." Writing in the journal *Criminal Justice and Behavior*, Robert B. Mills, professor in the criminal justice program at the University of Cincinnati, called the books "a seminal work, rich in new concepts of criminal treatment, which will be closely studied by correctional counselors in years to come."

Some observers consider the intense interest of prison officials to be one more sign of the bankruptcy of corrections as a discipline. "People are grasping at straws," said Simon Dinitz, an Ohio State sociologist who has done pioneering work in identifying organic sources of delinquency among juveniles. "The correctional system finds itself really without any motif," he said. "Almost all of the theories by which it has thrived are pretty well shot. And what [Samenow] is offering them is an excuse for failure [by saying] that you're dealing, after all, with cruel people who, while they are still young, tear the heads off cats, and whose thinking is all screwed up, and who are brutal and vicious."

To abandon the obvious sociological explanations for the failure of correctional treatment programs is folly,

Dinitz argued. "The major point, which they don't get anywhere close to," he added, "is that all of our major institutions are failing, and they're not only failing these people [criminals], they're failing a lot of other people, too. Nothing seems to work terribly well—not the schools, not families, not religious institutions. They're placing the blame back on the individual and his screwed-up thinking. And they can't even give you a good explanation for why his thinking is so screwed up."

Some critics of the study think it is simply a poor job of research. Samenow and Yochelson drew their conclusions from thousands of hours of interviews and therapy sessions. But according to Seymour Halleck, a professor of psychiatry at the University of North Carolina Medical School, their methods were less than rigorously scientific. Halleck, in an interview, said, "They haven't really used a control group. They don't have an independent and dependent variable. They don't give any data as to the number of people they saw, how they were classified, who they were compared with. It's not a piece of research.

"The best thing about the book," Halleck added, "is that it's a beautiful phenomenological description of antisociality. Phenomenologically, they learned a hell of a lot, a hell of a lot about how these people think. But they haven't proved a goddamn thing about the criminal personality."

Psychologist John Burchard of the University of Vermont, who reviewed the first volume for *Contemporary Psychology*, also criticized "the rather unsophisticated procedures that were employed to collect, analyze, and present their data."

Yochelson and Samenow's work infuriates prison reformers. "It's a clas-

sic piece of clinical claptrap," said Jerome Miller, the former commissioner of juvenile corrections in Massachusetts and Pennsylvania, who leads the movement to close juvenile correctional institutions. "It's the kind of thing that a lot of the old guard in corrections like to hear," Miller said, "because it confirms all of the biases of the institutional mentality—that we're dealing with the scum of the earth, and that they're incurable and no matter what we do we can't make them any better."

The study's conclusions fit in well with a general hardening of attitudes toward criminal offenders across the nation. The number of men and women in state and federal prisons has shot up 25 percent in the last two years, to a record high of 283,000. The public and its representatives in the courts and legislatures are apparently more inclined to see themselves, and not the criminals, as victims. Their demands for more and greater punishment can be backed with a mountain of studies showing that the efforts of social workers, psychologists, and psychiatrists to deal with criminals have had no effect.

If his work contributes to a less indulgent attitude toward criminals, it doesn't bother Stanton Samenow a bit. He believes harsh measures are called for against the hard core of habitual criminals who are, in his opinion, not amenable to treatment of any kind. "I am against warehousing people, and I am certainly against inhumane conditions in prisons," he said. "But society has to make some pretty hard choices. ... From my standpoint—this is a personal thing, now—given that I know what these people are like and the enormous damage they can inflict, I would as soon see them confined indefinitely, rather than out on the street."—M.S.S.

Police

2

Organized police as we know them in the United States came rather late in history. The first organized American police unit was established in New York City in 1844.

Over the past century we have developed a very complex pattern of police organization in America. There are 500,000 full-time law enforcement officers, serving in some 40,000 separate autonomous police agencies, at five levels of the government—federal, state, county, municipal, and what are referred to as *ad hoc*, i.e., special purpose, police districts. There are additionally more than one million auxiliary, reserve, and volunteer police, special deputies and officers, and uniformed personnel employed by private patrol services. This pattern has some advantages. It militates against the misuse of police power to seize control of the government and enables locally recruited and controlled police agencies to adjust their policies and operations to the widely varying needs of our huge and heterogeneous country. On the other hand, there are distinct disadvantages—non-uniform enforcement, competition rather than cooperation and coordination, local political interference and lessened economy and efficiency.

At the national level, the best known enforcement agencies include the Federal Bureau of Investigation, the United States Secret Service, the Drug Enforcement Agency, the Postal Inspectors, the U.S. Coast Guard, and the police units of the armed services. Each of the fifty states has a state police or a highway patrol and some have additional, more specialized policing units. Most of America's counties have elected sheriffs and an increasing number have large, modern, countywide police departments under professional rather than political administration. Municipal police departments in the more than 30,000 towns, villages, and cities of this country range in size from miniscule (having fewer than ten sworn officers) to large scale (having thousands of sworn officers) in the larger cities.

Some of the *ad hoc* policing agencies are among the largest and most professional in the country (e.g., the Port of New York Authority Police, the New York City Transit Police, and the National Park Police). These agencies supplement federal, state, and municipal police forces in areas of joint jurisdiction, in publicly operated transportation systems, in large public housing developments, and in extensive state and national parks. Very similar to these agencies, but lacking their public peace officer status, are the many uniformed private patrol services, industrial plant protection forces, and the sometimes very well-organized, trained, and effective private security operations.

American police at all levels face many problems, internal and external. Internal problems, although more manageable, have been remarkably persistent. They include corruption, brutality and denial of constitutional safeguards, political interference in policing, and, more recently, the politicization of the police.

External difficulties are less easily dealt with. In few countries of the world do police meet such open and widespread hostility and lack of cooperation from the public they are employed to protect. Crimes are not reported, witnesses do not come forward, victims decline to prosecute, and the communications media play up police scandals. The courts dismiss charges or award very lenient penalties to persons arrested after hard and dangerous work by the police. Police officers (and sometimes their families) find themselves abused, threatened, and occasionally prosecuted for carrying out their duties to the best of their abilities, often under highly stressful conditions for which society as a whole rather than the police might justly be condemned. Societies get the police, the level of police effectiveness, and the consequent levels of crime and disorder that they deserve.

POLICE
Under Fire, Fighting Back

Ripples set in motion by the urban upheavals of the 1960s are still being felt a decade later. New training methods, unions, "blue flu" and lawsuits against citizens are just part of the story.

From the cops on the beat in big-city slums to the deputy sheriffs who patrol the back roads of the rural South, the nation's police are in the throes of change.

Police officers are under unprecedented pressure to upgrade a profession that critics accuse of being out of touch with the times. In city after city, police are facing charges of incompetence, lawsuits accusing them of brutality and racial and sexual bias, indictments alleging corruption, and cuts in their budgets.

In return, police are making unprecedented demands of their own on the taxpayers they serve. They are unionizing to win higher pay and other benefits, and are striking if their demands aren't met. They are suing citizens who file complaints against them, and they are fighting to reduce political influence over their jobs.

Despite all the strife, police are finding that many people are on their side. They are winning sympathy for doing a job that many citizens and police alike consider to be more difficult and demanding than ever before.

The country's 500,000 police officers "have become subject to much closer scrutiny and to much more frequent challenge than at any time in the past," declares Herman Goldstein, a former Chicago police official now on the faculty of the University of Wisconsin.

The police have long been criticized for failing to solve crimes, but it has been only during the last decade that their problems have been almost constantly in the public spotlight. The social unrest of the 1960s—and the inability of many police departments to cope with it—prompted a new look at the role of police officers in society. During urban riots and antiwar demonstrations, "too many groups found themselves on the wrong side of the police and did not like what they saw," says Gerald Caiden, a professor at the University of Southern California who has studied law enforcement.

The result has been a movement to change the police from strictly law enforcers into service workers capable of handling a broad range of social problems. Says Houston Police Chief Harry D. Caldwell: "Policing used to be a fairly simplistic trade. It was deputize the posse, jump on the horses and go after the bad guys. Now it requires much greater response to the human condition."

The Crime War

After years during which criticism tended to be focused on the failings of individual policemen, now it is the efficiency of entire police forces that is being challenged. For a time, steadily rising crime rates made it possible for police departments to obtain an enlarged share of the tax dollar. But along with more money came an increased tendency for elected officials to question whether the police were making the best use of the funds they were getting.

What they found was often not flattering to them. A federally financed report by the Rand Corporation concluded that detectives—long glamourized on movie and television screens for their knack for cracking tough cases—really weren't so effective after all. The Rand survey of 25 police departments found that the time of most detectives "is largely consumed in reviewing reports, documenting files and attempting to locate and interview victims on cases that experience shows will not be solved." The report said that half of the detectives' work could be "eliminated or shifted to more-productive uses."

Police also were criticized for making many arrests that didn't stick. To get at the root of the problem, the Institute for Law and Social Research studied the records of 17,000 arrests made by Washington, D.C., police in 1974 for serious crimes. It found that more than 70 percent of the arrests did not lead to convictions. Chief reason for the low conviction rate: police failure to find witnesses and evidence.

Other critics fault police for doing too little about organized crime and for failing to detect white-collar crimes such as frauds involving computers or credit cards.

Many seasoned cops insist that this kind of criticism of police competence is overdrawn. They say they cannot ignore a case just because the chances of solving it are slight. They complain, too, about judges who dismiss cases for what police call "technicalities."

Nevertheless, the police are

New York police are circulating 100,000 of these posters in a drive for a pay increase.

From *U.S. News & World Report*, April 3, 1978. Copyright © 1978 U.S. News & World Report, Inc.

In Los Angeles, the back lots of film studios are used to demonstrate techniques for police cadets.

taking criticism of their competence seriously enough to take the lead in efforts to increase the effectiveness of law enforcement.

More and diversified instruction. On almost every force, better training is a top priority. A 30-year veteran of the Boston police force, Daniel J. MacDonald, recalls that "in my day, we received four days of training, were given a gun and told to get out onto the street." Now, most states require that all police officers be given several hundred hours of instruction.

The nature of the instruction has also changed. It once focused on such matters as how to use guns and handcuffs. Training today deals as well with the use of computers in analyzing crime patterns, hypnosis as an aid to solving crimes, suicide prevention, the need for discretion in making arrests and a host of other topics.

More emphasis is being given to teaching officers to understand the people they encounter on their beats and how to communicate with them. One example: Los Angeles recruits must now study conversational Spanish because nearly half the city's population is Spanish-surnamed.

Instruction is also being provided in more-realistic settings than the classroom. New San Francisco officers play the roles as suspects, victims and witnesses in mock crimes acted out on the street with the help of former convicts.

Many police departments, too, are experimenting with changes in the kinds of work their officers do. Patrolmen traditionally were assigned to drive around and await trouble calls. When they came upon a serious crime, the case usually was turned over to those on the burglary, homicide, or missing-persons squads or other specialized units.

Nowadays, some cities are trying "team policing" in which patrolmen and specialists are assigned to work together to handle all the crimes in a relatively small area. Other departments have upgraded the role of patrol officers to give them much of the work formerly done only by detectives. The Law Enforcement Assistance Administration, which has provided funds to help 31 cities set up such programs, says that "in all too many cases, the patrol officer has very little investigative responsibility, even though he is first on the scene and best able to take down timely, relevant information before it fades from memory or concern."

One city involved is Portsmouth, Va., where the crime rate has dropped since patrolmen started doing their own investigations instead of turning them over to detectives. "Everyone thought it took Kojak to arrest a homicide suspect, but it doesn't," says Sgt. Rick Gaddis.

Police also are concentrating more on winning convictions, not just making arrests. This usually involves working more closely with prosecutors and receiving legal training in order to learn what kind of evidence is necessary to sustain convictions. Police in Washington, D.C., now receive instruction on videotape in how to interrogate witnesses and encourage them to cooperate in a prosecution.

In New York City, the concern of Edward Koch, the new mayor, about failures to win convictions played a part in the appointment of a former prosecutor, Robert McGuire, to head the city's Police Department. Said Mayor Koch: "What good does it do to arrest someone if the case is thrown out in court because you've screwed it up?"

Blacks and Women

While the police try to fend off complaints that they are incompetent, they also face growing criticism about the underrepresentation of minorities and women in their ranks. The roots of this problem go back many decades to the days of mass immigration in the 19th century, when police jobs became havens for certain ethnic groups.

Robert Fogelson, an expert on police history, remarks that up to several decades ago "in Boston and several other cities, the Irish Americans enjoyed a virtual stranglehold on the police force and exploited their political influence and bureaucratic know-how to exclude blacks and other newcomers." In some other cities, Italian Americans and German Americans dominated police forces.

As recently as a decade ago, nearly all police jobs still were held by white males. Since then, things have changed gradually. By 1975, about 7 percent of the nation's patrol officers were black and about 4 percent were women. Persons of Asian, Mexican and Indian descent accounted for minuscule proportions. No new nationwide compilation has been made, but experts believe that the number of minority officers has continued to inch upward.

"Nothing but occupational forces." Drew S. Days, head of the Justice Department's civil-rights division, says that the lack of black policemen "can only reinforce the views of the young, the poor and racial minorities that police departments are nothing but occupational forces, insensitive to their needs and concerns."

Can women be effective in police work? Many male officers have long been skeptical. The Vera Institute of Justice, a private research agency based in New York City, says that opponents of women as police argue "that when faced with danger, female officers would tend to panic, that they would be more likely to use a gun when threatened, and that they would lack the stamina and strength necessary to chase a suspect for several blocks or to carry an injured person." After comparing the performances of male and female officers in New York City, the institute found that "the women's style of patrolling was almost indistinguishable from the men's."

To get more minorities and women into police work, civil-rights groups and the Justice Department have filed dozens of suits in recent years accusing police executives of violating civil-rights laws. The suits have helped push minority and female hiring rates upward, but most police departments are still far short of reflecting the general work force in the community they serve.

Some cities that have added blacks to the police force at a rapid rate report that the change has had both good and bad consequences. Detroit is one example. The number of black officers has more than doubled in the last four years, rising from 15 to 35 percent of the force. Chief William Hart says that "with more black officers, we get more cooperation from the black community." The department also is getting fewer complaints about police misconduct.

Yet racial tensions are running high among Detroit cops. One white officer complains: "Why should we do any work when the black guys get the promotions?" Another white contends that his black superior "can barely read or write." The city's Police Officers Association won a court ruling recently voiding the Police Department's affirmative-action plan—the policy that opened the way for the influx of blacks. The group successfully argued that the plan discriminated against whites. The case is on appeal.

The presence of women in patrol cars also has provoked tensions. Some wives of male officers are upset because their husbands spend eight-hour shifts with policewomen. Some male officers themselves are uncomfortable with fe-male partners; they fear that a woman might not be able to back them up in a situation requiring brute strength.

The Litigation Flood

Employment discrimination isn't the only issue that brings the police into court as defendants. Greater awareness of civil rights has prompted an upsurge in lawsuits accusing police of various kinds of wrongdoing.

Americans for Effective Law Enforcement, a nonprofit group that often helps officers to defend themselves in such cases, estimates that civil suits against police have jumped from under 2,000 in 1971 to more than 6,000 last year.

Wayne W. Schmidt, an official of the group, attributes the flood of litigation largely to the increased willingness of lawyers to listen to complaints about the police. "There used to be an unwritten rule among lawyers not to sue police officers, but as more suits are successful, they become less reluctant," Schmidt says. The most frequent charges: improper arrest, excessive use of force, or both.

A federal jury in New York awarded 1.2 million dollars on March 7 to a physician who charged that two parkway police officers beat him after they stopped his car and falsely accused him of drunken driving. The award was one of the highest ever in a police-brutality suit.

Police lose only a small fraction of these cases, but they

Day on the Beat: "A Decent Way to Make a Living"

BALTIMORE

Far from their television image as swashbuckling law enforcers who arrest narcotics kingpins and shoot it out with robbers, patrol officers spend most of their time on much more mundane tasks.

Baltimore Police Agent James M. Miller learned that when he joined the police force three years ago. He is assigned to a high-crime area in the city's eastern district, working the day shift. Yet he deals with only a half-dozen serious crimes each month in his eight-square-block post.

Much of Miller's work comes down to helping someone solve an everyday problem, whether it is finding a missing welfare check or locating a street address. Often the order of the day is breaking up family quarrels—a job Miller handles with caution. "Some people think that we're bouncers," he says. "But that type of policing has gone out. I try to settle things verbally."

When the 26-year-old policeman does get involved in a major case, it may be promptly taken out of his hands. Recently, he headed off to question workers at an auto-parts store on his beat that had been robbed a few days earlier by three armed men. But he found that a detective had been there the previous day. "You do something, and you turn around and find that the detectives are doing the same thing," Miller complains.

Miller's political-science degree from a Pennsylvania college qualifies him to be one of 134 agents on the Baltimore force, a step up from patrolman in status and salary. "My college courses gave me a lot more insight into how people act," he says.

The young policeman isn't disappointed about the lack of constant action on his beat. "The job has its ups and downs," he admits. But the variety of assignments and the opportunity to help all kinds of people has led him to conclude: "I could stay on the street all the time."

Police work also is drawing an increasing number of young women. Jennifer Wehr, 25, turned to a police career in Baltimore after studying dance at Goucher College and later being "really bored" as manag-

Jennifer Wehr

er of a store. "It's a decent way to make a living," she says. "When something happens, you're there and you can help. It makes you feel good."

Wehr, one of 60 women on the city's 3,200-member force, says she took up police work without any illusions that it would be as dramatic as television viewers might expect it to be. "This is not a beat-'em-up, shoot-'em-up job," she declares.

Like other Baltimore officers, Wehr patrols alone in her squad car. She believes that the setup is more efficient than the two-officer cars used in many cities because it allows more cars on the street. But officers must be quick to aid each other when trouble occurs.

On a recent night in Baltimore's southwestern district, Wehr devoted much of her shift to writing reports on auto accidents and standing by until tow trucks arrived to remove disabled vehicles. Among other tasks: checking on a woman whose daughter couldn't reach her by telephone, lecturing a youth who had tossed an ice ball at a city bus, escorting a female prisoner to a police-station bathroom, waiting outside the scene of a family disturbance in case the officer handling the call had trouble, and checking on a passenger who fell out of a car.

Is it tough for a woman to get along in a largely male profession? Her answer: "You get a lot of teasing, but once you prove yourself, you're accepted."

James M. Miller

must spend time and money defending themselves. This has made firms that insure officers jittery, often to the point of canceling policies. The American Home Assurance Company, which formerly sold liability coverage to more than 1,000 police departments, now insures only 370. Rates for some cities have risen as much as 700 percent in recent years. A typical charge: $200 per officer each year.

Meanwhile, criminal charges or disciplinary actions accusing law-enforcement officers of brutality or corruption show no sign of abating. The U.S. Commission on Civil Rights reports that last year it received "an increasing number of citizen complaints and reports indicating that police misconduct remains a widespread phenomenon that has, in some cities, become so pervasive as to appear officially sanctioned."

The Justice Department logged some 12,000 complaints last year about police officers' excessive use of force. About 70 officers were charged during that period with violating the civil rights of citizens.

In Philadelphia, three brutality cases were filed, involving a total of 19 officers, and a dozen more are under investigation. So far, six have been convicted and three acquitted. In another case that received wide attention, three former Houston officers were found guilty in February of violating the rights of a Mexican American who drowned while in their custody. During the same month in Louisiana, a federal grand jury indicted the town marshal of Bonita on charges of beating and Macing two suspects and charged two policemen from Bossier City with administering electric shocks to two prisoners.

Curbing payoffs. As for corruption, no one keeps count of exactly how many officers are implicated each year. But it is clear that the problem is still widespread. In recent years, there have been major police-corruption probes in Chicago, Indianapolis, Cincinnati, Denver and Atlanta, among other cities. In New York City, a special commission uncovered widespread payoffs to police in the early 1970s, and corruption charges have flared up from time to time ever since. New York officials disclosed in February that one inquiry alone resulted in 67 police employes' being charged with violating gambling and narcotics laws during the last two years.

Despite the flurry of police scandals, many experts doubt that crookedness and other types of misconduct by police have increased in recent years. In fact, some believe there may be less misbehavior now that police salaries and hiring procedures have improved. They contend that police misconduct only seems like a bigger problem today, because federal officials and news reporters alike are working harder at exposing it than ever before.

Hitting the Bricks

As the public steps up demands to improve police practices, the police are more aggressively pressing demands of their own. At the head of the list: better salaries and fringe benefits. The average annual pay for rookie officers around the country increased from about $7,500 in 1971 to nearly $10,350 five years later, according to one survey. But many police officers argue that the dangers they face, their irregular working hours and their broad responsibility for everything from breaking up barroom brawls to delivering babies entitles them to more.

To put muscle behind their demands, police increasingly are turning to unionization and collective bargaining. Most states prohibit police officers from striking, but that hasn't stopped police from Cleveland to Tucson from doing just that in recent years, often by calling in sick. And James VanDevender, president of the Detroit Police Officers Association, predicts that "the public can expect more outbreaks of blue flu in the next couple of years."

Estimates vary, but it is believed that at least two thirds of the nation's police officers belong to unions with collective-bargaining powers—up from only about 25 percent 15 years ago. Increased police militancy is due in part to lessons police learned while dealing with the civil-rights movement and antiwar demonstrations of the 1960s. "Cops saw that confrontation politics worked," says Richard F. Mayer, a labor-relations specialist for the International Association of Chiefs of Police.

Because it is relatively new, the police labor movement is still fragmented. Among major organizations are the International Conference of Police Associations, the Fraternal Order of Police and the International Brotherhood of Police Officers. The Teamsters Union and the American Federation of State, County and Municipal Employes also have recruited police members, with limited success.

Besides concerns over police paychecks, the unions and other police-support groups are involved in many other efforts to improve the lives of their members.

Seeking evidence of a crime can be dirty, uncomfortable work.

To aid police in taking the offensive against groundless accusations of misconduct, Americans for Effective Law Enforcement is publishing a newsletter on the subject. "Tired of being a civil defendant?" the group asks in one of its issues. "Read how other law-enforcement officers and agencies are filing suits." One example offered: A California highway patrolman won a $28,000 award from a jury in a lawsuit accusing his neighbors of falsely reporting that he had harassed them.

"Bill of rights." The police are fighting, too, against charges directed at them by their own superiors. They are asking Congress and state legislatures to enact a police "bill of rights" that would help officers to defend themselves in disciplinary cases. Five states have adopted it so far.

Part of the drive for police rights is an increasing tendency of police to challenge the influence of politicians

2. POLICE

on promotions, assignments or other internal police matters—a problem that long has been the bane of certain departments. One case in point: A Fort Wayne, Ind., patrolman was transferred because he criticized the city's new mayor. The patrolman got his job back only after a public campaign by business owners on the beat.

Police also are taking action to deal with the threats their work poses to their physical and mental health. The Federal Bureau of Investigation reports that 111 law-enforcement officers were killed and nearly 50,000 assaulted in 1976. Many of the deaths and injuries result from attempts to make arrests, but family quarrels account for a lot of this violence; nearly one third of the assaults occurred as officers responded to "disturbance" calls.

Because police in some areas had only meager death benefits, Congress passed a law in 1976 providing a $50,000 payment

As civil-rights groups press hiring demands, minority and female officers are being seen more often in patrol cars around the nation.

for survivors of officers who die in the line of duty. In the 18 months since the measure went into effect, the Justice Department has approved 148 claims for benefits. Most of the cases involved gunshot wounds and automobile accidents. In 1977, police groups persuaded Congress to pass legislation setting up a group-life-insurance program for them.

Love and Marriage

The stress caused by police work also is getting more attention. It is being blamed for divorces, alcoholism, nervous breakdowns and suicides. Last year, 27 of the 66 Los Angeles police officers who received disability pensions cited psychological causes. "Police see the seamy side of life. They become cynical, suspicious and depressed and begin to think the whole world is that way," says James C. Parsons, police chief of Birmingham, Ala.

Police departments are increasingly making psychiatric help available to their officers. And the Boston Police Department has started a program in which officers themselves counsel colleagues who come to them with problems. The unit was formed because policemen with difficulties have traditionally "put up a blue wall" and refused to confide in outsiders, explains Edward C. Donovan, the unit's assistant director.

More police departments, too, are using psychological testing to screen out unsuitable candidates before they enter police work. More than one third of police officers are unsuited for police work and are "untreatable," declares Dr. Edward E. Shev, a psychiatrist who has worked with police departments in California. "The actions of this minority are usually responsible for the bad reputation of police in many communities."

As police experts look to the future, they see somewhat contradictory trends. The educational level of those seeking police jobs has jumped dramatically in the past decade. Helped by an infusion of 250 million dollars in federal aid to 300,000 law-enforcement students under a program that began in 1969, the number of police officers with at least some college education more than doubled between 1960 and 1974, from 20 to more than 46 percent.

Yet the expansion of the job market appears to be slowing. A report prepared last year for the Law Enforcement Assistance Administration concluded that the growth of police departments will slow considerably in coming years "as the combined result of a projected slowdown in crime

rates and of tighter state and local-government budgets." Cutbacks so far have been concentrated in the big cities. New York City will eliminate 976 police jobs by attrition during the next 15 months. The resulting 23,400-member force will be nearly 8,000 smaller than the peak strength of the early 1970s. In Washington, D.C., the police force has dropped from 5,100 to 4,150 since 1972.

But as large urban departments are trimmed back, many suburban departments are expanding. For this and other reasons, the Department of Labor predicts that an average of 32,000 police jobs will open each year through 1985, a higher rate than for many other occupations.

Because of the tightened job market, police executives will be able to choose recruits more carefully than in the past, usually favoring better-educated applicants. Maurice J. Cullinane, who retired recently as police chief of Washington, D.C., says that this trend is a contrast to previous decades, when the ideal policeman was regarded as someone with "a large physical stature who could enforce the law because he was a powerful individual." Cullinane adds that "now the emphasis is on the opposite"—knowledge and training.

Most police chiefs agree that the officer of the future will be required to do a lot more than fire a gun and collect fingerprints. The typical police officer is "the guy who intervenes in the family dispute and who picks up the drunks from the city's streets," says Charles R. Gain, San Francisco's police chief. "Less than 10 percent of his time is spent chasing armed robbers or tracking down burglars."

How the public feels. Despite frequent criticism of police wrongdoing, the public regards the police well. Federally financed surveys in 13 big cities showed that the percentage of those questioned who believed that police performance was "good" or "average" increased from 79 to 81 percent between 1972 and 1975.

In spite of the throes of change rocking America's police profession, many officers still find their work highly satisfying. They predict that there will be no shortage of young people eager to take their places when they retire. Says Bobby Joe Dale, a Dallas police officer for 24 years, "At the end of the day there's a feeling that I've done the best I could and somebody benefited from it. You've taken an obstacle out of the way for society. It's a feeling you can't get anywhere else."

Associate Editor Ted Gest wrote this article, with reporting assistance from the magazine's eight domestic bureaus.

Integrated Professionalism: A Model for Controlling Police Practices

Barbara Raffel Price

Barbara Raffel Price is an associate professor of law and police science at John Jay College of Criminal Justice and holds a doctoral degree in sociology. She has served as research supervisor of the Police Executive Development Program and as director of the Police Supervisor In-service Training Program. A member of both the board of editors of *Criminology* and the executive board of the American Society of Criminology, she has also been executive secretary of the American Society of Criminology. She has authored articles on police personnel and jail services and practices for such journals as *Criminology, Criminal Justice Review, Journal of Police Science and Administration, The Police Chief,* and *Federal Probation.* Dr. Price is also the author of two books: *Jails and Drug Treatment,* coauthored with Charles L. Newman, and *Police Professionalism: Rhetoric and Action.*

Since the establishment of the first police department in America, the public has intermittently been critical of the police. Police are periodically berated for both real and imagined abuses of their power and authority. Attacks on the police reflect the public's generally ambivalent stance toward its institution of social control. On the one hand, the citizenry fear disorder and crime (especially predatory crime) and recognize their dependency on the police for protection. On the other hand, the public fears the police, with its monopoly on force, and is particularly fearful that police power might get out of control. These citizen fears have historical roots which go back to our ancestors' experiences of subjugation by military and police forces in their European homes. In modern times, distrust of the police has continued as we witness political coups in other countries and the emergence of police states. Within our own country, concerns over police abuse are not without foundation—we need only consider disclosures of break-ins into private residences, spying and other criminal acts by the FBI, or charges against city police of brutality, beatings, and the murder of citizens.

Highly publicized examples of police abuse may represent occasional cases of malpractice;

nonetheless, policing today needs to develop more effective ways to curtail its own illegal activities. What strategies might control and prevent police deviance? Do we need more punitive measures, more formal charges, and court trials; or is there a more positive way to approach the problem? Does professionalism offer a promising model to counter police deviance?

The police occupation frequently claims to be a profession. If we listen to police administrators, particularly those who speak for the occupation, we hear that policing has already achieved a certain professional status. Police rhetoric makes claims to professionalism, and it is that rhetoric that gives us a rough approximation of where police are in their actual professional development. The rhetoric depicts police interest in "acting like" professionals, and it also provides clues as to how the actual professionalism can work for the occupation. In what follows, the potential of integrated professionalism for preventing police abuses and illegal actions will be described. Integrated professionalism means that professionalism prevails throughout the department at the administrative, management, and line levels.

Reprinted by permission of the *Journal of Police Science and Administration,* copyright 1979 by the International Association of Chiefs of Police, Inc., Vol. 7, No. 1, pp. 93-97.

2. POLICE

THE PROBLEM: INSTILLING
SELF-CONTROL IN POLICE

By law police are implementors of violent force. They have the potential to wield extraordinary power. Of all criminal justice actors, the police are the most powerful, largely because of the great amount of discretion available to them.[1] They can deprive individuals of freedom, and under certain circumstances, society permits them to injure and, indeed, even kill. Although we give these special powers to the police, we also want to control their use. The American Bar Association has said:

> The continuing failure to devise and implement necessary procedures and sanctions to deal with police abuses is one of the most critical problems now confronting our society.[2]
> [The] courts are ill-equipped to control police conduct.[3]
> The need is for more effective administrative control.[4]

If we are willing to accept the possibility that police, as an occupation, have the ability to control themselves, and if we can imagine them acquiring, or in some cases already possessing, the managerial skills to exert administrative control, then the challenge lies in developing a system of control over improper use of authority and in instilling in police an appetite for participating in that task. The need is for developing voluntary self-control in the police, and that is where professionalism's strength lies. Because professionalism actually promotes a system of beliefs supportive of self-control, it generates self-regulation. Professionalism fosters responsibility (both for the individual and the occupation); it fosters objective standards in decision-making; it puts attention on ends as well as means, and it promotes self-evaluation.

If we look to the professional model and the fundamental traits of professionalism, we see that for an occupation to call itself a profession, it must exhibit a unique and specialized body of knowledge that is written down and can be transmitted abstractly, a dedication to service, self-regulation, performance neutrality, standards governing internalized decisions, and a code of ethics. In addition to these attributes, a mature profession also pays as much attention to the processes by which ends are achieved as it does to the ends themselves. When the role and importance of process is accepted by the mem-

bers of an occupation, and when the reward structure of the occupation recognizes the process, then the issues of self-control and structuring constituted authority should become manageable.

Assume for the moment that the professional model is the appropriate system for control of police activity. To be effective it must operate in two fairly distinctive ways. First, the professional model must operate at the administrative level; and, second, it must be present at the line level. Each of the police roles will be considered separately as they affect self-regulation.

THE POLICE ADMINISTRATOR

We know that external remedies to police abuses, such as exist through the courts or through government liability for officer misconduct, provide insufficient deterrence, largely because they react to an event rather than anticipate future events. The more immediate proactive strategies to meet the problem of police abuses have tended to be the responsibility of police administrators. Through leadership, they can (1) articulate clear standards of police conduct, (2) establish the necessary internal rules and procedures, (3) develop appropriate sanctions, and (4) set a climate of respect for the law.

One of the reasons that administrators do not aggressively control officer conduct is because the organizational structure of the criminal justice system works against it. As the system is organized, police must share their own self-regulation responsibility with two other sectors, the courts and political superiors. Where shared authority exists, it generally tends to be abdicated by all parties, but it is most often abdicated by those who view themselves as lower in the status hierarchy. The police consider themselves inferior in status to the judiciary. Their assessment is realistic, based on such differentials as salary, educational level, and public prestige. Until police administrators see themselves as the professional equal of others in government, they are unlikely to fully assume the self-regulation responsibility. The *Task Force Report: The Police* issued in 1967 by the President's Commission on Law Enforcement and Administration of Justice commented as follows on police deference to the courts:

> Unlike internal matters over which the police administrator has complete control, much of what the police do relating to crimes and criminals is dependent for approval upon the decision of non-police agencies.[5]

---

[1] Lawrence W. Sherman, "The Sociology and the Social Reform of the Police," *J. Police Sci. & Adm.,* 2(3) (1974), 259.
[2] American Bar Association, *The Urban Police Function* (1972), 120.
[3] ABA, 152.
[4] ABA, 152.

[5] President's Commission on Law Enforcement and Administration of Justice, *Task Force Report: The Police* (1967), 193.

As the police increasingly professionalize, they should also be able to increasingly deal on an equal basis with other sectors of the criminal justice system as well as with the political sector. Professionalism enhances one's self-image. As administrators' self-confidence improves, they will be better able to accept their role of controlling their department and will resume some of the responsibility which has by default fallen to other external control units. Thus, one way professionalism can indirectly control police practices is by improving the self-image and self-confidence of the occupation and its incumbents. [6]

Elsewhere this author has argued that a case can be made for progress in police professionalization over the last 100 years by using evidence from police rhetoric. [7] This rhetoric of administrators is especially visible when police defend themselves from a critical public. We hear: "Who are they [the public] to judge us, the professionals?" and "We are true professionals." Data exists that indicate police have become increasingly professionalized as measured by the broadening of professional interests from basic concerns about salary to attention to the technology of policing to, most recently, justifying the occupation's contributions to the social good. [8] Over the years the earlier police concerns remained, and new ones have been added so that the rhetoric has become increasingly rich, diverse, and sophisticated. But by whatever yardstick we care to use, there is no doubt that the professionalizing process is accelerating. In the last decade, there has been a substantial increase in the body of special knowledge; training has become longer and more complex; higher educational standards are being imposed at entrance. Police rhetoric reflects all of these changes, and it is freely used by chiefs.

Professionalism rhetoric plays a positive role for the police as a response to criticism. It helps to protect the occupation. However, it is also the case that the rhetoric had, and still has today, serious dysfunction: it enables police leadership to limit reform. By talking in ways that are acceptable to their superiors in the political sector, and by reassuring their own subordinates of their professionalism, police are able to substitute words for action. In effect, in rhetoric, the status of professionalism was assumed by the police administrator long before the reality of professionalism existed. In addition to this negative consequence of the rhetoric, many aspects of professionalism, described in the next section, lead to resistance from administrators.

WAYS THE PROFESSIONAL MODEL CAN CONTROL POLICE PRACTICES: THE LINE LEVEL

Professionalism encourages utilization of discretion by the street officer. It fosters lower-level decisionmaking, because training and education are high priority items in the professional model. Once people have been trained and socialized for a job, they expect to be given the opportunity to use their skills. In law enforcement, operations-level work involves continuous decisionmaking. Citizen calls for service require fresh determinations by the officer as each event occurs. The professional model anticipates that substantial discretion and authority will be exercised by the line level and that these professionals will have internalized, through socialization and training, skill in making legal and appropriate responses to citizens.

In conjunction with expanded line-level discretion, professionalism encourages rolemaking by subordinates rather than the more traditional roletaking from the organization. In rolemaking, work expectations are defined more by the officer than the department, which means the burden of responsibility for these activities is on the line level. Team policing enhances this aspect of professionalism in that each team develops special definitions of tasks to be accomplished and objectives to be met. Decentralization, through giving teams authority, requires that a greater degree of accountability be assigned to officers.

Further, professionalism can control police practices because it undermines organizational loyalty of police by encouraging members of the occupation to identify with the larger occupation. As this occurs, incumbents look outside the department for guidance and performance standards. This leads to the emergence of occupationwide standards; and, in turn, these standards reinforce the shifting of identification beyond the department and its own less rigorous standards. As police replace department norms with occupationwide standards, they tend to identify more with the sanctioning of abusive police practices and adherence to high ethical standards.

[6] The danger of partial professionalization has been demonstrated in the case of the FBI. For years the organization fostered a professional image which the public believed. FBI rhetoric was that of the professional, but it had not adopted the behavior of professionals. Members neither accepted individual responsibility for their actions, nor did they have sufficient independence to act with "right conduct." However, the public acknowledged their professionalism and had confidence in the organization. As a result, the FBI was permitted an enormous amount of autonomy.

[7] Barbara R. Price, "The Rhetoric of Professionalism: A Comparative Study of Police in Three Historical Periods" (Ph.D. diss., Pennsylvania State University, 1974), and *Police Professionalism: Rhetoric and Action* (1977).

[8] R. M. MacIver, "The Social Significance of Professional Ethics," *Annals of the Am. Acad. of Pol. & Soc. Sci.*, 297 (1955), 118-124.

Another aspect of professionalism breaks down the traditional secrecy of the police organization by encouraging more opening up of communications within the department as well as with the outside. Changes in police practices (such as informing the public about crime problems and police capabilities to respond) can create changed expectations and eventually more realistic demands from the public. In opening up communications, it may become possible to develop interdepartmental review boards and other activities to reassure the public by giving clear evidence that police are, in fact, engaged in self-regulation.

Improved self-image, increased internalized performance accountability, more roletaking and less rolemaking, less loyalty to the department and more to the occupation at large, and decreased secrecy of operations are all ways that the professional model can foster control of police behavior. Administrators are understandably ambivalent about these changes because they undermine direct executive control and require placing greater trust in their subordinates. However, the line level can see the advantages in their own commitment to professionalism (1) as administrators support the changes in the context of providing appropriate training, (2) as chiefs establish sound systems of accountability for checking on performance and establish detailed descriptions of appropriate and inappropriate conduct, and (3) as they create a fair hearing and review structure for alleged officer violations. We know that the "right conduct" (i.e., abiding by legal and organizational rules) of the line level cannot just be mandated by administrative policy. Moreover, use of peer pressure and the setting of an appropriate climate by administration and even direct supervision cannot assure good policing given a dispersed command structure. But the professional model offers a promising approach to police malpractice because under it officers are socialized to conduct themselves within legal constraints. Concurrently, administrators must encourage and reward such behavior.

Only with line level acceptance of their role in controlling police abuse can police malpractice be reduced, and this can happen as the police officer accepts professionalism's demands for internalized standards of behavior, devotion to service, neutrality, and objectivity. The police officer will also have to accept the notion that the process of enforcing the law is as important as the enforcement itself. When officers recognize that how an arrest is made is as critical as the arrest itself, and when they assume the responsibility for the discretion they exercise, policing will be a profession. At the line level there must be as complete a commitment to professionalism as at the administrative level.

If it is the case that the officer is a key factor in creating an internal system for controlling police malpractice, and if that control cannot be assured by direct observation and supervision, then a model of integrated professionalism in which both management and line level are professionally committed may be the most successful control strategy. As the officer professionalizes, independence in decisionmaking will be guided by both a code of ethics and the systematic application of a body of knowledge.[9] This use of law enforcement expertise in conjunction with ethical standards means that police apprehensions will be lawfully executed and the potential of endangering other citizens or the police themselves in the process will be minimized.

SUMMARY

Integrated professionalism implies that professionalism permeates the police occupation at all ranks. Administrators would still retain final responsibility for the conduct of subordinates, but under integrated professionalism, they would not be placed in the impossible position of sole enforcer of police behavior. The proposed model encourages a collaborative effort within police departments for providing community social control and protection through the responsible use of decentralized police authority. When police have a true stake in devising necessary procedures to deal with police abuses, the problems of administrative rulemaking and internal procedures will diminish.

This article began by noting that criticism of police in America has become virtually a chronic state of affairs. Breaking the pattern requires a new model with built-in incentives for reduction of police abuse. The model proposed here has these incentives in that it gives additional autonomy to line-level police while providing for its judicious exercise. For administrators it holds out the prospect of exchanging public dissatisfaction with their organization for public approval of both the department and the administration. Professionalism implies voluntary compliance; it holds promise for both technical proficiency in law enforcement and protection of individual liberties within a system of social order.

[9] E. Mintz and G. Sandler, "A Service Model for the New York City Police Department" (unpublished, NYPD, 1973).

POLICE FOR HIRE

Fear Pays a Dividend To Those Who Guard

Bruce Cory

Bruce Cory is a free-lance writer based in Houston, Texas.

EVERY April, George Wackenhut performs what undoubtedly is a most enjoyable duty. He reports to his stockholders.

At the 1978 general stockholders meeting, held in Coral Gables, Fla., where the Wackenhut Corporation is headquartered, he announced a record 20 percent increase in profits for the previous year. This year's annual report showed a more modest twelve percent rise in 1978 profits. But that still put the company's after-tax revenue over the $3 million mark, another year-end record.

George Wackenhut, a former special agent for the FBI, is the president and chairman of the board of the nation's third largest private security company. Founded just 25 years ago, the Wackenhut Corp. now employs more than 20,000 guards in the U.S., Europe, South America and the Middle East. Much of Wackenhut's success springs from the company's consistent ability to land major government security contracts, such as its current $4.7 million-a-year agreement to protect the Cape Kennedy Space Center. By a remarkable coincidence, the company's board of directors is studded

with the names of retired civilian and military intelligence executives. But the Wackenhut Corp. also has prospered because the industry it is part of has prospered. And there is no end to the industry's growth in sight.

The New York Times recently estimated that $12 billion is spent on private security in the U.S. annually. Despite the proliferation in recent years of increasingly sophisticated closed-circuit television and burglar alarm systems, 50 to 60 percent of the industry's revenues still comes from the services it originated in the 1850s: private detectives, guards, courier services and armored-car deliveries.

The growth in the private security industry has produced a steady stream of new companies entering the field. *Entrepreneur* magazine estimates that a security company offering neighborhood patrol service can gross as much as $100,000 its first year on an average cash investment of $14,000. The magazine candidly urges would-be security operators to scare customers into doing business with them. It advises mailing out advertising brochures headlined with phrases like, "Protect your loved ones!" and which should "trumpet local crime statistics." The mailing, it continues, should be followed by telephone sales pitches that "capitalize on fear." The article also urges security operators to hire police department applicants who are on long recruit wait-

ing lists, or applicants who "wash-out" for other than psychological reasons.

Police officers themselves, of course, frequently take second jobs in security. Most major police departments prohibit their officers from running security firms, or from doing private investigatory work, in order to prevent conflicts of interest. But individual private guard service is another matter. *The Other Police*, a 1975 study of private security in Cleveland, estimated that between 20 and 35 percent of local law enforcement officers worked second jobs in security. In Houston, Police Chief Harry Caldwell has estimated that as many as 80 percent of his officers hold second security jobs. This widespread moonlighting is frequently viewed with resentment by private security operators, who see police as unfair competition for the private security dollar.

No one is sure just how many people work in private security. Marketing studies made in the mid-1970s put the figure at about one-half million, or about as many as are publicly employed in law enforcement or protection of government property. But the industry's rapid growth has made even such recent estimates obsolete. In New York State, according to *The New York Times,* the number of private guards has more than tripled since 1973 to roughly 200,000, or about four times the number of police officers in the state. In many cities, private security guards outnumber public police officers by two-to-one or better. A 1975 study found 8,900 private guards and detectives working in Cuyahoga County (Cleveland), Ohio, compared with 4,150 sworn law enforcement officers. That same year, another study identified 4,187 licensed private security guards in New Orleans, compared with 1,413 police officers.

"Our biggest problem now is finding manpower," said E.J. Criscuoli, executive director of the American Society for Industrial Security (ASIS), the largest of more than 30 national security trade associations. ASIS membership, which is limited to owners or managers of security systems or companies, has doubled to 12,000 in the last four years. Those 12,000 people run an estimated 4,000-plus private security firms, ranging from multinational giants like Wackenhut to "mom and pop" operations of three employees or less. During hearings last April before the U.S. Senate Subcommittee on Criminal Laws and Procedures, Criscuoli's testimony prompted one subcommittee staff analyst to question whether "we have created a situation which has, unintentionally, started turning the United States into a garrison state."

Although it has only been in recent years that the security industry has emerged as a multi-billion dollar giant, the use of private guards and detectives in the U.S. is hardly new. Allan Pinkerton founded the nation's first private detective agency in the 1850s. Through the turn of the century, and before the formation of the Secret Service or FBI, "the Pinkertons" were the only detective agency capable of mounting nationwide manhunts. One of the best-known moments in the movie *Butch Cassidy and the Sundance Kid* came when Paul Newman, as the fleeing Cassidy, looked over his shoulder at his pursuers and muttered, "Who are those guys?" "Those guys" were Pinkerton's agents.

Pinkerton detectives also gained an unsavory reputation as strikebreakers and spies during the great union organizing drives between the 1870s and 1930s. In 1939, a U.S. Senate Select Committee on Violations of Free Speech and Rights of Labor issued a report condemning the "ruthless and brutal activities of armed guards to

prevent union organization." State and federal legislation has since restricted the use of private guards during strikes to the protection of private property. But anti-strike activity still plays a major role in private security operations.

In his 1978 stockholders report, George Wackenhut noted that "our total support services, which assist companies in maintaining operations during labor disturbances, had a banner year in 1977." A company brochure on "emergency support service" describes how the Wackenhut Corp. provides meals, bedding, laundry service and ping-pong tables for supervisory workers confined to a factory or mine during a strike. And at least one of the major security companies has been accused of an anti-union attitude toward its own employees. Henry Applen, vice-president of the 50,000-member United Plant Guard Workers of America, said his union has contracts and a "pretty good relationship" with all the major guard service companies except Pinkerton's, Inc. "They're just an anti-union outfit," he said.*

In 1909, a second national detective agency was founded by former Secret Service agent William J. Burns. Burns International Detective Agency, with 38,000 employees, ranks just behind Pinkerton's, with 40,000 employees, as the nation's second largest guard service. World War II and defense contracts mandating plant security systems boosted the number of private guards and sparked the formation of more security companies. The advent of the Cold War kept American industry on a tight security footing. But the greatest impetus to the security industry's growth was the climbing crime rate in the 1960s. By 1968, Solomon Baker, chairman of the board of Baker Industries, a major manufacturer of alarm systems and the parent company of Wells Fargo Security Services, announced that his company's sales had nearly quadrupled in the previous four years. "The industry," he said, "is geared toward several central and contemporary factors of our society, in-

*Applen said about 70 percent of his union's members are "proprietary" — that is, in-house — guards, most of them employed in industrial plants in the East and Midwest. The number of proprietary guards in the U.S. has dwindled slightly since the early 1960s, while the use of contract guard services has skyrocketed.

cluding the increasing crime rate and resulting demands for law and order." Although much of the private security industry's work is in fact geared toward preventing employee pilferage, industry spokesmen constantly stress "crime in the streets" as reason for their existence. "The day we live in," wrote John Peel, author of *Fundamentals of Training for Security Officers,* "with its unremitting parade of viciousness, depravity and wanton savagery, makes the private security officer a person of immense importance."

By the early 1970s, uniformed and, frequently, armed security officers were being assigned to guard public places where they had never been seen before. In St. Louis, where the number of private security personnel increased by 263 percent between 1960 and 1975, the number of guards employed in industrial protection actually declined. Dramatic increases occurred in the number of guards working at colleges and schools, private hospitals and in retail stores.

As budget cutbacks and hiring freezes continue to plague big-city police departments, the number of security guards is likely to increase. Indeed, grocery shopping at some inner-city Detroit supermarkets is an excursion into the garrison state. In some stores, the business office is a cage made of bullet-proof glass, suspended from the ceiling, and armed guards patrol the checkout areas.

In Philadelphia, private security has played an important role in that city's downtown "renaissance." "It has filled an enormous vacuum," said Ian Lennox, director of the Philadelphia Crime Commission, a crime prevention group funded by the chamber of commerce. "When the tax dollars [for city police] got short, the business community turned to private security." A court-imposed hiring freeze during a mid-1970s sex discrimination suit against the Philadelphia Police Department also spurred the use of private security agencies, he said.

As a result, the city's massive new shopping mall, the Gallery, is patrolled entirely by private guards. "The city police," Lennox said, "don't come within its walls." Armed campus security guards have also regularly patrolled four subway stops near Philadelphia's Temple University since a student was attacked and killed at one of the stops more than a year ago.

The increased use of contract security guards in new and highly visible assignments disturbs many observers. Little is known about the largely unregulated private security industry, and what is known is disquieting. The authors of the Rand Corporation's pioneering 1971 study, *Private Police in the United States,* noted: "To an extent of which the public is unaware, licensed private detectives often engage men of scant ability and little stability." The typical private guard, the Rand researchers found, "is an aging white male, poorly educated, usually untrained and very poorly paid," earning the minimum wage or only slightly more. Frequently ignorant of the law, often possessed of exaggerated notions of their own legal authority to use force or make arrests, most private guards received less than two days of pre-work training before being assigned to their posts, the Rand researchers found. "The majority of the private guard forces in the United States do not have any formal training program or any specified curriculum," they wrote. The annual turnover rate among security guards was estimated at 200 percent.

Lax personnel screening and hiring have plagued the private security field. A Philadelphia prosecutor told CBS's *60 Minutes* in 1975 that "one of the biggest problems we have with private security guards is that they end up stealing things. ... Hardly a month goes by that we don't get a complaint from a security agency somewhere, or from a store, that security agents within the store have been caught stealing things." It is a problem that persists. In May 1977 a private guard previously convicted of sexually abusing a child was arrested for the murder of an eight-year-old Brooklyn boy at the apartment complex the guard was assigned to protect. That same year, more than 10,000 of the 37,000 new guards in New York State were found to have arrest or conviction records.

The exact number of armed private security guards in the U.S. is unknown, with estimates running anywhere from 75,000 to 175,000 or more. Firearms training for private guards has varied greatly from state to state and from company to company. The larger firms provide in-house training. Other

guards have often received no firearms instruction. A 1974 study by the Institute for Local Self Government in California found that 55 percent of the security employees surveyed sometimes carried firearms on the job, but only eight percent had received firearms training at their current jobs. The Rand report speculated that 49 percent of the nation's security officers carried firearms, but only 19 percent had received any training.

Although a few police departments regulate the private police in their cities (as the St. Louis police have for more than 100 years), the licensing and regulation of private detectives and guards is most often overseen by state agencies. A few mostly rural states still do not license private security agencies. A few others license them only to raise revenue. But within the last five years, many of the larger states, including Ohio, Pennsylvania, Texas and Virginia, have adopted or strengthened laws requiring the training of armed private security guards. In 1978, Virginia adopted legislation requiring 80 hours of training for armed private guards. And several bills have been introduced in the current session of the Texas legislature to require 80 hours of training and psychological screening for security guards commissioned to carry sidearms.

The American Society for Industrial Security and security company executives have generally applauded the trend toward tighter regulation of their trade. Stan Schrotel, a former Cincinnati police chief who is now director of "corporate risk management" for the Kroger Co. supermarket chain, said stricter training standards for private guards are needed to help "overcome an image that has been rather indelibly imprinted of the security guard as not very much more than a vegetable."

But former Washington, D.C., police chief Jerry Wilson, now the president of his own private security firm in Bethesda, Md., questions how high the standards for private guards really need to be. "I'm all for strict requirements for armed guards," he said. "But does someone who is guarding a junkyard as a fire watch really need a high school degree?" In 1976, the National Advisory Commission on Criminal Justice Standards and Goals, on which Wilson sat, recommended that all pri-

vate guards be required to have a high school diploma or its equivalent before being hired. Wilson said some of the committee's most heated debates were generated by such proposed standards for the private security industry. "The reason was that the private security task force, which was very much in favor of strong regulation, was heavily weighted with representatives of the major security firms," he said. "And when people within an industry start talking about the need for professionalism, you can be sure that part of what they're doing is trying to set standards to exclude everyone else from getting in." The trend toward higher standards, Wilson predicted, will drive small operators out of business and concentrate the security trade in the hands of the major national firms.

Other observers concede that tighter regulation may close down small security operations, but view that as the price of progress. "It's usually the small, fly-by-night companies that give security a black eye," said Hal Hendricks, a public relations executive with Wackenhut. "I suppose it will force out of the market those who are in the market for a buck," said E.J. Criscuoli of ASIS, "and that, as a by-product, the big ones [companies] will get bigger." How much bigger is hard to tell. In the 1977 edition of their textbook, *Security Administration,* Richard Post and Arthur Kingsbury estimated that Pinkerton's, Burns, Wackenhut, Guardsmark and Globe Security Systems already account for a combined total of 50 percent of the security industry's annual revenues.

Hospital security has been one of the fastest growing fields in the security industry in the last ten years. A 1977 U.S. Commerce Department report, *Crime in Service Industries,* noted that the daily use of the nation's hospitals by more than a million patients, visitors and staff makes the potential for crime in hospitals "phenomenal." Estimates of the amount of property lost to hospital theft vary. Nationally, one industry source has speculated that such theft losses amount to about $1,000 per hospital bed annually.

Providing protection from violent crime to hospital users and employees is also a major security problem.

But hospitals around the country have had great difficulty finding private security firms that they trust. Pittsburgh, Pennsylvania's Mercy Hospital thinks it has solved this problem by bringing in five retired police officers to supervise its private guards.

Until mid-1976, a force of 15 unarmed Wackenhut Corporation guards had been solely responsible for security at Mercy, a 600-bed hospital on the edge of Pittsburgh's downtown black ghetto, known as "the Hill District." The former officers, who were brought in to supervise the contract guards through a "watch commander" system, all carry sidearms.

In three years the hospital's watch commanders have never fired their guns, or even drawn them. They have relied more heavily on their experience in dealing with distraught and disturbed people than on force or coercion of any kind. "These men have developed the equivalents of Ph.D's on the street," said Les Stone, an assistant administrator at Mercy. "They have given us what we wanted, a soft but extremely firm approach."

Like many of the nation's older hospitals, Mercy Hospital serves a broad social and economic cross-section of the Pittsburgh area from one of the city's most blighted high-crime neighborhoods.

The hospital buildings cover five city blocks; there are 26 entrances to the interconnecting buildings and most of them are unlocked 24 hours a day. The hospital stocks huge inventories of drugs, linens, food, medical equipment and other supplies that are, to varying degrees, attractive or accessible to potential thieves. (Drugs, the most attractive of such items, are the least accessible.)

Wackenhut assumed the contract for security at Mercy Hospital in 1969, and, said Mercy's associate executive director Hileman, provided better service than had been provided by a locally owned firm before them. "But their turnover rate has been astronomical," he said, "and frankly, some of them [the guards] have been little more than warm bodies." (The current starting wage for Wackenhut guards at Mercy is $3 per hour.) In 1976, the hospital hired Richard Ehland, a 26-year veteran of the Pittsburgh Police Department with most of his experience in the Hill District, to take over hospital security. "I told them they would have to pay the price and hire professionals," said Ehland, now director of security for Pittsburgh's transit authority. (The hospital's watch com-

manders currently earn about $15,000 per year.) "The contract type of security does not, and never will work," he said. "Most of the time, you're adding problems with them [contract guards] instead of solving them."

For that reason, Ehland chose for his watch commanders former city police officers with long years of duty in the Hill District.

Future security plans at Mercy Hospital call for a reduced reliance on contract guards; the hospital has already taken bids to install a closed circuit television system in its eight-story parking garage, a move that will eliminate one of the security system's five regular guard posts. Warren Brevard, the security director, speculated that closed-circuit television and electronic sensors in other parts of the hospital will probably cut further the number of contract guards within the next ten years. But the pace of this automation will depend on how much the hospital's board of directors is willing to spend on security; rising expenses in other departments will probably cause such automation to be postponed. In the meantime, the hospital will probably continue to use its unusual but effective alloy of contract guards and retired city police.

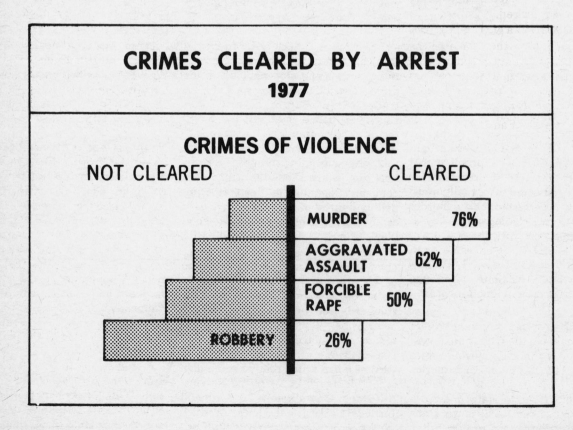

The nun who became a cop

Mary Ellen Beekman
as told to Susan Kuklin

Mary Ellen Beekman, 33, was born and raised in the Bronx. After graduating from St. Helena High School she became a nun. She majored in education at St. Thomas Aquinas College in Sparkill, N.Y., and taught fifth grade. She has been on the police force for three years.

Civil service runs in my family. My father and brother are firemen. My sister works with Health and Hospitals and my mother was a nurse. My uncle was a cop. I lived in the city all my life. I was born and raised in the 4-3 (43d precinct in the Bronx). I still live in the 4-3. Originally I wanted to save the world just like any other idealistic 18-year-old. I became a nun.

I gave five years of my life to what I considered a good cause, but then it was time for a change. It wasn't an overnight decision. It took a year to decide to give up the convent. I was scared. I felt guilty about my feelings but I didn't want to be a grammar school teacher all my life. Ultimately it was the general living conditions that made me make up my mind to leave. In the convent we had to do exactly as we were told. We needed permission for everything. It was as if they didn't trust us.

That was a really bad time for me. When I left the convent my mother and father came for me and brought me a dress that I had had a long time ago. I felt very sad but I never regretted my choice.

Believe it or not, there are great similarities between the politics in the convent and the politics in the police force. The gossip and everything else. In both places you need a hook (someone higher up who will get you a better position). Putting on a habit is like putting on a uniform. In both uniforms people have a little more respect for you than they do the ordinary citizen. When people found out that I had been a nun they thought that certain things would shock me. They didn't realize that I had seen the end result of a lot of violence: Children from broken homes, parents who didn't want them, who beat them. As a nun, I worked in areas just as bad as this one.

I didn't jump from being a nun to being a cop. It didn't happen that way. After I left the convent I had a job as a teacher in a Catholic school in Spanish Harlem. I taught for a year and a half. I left because the pay was bad. I worked in an insurance company. It was so boring. I quit and took the police exam. After two and a half years as a police officer I was laid off. I was out of work for eight months. That was a very rough time. When I turned in my shield, badge and gun I had the same feelings that I had when I took off the habit. The shield meant more to me than anything else. Then I worked as a sex-crime investigator in New Jersey. I hated that, dealing with sex crimes against children. I worked for a while as a security officer for AT&T, but when I had a chance to get back on the force, I took it, even though it meant less salary. I guess I hadn't gotten it out of my system yet.

The 4-2 is probably the best place I've ever worked— as far as people go. You have your oddballs here and there but most of the guys are really topnotch.

The thing with cops is to be there, to be where the action is. That's what most cops crave. Even guys who don't want to work on the street, when something happens, they want to be there. It's sort of like having a front seat on life and I'm a very nosy person.

One thing my partner Terry and I both share is that we do not work for the police department or for some captain, but for people. My faith is put to the test out here. I have more faith in God now than I ever did before because everytime I go out there I'm in His hands. If this is the night, that's it. There's nothing I can do about it.

I have always been able to do what has to be done, no matter what it is. When the moment comes I act, no matter how dirty. Last week we rushed a 12-year-old boy to the hospital. I see the blood but I try not to think about it. When a tough job is over and I go home I'll either laugh or have a drink. Sometimes I think, "Gee, I coulda gotten killed." Usually I don't think about it. My mother worries about it, so I say at least I'll die happy.

I never thought that having a special partner was such a big deal. But every day I would arrive at work and be assigned to a different partner. One day I got a little disgusted about that and went to "Roll Call" to complain. They said, "Why don't you find a steady partner?" I asked one guy but he said he didn't think his wife would go for it.

When I asked Terry he said he'd have to talk it over with his wife. He did and she approved. His wife and I have a lot in common. We're both ex-nuns and we both have master's degrees. Terry is the shortest guy in the

"The Nun Who Became A Cop," by Mary Ellen Beekman and Susan Kuklin, *Sunday News Magazine,* December 2, 1979. Reprinted by permission.

precinct and the other fellows say the only reason he took me as a partner is that I'm shorter than he is. They call us the "4-2 Donny and Marie." A lot of times when we show up at a job everybody laughs. They say, "But we called for cops!"

Having a steady partner is the most crucial thing to a cop. I've seen guys really frightened because they were separated from their partners for one tour. I was trying to think of one word that would properly describe the relationship between partners: Marriage. There's a chemistry that exists that is similar to a man and wife, even between guys. Partners become very dependent upon one another. Most cops can't admit that they love one another, but I think they do. They must.

This is my first experience with a steady partner and it's the best thing that ever happened to me. My confidence on the street is so much stronger. I'm more effective. When we work together I know that one of us is going to talk to the guy, not smack him and lock him up.

Terry was telling his wife that in a way it's better to be working with a woman because he's more cautious. He feels that he has to protect me but I tell him that we make the same money and if anybody has to get hurt it should be me because I'm single and he's got three kids.

Lillian (officer Lillian Hogan) and I were once on call and went to the house of a guy who was having an argument with his wife. Our backup happened to be two more policewomen. When the guy saw four police-women walk in he threw up his hands and yelled, "I give up!" and walked out. He couldn't deal with four more women. He was having enough trouble with one. In cases like this it is important to separate the couple. I'll put my arm around the female and say, "Let's go in the other room and talk it over." Then Terry is able to stay behind and calm down the male.

When I did undercover work I acted as a prostitute and used the name "Rose." This happened just after I graduated from the police academy. I was working in the 4-6 (46th precinct in the Bronx) and the Youth Gang Task Force had a 16-year old girl who was working the street. She was from the South and slightly retarded. Her pimp was bringing mentally retarded girls up here to work as prostitutes and we wanted to get him. We drove her all over the Bronx in a squad car looking for the pimp.

Usually when you work with a prostitute a police-woman is used so that male cops don't get into trouble. After 11 o'clock "Roll Call" decided to put me out on the street with her to try to lure the guy in. Believe it or not, I had a black vinyl raincoat, black slacks and black high heels in my locker so I really looked the part. I had long blond hair then also. We were walking together and Diane (the prositute) said to me, "You know you could probably make a lot of money down here. You really look good."

People would approach us in cars and ask if we were working. Obviously I couldn't get in so I kept raising the price. Most of the girls were going for $25 so I kept saying $50. Then I began getting takers for $50 so I raised it to $100. One guy—a short, fat, bald dude—got out of his car and showed me his $100. I said, "If you have $100 you must be a cop!" (laughs). Another prositute was near me and kept yelling, "Take it! Take it! Are you crazy!" The Youth Gang Task Force was backing me up. They were riding around in a cab while one man stood across the street and another was on the curb near me.

I don't particularly care for what the police depart-ment is trying to do right now. All of a sudden somebody got the idea that since women cops want to be equal with male cops we should be made to look like men. So they took the male's uniform and made it smaller and put it on us. They're trying to make little men out of us but I knew that I could not model myself after a male patrol officer.

There are a lot of things I don't do as well as a male cop but then there are a lot of things I do better. I feel I'm more compassionate. I do better with family crisis cases. I try to talk my way out of things rather than get involved in a confrontation. When I was working with Lillian we talked our way out of lots of things. One day we talked a couple of kids into being arrested (laughs). We brought two kids in. One was only 5'8", he wasn't too bad, but the other was 6'4". We talked them into being handcuffed. They were nice about it. In fact they thought it was really great. We walked into the station house. The two of us with two big dudes. We didn't tell the fellas that we just talked the prisoners into it.

A lot of women cops are losing their femininity. They think that in order for them to achieve they have to become masculine. I strongly disagree. I don't have to become a man. I don't have to act tough or be aggres-sive. My philosophy is that we're equal but we still maintain our differences. Out here on patrol I feel I'm still a woman and I want to be treated like a woman. I don't want to be one of the guys. My equality comes from the fact that I am a cop. But I am not a male cop. I'm a female cop.

BURNED-OUT COPS AND THEIR FAMILIES

Dealing with stressful human conflicts every day, policemen—like other "people-workers"—sometimes develop symptoms of emotional exhaustion that include cynicism and suspiciousness toward others. A study by two psychologists describes the impact at home.

Christina Maslach
Susan E. Jackson

Christina Maslach is an associate professor of psychology at the University of California, Berkeley. She is coauthor of *Influencing Attitudes and Changing Behavior* (Addison-Wesley, 1977) and *Experiencing Social Psychology* (Knopf, 1979), and is currently writing a book on her burnout research.

Susan E. Jackson is a graduate student in the psychology department at Berkeley. In addition to her work on burnout, she has been conducting research on the nature of social identities.

You change when you become a cop—you become tough and hard and cynical. You have to condition yourself to be that way in order to survive this job. And sometimes, without realizing it, you act that way all the time, even with your wife and kids. But it's something you have to do, because if you start getting emotionally involved with what happens at work, you'll wind up in Bellevue [psychiatric hospital].

—Police officer, New York

I can't understand how seemingly normal husbands turn into such 'machos.' Arguments end in 'Because I said so.' Our children feel as though they really can't discuss problems with their father because he relates in terms of the law and logic, and not the emotions involved. Sometimes I feel that if I don't do what he wants, I'll be arrested.

—Police officer's wife, California

If a public-opinion poll asked what type of work is most stressful, a large number of people would be likely to say "being a cop." If asked to give their reasons, they might point to

the physical dangers involved: the risk that a man may be injured, or perhaps killed, in the line of duty.

Police work *is* highly stressful. However, recent research suggests that the stress is due more to psychological than to physical risks. The ambiguity and conflicting values surrounding the job, the responsibility for other people's lives and their well-being, the long hours of inactivity mixed with unpredictable crises, the frustrating encounters with the court system and the police administration, the negative public image of cops in general—those factors are often more debilitating than the physical hazards of the job.

How does the policeman's struggle to cope affect his own emotional health and his relationships with other people—not only the public he deals with, but his family and friends as well? Our approach to those issues makes use of the concept of "burnout," which we and our colleagues at Berkeley have been studying for the past five years. Burnout refers to a syndrome of emotional exhaustion and cynicism that frequently occurs among individuals who do "people-work"—who spend considerable time in close encounters with others under conditions of chronic tension and stress. Whether a person is a social worker struggling with an unmanageably large case load, a therapist working with disturbed patients, or a nurse caring for children with terminal illness, he or she sometimes finds that contact with others is charged with feelings of anger, embarrassment, frustration, fear, or despair.

Over time, a person working in such a constantly stressful situation

may begin to distrust and even dislike his or her clients, and to wish they would "get out of my life." This detached and even callous response is, in part, a protective device: it reduces the amount of emotional involvement and consequent stress, but it also seriously impairs the quality of the human contact.

In addition to feeling negative about others, many people-helpers begin to feel negative about themselves. Burnout may also be accompanied by physical exhaustion, vulnerability to disease, or by psychosomatic symptoms (for example, ulcers, back tensions, headaches). Alcohol and drugs may be used more frequently to cope with the stress. At an institutional level, burnout can contribute to low morale, impaired performance, absenteeism, and high job turnover. We the public, who are personally mistreated or given the institutional runaround by public servants under stress, may in turn develop disrespect not only for those individuals themselves, but also for the institutions that they represent.

The Study: A Family Perspective

In our early research, we found that people experiencing burnout talked about increased difficulties with their families; some felt it was implicated in marital discord that led to divorce. However, the evidence was only suggestive, and we lacked corroborating information from the families. Therefore, we decided to collect more systematic data, as well as to get a different perspective by looking at burnout from the spouse's viewpoint.

2. POLICE

We began with a preliminary study of police officers in a South Bronx precinct of New York City, riding with two of the men in a patrol car to get a sense of the stresses in a routine tour of duty, and interviewing others at the precinct house. The questions were open-ended and exploratory, focusing primarily on the emotional demands of the work and its effect on the officers' personal lives.

Combining what we learned in those initial interviews with other data on policemen's lives, we developed two questionnaires, one for officers and one for their wives. We gave the questionnaires to a sample of about 130 police couples from all parts of California whom we contacted from a list of delegates and alternates to a 1977 California convention of clubs for police officers' wives. The couples came from both urban and rural parts of the state. The officers represented all ranks, from patrolmen to command officers, had an average of 12 years of experience in police work, and ranged in age from their early 20s to late 40s. Almost all of the couples were white, and the vast majority (90 percent) had at least one child. They had been married for an average of 10.5 years; in more than half the families, the wife had a job.

We asked each of the men to answer the Maslach Burnout Inventory (MBI), which consists of 25 statements about personal feelings, attitudes, and perceptions of both self and "recipients" (a general term referring to the particular clients or people one deals with). Each statement is rated twice, once for frequency of occurrence ("Never" to "Daily") and again for the intensity of the experience ("Very mild" to "Very strong").

The MBI measures four dimensions that are independent of one another: emotional exhaustion (for instance, "I feel emotionally drained by my work"); negative, cynical attitudes toward recipients ("I've become callous toward people since I took this job"); negative evaluation of the subject's own strengths and accomplishments in working with others (reflected in a low score on such items as "I feel I am positively influencing other people's lives through my work"); and the subject's sense of closeness to clients ("I feel personally involved with my recipients' problems").

The questionnaires we devised for our sample of police couples were more elaborate than the MBI. The officers were asked about their work conditions and satisfaction (for instance, whether they would want to change occupations); their family relationships (for instance, how often they shared feelings with their spouses); and which techniques they employed for coping with stress (smoking, drinking, medication, going to church, seeing a therapist, and so on). The questionnaire given the wives asked them to rate statements about their husbands' work ("His work is a source of pride and prestige for the family," and "His work is a source of discomfort and embarrassment") and his behavior at home ("He comes home feeling upset or angry," or "Children feel emotionally close to/distant from father").

The officers' scores on both the questionnaire and the Burnout Inventory were placed along continua ranging from low to high. Although those values were thus only relative to one another—and did not yield an absolute measure of burnout and tension—we could compare each man's scores with his wife's responses on her questionnaire. Perhaps not too surprisingly, we found that high burnout scores are associated with domestic strains that are absent or mild in the families of low scorers. It appears that the officers on the top third of the burnout continuum—and their families—are at some risk for emotional and behavioral problems and could use some support or counseling. And younger officers, who tended to score higher than others on burnout, seem to be in the greatest jeopardy. From the responses to the specific questions, and from our interviews with men in New York and California, we obtained a detailed picture of tensions in police families, and what might be done about them.

Coping with Everyday Horror

The police officer usually has to deal with people under adverse, even traumatic, circumstances. His intervention often comes when emotional feelings are most intense (as in a fight or family dispute). Furthermore, the painful aftermath of crime, in terms of the victim's loss, suffering, or even

death, is seen and experienced more directly by the police officer "at the scene" than by anyone else in the criminal-justice system. Indeed, the policeman is often confronted with the discrepancy between the horror of his personal observations and the sanitized version that is presented by lawyers for the defense. The negative quality and the emotional intensity of many police-citizen encounters is vividly described by George Kirkham, a Florida State University criminology professor who worked as a police officer for five months:

"As a policeman, I found myself forced to deal with other people at their worst, day in and day out—to mediate interpersonal conflict in situations where the disputants were crying, kicking, screaming, threatening, bleeding, drunk, or enraged. Let me assure you that it is quite a different thing to discuss Jones's chronic temper outbursts in a counseling setting, and to face the same man after he has just smashed his wife's face with a fist and is angrily proclaiming his readiness to do the same to you!"

How does a person confront and survive those unpleasant and tense situations on a continual basis? Some policemen overcome intense feelings through a process of habituation. "When I first came on this job, I couldn't look at blood, I couldn't stand it. And the first times, I really got sick. But you've got to keep going back, and now it doesn't bother me." This cool, unemotional stance is considered critically important for good police work, because it may be the only way to do a necessary job under emotionally stressful circumstances. Consider the cop who has to investigate and report on a fatal shooting:

"You don't look at a dead body anymore as a human being. You're looking at it now from a job aspect—what happened to this guy, how did it happen to him, where did he get shot, did the bullet stay or did the bullet come out—these are things you have to do. You have to look at it objectively, it's your job. This guy—we don't know who he is, I don't even know what his name is—it's a total stranger. So there's nothing personal there, and it's just a job."

However, there are times when things do get more personal (even with total strangers), and then great cracks appear in the policeman's emotional armor. The more often a police officer deals with either very young children or the elderly (usually as victims of abuse or neglect), the more likely he is to suffer. As one cop told us, "You shouldn't let anything get to you, but when it's kids or old people—you see your own mother and your own kid. It really cuts you—and you do go home and dream about it, you think about it."

Police working with very young children scored high both on our emotional-exhaustion index and on the dimension of closeness to recipients, and low on negative feelings toward children. The picture is reversed for police who deal frequently with teenagers; they report negative feelings toward them, and little sense of closeness. Interestingly, several wives reported that their husband's relationship with their own children was most difficult during the teenage years. While those problems are true of many families and not just of police families, the cop who must struggle on the job with youthful criminals, when he has problems with his own adolescents at home, is getting a double dose of upsetting experience.

Living with a Burned-Out Cop

It is almost impossible for policemen to avoid bringing work attitudes home when they leave the station, however valiantly they may try. For one thing, a cop is always a cop, even when off-duty. He is expected to respond appropriately to any emergency or crisis situation, even when in civilian clothes. More subtle, and yet more important, is the policeman's carefully developed tough skin—his emotional cool, his suspiciousness, and his sense of caution—which cannot be taken off and put away as easily as his uniform. Those qualities become second nature to him, an integral part of relating to all people—including his wife and children. Over time, many wives report, he unwittingly becomes more tough and aggressive when dealing with his family, questions them more often, and appears to mistrust them; he may become more rigid in deciding what's "wrong" or "right," and less capable of getting emotionally involved with his family.

This last problem can be compounded by the policeman's unusual working hours, which can disrupt family routines and minimize his contact with his wife and children: "Lately, I've been very depressed about the hours," one wife told us. "Unfortunately, it's beginning to test what has been a very good marriage. Our children have been raised with 'Be quiet,' which has been converted to a rude 'Shut up,' or 'No, your friend cannot come over because Daddy is sleeping.'"

The higher a man's score on our emotional-exhaustion subscale, the more likely his wife was to report that he comes home feeling physically exhausted, tense, upset. His wife was also more likely to say that he complains more about his work, gives less time to pleasant conversations with his family, and has difficulty sleeping. His wife generally feels depressed and describes their children as feeling anxious, irritable, and isolated. He himself may recognize that he has come to have a short fuse, and he observes his children respond to his anger by withdrawing from him.

In the high-burnout cop's family, the children are four times as likely to look exclusively to their mother for support (according to the wives' reports). The man is twice as likely to report feeling distant from his kids; he and his wife are nearly twice as likely as other police couples to disagree about discipline of the children. As one police wife summed it up: "His work created a distance. We were a family—he was a stranger."

The growing distance between a burned-out cop and his children is often mirrored by a similar alienation between him and his wife. The high-burnout cops report (twice as often as more moderately affected policemen) that their wives fail to understand the problems and stresses of the job—and their wives generally agree with that assertion. In many cases, though, the wife's lack of understanding is not for want of trying to get information from her husband (or other sources), but from his refusal to discuss the job with her. "I never tell my wife what I'm doing—never," one man said. "And we're always having conflicts about this. She comes home from work, and all she does all night long is tell me about the kids she teaches and what went on in school. And she says,

'You never tell me about what you do, you never talk to me about it.' Because I don't *want* to talk to her about it. I don't want her to know what I do here—it would just make it worse."

Although the policeman says he wants to protect his wife from the grim realities of his job, it may be more accurate to view him as trying to protect *himself* by not reliving the stress he has already undergone and by keeping its ugliness from contaminating his home. With such a strategy, he can also avoid having to deal with her anxieties about police work. Such a self-protective device can have detrimental side effects on the marital relationship, ironically, by creating barriers to an open, trusting, sharing partnership.

When the policeman's burnout hits the phase of negative self-evaluation, his isolation from other people becomes even more pronounced. Not only does he feel distant from his children, and either unwilling or unable to share his feelings with his wife, but he also has fewer friends and is more likely to shun social activities for solitary ones. This self-imposed isolation may be seen in part as a way of coping with the daily overload of stressful contact with people. He may simply want peace and quiet, uninterrupted by *any* human being and especially one with a problem. Or he may feel he is not working well with people and may thus want to avoid any further evidence of his ineffectiveness by minimizing the number of involving relationships he has with others. Finally, he may anticipate (sometimes correctly) that his off-duty contact with people can be just as upsetting as the on-duty work because of the social stigma he thinks is attached to being a cop:

"If I go to a party, the first thing I tell the host is, 'Don't tell anyone I'm a cop.' Because if people find out, then they start bitching about some traffic ticket or tell me about the hard time some stupid cop gave them—and before you know it, your night is ruined. After a while, you don't go out to parties unless you go alone or you go with another cop and you stay together and stay on the side. You don't get involved with people. You don't want to bother getting involved, because you know what's going to happen."

Stress Inoculation

Faced with those emotional stresses, how do policemen and their families cope? "A beer helps," according to one cop, and indeed, more frequent use of alcohol and tranquilizers was correlated with burnout. Use of medication and marijuana was very low in our sample, but may have been underreported. Wives were most likely to report using alcohol to cope with stress when their husbands scored high on feeling distant from clients.

For the cop, having a drink with his buddies after work may be a "decompression routine" offering a chance to unwind from the emotional pressures of the job, talk over worries and problems with trusted friends, and just laugh and have some fun. The important social function of "drinking with the guys" is often recognized by wives, although they sometimes long for alternative mechanisms that don't run the risk of alcoholism: "They need encounter groups besides the bar," as one wife put it. And, of course, when they are with the guys, they are not with the family. There are other types of decompression routines, and some involve · sports or other physical exercise. "The guys need to have a place to go cool off or work out, but it's hard to find something to fit in with their odd hours."

One clear difference between officers and wives in their coping responses is that 80 percent of the wives seek out organized activities as a source of help and social support, but only 10 percent of the men do. An example of a support group used by the women is the police officers' wives club, which is often designed to give women a chance to discuss their difficulties and find new ways of dealing with the impact of the police job on their family life. For many wives, the most important benefits lie in realizing that they are not alone in their problems, and in getting a different perspective on the source of their troubles. "I need to know that it's the job, and not the man, creating these problems," said one wife. A majority of wives also listed talk with intimate friends as an important support.

Some policemen are reluctant to expose their feelings and anxieties, partly because they view them as unmasculine, a sign of weakness. Yet a dozen or so of the larger police departments have psychologists on staff for the development of stress-reduction programs, and are available for counseling police officers and their families as well. The Los Angeles Police Department reported some 1,400 sessions in the past year. But many observers believe that most cops and their wives will not take advantage of such services unless they can be assured that word of their visits will not leak back to their fellow officers and superiors—or onto their records. Unfortunately, the attitude of many policemen toward seeking professional help is, "if you need it, you're unfit for this line of work."

There are signs of some changes in attitude. As one wife said to us, "Ten years ago, you could not have gotten any of these men to fill out your questionnaire and talk about their personal feelings. So the fact that they are willing to do so now represents a big step for them."

The next step would be to acknowledge that the burnout syndrome is a common frailty of many people whose jobs require them to give too much, too often, to other people in need. Then, both the institution and the individual can begin to reexamine and perhaps restructure the job itself to better control the intensity and exposure to emotional stress. Similarly, the public should recognize the potentially destructive impact of job burnout on the people who serve some of our most basic human and social needs.

For further information, read:

Maslach, C. "Burned-out," *Human Behavior*, Vol. 5, 1976.

Maslach, C. "The Client Role in Staff Burnout," *Journal of Social Issues*, Vol. 34, No. 4, 1978.

Kroes, W. H. *Society's Victim—the Policeman: An Analysis of Job Stress in Policing*, Charles C Thomas, 1976, $9.95.

Kroes, W. H., J. J. Hurrell, eds. *Job Stress and the Police Officer: Identifying Stress Reduction Techniques*, December, 1975, #017-033-00149-9, U.S. Government Printing Office, Washington, D.C. 20402.

CRIMES CLEARED BY ARREST
1977

CRIMES AGAINST PROPERTY

NOT CLEARED · CLEARED

BURGLARY 16%

LARCENY-THEFT 20%

MOTOR VEHICLE THEFT 15%

Protecting Thy Father And Thy Mother

"... Special New York police squads were created two years ago to concentrate on crimes against the aged and defenseless ..."

Randy Young

Old is what everybody thinks about. Will the sounds of life slip away from me? Will I be unlovely? Will I be safe? God, will I be alone? Cops can't be expected to have all or even most of the answers, but the New York City Police Department has been thinking about old, about the safe part. And so it has created special anti-crime squads to concentrate on the violence that seems so often to sneak around corners and land on the elderly.

Statistically, persons over 60 (about 18 percent of New York City's population) are no more likely to become victims than anyone else. But certain kinds of crimes—purse snatchings, indoor robberies, con games—are the stuff that older people go through. Consequently, that golden 18 percent is possessed of the mini-fortress mentality; they spend their time locked up in their own apartments or rooms behind chains, metal plates, and ugly bars. Much more so than the rest of us. Many are without families and friends, existing on Social Security checks or the fruits of whatever plans they were able to make in the strength of their springtimes. Now it is dead winter.

Freddy Foster was not your average commuter. But he did ride the bus every morning from his home in Yonkers to 178th Street in Manhattan. Then he took the IND to 125th Street and then he walked the rest of the way to 110th. No office or desk awaited Foster (not his real name), only lines of elderly people moving slowly along uptown sidewalks, sometimes in

pairs but more often alone. He watched them closely, beginning the selection process: not whites, because (he later told authorities) "I might get busted in a white neighborhood." No young people, obviously. There were so many old ones; there, for example ...

Joseph Fornabaio is commanding officer of the new Manhattan North Senior Citizens detail. He oversees an eighteen-member unit working out of the city's 24th Precinct. He says, "We're dealing with a group that is basically helpless and rarely offers any resistance. And it's a group that can't afford to be victimized; it's not like some guy making $50,000 a year and gets his battery lifted." That's part of it. Another part, says Fornabaio, is this about old people: "They may have faulty eyesight, bad memories, and other signs of senility. We've had cases where we picked up a guy we knew was guilty and had to release him because the victim couldn't make the right identification."

Many of the crimes against the elderly are what police call "push-in jobs," which are exactly like that sounds. Follow the victim to her apartment, wait until she turns the key, push her in, and rob her. Beat her, rape her, perhaps kill her. Two years ago, it appeared that an unusual number of attacks were being made upon older people, and that led to the formation of the special police groupings, lamentably called "Senior Citizens Robbery Units." (A pilot project in the Bronx had been successful since 1974.)

There are 18,000 police officers in New York City, but it is fair to say that none (with the possible exception of the bomb squad) has more delicate tasks facing him daily: victims whose memories or eyesight fail them, citizens too embarrassed to talk, people so frightened that their assailants will return that they won't open their doors even to uniformed officers.

It is just the way of life, as members of the seven units concerned with crime against the elderly have learned, that aged victims are resigned to, bearing their pain in silence. Police say that as few as one in fifteen violent acts against the elderly ever reach police blotters. The police are right; a recent study by the Senior Citizens Crime Prevention Program (a federally funded project administered by the New York City Department for the Aging) bears them out. The program surveyed persons over 65 years of age who had applied for replacement of their Reduced Fare Transit Cards; 10 percent of them had lost the originals in robberies, and almost all had failed to report it to the authorities.

Foster would stalk them at a safe distance to their apartment buildings. At the right moment, he would jump at them, brandishing a hunting knife. "Give me the money," he'd scream; shrillness was important, as it made him sound out of control, more menacing. There was one woman, however, to whom he was actually polite. She was 71, and the police said she was small, but everyone except John Wayne looks small at 71. Foster held a door for the woman as she lugged a shopping bag into the apartment-building lobby. Then he accepted more than her thanks. He grabbed her pocketbook and ran away. On 115th Street he bought his daily bread, the drugs that were the point of the whole exercise, and sailed away to Yonkers.

Because the cops in these special units are not assigned the huge case loads that other police officers are forced to grapple with, they can—and apparently do—get closer to the people they deal with. They routinely visit victims' homes, help them fill out mountains of forms, aid them in the mysteries of recovering stolen Social Security and senior citizens' discount-fare cards, even help them find housing in places that are not prisons. They lecture on crime prevention at clubs and centers for the aged.

At the 28th Precinct house, with Foster safe back in Yonkers, the cops had blue dots over a street map on the wall. Each dot represented a robbery against some old person, and most of the dots were clustered in the area between 110th and 125th streets. The dots just grew and grew in number, 24 new ones in the month of January alone, and that was the highest of any precinct in the city.

A certain macabre satisfaction, cop satisfaction, was taken in the descriptions that went along with the dots. Almost without exception: five feet nine or a little better, 160 to 175 pounds, a green jacket and dark-green ski cap. A picture was forming.

Detective Jerome Harvey of Manhattan North was visiting every elderly victim in the precinct. Most of them lived in single-room apartments in old brownstones and tacky high rises. Security, if it existed at all, was lax. He and his colleagues, Al Genova and Denis O'Sullivan, didn't do very well. Foster, as they were discovering, had no record in New York, and so no mug shots, and so no one could "make" him, even if they were inclined to, and the old people were notably uninterested.

Better than 90 percent of all arrests made last year by the special units resulted in convictions. In all, 10,000 complaints were lodged with the units and 651 arrests made. No one is quite sure why, but the number of complaints was down 26 percent from the previous

year, and the drop may be directly attributable to the effective work of the special branch.

Breaks, breaks. You take the smartest detective in the world and give him a break—a fat piece of luck—and he'll solve the disappearance of Judge Crater. In the Foster case, two breaks came together: First was discovery, through hard work, of a "younger" victim, 54 years old (Harvey and his men had cleverly decided to talk with the less advanced in years, perhaps there to discover better memories, clearer eyes). He was a Postal Service worker and had been robbed twice by the same man—a man whose description was awfully close to the police impression of Foster.

Break number two: At 11:45 P.M. Friday, February 17, a cop collared a man for drug possession up in the 28th Precinct. The cop remembered Harvey's many trips around with his composite and his talk, and he said the man he had in tow fit pretty well. Harvey, Genova, and O'Sullivan went over, and sure enough the man—quiet to the point of sullenness—looked the part. They took some Polaroid pictures of him.

Harvey took his photograph back to break number one, the postal worker, and showed it to him—together with Polaroids of six other men. Without hesitation the postal worker pointed to the picture of Foster.

The federally funded Crime Prevention Program is not at all satisfied with what is available to elderly victims of crime in New York. What is most needed, believes Elaine M. Walsh, director, is guaranteed immediate financial relief to needy crime victims. (A Crime Victims Compensation Board does exist, but it is viewed by police and social workers alike as ineffective when it comes to the elderly.)

Harvey and his colleagues were back on the street at 8:30 the next morning, once more knocking on the doors of the elderly victims. Bingo. Foster's picture was pulled from the spread of photographs by nearly everyone. Now the officer had the tough job—tougher by far than the make—of holding the case together, realizing that from this point on great agony awaited the victims.

Victims fear reprisals if they agree to testify. The long trips to precinct houses are difficult and confusing. The trips to

courtrooms can be longer and more traumatic. Who wants to sit all day in a stuffy oak room, maybe right across the aisle from a man who assaulted you, and wait and wait for the case to be called? Hardly anyone.

Someone. Fifteen people, in fact, responded to the entreaties of Harvey and his gang. Cops went out and picked each one of them up to go to the 24th Precinct house. It was a 2 P.M. screening. Soon they were filing slowly through the front doors of the station house, looking for all the world like a tour group to be shown the police chief's office or the remodeled cell block.

Right out of a movie. They were ushered into a room one wall of which was decorated with a mirror; you guessed it—one-way. And those old people looked through to a lineup that included Foster and six imitation bad guys who had been paid $5 apiece to stand there in ski caps. Of the fifteen victims, twelve made what the police like to call positive identifications of Foster.

A grand jury indicted Foster on ten counts of first-degree robbery, which could land him up to 25 years in prison on conviction. He has been arraigned and has pleaded not guilty to the charges, which are felonies. He could not make the $25,000 bail, and he was sent to Riker's Island to await trial; he is there today.

Foster is 24, hooked on a $70-a-day heroin habit. He hasn't said much to the police since his arrest, but Harvey and his fellow officers feel they can link him to at least 40 robberies and assaults in Harlem and Manhattan earlier this year. Foster has not been entirely silent: He has offered to own up to nine robberies (in which positive identifications have been made, police say), provided the cops do not go back any farther. No deal.

Director Walsh of the Crime Prevention Program says just catching criminals may be only part of the task. The toughest, she says, may be relieving the fears and frustrations that exist among a generation of city dwellers that has come to expect so little of its public guardians. "I hate getting involved in anything like this," said a 76-year-old man who was one of those who picked Fred Foster out of the police lineup. "But these people are taking really good care of us. I'm gonna sit down and write somebody a letter."

THE NEW TRUTH MACHINES

The inventors of a new lie-detection device
called the voice-stress analyzer say it could help
make the country a little more honest. Critics say it's
less accurate than the polygraph—and more menacing.

Berkeley Rice

THROUGHOUT HISTORY, men have tried various ingenious methods for sorting out truth-tellers from liars. A medieval "truth by trial" technique called for thrusting a suspect's hand into a fire; if it was not burned, he was judged innocent. An ancient Chinese test required a suspected wrongdoer to chew rice powder while being questioned. If the powder was dry when he spit it out afterward, the man was condemned—on the theory that the tension of lying had blocked his salivary glands, producing a dry mouth.

Modern techniques of lie detection are more sophisticated, although critics say their accuracy has not improved much. Since its invention in the 1920s, the polygraph has become a standard tool for police, military, and private investigators. And in recent years, lie detection has gained increasing popularity in industry and retail businesses. Depending upon whose figures you believe, American businessmen are losing from $5 billion to $50 billion a year to dishonest employees. To combat the loss, they have turned increasingly to lie-detection devices to screen out potential thieves, as well as junkies, alcoholics, the emotionally unstable, and the politically extreme.

Now they have a new device, called the "voice-stress analyzer" or "psychological stress evaluator," that threatens to replace the polygraph: it's simpler, quicker to operate, and less threatening because it doesn't need wires connected to the body. Like the polygraph, the voice analyzer detects stress—not lying—by measuring certain psychophysiological responses of the person who is being questioned. By properly structuring his interrogation, and interpreting the machine's results, a trained operator can supposedly tell whether the subject's stress indicates

deception, lying, or guilt. While the polygraph records blood pressure, breathing, and skin conductivity, the voice analyzer picks up fluctuations or "modulations" of a "microtremor" in the voice that varies according to the degree of stress.

While the voice analyzer is portable and convenient, its critics say it's less accurate than the polygraph (whose own accuracy is debatable) and more menacing because there's no way of knowing when one is being used covertly. Job interviews, theft interrogations, or any telephone conversation can easily be taped and later run through the machine without the subject's knowledge. Dozens of insurance companies—who prefer anonymity in the matter—now use voice analyzers to check taped interviews with people filing suspicious claims for damage or loss. Last year, the Congressional committee investigating the Kennedy assassination planned to buy two voice analyzers and two mini-recording devices to secretly tape and evaluate interviews with potential witnesses. When Rep. Don Edwards, chairman of the House Judiciary Subcommittee on Civil and Constitutional Rights, learned of the plan, he denounced it as "wrong, immoral and very likely illegal."

Spurred by such fears, and the growing potential for abuse by both private and public agencies, Congress is now considering legislation that would essentially ban the use of lie-detection tests by employers. A Senate subcommittee headed by Birch Bayh will hold hearings on such a bill this summer. Bayh has summed up the problem this way:

"Each year in this country hundreds of thousands of ordinary workers and job applicants are forced to submit to mass lie-detector sweeps of the plant or shop where they are employed or seeking employment. These truth-

testing sessions are not necessarily the result of a specific theft or loss, or even of suspicion of such crimes. Rather, they represent the indiscriminate and random intrusion of so-called truth-testing machines into the daily lives of Americans. Failure to submit to these tests, or unsatisfactory responses to questions, are often punished by loss of employment, or summary transfer to a less desirable position."

A cabdriver in Washington, D.C., who took me to my first look at a voice analyzer, provided an example of what Bayh means. Hearing the purpose of my trip, he said, "You Americans are crazy about this lie-detector business." A native of Sierra Leone, he had applied for a job with the 7-11 food-store chain soon after arriving in Washington. He passed his employment interviews until they told him he would have to take "one of those lie-detector things. I say, 'No way, man' and I walk out of there."

How It Was Invented

Like some other marvels of modern technology, the voice analyzer grew out of research by the Army during the Vietnam war. Army intelligence officers were looking for a simpler, ideally covert alternative to the polygraph for interrogating prisoners. For a while, body odor seemed promising: everyone apparently gives off a distinct odor when under stress. But body odors turned out to be too numerous and too easily dispelled or adulterated for accurate measurement.

Lt. Col. Allan Bell, a career intelligence officer with a background in electronics, learned that certain vibrations or "microtremors" in the voice change when the speaker is under stress. The stress somehow triggers the autonomic or involuntary nervous system, which changes the frequency of the microtremors. All Bell needed was a device sensitive enough to pick up and chart the inaudible fluctuations of these vibrations, the way an EKG machine charts the beating of the heart.

He and Lt. Col. Charles McQuiston, an Army polygraph expert, set out to design such a device. But the Army's lack of enthusiasm for their idea, and the red tape of military bureaucracy, became intolerable. In 1970, both men retired from the Army and set up shop on their own. Working out of his basement, Bell invented the "psychological stress evaluator," or PSE, and McQuiston designed the related charts and training methods. With several other former Army colleagues, they founded Dektor Counterintelligence and Security, which started producing PSEs.

The advances in audioelectronics that made the PSE possible also enabled Fred Fuller, another inventor with Army funding, to design a similar gadget, now called the Mark II voice analyzer. "We did the original work back in 1963," he recalls. "It could have been built back then, but it would have been 10 feet long. We had to wait for the state of the art in electronics to catch up with us before we could design this thing as it is now."

Fuller's Mark II is now sold by Law Enforcement Associates, a police and industrial security supply outfit in Belleville, New Jersey. LEA also offers wiretapping and debugging equipment, phone scramblers, bomb detectors, vehicle monitors, wrist transmitters, and other electronic exotica.

The Mark II is even simpler than the PSE, and, to the people at Dektor, less accurate for that reason. The PSE requires a multispeed tape recorder because the tape must be played back into the machine at one-quarter speed, to pick up and chart the patterns of the voice microtremors. The quarter-speed playback, and the complexity of the PSE's chart interpretation, require considerably more time than Fuller's Mark II, which produces an immediate numerical measure of stress on both a digital display and a bar-graph chart. The Mark II fits into a single portable case, while the PSE comes in two cases: one for the voice analyzer itself, and one for the relatively bulky Uher recorder. Both machines sell for about $4,000, roughly twice the cost of a standard polygraph. Dektor claims to have sold 1,300 units so far, and LEA 300.

Competition for the growing lie-detection market leads to some cattiness between the two companies. Edward Kupec, Dektor's marketing vice-president, told me, "They try to make

the Mark II sound like it does the same thing as ours, but I'd say it's only about 70 percent as accurate." Fred Fuller returns the compliment: "I have nothing against the PSE, but basically it's a dinosaur compared to ours in the sense of technological growth."

What It Can Do

Because it can be used on tapes, telephones, TV or radio broadcasts, the voice analyzer offers some intriguing opportunities. Cynical citizens might use it to evaluate the honesty of elected officials and other public figures. A free-lance writer used one to check tapes of Lee Harvey Oswald's statements after his capture in Dallas ("I didn't shoot anybody, no, sir," Oswald said) and concluded he was innocent. Others have used the devices to evaluate the truthfulness of John Dean, Howard Hughes, Patty Hearst, and Richard Nixon. The makers of the PSE used it to test contestants on the TV show "To Tell the Truth," and claimed 95 percent accuracy in spotting the real McCoy.

> "Some large industrial and retail companies run annual or even monthly lie-detector tests on all employees."

Three years ago, the revived *Saturday Evening Post* published a highly flattering article on the PSE, inviting anyone who thought they had been falsely accused of a crime to contact the magazine. The *Post* promised to arrange a PSE test via telephone for people who wanted to prove their innocence. When I called the magazine to find out how its humanitarian offer turned out, a spokesman told me they had been forced to drop the project: "We thought it was a good idea, but it kind of got out of hand. The mail just came in in truckloads. We got so many letters we had to quit, because we couldn't go through them all and still put out the magazine. Part of the problem was weeding out the nuts."

While the public tends to associate lie detectors with criminal investigations, most of the new voice analyzers—like most polygraphs today—are being used by large industrial and retail companies to screen applicants for employment and to investigate in-

house thefts. A Dektor handout lists such satisfied PSE users as Cumberland Farms Dairy Stores in Massachusetts, Li'l General Stores in Florida, Jim Dandy Fast Foods in Texas, and Shopwell Supermarkets in New York. The "director of loss prevention" for Gray Drug Stores, a 275-unit Ohio-based chain, says, "Our gross profits are up for every division because pilferage has been reduced. . . . We do hire quite a number of people who have had problems such as minor drug use or minor thefts from former employers. But with the PSE, they put us on notice so we can watch them."

Employees may not enjoy the sensation of being watched, but many companies feel the threat of periodic "sweeps" acts as a deterrent to those who might be tempted. Some companies run annual or even monthly lie-detector tests on all employees ("all" generally means lower level, not executives), while others run tests only when specific losses occur.

Sheldon Levine, head of security for Waldbaum's, a 125-store grocery chain based in New York, formerly used the polygraph, but has switched to the PSE because "people feel more comfortable with it." His office runs an average of 50 tests a week on job applicants for store managers and department heads. "It isn't really a lie-detection test," Levine told me. "We just want to find out if they've been truthful on their applications, or if they've left something important out, like being fired for dishonesty. After all, we're entrusting them with responsibility for our stores, our merchandise, our safes. We're entitled to know whether they're honest." Levine doesn't believe in periodic testing of nonsuspects, although he knows lots of other companies do it. "In my eyes they're wrong," he says. "I don't believe in witch hunts. We only do it if we have a specific loss."

Some companies hire lie-detection agencies to conduct annual sweeps or "fishing expeditions," in which they run hundreds of employees through 10-to-15-minute exams. Even Dektor considers such brief examinations inadequate; a thorough exam can take an hour or more. Prices range from $25 to over $100 per exam, depending on the length.

Preemployment tests generally check information the applicant has given the company about previous employment, and try to discover whether the person has stolen before. Officials of the lie-detector industry justify such tests by claiming that three out of four applicants have in fact stolen money or merchandise from previous employers. But according to complaints to the American Civil Liberties Union, uninhibited examiners use lie-detection tests to probe for marital, sexual, or emotional problems.

Although private industry is the most lucrative market for the new voice analyzers, Dektor and LEA also push sales to law-enforcement agencies. Several hundred police and fire departments and county sheriffs now use the machines in criminal investigations. And while the results of voice-analyzer tests—like those of polygraph tests—are still inadmissible in court, the machines have apparently proven effective in some criminal investigations.

A Florida police official calls the PSE "a great time-saver" because it helps "eliminate the suspects and cut down on the man-hours of investigating a case." A detective in North Dakota finds that subjects under investigation "will consent more readily to the PSE than to the polygraph." He is convinced the machine "indicates quite accurately if the subject has a knowledge of the crime."

Like the polygraph, the voice analyzer is also quite effective in eliciting confessions. When confronted by a skillful examiner with the machine's seemingly conclusive "evidence" of guilt, many suspects break down and admit to the crime. Police officers thus refer to the voice-analyzer test as "a painless third degree." Critics call it a "psychological rubber hose."

Claims and Counterclaims

Since the Army had been instrumental in developing both the PSE and the Mark II, I had expected to find that federal agencies were making use of them. Several of these agencies have used the polygraph for years for interrogation, and to test employees who require security clearance. However, neither the military nor other government agencies are buying voice analyzers. Dektor claims it simply hasn't pushed such sales, but when I checked around, I got a different story. Those customers simply don't believe the new machines work.

Various military and other intelligence agencies did buy and test a few voice analyzers when they first came out in the early 1970s. But most of

those machines have since been discarded, dismantled, or destroyed. The Pentagon's National Security Agency tested both devices and found them "insufficiently reliable." The Air Force's Office of Special Investigations conducted 60 tests of the PSE and found it "not useful." The Army commissioned a comparative study of the voice analyzers and the polygraph in which the voice machines achieved an accuracy rate barely equal to that of pure chance.

> "Uninhibited examiners use lie-detection tests to probe for sexual, marital, emotional, or political problems."

After examining the evidence of various federal agencies, including the CIA and the FBI, the House Subcommittee on Government Information and Individual Rights concluded in 1976:

"The nature of research undertaken . . . and the results therefrom have done little to persuade the committee that polygraphs, psychological stress evaluators, or voice stress analyzers have demonstrated either their validity or reliability in differentiating between truth and deception, other than possibly in a laboratory situation."

Since the voice analyzer appeared in 1970, there have been only about two dozen studies of its accuracy by disinterested researchers. Amazingly, no one has tested its accuracy in pre-employment exams, although that is by far its most common use. Most research has taken the form of small-scale laboratory studies by academic researchers using college students in simulated crimes or prearranged lies. When the results achieve reasonable levels of accuracy, the makers of the machines are quick to cite such evidence as convincing. When the results are inconclusive or negative—which occurs more often—they are just as quick to argue that laboratory studies are meaningless; research under simulated conditions, they say, does not create the real jeopardy necessary to produce enough stress for accurate measurement.

Most studies of the voice analyzer compare its accuracy with that of the polygraph, as though that instrument's

accuracy were beyond doubt. It isn't. Despite frequent claims of near-infallibility by spokesmen for the American Polygraph Association, there have been few reputable studies to support such claims. Noting that government agencies engaged in security investigations routinely use the polygraph, a recent Justice Department report deplored the "conspicuous lack of reliable data" on the machine. The report found that figures of 98 or 99 percent accuracy often cited by polygraph examiners were "unsubstantiated."

Compared with the polygraph, the accuracy of voice analyzers ranges from pure chance to roughly equal. In reputable studies of actual criminal suspects, whose guilt or innocence was later determined by confession or trial, voice analyzers have proven accurate in only 50 to 60 percent of the cases, a bit better than chance. They apparently do a pretty good job of identifying guilty suspects; but they have a troublesome tendency to identify innocent suspects as guilty also.

Frank Horvath, a lie-detection researcher at Michigan State University's School of Criminal Justice, says of the voice analyzer, "In my opinion, it simply does not work. It doesn't do what they say it does." David Lykken, professor of psychiatry and psychology at University of Minnesota's Medical School, and generally regarded as the country's foremost authority on the subject of lie-detection research, told me, "I review most of the articles on the voice analyzer for the professional journals, and I haven't seen the slightest bit of credible evidence to support its validity."

Despite such low opinions of their machines, the manufacturers of the PSE and the Mark II make frequent claims of 95 to 99 percent accuracy. In conversations with skeptical journalists. they are careful to point out that the machines are not lie detectors but stress detectors; they say the rest is up to the skill of the operator. In their ads, however, which appear regularly in such publications as *Security World* and *Law Enforcement Communications*, the two companies are noticeably less modest. Dektor offers "To Catch the Truth," describing the PSE as "proven by over 2,000 examiners in thousands of field tests." LEA's ads for the Mark II call it "The Truth Machine," and claim it produces "an accurate measure of truth or lies."

When I asked for proof of the Mark II's validity, Law Enforcement Associates sent me a packet of 10 studies that purport to show it is highly accurate at measuring both stress and deception. The studies are unpublished, and only two cite the name of the researcher—an apparently independent testing firm called Technical Development Inc. I checked out TDI, and discovered that its president is none other than Fred Fuller, the inventor and owner of the Mark II. When I asked him who had done the rest of the Mark II studies sent by LEA, he replied cheerfully, "I did. I did them all."

Dektor's president Allan Bell scoffs at negative studies of the PSE by academic psychologists, calling them "conservative almost to the point of being immobile." When Dektor is pressed for evidence to support its claims for the PSE, it, too, produces studies—many of them unpublished—which show the machine has supposedly achieved accuracy levels of 95 percent or more.

Dektor leans heavily on two unpublished "independent" studies. One was conducted by Michael Kradz of the Howard County Police Department in Maryland, who achieved a remarkable 100 percent accuracy with the PSE in determining the guilt of 36 criminal suspects. The other was by John Heisse, a private researcher in Burlington, Vermont, who repeated the Army-sponsored PSE study that produced 33 percent accuracy, and came up with a much more impressive figure of 96 percent.

Both of these researchers are undoubtedly men of integrity, but their independence is open to question. Shortly after completing his study, Lieutenant Kradz joined Dektor as its chief instructor. Heisse now serves as a consultant to Dektor in developing new PSE equipment. And his frequent testimony in defense of the PSE at legislative hearings has earned him a reputation as "Dektor's bulldog."

The Training of Diogenes

John Heisse, M.D., is a busy man who juggles several overlapping careers with agility. Trained as an otolaryngologist, he has had an active ear, nose, and throat practice for years. But the discovery of the PSE awakened in him the fervor of a moral crusader. He soon acquired proficiency in its use and carried out several studies of its validity and reliability. He then founded and is currently president of the International

TIPS ON INTERROGATION

Some employers use voice analyzers to check on whether job applicants have been truthful in filling out personnel forms and to spot such problems as drug abuse, alcoholism, and stealing from previous employers. To identify topics that arouse significant stress, a typical test contains three distinct types of questions:

1. *Emotionally irrelevant questions* are used to relax the subject by reducing extraneous or situational stress, caused perhaps by the threat of the test itself, or by some temporary family problem. Such "throwaway" questions take the form of: "Do they call you Tom? . . . . Do you live in Chicago? . . . Is today Tuesday?"

2. *Control questions* are designed to arouse a mild level of anxiety that provides the examiner with a comparative or "base level" of stress. Many people respond with white lies to such questions, which might be: "As a child, did you ever steal anything of value? . . . Did you ever lie to your wife? . . . Did you ever think about anything so bad that you couldn't tell others about it?"

3. *Relevant questions* apply directly to the job, and are thus the critical part of the test. When stress rises significantly above the base level in response to those questions, it supposedly indicates deception. The examiner might ask; "Have you used any hard or illegal drugs recently? . . . Do you have a serious drinking problem? . . . Did you actually complete four years of college? . . . In your last job, did you really earn $12,000? . . . Did you ever steal more than $10 in money or merchandise from a previous employer? . . . Were you ever fired from a previous job? . . . If hired, do you have any plans to quit the job?"

In interviews after the tests, the responsible examiner goes over the results with the individual and gives him a chance to explain why he might have shown stress in response to particular questions. These interviews are particularly important in investigations of employee thefts, and often end in confessions.

A recent newsletter from the International Society of Stress Analysts offered the following advice from one analyst on how to interrogate theft suspects:

"The interrogation of a subject begins in the pretest interview. Here you obtain a wealth of information about the subject in both general questioning and 'idle conversation.' It is at this time you should discuss his family, prior work history, children, schooling, military history, medical history, drug use, arrests, debts . . . marital problems, gambling, drinking, etc.

"Once you have obtained deceptive charts from your subject, you should immediately proceed with an interrogation . . . in an attempt to obtain a confession or admission from him. . . . Your subject's emotions are at a peak, you have the desired privacy, and you are alone.

"I would suggest not showing the charts to the subject unless the deceptive responses are truly dramatic. It is too easy to get into an argument with a subject about the varying degrees of patterns, and no purpose is served by such a debate. Remember—you have the top hand, not him.

"The emotional offender . . . usually has feelings of remorse or mental anguish. His conscience may bother him, and he has a sense of moral guilt. Don't bully him! Convince him you know he is guilty! Point out all the evidence against him, such as his own physiological and psychological symptoms of guilt, such as a dry mouth, blood pounding in his head, upset stomach, hands shaking, etc. Give him plenty of sympathy, and minimize the gravity of the crime. Urge him gently to tell the truth. Cite examples of others who have done the same thing. Tell him how good he will feel to finally get this horrible burden off his mind or conscience.

"The nonemotional offender . . . is not bothered by pangs of conscience or moral guilt feelings. Appeal to his common sense rather than his emotions. You should point out the futility of his resistance to tell the truth. Let him know that there is no doubt about his involvement, and eventually the truth will come out.

"Rationalize the offense by helping him blame others. Minimize somewhat the seriousness of the offense. Justify his act; blame the victim, his accomplice, his wife, parents, partner, or anyone. . . ." —B. R.

Society of Stress Analysts (ISSA), which has about 360 members who work with voice analyzers.

Heisse also founded and is codirector of a commercial PSE training school called Diogenes Associates ("We're looking for an honest man"). Diogenes offers a two-week course for $1,000 that leads to membership in ISSA. As president of ISSA, Heisse speaks often about upgrading the skills and standards of voice-stress analysts, and ISSA's monthly newsletter devotes considerable space to the need for continuing education and workshops offered by Diogenes Associates.

Heisse also finds time to conduct his own thriving lie-detection service, handling everything from rape and murder cases for the local police to insurance claims and employee theft. He told me of one recent job for a large retail chain which had been losing $500,000 a year until Heisse ferreted out 238 dishonest employees.

Like most reputable practitioners of lie detection, Heisse readily admits the machines cannot detect guilt, only stress. As both proponents and critics of these devices kept telling me, the technique of lie detection is only as effective as the person conducting the interrogation. Or as computer programmers put it, "Garbage in, garbage out." But given the almost total lack or enforcement of standards in the trade, this disclaimer is hardly comforting.

The measurement and interpretation of stress involves complex physiological responses that have puzzled generations of scientists. Those who study psychosometrics and psychophysiology generally spend several years acquiring a professional level of knowledge. Even allowing for a certain amount of unnecessary academic credentialism, it seems odd that literally anyone can buy a voice analyzer and set up shop to test psychological responses, interpret results, and make judgments that can damage lives and reputations.

Consider just three human variables that might affect and therefore distort the measurement and interpretation of stress: some people may be simply more emotional and thus more subject to stress than others; some people may have greater confidence than others in the lie-detection apparatus and technique, which could increase the degree of stress they feel during an exam; and some people might have greater fear—and thus more stress—at the prospect of losing their job. Lie-detection

examiners claim they can allow for all these variables, by using "control" questions that establish individual "base-line levels" of stress. Critics doubt the precision of such techniques.

Many of those who use the PSE and the Mark II are former polygraphers, which would be reassuring except that several leading members of that profession admit that only a few of their colleagues are truly competent. The security officer of a Chicago bank that regularly hires polygraphers to test its employees remarked, "I've seen operators that I wouldn't have enough faith in to ask if it's raining outside."

"Voice analyzers do a good job of identifying guilty suspects, but they tend to identify innocent suspects as guilty also."

As David Lykken explained to me, "About 99 percent of the people in this industry are nonpsychologists and nonscientists. They're mostly ex-policemen and entrepreneurs who've gotten into it because of the money. They're generally people with limited education. And as for their training, a weekend or a week or even six weeks is really just superficial. It would be just a bad joke if it weren't for all the victims who get screwed out of their jobs."

While the standard polygraph course takes six weeks and the Army's polygraph school runs 14 weeks—both followed by a six-month internship—the companies that sell voice analyzers put customers through a mere three to five days of training (at roughly $100 per day), depending on their previous lie-detection experience. The companies say that's long enough because their machines are much simpler to operate than the polygraph (true), and the results easier to interpret (debatable).

A School for Voice Analysts

Dektor claims it won't sell a PSE to anyone until the person completes its own or some other "approved" training school. (Several have sprung up recently, under Dektor's supervision.) The Dektor school is located in the firm's manufacturing and sales headquarters in Springfield, Virginia, a suburb of Washington, D.C. The day I showed up, four students completing that week's course were taking their

"final exam." It consisted of trying to discover which of three Dektor secretaries had the instructor's car keys. All three denied possession; one was lying. Using the PSE, each student interrogated the three secretaries. Of the four students, only two picked the real culprit. One had recorded on the wrong speed; and the other couldn't make a guess on the basis of his charts. Nevertheless, they all received their diplomas, and their shiny new PSEs in simulated-leather attaché cases.

The four graduates that day were fairly typical of those who attend Dektor's training school: a Louisiana state police officer; a woman from a private security agency in Maryland; the head of security for a nationwide trucking company; and a private investigator of employee theft from Jackson, Mississippi, who calls the PSE "the greatest aid in history for private investigation because it saves you a lot of time by weeding out the innocent." The trucking-company man added, "The very fact that people know they're going to be tested each year can cut down on theft."

Dektor's PSE instructor is Mike Kradz, a veteran police officer reputedly expert in all phases of criminal investigation. When I questioned the wisdom of sending students out to determine guilt or innocence after only five days of training, Kradz assured me that any Dektor graduate puzzled by the PSE charts of a particular individual can send copies to the company or call and play the tape over the phone. Kradz will then tape it himself, run it through his own PSE, and, at no charge, give his own opinion. When I asked how he could be sure his former students would check with him, he shrugged.

Dektor's president, Allan Bell, feels the five-day training session is quite sufficient. He thinks the six weeks required for polygraph trainees is unnecessary, and designed to lend a "certain amount of dignity to the profession. It's a bit like requiring M.D.'s of all psychiatrists."

Bell feels voice-stress analyzers should, and someday will, play a more important role in criminal proceedings, including the trial itself. "I do feel they're more accurate than eyewitness reports and juries. But I don't know if society is ready for that yet."

Despite such confidence, Bell made the usual disclaimers. "It's simply a thermometer of stress," he said about the machine. "It doesn't tell why you have the temperature. For example, if I brought a shapely secretary in here now, and had her strip to the waist in front of you, you'd probably show stress. But the stress doesn't indicate whether you're a heterosexual or a homosexual or whatever. People want to look at the PSE as the ultimate magic, but it's just not that simple."

When confronted by ethical questions about the covert use of the PSE, Bell retorts, "Which is immoral—for a person to lie or for a lie to be uncovered?" ISSA president John Heisse admits he's "unhappy" about the potential for covert abuse, but feels it could make the country a little more honest. "It might not be a bad idea if politicians, newspaper people, and others who influence public opinion were checked occasionally for honesty."

As a journalist, I naturally find that prospect chilling. But if you hang around with people engaged in lie detection long enough, as I did, a certain amount of paranoia begins to set in. You begin to wonder if people are telling you the truth, or if they are secretly taping your phone conversations and testing them for honesty.

Lie Detectors of the Future

In order to protect the individual's right to privacy, opponents of lie detection are beginning to fight back, and are making some headway. Several state legislatures are currently considering restrictions on the use of voice analyzers for pre- or postemployment testing. New York State recently passed a law prohibiting employers from "requiring, requesting, suggesting, or knowingly permitting" employees or applicants to take or be subjected to lie–detector tests on voice analyzers. ISSA's John Heisse

"Literally anyone can set up shop to do voice tests, and then make judgments that can ruin people's reputations."

strenuously opposes such legislation, calling it "the guaranteed right to steal."

On the national level, the Federal Privacy Commission recently recommended a ban on all lie-detector exams by private businesses. Senator Birch Bayh, chairman of the Senate Judiciary

HERE COMES THE HAGOTH

The voice analyzer already comes in a handy home or office model called the Hagoth, the creation of a genial, fast-talking promoter named Rick Bennett. The Hagoth is much smaller and simpler to operate than the Psychological Stress Evaluator, or the Mark II, and at a price of only $1,500 (versus over $4,000 for the larger machines), it looks at first like a bargain. Bennett claims he's sold thousands of Hagoths so far, mostly to top executives who he says use it when engaged in million-dollar deals over the phone.

The Hagoth is roughly the size of a flattened cigarette carton, weighs only two pounds, and can easily be concealed in a desk drawer or an attaché case. It picks up the voice with a standard microphone or telephone attachment, and gives an instantaneous measure of stress on a row of eight green lights (low stress) and eight red lights (high stress). Once the voice stops, the lights stop flashing also, leaving no graph or chart or other tangible record. The Hagoth has a built-in recorder, however, that can tape the voice and play it back later to check the lights again.

Because the Hagoth is much simpler to operate than its larger competitors, Bennett says that "any fool can use one" after a weekend of practice. Like the inventors of the larger models, he carefully explains that his device really detects stress, not lying. But his ads claim it enables the user to "flawlessly pinpoint deception," and "to unerringly spot a liar."

Most people in the lie-detection field say the Hagoth simply doesn't work. They cite the difficulty of getting a clear reading from the flashing lights and the lack of any permanent measure of stress, like a chart or graph. Psychologist David Lykken,

who carefully monitors all research on voice analyzers, calls the Hagoth "a gimmick, a Rorschach test. You can read into it anything you want."

Bennett casually dismisses such criticism, pointing out that few of his customers have taken up his money-back guarantee of satisfaction. And when doubters ask for studies proving the Hagoth's accuracy, Bennett says, "I give them my banker's phone number. That's my study."

When Bennett tried the Hagoth on me, he had me choose a number from one to five, and then asked, "Is your number one? . . . Is your number two? . . ." and so on. I replied "No" to each question, and he watched the flashing lights on the Hagoth to see when I lied. It worked once, but failed the next time. The same thing occurred when I tried the test on him. My biggest problem—and one that has plagued many people who have tried the Hagoth—was that it wasn't always clear whether the red lights flashed more than the green, or vice versa. On most responses, both colors seemed to light up almost randomly.

Because Bennett fears that state and federal legislation will eventually outlaw or seriously restrict most commercial use of voice analyzers, he will soon bring out a pocket-sized version, and his engineers are now developing a wristwatch model. "I truly believe we can come out with new technology faster than the bureaucrats can come up with regulations against us," says Bennett. "Technology is impossible to control. They'll never be able to regulate this thing, or at least they can't enforce the regulations. And if they do, we'll come up with another widget they can't detect."   —B. R.

Subcommittee on the Constitution, has introduced a bill (S-1845) that would essentially limit the use of lie detection devices to law-enforcement agencies.

At hearings held by Bayh's subcommittee last fall, the senator tangled several times with Dektor's Charles McQuiston, a bristle-haired man of military bearing and prickly pride. McQuiston argued that employers have civil rights also: "the right to expect an

honest day's work for an honest day's pay, without the right to steal everything within sight or reach." Because of a decline in public morality, he feels that today "trust must be earned," and the quickest method is obviously a PSE exam. He seemed unaware that the "opportunity" to prove one's honesty reverses the quaint notion that one should be presumed innocent until proven guilty.

McQuiston accused Senator Bayh of

trying to deny his means of livelihood, apparently unconcerned that lie detection is often the means by which others lose.theirs. He found it "incomprehensible" that a committee that required him to swear to tell the truth before testifying could call the use of lie-detection tests for employees immoral. Quoting Howard Beale, the newscaster in the film *Network*, he told Senator Bayh, "I'm mad as hell, and I'm not going to take this anymore."

If people of various opinions find themselves angry over the use of voice analyzers these days, just wait. Those in the trade think lie-detection technology is still in its infancy, and see marvelous advances "down the road." Researchers are now exploring the possibilities of using voice pitch, nonverbal gestures, and face temperature as means of detecting dishonesty. A Kent State psychologist has developed a lie-detection technique based on the responses of the pupil and retina. Researchers at Israel's Weizmann Institute have invented a "microwave-respiration monitor" now being used by Israeli police at airports and border crossings. It measures stomach palpitations caused by rapid breathing under stress, and can be used secretly and remotely.

Even the PSE's inventor, Allan Bell, says that his device "is to stress analysis what the Model T is to locomotion." He envisions a device that could pinpoint and monitor the specific area of the brain where stress originates. Dr. Heisse also says the PSE is "almost obsolete now. I think there will be computers that will do the chart analysis far more accurately than any human being." When I suggested that reasonable people might find that prospect frightening, he seemed surprised: "Frightening? Perhaps a little bit. But is telling the truth that bad?"

Certainly not, though I'm not sure I want a computer to decide who's telling the truth. But maybe I'm just old-fashioned. Most Americans are suckers for technological gadgets, and remedies for today's social ailments often come packaged in microelectronic circuitry. In a time of rapid social change, when people seem to know less about, and have less trust in, their neighbors, a handy home lie detector might attract a lot of buyers.

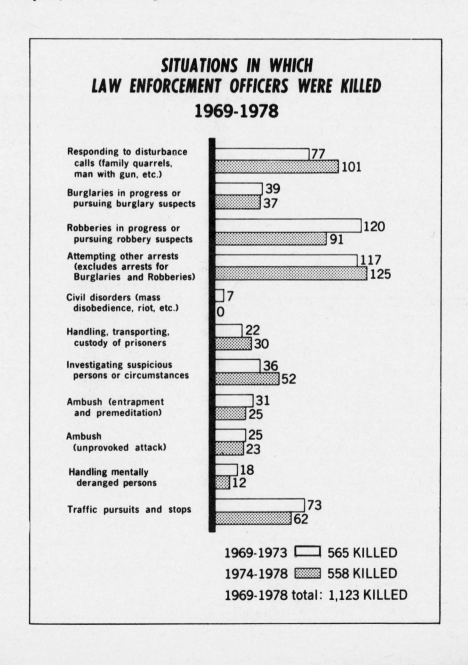

SITUATIONS IN WHICH LAW ENFORCEMENT OFFICERS WERE KILLED 1969-1978

Responding to disturbance calls (family quarrels, man with gun, etc.)
77
101

Burglaries in progress or pursuing burglary suspects
39
37

Robberies in progress or pursuing robbery suspects
120
91

Attempting other arrests (excludes arrests for Burglaries and Robberies)
117
125

Civil disorders (mass disobedience, riot, etc.)
7
0

Handling, transporting, custody of prisoners
22
30

Investigating suspicious persons or circumstances
36
52

Ambush (entrapment and premeditation)
31
25

Ambush (unprovoked attack)
25
23

Handling mentally deranged persons
18
12

Traffic pursuits and stops
73
62

1969-1973 ☐ 565 KILLED
1974-1978 ▦ 558 KILLED
1969-1978 total: 1,123 KILLED

Probes, trials and tribulations shake the LAPD

The Los Angeles Police Department, considered by many to be a model for effective policing, was rocked last month by a series of internal integrity problems, the most serious of which forced the agency to relinquish its authority over police shooting investigations.

In an interview with Law Enforcement News, a department spokesman noted that the city's politically appointed Police Commission would have ultimate say over disciplining officers who were involved in shooting suspects.

Quoting from the department's new 30-page directive on the matter, the spokesman said: "The Police Commission will have direct responsibility for adjudication of all officer-involved shooting incidents and will make the final determination on such cases."

While the fur is still flying over Mayor Tom Bradley's decision to put the five member commission in the driver's seat, other problems have cropped up to disrupt the routine of the LAPD. The city's District Attorney has mounted a full-scale investigation of a detective's charges that the force has been infiltrated by organized crime; an internal probe is being conducted in the force's Scientific Investigation Division, and a departmental trial has led to the temporary suspension of 28 officers who were charged with working short shifts.

However, the transfer of the department's shooting-incident authority to the civilian panel seems to have superseded all of the agency's other troubles, attracting the attention of the media, the public and the city's police officers association.

Sam Flores, the president of the Police Protective League, told Law Enforcement News that his group is ready to fight the new officer-involved shooting directive. "We feel that there may be improper administrative due process as far as the officers' rights are concerned," he said. "We do plan to file some action in the court regarding that."

The league executive noted that he is pushing for a system in which his group would be able to negotiate with the commission before any decision was reached regarding a police shooting. "That's a change they're contemplating," he observed. "By state law and by city law, we allege, they have to meet and confer with the affected employee organization and that's us. So that's one basis for our lawsuit."

Flores' proposal would inject another step into an already complicated procedure. "We have robbery/homicide investigators who compose the Officer-Involved Shooting Team," the department spokesman said, "Every time an officer gets involved in a shooting where there is a hit, they go out and gather all the data and all the information. They prepare a report for the Shooting Review Board, which presents its findings to the chief of police."

Under the new directive, Police Chief Daryl Gates would have to hand over the internal review panel's report on any questionable incident, along with his recommendations, to the Police Commission. The Protective League's planned lawsuit contends that the group should be consulted at this point.

Although the new policy states that Gates's "authority to impose discipline will remain unchanged," it gives the Police Commission the power to hire independent investigators in cases where there is doubt of an officer's conduct in incidents where a suspect is killed or injured.

The new directive was issued after weeks of municipal turmoil over a report released by the Police Commission concerning the January 3 shooting death of Eulia Love, who was killed by two police officers in a knife-throwing scuffle.

Although the LAPD's Shooting Review Board had cleared the policemen of any wrongdoing in the dispute, the Police Commission charged that the two had "violated policies of the Los Angeles Police Department governing the use of firearms and deadly force and that the officers made serious errors in judgment and in their choice of tactics which contributed to the fatal shooting. . ."

Reaction to the report from the officers' league came swiftly in the form of a "no confidence" vote against the commission. "We had almost 4,400 signatures and those were gathered in about three days," Flores noted.

Chief Gates, meanwhile, entered the fray with full force, contending that the members of the commission were "all too liberal." The charge was echoed by former chief Edward M. Davis, now a candidate for the U.S. Senate, who accused Bradley of "systematically destroying the police department through the police commission" by appointing "ultra-liberals."

While Bradley defended the civilian panel as being "balanced," Flores refused to get involved in the political implications of the situation. "I would characterize the commission as possibly acting unilaterally capricious in some areas," he said. "They should be meeting with us prior to any policy making because they are the department head. I don't know about their political philosohies."

As the Protective League prepares to go to court on that matter, Gilbert Carcetti, who heads the District Attorney's Special Investigations Division, has announced that he will conduct a comprehensive probe of alleged organized crime activity within the LAPD.

Garcetti declined to discuss the direction that his investigation would take, noting only that "it could take months."

The probe was touched off by Detective Donald Wicklund, who told a television news team that a deputy chief, demoted in 1976 for leaking police files to a movie producer, was allegedly tied to mob figures. Wicklund later took his charges to the Police Commission, but it was agreed that the situation could best be handled by the DA.

Although the detective's charges publicly focused on Deputy Chief George Beck, the commander of the LAPD's West Bureau, Wicklund indicated that he had information which points to possible mob connections in two other areas of the department.

Commenting on the investigation, the PD spokesman indicated that the charges were false. "There's no truth to this allegation that there is organized crime influence in this department," he said. "We're cooperating fully with the District Attorney's Office—anything they want, anything they need."

Flores took a more open stance on where the probe might lead. "We don't have a position on that because we don't know that much about it," he observed. "We haven't seen the evidence, if any, that this individual has."

The LAPD's probe of its Scientific Investigation Division elicited less comment from both the police official and the league president. The spokesman noted that "the investigation is still continuing," and Flores stated that "the matter has not been adjudicated yet."

Regarding the departmental trial of officers in the Metropolitan Division who were accused of leaving their posts early, the spokesman said that a lieutenant and a sergeant were exonerated, but that 28 officers, including several sergeants, "were found guilty of not cooperating with the investigation."

Noting that those found guilty were slapped with suspensions ranging from five to 40 days, Flores said that the men had "accepted the discipline because they apparently felt it was warranted."

In spite of the myriad difficulties that hit the LAPD last month, the spokesman noted that morale is "good from what I can see around here."

Speaking for the rank and file, Flores indicated that the worst was over. "Oh, it affected [morale] adversely during the time," he said. "But I think that's something that happened in the past and I think now we'll go on forward with our work."

Police leaders find FBI mandate is a flawed gem

Top officials of three of the nation's foremost police executive organizations went on record this month in support of the proposed FBI charter, but they offered differing views on tightening or loosening the nuts and bolts that hold the document together.

All three representatives—Gary P. Hayes of the Police Executive Research Forum, Glen R. Murphy of IACP and Ferris E. Lucas of the National Sheriff's Association—told the Senate Judiciary Committee that their groups recognize the need for a written legislative mandate for the FBI. They differed, however, about how restrictive the charter should be, particularly in regard to the bureau's interaction with state and local police agencies.

Hayes emphasized that the document should lay down the law on the extent of FBI power on the local scene. "Without being encumbered with too many details or specifics, the charter should make clear that the FBI, when assisting state or local units of government, recognizes the boundaries of local authority and independence," he said.

While Murphy acknowledged that some sections of the proposal were vague in regard to the FBI's jurisdictional limits, he indicated that the charter would not allow the bureau to run roughshod over local policing.

"As it is written, we do not perceive the proposed FBI charter as having any significant deleterious effect upon the capabilities of state and local law enforcement organizations," he noted. "Nowhere on the face of the legislation nor in any of the supporting documents is there evidence of any intent to enlarge the duties of the FBI in such a way as to impair the ability of state and local police departments to deal with characteristically state and local law enforcement problems."

Lucas, in a letter to committee chairman Senator Edward M. Kennedy (D-Massachusetts), also praised the current draft of the bill, S.1612, for not holding too tight a reign on the bureau's activities.

"If the proposed charter were more restrictive, I would be opposed because, when investigating crime and other such activities, a certain amount of discretion is necessary," he said. "If every necessary function were prescribed and every unnecessary function proscribed, it would render the FBI unable to function effectively."

A spokesman for the sheriff's association, Truman Walrod, declined to comment on whether his group's position was closer to that of IACP or PERF, indicating that the organization has set its own course on the matter.

"I haven't seen either of their positions," Walrod told Law Enforcement News. "We approved (of the charter) as long as there weren't any additional restrictions added that would hamper the FBI. Basically, Lucas agrees with FBI Director William H. Webster. I'm sure he would not like anything that restricted the FBI in its day-to-day operations."

In his testimony before the committee on November 2, Hayes made a point-by-point analysis of the portions of the charter that PERF finds objectionable. Quoting from section 535d (4), he noted that the charter would allow the FBI to "provide investigative assistance to other Federal, state or local law enforcement agencies in criminal investigations when requested by the heads of such agencies if the Attorney General or his designee finds that such assistance is necessary and would serve a substantial Federal interest."

PERF's executive director complained that such phrases as "when such assistance is necessary" and "substantial Federal interest" were too cloudy, and he called for the inclusion of a set of guidelines that would better define the FBI's authority in the area.

"If interpreted too broadly, the section could leave police administrators subject to political pressures to call for FBI help in cases of a locally sensational or sensitive nature when FBI intervention would be inappropriate," Hayes testified. "If interpreted too restrictively, this section could preclude help when it is genuinely needed by local law enforcement."

IACP took an opposing position on the clause with Murphy acknowledging that the words "substantial Federal interest" were hazy but maintaining that the overall section is valid. "It provides for FBI assistance at the request of state or local authorities, yet limits the ability of regional organizations to do so by requiring the approval of the Attorney General, thereby insulating state and local law enforcement authorities from political pressure to request FBI assistance," Murphy said. "On the other hand, this section also protects state and local law enforcement organizations from unwarranted FBI intervention in that no such activity may be engaged in absent a request for assistance."

Murphy and Hayes were closer to accord regarding a section which authorizes the FBI to establish and conduct "education and training" programs for state and local agencies. The PERF executive said that the section is too broad ranging and suggested that it be amended to include wording from the Omnibus Crime Control and Safe Streets Act.

That statute, which makes up the enabling legislation for LEAA, states that the assistance agency's programs "shall be designed to supplement and improve rather than supplant the training activities of the state and units of general local government." A related section of the act notes that FBI training should be made available "at the request" of outside agencies.

Speaking for the IACP, Murphy agreed that restrictions should be placed on the range of FBI training, but he seemed less adamant about it than Hayes. "Although we would prefer the inclusion of such (restrictive) language, we do not believe that the charter evidences any intention to local governments," he said. "As a practical matter, FBI support resources are limited and are ordinarily only made available where they have been sought."

The IACP executive made similar comments about Secion 536(b) of the charter, which defines the bureau's role in providing technical assistance. Murphy noted that the article "does contain limiting language" that allows states and localities to choose whether they want FBI aid.

But Hayes indicated that the section does not go far enough in its restrictions. "The forum believes that guidelines should be developed cooperatively by the Attorney General, the director of the FBI and an advisory committee of state and local government so that local government has a full voice in determining aspects of this assistance," he observed.

PERF also challenged a portion of the charter dealing with the bureau's research and development function, noting the section should stress that LEAA "remain the major source of support for Federal research in the areas" of criminal justice and law enforcement.

Commenting in general tone of the proposed charter, Murphy said passage of the document would build public confidence in the bureau which might "filter throughout the nation's law enforcement system. Furthermore, the success of such a charter may encourage state and local authorities to enact or promulgate similar guidelines," he added.

The sheriff's association offered a more cautious view on the regional adoption of the standards contained in the charter. Lucas noted that while the FBI is equipped to handle the "high level approval requirements" of the guidelines, local agencies would have trouble in living up to them.

"Similar requirements at the local level could frequently present great operational difficulties in effecting prompt criminal investigations," he said. "Consider the situation of a deputy sheriff located many miles from his superiors with only one overloaded radio channel available to him."

While the PERF testimony called for additional detailed limitations on the bureau's jurisdiction, Lucas noted that the one "weakness" in the charter is Section 533b, which standardizes FBI investigations in the areas of general crime, terrorism and organized crime.

"Section 533b details specific restrictions which, if necessary at all, should be in guidelines—not the statute—so changes can be more easily made when future conditions require such action," Lucas told the committee. "The purpose of my comments is to point out that if changes are to be made, there should be fewer rather than more specific restrictions in the statute."

In spite of the discrepancies in the views expressed by the police groups, Senate aide Bob MacNamara noted that the Judiciary Committee reacted "fairly favorably" to the testimony.

"I think individual law enforcement people focused on specific kinds of concerns that they had and that's what we really were interested in," MacNamara told Law Enforcement News. "It may have taken a different perspective—like the sheriffs' association was a little different from the police forum. But I don't think there's any concern about it. All the issues they raised are what the committee is going to take a look at later on."

The Senate aide said the panel is aiming for an early February markup date for the charter bill, with floor action to follow in March. "That could be set back, depending upon how long the markup takes," he explained.

In general, MacNamara gave high marks to the way the police representatives presented their views on Capitol Hill. "They focused on the areas that we were concerned in that hearing," he said, "which is the FBI's assistance to state and local law enforcement. They were very positive about it; they were concerned to a certain extent about whether or not it would continue and making sure that there's a two-way street—a cooperative venture both ways."

CITIZEN COPS

The policeman's lot is a happier one, and you may be safer, thanks to volunteers.

Norman Sklarewitz

Norman Sklarewitz was a police reporter in Chicago for several years and enjoyed riding with the volunteer lawmen in Los Angeles while covering this story.

Before the start of the evening watch at the old Lennox sheriff's station at the southern end of sprawling Los Angeles County, the arriving deputies drifted into the grubby locker room to change from street clothes into uniforms. From a battered, steel wall locker, Ted Naimy pulled out green uniform slacks, khaki shirt, boots, and lightweight body armor, and in their place he hung up his natty three-piece, pin-striped business suit.

As they dressed, the deputies exchanged the usual banter that is part of the ritual of going to work. Naimy buckled on his leather equipment belt, already heavy with handcuffs, tear-gas container, and ammunition pouches. He next slipped his .38 caliber Smith & Wesson Combat Masterpiece revolver into a quick-release holster.

Finally, he tucked his patrol box stuffed with reporting forms and his traffic-citation book under his arm and joined the rest of the oncoming shift at the station training room for the watch briefing. The sergeant in charge went through a list of administration notices, passed around mug shots of a gang of burglars working the area, and then read off the radio patrol-car assignments for the shift about to start at 3 P.M.

This winter evening Deputy Allan Senkow, a five-year veteran, would drive the car — that made him the "wheelman." Naimy would take care of the log and file the necessary reports required for the eight-hour shift ahead — that made him the "bookman."

The two men hadn't worked together in some time, so as the black and white patrol car rolled out of the station parking lot, Naimy introduced himself in a way distinctive to experienced lawmen: He told his partner where he kept his extra shotgun shells. If a felony auto stop should take place, he offered to handle the 12-gauge shotgun cradled on the floor at his feet.

The partners discussed the way they would handle any foot pursuits and set procedure to check out vans. "They're all bad," grunted Senkow, an observation based on the fact that such closed vehicles easily conceal passengers who might be armed.

With those necessary police basics out of the way, the pair moved into the routine of patrolling their sector of the Lennox district and responding to assignments that crackled from the radio. That night, they would find themselves warily moving with revolvers drawn, through the blackness of a schoolyard, searching for an armed man who had just robbed, then shot, a woman nearby.

Later they apprehended and locked up a man charged with threatening a state offical earlier that day. Finally, just as the shift was to end, the pair joined in a wild pursuit of a suspect in a car. The chase took them with siren screaming through heavy traffic on the San Diego Freeway at speeds up to 100 miles per hour.

All in all, it was the kind of night familiar to most big-city cops. But Ted Naimy, while armed and authorized with full police powers, is an unpaid volunteer — a member of a uniformed unit, the Reserve Forces Bureau. Sheriff Peter J. Pitchess looks on this unit as the finest and best-trained outfit of its kind in the country. With 867 members, it is also the largest such law-enforcement organization in the United States.

Members of the uniformed reserve unit — which now includes nearly 100 women — wear the same uniforms as paid deputy sheriffs. They do the same work as regular deputies and run the same risk. But they receive only $1 a year in order to qualify for workers' compensation insurance should they be hurt on the job. And volunteers must pay for such desired accessories as spare guns and extra handcuffs.

The unpaid lawman is by no means a new figure on the American scene. Back on the western frontier, it was common for a sheriff or federal marshal to deputize townsmen or ranch hands if, say, an outlaw gang was heading for town. Later, a short-handed rural sheriff would often form a posse of local residents to hunt for a suspect.

In recent times, however, the practice of deputizing friends or political cronies has been far less justified. Such "honorary" deputies are sometimes inclined to use their badge more for personal than public good. "Some of those deputies ought to have been wearing white sheets instead of police blue," says one source familiar with occasional excesses practiced by some self-styled lawmen. Now, however, civil-rights legislation and a far more responsible attitude toward arming untrained civilians has reduced most of the charges of vigilantism.

The alarming rise in the crime rate, not only in big cities but in once-tranquil suburbs and farms, has strained the resources of many law-enforcement agencies. And with the relentless pressure of inflation on municipal, county, and state budgets, not to mention public opposition to higher taxes, it has become hard enough these days to keep the

> 'No two calls are the same; there's always something different happening.'

same number of uniformed men and women on the streets let alone increase force levels.

Faced with those twin pressures — increased crime and spending ceilings — more and more communities have turned to volunteers. When properly trained and supervised, these part-time law officers make significant contributions to their communities.

"Having a couple of reservists available each night means we can put another car on the street," says one Los Angeles station commander. That is significant as there are 17 such stations. And reservists don't take work away from regulars, either, it is argued. With limited funds to pay overtime, a regular might be forced to work alone if his salaried partner is out sick or on leave. With a reservist available to fill in, the regular doesn't have to go out alone — something few care to do these days.

Volunteer lawmen are often the object of considerable discussion and controversy. Plenty of cities and counties still won't use volunteers in any capacity; others can't because of legislative prohibitions. Some restrict volunteers to such duties as directing traffic or handling crowds, and they do not permit these officers to be armed.

But overall, there's a definite trend toward greater and greater use of volunteers in all aspects of law enforcement. Otto M. Vehle, national director of the Reserve Law Officers Association of America in San Antonio, Texas, estimates that there are about 350,000 such volunteers, variously called reserves, auxiliaries, or possemen. And Vehle foresees a significant increase in their number.

In a survey of 15 major American cities, *Police* magazine last year found that all but 5 have formal police-reserve programs. Those without such units by choice are Atlanta, Chicago, Boston, and Cincinnati. Philadelphia disbanded its force three years ago under a superior court ruling. New York City has 5,000 auxiliaries, but they are unarmed and do not have the power of arrest.

Los Angeles, St. Louis, Phoenix, and Denver are among the major cities with reservists who have mostly the same duties, authority, and responsibilities as sworn, paid officers. Smaller towns, cities, and counties around the country are also being attracted to the volunteer concept with generally good results.

In Freestone County, Texas, for example, the sheriff's reserve unit at Fairfield works weekends so that the regulars can be off. Units in Loveland and Larimer County, Colorado, were cited by the Reserve Law Officers Association for their disaster-relief work during the Big Thompson Canyon

flood in July, 1976, and many reservists, by virtue of their first-aid and cardio-pulmonary resuscitation (CPR) training, have saved the lives of accident victims.

While the uniformed reservists riding patrol make up the largest unit of the sheriff's reserve forces in Los Angeles County, it isn't the only one. There are two other components of the total force of some 1,300 men and women volunteers. One is the mounted posse composed of approximately 320 men and women who ride their own horses in areas of the county inaccessible to vehicles, search for lost people and evidence, and aid in crowd control. The other is the mountain search and rescue unit made up of some 100 highly skilled mountaineers with such additional abilities as scuba diving. Team members are called out to hunt for and then bring out lost, stranded, or injured hikers or motorists in the rugged mountains of Los Angeles County.

Ordinarily a Los Angeles County reservist will ride patrol with a regular deputy, but it's not at all uncommon for two reservists to ride together. If they do, their car is given a special radio code designation so that the dispatcher may or may not elect to send the unit in as the primary car on a "hot" or potentially dangerous call. However, a regular deputy with a reservist as his partner will be assigned to tackle anything. A reserve car might be dispatched to the scene of a "211" (armed robbery) or a "459 now" (burglary in progress). And there's no hesitation about using two reservists as the "will assist" unit to back up regulars on a hot call.

Without giving the subject too much thought, most people probably would assume that the typical volunteer cop would be young, single, on the rugged side, and have as his occupation something equally robust — perhaps a construction worker or truck driver. In the Los Angeles sheriff's uniformed reserve unit, that profile doesn't fit at all.

That's because, in part, only those with above-average incomes can afford to donate large blocks of their personal time to community service. Far from being hard-hat types with gnarled hands, most Los Angeles reserve deputies are quite comfortable ordering in French from a gourmet-restaurant menu, but they are equally at home using the hood of a prowl car as a table while wolfing down a greasy meatball sandwich ordered from an all-night diner.

While there are some blue-collar workers in the ranks of the uniformed reserve forces, the majority are corporate executives, professionals, schoolteachers, and successful businessmen. Naimy is a lawyer with a

What It Takes

To be a member of the Los Angeles County Sheriff's Department uniformed reserve unit, a candidate must pass a screening that includes interviews and psychological tests. If accepted, the candidate attends the Sheriff's Academy for a special five-month course that is conducted all day each Sunday and on Monday evenings. "You can kiss Monday night football good-by when you join us," quips Captain Richard Winter, the regular officer in charge of the reserve forces.

The training calls for about 300 hours at the academy with courses in patrol procedure, criminal investigation, physical fitness and defensive tactics, weapons, marksmanship, and special lectures in such topics as "Management of Stress in the Police Environment" and "Emergency Aspects of Childbirth."

"In terms of quality, this training for reservists is as good or perhaps better than any available anywhere," says Lieutenant Anthony Toomey, academy cadet-training officer who, with Sergeant Lee Lanzini, oversees the process of turning volunteers into street cops.

Not all make it; there's a loss of at least 25 percent out of each class of some 80 candidates. Once graduated, the rookie reservist is by no means turned loose as a crime fighter. Ahead are some 200 more hours of advanced training at a regular station.

The total formal and on-the-job training given these uniformed reservists is actually greater than that given full-time paid police officers in many communities. Even so, the work is not for everyone. Tommy Thompson, Reserve Forces Bureau chief of staff and a veteran volunteer himself and Captain Winter drop up to 10 percent of the volunteers each year, mainly for failing to put in the required minimum time. But anyone who uses his authority improperly is also out.

practice that involves negotiating contracts for big-name professional football stars and entertainers. Jerry Goddard is another lawyer who finds time to teach American government in a high school and serve as a Redondo Beach City councilman. Steve Pair is a network television engineering supervisor and Peter Gruenberg is a psychiatrist. Garnet Cumming is executive vice-president of a real-estate development company and Richard Olson is flexible-tubing division sales manager for a major conglomerate. When any one of them slides into the seat of a black and white patrol car,

Volunteer lawmen are often the object of considerable discussion and controversy.

however, he's a deputy sheriff and nothing else.

There is nothing here for the dilettante. While only two rides a month, or roughly 200 hours a year, are required of reservists, that's not considered enough to remain street wise — to know, as one deputy puts it, "which addresses are good ones, which are bad ones, where the ambushes can come, and who the bad guys around are." So the actual average of working time is closer to 300 hours, and many volunteers work longer. Riding four or five times a month is not uncommon, and that adds up to more than two 40-hour weeks of unpaid work a year. In Los Angeles County last year, reservists donated time valued at nearly $4.9 million.

But why would anyone, and particularly someone with a family, leave the comfort and security of home to take verbal abuse from an angry motorist stopped for reckless driving, to get roughed up in the course of wrestling some burly drunk wielding a switchblade knife, or literally to risk death in a back-alley shoot-out?

Some will say they want to help make their city a safer, better place to live. Others offer the philosophy that each of us has a responsibility to share the burden of fighting crime. But most admit candidly that being a cop as a part-time hobby is just plain fun. For example, Leo Manahan, 45, who owns and operates a commercial-art studio, says:

"This work is super exciting. After a long day battling with clients and suppliers and worrying about the payroll, you go out and ride at night and you're totally absorbed. It's recreation in the truest sense. You come off the night shift exhausted, but you're sure never bored."

David Simon, who owns his own public-relations company, says: "Patrol work is fascinating. It's a wholly different kind of existence. You get a view of how society functions that the average person never sees. You read about law enforcement or crime or the courts, but on the streets you get a view that changes your whole perspective. No two calls are ever the same; there's always something different happening. It's challenging, stimulating, exciting."

Jerry Ludwig, 43, who is president of a chain of 63 restaurants, joined the Sheriff's Reserve Forces Bureau seven years ago because he was interested in penology and in oppressed people: "There's a lot of good that can be done on the street. You can counsel people, maybe not in a professional way, but in a small way that could help change their way of life."

Sums up Naimy: "Patrol work gets everything else out of my mind; it's fun; it's therapeutic. Police work is a real intellectual challenge, too. You have to use good judgment when you get into sticky situations or you can be in deep trouble." Naimy calls the professional policeman a member of the "last warrior class," and says being a deputy is much like being a professional soldier: "All of these reservists deep down are romantics."

The average volunteer, he contends, has a sense of duty and courage. But the bottom line, in his opinion, is: "There's nothing in the world as exciting as working the streets in a patrol car. Hell, if he asked me, I'd pay the sheriff to let me work."

Few People Arrested Go to Prison— THE RECORD IN 6 CITIES

Based on latest figures available in six large cities or metropolitan counties:

Of All Persons Arrested on Felony Charges—

	Convicted	Sent to Jail or to Prison
Washington, D.C.	33%	18%
Chicago	26%	15%
Baltimore	44%	28%
Detroit	58%	20%
Los Angeles County	46%	28%
San Diego County	34%	14%

Source: Institute for Law and Social Research. "Felony Justice" to be published this fall by Little Brown & Company, California Bureau of Criminal Statistics.

The Future of Local Law Enforcement in the United States
The Federal Role

David J. Farmer *Director, Police Division, National Institute of Law Enforcement and Criminal Justice, U.S. Department of Justice*

Almost ten years have passed since Lyndon B. Johnson, questing for the Great Society and facing the reality of civil disorders and rising crime rates, signed into law the Omnibus Crime Control and Safe Streets Act of 1968. The Act established the Law Enforcement Assistance Administration (LEAA) as the principal federal agency concerned with state and local law enforcement and provided for criminal justice planning agencies in every state.

In 1960, when John F. Kennedy defeated Richard M. Nixon, crime had been regarded as a purely local issue.[2] By 1968 it had become a national priority. The America that could place a man on the moon could certainly ensure the safety of its citizens on the streets. As the President's Commission on Law Enforcement and Administration of Justice concluded in its 1967 report, ". . . American can control crime if it will."[3] On that note of confidence, LEAA was created[4] to lead the war against crime, and it came to account for five per cent of the criminal justice budget.[5]

Unfortunately, the rhetoric that succeeded in launching the "War on Crime" was not as easy to achieve on the battlefield. Ten years and six billion dollars later, there was discontent about the results, and the red tape. Although there had been many successes, there also were numerous failures. Social problems did not appear to be as tractable as the technology of space travel. The discontent was felt particularly by the cities, which were becoming increasingly strangled by financial shortages and increasingly resentful of the "cooperative feudalism" represented by federal assistance (and the inevitable companion guidelines) in all major domestic areas.

With the election of President Jimmy Carter, reorganization and reform of the Federal Branch of government has become a top priority. As part of that effort, the Federal element of the crime control assistance program has come under increasing scrutiny. Attorney General Griffin B. Bell has repeatedly cited what he perceives as the deficiencies of the Law Enforcement Assistance Administration, and has indicated his determination to take corrective action. A task force established by the Attorney General made its report [6] to Mr. Bell with two major recommendations and offering a number of options. Following a public comment period, the Attorney General submitted his report to the President. These recommendations are currently being coordinated with the work of the President's Reorganization Project. Thus, the future of federal involvement in crime control remains (at the time of

writing) to be determined, and readers of this article should bear in mind the historical position of the author.

This article looks beyond this period of reassessment to 1984 and the next half century. First, what do we want to achieve in the future in the area of law enforcement? Second, how do we get to that point? These two questions, looking first toward the future and toward the goals or the ideal that we seek, is the perspective of this article - a perspective that takes the viewer outside the limitations of current controversies and permits a longer view. However, the ideal is not one untempered by realism. Law enforcement is part of the weave of the nation's political life, and decisions about it will inevitably be made within a context of compromise among the various pressure groups and vested interests wrapped up in the present structure, and in light of other political realities. In the same way that budgeting cannot be viewed as an "arid subject, the province of clerks and dull statisticians,"[7] so decisions about the character of law enforcement will be made in an incremental and highly politicized fashion. Thus, consideration of what we want in the future might be more accurately stated as: "What can we reasonably expect?" OR "Given a favorable environment, what will be the probable and desirable outcomes?" The second question then becomes "How can the favorable environment be created?"

Looking ahead to the 21st century, what should we expect the general shape and character of law enforcement services to be? In particular, what functions should we expect law enforcement organizations to perform? What should be the general organization of law enforcement services? What kind of personnel should staff these services? What operational systems should be used? What management systems should be used? What should be the general condition of police science? Tentative answers to these questions are offered below.

What will be the general organization of law enforcement services in 2034 – 50 years after 1984?

Two extremes can probably be excluded. First, it is unlikely that the United States will have a national police force. The geographical size and the diversity of the country are the principal guarantees against this. Another is the nation's well-established conviction that the absence of a national police force is a barrier against tyranny. In part, this prejudice stemmed from J. Edgar Hoover. Conscious that his own Achilles heel might be that he wished to establish the Federal Bureau of Investigation as a national police force, Mr. Hoover consistently attacked the "national police force" straw man. He was successful, as the strength of public opinion attests.

Second, it is unlikely that the current parish-pump or atomistic system can survive. Certainly it *should* not. There are more than 17,000 police departments in the United States, ranging from one department which at, full complement had more than 30,000 officers to entirely part-time and volunteer departments. If there is any doubt about the confusion and the unsystematic character of the proliferation, one need only reflect that the 1967 President's Commission on Law Enforcement and Administration of Justice reported the total number of agencies to be 40,000. This erroneous belief was universally held until 1975 when the statistical error was discovered and the lower figure became known.[8]

The principal intellectual advocate of localism is a perceptive scholar, Dr. Elinor Ostrom, whose deep understanding of the police function must give any conscientious consolidationist pause.[9] Logic, however, seems to argue persuasively against this proliferation.[10] With a population of some 46 million, England has 39 police forces; with a population of some 58 million, France has two police forces. In comparison, the number of police departments in the United States – with a population four or five times as great – has an Alice-in-Wonderland quality. Robert DiGrazia, a former Police Commissioner of Boston and currently Police Chief of Montgomery County, Maryland, has recommended that the country should have 300 – rather than some 17,000 – police departments.[11] While the precise number cannot be predicted, it is reasonable to assume that the common sense of reducing the number of departments will be realized by 2034.

What functions will law enforcement organizations perform in 2034?

Today, as always, police departments do what police departments do. Their functions are many, varied, and undefined.[12] The number and variety of these functions is indicated by the title of a polemic published by the New York City Patrolman's Benevolent Association, *The One Thousand and One Hats of Officer Jones*. The confusion about definition can be seen in the absence of any definitive publication on the subject and in the widespread public misconception of the police officer's role. While television and popular mythology depict the police officer as the great crime-fighter, many point out that the typical police officer spends only a small percentage of his time on crime-related activities.[13]

It is likely that police agency functions will be more precisely defined by 2034. The growing popularity of systems thinking, general increases in the educational level of the public and of police officers, the increasing professionalism of police managers, and the development of police science[14] as well as other urban disciplines: all these factors will lead to demands for greater specificity of purpose, despite the difficulties and complexities. It is likely, too, that circumstances will require police agencies to take a more active role in areas other than street crime. White collar crime,[15] for example, inevitably will grow as computers become increasingly ubiquitous. It is also probable that the service functions of police will be emphasized.[16] There is a growing recognition that the police are the only available 24-hour-a-day social service agency, and providing quality social services may facilitate greater citizen cooperation needed for crime control (both arrests and convictions). Police will also become more involved in following through on court activities, by such means as transporting witnesses to court and explaining court processes to victims and witnesses.[17]

What kind of personnel will staff police services in 2034?

In addressing this question, let us focus on each end of the spectrum - the patrol officer (or private) and the police chief. The most significant change that has been occurring at the patrol officer level in the past decade is that the officer is becoming more than just a person with white socks: now he usually has an extension school degree. Much valid criticism can be levelled against the criminal justice education courses (for example, see notes on the subject in the 1976 edition of the *Police Yearbook*).[18] But, due to the impetus of the Law Enforcement Program (LEEP), a revolution has been started in police agencies and there is no reversing the clock. The current problem, however, is that police departments have made no effective provision for the educated officer. Thus, most of the best leave for occupations that promise greater (*à la* Maslow) self-actualization. The grinding down effect of a paramilitary bureaucratic organization at the patrol officer level is incompatible with education. It is likely that more effective organizational arrangements will be made for the educated officer by 2034. This process will be spurred primarily by the community need for better police service and by growing police professionalism. It will also be encouraged by the opening of police job opportunities to people such as women who will not perpetuate the traditional image. It is likely that this provision will include redefinition of the general duty police officer – more toward the "community manager" concept.[19]

At the chief executive end of the spectrum, 2034 will probably see improvements in two major areas – selection and training. Currently, the typical qualifications for the position of Police Chief are *not* an advanced degree in public or business administration coupled with extensive police command experience in a variety of settings. The essential qualifications of the successful applicant include being born and raised in the community he serves and having spent all his working life in that one police department. While some lateral movement does occur at the chief level, parochialism is the rule. Compared with the English and the French systems, we do little to prepare police chiefs for their responsibilities. Because the job is the most difficult in the department, the position of police chief thus is usually the weakest link. By 2034, the United States will surely have its equivalent of Britain's Bramshill,[20] providing adequate management and administrative training to equip chiefs and other managers to use modern management approaches such as long-term planning.

What operational systems will be utilized in 2034?

Police agencies are at the beginning of a revolution in operating practices. The question is not whether the revolution will occur but how long a period is required for percolation. Research has shown the opportunity and the need for a radical restructuring of police field service delivery systems. Three studies, two funded by the Federal Government and one by a private foundation, are particularly significant. The

Kansas City Preventive Patrol experiment,[21] despite some methodological limitations,[22] has cast significant doubt on the efficacy of traditional preventive patrol as it is now practiced. The key words in this sentence are "as it is now practiced". There may be a high level of manpower saturation where crime is deterred or displaced and a low level where criminal activity is encouraged. But the study suggests that, within these parameters, manpower variations are irrelevant. The study indicates that what is usually done now by police departments under the heading of preventive patrol does not produce the results traditionally expected, and that police commanders have far greater flexibility in deploying resources than they usually suppose. The Response Time Study,[23] conducted in the same city, reconceptualizes response time, indicating that police response time alone is an insufficient concept. Citizen mobilization (the time between observation of the crime and the reporting to the police) is a relatively large part of the total response continuum. It also questions the belief that police departments must be geared up to respond rapidly to all calls. Rapid response does not have great significance in making apprehensions in most cases, and citizen satisfaction is more a function of expectations (which can be affected by the police agency itself) than merely of quick response. The study of the Criminal Investigation Process,[24] conducted by the Rand Corporation, did not surprise informed police administrators, but it did question the popular conception of the great investigator. Among its conclusions: the most important determinant of whether a case is solved is the information gathered by the immediately responding patrol officers; of the remaining cases that are solved, the solutions usually come from routine police procedures. While the study's recommendations may have stretched beyond its data base,[25] the conclusions seem accurate. Taken together, these studies should result eventually in a complete re-thinking and re-structuring of field operations, as cities continue to experience financial pressures and as the public realizes the enormous cost of law enforcement.[26] Some departments are already beginning to change – for example, with directed patrol,[27] split force patrol[28] and the greater use of anti-crime (or blending and decoy) strategies.[29]

The direction of the operational revolution will probably be toward wider use of the systems approach in police operations. This will involve more complete and effective analysis of police problems and identification and evaluation of alternative solutions. Illustrative examples would include approaches that focus on the problem of policing prostitution not merely by arresting prostitutes but by concentrating on pimps and appropriate hotel owners; that focuses not merely on burglars but mainly on fences; and that relies not only on preventive patrol as a method of reducing auto thefts but also on urging regulations requiring improved auto anti-theft devices and so on. A systems-oriented approach will require, among other things, upgrading of both the police crime analysis and intelligence functions.[30] It will also include the development of more purposeful police activity: a possibility is a system for working officers similar to Management-by-Objectives but without the usual concomitant paperwork. Operations will have developed to the point where a differential response pattern will be

used. Rather than responding to all calls as if they were of equal urgency, a structured plan will be used. The fact is that not all police calls require equal types of response. Some require the emergency "sirens and lights" dispatch of a police unit; some can be handled on a planned delay basis ("An officer will be there in 30 minutes.") Some can be handled over the telephone; and others can involve a visit by the callers to headquarters.[31] Perhaps some patrol officers will operate like insurance agents or detectives responding to appointments and operating from desks rather than from cars prowling aimlessly throughout the community.

What management systems will be used in 2034?

Here the stirrings of change are being felt, but the shape of the change has not yet been adequately formulated. In the operations area, ground-breaking studies have been completed, but the management area remains uncharted, and thus the direction of change is difficult to predict. A number of police chiefs realize that the traditional reactive management-by-crisis mode of police administration is inadequate, a fact that will become even more apparent as the changes in police operations demand accompanying managerial adjustments. But the strongest pressure for change will come when a sound police program performance system is developed.[32] Currently the police community does not have a meaningful system for evaluating police programs, and the result is that police chiefs are essentially unaccountable for the quality of their agency's performance beyond handling the public relations aspects of sensational incidents or other problems that get out of hand.

Traditional police management textbooks owe much to the mechanistic view of management represented by POSDCORB,[33] discussions of organization charts and the like. This is changing as instructors incorporate the behaviorist and psychological views in police management courses and police organizations are increasingly examined not only in terms of structure but also of the work-flow and the human perspectives. Discussions about Theories X and Y and references to Alderfer are now not uncommon in police administration.[34] New management concepts are indeed available and will be increasingly tailored to the police situation. An example is the matrix approach, where department-wide policy is determined by teams of officers cutting across divisions and ranks. Also appearing anecdotally on the horizon is a perspective of police management as an exercise in interest group politics – along the lines described for government as a whole by David Truman[35] in 1952 and subsequently widely discussed by others like Lowi.[36] Perhaps the police management theory of 2034 will have effectively synthesized these approaches. Certainly, it seems necessary.

As the foregoing indicates, the police service should not be expected to remain static. Law enforcement in 2034 should – and probably will be – significantly different. Our grandchildren will probably look at police organizations of 1977 with much the same wry amusement as we do when we look at pictures of Victorian cops with tall hats and wide moustaches. In 2034, however, the gap will be much wider. The 2034 projection in this chapter may be viewed as unimaginative. It envisions no robots, nor

2. POLICE

the inevitable computer wonders, for example. Nor does it discuss possible radical changes in the environment of police work: increasing urbanization toward the world city, and the like. In looking toward the future of law enforcement, this article has been deliberately conservative. The point is that, even assuming minimal change, dramatic advances should be expected and sought.

To reach such a level of achievement by 2034 will require significant advances in both research and action programs. While federal and state governments have no monopoly on either wisdom or ability, it would take a bold prophet to proclaim that police agencies and local authorities have the objectivity and capability to provide self-leadership. The change must be effected in (and by) local government, but it will require a driving force, an entity dedicated to forward movement and capable of providing appropriate leadership and support. Bootstrapping into the future is likely to slow law enforcement progress and risk the failure to achieve the more effective performance possible from more rapid change.

The questions, then, are whether and how state governments can give the required leadership? In the area of research, it seems inappropriate to have 50 entities attempting to sponsor or undertake research. Such an approach is possible, but it exacts a price in terms of the inefficiency of inevitable duplication and the ineffectiveness of a lack of national focus in research activity. In the area of implementation, it would be very logical and within the Constitutional framework – where localities are creatures of state government – for the states to take the lead. Given the comprehensive statewide planning on the lines contemplated in the 1968 Act, there is no substitute for effective state action in securing the implementation of criminal justice improvements. But the fact is – on both research and implementation – no state has yet provided this leadership. This is reflected in the report of the Department of Justice study group [37] and elsewhere.[38] "Few states and local governments planned for all criminal justice expenditures at their respective levels".[39] System-wide criminal justice planning, the report notes, has not taken place at the state level, "except on a very limited scale and only on an exception basis."[40]

In the interests of effective law enforcement, the Federal government should continue (and improve) its supportive activities until the states provide the appropriate leadership. Even if state-level research were significantly upgraded, the central government should continue (and improve) its research activity. As long as enough crucial states fail to provide leadership in fostering and persuading local agencies to improve their operations, continued and improved Federal activity would also seem desirable in the action area. The principal Federal thrust should be to encourage and persuade the states to take a more positive leadership stance; the Federal role would then be to support state initiatives in the reform area by such means as program, organizational, personnel and financial assistance.

This article has examined the future role of the federal (or state) government in the crime control process from the viewpoint of the future of law enforcement. Other perspectives are, of course, feas-

ible. One could begin by analyzing existing arrangements to determine strengths and weaknesses, and then to suggest improvements. This is typical of many contemporary discussions about the Federal (or state) government role in the crime control process, because the experience of LEAA has been so extensively debated [41] in the Congress and in the press. This article has avoided this well-trodden path. Such discussions – overly influenced by present problems – often lead to the creation of the horseless carriage rather than the automobile.

The context of this discussion has been law enforcement, concerned only with government's responsibility for the crime control function. In other words, the specialist viewpoint. Another discussion might choose to consider the overall pattern of governmental involvement in the full range of program areas such as housing, energy, environmental affairs and other domestic issues.[42]

The future role of the Federal government in the crime control process undoubtedly will be resolved in the general context of issues of intergovernmental relations and (except to the extent that special circumstances can be demonstrated for crime control) in response to general basic principles and pressures. Clearly, this is a valid approach, but it, too, has been widely discussed.[43]

In looking at future improvement opportunities – rather than being obsessed with past mistakes or enmeshed in the larger question of intergovernmental fiscal relations – it is possible to put the Federal role in sharper focus. The question is not whether the Federal role should be abolished. Rather, it is "How can it be strengthened? How can it be increased in both quality and quantity? How can the Federal government energize the other levels of government – and, in particular, persuade the states to fulfil their leadership role in implementation?" Without appropriate leadership, the type of change described in this chapter is unlikely to be realized. The prospect then would be a deterioration of the crime situation, with a corresponding decline in the quality of American styles of living. That is a prospect the nation would be reluctant to contemplate.

Footnotes

1. The author is currently Director of the Police Division at the National Institute of Law Enforcement and Criminal Justice. However, this chapter is written as by a private citizen, and points of view or opinions in this chapter are those of the author and do not necessarily represent the official position or policies of the U.S. Department of Justice or LEAA.
2. See Caplan, Gerald, "Reflections on the Nationalization of Crime, 1964-1968," *Law and Social Order*, pp. 583-635, 1973.
3. President's Commission on Law Enforcement and Administration of Justice, *The Challenge of Crime in a Free Society*, U.S. Government Printing Office, Washington, D.C., 1967, p. 291.
4. The establishment of the Law Enforcement Assistance Adminstration in 1968 followed the creation by the Federal Government in 1965 of the Office of Law Enforcement Assistance (OLEA) and the 1967 President's Commission on Law Enforcement and Administration of Justice.
5. The functions of LEAA were to (a) support statewide criminal justice planning by the creation of state planning agencies (b) supply states and local governments with block grants to improve their criminal justice systems (c) to make discretionary grants (d) to sponsor and evaluate research and (e) supply money for the training and education of criminal justice personnel.

6. The Department of Justice Study Group, *Restructuring the Justice Department's Program of Assistance to State and Local Governments for Crime Control and Criminal Justice System Improvement*, U.S. Department of Justice, Washington, D.C., June 1977. The study group recommended a major restructuring of the program designed to (a) refocus the national research and development role into a coherent strategy of basic and applied research and systematic program development, testing, demonstration and evaluation and (b) replace the present block/formula portion of the program with a simpler program of direct assistance to State and local governments with an innovative feature that would allow State and local governments to use the direct assistance funds as "matching funds" to buy into the implementation of national program models that would be developed through the refocused national research and development program.

7. Wildawsky, Aaron, *The Politics of the Budgetary Process*, Little, Brown and Company, Boston, Massachusetts, 1964, 1974, p. xxiii.

8. See President's Commission on Law Enforcement and Administration of Justice, *The Challenge of Crime in a Free Society*, U.S. Government Printing Office, Washington, D.C., February 1967, p. 91 for the 40,000 figure. See the Law Enforcement Assistance Administration, *Criminal Justice Agencies*, U.S. Government Printing Office, Washington, D.C., for figures of 17,464 general purpose and 987 special police agencies. The 17,464 includes all major enforcement agencies, including state police, separate bureaus of identification, county sheriffs and police departments and municipal and township police departments. Special police includes park rangers, harbor police, housing police and campus police. Richard W. Velde, former LEAA Administrator, indicates that the error between the 40,000 and the approximately 17,000 figures was clerical. A statistician had a column entitled "jurisdictions with no police officers," and this was added to the number of police agencies.

9. Ostróm, Elinor, et al., *Policing Metropolitan America*, U.S. Government Printing Office, Washington, D.C., 1977.

10. e.g., see Skoler, Daniel L., *Organizing the Non-System*, Lexington Books, Lexington, Massachusetts, 1977.

11. Remarks delivered at a Police Foundation conference on "Upgrading the Police," April 1976. On this occasion, Commissioner DiGrazia also referred to police chiefs as "pet rocks."

12. Herman Goldstein, in his *Policing a Free Society*, (Ballinger Publishing Company, Cambridge, Massachusetts, 1977) argues that "the whole reform movement in policing has been short-sighted in focusing almost exclusively on improving the police establishment without having given adequate attention to some serious underlying problems that grow out of the basic arrangements for policing in our society." Among the publications which cast light on the functions of policing are Wilson, James Q., *Varieties of Police Behavior*, Harvard University press, Cambridge, Massachusetts, 1968; Bittner, Egon, *The Functions of the Police in Modern Society*, U.S. Government Printing Office, Washington, D.C., 1970; Niederhoffer, A., *Behind the Shield*, Anchor Books, Gordon City, New York, 1967; Reiss, Al, *The Police and the Public*, Yale University Press, New Haven, Connecticut, 1971; and Roberg, Ray R., *The Changing Police Role*, Justice Systems Development, Inc. San Jose, California, 1976.

13. The actual percentage of time spent by police officers on crime-related activity clearly varies by geography and by time, and there are definitional and measurement problems in allocating police time among crime-related and non-crime related activities. Among the numbers which are given are 32 per cent (President's Commission on Law Enforcement and Administration of Justice, *Task Force Report: Police*, Washington, D.C., U.S. Government Printing Office, 1967, p. 121), less than 30 per cent (The National Commission on Productivity, *Opportunities for Improving Productivity in Police Services*, National Commission on Productivity, Washington, D.C., 1973, p. 27.) See Reiss, Albert J., *The Police and the Public*, Yale University, New Haven, Connecticut, 1971, p. 96 for his report on the Chicago Police Department that "only 3 per cent of all time spent on patrol involves handling what is officially regarded as a criminal matter."

14. Contrary to some impressions, there is a body of helpful research in the police area. For example, see the account in Farmer, David J., "Fact v. Fact: A Selective View of Police Research in the United States," *The Police Journal* , Vol. XLIX, No. 2, April - June 1976, pp. 104-113.

15. For a general account, see Edelhertz, Herbert, *The Nature, Impact and Prosecution of White-Collar Crime*, U.S. Government Printing Office, Washington, D.C., 1970.

16. e.g., see San Diego Police Department, *Community Profiling and Police Patrol: Final Staff Report of the Community Profile Development Project*, San Diego Police Department, San Diego, California, 1974. The Community Profile project represents a community-oriented approach to policing that emphasizes increasing the individual officer's awareness and understanding of his community and improving officer response to area problems. An experimental group of 24 patrol officers and 3 patrol superiors was given training in methods of community analysis, decisiin making, patrol goal setting, community organization and interpersonal relations. An experimental and a control group spent ten months working alternating shift schedules on the same group of patrol beats. The major conclusion of the project was that the experimental group changed their attitudes about patrol work and their communities. The experiment was however flawed by some evaluation problems, e.g., turnover problems in the group, lack of a community attitude survey, and the experimental group may have been provided with handi-talkies and overtime pay.

17. see Knudten, Richard D., *Victims and Witnesses: Their Experiences with Crime and the Criminal Justice System* , U.S. Government Printing Office, Washington, D.C., 1977. This study documents victim and witness problems, and discusses implications for policy. Among the new approaches discussed for meeting victim/witness needs are victim reporting fees, equitable witness fees, and the concept of an office of justice advocate. A conclusion of the study is that "extensive victim/service programs are not needed by most victims and witnesses. What is needed is greater knowledge about the coordination of already existing community services, increased public and private agency willingness to service these client groups, designation of responsibility to some person or group for victim/witness concerns (probably with legal power), lessened competition among the various elements constituting the criminal justice system, and increased desire by system operatives to respond to victim/witness problems."

18. Farmer, David J., "Education and Practice – Operational Relations and the Development of Quality Control: Remarks," *The Police Yearbook*, International Association of Chiefs of Police, Gaithersburg, Md., 1976, pp. 227 - 228.

19. Bordua, David J., "Comments on Police-Community Relations", *Law Enforcement Science and Technology II*, Port City Press, 1969, p. 118. The reference is to police as "community managers and monitors of social change."

20. Bramshill is the staff training college for the British police service. See the March 1978 issue of *Police Studies*, vol.1, No.1, pp. 5 - 12.

21. Kelling, George L., et al. *The Kansas City Preventive Patrol Experiment: A Summary Report and a Technical Report*, The Police Foundation, Washington, D.C., 1974. The Kansas City Preventive Patrol experiment has cast serious doubt on the effectiveness of traditional preventive patrol. In the words of former Kansas City Police Chief Joseph McNamara, it has shown that "routine patrol in marked police cars has little value in preventing crime or making citizens feel safe," and that the substantial amount of time spent on routine preventive patrol might be devoted to more productive assignments.
A 15-beat segment of the city was used for the experiment. Five of the beats were designated as reactive: officers responded only to calls for service and preventive patrol was discontinued. Five matched beats were control areas: preventive patrol was maintained at normal levels. Five were designated as proactive areas: preventive patrol was increased up to three times the normal levels. Victimization surveys were conducted to measure unreported crime. Community surveys were undertaken to assess citizen and business satisfaction. Reported crime and other data were analyzed. In general, the differences between the three types of beats (i.e., the three levels of patrol coverage) were not significant in terms of reported and unreported crime, of citizen satisfaction, and of citizens' perceptions of their own security.

22. It should be noted that the validity of the Kansas City Preventive Patrol experiment has been questioned. The most significant criticisms concerned the location of the cars withdrawn from reactive beats when not responding to calls for service; the small sizes of the beats, presenting uncertainty concerning public perceptions of variations in patrol levels; and the small sample sizes utilized in the surveys. (For an assessment of the study, see the report of the National Evaluation Program Phase I study, *A Review and Assessment of Traditional Preventive Patrol*, University City Science Center, Philadelphia, Pennsylvania, 1975).

23. Bieck, William, et al, *Response Time Analysis Report*, Executive Summary, Kansas City Police Department, Kansas City, Missouri, 1977. Bieck, William et al, *Ibid*, Vol. I Methodology. Bieck, William et al, *Ibid*, Vol. II Analysis.

Through the use of civilian observers, analyses of the communications center's tapes, and interviews with victims and witnesses, the project has assembled a wealth of data. At the time of writing, only the data on some 949 Part I crimes have been analyzed, and the above reports refer to the Part I figures alone. The remaining data is on Part II crime calls, potential crime calls (e.g., disturbance, prowler, suspicious persons), and general service calls. Unlike earlier studies of police response time (e.g., Isaacs, 1967; Furstenberg, 1971) this study did not rely upon officer self-reporting for the data. This and the meticulous methodology give significant confidence in the results.

The results of the Part I data analysis include the findings that: arrests occurred in only a small percentage of all Part I crimes; rapid citizen reporting had a greater effect on suspect apprehension than did police response; police responded faster to calls involving serious injuries than those with minor injuries, although citizens took longer to report incidents involving serious injuries than incidents involving non-serious injuries; citizen mobilization time was the major determinant of witness availability; in 76 per cent of all cases, citizens encountered problems in reporting crime to the police; in 75 per cent of all cases, citizens were responsible for the most common cause of delays; many talked to at least one other person before calling the police; and citizens did not use special emergency numbers for reporting only emergency calls.

Among the implications which the authors draw from their findings are:

> Because of the time citizens take to report crimes, the application of technological innovations and human resources to reducing police response time will have negligible impact on crime outcomes.

> If procedures can be developed to discriminate accurately between emergency and non-emergency calls, more productive response-related outcomes can be achieved if coordinated with patrol resource allocation.

> Direct rapid response to robbery incidents by other than dispatched officers may be less effective in achieving response-related arrests than interception patrol away from the location at which a robbery occurred.

24 *The Criminal Investigation Process*, The Rand Corporation, Santa Monica, California, 1976. See also Greenwood, Peter W. et al, *The Criminal Investigation Process*, Rand Corporation, Santa Monica, California, 1977. Among the principal findings are: more than half of all serious reported crime receives no more than superficial attention from investigators; an investigator's time is mainly taken up in work on cases that experience indicates will not be solved; for solved cases, the investigator spends more time on post-arrest processing rather than the pre-arrest phase; the single most important determinant of whether a case will be solved is the information the victim supplies to the immediately-responding patrol officer; of solved cases in which the offender is not identifiable at the time of the initial report, almost all are cleared as a result of routine police procedures; and in many departments, investigators do not consistently and thoroughly document the key evidentiary facts, with untoward consequences for prosecutors.

25. See National Institute of Law Enforcement and Criminal Justice, *The Criminal Investigation Process: A Dialogue on Research Findings*, U.S. Government Printing Office, Washington, D.C., 1977.

26. Many still think of a police car as costing something like $3,000. This is incorrect. It takes about 5 officers to staff a police car round-the-clock seven days a week all year round, because individual officers do not usually work more than 40 hours per week and they have vacations and holidays. Considering salaries and fringe benefits, a one-person patrol car thus cost over $100,000. A two-officer patrol car costs not $3,000, but in excess of $200,000.

27. Unlike traditional patrol where officers patrol their beats entirely at their own discretion, directed patrol is structured preventive and apprehension activity – involving goal-setting and task assignment by management. Rather than a mode of merely responding to problems, the emphasis is on planned and purpose-oriented activity. See Gay, William G., *Improving Patrol Productivity, Volume I Routine Patrol*, U.S. Government Printing Office, Washington, D.C., 1977, pp. 13-14.

28. Split-force patrol is an approach in patrol specialization, based on separating the call-for-service response and the crime prevention functions of police patrol. This contrasts with the traditional generalist pattern whereby police patrol officers handle all aspects of patrol. See Tien, James M., *An Evaluation Report of An Alternative Approach in Police Patrol: The Wilmington Split-Force Experiment*, Public Systems Evaluation, Cambridge, Massachusetts, March 1977. The experiment showed that the split-force approach in Wilmington caused significant increases in both call-for-service response and arrest productivity and for an increase in police professionalism and accountability. The report notes that the very act of forming a dedicated prevention-oriented unit leads to more efficiency, and it attributes the increase in arrest-related productivity primarily to the immediate incident-oriented investigation conducted as a result of the split-force approach. Among the other findings is that there may be an opportunity for police agencies to manage the demand of the public for police services – "inasmuch as 86% of all calls for service are non-critical in nature and citizen satisfaction is a function of expectation." The Wilmington Bureau of Police is now experimenting with this notion of managing the public demand for police services. For another form of split-force, see also Tien, James M., *An Evaluation Report of the Worcester Crime Impact Program*, Public Systems Evaluation, Cambridge, Massachusetts, 1975. Worcester utilized civilians who assumed traditional police roles, and the civilians (police service aides) were deployed on patrol to respond to service calls and to assist police officers. Thus, this civilianized split-force approach involves the civilians focusing on service calls and the police on the more serious criminal-type calls.

29. See Schack, Stephen, *Improving Patrol Productivity, Volume II, Specialized Patrol*, U.S. Government Printing Office, Washington, D.C., 1977 for an excellent overview and see Halper, Andrew et al., *New York City Police Department Street Crime Unit*, U.S. Government Printing Office, Washington, D.C., 1975 for an account of the New York experience. Blending and decoy are the two principal approaches used in anti-crime or casual clothes squads. Rather than uniformed high-visibility patrol, officers wear street clothes to blend into situations or adopt disguises to serve as decoy victims. A distinguishing feature of the New York operation is the relative size of the anti-crime operation in relation to the total patrol force. The approach has been very productive in terms of felony arrests. However, at the time of writing, a comprehensive and independent evaluation has not been made of the strategy, considering not only felony arrest productivity but also factors such as citizen satisfaction.

30. See Reinier, Hobart G., *Crime Analysis in Support of Patrol, National Evaluation Program Phase I Summary Report*, U.S. Government Printing Office, Washington, D.C., 1977. The problem lies not only in the undeveloped state-of-the-art of both crime analysis and intelligence, but also in the problem of communicating the results of such analyses in a timely and useable fashion to operating personnel.

31. A comprehensive study of alternative police strategies for responding to calls for service is being undertaken by the City of Birmingham Police Department, and an experiment in this area is being conducted by the City of Wilmington Bureau of Police. Other departments are also experimenting with non-traditional methods for responding to calls for service, e.g., Portland, Oregon.

32. Farmer, David J., "Fact v. Fact: A Selective View of Police Research in the United States," *The Police Journal*, Vol. XLIX, No. 2, April - June 1976, pp. 108-109. Among the deficiencies of systems relying on crime and clearance rates is that, as is widely understood, they take no account of unreported crime; they are subject to manipulation and classification problems, and they lump together major and minor crimes under the same headings. In fact, they distort activity because they emphasize arrests. These lead to neglect of such factors as recovering stolen property, and give no consideration to elements such as the fear of crime. A sound performance measurement system must utilize the concept of indicators – on the same lines as economists use in describing the performance of the economy. It should also collect information on citizen perceptions of safety and of police performance, as additional indicators.

33. As is noted in Wilson, O. W. and Roy McLaren *Police Administration*, McGraw-Hill, New York, New York, 1977, p. 60, "Administration has been classically defined by Luther Gulick in his famous acronym POSBCORB, which stands for the initial letters in Planning, Organizing, Staffing (or personnel management), Directing, Coordinating, Reporting and Budgeting. In a text on police administration, naturally these functions of administration and management are fundamental."

34. see Huse, Edgar F and James L. Bowditch, *Behavior in Organizations: A Systems Approach to Managing*, Addison-Wesley, Reading, Mass., 1973.

35. Truman, David B., *The Governmental Process: Political Interests and Public Opinion*, Alfred A. Knopf, New York, New York, 1951, 1971.

36. Lowi, Theodore J., *The End of Liberalism*, Norton, New York, New York, 1969.

37. The Department of Justice Study Group, *op.cit.* The report indicates (p. 10) that "the lessons of the past nine years of the LEAA program have been mixed." On the positive side, for example, the Group quoted the report by the Advisory Commission on Intergovernmental Relations (*Safe Streets Act Reconsidered: The Block Grant Experience 1968-1975*, Washington, D.C., 1977, pp. 187-190) that block grant funds have supported many useful criminal justice activities and projects and that the block grant assistance has established a process for crime control and improvement of the administration of justice. However, it does note that system-wide criminal justice planning has not been taking place at the state level, except on a limited scale. "Few state and local governments planned for all criminal justice expenditures at their respective levels. Most planned only for the 3% to 5% of their expenditures that were derived from the LEAA program" (p.7). Even the planning done for the use of the LEAA block funds often amounted to little more than a paper-work exercise required by statute and guidelines in order to qualify for the funds. Further, "the national leadership role for LEAA in the research and development of new and innovative techniques for responding to the crime problem and for possible transfer to State and local governments simply has not materialized on the scale envisioned under the 1968 Act."

38. For example, see Twentieth Century Fund Task Force (*Law Enforcement: The Federal Role*, Twentieth Century Fund, New York, N.Y., 1976) and the series of reports produced by the Center for National Security Studies (Sarah Carey, *Law and Disorder*, 1969; *Law and Disorder II*, 1970; *Law and Disorder III*, 1973 and *Law and Disorder IV*, 1976.)

39. The Department of Justice Study Group, *op. cit.*, p.7.

40. *Ibid*, p. 7.

41. See footnotes 37 and 38 for references.

42. Other context choices include the decision whether to view the discussion from the viewpoint of the police (or other element of the criminal justice system) or the criminal justice system as a whole.

43. e.g., see Advisory Commission on Intergovernmental Relations, *Fiscal Balance in the American Federal System*, U.S. Government Printing Office, Washington, D.C., 1967 or Maxwell, James A., *Financing State and Local Government*, The Brookings Institute, Washington, D.C., 1969. Another entertaining book on the subject is Reiss, Henry S., *Revenue-Sharing: Crutch or Catalyst for State and Local Governments*, Praeger Publishers, New York, N.Y., 1970. Involved are such questions as - Will the Federal government continue to dominate the lion's share of the country's tax resources, while the localities (manacled by state fiscal restraints such as those on property taxation) bear such a large proportion of the problems? Will the fiscal-needs imbalance be adjusted by some form of revenue sharing? Will the mechanism for money transfer between the layers of government be improved? Will the relative roles of the several layers of government remain as at present? Will the system be more rational than at present? What will, or can, be done to rationalize the crazy-quilt pattern of local government – and in particular, the proliferation of governments in the metropolitan areas? Within the setting of interest group pressures and in response to the realities of accelerating problems in the variety of domestic areas, such overall questions will be addressed.

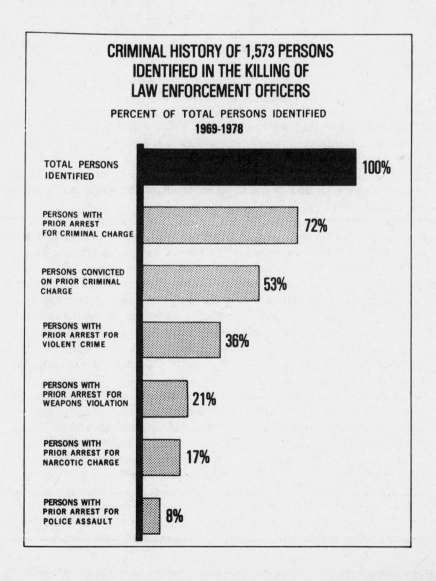

CRIMINAL HISTORY OF 1,573 PERSONS IDENTIFIED IN THE KILLING OF LAW ENFORCEMENT OFFICERS

PERCENT OF TOTAL PERSONS IDENTIFIED
1969-1978

- TOTAL PERSONS IDENTIFIED — 100%
- PERSONS WITH PRIOR ARREST FOR CRIMINAL CHARGE — 72%
- PERSONS CONVICTED ON PRIOR CRIMINAL CHARGE — 53%
- PERSONS WITH PRIOR ARREST FOR VIOLENT CRIME — 36%
- PERSONS WITH PRIOR ARREST FOR WEAPONS VIOLATION — 21%
- PERSONS WITH PRIOR ARREST FOR NARCOTIC CHARGE — 17%
- PERSONS WITH PRIOR ARREST FOR POLICE ASSAULT — 8%

Discipline in American Policing

Donal E.J. MacNamara

John Jay College of Criminal Justice
City University of New York

Police discipline is the most publicized, yet least researched area of American police administration and management. Certainly any analysis of police news (in newspapers, popular periodicals, on radio and television) will document the disproportionate coverage of charges of police corruption, brutality, discrimination against minorities, and violations of constitutional protections. The crimes and peccadilloes of police officers are heavily reported compared either to the attention given these matters by police textbooks and professional journals or the attention given by the media to similar infractions by physicians, lawyers, public officials, businessmen, and blue-collar workers. Perhaps this occupational inequity is understandable on the basis of the "man bites dog" yardstick of the media, but the reluctance of those who undertake to educate the law enforcement officers and commanders of the future to come to grips clearly and forcibly with this important problem of police management and community relations is obviously less defensible.

The very nature of the police officer's job (its responsibilities, powers, opportunities, temptations, dangers, pressures, and frustrations) creates disciplinary problems unlikely to develop in most other occupations. Acton tells us that "power corrupts," and the individual police officer at the very base of the command hierarchy exercises, for the most part unsupervised, a degree of direct power (discretion) over the lives, liberties, reputations, behaviors, and incomes of thousands of his fellow citizens unequaled by many with much more imposing titles and at much higher levels of the public and private power pyramids.

Alexander Pope tells us that "vice is a monster of so frightful mien. . .that to be hated needs but to be seen. Yet seen too oft, familiar with her face, We first endure, then pity, then embrace." One would have to scan the *Dictionary of Occupational Titles* at great length before discovering a calling so continually exposed as that of the police officer to man at his most vicious, immoral, dishonest, and unethical worst, and the police officer is not exposed to just a small and easily identifiable criminal element but all too frequently to public officials, professionals, and esteemed citizens of the community. Certainly no other occupation combines so maximally temptation with opportunity—and at least until very recently little risk of exposure and punishment.

Perhaps we should not ask ourselves why some police officers embrace vice but rather how it is that so many of our more than 500,000 full-time police officers remain faithful to their oaths of office and with courage and dedication protect the lives and properties of their more than 200 million fellow citizens.

There are to be sure two perspectives: the first, favored by most police or police-oriented writers, is the "bad apple" school which avers that the rogue cop is the atypical exception and that once we identify and eliminate him the problem is solved; the second perspective is from the increasing number of critics from outside the police establishment, with some support from mavericks within. These critics see a more systemic infection communicated to succeeding generations of police officers through a process of in-group socialization, with ostracism and sometimes harsher penalties visited on those whose consciences do not permit them to participate or to consent by their silence.

Fragmentation of American Police

It might be best once again to emphasize the decentralized character of the American police operation. In no other country has the shibboleth of local autonomy and the fear of strong central authority combined to produce so anarchic a police structure. There are some 40,000 police agencies (many with only a handful of officers) on five governmental levels. They frequently have overlapping jurisdictions with no formal machinery to provide inspection and supervision, to mandate coordination, or even to promote cooperation.

Among these many agencies and departments, there are always some officers who maintain the highest of ethical standards and uncompromising disciplinary codes and others in whom brutality, corruption, discrimination, and job-shirking are minor. Still others (and not always just the highly publicized big-city forces) are so undisciplined, standards are so low, and supervision is so lax that they are involved in scandals. They often create headlines just as the participants in a previous scandal are being transported to the penitentiary (or in all too many cases drawing the first pension checks of an ill-earned retirement).

No specific agencies, bureaus, or departments will be mentioned in this essay, nor will any invidious comparisons between federal and state levels, sheriffs and county police, or big-city and small-town law enforcement be attempted. There are outstanding police agencies at all levels, of all sizes, and in all geographical regions of the country, and there is blame enough and to spare for police agencies in each category which have either throughout their history—or more frequently, for limited periods—failed to measure up to the standards of police conduct which both their fellow police officers and the citizenry have every right to expect.

Approaches to Police Discipline

An analysis of the infrequent discussions of police disciplinary problems in the professional literature reveals three major approaches to discipline: the *preventive*, the *positive*, and the *punitive*.

Preventive discipline emphasizes (1) the recruitment and probationary processes to prevent the appointment or tenuring of potentially troublesome officers, (2) alert supervision to detect difficulties in time so that they can be dealt with before they reach unmanageable proportions, and (3) the elimination of as many temptations and opportunities as possible. Included among the preventive disciplinary techniques are: intensive character and background investigations of recruits; polygraph and psychiatric screening; relatively long probationary periods under intensive supervision with rigorously administered separation proceedings against those who fail to measure up; and deterrent attention during recruit training to the ethical code and the punitive consequences of violations. Douglas Kelley and others have documented that a great number of the disciplinary infractions involve a relatively small percentage of the total police work force. Early identification and elimination of those unsuited for police duties and responsibilities should reduce the overall disciplinary problem to more manageable proportions. In the past decade, partly as the result of efforts to open police ranks to a greater number of minority officers (a goal with which I am in complete sympathy), the effective use of the recruitment and probationary processes to prevent the appointment and tenuring of officers with criminal records, emotional difficulties, deviant lifestyles and other potentially troublesome characteristics has been curtailed—and, as we shall see, their later elimination from police agencies even after serious overt misbehavior has become much more difficult.

Positive discipline emphasizes training, leadership, example, development of esprit de corps, professionalism and a system of rewards and recognition. Modeled on the military approach, it entails command interest in the morale and well-being of the force (including their pay and fringe benefits, working conditions, and family welfare) and highly publicized incentives for valued behavior (commendations, medals, extra days off, desirable assignments, and promotions). Special attention is given to the example (appearance and behavior) set by supervisory and command officers and to their training in leadership techniques. Opportunity and encouragement (salary increments, additional promotion credits, time off, and tuition reimbursements) are provided for officers seeking college degrees, and police personnel are encouraged to identify themselves as professionals—not workers. While there is little doubt that the *positive* approach has many values both to the agency and the individual officers (and indeed to the community), it is equally obvious that overreliance on this optimistic view of human reaction to good leadership, good example and good treatment rests on undemonstrated psychological hypotheses and may open a department to serious misbehavior by a perhaps small minority of officers who would interpret such a positive disciplinary emphasis as naiveté or command weakness.

Punitive discipline is by far the most widespread disciplinary approach. Here, there is an emphasis on rules and regulations, on attempts to surprise (or even entrap) officers in violations, on intensive investigation of complaints, and on the imposition of penalties for disvalued and nonconforming behaviors. Although only a few police administrators publicly acknowledge that this is their principal disciplinary model, examination of many administrators' procedures and records—and interviews with their police officers and union delegates—make abundantly clear the predominance of the punitive approach to the discipline of police personnel. Comparison of the number of commendations with the number of charges and penalties recorded in a department over a one- or two-year period will convincingly demonstrate its dependence on negative, punitive disciplinary measures.

Disciplinary Responsibility of the Police Administrator

The chief executive of a law enforcement agency is as responsible for its discipline as for its effectiveness; the two are related but neither is synonymous nor wholly interrelated. This is not to say that every police administrator is accorded either the legal authority, the political support, or the necessary facilities to effectively carry out his disciplinary responsibilities. Civil service laws, veterans' rights, police unions, political interference, public pressures and, paradoxically, the *occasional* opposition of the communications media at times severely limit his capacity to discipline or remove undesirable officers; and criminal charges all too frequently fail for want of aggressive prosecution, technical difficulties with the proofs, or overly sympathetic juries whose members will later decry police dishonesty.

Police administrators often sit uneasily atop pressure boilers with no warning or cut-off valves. Although they have great need for information as to what is going on in the ranks below, they are frequently last to know of a developing scandal, learning of it only when the headlines blazon a grand jury investigation and their jobs and reputations are in jeopardy.

While in some instances the police chief is the victim of a conspiracy of silence among his subordinates, more frequently, he is self-victimized, neither seeking nor welcoming unpleasant information. Many chiefs neither read the papers nor have a staff aide abstract news relating to their departments;

others do not cultivate contacts either with their colleagues in the criminal justice system or with those knowledgeable about community affairs; some cut themselves off from communication with their subordinate officers; and others unfortunately are themselves part of the problem because they are brutal, corrupt, and contemptuous of the Constitution, court decisions, and legislative fiats.

Police Disciplinary Offenses

The components of the police disciplinary problem might well be classified into four general categories:

1. Offenses committed by an officer in a personal, nonjob-related capacity (wife-beating, assaulting a neighbor, drunken driving, adultery, nonpayment of debts, smoking marijuana, or shoplifting);
2. Administrative offenses (late report, drunk on duty, off post, improper uniform, disrespect to a superior);
3. Excess of zeal (use of excessive force, warrantless search or seizure, coercive interrogation, illegal detention—where no malice or personal profit was involved);
4. Abuse of police status (extortion, prejudiced actions against minorities, deliberate false arrest or false charges, faked evidence, perjury, selling, destroying, or divulging police information).

There are some who hold that an officer's nonjob-related personal offenses are not cognizable by the police disciplinary system, but maturer reflection on the disproportional publicity accorded a police officer's misdemeanor or felony and the resultant negative impact on the good name of the department and profession should convince us that a police agency, not unlike the military services, must insist on a standard of personal conduct somewhat higher than that perhaps required of a worker in private industry—or a public employee not empowered to enforce the laws against his fellow citizens.

A much more difficult disciplinary problem to deal with concerns the tradition of "professional courtesy," which is either limited to members of the local department or extended rather broadly to all who carry police identification. While such "courtesy" is usually restricted to minor violations (traffic offenses, drunkenness, disorderly conduct), in some cases it is rationalized as necessary to maintain good interdepartmental working relationships. It should be obvious that such preferential treatment of police officer violations is illegal, illogical, unprofessional, and likely to exacerbate police—community irritations.

Violations of departmental rules constitute by far the greatest number of disciplinary infractions (in some departments almost 100 percent). These are usually handled within the chain of command, and only in unusual circumstances do they arouse widespread public interest. However, failure to monitor this important disciplinary area will soon produce a sloppy, inefficient, undependable force with low morale, no sense of professional pride, and a vulnerability to much more serious infractions.

Excess-of-zeal offenses can result from many different causes: inadequate training and supervision; undue pressure on officers for speedy results; pressure to meet quotas; improper personnel assignments; a perception among officers that administrators and commanders are giving only lip service to the constitutional limitations on police procedures; and occasionally an overly judgmental, moralistic, almost missionary zeal (or highly competitive instinct) in a police officer. While policemen must necessarily be encouraged to zealously pursue their sworn duties to enforce the laws, apprehend offenders, control disorders, and faithfully fulfill their many responsibilities, commanders must equally insist that officers scrupulously observe the limitations imposed on their choice of methods and procedures by the Constitution, the legislature, the courts, and the agency's policies—even if such limitations are in their opinion undesirable, unnecessary, unwise, or make the officer's tasks more dangerous, difficult, and time-consuming. When excessive zeal is repeatedly and selectively utilized against persons of a particular minority (e.g., ethnic, ideological, or lifestyle groups) to the extent that it is demonstrably a manifestation of an officer's bias or prejudice against that minority, the offense must be reclassified into the much more serious "abuse of police status" category of disciplinary infractions.

Abuse-of-police-status offenses constitute the most serious disciplinary problem because they are subversive of the essential and fundamental mores of the police service. There should be little doubt or controversy as to the need for prompt, rigorous disciplinary action in the following offenses by law enforcement officers: shakedowns of numbers runners, bookies, dope pushers, afterhours clubs, peddlers, pimps, and prostitutes; operation of systematic "pads" to give protection to continuing illegal activities; cooperation with organized crime by destroying records, divulging information, and providing warnings of impending raids or arrests; changing testimony in criminal prosecutions; maliciously framing innocent persons or protecting guilty ones; and burglarizing premises on their patrol beats instead of protecting property.

Brutality, Corruption, and Discrimination

The three serious charges repeatedly leveled against police officers and/or agencies over the past decades might well be subsumed under this heading—with perhaps, as regards certain agencies, the additional allegation of arrogant invasion of constitutional protections. That many of these charges are self-serving, exaggerated, false, even malicious, is demonstrable. That all too many have been amply documented by official investigations which resulted in criminal penalties and civil damages is equally incontestable.

The overuse of force (or the use of any force in situations not authorized by law), discriminatory actions against minorities, and invasions of constitutionally protected rights are often interrelated and stem in the opinion of some commentators from identifiable police attitudes and ideologies. Without attempting to psychoanalyze or stigmatize so large, so varied, and on the whole so competent and dedicated an occupational grouping, some studies have indicated that police, as compared to other occupational cohorts, tend to be more conformist and conservative, more judgmental and moralistic, more intolerant of deviation and more resistant to change than many if not most of those with whom they at times come into adversary contact (civil rights and antiwar demonstrators, hippies and college students, rock fans and nude bathers, gay liberationists, and left-wing ideologues). They also have been found to share to a greater or lesser extent the antiminority prejudices of the lower middle-class blue-collar families from which so many of them originate. Thus oriented, they are easily irritated and angered by the often deliberately provocative conduct of their adversaries. The police at times overreact physically.

This tendency to physical overreaction to stress situations is complicated by the fact that, unlike the military, most police officers are neither experienced in nor trained for small unit tactics in controlling crowds, mobs, demonstrators, pickets, sit-ins, passive resisters, and/or mutinous prisoners. Nor are they used to acting under verbal commands from on-the-scene superior officers. The police officer's experience is in acting alone or with a long-time partner without supervision; confronted with a hostile crowd, and sometimes incompetently commanded by superior officers not personally known to him (or perhaps from another police agency), he quite humanly at times out of anger, hate, frustration, and perhaps even fear, lashes out with fists or night stick against those whom he perceives as his tormentors, his enemies. With a few notorious exceptions in recent decades, his violent reaction has rarely included the misuse of firearms.

Corruption, however, is quite different, both as to the type of police likely to be involved and as to the circumstances in which it flourishes. Here, the adversary confrontation between the forces of social protection and the enemies of society breaks down, and an unholy alliance between good and evil is negotiated. The officers involved may be inherently dishonest (we have no validated screening devices for identifying such a character weakness in prospective police recruits), or they may have developed what might be called a situational dishonesty stemming from a negative socialization by their police peers into the mysterious distinction between "clean" and "dirty" graft. They may be following the herd instinct ("everybody does it"), or they may be participating because they fear peer pressure, the threat of ostracism, or, worse, being identified as a stooge for the bosses. Or they may have over the years become cynical of society's commitment to honesty, having witnessed the "best and the brightest" grab with impunity; and they may have noted the few rewards for resisting the temptation of immediate and sometimes very lush payments for breaking one's oath of office. Recurrent disclosures of widespread corruption in police agencies of all sizes and in all areas have moreover not been consistently followed up with policies and procedures designed to eliminate this evil.

Sources of Complaints and Agency Attitudes Toward Complainants

Complaints of police misconduct may be initiated by widely divergent sources, and the source of the complaint rather than its nature or its seriousness frequently influences agency response, as does with some lesser frequency the identity or rank of the officer complained of. One might classify sources as *internal* (police supervisors, commanders, special inspectional or disciplinary control units, and, very rarely, fellow officers) or *external* (the victim of the abuse complained of, pressure groups, politicians or public office holders, civil liberties organizations, journalists, prosecutors and other officers of the criminal justice system, and occasionally disinterested citizens who claim to have witnessed the misconduct). By far, the greatest number of disciplinary actions are initiated by police superior officers who have observed misconduct on the part of a subordinate or who have had a violation of the rules, regulations, or procedures brought to their attention. Analysis of complaint files (where they exist) indicates only a minimal number of external complaints, yet it is these complaints which all too frequently elicit an aggressively hostile agency response which might be characterized as harassment of the complainant rather than investigation of the complaint.

It is axiomatic that some complainants (individual and organizational) are antipolice or out to "get" an individual police officer, that some politicians and pressure groups seek publicity and advantage in making false or exaggerated charges, and that sensational newspapers disproportionately headline undocumented and unproved scandals. However, these abuses do not justify negative agency response. The ulterior motivations of the complainant are less important than the substance of the complaint.

Departmental Handling of Complaints

Every complaint, from whatever source, should be *acknowledged, recorded, investigated, reported on*, and if found valid, *acted on* to prevent reoccurrence. Few agencies until recent years maintained satisfactory complaint and disciplinary files . . . complaints were often ignored, "lost," bucked from one unit to another with little possibility of fixing responsibility.

Annual reports contained inadequate information for either chronological or cross-departmental disciplinary comparisons, and the individual files of police personnel often were so cavalierly secured that information about disciplinary matters could easily be altered or removed.

I devised a very simple disciplinary record system many years ago. It is now employed by many smaller police departments, with some larger departments adapting it to fit their more complex needs. Basically, it consists of three things. There is a *complainant's file card* (a 5 × 8 card made up for each complaint source, i.e., individual, organizational, or anonymous) recording the following in columnar format:

—Date of complaint
—Complainant's name, address, and identifying material
—Officer or unit being complained about
—Date acknowledged
—Nature of the complaint (brutality, shakedown, drunk on duty)
—File number assigned
—Investigating officer
—Result of investigation (unfounded, upheld, etc.)
—Disposition

There is also an *officer's* or *unit disciplinary record card* (also in columnar format) which will show the following at a glance:

—Number and type of complaints against the officer
—Identity of the complainants
—Disposition in each case

The third record is an *offense record card* showing the following for each type of offense (discrimination, late report, unnecessary use of firearm, etc.):

—Number of such complaints
—Repeat complainants
—Repeat offenders
—Level of validity (founded complaints) for or against each

Analysis annually would clearly identify complainants who repeatedly level false or exaggerated charges or who are out to crucify an individual officer. It would also reveal which officers should be retrained, reassigned, or separated from the department, and which areas require intensified command and supervisory attention. Agency policy should provide for a "statute of limitations" so that after an appropriate period (perhaps three to five years) complaints might be removed from an officer's disciplinary record.

"Quis Custodiet Ipsos Custodes?"—Juvenal*

While the departmental or agency chain of command is usually quite adequate and efficient in investigating and processing internal complaints of minor misconduct, a more formal system and more specialized mechanisms have proved necessary to ferret out corruption and to process complaints of serious misconduct. Many large agencies have set up internal security or intelligence units to police their police officers; some have appointed carefully selected integrity officers to report serious offenses by officers within their units (and a few departments have encouraged turnarounds by apprehended rogue police officers who escape severe punishment by informing on their fellow officers). In other areas the processing of certain types of complaints has been turned over to special prosecutors, grand juries, crime commissions, and/or civilian complaint units. No method has proved so demonstrably successful as to merit a recommendation for general acceptance. Indeed, the per-

*Who watches the watchman? Who polices the police?

sonality, integrity, determination, and ability of the agency head, rather than the organizational structure or the tactics employed, seem to be the key to the elimination of abuses.

Rights of Police Officer Defendants in Disciplinary Cases

The emergence of strong police organizations (unions in fact if not in name) and the cumulative effect of judicial reviews of administrative disciplinary proceedings have eliminated the grosser violations of due process which until a decade ago characterized the trials of police officer defendants. Today, by law or by policy, the police officer charged with an offense is entitled to timely, written notice specifically setting forth the charges of misconduct. He may be represented by counsel. He is entitled to process for securing witnesses and records necessary for his defense. He may cross-examine the complainant and witnesses against him (even impute discreditable motives or actions on the part of a superior officer). He is entitled to a record of the proceedings and to an avenue of appeal from its determinations. Summary dismissals and punishments are now seldom encountered, and the tribunal (whether a trial commissioner or administrative judge, a civil service panel or the public safety committee of the municipal legislature, a court-martial-type board of superior officers, or a specially appointed hearing officer) is well aware that the record will have to support the findings and disposition.

Nevertheless, there are many problems which continue to cause difficulty. Space precludes consideration of all of them but certainly several demand attention:

—Suspension of police officer defendants
—Double jeopardy
—Impact of administrative proceedings on possible civil action against either the governmental unit or the individual officer
—Waiver of immunity
—Employment of the polygraph or psychological stress evaluator

Suspension of a police officer against whom serious charges have been brought seems at first consideration to be proper and necessary. Yet, maturer consideration raises some questions. Suspending a police officer increases the burdens on his fellow officers and, if the suspension is without pay, punishes his family. If the suspension is prolonged (and even administrative proceedings can take weeks or months), not only are these conditions exacerbated, but should he be exonerated, the police officer will have to be paid in full for all the period of his suspension. Depending on the nature of the charges and the potential for separating the defendant officer from the force, it might be better to find some assignment for him, pending the final disposition of his case, which will not bring him into direct contact with the public nor entail the employment of his police authority.

Should the nature of the charges indicate that the defendant officer might face indictment and a criminal trial, as well as administrative disciplinary action, some jurisdictions postpone the latter until final disposition of the case in the criminal justice system, rationalizing that a finding of guilt in the disciplinary hearing might prejudice the officer's defense in the criminal trial. It should be quite clear that separate determination of the administrative charges and the criminal indictment (even if they grow out of the same alleged misconduct) does not constitute double jeopardy, and it seems quite clear to me that the agency should process its case independently and with dispatch. A finding of guilt by the agency does not bind the criminal court, nor does an acquittal in court preclude agency disciplinary action.

Much the same reasoning applies to situations when either the municipality or the defendant-officer faces the prospect of civil action for damages growing out of the alleged misconduct. Civil trials in many jurisdictions take even longer than criminal court cases and with appeals may go on for years. To delay resolution of administrative disciplinary charges until final disposition in such a case would entail either long-term suspension of the officer, months or even years of limited duty assignment, or dismissal of the complaint for violation of the speedy-trial requirement.

Some jurisdictions require public employees against whom charges have been brought to waive immunity at least insofar as their testimony (before a grand jury or other official investigating commission) relates to their official duties. Such jurisdictions provide for dismissal of officers who refuse to sign a waiver. While there is some dispute as to the constitutionality of such involuntary waivers, there is a strong case in law, logic, and necessity for retaining the requirement that a public officer must answer before any lawful tribunal for his stewardship or forfeit his public office or employment. This can be distinguished from the compulsory self-incrimination prohibited by the Constitution in criminal cases.

Many law enforcement agencies employ instrumental detection of deception in connection with their investigations of criminal charges against non-police officers. Yet, there is strong opposition to employing either the polygraph or the psychological stress evaluator to assist in determining whether a police officer took a bribe, committed perjury, or engaged in other alleged misconduct. Without addressing the scientific arguments as to the validity of instrumental detection or the legal arguments as to its admissibility in criminal trials, I must confess a strong leaning toward a contractual waiver which would require as a condition of continued employment in a police agency submission to polygraph interrogation, under full safeguards, in specifically designated cases of serious misconduct. The imperatives of the public good and of the agency's needs in such cases seem to me superior to the alleged malefactor's individual interests.

Penalties for Officers Adjudicated Guilty

The penalties which may be imposed on law enforcement officers adjudicated guilty in an administrative disciplinary proceeding range from dismissal to an admonition or reprimand. Among the interpolated penalties are monetary fines (in a recent case as high as $30,000), demotion (seldom used), suspension without pay for definite periods, disciplinary transfers (a questionable penalty with grave administrative consequences), forced retirement or resignation, removal from promotion consideration, and extra duty (assignment to work on holidays or loss of vacation). Penalties should, of course, be proportionate to the offense and should, as Beccaria tells us, be swift, certain, and consistent. They should, however, also have some positive attributes, either deterring reoccurrence of the offense by the defendant-officer or by the example of his punishment deterring others. Sentencing authorities should consider, either as alternatives or as additions to the penalty imposed, recommending counselling (particularly in cases related to alcohol abuse or family troubles), retraining (especially in cases of excessive zeal or ignorance of proper procedures or techniques), restitution (in cases involving injury, property damage, or monetary loss growing out of the officer's misconduct), special supervision, and/or a period of special probation. By and large, despite the stereotype of the tough police administrator and the general police paranoid perception of themselves as a persecuted minority, penalties in police disciplinary procedures are heavily skewed to the lenient end of the punishment spectrum.

Concluding Remarks

Although the decades from August Vollmer through J. Edgar Hoover and O.W. Wilson to Pat Murphy, Ed Davis, Frank Rizzo, and Tony Bouza have produced reams of rhetoric on police professionalism, codes of police ethics, tens of thousands of college-educated law enforcement officers, judicial and legislative limitations on the police abuses of the past, and an alert and intelligent public appreciation of the need for a controlled and disciplined police, the reality is that the battle is far from won. Police officers are human beings subject to the weaknesses inherent in the human condition. They are subjected to strong temptations and enjoy unique opportunities to succumb. Their work requires them to deal with criminals, and their authority induces those who wish to cut corners or operate outside the law to attempt to purchase favorable treatment. They observe others of higher station, with greater perquisites (the white-collar criminals) stealing millions with impunity; and they frequently see the moral lapses of those who hypocritically condemn what seem to the police either necessary circumventions of the law (wiretapping, excessive force, or warrantless searches) or minor peccadilloes (sharing the profits of the bookmaker, numbers runner, or afterhours bar). They also see the many unnecessary and unenforceable laws enacted by legislators anxious to win votes and the resistance of pressure groups to decriminalizing conduct which the mores and folkways of the society have decreed acceptable. In many jurisdictions they also experience public hostility and noncooperation, neglect of their legitimate needs for increased pay and fringe benefits, little recognition of their courageous and dedicated service, and overreaction to their failings, and within their own agencies, preferment and promotion are given to those whom they know to be untrue to the ethics of the profession.

No approach to police discipline and the elimination of abuses of police authority will be effective if it concentrates on sporadic investigations, emphasizes changes in organizational patterns and personnel assignments, makes an example of a dozen or a score of low-ranking scapegoats, and ignores the very real truth that a police agency stems from a societal milieu. The police agency is in itself a microcosm of that society and is unlikely to ever exhibit a higher standard of dedication, ethics, morals and professionalism than is the mode for the population it controls and protects.

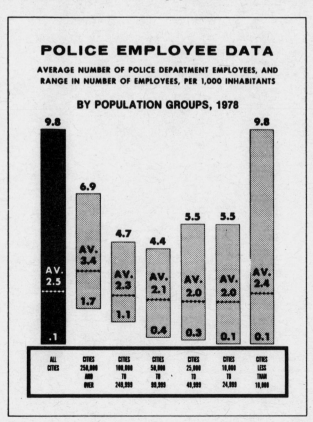

POLICE EMPLOYEE DATA

AVERAGE NUMBER OF POLICE DEPARTMENT EMPLOYEES, AND
RANGE IN NUMBER OF EMPLOYEES, PER 1,000 INHABITANTS

BY POPULATION GROUPS, 1978

The Judicial System

3

The system by which we determine the guilt or innocence of those charged with crimes might better be termed the *adjudicative* system since it involves many who are not members of the judiciary such as prosecutors, members of grand and petit juries, defense counsel, probation officers and of course complainants, witnesses, and defendants. Our criminal trial is an *adversary* procedure somewhat different in philosophy and process from the *inquisitorial* approach of such countries as France, Germany, Italy, and those in Latin America. Because it is adversary, there are necessarily many rules by which all participants must abide, violations of which may permit a guilty defendant to escape punishment on appeal. These rules include the *Miranda* warning at the time of arrest, the *Mapp* rule on searches and the seizure of evidence, and the *writ of habeas corpus* to test the lawfulness of holding the accused in custody. Included also is the rule against excessive bail, the non-discriminatory selection of grand and trial juries, the divulgence by the prosecutor of evidence favorable to the defense, the very complex pattern of rules governing the admissibility of the various categories of evidence and of course the necessity that the prosecution establish guilt *beyond a reasonable doubt.*

Much of the responsibility for making this complex process work justly and effectively rests on the trial judge. It is the criminal court judge who has been increasingly condemned in recent years by police and prosecutors, victims and defendants, press and public, civil libertarians and reactionaries, and even at times by fellow jurists, including justices of the highest appeals courts. S/he is, depending on the critic, too harsh or too lenient, too ignorant of the law or too aware of legal technicalities, too puritanical in dealing with prostitutes, homosexuals, and pornography or too permissive. S/he is too subservient to public pressures or too resistant to the demands of the critical group, and finally too offender-oriented, too victim-oriented, but seldom too society-oriented.

Since we have many thousands of judges trying criminal cases, it is probable that all or most of these criticisms are justified for some judges in some cases. While the caliber of criminal court judges might well be improved by better selection, training, and supervision, simplistic, invidious comparison with the judiciary of other countries is self-defeating. Equally discouraging are the simplistic demands for changes in the criminal justice system designed by their proponents to restore the equilibrium between prosecution and defense which, in their opinion, is heavily weighted in favor of the latter.

The ills of our criminal justice adjudicative system are largely managerial and structural. The former is a result of our attempt to process the hundreds of thousands of criminal cases through a complex series of processes developed in England during the 16th and 17th centuries. We have neither sufficient manpower, physical facilities, nor the developed technologies to prevent the backlogging of cases and unconstitutional delays of sometimes more than a year between arrest and trial. The structural ills stem from our federal system of government's fifty sovereign states, each with its own penal code, code of criminal procedure, and network of trial and appellate courts. In both cases, some progress toward a rational system is being made slowly, since many diverse interests are involved.

A DECADE OF CONSTITUTIONAL REVISION

Sidney Zion

Sidney Zion, a regular contributor to this Magazine, has written extensively on the law during the past 15 years. He is a former legal reporter for The Times. He is also a member of the Bar in New York and New Jersey, and was an assistant United States Attorney.

It seems safe to say that, until fairly recently, most Americans believed they possessed certain rights that were so fundamental no governmental authority would dare challenge them, much less take them away. They went without saying, these beliefs—they were the "givens" of our American heritage:

● That all people who were accused of crimes were entitled to trials by juries of 12; that in every case the trial judge was required to instruct the jury that the accused was presumed innocent until proven guilty; and that no jury could convict an accused person unless its verdict was unanimous.

● That the courts belonged to the people, and that the public and the press alike had the constitutional right to enter the halls of justice of our cities, our counties, our states and our nation.

● That indigent defendants who were charged with nonpetty crimes had the right to free legal counsel.

● That bank and telephone records were private, and could not be seized by government agents without a person's knowledge and consent.

● That the police could not legally ransack newsrooms, and that reporters could not be jailed for protecting their confidential sources of information.

● That a person's good name and reputation were sacred, and were secured by the Constitution against wrongful assaults by public officials.

But in every instance these beliefs, these "givens" of our heritage, were wrong. We do not have the rights we thought we had. Indeed, we are told we did not have them in the first place. And we are told this by the men with the power to make their opinions prevail: the justices of the United States Supreme Court.

□

A decade ago, the Supreme Court would have been the last place where these rights were called into question. Under Chief Justice Earl Warren, the Court protected and expanded civil liberties to a degree that had never before been approached. "The essential scheme of our Bill of Rights was to take the Government off the backs of people," Justice William O. Douglas wrote in 1972. In large measure, the Warren Court enforced that purpose.

But the Court that Earl Warren left 10 years ago last June was markedly different from the one that his successor, Chief Justice Warren E. Burger, called to order on the opening of its new term last month. Gone, along with Justice Warren, were Justices Douglas, Hugo Black, John Harlan and Abe Fortas. In their place were four men appointed by President Nixon: Justices Burger, Harry A. Blackmun, Lewis F. Powell Jr., William H. Rehnquist; and one Justice, John Paul Stevens, appointed by President Gerald Ford. Remaining from the Warren Court are Justices William J. Brennan Jr., Thurgood Marshall, Potter Stewart and Byron R. White. Of the latter, only Justices Brennan and Marshall were consistently part of the libertarian march that characterized the Warren era. That march has been largely turned back by the Burger Court. The broad-scale revision may be summarized this way:

● The criminal-justice revolution forged by the Warren Court has been virtually dismantled through a series of decisions that have sharply limited the rights of suspects—in the street, in interrogation rooms, in police lineups and in the courts. This has been accomplished by narrow interpretations of the Warren Court's landmark rulings, rather than by outright reversals.

● Conflicts between an individual and the Government have been resolved mainly against the individual. For a Court that was heralded as "conservative," as a counterbalance against the power of government, this is ironic. So, too, is the fact that the Burger Court has proved to be as "activist" as the Warren Court.

● Conflicts between an individual and the press have been resolved mainly against the press. This includes conflicts beween the criminally accused (even the criminally convicted) and the press. Thus, an apparent paradox: the Burger Court, far less concerned about the rights of suspects than the Warren Court was, has been far more concerned about their rights when press has been on the other side.

● In response to all of this, a small important trend has been emerging, the state courts, where—instead of relying on the Supreme Court—judges are looking to their state constitutions to protect individual rights.

□

Despite this wide-scale revision, the Burger Court has been pictured by many in recent years as non-ideological and unpredictable. This was not the case in the earlier years of the Burger Court, when it was generally viewed as a "conservative" bench bent on substantially altering the constitutional jurisprudence of the Warren Court. As we shall see, the Burger Court has changed little from its early days; its stance has been essentially consistent. But the perception of it by some of those in the news media has changed considerably.

Chief Justice Burger has probably had much to do with this development. In a rare news conference three years ago, Justice Burger astonished civil libertarians by stating that there had been "no significant changes in the Court's attitude toward the rights of criminal defendants." In the ensuing years, Chief Justice Burger —who declined to be interviewed for this article—has repeated this theme, and more and more it has been picked up by various law professors around the country. These professors have found a receptive audience largely because none of the Warren Court's landmark rulings have actually been overruled by the Burger Court. However, legal scholars know that a case may be as effectively undermined by interpretation as by reversal. That some of them choose not to point this out is not so surprising as it may seem. Few law professors make a habit of criticizing the Supreme Court in the mass media. They need the Court for various reasons: they wish to have their articles cited by the Court, they vie to place clerks with the Justices, and some even argue cases before the Court.

Moreover, the professors generally resent what they consider to be "simplistic" reporting of legal matters. By nature they prefer complexity and the examination of small distinctions to anything resembling a sweeping overview of the work of the Supreme Court. Indeed, some of them deny that there is even such a thing as the Burger Court.

These legal scholars point to cases where, for example, President Nixon's appointees have not voted as a bloc. How, they ask, could there be a "Burger Court" when sometimes Justice Blackmun, or sometimes Justice Powell, do not go along with Justices Burger and Rehnquist, even in criminal cases, even in press cases? It is altogether too complex to be labeled, they say.

But this analysis is in itself simplistic. As legal scholars know, Justices White and Stewart had dissented from most of the Warren Court's criminal-justice decisions, and they vote with the majority in most of the Burger Court criminal-justice rulings. Thus, it makes no difference that, occasionally, one or another appointee of Mr. Nixon breaks away from the majority —so long as, in the end, there *is* a majority to eviscerate the Warren Court holdings.

Those who say that there is really no such thing as a "Burger Court" are hard pressed to explain why Justice Brennan, a bulwark of the Warren Court, and Justice Marshall, a late Warren Court arrival who upheld the traditions of that Court, now nearly always find themselves dissenters in civil-liberties cases.

In the few instances when they are in the majority, the Court is almost invariably involved in striking down police procedures that are so flagrant—like the random stopping and searching of automobiles—that they would probably not have been attempted by the police, and surely not defended by prosecutors, without the earlier encouragement of the Burger Court. It is mainly in these kinds of cases that the justices appointed by President Nixon split; that is, where Justices Burger and Rehnquist take pro-police positions that are considered too extreme for Justices Blackmun and/or Powell, not to mention Justices White, Stewart and Stevens.

Still, the Burger Court is looked upon as a "moderate" one by many, and in some quarters even as a "progressive" force.

Meanwhile, the libertarian critics of the Court have generally been relegated to the law reviews or to the small journals of opinion. Criminal suspects have never had much of a constituency. The media, which obviously has a voice, more often than not refuses to challenge the Court's press rulings on the grounds that to do so would be "self-serving."

□

But there is a Burger Court, and nobody knows this better than the prosecutors and the police. They feel they have a friend in the Burger Court, no ambiguity about it, and they express their appreciation in the most eloquent, effective way they can: by never blaming the Supreme Court for fostering crime.

In the 60's, hardly a day went by that some police chief or district attorney did not blast the Warren Court for "coddling criminals" and encouraging "crime waves." Decisions that many believed breathed life into the Fourth Amendment's proscriptions against unreasonable searches and seizures, the Fifth Amendment's guarantee of trial by jury and protection against self-incrimination, the Sixth Amendment's pledge of assistance of counsel, and the Eighth Amendment's prohibition against cruel and unusual punishment, were often bitterly denounced by law-enforcement people. More often than not, these attacks were joined in by some of the press and the public, which provided a kind of rhythm section to an omnipresent chorus of policemen and prosecutors.

Although the Burger Court has not stemmed the rate

of crime, its rulings have served to keep the police and the people off the backs of the justices. This is as it should be. Whatever one may say about the Burger Court, one may not say that it is responsible for the rising crime rate.

Nor was it fair to pin that responsibility on the Warren Court, a point underscored, albeit inadvertently, by the record of the Burger Court. For if that record teaches anything, it teaches that the Supreme Court can have no appreciable effect on crime.

Yet the Burger Court has continued to eviscerate the holdings of the Warren majority, as if to vindicate Mr. Nixon's 1968 campaign oratory that the Warren Court had "tended to weaken the peace forces as against the criminal forces in this country."

On the other hand, the Burger Court has continued to press for school desegregation and has attempted, most legal scholars believe, to strike a fair balance in the so-called affirmative action, reverse discrimination cases. This article does not study the affirmative action cases, or the sex-discrimination cases, because in these areas the Burger Court was writing on a relatively clean slate, and there was little question of revising the Warren Court rulings.

This piece surveys the two landmark areas that span both the Warren and Burger Courts—criminal justice and freedom of the press, which are at the core of the civil liberties guaranteed by the Bill of Rights.

Prof. Yale Kamisar of the University of Michigan Law School, one of the pre-eminent scholars in the field of criminal procedure, observed recently: "Reading the criminal law decisions of the Burger Court is like watching an old movie run backward." Here are some of those movies—involving the Burger Court's interpretations of the Fourth, Fifth and Sixth Amendments—run forward.

The 5th and 6th Amendments: CONFESSIONS

The Warren Court delivered its landmark ruling on confessions in 1966, in *Miranda v. Arizona.* The Court held that when police have a suspect in custody, they may not interrogate him without first warning him of a number of things: that he has a right to remain silent, that anything he says may be used against him in a court of law, that he has the right to the presence of an attorney, and that if he cannot afford an attorney, one will be appointed for him prior to any questioning if he so desires.

The purpose of the ruling was to secure for suspects, in a meaningful way, the Fifth Amendment's protection against self-incrimination and the Sixth Amendment's guarantee of assistance of counsel—both of which, previously, had been held by the Warren Court to apply to the states through the 14th Amendment (". . .nor shall any State deprive any person of life, liberty or property, without due process of law").

Before the *Miranda* decision, no admonitions to a

suspect were necessary. Confessions, or other statements damaging to a defendant, were admitted into evidence at the trial if they were found to be "voluntary." And the courts had held that the determination of voluntariness depended on the "totality of the circumstances" surrounding the taking of the statement.

Under this standard, however, statements elicited by virtually every method short of the third degree were held to be "voluntary."

The effect was the establishment of a double standard: one for the interrogation room of the police station, where the defendant's rights were often honored in the breach; another for the courtroom, where his rights were scrupulously honored. However, once a case got to court it no longer really mattered, because once a person confessed, it made little difference how properly he was treated in court, for the confession sealed his fate.

In the *Miranda* case, the Warren Court sought to narrow, if not entirely abolish, this double standard. A suspect could still be questioned, without the presence of a lawyer, but only if he waived his rights, "voluntarily, knowingly and intelligently."

The decision created an uproar among law-enforcement officials, in judicial circles and in much of the press. High-ranking police officials across the country, arguing that some 75 percent of reported crimes were solved by confessions, threw up their hands en masse.

But various studies, including one by the Los Angeles District Attorney's office, showed that the importance of confessions had been grossly exaggerated. (Most cases are not solved at all; but the vast majority of the cases that *are* solved employ means other than confessions—by catching the culprit red-handed, by relying on information from eyewitnesses, or by employing ordinary detective work.) Although confessions "cement" a case, they proved necessary in less than 10 percent of the cases studied by the District Attorney's office.

That the *Miranda* warnings themselves have had a minimal impact on police effectiveness is perhaps best indicated by the fact that the police outrage over the decision had largely died down by the time the Burger Court first considered the implications of the case in 1971.

That year, in *Harris v. New York,* the Burger Court ruled that if statements have been obtained from a suspect in violation of the *Miranda* safeguards, those statements can be used to "impeach his credibility" when the suspect testifies at trial. Thus, if the defendant takes the stand and says anything that contradicts what he told the police, the prosecution can bring to the attenion of a jury an otherwise inadmissible statement.

Of course, if he does not testify, the statement cannot be used. But as every lawyer knows, a defendant who does not take the stand in his own behalf is far more likely to be convicted than one who is willing to explain his alleged actions. By offering this Hobson's choice to a person who has been unconstitutionally questioned by the police, the Burger Court has undercut the fundamental purpose of *Miranda*. Or, as Justice Brennan wrote in dissent in the *Harris* case: "The Court today tells the police that they may freely interrogate an accused [person] incommunicado and without counsel, and know that although any statement they obtain in violation of *Miranda* cannot be used on the State's direct case, it may be introduced if the defendant has the temerity to testify in his own defense."

The court was also telling something to state and Federal judges. As Professor Kamisar wrote at the time: "After [the] *Harris* [case], a lower court judge unhappy with *Miranda* has cause to believe that almost no emasculating interpretation of *Miranda* may be too outrageous."

Before the Burger Court decided the *Harris* case, 23 courts faced the precise issue of "impeachment," and 20 of them held that statements obtained by the police in violation of the *Miranda* rules could *not* be used against a defendant who took the stand in his own defense. The main reason the courts cited: The Warren Court, in the *Miranda* case itself, had specifically said that such statement could not be used for impeachment purposes. Therefore, the argument that *Miranda* could be so easily circumvented was considered too outrageous, no matter what the judges might think of the *Miranda* decision.

It was not too outrageous for Chief Justice Burger. Writing for a 5-4 majority in the *Harris* case, he said that *Miranda's* discussion of the issue "was not at all necessary to the Court's holding, and cannot be regarded as controlling." That is to say, according to Chief Justice Burger, *Miranda* could have been written without reference to the possible use of a statement for impeachment purposes.

Generally speaking, the same thing could be said of all precedents—since, techincally, all that is "necessary" to a decision is what was directly before the Court. But *Miranda* was specifically structured to canvass a wide range of problems that were not directly raised by the case, in order to "give concrete constitutional guidelines for law enforcement agencies and courts to follow."

In any event, the Burger Court has never held a single item of evidence inadmissible on the authority of the *Miranda* case. Furthermore, Geoffrey R. Stone, associate professor of law at the University of Chicago, pointed out in a definitive article in the Supreme Court Review:

"Despite the relative frequency and complexity of these decisions, neither Justices White or Stewart, both of whom dissented in *Miranda,* nor any of the four justices appointed by Richard Nixon, has found it necessary to cast even a single vote to exclude evidence because of a violation of *Miranda.*"

The Burger Court's decisions in the dozen-plus cases it has taken up—not to say the scores of lower-court rulings it has left standing—indicate a desire to discount the *Miranda* holding and return to the old "voluntariness" test for confessions.

Indeed, five years ago in *Michigan v. Tucker,* the Court appeared to have done just that. Speaking for the majority, Justice Rehnquist took the position that the *Miranda* warnings were not themselves "rights protected by the Constitution," but were merely "prophylactic rules" designed to "provide practical reinforcement" for the constitutional privilege against compelled self-incrimination.

Therefore, Justice Rehnquist said, the failure of police to give the full *Miranda* warnings does not violate the Fifth Amendment's self-incrimination clause; in order for such a violation to occur, the ensuing admissions must be involuntary, "as that term has been defined in the decisions of this Court."

As Professor Stone has observed, Justice Rehnquist's reading of *Miranda* is an "outright rejection" of its core premises. *Miranda* was anchored squarely in the Fifth Amendment. Had it not been, the Supreme Court would have been powerless to reverse *Miranda's* conviction. The High Court has no supervisory powers over state police practices; it can only strike down procedures that violate some Federal constitutional guarantee.

Justice Rehnquist would strip *Miranda* of its constitutional basis, and leave the case in an analytical vacuum. Had he stopped there, *Miranda* would have been interred. But, for whatever reason, Judge Rehnquist ultimately found a narrower ground to hold against the defendant without overruling *Miranda*.

Since then, the Court has continued to dismantle the case in a piecemeal way, and most observers believe the Court will always stop short of a direct reversal. In any event, the case has already been so confined by the Court to its basic facts that, some have said, now only Ernesto Miranda himself could take advantage of it. And Ernesto Miranda himself is dead.

The 4th Amendment:
SEARCHES AND SEIZURES

What of the individual's protection against the unreasonable incursions of Government? Before the *Miranda* case came along, the Warren Court's most controversial criminal-procedure ruling was *Mapp v. Ohio,* decided in 1961. There, the Court required state judges to bar from trials any evidence that had been seized in violation of the Fourth Amendment's proscriptions against unreasonable searches and seizures. Previously—in 1941—the Court had applied this sanction, known as the "exclusionary rule," to Federal courts. Now, through the Due Process Clause of the 14th Amendment, the exclusionary rule was made applicable to the states.

The reasons for this were clear and simple. If a court could not sanction a search or seizure before the event—because, for example, the police lacked sufficient cause to make the search, or were unable to describe the items they sought with the particularity required by the Fourth Amendment—then a court could not, or at least should not, affirm or sanction the search or seizure after the event. To do otherwise—to permit into evidence items unconstitutionally seized by the police—would violate the imperative of judicial integrity by making the courts partners in police lawlessness. The Court quoted the famous remark of Justice Louis Brandeis:

"Our Government is the potent, the omnipresent teacher. For good or ill, it teaches the whole people by its example. If the Government becomes a lawbreaker, it breeds contempt for law; it invites every man to become a law unto himself; it invites anarchy."

Without the exclusionary rule, the Warren majority concluded, the Fourth Amendment would "remain an empty promise," for the privacy rights protected by it would be "revocable at the whim of any police officer who, in the name of law enforcement itself, chooses to suspend its enjoyment."

The *Mapp* case was met by a firestorm of protest comparable to the one that later greeted *Miranda*. Enforcement officials—ignoring the fact that the Federal Bureau of Investigation had operated effectively throughout its existence under the dictates of the exclusionary rule, and that 26 states had imposed the rule on themselves—cried out that they could not protect the citizenry with the new handcuffs that had been clamped on them by the Warren Court. Paraphrasing a line out of an old New York Court of Appeals opinion by Benjamin Cardozo, the police asked rhetorically: "Should the criminal go free because the constable has blundered?"

It was hardly a matter of "blundering," however. The police systematically ignored the Fourth Amendment in those states that had no exclusionary rule, a point implicitly conceded in the outraged reactions of the police, as well as in the broad-scale efforts undertaken after *Mapp* to "retrain" officers in their understanding of the law of search and seizure. Sometimes the concession that the Fourth Amendment had been ignored was explicit. At a post-*Mapp* training session in New York City, Leonard Reisman, then the Deputy Police Commissioner in charge of legal matters, said, "The *Mapp* case was a shock to us. We had to reorganize our thinking, frankly. Before this, nobody bothered to take out search warrants. Although the Constitution requires [search] warrants in most cases, the Supreme Court had ruled that evidence obtained without a warrant—illegally, if you will—was admissible in state courts. So the feeling was: Why bother?"

Mapp was the Warren Court's answer. But its effort to rescue the Fourth Amendment from its steerage-class status has been gutted by the Burger Court—despite the lack of evidence that *Mapp* has substantially curbed the efforts of the police, and against the clear knowledge that state-court judges seldom grant motions to suppress evidence that has been gathered in alleged violation of the Fourth Amendment.

Last spring, in response to a request by the Senate Judiciary Committee, the Comptroller General of the United States produced a study showing that evidence was suppressed on Fourth Amendment grounds only in about 1 percent of Federal cases; motions to suppress were made in only 10.5 percent of the cases studied. Nonetheless, many legal experts predict that the Burger Court will soon emasculate the exclusionary rule by requiring defendants to prove that police officers did not act in "good faith" when conducting otherwise unconstitutional searches and seizures.

In the meantime, the Burger Court has conducted a substantial watering down of the Fourth Amendment itself; and so, it has often managed to get around the exclusionary rule without purging it of all significance.

This has been accomplished by sharp limitations on the meaning of "probable cause," the constitutional standard upon which arrests, searches and seizures are permitted; by a dramatic expansion of the concept of "consent searches," wherein suspects "voluntarily" consent to searches that would otherwise be illegal; by narrowing the scope of the exclusionary rule through holding that it does not protect grand-jury witnesses; by depriving defendants of the right to test the legality of searches in Federal habeas corpus proceedings once the state courts have ruled against them, and by holding that some things are outside the purview of the Fourth Amendment—that they may be seized by Government agents without a warrant, without probable cause and without the knowledge and consent of the individual.

Here are the examples of some of the above; the last concept will be dealt with first, because of its potential for "Big Brother" abuse:

Outside the Fourth Amendment: In 1976, the Burger Court rules that the Government can subpoena from banks a person's checks, deposit slips and financial statements without regard to the Fourth Amendment. The reason: a depositor has no "legitimate expectation of privacy" in his accounts because, by dealing through a bank employee, he has "revealed his affairs to another" and thus has "assumed the risk" that they "will be conveyed by that person to the Government." And this, "even if the information is revealed on the assumption that it will be used only for a limited purpose, and [that] the confidence placed in the third party will not be betrayed."

Since it is next to impossible to survive in today's world without having a bank account, the Court leaves a person with no choice but to "waive" his privacy—unless he decides to deal only in cash, and to keep his money under the pillow.

Moreover, as Justice Douglas once observed: "In a

sense, a person is defined by the checks he writes. By examining them, the agents get to know his doctors, lawyers, creditors, political allies, social connections, religious affiliation, the papers and magazines he reads, and so on ad infinitum."

If bank records do not provide the Government with all its needs to know about a citizen, the names of the people he calls on the telephone may help to bridge the gap. Last term, the Burger Court held that a phone company's installation and use, at police request, of a "pen register" to record the numbers dialed from a telephone at a suspect's home did not constitute a "search" within the meaning of the Fourth Amendment. (The "pen register" is a device that records the numbers dialed from a particular phone; the original instruments, now obsolete, used a pen to mark coded dots on tickertape paper.) This, the Court said, was because the pen-register device does not record conversations, but only makes a record of the numbers dialed from a given phone, and a record of the time the number was dialed.

As in the bank-record case, the Court ruled that a person has no "legitimate expectation of privacy" in the numbers he or she dials, for the person has "voluntarily conveyed to the [phone company some] information that it had facilities for recording, and that it was free to record." Thus, the person "assumed the risk that the company would reveal to the police the numbers he dialed."

The dissenters argued—there were two dissenting opinions, one by Justice Stewart (joined by Justice Brennan), the other by Justice Marshall (also joined by Justice Brennan)—that it could not be said that the defendant voluntarily turned over any information to "third parties." As a practical matter, a person had no alternative if he or she wanted to use the phone. Wrote Justice Marshall: "Unless a person is prepared to forgo use of what for many has become a personal or professional necessity, he cannot help but accept the risk of surveillance." The majority's "assumption of risk" analysis, Justice Marshall said, is therefore out of place. The question instead should be: what risks should a person "be forced to assume in a free and open society."

Journalists must assume the risk of Government surveillance when using telephones quite as much as those persons engaged in criminal activity. In 1974, the Reporters Committee for Freedom of the Press sued the American Telephone and Telegraph Company, contending that both the First and Fourth Amendments require the phone company to give newsmen prior notice before turning over their long-distance telephone billing records to law-enforcement officials. This modest demand was rejected by the Circuit Court, and, in 1979, the Burger Court refused to review the ruling.

While such a refusal—known as a denial of certiorari —does not put the Supreme Court's imprimatur on a decision, there is little reason to believe that the Court will, in the future, put a stop to this kind of surveillance, given its reasoning in the pen-register case, and its general view that the press stands in no better position than any other citizen, the First Amendment notwithstanding.

The implications for freedom of the press are serious, to say the least. By checking long-distance numbers— and in the "pen-register" case the Court rejected any distinction between long-distance and local calls, so both can be seized—Government agents are in a good position to discover confidential sources of information. The Burger Court, as we'll see in Part II of this article, has effectively held that the First Amendment does not give reporters a privilege to protect these sources. So the seizure of phone records provides another—and less politically sensitive—route for Government to uncover "leaks" and to otherwise induce a chilling effect on a robust, investigatory press. It also allows a kind of end run around the state "shield laws" that are designed to protect sources; it does this by permitting agents to search out the leakers without giving notice to the reporter, thus preventing the reporter from protecting the sources with the shield law.

Consent Searches: The easiest, most propitious way for the police to avoid the myriad problems presented by the Fourth Amendment is to obtain the consent of a suspect to a search of his person or his premises. Once consent is given, the search is legal, and any contraband it turns up will be admitted into evidence, even if there was no probable cause to make the search. This is because the suspect (or any other person on the suspect's property who can give consent for the suspect, in what is known as "third-party consent") is deemed to have waived his right to privacy.

But the question the courts must decide in such cases is whether the alleged consent was that of a free and intelligent choice, or whether it was coerced; or, to put it in nicer words, whether it was a "true consent" or a "peaceful submission to authority."

In 1973, the Burger Court dealt a crippling blow to the nature of consent. In *Schneckloth v. Bustamonte,* the Court ruled 6-3 that a person can consent to an otherwise unconstitutional search—even though he didn't know, or wasn't told, he had the right to refuse the search.

The facts were simple. A police officer stopped a car in Sunnyvale, Calif., because one headlight and the license plate light were burned out. There were six men in the car, and they were asked to get out. As soon as they did, two other policemen appeared on the scene. The officer who stopped the car asked one of the men if he could search it. The answer: "Sure, go ahead." The search produced three checks that had been stolen from a car wash; they were wadded up under the left rear seat. The admission of these checks into evidence resulted in Bustamonte's conviction. Although he was in the car at the time, he was not the man who "consented" to the search. This was a "third-party consent," but it is not what makes the case important.

The crucial point was the Court's holding that the police need not tell a person that he has the right to say "no," when that person is asked to consent to a search that would otherwise violate his Fourth Amendment rights. Consent, the Court majority said, "cannot be taken literally to mean a 'knowing choice.'" It is enough that the consent was "voluntary," i.e., free of coercion. The prosecution therefore need not show that the person made an "intelligent waiver" of his rights, only that the police didn't force him to waive them.

In dissent, Justice Brennan declared: "It wholly escapes me how our citizens can meaningfully be said to have waived something as precious as a constitutional guarantee without ever being aware of its existence."

But the majority opinion makes it clear that the Burger Court does not consider the Fourth Amendment a "precious" guarantee. The opinion agrees that to establish the waiver of a constitutional guarantee—according to the dictates of a 41-year-old Supreme Court decision—the state must prove "an intentional relinquishment or abandonment of a known right or privilege." But the majority said that this doctrine was only meant to protect a defendant's right to a fair trial:

"There is a vast difference," the Court said, "between those rights that protect a fair criminal trial and the rights guaranteed under the Fourth Amendment."

Like the old movie running backward, the Burger Court thus went a long way toward again demoting the Fourth Amendment to its steerage-class status.

"The holding today," Justice Marshall wrote in separate dissent, "confines the protection of the Fourth Amendment against searches conducted without probable cause to the sophisticated, the knowledgeable, and, I might add, the few.

"In the final anaylsis, the Court now sanctions a game of blindman's bluff, in which the police always have the upper hand, for the sake of nothing more than the convenience of the police."

Ironically, the *Bustamonte* case might not even have reached the Supreme Court today, for Bustamonte's bid—to suppress the evidence the police had found against him—had been denied by the California state courts. His conviction was subsequently reversed by the Federal Court of Appeals on a writ of habeas corpus, a judicial procedure for testing the legality of a person's detention. The Burger Court reinstated the conviction, but, three years later, it barred Federal habeas corpus relief for prisoners who had previously been afforded a opportunity for "full and fair litigation" of their Fourth Amendment claims in state courts. The practical impact appears to be that prisoners can no longer rely on lower Federal courts to overturn their convictions on Fourth Amendment grounds.

This habeas corpus ruling was a startling decision even for the Burger Court, for it orphaned the Fourth Amendment, making it the only provision of the Bill of Rights (so far) which may not be vindicated by habeas

corpus—the Great Writ, so-called because it is considered to be the single most important safeguard of personal liberty known to Anglo-American law.

"This denigration of constitutional guarantees and constitutionally mandated procedures," Justice Brennan wrote in a long, bitter dissent, "must appall citizens taught to expect judicial respect and support for their constitutional rights."

What was the Court's reason for this "denigration?" The same reason for its antipathy to the Fourth Amendment and to the exclusionary rule that enforces it and keeps it from being an "empty promise." When police make an illegal search and find stolen goods or guns or drugs, they nearly always have the guilty party. Shall the criminal go free because the constable has blundered—or even *plundered*—his rights?

But the fundamental purpose of the Fourth Amendment—of the Bill of Rights, in general—was to protect the guilty as well as the innocent.

As Justice Brennan added in his dissent: "Even if [the] punishment of the 'guilty' were society's highest value (and procedural safeguards [were] denigrated to this end) in a Constitution that a majority of the Members of this Court would prefer, that is not the ordering of priorities under the Constitution forged by the Framers, and this Court's sworn duty is to uphold that Constitution and not frame its own."

The 6th Amendment:
THE RIGHT TO COUNSEL

The Burger Court has emphasized, in Fourth Amendment cases, the "vast difference" between (1) a person's rights that are protected by the prohibition against unreasonable searches and seizures and (2) "those rights that protect a fair criminal trial." One would think then, that when the very question of guilt or innocence is involved, the Court would be especially concerned with a person's right to a fair trial. It might be expected that the Court would lend a sympathetic ear to a defendant's allegation that the police nabbed, and the jury convicted, the "wrong man."

It hasn't turned out that way, even in the area that legal experts universally deem the most suspect of all: eyewitness identification. In 1967, the Warren Court, noting that "the annals of criminal law are rife with instances of mistaken identification," ruled in *United States v. Wade* that an arrested suspect has a constitutional right to have his lawyer present when he is paraded in a police lineup before possible eyewitnesses. The major reason: to protect him from the suggestive techniques that are often employed by police and Federal agents (for example, when the accused may be the only black person, or the only tall or short person, in the lineup). Such suggestion, once accomplished, may be irretrievably devastating.

"It is a matter of common experience," the Court said, "that once a witness has picked out the accused at the lineup, he is not likely to go back on his word later on, so that in practice the issue of identity may. . . for all practical purposes be determined there and then, before the trial.''

Unless the lawyer for the suspect is present at the lineup, he can neither guard against improper suggestion, nor even know what really happened there. At a trial, this, in turn, deprives the accused of "that right of cross-examination which is an essential safeguard to his right to confront the witnesses against him." The lawyer must conduct the cross-examination in the dark, so to speak, making the assistance of counsel, guaranteed by the Sixth Amendment, an empty right.

In 1972, the Burger Court, in *Kirby v. Illinois*, had its first opportunity to interpret the Warren Court's *Wade* case. In the *Kirby* case, the lineup took place before the defendant was indicted. In *Wade*, the lineup took place *after* the indictment. The Burger Court chose to make the fact of the indictment the controlling distinction— the fact that determined the court's decision—and therefore ruled that Kirby was not entitled to counsel at his lineup.

Justice Brennan was in a peculiarly good position to say whether Wade's indictment had anything to do with the decision in that case, since he wrote the opinion for the Warren Court. He said the fact of the indictment was "completely irrelevant," and that "even a cursory perusal" of the *Wade* decision "reveals that nothing at all turned upon that particular circumstance." But now, in 1972, Justice Brennan was writing in dissent.

It is instructive to compare the Burger Court's use of distinctions—those facts that are crucial to a ruling—in the *Kirby* case with its treatment of the *Miranda* case. In the Burger Court's *Harris v. New York* decision, statements taken illegally from a suspect were allowed in to "impeach his credibility" when he took the witness stand. The Burger Court said that while the *Miranda* decision had barred the use of such statements, it was not a "controlling" precedent because "it was not at all necessary to the Court's holding."

Whatever one may say of that viewpoint, one can only wonder at a Court that would, one year later, create a constitutional distinction out of a mere description of a defendant's status—i.e., whether he was in a lineup before or after his indictment. And one wonders at a Court that, in creating such a constitutional distinction, has signaled the police that there is an easy way to circumvent *Wade*: by holding lineups before filing formal charges.

In subsequent eyewitness identification cases, the Burger Court has moved step-by-step toward what Justice Brennan calls "the complete evisceration of the fundamental constitutional principles established . . . in *United States v. Wade*."

This development, says Professor Kamisar, is "in some ways more depressing than anything else the Burger Court has done in the criminal-procedure area." Why? "Because unlike *Mapp* and *Miranda*, which

furthered societal values not usually—certainly not always—related to guilt or innocence, the Warren Court's 1967 lineup cases were explicitly designed to protect the innocent from wrongful conviction. What is more important than that? And where is the countervailing balance? The defense lawyer's presence in the interrogation room may well cut off police questioning altogether, but the defense lawyer's presence at a lineup will not—and cannot—eliminate lineups, only discourage the holding of *unfair* ones. How does that harm effective law enforcement? In fact, it helps it; if the wrong person is convicted, the system has failed and the real culprit is still at large. Even if one is convinced that the Warren Court substantially weakened the 'peace forces'—I'm not, but some justices evidently are—the Burger Court's retreat from the 1967 lineup cases is not responsive to that need."

In the lineup cases, as in some of the confession cases and the search-and-seizure cases, the Burger Court has reached out to reverse the actions of lower courts that have read the Bill of Rights more liberally than is to the High Court's liking.

This is the opposite of the situation that prevailed during the halcyon days of the Warren Court, when that Court continually patrolled the state and Federal courts, which not only gave niggardly interpretations to its rulings, but often fought the Court in the press.

During the past few years, however, a trend has developed. In response to the Burger Court's reluctance to afford what they consider proper protections to the criminally accused, a number of state courts have dusted off long-ignored state bills of rights. Since the United States Supreme Court may only set minimum standards of justice, the states are free to grant their citizens more extensive rights. In cases in which they wish to afford such rights, in order to foreclose reversal by the Burger Court, the state courts need only say that they have based their rulings on state law, rather than on the Federal Bill of Rights.

This development, which has reportedly annoyed and occasionally frustrated the Burger majority, is an event in the law. The trend is in its infancy, and has been taken up by only a handful of state courts—most notably those in California, Michigan and Pennsylvania. In the large majority of states, the judges seem only too happy to go along with the Burger Court and to accept its "signals," and go even further. But the new movement the other way is not without significance, and it has been encouraged by Justices Brennan and Marshall, dissenters in the tradition of Justices Holmes and Brandeis, and of Justices Black and Douglas.

In 1977, Justice Brennan published an article in the Harvard Law Review "saluting" those state courts that chose to use their own bills of rights to vindicate liberties no longer recognized by his Supreme Court brethren.

At age 60, John McNulty, the great Irish-American journalist and author, wrote to his old boon companion,

3. THE JUDICIAL SYSTEM

James Thurber: "Dear Jimmy, I think that maybe threescore years and 10 is subject to change without notice."

It turned out that way for Mr. McNulty, who died a few days later. In the law, it is supposed to go the other way: the older the precedent, the less subject it is to change without notice. But in the matter of the Burger Court, this comfortable maxim has not held true.

President Nixon's appointees to the Court were heralded by him as apostles of "judicial restraint," men who would adhere to precedent, "strict constructionists" who would not allow their political, social and economic views to influence their decisions. These themes dominated the Senate confirmation hearings, at which each of the four swore his dedication to such principles.

Here, though, are a few examples of how these principles have been practiced:

The Presumption of Innocence:

In 1895, the Supreme Court, tracing the venerable history of the presumption of innocence from Deuteronomy through Roman law, English common law, and the common law of the United States, wrote: "The principle that there is a presumption of innocence in favor of the accused is the undoubted law, axiomatic and elementary, and its enforcement lies at the foundation of the administration of our criminal law."

On May 14, 1979, the Burger Court said that the presumption of innocence has "no application to a determination of the rights of a pretrial detainee during confinement before his trial has even begun." In so holding, the Court reversed two lower Federal courts in New York, which had granted relief to inmates awaiting trial while housed at the Metropolitan Correctional Center. The inmates complained that they had been treated as convicts rather than as persons presumed innocent until proven guilty. They were subjected to body-cavity searches, following visits from friends and relatives; they were forced to "double-bunk" in rooms built for single occupancy; they were prohibited from receiving books unless the books were mailed by the publishers or by book clubs or bookstores; they were forbidden to receive food and personal items from outside the institution.

The lower courts enjoined these practices as unconstitutional. They relied primarily on the presumption of innocence as the source of an inmate's right to be free from these sorts of conditions. In a lengthy opinion by Justice Rehnquist, the Supreme Court lifted the injunctions of the lower courts, stating, among other things, that the presumption of innocence provides "no support" for the relief that was granted to the prisoners by the lower courts.

"Without question," Justice Rehnquist wrote, "the presumption of innocence plays an important role in our criminal justice system." But that role, he said, is confined to the trial itself.

One week later, on May 21, 1979, the Burger Court held that, at the trial itself, a judge could refuse a defendant's request to instruct a jury that he was presumed to be innocent until proved guilty beyond a reasonable doubt. So, now a jury need not be told that a defendant starts a trial with a clean slate, a right that was considered fundamental even in biblical days.

"No principle is more firmly established in our system of criminal justice than the presumption of innocence that is accorded to the defendant in every criminal trial," wrote Justice Stewart. But now, this principle was relegated to a dissent, and Justice Stewart was joined by only Justices Marshall and Brennan.

Trial by Jury: In 1952, Justice Felix Frankfurter, in delineating for the Court those provisions of the Bill of Rights that have a "rigid meaning," as opposed to those without a "fixed technical content," wrote: "No changes or chances can alter the content of the verbal symbol of 'jury'—a body of 12 men who must reach a unanimous conclusion if the verdict is to go against the defendant."

By 1970, the Burger Court, saying it was unable "to divine precisely what the word 'jury' imported to the Framers," ruled that six-person juries were constitutional in criminal cases. Two years later, the Court held that a 12-man jury need not reach a unanimous verdict to convict a defendant, upholding votes of 11-1, 10-2 and 9-3.

Indigent Defendants: Last term, the Burger Court ruled that an indigent defendant charged with a crime carrying a possible one-year prison sentence was not entitled to free legal counsel as long as the judge did not sentence him to jail.

This was a real surprise to the dissenters who had assumed—as did most lawyers and even most states—that at least when a person had a right to a jury trial he had a right to free counsel. Since the Supreme Court had already held that any crime punishable by more than six months in prison carried with it a right to trial by jury, it was natural to expect that it also required a lawyer—especially in view of the Court's earlier holding that the right to counsel occupies a higher constitutional status than the jury-trial right.

But Justice Rehnquist, writing for a 5-man majority, said no, arguing in part that such a rule would economically burden the states.

In dissent, Justice Brennan termed the ruling "intolerable," noting that the crime that was involved—theft—carried a "moral stigma" indicating "moral depravity" and was therefore by no means petty, whether or not a prison sentence was applied. As to the economic burden argument of the majority, Brennan pointed out the 33 states provided for counsel in such cases and that, in any event, the argument was "both irrelevant and speculative."

Judicial Immunity: This is the one area in which the Burger Court has managed to divine an absolute right for a class of people—namely judges—despite the fact that the Constitution nowhere makes any provisions about judicial immunity.

In 1978, the Court ruled on a case involving a judge who signed an order to sterilize a 15-year-old girl—without a hearing and merely at the request of the girl's mother, who said she was "somewhat retarded" and had been staying out overnight with "older youth or young men." The Court held that the judge was immune from a subsequent lawsuit by the girl—who was now a young woman—and her husband.

The girl was attending a public school at the time of the sterilization—despite the "retarded" appellation—and was told that she was going to the hospital to have her appendix removed. Instead, the doctors, acting in accord with the judicial order, performed a tubal ligation.

Two years later, the girl was married. Her inability to become pregnant led her to discover that she had been sterilized. She and her husband sued the judge. The Federal District Court in Indiana dismissed the action on grounds of judicial immunity, but the Circuit Court reversed, holding that the judge had forfeited his immunity due to "his failure to comply with elementary principles of procedural due process." The Burger Court reversed, by a 5-3 vote (Justice Brennan took no part).

Citing an 1872 ruling by the Supreme Court, the Burger majority held: "A judge will not be deprived of immunity because the action he took was in error, was done maliciously, or was in excess of his authority; rather, he will be subject to liability only when he has acted in the 'clear absence of all jurisdiction.' " The Court found jurisdiction in the sweeping language of the Indiana judicial code, which conferred jurisdiction "at all cases at law or in equity."

In sharp dissent, Justice Stewart (joined by Justices Marshall and Powell) wrote: "A judge is not free, like a loose cannon, to inflict indiscriminate damage whenever he announces that he is acting in his judicial capacity."

What gave a judge this freedom, according to the Burger majority, was the doctrine of judicial immunity. Where did that come from? From the Supreme Court itself, surely not from the Constitution.

It is quite remarkable, to say the least, that the same justices who disparage the exclusionary rule of the Fourth Amendment as "merely judge-made," think differently when judges are defendants in civil-law suits. But as it is said: "Where you stand often depends on where you sit."

Article 25

Are Grand Juries Getting Out of Line?

Not only minorities say that the answer is "Yes." Pillars of the establishment, too, are beating the drums for reform.

A centuries-old bulwark against government oppression—the American grand-jury system—is coming under increasing fire both in state capitals and in Congress.

The result is a drive by critics to abolish or reform an institution that is misunderstood by millions of Americans. Many people believe the sole job of grand juries is to bring criminal charges against possible wrongdoers. What they often forget is that grand jurors have another, equally vital, task: to shield fellow citizens from being unjustly subjected to a criminal trial.

In recent years, this shield has slipped badly, according to critics, who include judges, lawyers and religious groups. Grand juries are accused of acting too often as "rubber stamps" for overzealous or unscrupulous prosecutors who:

■ Bludgeon witnesses into providing information the government isn't entitled to.

■ Gather flimsy, insubstantial evidence that sometimes is leaked to the press, sometimes is made the basis for prosecutions with little chance of success.

■ Harass or intimidate racial or political minority groups.

■ Unnecessarily invade the privacy of witnesses.

"Total captive." Grand juries, normally made up of 23 persons without special skills in the law, have long been vulnerable to manipulation by prosecutors.

The problem has been growing worse in recent years because of the increasing complexity of criminal statutes and criminal cases. "Today, the grand jury is the total captive of the prosecutor who, if he is candid, will concede that he can indict anybody, at any time, for almost anything, before any grand jury," declares U.S. District Court Judge William J. Campbell of Chicago.

In past decades, complaints of abuses by grand juries came most frequently from political radicals, civil libertarians and others out of step with the majority of citizens. Today, complaints are still coming from these groups. But new voices have been added. Some of the country's leading corporations have protested grand-jury actions, and such pillars of respectability as the National Council of Churches and the American Bar Association are backing a push in the states and in Congress for a spate of reforms.

Many prosecutors and judges are resisting the reform move. They warn that new limits on grand juries would undermine le-gitimate crime fighting. But both opponents and backers of reform agree that grand juries sometimes abuse their powers. Cited as examples are cases in recent years involving a wide range of people from corporation officials to civil-rights and religious activists.

One celebrated case involved a potential misuse of the criminal powers of a grand jury to aid the government in a civil case against a major company. The dispute stemmed from General Motors Corporation's 1972 income-tax return—audited by the Internal Revenue Service in 1975. After many months of wrangling with GM, an IRS attorney active in the dispute convinced the Justice Department to begin a criminal tax investigation. The trouble came when the same IRS employe was designated by Justice officials to help direct the grand-jury probe.

In April, a three-judge federal appeals panel stopped the investigation. The judges, in a 2-to-1 ruling, concluded that the arrangement was an invitation to misuse grand-jury powers. The court noted GM's concern that the IRS employe "has an ax to grind and is more interested in justifying his previous investigations, his recommendations and the conduct of IRS agents than in protecting GM against unfounded criminal prosecution."

A Blizzard of Indictments

Political corruption, whether real or merely suspected, has been an even more fertile field for aggressive prosecutors and grand juries in recent years. Many investigations of public officials have been conducted responsibly and led to the conviction of scores of crooked officeholders. In other instances, critics charge, grand juries led by egotistical or politically ambitious prosecutors have churned out indictments supported by only the flimsiest underpinnings of evidence.

The record of the New York special prosecutor's office is sometimes cited by critics of grand-jury practices. Between the establishment of the office in 1972 and 1976, the grand

Grand juries, which usually consist of 23 persons without legal training, are easily controlled by overzealous prosecutors, critics charge.

114   From *U.S. News & World Report*, June 19, 1978. Copyright © 1978 U.S. News & World Report, Inc.

jury working with the special prosecutor approved a steady stream of indictments against officeholders. More than 250 persons were charged, but only 17, almost all of them low-level police officers, were convicted and served sentences. All other cases, including those against 10 judges, ended with dismissal of the charges, acquittals or reversals of convictions by appeals courts.

On top of the harm to reputations caused by the prosecutions, there have been frequent leaks of grand-jury testimony to the press. One celebrated leak, occurring in the midst of the 1973 mayoral race, is blamed for severely damaging the campaign of a leading candidate, Representative Mario Biaggi (D-N.Y.).

Targeting Minorities

In other instances, the targets of alleged grand-jury harassment are minorities or dissidents whom the prosecutors, and perhaps the grand jurors themselves, find abhorrent.

A recent case in point occurred in Byhalia, Miss. Members of a black civil-rights group, the Marshall County United League, protested the fatal shooting of a black man by police and denounced as a "farce" the grand-jury investigation conducted by a local prosecutor.

When a judge ordered a second probe, the grand jury summoned members of the black group to testify. The grand jury disposed of the shooting incident with a few perfunctory questions and then quizzed the black witnesses at great length about their organization's membership and its activities.

Complaints of grand-jury harassment come most often from minorities and political dissidents.

A federal appeals court in March found that these questions were asked solely to harass group members. "This abuse of the grand-jury process cannot be tolerated in a free society," the court said, adding: "It would be a sorry day were we to allow a grand jury to delve into the membership, meetings, minutes, organizational structure, funding and political activities of unpopular organizations on the pretext that their members might have some information relevant to a crime."

In some cases of alleged harassment of dissident organizations, citizens have decided to go to jail rather than testify about colleagues. This is what happened in a case involving two women lay ministers of the National Commission on Hispanic Affairs, a New York organization funded by the Episcopal Church. Last year, the two were subpoenaed before a federal grand jury investigating bombings and other activities of a self-styled Puerto Rican terrorist group.

The women said publicly that they had no knowledge of the terrorist group. At the same time, they refused to testify about Hispanic-commission activities, contending that their testimony would violate the trust of community people working with the commission.

For this refusal, at the request of a federal prosecutor, the women were jailed for contempt of court in March, 1977. They were freed last January after winning a court order for their release. Seven other persons were jailed for an average of seven months after denying any knowledge of the terrorist group and refusing to answer questions before the grand jury.

This investigation, which is still under way, prompted the governing board of the National Council of Churches to pass a resolution last year condemning misuse of grand-jury powers. William P. Thompson, council president, observes: "It is not the hardened criminals, nor even those with knowledge about crimes, who are the main victims of the modern grand jury, but often idealistic members of ethnic groups or dissident movements who for reasons of principle or loyalty refuse to name their associates—who in most instances have no connection with any crime. They are the ones who sit in jail rather than betray their friends."

Numerous groups with unorthodox or unpopular political views have charged they have been targets of improper grand-jury actions in recent years. Among them: the Vietnam Veterans Against the War, the Black Panther Party, the Irish Northern Aid Society, left-wing Catholic groups, the women's movement and labor organizations.

Roots of Reform

Despite the documented cases of abuse, changes in the grand-jury system have been slow in coming.

For many years, grand-jury critics relied entirely on the courts to check injustices. Judges, who have the power to halt or overturn improper grand-jury actions, sometimes act quickly to correct the most blatant abuses, as in the GM and Mississippi cases. But critics contend that judges far too often take a hands-off approach.

"The courts don't exercise enough authority over grand juries, either because they're not concerned or because they're reluctant to go up against the prosecutors," says Seymour Glanzer, one of the original Watergate prosecutors now in private law practice.

Making matters worse, from the critics' standpoint, the Supreme Court has cut back the rights of grand-jury witnesses in a series of rulings since 1972.

Faced with this trend, grand-jury critics have headed in two directions: abolition and reform.

A minority of the critics favor abolition. They note that England, where the grand-jury concept originated in 1166, eliminated grand juries in 1948. Even some grand jurors have joined the cause of abolition. Last year, for example, members of a Maryland grand jury—charging that they were merely "pawns" of the prosecutor and a "token citizen involvement" in the judicial process—urged that their role be abolished.

Actually, as things stand today, most states use grand juries mainly for major criminal investigations. Twenty-nine states, including California and Illinois, allow charges to be brought without use of the grand jury. In routine cases in these states, prosecutors file a charge. A judge, after giving the defendant and his lawyer a chance to oppose it, decides whether a trial should be held.

Five states, Michigan, Wisconsin, Connecticut, Kansas and Washington, use another method, "one-man grand juries," each consisting of a judicial officer who has most of the usual grand-jury powers.

The Federal Picture

Adopting such procedures at the federal level, however, would be difficult. It would take a constitutional amendment to nullify the Fifth Amendment's requirement that all serious federal charges be heard by a grand jury.

Most critics aren't interested in abolishing grand juries. What they want are new safeguards against the misuse of their powers.

Proposals being pushed in the state legislatures and in Congress would require that:

■ Grand-jury witnesses be told what the investigation is about and given a list of their rights.

■ All subpoenas be approved formally by a majority of the grand jurors, not through informal assent to the prosecutor's wishes.

■ Prosecutors tell the grand jury about evidence that might favor the defendant.

■ Judges instruct new grand jurors that they have the authority to call their own witnesses and to make an inquiry independent of the prosecutor.

■ A transcript be made of everything that occurs in a grand-jury hearing, including remarks by the prosecutor, a practice already followed in 31 states.

The key issues, however, in the view of reformers, are two other proposals. One would give a witness the right to be accompanied by a lawyer when appearing before a grand jury. Reformers argue that without a lawyer by their side, witnesses often are vulnerable to a prosecutor's trick questions and high-pressure tactics.

The reformers have made impressive headway in the states on this question. The right to a lawyer now is provided in 11 states, 10 of which have acted since 1970.

The other key proposal being pushed by reformers is to impose new limits on the state and federal procedures through which witnesses can be given immunity from prosecution. Under the current system, grants of immunity are to be used to obtain testimony that a witness otherwise could withhold by invoking the Fifth Amendment's protection against self-incrimination.

If a person given immunity still refuses to answer questions, he or she can be jailed for contempt of court. All too often, critics charge, this threat is employed by prosecutors to force witnesses to talk about personal associations and other private matters that may go well beyond the legitimate scope of the investigation. It also can be used in conjunction with an effort to confuse witnesses into giving answers that may technically constitute perjury.

Accordingly, many critics of grand-jury practices want to require that a grant of immunity be given only with the consent of the witness.

Those pushing for changes of various kinds in grand-jury practices have swelled in recent years from a small band of civil libertarians into a movement that includes not only powerful groups, like the American Bar Association and the National Council of Churches, but also many prominent judges and prosecutors. At the center of the drive is the Coalition to End Grand Jury Abuse, a national alliance of 21 legal, civil-liberties, labor and religious groups.

Are Critics Overreacting?

Arrayed against these forces are other powerful and respected forces, including not only many federal and state prosecutors and judges but the Justice Department as well.

Lawyers in the grand-jury room, they contend, will disrupt and delay proceedings by repeatedly objecting to questions. Judges will have to rule on these objections, and "minitrials" will result. Attorney General Griffin Bell denounces the proposal as "the lawyer's relief act."

Restricting immunity, prosecutors argue, would greatly impede investigation of organized crime and other conspiracy cases.

"We should be careful to avoid an overreaction to past abuses in a way which unduly hampers efficient, fair lawenforcement efforts in the future," warns Robert J. Del Tufo, U.S. attorney for New Jersey.

Del Tufo and other prosecutors argue that law-enforcement people can prevent abuses by writing and enforcing guidelines of their own. When he was a New Jersey official, Del Tufo helped draft such rules. Other states have done this, too, and the Justice Department issued regulations last December barring techniques that might smack of harassment.

Despite action in some of the states and steady pressure from those demanding reforms, Congress has been moving slowly. A House subcommittee has held extensive hearings over the last two years, but the Senate Judiciary Committee has given the matter no attention. Reform advocates are optimistic, however, that the picture will quickly brighten next year when Senator Edward M. Kennedy (D-Mass.), a staunch reform advocate, is scheduled to become committee chairman.

In the meantime, backers are doing their best to organize grass-roots support. They see citizen interest as crucial.

U.S. District Judge Marvin E. Frankel and Gary P. Naftalis, a former New York prosecutor, conclude in their recent book on grandjury reform: "The most important link of all is the one between the grand jury and the citizen who both staffs it and is touched by it. The safeguard of paramount value, for the grand jury, as for other agencies of a democratic society, is the steady concern and attention of the people."

This report was written by Associate Editor David F. Pike.

Publicity from flimsy indictments or leaks of grand-jury testimony to the press can damage the reputations of officials or citizens.

Advocacy and the criminal trial judge

Hugh F. Keefe

Hugh F. Keefe is a practicing attorney in New Haven, Conn.

Recently, many criminal court trial judges seem to have become more impatient than usual with defense attorneys who insist on challenging jury selection processes, file numerous pre-trial motions, and insist on fighting the cause of their clients to the hilt. Sporadic outbursts of judicial temper, criticisms and thinly-veiled threats — all aimed at defense counsel — intimidate many lawyers into unnecessary plea bargaining and many defendants into coerced pleas of guilty. Is the proud spirit of advocacy being broken by a mountain of congested calendars and overcrowded courts?

It is a fact that some judges are simply ill-suited to truly understand or accept the function of the advocate in a criminal case. One of the principal reasons for this problem is undoubtedly a lack of personal criminal trial experience on the part of many judges. A true understanding of counsel's unique role should begin with the minimum required as Sixth Amendment "effective assistance of counsel" by the courts.

Justifiably, the traditional rule that "effective assistance of counsel" simply meant a defense effort that amounted to something more than a "farce or mockery" has been much criticized.[1] And deservedly so. It is gratifying that the standard is finally being abandoned in a growing number of federal[2] and state jurisdictions.[3] Although the semantics differ, the new test is generally articulated along the following lines:

"Defense counsel's performance must be reasonably competent or within the range of competence displayed by lawyers with ordinary training and skill in the criminal law. The defendant's burden is to show that his counsel's conduct fell below that standard and that the lack of competency contributed to the conviction."[4]

In *Beasley v. United States,* Judge Celebreeze articulated it well: "Defense strategy and tactics which lawyers of ordinary training and skill in the criminal law would not consider competent deny a criminal defendant the effective assistance of counsel, if some other action would have better protected a defendant and was reasonably foreseeable as such before trial ... We hold that Petitioner did not receive the effective assistance of counsel before and during trial ... Harmless error tests do not apply in regard to the deprivation of a procedural right so fundamental as the effective assistance of counsel."[5]

Certainly, the new requirement is not earthshaking, but even this minimum representation standard would seem to require a zealous advocacy from the beginning lest unaware counsel could find himself a witness in a habeas corpus hearing or a defendant in a legal malpractice suit, an area being looked at with renewed interest.

WHAT IS ADVOCACY?

In *Gulliver's Travels,* Jonathan Swift offered a lowly, albeit popular, opinion of us when he said lawyers are: "A society of men bred up from their youth in the art of proving by words multiplied for the purpose that white is black and black is white according as they are paid."

We have all heard such opinions along with the inevitable cocktail party question, i.e., "How can you defend a man you know is guilty?" The easy answer, of course, is that under our system, a man is not "guilty" until the jury foreman says he is and even then not until the appellate courts agree. Or we could answer as Brandeis did: "As a practical matter, I think the lawyer is not often harassed by this problem partly because he is apt to believe at the time in most of the cases that he actually tries, and partly because he either abandons or settles a large number of those he does not believe in."[6]

Or we could simply look the questioner in the eye and say: "Why shouldn't I defend a man who is blatantly guilty? It is his constitutional right and my professional duty." The defendant is presumed innocent, the burden is on the prosecution to prove guilt beyond a reasonable doubt, and even the guilty accused has an "absolute constitutional right" to remain silent and to put the government to its proof.[7] There should be no hesitation on the part of the trial lawyer. As Justice White commented, "Our system assigns him a different mission ... we ... insist that he defend his client whether he is innocent or guilty."[8]

And our judiciary would be well counselled to remind themselves of the pure role of the advocate:

"He does not profess to present his own point of view or his own beliefs to the court. He is there as the mouthpiece of the client to say for him what he would wish to say for himself, were he able to do so with knowledge and understanding.[9]

"Advocacy requires a lawyer to start with something to be proved and this is as true of facts as it is of proposition of law. When he goes to interview a witness as well as when he goes to the law library, he goes to get something. He will waste a lot of time if he goes with an open mind. He must, of course, first formulate the issue in his mind, but he does this only to make it the easier to find what lies on his side of the issue. He fixes on the conclusion which will best serve his client's interests, and then he sets out to persuade others to agree.

"It is profoundly true that the first person a lawyer persuades is himself. A practicing lawyer will soon detect in himself a perfectly astonishing amount of sincerity. By the time he has even sketched out his brief, however skeptically he started, he finds himself believing more and more in what it says, until he has to hark back to his original opinion in order to orient himself. And later, when he starts arguing the case before the court, his belief is total, and he is quite sincere about it. You cannot very well keep your tongue in your cheek while you are talking. He believes what he is saying in a way that will later astonish himself as much as it now does others."[10]

3. THE JUDICIAL SYSTEM

PASSIVITY SHOULD BE DISCOURAGED

In trying a case recently as a special public defender for a particularly obstreperous client, I was confronted with a trial judge who was obviously upset that my client would not plead guilty, notwithstanding an offer by the prosecutor to reduce the charge and recommend a relatively light prison sentence. Though the jury ultimately acquitted him, that did not lessen the judge's dissatisfaction with me. To this day, I am certain he is convinced that I could have "controlled" the defendant and "sold" him the disposition offered. If it ever did exist, the day of the passive, "controllable" criminal defendant is long gone. And good riddance! Now, more than ever, the 1883 analysis of Sir James Stephen is true: "A criminal trial is a substitute for private war, and is and must be conducted in a spirit which is often fervent, and even passionate. No man will allow himself to be deprived of character or liberty or possibly of life without offering the most strenuous resistance in his power, or without seeking, in many cases, to retaliate on his opponent and his opponent's supporters. A trial of any importance is always more or less of a battle."[11]

Those of us who had occasion to be around the criminal courts during the Black Panther, draft-resister, and/or antiwar demonstration trials of the late 60's and early 70's, know the literal meaning of the "battle" syndrome. Anger and hostility toward the advocates for both sides were constantly in evidence. And this is not a recent phenomenon.

"The hostility toward an unpopular defendant, more often than not, has been visited upon his counsel. Such was Erskine's fate when he defended Thomas Paine; such was John Adams' portion when he became counsel for the British soldiers charged with the Boston Massacre. Such was the reward of William Seward, when a hundred and eight years ago, in a little crowded courtroom, he stood up to defend a Negro by the name of Freeman on a charge of murder. His client was an emancipated slave. The man was deaf and obviously insane, but this, far from creating sympathy, seemed to accentuate the community's hostility for the poor Negro."[12]

Finally, a word should be said about integrity and the advocate. No profession is more concerned with integrity and no profession is more slandered for not having any. Again, much of the criticism can be attributed to the public's ignorance of the true role of the advocate and the consequent confusion in distinguishing the lawyer from his client and his client's interest.

In 1954, in a dinner address, the Right Honorable Sir Norman Birkett, an English Lord Justice of Appeal, stated it incisively: "The advocate has a duty to his client, to the Court and a duty to the State; but he has above all a duty to himself that he shall be, as far as lies in his power, a man of integrity. No profession calls for higher standards of honour and uprightness, and no profession, perhaps, offers greater temptations to foresake them; but whatever gifts an advocate may possess, be they ever so dazzling, without the supreme qualification of an inner integrity, he will fall short of the brightest."[13]

CONCLUSION

Judge Parry, in his *Seven Lamps of Advocacy,* wrote: "Without a free and honorable race of advocates, there would have been little of the message of justice. Advocacy is the outward and visible appeal for the spiritual gift of justice. The advocate is the priest in the temple of justice, trained in the mysteries of the creed, active in its exercises."[14]

And so, it is submitted that the age of advocacy in our criminal courts is not over, nor should it be. Rather, zealously representing a client, asserting his every right, guarding his liberty and if need be, his life, is the privilege, duty and responsibility of every member of our profession.

As the ancient Romans were fond of saying, "Fiat justitia, ruat coelum" — "Let justice be done, though the heavens fall."

NOTES

1. Finer, *Ineffective Assistance of Counsel,* 58 Cornell L. Rev. 1077, 1079 (1973).

2. *Moore v. United States,* 432 F. 2d 730 (3d Cir.) (en banc); *Coles v. Peyton,* 389 F. 2d 224 (4th Cir.), cert. denied, 393 U.S. 849, 89 S. Ct. 80, 21 L. Ed. 2d 120; *Herring v. Estelle,* 491 F. 2d 125 (5th Cir.); *Beasley v. United States,* 491 F. 2d 687 (6th Cir.); *United States v. DeCoster,* 487 F. 2d 1197 (D.C. Cir.); but cf. *Moran v. Hogan,* 494 F. 2d 1220 (1st Cir.); *United States v. Ramirez,* 19 Cr. L. 2141 (CA1 April 21, 1976); *United States v. Yanishefsky,* 500 F. 2d 1327, 1333 n.2 (2d Cir.); *United States v. Garguilo,* 324 F. 2d 795 (2d Cir.); *Thomas v. Pate,* 493 F. 2d 151, 157 n.4 (7th Cir.), cert. denied, 419 U.S. 879, 95 S. Ct. 143, 46 L. Ed. 2d 110; *McQueen v. Swenson,* 498 F. 2d 207 (8th Cir.);

United States v. Steed, 465 F. 2d 1310 (9th cir.), cert. denied, 409 U.S. 1078, 93 S. Ct. 697, 34 L. Ed. 2d 667; *Johnson v. United States,* 380 F. 2d 810 (10th Cir.).
3. *Risher v. State,* 523 P. 2d 421, 424 (Alas.); *State v. Merchant,* 10 Md. App. 545, 271 A. 2d 752; *Delle Chiaie v. Commonwealth, Mass.,* 327 N.E. 2d 696; *People v. Lewis,* Mich. App., 235 N.W. 2d 100; *Thomas v. State,* 516 S.W. 2d 761, 765 (Mo. App.); *Rook v. Cupp,* 526 P. 2f 605 (Ore. App.); *Commonwealth v. Nole,* Pa. 336 A. 2d 302; *Baxter v. Rose,* 235 Tenn., 523 S.W. 2d 930, 936; *Ex Parte Gallegos,* 511 S.W. 2d 510, 512-13 (Tex. Crim. App.); *In Re Cronin,* 133 Vt. 234, 336 A. 2d 164; *State v. Thomas,* W. Va., 203 S.E. 2d, 445, 461; *State v. Harper,* 57 Wis. 2d 543, 552, 205 N.W. 2d 1; *State v. Clark,* _____ Conn. _____ (1976).

4. _____ Conn. _____ (1976) (36 Conn. L.J., NO. 36, pp. 4-5).
5. 491 F. 2d 687 (CA6 1974).
6. Brandeis, *The Opportunity in the Law,* 39 Am. L. Rev. 561 (1905).
7. *Escobedo v. Illinois,* 378 U.S. 478 (1964).
8. *United States v. Wade,* 388 U.S. 218 (1967) (dissenting opinion).
9. Birkett, *Advocacy,* (1954). Reprinted in *Holdsworth Club Presidential Addresses,* 1950-59. Published in the Holdsworth Club of the University of Birmingham.
10. Curtis, *The Ethics of Advocacy,* 4 Stan. L. Rev. 3 (1951).
11. Stephen, *A History of the Criminal Law in England,* (1883).
12. Stryker, *supra* Note 3.
13. Birkett, *supra* Note 10.
14. Parry, *Seven Lamps of Advocacy,* Quoted in Stryker, Note 3.

Justice for Whom?

Plea bargaining, the latest scapegoat in
the justice game, can often be the human
side of the law, particularly when it comes
to weighing a life against a death.

Steven Phillips

Steven Phillips graduated from Williams
College and received his law degree from
Columbia Law School in 1971. For the
next five years he served as an assistant
district attorney in Bronx County, New
York, where he specialized in the investigation and trial of homicide cases. Now
employed by a New York City law firm, he
is the author of No Heroes, No Villains, an
account of a murder trial, published by
Random House.

HE WAS ON HIS WAY HOME from a schoolyard pickup basketball game, dribbling
his ball down Arthur Avenue in the
Bronx, when a white teenager walked
up and stabbed him once in the abdo-
men. The black boy was dead before he
hit the ground. The assailant turned and
fled, leaving his victim sprawled face
upward on the sidewalk. From start to
finish, the killing took no more than
five seconds.

It took the detective almost a month
before he broke the case. At first it was a
total mystery, with no apparent motive
for the killing and no decent leads to
work on. In fact, several days passed
before the detective even learned the
victim's identity.

When they undressed the boy at the
morgue, all the detective found were a
set of keys and a dollar and a half in
change. There was no wallet and no
identification cards. He fingerprinted
the corpse and ran the prints through
the computer, but drew a blank. The
dead boy had never been arrested. Finally, the detective took photographs of
the victim's face, and distributed copies
to the desk officers and detective squads
of all the neighboring precincts. He
hoped someone reporting a missing person would identify the photo. As it happened, the boy's parents had reported
him missing on the day of his death.

Four days had passed, however, before
anyone remembered to show them a
copy of the morgue photo. He was 17
when he was killed, a senior in high
school.

For two weeks the detective got nowhere. The boy had no enemies, he had
not been robbed, and no clues had been
found at the scene of the crime. A canvass of the scene had produced only one
eyewitness, a middle-aged black gas-
station attendant who had seen the killing from about half a block away. He
described the assailant as a white teen-
ager of about average height and weight,
with dark hair. He did not remember
what the youth was wearing, or anything else about him.

The detective interviewed students
at the dead boy's high school, where he
had been an honor student. He also
questioned members of the local youth
gangs. But he made no progress. As the
investigation stretched into its third
fruitless week, the detective's squad
commander began to talk about pulling
him off the case. Summer was ap-
proaching, the homicide rate was
climbing as fast as the temperature, and
vacation schedules were cutting into
available police manpower. The commander figured it made no sense to
waste a good man on what appeared to
be a hopeless task. They talked it over
and decided to give the case one more
week.

A lead on the killer. On the final day of
that third week a lead finally developed.
The gas-station attendant called and
told the detective that a kid driving an
old souped-up Thunderbird had been
around the gas station several times
asking what he knew about the homicide. The attendant decided these questions were suspicious. Although the
driver did not resemble the killer, he
took down the license-plate number
and passed it along to the detective.

It took the detective a day and a half
to track down the driver of the Thunderbird. He was the kind of street tough
who had been in and out of minor trouble since he was 13. The youngster denied all knowledge of the killing. In a
whining, plaintive voice he asked why
he had been brought in. The detective
then took his cigar out of his mouth, put
his face close to the boy's and grabbed
him by the shirt front with both hands.
Like the Marine noncom he had once
been, he told the boy the facts of life.
"Now you listen to me, you punk. This
isn't an auto larceny of a burglary I'm
investigating, it's a goddamn murder.
And I know that one of your punk
friends did it! You're going to tell me
who did it, 'cause if you don't I'm gonna
lock your ass up for hindering prosecution! And you'd better believe I'm
gonna make it stick! I'm gonna send you
upstate for sure. You understand?"

The detective left the boy alone in the
squadroom to think that over. Within
an hour, he told the detective everything he knew. He had not been an eyewitness to the killing, and his
knowledge was second-hand. The killer
was an 18-year-old who worked as a delivery boy for a local pastry shop. The
detective also learned the names of a
number of youngsters who had actually
witnessed the stabbing.

There was no need to run right out to
arrest the suspect. The detective knew
from long experience that if the boy had
not already vanished after three weeks,
he was not about to. Instead, the detective rounded up all the eyewitnesses (an
easy task, since they were all attending
local high schools), and brought them
back to the station house. He kept them
separated, and spoke to each one individually. A half hour later he had six
signed eyewitness statements identifying the killer. The time had come to
make the arrest.

3. THE JUDICIAL SYSTEM

The suspect lived with his aged parents in a two-bedroom apartment over a shoemaker's shop, not four blocks from the scene of the killing. The apartment was immaculate, and had a warm, old-world immigrant flavor the detective knew all too well. He had grown up in such a home himself. In the entrance hallway were framed pictures of Pope John, John Kennedy, and the Virgin Mary.

"I didn't mean to do it." The boy's father answered the door. He was a frail but intense white-haired man in his 60s, and he spoke with a heavy Italian accent. Asked what he wanted, the detective said, he had to speak to the boy about a crime that had been committed. As he stood there, the detective was embarrassed by the old man. He could see that the boy's father did not have the slightest inkling of what this was all about, and the detective had little stomach for what he knew was about to happen. Grimly he pushed on.

"Where is the boy?"

"He's in his bedroom, studying," the father replied. "I'll call him, but first you tell me what crime this is you want to talk to him about."

"It's a murder. A black kid was killed up on Arthur Avenue three weeks ago. I've got to talk to him about it."

"Are you here to arrest my boy?"

"Yes, I am," the detective said softly.

The old man looked hard at the detective, and began to shake. His eyes widened, and he began to look a little wild. But then, just as suddenly, he seemed to regain control of himself. He called out the boy's name.

The boy emerged from his bedroom and walked up to his father and the detective. He was short and slender, almost fragile in build, dressed in blue jeans and a white T-shirt. He was smooth-cheeked, and the detective was struck by the boy's eyes. They were large and dark and liquid, the sort of eyes you would expect to see on a beautiful woman. The boy looked straight at the detective and then lowered his eyes. He knew what this was all about.

The old man spoke first.

"This man says you killed a black kid up on Arthur Avenue three weeks ago."

The boy hung his head and began to cry. "Papa, I did it. I didn't mean to do it, and I wanted to tell you, but I couldn't. It just happened, and I'm sorry." The old man was in a state of shock. The three of them stood silently, and then the old man too began to cry. The detective waited a minute and then put the boy in handcuffs and led him away.

It was almost 24 hours from the time of arrest until the boy was arraigned. They spent it waiting for transportation, waiting for the Correction Department red tape at Central Booking, and finally, waiting for the court. The boy and the detective chatted to kill the time. The detective found that he liked his prisoner, and it bothered him. As he reflected upon what was in store for the boy in prison he felt sick. For the first time in his career he found himself wishing he had not broken a case.

By the time the boy was arraigned, his father had spoken to his neighbors, and a delegation of them went with him to the Bronx Criminal Court Building on Washington Avenue and 161st Street. When his case was called, they all stepped forward to vouch for the boy, his character, and his family. Impressed by this unusual show of neighborhood solidarity, and by the impeccable character of the local merchants who spoke up for the boy, the judge set bail at the modest sum (for a murder) of $15,000. It was raised within the hour. The boy walked out of the court after spending only one night in jail, and the case was referred to the grand jury.

There were over 400 homicides in Bronx County that year. Almost 350 were solved by the police, leading to arrests that were turned over for prosecution to the 12 of us in the Homicide Bureau of the District Attorney's office. The death of the black boy on Arthur Avenue was only one of these homicides.

An airtight case. It was bound to be a low-priority case, with the defendant out on bail at a time when we had prisoners who had been languishing in jail for up to two years awaiting trial. This case had to be put on a back burner. Besides, with six eye-witnesses, an oral confession, and a vicious, senseless crime to work with, any trial of the case was bound to result in a murder conviction and a mandatory life sentence.

From the very beginning, when I was first assigned the case, I knew no defense attorney would risk taking it to trial. It was foreordained to result in a plea bargain. The grand-jury presentation took a little less than 15 minutes. Two of the eyewitnesses and the detective testified, and I read from the medical examiner's report. The grand jury deliberated about 30 seconds before handing up a murder indictment.

It was two months or so before I heard from the boy's defense attorney, a man I had dealt with before and respected. Late one afternoon, several days later, we met in my office. Although I was eager to avoid a trial, there wasn't much I could offer the boy as a plea bargain and I said so. I had close to an airtight case, one that was bound to lead to a murder conviction. The crime itself was both shocking and senseless, and the defendant, then 18 years old, would be treated as an adult rather than a juvenile. I saw no reason why I should not take a very hard position.

The defense attorney listened, and then asked me what I would offer the boy. I thought for a minute, and told him I would agree to a plea to manslaughter in the first degree. I added that at the time of sentence I would ask the judge to impose a very lengthy jail term with a fixed minimum to guarantee that substantial time would actually be served.

The defense attorney was candid in his response. He acknowledged right away that his client was guilty and admitted he didn't dare take the case to trial. He had to plead his client guilty, and did not care what particular crime he pleaded to so long as it was not murder, which carried with it a mandatory life sentence. What he did care about was the sentence his client would receive, and in this regard he had two requests. Before discussing the question of sentencing he asked me to read a report on his client prepared at his family's request by a forensic psychiatrist. Then he asked me to meet the boy myself and size him up. I agreed.

Killer on the couch. The psychiatrist's report read, in part, as follows:

... Although I am unable to state that [this young man] was unaware of the nature and consequences of his actions, or that he was unaware of the fact that his conduct was morally wrong, I do believe that there are circumstances that should weigh heavily in determining the disposition of his case.

... [he] is the only son of immigrant parents and was born at a time when his parents were already on the brink of middle age. Since early childhood he has been overprotected and overindulged by his mother who has made him the central focus of her life. His father, a stern disciplinarian, has always attempted to instill in [this young man] his own rather rigid set of values. Needless to say, this interparental conflict over the nature and style of his

120

rearing, has left [the boy] with an ambivalent and deeply troubled attitude toward his parents.

This ambivalence was exacerbated by a phenomenon that is rather common in the first general offspring of newly arrived immigrants. [The boy], whose English is, of course, fluent and unaccented, and who is very much a product of this society, is ashamed of his parents' heavy accents, and what he described as their "foreign ways." He is reluctant to bring friends into the house for fear that his parents might embarrass him, and is equally reluctant to share his "American" school or "street" life with his parents, for fear that they would misunderstand or disapprove of things he has come to cherish as he struggles to find his own identity. On the other hand, [the boy] loves his parents deeply, and has great difficulty coping with this shame over their "old fashionedness."

...[He] has also had serious trouble in coping with peer-group pressure which is, of course, a particularly intense force in late adolescence. The young people in [his] neighborhood place great emphasis upon a young man's having "machismo," e.g., on being both sexually and physically powerful. These values directly conflict with the overprotected and unyielding values the boy has learned at home. In addition, [the boy] has gone through a relatively late puberty, and to this day is relatively small and frail for his age. He does not yet need to shave frequently, and his boyish appearance makes him the butt of a considerable amount of peer-group teasing. He has had considerable difficulty dealing with these pressures both in school and at play in the streets. In view of this it is quite remarkable that he has done as well as he has in his studies. He is a B student, a fact that reinforces my own impression that he is both a sensitive and an intelligent young man.

...There is no gainsaying the fact that he has committed a most horrible crime, and it is not my purpose to in any way diminish or make light of his offense. Nevertheless, it must be understood that [the boy] acted as he did out of a kind of neurotic desperation, from a terrible need to win acceptance from his peers, and to rebel against the strict morality of his parents. In [his] mind, the grotesque action of taking a baking knife and stabbing a strange black boy in the presence of his friends became a

means of showing them, and himself, that he could outdo any of them in both violence, and at least symbolically in sexuality. The use of the knife as a chosen weapon is significant, for it is phallic substitute, and was used to assuage doubts that he had developed about his own masculinity. I am not suggesting that [he] did not know that what he was doing was wrong. What I do find though, was that [his] actions were not wholly voluntary, but were precipitated by conflicts between intense psychological forces over which he ultimately lost control.

... I have been seeing [him] for two months now on an intensive basis, and even in this short time there has been extraordinary progress. He has begun to discuss his feelings and has begun to face directly the ambivalences that have so deeply disturbed him. His parents, who are deeply concerned, have cooperated fully in his therapy, and my sessions with them and the boy have been particularly fruitful.

While no one can ever pretend to predict these things with certainty, it is my strong feeling and my professional judgment that with continued care [this young man] will become a well adjusted and valuable member of society. I view with horror the prospect of his going to prison. Such an eventuality would hopelessly undermine all hopes of effective treatment, would exacerbate his problems, and would most likely destroy him as an individual. Sending this young man to prison in his present psychological state would be a tragedy...

As I read the report, I realized it was a partisan document prepared at the defendant's expense. Nevertheless, I could not completely discount what it contained. The psychiatrist's comments seemed both thoughtful and sincere.

"A pretty good kid." Two weeks later the lawyer brought the boy and his parents to my office. They were dressed in their Sunday best and obviously ill at ease. Their discomfort made me feel uncomfortable too. The defense attorney's purpose in arranging this meeting was not hard to divine. He wanted me to meet his client so that I might develop some sympathy for him and his family. He knew his only real hope for obtaining lenient treatment for the boy lay in winning my acquiescence.

I did find myself feeling sorry for the boy. He looked so terribly frail, young and insecure, completely unlike what I

had expected. He was polite, and had soft, almost effeminate features that could not be squared with the conventional image of the vicious killer. In talking to him, I came to understand what the detective had meant when he had told me the boy was "a pretty good kid, who shouldn't get hit too hard."

The boy asked me for permission to go see the parents of the boy he had killed. He wanted to seek their forgiveness, to tell them how terribly sorry he was for what he had done. It was a pathetic request. The whole thing was pathetic. But I believed he was sincere. I kept reminding myself that I was talking to a vicious killer who had taken a human life for no reason at all and then calmly gone about his business for three weeks. He had come very close to getting away with murder. I knew it was possible that he was trying to con me into feeling sorry for him, but somehow I just did not believe it. The boy was not putting on an act.

I talked to the boy's parents briefly. They were restrained and subdued, and seemed to be good people. I could see that the prospect of losing their only child to prison was taking a terrible toll on them, and it was impossible not to sympathize with their plight. I thought about the boy's request, and then told them that it would be unwise for him to try to see the dead boy's family.

That afternoon I spoke to the dead boy's father on the telephone, and arranged for him to come to my office the following day. When I arrived that morning at 9:00 I found him already waiting for me. He was a dark-skinned, hefty man with a receding hairline. We shook hands firmly and he met my gaze with unwavering eyes. I ushered him into my office, and he sat down in the same chair where 24 hours earlier the other boy's father had sat.

I offered my condolences, and then, before asking him the questions that were on my mind, I tried to make my position clear. I was not his lawyer. I worked for the State of New York and my responsibility was to the people of the state and not to any particular individual. I wanted to talk to him about his son's death and I wanted his opinion about the treatment his son's killer should receive. But in the end, he had to understand that whatever he might feel and whatever he might think, I had to be the one to decide how the case was handled. When I asked him if he understood, he continued to look levelly at me, and answered, "Yes, I do."

I went on to outline in some detail the results of the detective's investigation. He learned that I had a powerful case, and that a trial was almost certain to result in a murder conviction with a mandatory life sentence for his son's killer. I also told him what I had learned from the psychiatrist's report and described the interview in my office the preceding day. I described my problem to him. In about a week the case was scheduled to come up on the court calendar, and I would be obliged to make a recommendation to a judge on the question of plea and sentence. The judge would most likely follow my recommendation. The defense would have no choice but to go along with my offer, and in the final analysis I would bear a heavy responsibility for what would happen. I asked the man for his help in reaching a decision. He sat silently, pondering what I had said.

When he spoke, it was with great force. There was a lot bottled up inside him and he had come to my office to get it off his chest. He was blunt. He said he was not about to make things easy for me by telling me not to go hard on the white boy. As far as he was concerned "that white boy" had to go to jail for a long time and the longer the better. He told me his wife had planned to come with him to my office, but at the last moment she had broken down and couldn't come. Their son's death had just about killed his wife. The death had made her old before her time and he knew she would never be the same again.

And then there was their younger son. He had been doing really well in school, almost as well as his dead brother had been doing. But ever since the murder, the knowledge that his brother's killer was free had been eating at him. The parents did not know what to say to him. He was turning bitter, neglecting his studies, and for the first time had begun to get into trouble with the law. Was it right that their only remaining child be condemned to grow up with such hatred?

Then there was the question of race. He asked me whether a black kid who had senselessly killed a white honor student would be out on bail receiving such gentle treatment. It was a rhetorical question, and he supplied his own answer. He knew damn well that if the tables were turned his son, or any black boy, would be rotting in jail facing a

certain life sentence. I listened quietly and didn't argue. I let the man talk himself out and then thanked him for coming to see me and for speaking so candidly. Then we parted.

The case got some minor press coverage, especially in the local newspapers serving the black community. We had received some mail on the case and there was one editorial highly critical of the way the criminal justice system was handling it. Here was an extraordinary young black senselessly cut down by a youthful white racist, and nobody was doing anything about it. There were letters calling for the defendant's head, and many of them were rational and forceful. It was reasoned that the failure to punish the white killer severely was a clear signal to other white youths with similar inclinations that black life was cheap and could be taken with impunity. Similarly, it told someone in the black community that there was no justice in the courts, and that recourse to justice in the streets was a wiser alternative. The newspaper clippings, the editorial, and the letters all found their way into the file. I read them, and found that I could not ignore the message they contained.

By the time the case came up for a pretrial conference I had decided unheroically to pass the buck. The judge, I thought to myself, was elected by the people, and is paid about three times as much as I am to make these tough sentencing decisions. I decided to recommend a plea to manslaughter one and take no position on the question of sentence. This would give the judge latitude to choose anything from a 25-year sentence down to no sentence at all. Let him read the presentence report, talk to both sets of parents, and decide what to do with the boy. That's his job really, not mine.

It did not work out that way, and deep down I had known it wouldn't. The judge listened courteously enough while the defense attorney and I outlined the facts of the case. Then I proposed the open plea to manslaughter in the first degree with the question of sentence left entirely in the judge's hands. The proposal was turned down on the spot.

"What, are you out of your mind?" the judge asked. "You want me to stick my neck out all alone on a case like this? No way! Here's what I'll do. I'll adjourn the case for one week. If, at that time, the district attorney's office is pre-

pared to make a recommendation on sentence, I will accept the plea and follow that recommendation. If not, I will set the case down for trial."

As we were leaving the courtroom the defense attorney called me inside. He was angry and spoke harshly. Again I was asked rhetorical questions. Didn't I know what was going to happen to the boy in jail? A soft, good-looking kid like that would certainly be gang-raped by homosexuals in prison. He would almost certainly end up becoming a homosexual himself, and probably would become the "wife" of some stronger inmate just to obtain protection. Hadn't I read the psychiatrist's report? Didn't I know what the prisons were like?

I did not reply to the defense attorney's outburst. There was nothing I could say. I did know what the prisons were like and I had read the psychiatrist's report. I didn't need the defense attorney to remind me of these realities. They had been nagging at me all along. The defense attorney paused a minute waiting for an answer. When I said nothing, he went on. Didn't I know that 80 percent of the prison population was black or Hispanic? Once they find out what the boy is in jail for they would probably cut his throat. He said his client would never survive a lengthy jail term.

I did not argue with the defense attorney as he said this. I too had considered this possibility, and frankly, I just did not know whether he was right or wrong. I heard him out, and then excused myself. It was a bad week for me. The case would not leave my mind, and the more I thought about it, the more impossible it seemed to reach a sentencing decision. I would have liked to have had more information about the boy before making a decision. But with our crushing caseloads, neither I nor the detective could possibly devote more time to this particular case.

I turned to my colleagues for advice, but, as I expected, they showed no inclination to make the decision for me. This was only one case among many, and only I had any knowledge of its complexity. The advice I got was both wise and useless. "Do the right thing, and don't worry," I was told.

The trouble, of course, was that I did not know what the right thing was, and I could not stop worrying. I wanted to reach a just result, but justice, I quickly came to realize, was a relative thing. It all depended upon your perspective. Justice for an emotionally disturbed boy, gripped by psychological forces partially beyond his control, or for his aged parents, faced with the loss of their only son? Justice for the dead boy, senselessly cut down in his youth, or for his family, grief-stricken and embittered by their loss, and by the seeming indifference of the judicial process? Society needed justice too. But what kind? Stern justice to clearly show that racial violence would not be tolerated? Or a more humane justice that sought to heal and rehabilitate rather than punish?

There was no end to the conflicting values at stake, and the conflicts, such as they were, would not resolve themselves in my mind. I had no difficulty articulating the arguments to justify either harsh or lenient treatment. But in the end, I came to realize that the arguments were pointless. Each one was based upon a different assumption about the purpose of punishment; and in effect, in making the argument, the unspoken assumption would dictate the conclusion reached. For example, if the purpose of punishment was retribution, then the very seriousness of the boy's offense, independent of all other considerations, required harsh punish-

ment. But if the idea was rehabilitation rather than retribution, then I had a boy who most probably could be transformed through sympathetic and therapeutic, i.e., lenient, treatment into a valuable member of society.

If, on the other hand, punishment was designed to be exemplary, if it was to teach and to deter, then harsh treatment was necessary to demonstrate that racial violence would not be tolerated.

Retribution, rehabilitation, and deterrence, they all have a certain validity, and I could not easily choose between them. Besides, I was haunted by the images of the two families, and concerned about the impact of my decision upon all of these decent and innocent people.

I tried to take a pragmatic approach and asked myself what was to be gained by sending the boy to prison. It wasn't going to bring the dead boy back, and it wasn't really going to end racial violence or make the streets of the Bronx any safer. In one way or another, prison would probably destroy the boy, and in the final analysis, wasn't it more important to save this life, then to bow to the imagined dictates of abstract social justice? The boy was so young, and in a

sense he was the victim of powerful social and psychological forces that were beyond his control. Was it right to make him pay as an individual for a crime that found its origins, at least in part, in peer-group pressure and the collective racial attitudes of society in general? I toyed with all these arguments, but I could not escape the idea that the boy, however young, bore an individual responsibility for his actions, and had to answer for that responsibility.

A decision had to be made, and one week later I made a sentencing recommendation. Later, at the time of sentence, the judge followed it. Whether or not I did the right thing I shall never know. No doubt reasonable people will differ about the rightness of my decision and what ought to have been done.

The boy is currently serving a 15-year term in state prison. He will be eligible for parole in three years. Two months after sentence, the white youth's father suffered a stroke. He is now an invalid. The dead boy's brother is now under indictment, charged with armed robbery. There has been no noticeable decrease in the amount of crime or racial violence in the Bronx.

Preventive Detention
A Matter of Balance

Philip Baridon
St. Elizabeths Hospital

Philip C. Baridon is chief of research, Division of Forensic Programs, St. Elizabeths Hospital. He has worked as a police officer and taught at The American University. His most recent publication is Addiction, Crime and Social Policy *(Lexington: D.C. Heath 1976).*

Thomas McEwen
PRC Public Management Services, Inc.

J. Thomas McEwen is a vice-president with PRC Public Management Services, Inc. in McLean, Virginia. He was previously employed at the St. Louis Police Department, where he was involved in numerous research activities.

The authors suggest that the probability of an arrestee engaging in violent crime before trial should be recognized as an independent and legitimate concern of the courts. Some of the major practical and legal considerations in implementing a pretrial detention option are discussed. A model is proposed which would give prosecutors a uniform basis for the decision to request a judicial order to detain pending trial. The model is based upon a modification of the Sellin-Wolfgang index of seriousness.

The Sixth Amendment guarantees every citizen charged with a crime the right to a speedy trial. Unfortunately, delays of more than six months from arrest to trial are not uncommon, especially in major urban centers. The reasons for delay are not hard to find. Overworked prosecutors are less inclined to object to defense motions for a postponement on various grounds. Delay serves the defense since complainants and witnesses become less interested in prosecution, are more vague on the details of an event, and are bewildered about the entire criminal justice process. During a delay the accused may be held without bail (for some capital offenses) or may be unable to post bond. More often than not, the accused is released on a surety bond, to third party custody, or on his own recognizance. Approximately 35 states and the District of Columbia now have some type of "release on recognizance" (ROR) program (National Advisory Commission, 1973: 108).

The only purpose of bail is to assure the appearance of the defendant at later proceedings (Newman, 1975). It is a protection against flight. Other forms of pretrial release share the same objective. ROR investigations are designed to assess the probability that the defendant will be present for pleading and trial. Willingness to appear on previous charges (if any) and strong community ties are the keys to the rather recent empirical development of an adequate base expectancy approach to prediction. Such a probabilistic approach to pretrial release has seen rapidly expanding use during the last ten years. It is now considered relatively simple, efficient, reliable and valid—all necessary criteria for any predictive effort (Mannheim and Wilkins, 1970). While it cannot be denied that only a small percentage of released defendants fail to appear as required, there is growing concern by many that a small core of these releasees are confirmed recidivists, and, as such, pose a considerable threat to the safety and well-being of the community.

Data have been compiled in at least one major city which tend to support such concerns. During calendar year 1975, 9,053 people were arrested in Washington, D.C. for a serious offense.[1] Twenty-six percent or 2,328 of these individuals were free while facing the same or other charges (District of Columbia Police Department). Although the usual arguments may be made that arrest does not correspond to legal or even factual guilt, the probability of such an overlap occurring by chance approaches zero. Since there is nothing to suggest that the habits of Washington criminals are unique, a problem has clearly presented itself for our examination. We posit as a given that there is a numerically small but seriously deviant group of individuals in our major cities who, at some given time, find themselves in a period of intense and regularized criminal activity. Then the issue becomes what effective and just response, if any, may be made to this identifiable situation.

Unfortunately, when the judicial system encounters a person who seems to symbolize this threat, the response is usually to set bail at a very high sum. Not only does this violate Eighth Amendment requirements, which prohibit excessive bail, it is also fundamentally discriminatory. Potentially dangerous criminals with financial means are freed, while those not so well off remain incarcerated. The pernicious effects of pretrial detention extend beyond the individual and his family to limit the effectiveness of defendant and counsel in preparing an adequate defense. Accordingly, the very serious decision both to confine and handicap a defendant should not be left to the vagaries of financial wealth or subjective assessments.

To summarize, there are two possible reasons why a judge or magistrate might wish to order pretrial detention: (1) to assure the appearance of the defendant for pleading and trial, and (2) to prevent the release of someone whom he considers dangerous to the community. In the majority of states some type of

ROR program has been established which effectively meets this first requirement. For the second consideration, high bail has been and still is the only route open to a judge for someone charged with a noncapital offense.[2] A few of the constitutional, moral, and methodological problems related to this use of bail have been discussed. Proper use of bail would restrict it to the prevention of flight in communities which have not developed some type of ROR program.

It seems to us that the potential dangerousness of the arrestee must be recognized explicitly as an independent and legitimate legal concern. With this recognition must come a fair and efficient means of making such a determination. Those found very likely to continue a pattern of serious crime should be incarcerated pending trial. This finding must be entirely separate from any assessment of the defendant's likelihood of appearing in court as required. It must be emphasized that these determinations in no way compromise the presumption of innocence. While there may be some empirical basis for the belief that more "dangerous" defendants will flee, there is no necessary connection between the two. "Dangerous" defendants routinely appear for trial while "nondangerous" defendants fail to appear. Conceptual clarity is important for pragmatic and constitutional reasons. A determination of "somewhat dangerous" and "somewhat likely to flee" should not be combined, either formally or informally, to justify a decision that would impose pretrial detention.

The District of Columbia is the only jurisdiction to attempt to identify and detain the "dangerous" adult defendant through special legislation. A provision of the Court Reform and Criminal Procedure Act of 1970 allows the pretrial detention of an arrestee for up to 60 days following a judicial determination that release would pose a significant threat to the community (23 D.C. Code §§1321-1322).

The most salient fact about this law is its lack of use. The U.S. Attorney in charge of federal prosecutors reports that preventive detention has been sought an average of only 20 times a year. Several problems contribute to this disuse. One of the most important is the fact that an overworked prosecutor's office must initiate the request and present witnesses and evidence at a judicial hearing. This procedure is very time consuming, allows discovery of incriminating evidence, and poses a real threat to prosecution witnesses if the motion is denied. While this procedure does seem to meet the requirements of due process, it is so cumbersome and infrequently used as to be ineffective in meeting community expectations of reasonable protection. System pressures for "production" are such that, if the concept of preventive detention is to be operationalized, a more practical and efficient approach must be found which is objective in nature and satisfies due process requirements.

In the following section we propose a model as an alternative solution. The model could be applied by a prosecutor in the decision to request a preventive detention order from a judge. The model is based on a modification of the index of delinquency developed by Drs. Thorsten Sellin and Marvin Wolfgang in the early 1960s.[3] For the prosecutor's decision we are suggesting that certain categories in the index be deleted and others added. Actually, the following section is more a call for research than a fully developed procedure. For example, a weight needs to be developed for a new category added to the

index. Such scores could be developed in a variety of ways from the procedure originally used by Sellin and Wolfgang to an analysis of prosecutor and court records. In order to illustrate the use of the model, we suggest specific numbers for each category.

A MODEL FOR PREVENTIVE DETENTION

The Sellin-Wolfgang index ignores legal classifications and examines the specific elements that constitute a criminal event. It was developed by having a group of approximately 800 policemen, students, and judges score a series of events for seriousness. An analysis of these scores led to the index. Since that time the scaling operations have been replicated by other researchers with essentially the same results. At the present time, an application of this index is being used in numerous major cities under the acronym of PROMIS (Prosecutor's Management Information System). The objective of this segment of PROMIS is to screen and rate cases according to their seriousness and the gravity of the defendant's criminal history.

As originally devised, the index was intended to measure the total seriousness of any criminal event, including property stolen, damaged, or destroyed. Our purpose is much narrower: to develop a model which focuses on violent behavior and produces a cumulative "violence score" based upon known specific acts and upon known special factors. We suggest that the cumulative "violence score" be derived from an analysis of three types of events: present criminal charges, pending charges, and convictions—not arrests—within the last five years. Excluding special factors, which will be discussed shortly, the scoring system is designed to examine the specific elements of all criminal acts in which the defendant is accused or was convicted of a crime involving evidence of violent behavior. The "violence score" does not consider victimless or property offenses. The basic scoring system developed by Wolfgang and Sellin is presented in Figure 1 with modifica-

Elements Scored 1	Number 2	X	Weight 3	Total 4
I. Number of victims of bodily harm				
a. Receiving minor injuries			1	
b. Treated and discharged			4	
c. Hospitalized			7	
d. Killed			26	
II. Number of victims of forcible sex intercourse			10	
a. Number of such victims intimidated by weapon			2	
III. Intimidation (except II above)				
a. Physical or verbal only			2	
b. By weapon			3	
IV. Carrying a dangerous weapon			3	
			TOTAL RAW SCORE	

SOURCE: Adapted from Sellin and Wolfgang. Constructing an Index of Delinquency: A Manual (1963).

Figure 1: Scoring System

tions for our purpose. Two changes have been made. First, all property categories have been deleted. Second, a new category

3. THE JUDICIAL SYSTEM

has been added which corresponds to an offense category: carrying a dangerous weapon.

For illustrative purposes we have given a score of three to the element called "carrying a dangerous weapon." All other weights are the same as the original Sellin-Wolfgang index. A total raw "violence score" is obtained for each event which is either a present or pending charge or a prior relevant conviction. Although we have been speaking of behavioral rather than legal classifications, the following offenses are expected to be those most closely associated with this approach: robbery, rape (forcible sex), assault, nonnegligent homicide, carrying a dangerous or prohibited weapon, arson, kidnapping/hijacking, and terrorism.

SPECIAL ADJUSTMENTS PRIOR TO FINAL SCORING

Previous Convictions. If charges were consolidated on previous convictions, only the actual charges on which the defendant was found guilty or pleaded to should be used.[4] Points should be subtracted for each year since conviction, or if incarceration was ordered, since release from prison. In other words, time not in confinement is used to erase points. We suggest that points be subtracted at the rate of three per year for a maximum of five years or until all points are removed.

The choice of three points per year and five years is, of course, arbitrary and would need to be examined more carefully in a research design. However, the concept is an important one in terms of fairness to the person arrested. The time period of five years seems a reasonable period to examine any pattern, and it should suffice until more empirical data either disrupt the assumption of linearity or the notion of what is a reasonable and proper time for purposes of prediction. As for use of time in prison for prediction, it can offer nothing since there are no conventional opportunities for or pressures toward crime.

Victim/Defendant Relationship. Points should also be subtracted if the victim was closely related to the defendant, e.g., cohabitee, ex-spouse, common law spouse, or boyfriend/girlfriend. While the seriousness of any assault is not to be minimized, the value for prediction is low. We suggest that perhaps one-half of the points for that event could be subtracted.

Victim Precipitation. Points also should be subtracted when there is reliable evidence of provocation by the victim. Violent crimes sometimes begin as an exchange of taunts or a test of wills. What often follows has been described as a "degenerating sequence" in which both parties may feel trapped by their roles in the exchange. Such elements are difficult to assess later but are important in establishing the level of victim-precipitation or provocation. In some cases, for example, both victim and defendant may have been armed. We again suggest that perhaps one-half of the points for such events could be subtracted.

Aiding and Abetting. Except for accessory after the fact, a principal in a crime is liable for the same charges as any other principal. This would not change except for the accrual of points. The degree of involvement and level of personal participation in the violent event should be factors in the release decision. If there is reliable evidence that the defendant was

only an aider or abetter, we suggest that one-half of the points for that event should be subtracted.

HOW THE MODEL WORKS

Referring back to Figure 1, the reader will note that under the first major heading there are three scores (excluding "killed") which correspond to some type of bodily harm or injury sustained. Points for these injuries may be accrued as the result of a rape (II) or a robbery (III—Intimidation) or merely from an assault by an acquaintance or spouse. A single act which is legally classified as one crime may vary widely in scores depending upon the violence of the event. Rape, for example, can vary from 11 (II + Ia) to 19 (IIa + Ic). Of course, the victim could be killed (26).

As the prosecutor papers the case, a total "violence score" for that defendant will be calculated using the relevant behaviors and their weights and taking into account the special adjustments discussed in the preceding sections. The prosecutor will also make, as part of the charging process, an assessment of the evidence: ranging from somewhat marginal to a very strong case. This evidentiary assessment will also affect the final "violence score" as demonstrated in the matrix shown in Figure 2.

To give an example, a man is arrested for two counts of burglary, one rape, and robbery while armed. Assume that

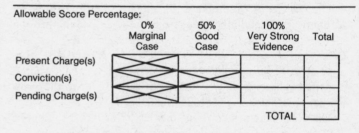

Figure 2: Postadjustment Violence Score

the person raped was treated and discharged (14) and the robbery victim was not injured (4). Also assume that the defendant was convicted of armed robbery four years ago, has served two years, and has been on parole two years. If the prosecutor thinks that the evidence is "very strong" for these present charges, the total violence score is 18 (14 + 4). Since the defendant has been on parole for two years, his old score of four (4) has been erased. The burglary charges are not relevant to the scoring system.

Although this model focuses on behavior rather than legal classification, it must be responsive to the realities of the charging process in American courts. Offense categories tend to suggest a range of scores, and the serious decision to detain someone before trial must reflect a consensus of the people as they view the gravity of crimes in familiar categories. To bridge the gap between this behavioral orientation and the more familiar legal classifications, Figure 3 is offered. These scores are based on one victim and one offense in the event. We suggest that a total "violence score" of 18 be required before the prosecutor requests a preventive detention order from the judge. Several factors should influence the location of this cutoff point.

From Figure 3 it is evident that only homicide without mitigating circumstances and the most violent type of rape can reach the score of 18 on one single offense. This is as it should

Offense	Range	Mean
Robbery	2-11	6
Rape	11-19	15
Assault	1-7	4
Non-Neg Homicide	26	N/A
Carrying a Dangerous Weapon	3	N/A

Figure 3: Score Variations for Common Violent Crimes

be. A pattern of violence must be established which has the practical effect of shifting the burden to the defendant to remonstrate that this conduct before adjudication will not continue to be socially predatory. A decision to detain prior to trial does not deny the presumption of innocence, nor is it admissible as any type of character evidence. It merely reflects a collective recognition that a pattern of behavior is so threatening to the safety of the people, that pretrial detention becomes the only interim solution.

Regardless of the cutoff point chosen on the "violence score," there are two types of interacting errors that can be made in the decision to detain or release. The value chosen, however, does impact heavily on which of these errors is considered more serious. Clearly, the operational hypothesis is that the defendant is dangerous and will continue his pattern of violence if released. For any given case, the first type of error is to reject this hypothesis and release a truly dangerous offender. The second type of error is to accept the hypothesis as true and detain someone who poses no *further* threat to the people.

Unfortunately, the first error is highly visible while the second is not. Any resulting temptation to lower the score accordingly must be resisted. While the first error is more visible, the second is more insidious. A relatively high cutoff insures that the established tradeoff weighs heavily in the defendant's favor.

This model is not intended as a prediction device to identify all dangerous offenders. Its purpose is to provide an objective and practical method of identifying only those who, by their own behavior, have demonstrated a strong propensity for violent crime. Subjective assessments and uneven applications of the law are thus avoided. This does not imply that discretion will be, should be, or even can be eliminated by this approach.

Discretion would continue to exist at two points within the system. The evidentiary assessment needed prior to final scoring must be done by the prosecutor. He is the most qualified for it and now makes equivalent judgments on a routine basis. The second point of discretion is judicial. When a high "violence score" is produced by a defendant's activities, the prosecutor would recommend detention to the judge at initial appearance. The judge may accept or reject the recommendation. A special hearing should be available to consider unusually complicated or extenuating circumstances.

Should the judicial decision be to detain pending adjudication, a speedy trial rule of either 30 or 60 days should be enforced without exception. In seeking preventive detention, the prosecutor must share with the court the burden of expediting the preparation and trial of these special cases.

SUMMARY

In this paper we have suggested that "danger to the community" should be recognized formally as an independent concern in the decision to release before trial. The present use of high money bail for cases in which danger rather than flight is clearly the issue is both discriminatory and legally improper.

Accordingly, we offer a model which could be used by prosecutors in requesting a judicial order for pretrial detention. The model is based on a modification of the Sellin-Wolfgang index which examines the specific elements that constitute a criminal event. Release decisions would be based, in part, upon a cumulative "violence score" for each defendant.

NOTES

1. Aggravated assault, auto theft, burglary, homicide, larceny, rape, and robbery.
2. The District of Columbia has an ineffective preventive detention law, which will be discussed shortly.
3. A detailed discussion of the initial effort appears in the Wolfgang and Sellin book, The Measurement of Delinquency (1964).
4. With the passage of time and routine plea negotiation, some relevant details about prior violent behavior may not be available. To whatever extent this information is lost, it is an error that favors the defendant.

REFERENCES

MANNHEIM, H. and L. WILKINS (1970) "The requirements of prediction," in N. Johnston, L. Savitz, and M. Wolfgang (eds.) The Sociology of Punishment and Correction. New York: John Wiley.

National Advisory Commission on Criminal Justice Standards and Goals (1973) Corrections. Washington, DC: Government Printing Office.

NEWMAN, D. (1975) Introduction to Criminal Justice. Philadelphia: J. P. Lippincott.

PROMIS Briefing Series (1975) Crime Analysis Worksheet. Washington, DC: Institute for Law and Social Research.

Verdicts on Judges

Increasing numbers of bar groups are polling members on the performance of the federal judiciary. But the judges haven't exactly embraced the idea. Their customary response to the polls' results remains, "Who asked you?"

Marlene Adler Marks

Marlene Adler Marks, a freelance writer based in Los Angeles, is a regular contributor to Juris Doctor.

When a lawyers' group polls its members on the performance of federal judges, a number of interesting questions arise, the most revealing being, Who asked for your opinion, anyway? The answer, of course, is no one.

Nothing in the blueprint of the federal legal system expressly calls for attorneys' reflections on how judges are fulfilling their responsibilities. As R. Clark Wadlow of the American Bar Association's Young Lawyers Section puts it, "Federal judges, who are appointed for life, on good behavior, are particularly isolated from constructive criticism." But in the aftermath of the last decade's political reform movements, no one, and no institution, is above close scrutiny. Poll-taking is a way for attorneys to indicate publicly where they feel changes must be made, as well as to vent their frustrations at the unapproachable judiciary.

So whether judges like it or not, attorneys who practice in federal courts are beginning to voice their opinions in a growing number of surveys around the country. The Washington state bar, the Barristers of the Beverly Hills bar, and bar associations in Atlanta, Cleveland, San Francisco, and Dallas are among the numerous groups that have queried local attorneys since the Chicago Council of Lawyers survey—the big daddy of these polls—was done in 1971.

Though the styles and questions of the surveys vary, judges usually emerge with their pride intact and their reputations well applauded; perhaps one judge in each jurisdiction is singled out for inadequate skills or decorum. However, the favorable response does not mean that the surveys are noncontroversial or even generally accepted.

Polls are regarded with great foreboding. Although judges deny feeling personally threatened, a few have used their considerable influence with the bar to try to stop a poll, on the grounds that polling tampers with the independence of the federal judiciary. The new surveys are threatening, perhaps, because their goals are relatively unspecific. Pre-election polls and plebiscites on state judges, which have been used for quite a while by some bar associations, help newspapers to make their endorsements and the public to know where to place a vote. Federal judge performance polls, on the other hand, try to expose and improve an area of government heretofore shrouded in mystery. No wonder judges see the polls as aimed purely at their public humiliation.

Many attorney-pollsters themselves are ambivalent about how to use a poll. The Washington bar, for example, does not make its survey results public; rather, it consults individually with each judge and tells him where it thinks he is lacking.

Other attorney groups have steered clear of polling altogether in favor of more cautious mechanisms. The New York City bar association has for several years been rejecting calls for a poll, but it does keep files of anonymous complaints from its members and the public for use if a judge is seeking elevation. "We like to keep a good relationship with the judiciary," explains Ronald Monroe, the New York City bar association's assistant director. "We feel that if the judges think we are busily trying to get information on them—like the CIA —they won't like us. Not that it matters if they don't like us, but it [poll-taking] seems to be inviting a lot of comment from those who lost cases. It's counterproductive."

The San Diego bar association, which recently decided against a membership poll, goes a different route. "We want to maintain anonymity," says bar member J. Michael Reed. The group opted for a committee to receive and investigate complaints, which will then be discussed, not with a judge himself, but with a judge's close friend.

In light of the fear and awe with which attorneys' groups apparently hold the federal judiciary, the decision to run a poll must be seen as a risky act. To get an idea of the pressures and dynamics bearing on such a decision, *Juris Doctor* took a longer look at a survey recently conducted by the Barristers of the Beverly Hills Bar Association. The Barristers' project, one of the most protracted endeavors ever undertaken by the association, won them an American Bar Association Achievement Award.

The Barristers, all under age 36, are hardly the type of young lawyers who will go out of their way to create a political ruckus. They work for conservative, mostly corporate firms and consider themselves innovative rather than radical. The group had nothing more specific in mind than "improving the judicial process," says former Barristers President Robert Frandzell. "We wanted the judges to know that if they were doing something great, they should continue, but if they were doing something poor, they might change."

In designing their survey, the Barristers worked with Ph.D. candidates in statistics at Claremont College in Pomona, California. The attorneys were cautioned against rating judges as "good," "bad," or "indifferent" on various judicial questions. Such ratings, according to Joseph Zadny, project director and professor of statistics at Claremont, "are virtually uninterpretable, clearly unverifiable, and therefore worse than useless in view of the expense of conducting a survey [more than $2,000]."

So the format called on the lawyers to choose among five different responses to each of 29 statements. For example, the item "The judge's procedural rulings are prompt and proper" offered the choices "strongly agree," "moderately agree," "undecided," "moderately disagree," and "strongly disagree." Every item also gave respondents the opportunity to admit having no basis for rating.

The statements all had a positive tone; for example, "The judge does not usurp the role of counsel in questioning witnesses" was used instead of the accusatory "The judge usurps. . . ." One Barrister remarked after the results were out, "We certainly did everything in our power to make them look good."

Even though it took a year—and several different versions—to insure the methodological integrity of the poll, some Barristers still withheld their approval. A number worried that the rights of their clients might be affected by judicial backlash against members of the association. Others saw no point in running the poll—what good would it do? Still others insisted that the mammoth Los Angeles County bar, representing 70 percent of Los Angeles-area attorneys, was the proper body to conduct or at least pay for it.

The county bar declined to assist the group for philosophical reasons, including the propriety of offering the results to the press. "Does making it public do any good?" wondered one Los Angeles bar official. And some bar members questioned how one might diplomatically criticize a federal judge. "There's a problem," notes the L.A. bar official, "in saying to a judge, 'Hey, we get a lot of complaints about you—you better clean up your act.'"

After thrashing these questions around in often heated debate, the Barristers' board of governors finally gave the poll a green light. It had taken the poll's proponents two years to get the unanimous vote they needed. With the decision made, the Barristers held several meetings with the judges, who sit in California's Central District, in an effort to smooth the inevitably ruffled feathers.

The judges were highly critical: Why, they wanted to know, weren't Superior Court judges to be evaluated, too? (Answer: Not enough money in the till.) Who should be questioned? How many attorneys? And how would the pollsters insure that the respondents had federal court experience? One judge suggested the only valid poll would be limited to names drawn from the federal dockets, apparently knowing the difficulty such a searching procedure would pose. The Barristers agreed, searched the dockets, and were later criticized for using only the top name on the dockets on the grounds that the lead firm name rarely appeared in court.

So despite the meetings, it was clear from the beginning that the judges were unhappy about the poll and would be difficult to satisfy. In fact, three sent letters to members of the senior bar of Beverly Hills urging that the project be halted.

"I see nothing to be gained by holding us up individually to public ridicule, which would be the inevitable result of the project if carried out as planned," wrote Judge Jesse Curtis.

Judge Andrew Hauk wrote, "However cleverly, though obviously jejunely, conceived, it calls for a childish 'numbers game' of hearsay opinions by anonymous pollsters who in the vast majority have not practiced in any of our courts, cannot judge the judges upon anything other than what they have heard from other faceless anonymities, a good many of whom may well be disgruntled if experienced, and uninformed themselves if not experienced."

And Judge Charles H. Carr, now deceased but once known for his arrogant dressing down of attorneys in open court,

tried to impress upon the senior bar that the poll would ultimately embarrass everyone involved with it. "I think that several of our judges are gravely concerned that if this program is carried out, serious problems will develop," Judge Carr wrote. "A published report may be construed as an attack on a particular judge, or on the court as a whole, without a stated ground or basis for the attack. In other words, it would be merely the opinion of anonymous persons, yet the report would carry the sanction of the Beverly Hills Bar Association."

Other judges on the 17-member court had their private reservations but were embarrassed by the actions of their more outspoken colleagues. "I knew there was nothing any letter could do to stop that poll if they wanted to do it," says Judge Manuel Real.

Perhaps in response to such judicial concern and a spate of pre-election polls, the California state bar and the Conference of California Judges issued a joint statement urging restraint in conducting judicial evaluation polls, questioning whether such polls were necessary, and insisting that the proper place for the investigation of errant judges was within the Judicial Qualifications Commission (which has jurisdiction only over state judges).

Such pressure had its effect on some of the young attorneys. "The letters scared the life out of a lot of people," one Barrister recalls. "A lot of others said, 'Piss on them—we'll do our own thing.' The letters made people sit back and consider what we were doing."

The questionnaire—eight green pages consisting of 35 questions printed in minuscule type—was eventually sent to 2,710 attorneys whose names had appeared on federal civil and criminal actions during the preceding five years. With 18 district judges to evaluate, it took almost an hour to complete. It also left a page for comments (which were not published).

Evidently many attorneys could not spare the time. When results were released last fall, the chief surprise was that, for all the private complaints about the federal bench, only 268 usable responses, or 10 percent, were returned. The respondents were mostly civil practitioners who claim to have appeared ten or more times in federal court during the 12 months prior to the survey.

The findings tend to reflect generally accepted wisdom; most of the judges were evaluated quite favorably, one received a noticeably poor appraisal on every question, several were criticized for bad tempers.

Despite the basically sanguine results, the poll caused quite a stir in the marble halls of the downtown Los Angeles court. Judge A. Andrew Hauk, the one who re-

ceived those low scores, publicly called the poll "a cheap shot" based on "shoddy, unscientific methodology." He implied that the entire affair was a personal vendetta against him by a disgruntled Barrister. "It really had no function except to make bad things worse," said another federal judge.

Says one federal court observer, "There's been a great deal of discussion here, and most of it's been critical." Despite his feeling that the results were quite accurate, this observer doubts the poll will have a salutary effect. "Judges don't want to be in a position to cave in to a survey."

The irritation of the judges has done nothing to cool the Barristers' enthusiasm for their project. They say the poll proves that attorneys are capable of expressing objective opinion outside the emotional context of whether they won or lost a case before a judge.

"People knew what they were responding to," says Tony Mohr, a member of the survey committee. "They thought about the questions. The poll shows a real trend in how the judiciary really is."

The Beverly Hills Barrister poll is "among the best I've seen," says J. Michael Reed of San Diego, a member of the California bar committee charged with setting up statewide guidelines on such surveys.

Nevertheless, there are questions, all of which originate with how one feels about such polls. The methodological problems are tricky enough to support any argument that polls prove nothing and are therefore a waste of time. Once you begin to look closely at the types of questions asked and the group that answered, the fabric begins to shred.

In the Barristers' poll, for example, some questions got no more than a 30 or 40 percent response. And then, since only about 59 attorneys, or 22 percent, practiced criminal law, the statistics on questions about sentencing and other criminal matters are difficult to regard as totally credible; with a sample that small, a few votes changed either positively or negatively have a major statistical effect.

The poll is a "travesty," says Richard Sherman, a local criminal attorney. "There's no civil attorney living and breathing who has appeared six times a year in federal court, and few criminal attorneys who do either. Private attorneys just don't go into federal court that often. So you see, the poll was answered by idiots, who based their response on a judge's reputation. They say they've been in court when they haven't."

Critics say the poll asks questions no attorney could answer, such as "The judge makes effective use of court time" or "The judge displays preparation for the case at hand." They laugh at the high rating given Judge Harry C. Westover, who had not served in open court for the past eight years.

"Here, I'll pick a question that is non-controversial to show you how uninformed the answers are," says Judge Manuel Real, who received his share of negative responses. "The judge sanctions and supports negotiated pleas. Thirty-six percent strongly or moderately agreed with that statement [216 did not answer]. Well, I told everyone interested I don't negotiate pleas. I've never, never taken a negotiated plea, so it just shows you the types of answers given."

Judge Real's major complaint about the poll is that only those who wanted to answer did so; therefore the answers reflect the bias of those with vested interests. "I don't object to the poll in principle," he says. "But I don't think this is adequate. The people who answered either like me or dislike me, there was no neutrality, and that's not the way a statistician does a survey. There's screening and random selection—not just people who want to answer it."

The Barristers acknowledge each of these criticisms. They nevertheless believe the poll results to be "worthwhile in their own right, but not the final barometer of opinion of local attorneys with respect to the Central District of California," according to a Barristers position paper.

The 10 percent response is indeed small for a mail survey, since 50 percent is a normal standard of reliability, the Barristers say. And they concede there may be bias in the respondents' very decision to answer the poll. However, the Barristers contend, such problems have been factors in bar polls from their beginning, and statisticians have still found the results reliable. Precedent was set when the 1971 Chicago Council of Lawyers poll, which brought in 529 responses from a mailing to

3,150 lawyers, was validated by the Political Research Laboratory at the University of Wisconsin.

"The 'representativeness' of the 529 respondents as a sample of the universe of lawyers practicing before the Chicago Federal Court is not important," the research laboratory concluded. ". . . The self-selection by practicing lawyers who accepted an opportunity to evaluate one or more judges guaranteed a sample of lawyers particularly concerned with the reputation of the court. The results indicate that the respondents were both fair and accurate in their perceptions of the Chicago judges."

Almost a direct response to the infamous trial of the Chicago Seven anti-war activists in the courtroom of Judge Julius Hoffman, the Chicago Council survey is a reminder of the political climate in which lawyers began speaking out on controversial issues.

Even by 1971, when that first survey was finally taken, polarization still marked national and local politics. The rank-and-file bar (the rival Chicago Bar Association) looked upon the council as "radicals" and therefore tried to dismiss the results. When the second poll was distributed in 1976, however, times had indeed changed. The major Chicago firms responded to a request for names of lawyers who practice in federal court, and 5,400 questionnaires were sent out.

Some things, however, had not changed. The bar still had a low opinion of Judge Hoffman. Of more than 400 responses, 92.9 percent thought Hoffman unworthy of advancement; only 21.6 percent thought him worthy of retaining. As Hoffman's performance had been similarly disparaged five years prior, these results bring up the question of what a poll can actually accomplish.

"A judge who does not want to listen will not do so no matter what lawyers say to him," one federal judge remarked.

The Chicago Council, however, like the Beverly Hills Barristers, is proud of its efforts and believes it has been influential in raising the level of judicial performance. A spokesperson for the council says that Senator Charles Percy now takes an interest in the poll when choosing judges for elevation to the appellate courts, and seems quite proud that his appointees to the trial bench are well regarded by the council's survey.

Attorneys seeking a "thank you" or some other way to judge the effectiveness of their travails may find one a long time coming. Dorothy Maddi, a social scientist with the ABA Foundation, says there is no clear way to gauge a poll's force. "There are some claims that a judge left office as a result of a negative poll," she says, "but these claims are difficult to substantiate. Perhaps he was going to retire anyway. But who knows? It may give the final bit of pressure to force someone out."

The early retirement of an unpopular judge, of course, is not the only measure of a poll's impact. Other effects may be less obvious; in Beverly Hills, for example, it was surprising to see formerly callous attorneys come to the public defense of a judge criticized in the poll. Who knows if that negative vote didn't make the local legal community reevaluate just what it expects of a judge?

It seems clear that the poll-taking trend is not geared to making radical changes in the federal judiciary, but has as its primary goal the unleashing of energy long trapped in frustration. However imperfect, the polls give attorneys a way to speak out. Sometimes those voices are unclear, but their intent is honorable.

Judging the Judges

An outsize job, getting bigger

By trappings and tradition, judges are a secular priesthood, oracles of the law, the embodiment of justice. Dressed in black robes, heralded into court by bailiffs crying "Hear ye! Hear ye! All rise!" and addressed as "Your Honor," judges are imposing, even intimidating. They are supposed to be: they have great power over people's lives, and increasingly, they use it.

But who are the judges? Former lawyers, former politicians. Most commonly, lawyers who knew politicians. Some rise above their own human limitations, but more do not. Mostly, they are ordinary men and women, coping fitfully with the failings of others, the endless procession of broken promises and brutal acts that are the daily business of the courts.

The system of justice is a huge and complex machine. Delicately balanced by counterweights, equipped with elaborate filters and safety valves, it is designed to sort the guilty from the innocent, restore rights, redress wrongs. In short, to do justice.

It is a wondrous invention when it works, but frequently it does not. Consider:

▶ Left a quadriplegic by a truck accident that was not his fault, Thomas Curtis, 57, waited five years before his personal injury suit went to trial in Modesto, Calif. A jury awarded him more than $2 million last January, but a judge reduced the damages to $350,000, and the case will probably be another three years on appeal before Curtis sees any money. Meanwhile, Curtis has lost his $25,000-a-year income and his house; his wife has divorced him and emotional problems have sent him to a psychiatrist.

▶ In Ohio last winter, Judge Neil W. Whitfield sentenced Robert W. Attwood, 20, who had stolen $10 worth of beer from a neighbor's garage, to four to 25 years in jail. On the same day, the same judge sentenced Mary Murray, a motor vehicles official, to five years probation for embezzling $8,000 in public funds.

▶ Last month in New York, the conviction of Eric Michael, 24, for robbery, burglary, rape and sodomy was overturned because he had been tried twice for the same crime. The first trial had been terminated by Criminal Judge Arnold G. Fraiman. Why? Because continuing the trial would have interfered with the vacation plans of the judge and some jurors. Judge Fraiman, who had once before ended a trial rather than forgo a holiday, this time offered to postpone his plans, but he did not order the jury to do so; instead, he declared a mistrial.

A Yankelovich, Skelly and White poll of the general public, judges, lawyers and community leaders last year ranked public confidence in state and local courts below many other major American institutions, including the medical profession, police, business and public schools. Too much law, too many lawsuits and too many lawyers have all combined to overwork the judicial machinery. But the final responsibility for the courts rests with the people who run them: the 28,000 state and local judges, 1,083 federal administrative law judges who hear disputed claims brought to the regulatory agencies, and nearly 700 federal judges charged with upholding the law. Too often it is a responsibility that judges fail to live up to.

The litigation explosion in the U.S. has not just created choked courts and endless delay. It also means more power for judges. Tocqueville's observation, made more than a century ago, that there is "hardly a political question which does not sooner or later turn into a judicial one" has never been truer. This is so not only in the U.S. Supreme Court, which is expected to be the final arbiter of the law, but in courts all over the country. By reading their own views into broadly worded statutes and vaguely defined constitutional rights, judges have assumed—some say usurped—unaccustomed roles. Increasingly, judges, state and federal, can be found ordering government boards and agencies to obey the law. When the boards balk, as they often do, judges end up running school boards, welfare agencies, mental hospitals and prisons. Just last month, for instance, a Boston judge placed 67 public housing projects into receivership under court control because they had been mismanaged by the Boston housing authority. Such decisions often require judges to rule on specific questions like garbage removal from tenements, proper bus routes for schoolchildren and minimum hot water temperatures for prison inmates.

Judges are quick to assert that they are simply enforcing the laws and the Constitution. "Judges, unlike Presidents, Congressmen and lawyers, cannot generate their own business," says Federal Judge Prentice Marshall, who halted discriminatory hiring and promotion practices in the Chicago police department despite Mayor Richard Daley's vow to fight the decision. Whether by default or design, the judiciary increasingly has the last word on important social questions.

Within their courtrooms, judges are virtual autocrats. Many will not even talk to the press; thanks to last month's Supreme Court decision in *Gannett* vs. *DePasquale,* they are now closing off their courtrooms. Already, at least 39 judges have banned press or public or both from pretrial hearings or trials.*

Lawyers, out of necessity, bow before the bench. "The job corrupts people," says Jack Frankel, executive officer of the California Commission on Judicial Performance. "The judge says, 'I'm going on vacation.' Everyone says, 'Fine, Judge.' The judge says, 'I'm coming in late.' Again, it's 'Fine, Judge.' Pretty soon it changes them."

Stories of judicial arrogance are commonplace. When a Japanese-American lawyer requested additional time for a trial, a federal judge responded: "How much time did you give us at Pearl Harbor?" Former Los Angeles Municipal Court Judge Noel Cannon, who painted her chambers pink, kept a pet Chihuahua by her side and was called the "Dragon Lady," once threatened to give a traffic officer "a vasectomy with a .38." While hearing a voting rights case brought by blacks in Al-

*In a rare interview, Supreme Court Justice Warren Burger told TIME last week: "The Gannett opinion was misunderstood. The case wasn't about a trial, only about a pretrial hearing." Burger blamed the press for misleading lower court judges on the scope of the high court's decision. Presumably local judges have not bothered to read the opinion.

abama in the '60s, Federal Judge William Harold Cox exclaimed, "Who is telling these people that they can get in there and push people around, acting like a bunch of chimpanzees?"

The bench is obviously the worst possible place to encounter that kind of prejudice. Nothing is so damaging to the stature of the judiciary as the common perception that punishment depends less on what a criminal did than on the biases or whims of the judge.

Some sentences should vary, of course, according to the character and prior record of the defendant. The fact that shoplifters usually go to jail if they get caught in Charlotte, N.C., whereas they get probation in Albuquerque, may just reflect different local mores. As New York Criminal Court Judge Harold Rothwax says, "Communities have a right to view crime differently." Mandatory sentences set by the legislature, which several states use for at least some crimes, can be more heavyhanded than evenhanded. Such laws cannot distinguish, for instance, between someone who steals to feed his family and someone who steals for excitement or easy money. But if discretion

"Vindicating" Rights in California

Federal Judge Irving Hill likes to recall that his uncle, a Ukrainian Jewish immigrant to the U.S., went to a railroad station in New York City, plunked down his savings and asked for a ticket west, as far as his money would take him. That turned out to be Lincoln, Neb. Hill's father, arriving from the Ukraine "with less than a buck in his pocket," followed, and it was in Lincoln that Hill was born and raised.

"Inbred in me is a concern for rights of the minority, no matter how unpopular," says Hill, 64. "Concern for religious and political freedom, human rights, just the right to practice a profession and get an education were things that were denied to my forebears." His roots have clearly helped to shape his judicial philosophy: "Whenever you can vindicate the individual against the government, consistent with your judicial obligation, you do so."

As the chief judge of a federal district court whose jurisdiction includes Los Angeles and 11 million people, Hill could hardly be in a better position to "vindicate" (a favorite word) individual rights. The great expansion of the "due process" and "equal protection" guarantees under the 14th Amendment over the past two decades has taken place largely in the federal courts, and it is to the federal district courts that people come first to assert their constitutional rights. Hill has struck down a California law barring aliens from certain public jobs, and is especially proud of his decision holding that to deny a black a job purely because of his

arrest record is discriminatory. His view that Chinese students have a right to a bilingual education, first expressed in a dissenting opinion, was later adopted by the Supreme Court. In an opinion in an obscenity case, he once wrote: "The censor and the illegal police raiding party are even less welcome in this country than the peddler of execrable sex materials, and with good cause."

Hill is mindful, however, of the limits to what he can do. When there is a "clear and unequivocal and recent decision" by a higher court, a judge is bound to follow it and not try to carve out new law. Hill also believes deeply in the concept of the judiciary that he learned "at the feet of Felix Frankfurter" when the late Supreme Court Justice was a teacher and Hill a student at Harvard Law School in the late '30s. Says Hill: "Frankfurter had a very strong and very well-thought-out concept of judicial restraint that would have kept the courts out of many political matters and out of the daily supervision of institutions." Hill is wary of judges who too willingly become custodians of prisons or school systems. He fears that they "dilute the moral force" of the bench, and he adds, "There are other judicial tasks, perhaps of equal importance, that are shunted aside."

Hill would have his colleagues pay more heed to administering their courts efficiently. "You have to have judges who take pride, not only in the quality of their work, but in their ability to move a reasonable number of cases." For Hill, that means reining in lawyers, who, he

says, "are most resourceful at thinking of superficially persuasive reasons" for creating delays. Hill believes in strict deadlines and backing them up with stiff sanctions. In his court lawyers who make too many frivolous motions must reimburse the other side—out of their own pockets, not the clients'—for the expense of answering them. If the abuses persist, he can throw out the lawyer's case.

Becoming a federal judge in 1965, says Hill, was "the achievement of my highest ambition." With his $54,500-a-year salary, Hill is not nearly as wealthy as he would have been if he had remained a lawyer, but he still lives comfortably with his wife in Los Angeles. An insatiable sports fan, he finds time to use the season tickets he holds to the games of half a dozen Southern California teams. Every night, he walks 1.2 miles with Los Angeles *Herald-Examiner* Sports Writer Mel Durslag. "Half the walk we talk about sports, and the other half we talk about the court," says Durslag. Hill is an unpretentious but firm man, with few illusions about judges: "We're human, the products of our own environments. Today, of course, every person or group with some cause for unhappiness or dissatisfaction with any governmental body, or even his neighbors, expects the judiciary to vindicate his rights and give him a remedy. In that sense we can't possibly meet everybody's expectations. But by and large," says Hill, "we sure try, and we try in good faith."

is something judges need to make the punishment fit the crime or the criminal, it is also something they too often abuse.

At the core of public trust is the belief that judges are impartial. New York Lawyer Simon Rifkind, a former judge, notes: "Impartiality is an acquired taste, like olives. You have to be habituated to it." Some judges never lose the attitudes they brought to the bench; lawyers complain that judges who were prosecutors favor the state, and judges who were defense lawyers favor the defendant.

Faith in the judiciary may be faltering, but that has not stopped people from going to the court in droves. Civil suits filed in federal courts, which outnumber criminal cases 4 to 1, increased from 87,321 to 138,770 between 1960 and 1978. Over 16,000 cases have been pending for more than three years in federal district courts, double the backlog ten years ago. "If court backlogs grow at their present rate, our children may not be able to bring a lawsuit to a conclusion within their lifetime," predicts Harvard Law School Professor Laurence Tribe. "Legal claims might then be willed on, generation to generation, like hillbilly feuds; and the burdens of pressing them would be contracted like a hereditary disease."

Laws that spew from legislatures at the rate of over 100,000 a year inevitably mean more lawsuits. Too many lawyers use their skills to drag out cases. The object may be to wear down a less well financed opponent, or put off an unfavorable judgment. Sometimes it is simply a matter of greed, of contriving any excuse to keep fees rolling in. Favorite devices include making endless pretrial motions on one or another point of procedure, obtaining postponements (continuances) from the court, requesting huge amounts of information from the other side in the pretrial discovery process, or just burying the case in paper work.

Judges share the blame for the courts' delay. In Pittsburgh, criminal judges have almost four times the caseload of those in The Bronx, but dispose of cases five times as fast. Why the difference? Because some judges take an active role in pushing a case along from the moment it is filed. They enforce strict deadlines on filing motions and papers and limit pretrial discovery; in short they stop lawyers from delaying. In other courts, judges sit back and let lawyers set the pace by handing out postponements freely.

"Moving the Business" in Philly

In Philadelphia, birthplace of American democracy, local judges are popularly elected. More accurately, they are chosen by the political party in power and then automatically voted in by apathetic voters. They are selected, says District Attorney Edward G. Rendell, not for integrity, legal ability or judicial temperament. "Instead," says Rendell, "these questions are asked: What has the lawyer done for the political party nominating him? What has he contributed to the party in time and money?" The result, say Philadelphia's lawyers, is "a sad bench."

Criminal Judge Thomas A. White was picked to fill a vacancy in 1977. Why? "I'm Irish," he says. "Of course, I'm qualified," he hastily adds, but he matter-of-factly explains that the Democratic Party needed an Irish judge to "balance the ethnic makeup" of their judicial slate. One of 16 children of an I.R.A. member who fled Ireland for the U.S. in 1928, White, who has six children of his own, is president of the Irish Society of Philadelphia, an American Legionnaire and a booster of a boys' club. He is also, he says, a "lifelong Democrat" who managed to be elected to the state legislature in the Eisenhower landslide. Redistricted out of his seat in 1954, he decided to go to law school and become a criminal defense lawyer. All the while, he stayed active in Democratic ward politics, and his loyalty was rewarded when he was

backed for a judgeship by Congressman Raymond F. Lederer, whom White describes as "a close personal friend."

White is a "waivers judge," which means that he tries defendants who have waived their right to a jury. In Philadelphia, defendants usually do not plea bargain—that is, plead guilty in return for leniency. Instead, they are apt to plead not guilty but waive their right to a jury trial because they know waivers judges will go easy on them. Too easy, complain Philadelphia prosecutors. In White's court, defendants convicted of shootings and stabbings get off on probation; attempted rape of a girl of 16 by three men with criminal records got the three only six to 23 months in jail.

Leniency does have one dubious advantage for an overloaded court system. It makes for speed. Trials without jury are brief; the more defendants who opt for them—and most do—the faster the Philadelphia courts can dispose of their huge case loads. Judge White likes to "move the business" right along; he hears three or four cases a day, disposes of 15 a week. The day begins at 9:30 or 10, when the judge, clad in his black robe, enters his small, drab courtroom through its single door. White says he deplores the lack of a private entryway to his chambers; it means he has to come in the same way as spectators, lawyers, witnesses, defendants, everybody. Only a few feet of space separates the lawyers from the bench. That is not enough for his-

trionics, but then there is no jury to sway. There is only Judge White, and he is more interested in a rapid recitation of the facts than impassioned pleas or oratory.

The only emotion on a busy summer day comes from a black teenage defendant and his mother. Though White prefers parole to jail for first offenders in order to give them a second chance, he is strict about parole violations. In this case, the teen-ager, convicted of robbery, has failed to report to his probation officer for a month. White revokes his probation and sentences him to jail for one to 23 months. Both mother and son burst into tears. "Judge, that's unfair, a child like him," cries the mother. The judge shuffles papers as the young man is led off, and the crying subsides. Then he calls the next case.

White is vexed only by interruptions in his schedule. He is clearly irritated one morning when a defense lawyer brings along eight witnesses to testify in a purse-snatching case. The judge complains that it will take him all day to try the case. "All day" turns out to be five hours. After hearing the witnesses, White says he cannot be sure whether the defendant is guilty or innocent, so he has to find him not guilty, using the "beyond a reasonable doubt" standard. The prosecutor says he has witnesses ready for another trial, but White curtly rebuffs him. It is 2:30 in the afternoon. The judge adjourns court.

3. THE JUDICIAL SYSTEM

Some judges simply cannot make up their minds. One California judge underwent psychoanalysis to get at the root of his inability to pass judgment. But a more fundamental problem is the way judges, particularly older ones, perceive their role. By training and tradition they are judges, not administrators or managers. That helps to explain why modern technology and management techniques have been almost totally ignored by the courts. "In a supermarket age we are like a merchant trying to operate a cracker barrel corner grocery store with the methods and equipment of 1900," said Burger in 1970. He spoke from experience. When he came on the court in 1969, he asked to have some papers duplicated. The clerk had to explain to him that the Supreme Court Justices had no copying machine. Burger and other bench and bar leaders have pushed with some success for more efficient administration. "There was a day back when a judge said, 'I'll start my court at 9 or 10 or 11 o'clock or whenever I want,'" Burger told TIME. "But that attitude won't work today." Still, judges are jealous of their fiefs and do not like to be told to change their ways, even by higher judges.

This is especially true in state and local courts, where most of American justice is meted out. "In some ways we now function just as we did in the days of Charles Dickens," says Judge James Lynch, chief justice of the Massachusetts Superior Court. The court hours—generally 10 to 4—have not changed since the 18th century when lawyers and judges were farmers and had to tend to their cows, says Boston Lawyer and Novelist (*Friends of Eddie Coyle*) George V. Higgins. "We do business in total and willful disregard for the telephone, the automobile and the computer. On opening day of a district court session, you can find 300 lawyers waiting around to get their cases scheduled, with their meters running." The trial date the judge wants often will not suit one or the other lawyer; when they finally agree, a witness will go out of town or fail to show up and trial will be further delayed. It is a costly cycle of inconvenience, frustration and ineptitude repeated in courts the country round.

There are exceptions. The courtroom of Erie County, Ohio, Judge James L. McCrystal is one. It is equipped with a videotape machine and television monitors. McCrystal does not need to bring all the lawyers, parties and witnesses into court at the same time for a trial. Witnesses can be questioned by lawyers

"Chewing on It" in Nebraska

In the Old West, judges rode the circuit on horseback with two indispensable tools of justice in their saddlebags: a copy of *Blackstone's Commentaries* and a flask of whisky. Today Judge Robert Moran, 52, travels the five counties of Nebraska's 16th judicial district in a battered 1972 Plymouth with 140,000 miles on it (his 1960 model died at 240,000). His tools are two loose-leaf binders with summaries of his case docket and a black bag stuffed with lawyer's briefs. His territory is his state's western panhandle. It is sparse ranch and farm country, though railroads hauling low-sulfur coal have made the local junction, Alliance (pop. 10,000), a boom town. The mean Midwest weather that Judge Moran encounters has not changed since Lawyer Abraham Lincoln rode Illinois' Eight Circuit. Carl Sandburg described it: "Mean was the journey in the mud of spring thaws, in the blowing sleet or snow and icy winds of winter."

The law has changed a great deal, and Moran's district court is the court of original jurisdiction for most serious criminal and civil cases. Just keeping abreast of the law means that Moran constantly reads as his driver, court reporter and general assistant, Mike Benitez, 22, ferries him from county to county, some 1,700 miles a month. In only a few days, in three different courts, Moran will change some child visitation rights, grant half a dozen divorces, hear pretrial motions on a first-degree murder charge, listen to motions on a complex home-construction case, sentence a drunken driver, a housebreaker and a cocaine peddler (90 days' probation). The legal issues and questions he constantly confronts hop from civil to criminal to constitutional.

When some American Indian activists occupied a building at Fort Robinson and threatened to burn it down, Moran sentenced them to five days in the county jail. Some whites denounced him for being a "bit soft on our Indian brethren." But in Moran's view, "shorn of emotionalism, what happened is nothing more than a slightly aggravated case of trespass." In another case he heard the murder trial of two white youths for beating an Indian who later died of brain damage. When Moran sentenced the boys—six years for the leader, two years for the other—some Indians were furious and tore down the American flag outside the courthouse. The judge's reasoning: the Indian's death was a "senseless act of hooliganism which was not intended to be criminal."

Though Moran knows all the lawyers who come before him, he keeps his distance. His regular golf game with an Alliance lawyer ended when he had to rule on a close case in his friend's favor. Moran, who has been on the bench for twelve years, is known for running a strict court; with 450 cases a year, he has to. "The way to irritate Moran," says the judge about himself, "is to ask for continuances." He is a one-man show: he does all his own legal research and wrestles with his hard decisions alone. "I can't bounce things off other people to help me," he says. "A judge lives a fairly lonely life." A practicing Roman Catholic, he has eight children. Child custody cases leave him drained. "We are asked to play God in these cases, and you can't be God. The touchstone is 'the best interests of the child.' Isn't that a lovely phrase? What does it mean?" Criminal sentencing sometimes sends him walking around town, "chewing on it like a dog with a bone. You drop it and pick it up again and chew on it."

Yet Moran clearly relishes his job. "I'm miserably happy with it," he says. As he drives around his district, he loves to tell of applying the law to life in the panhandle. He recalls the case of a thief who stole some unbranded cattle, put his brand on them and rustled them off to North Dakota. The owner pursued and identified his own cattle. But how, Moran asked, could he identify them? "Well," the man replied, "I just went up there and called out their names and they came right to me." Moran smiles broadly retelling the story. "You know, I went home that night and looked up the case law on identifying animals by their names, and there it all was."

and have their testimony video-taped at their convenience. One local law firm has fixed up a large mobile van with video-tape recorders so the court can come to the witness, rather than the witness to court. Judge McCrystal edits the film in his chambers or sometimes at home and shows it to a jury at trial. Result: McCrystal tries about three times as many civil jury cases as the average Ohio judge. He has been doing it this way for more than seven years, and he has never been overturned on appeal because of his use of technology. Yet the idea still has not caught on with other judges. Why? "Judges are the roadblock," says McCrystal. "They just say, 'I don't want anything new.' But only they can make this thing work."

Perhaps. But there are a number of other ways to better use judicial resources and help judges with their heavy caseloads. Among the most important:

▶ More judges. This is an obvious step. The federal judiciary clearly needed more judges to cope with its overwhelming load, and last fall it got them from Congress: 152 new judgeships, a 30% increase, the largest ever.

▶ Less law. Complex law makes for complex litigation. The hopelessly vague antitrust laws, for instance, have been a chronic problem for troubled courts since 1890 and produced a tangle of conflicting interpretations. The antitrust monster of *U.S.* vs. *IBM* is now ten years old and nowhere near resolution. Clarifying or simplifying labyrinthine laws would save millions of dollars in legal costs as well as free judges to work on other matters. Like regulatory schemes that do more harm than good by stifling competition, some laws might even be eliminated altogether.

▶ Getting cases out of court that should not be there to begin with. Some argue that no-fault auto insurance can help clear the civil courts by eliminating many lengthy personal injury suits. Decriminalizing so-called victimless crimes, such as vagrancy, drunkenness, gambling and marijuana possession —often randomly enforced—would ease the strain on criminal courts. Perhaps the most promising alternative is to arbitrate or mediate disputes rather than take them straight to court. Neighborhood justice centers set up by the justice department in Atlanta, Kansas City and Los Angeles have worked well, informally settling disputes like neighborhood squabbles and consumer complaints.

▶ Court reorganization. Fragmented or overlapping jurisdictions keep some judges underworked, others overworked, and still others doing the same work all over again. Seventeen states have adopted measures to streamline their court systems since 1970; reform came to Massachusetts in July, when its reorganization plan went into effect. No longer will criminal cases be tried *de novo*—from scratch—on appeal, and it will be easier to move judges around from court to court to even up work loads. Some courts have also improved efficiency by hiring professional administrators to set schedules and assign cases.

▶ Eliminate juries in civil trials that are too long and too complicated for laymen. At the Conference of State Chief Justices last week, Chief Justice Burger strongly urged judges to consider this proposal, pointing out that it can take "not hours, but days" for the judge to explain the legal issues to jurors, who then cannot always be expected to understand or remember what the judge said. Burger noted that Britain, which has less delay in its courts than the U.S., has successfully abolished juries in most civil cases.

▶ Speedy trial laws. Delay in the criminal courts means that many defendants languish in jail, whether or not they are guilty. Forty-one states have laws on their books requiring that defendants go to trial within a specified period. However, these laws do not always work: they are vague and ambiguous, and judges are lax in enforcing them. When the laws do work, there is a need for more judges to handle the load and civil cases are backed up. Lawyers complain that they do not have time to prepare their cases, and that means that some prosecutions simply get dropped. Because of such arguments, the Federal Speedy Trial Act, expected to go into effect last month, has been postponed by Congress for one year.

▶ Plea bargaining. This is the most common solution to delay in the criminal courts. It is frequently denounced. In theory, criminal courts determine guilt or innocence only by the most thoroughgoing "due process." In reality, justice is usually done by way of a deal: a guilty plea in return for a lighter sentence or reduced charges. The accused's "day in court" lasts only a minute or two. In one such case in California, a defendant pronounced guilty of assault with a deadly weapon exclaimed in bewilderment: "What? You mean I've been tried?"

Some critics of plea bargaining complain that criminals get off too lightly. Others insist that defendants get railroaded out of their right to a trial by prosecutors who "overcharge," *i.e.*, charge defendants with worse crimes than they committed, to force them into guilty pleas. What everyone agrees on is that plea bargaining is at best an expedient to lighten case loads. "Sheer volume almost mandates it," says Judge Rothwax, who is careful to make sure the defendant agreed to the bargain and that it is fair. In New York, according to District Attorney Robert Morgenthau, the sentence a defendant gets from pleading guilty is not much different from the sentence he would get by going to trial. But in many other courts, clearing the docket, otherwise known as moving the business, becomes almost an end in itself.

Six years ago, a national commission on criminal justice recommended that plea bargaining be abolished by 1978. Today, it is still the method by which the vast majority of criminal cases are handled. It helps reduce the case load, but it also reflects the fact that the system cannot handle the flood of litigation. Says a Sandusky, Ohio, attorney, Thomas Murray Jr.: "When you talk about one case in 50 getting to trial, the system is not breaking down. It has broken down."

The system cannot be repaired if the judges themselves are incompetent or corrupt. "The problems caused by unfit federal judges, whether from outright corruption, political favoritism or inability due to ill health or senility, amount to a hidden national scandal," testified Clark Mollenhoff, a Pulitzer-prizewinning former Des Moines *Register* reporter, at a congressional hearing on methods of disciplining judges. (Mollenhoff has been investigating the federal bench for three years.) The only way to remove federal judges now is by impeachment, a cumbersome process. Only four of the nation's federal judges have been tried and convicted by Congress in the nation's history, none since 1936. Convicted of income tax evasion, perjury, bribery, conspiracy and mail fraud in 1973, Federal Judge Otto Kerner resigned from the bench only five days before he was scheduled to enter prison. Federal Judge Herbert Fogel of Philadelphia, implicated in a scandal involving backdated documents to win a Government bid in 1970, took the Fifth Amendment when questioned by a grand jury. He resigned last year before any disciplinary action was taken against him. Federal Judge Willis Ritter, infamous for an abusive temper that led him to bully lawyers and to hale a postmaster and 29 aides into court because their mail-sorting machinery in the courthouse was too noisy, was allowed to stay on the bench until he died last year at age 79. Examples like these, not to mention frequent charges of senility and laziness, have spurred congressional interest in disciplining judges. A Senate bill, supported by Attorney General Griffin Bell, would set up a court on judicial conduct to remove unfit judges.

It is easier to weed out state and local judges. Since 1960, 48 states, plus the District of Columbia and Puerto Rico, have created commissions to discipline judges for wrongdoing. A few of these commissions are effective: since 1975, the New York commission has removed ten judges, censured 65, suspended four, and 73 have resigned. California is now witnessing the unique spectacle of a public investigation of the state supreme court. At issue is whether some members of the court delayed announcing politically controversial decisions before an election in order to save Chief Justice Rose Bird from being ousted by the voters; so far the inquiry has shown less evidence of conspiracy than pettiness and distrust among the court's seven justices. In many other states, accountability commissions exist in name only. Sanctions can be very mild. Massachusetts Judge

3. THE JUDICIAL SYSTEM

Margaret C. Scott was reprimanded last February by the state's highest court for "violating the rights of indigents and others" in some 40 cases. Her punishment: she was barred from judging for a year, but she still collects her $40,000 salary.

Totally exempt from discipline are what Frank Greenberg, past president of the Chicago Bar Association, calls "the gray mice": judges who "lack the scholarship, the temperament, the learning" and are "simply in the wrong occupation." Says Greenberg, a member of the Illinois Judicial Inquiry Board: "There is not a damn thing the discipline system can do about them."

That is a convincing argument for getting better judges to begin with. In about half the states, most judges are elected. The rationale has always been that voters should have a say in choosing the people who resolve their disputes and enforce public law. But most voters do not know much about the candidates for whom they are voting. A Texas poll in 1976 found that only 2% could even remember the names of the county judges on the ballot. A campaign for office is an inexact gauge of how a judge will behave if elected. New York Court of Appeals Judge Sol Wachtler made a TV commercial showing him, dressed in his robes, slamming shut a jail door. This tough-on-crime approach was good politics, but voters favoring a law-and-order man were probably disappointed. Wachtler turned out to be, if anything, defense-minded. To get on a partisan ballot often requires a financial contribution to a political party. A New York judge remembers one candidate coming to him in tears because he could not come up with the necessary $25,000.

Over the past 40 years, half the states have turned to so-called merit selection for at least some judges. Typically, a judicial "selection committee" nominates several names, the Governor picks one, and the judge runs unopposed on a yes-no "retention ballot" after a year or more. The system can produce a higher quality bench, if politics does not creep back in. "The big problem," says Stanford Law Professor Jack Friedenthal, "is the selection of the selectors."

Political patronage has been the traditional way to fill the federal bench. Presidents appoint federal judges, but since Senators can blackball any candidate from their home state, they have the real power of appointment. Sheer embarrassment is about the only check. When Senator Ted Kennedy tried to nominate Family Retainer Francis X. Morrissey for a federal judgeship in 1965, other lawyers began joking that Morrissey was boning up for the job by reading the *Federal Rules of Civil Procedure*, the rough equivalent of preparing for surgery by looking at Gray's *Anatomy*. Kennedy eventually withdrew Morrissey's name.

Still, the surprising thing about the process is that it has worked relatively well. Says Mollenhoff: "Most observers agree that 90% of the nominees have gone on to become excellent federal judges. But another way of putting it is that 70 out of 700 federal judges should not have been put on the bench. That is way too many."

The creation of 152 new judgeships last year gave President Carter the chance to fulfill his campaign promise: "Why not the best?" He has managed to make Senators use "merit" selection committees in 24 states, the District of Columbia and Puerto Rico, but some flatly refused. Maryland's Senator Paul Sarbanes selected his former law partner; another, North Carolina's Robert Morgan, nominated his campaign manager. Carter has also diversified the bench to make sure the judges' backgrounds and attitudes more closely reflect the population's. When he took office, only 1% were female and only 5% were black or Hispanic. So far, a third of his appointments are women or members of a minority group, or both, like Amalya Kearse, 42, a black woman. She will sit on a U.S. Court of Appeals in New York, after the U.S. Supreme Court perhaps the most powerful bench in the country. One thing that has not changed:

95% of Carter's appointments are Democrats, just as 92% of Nixon's appointees were Republicans.

Selection committees generally keep out the clearly unqualified. But they also will settle for what Senator Adlai Stevenson calls "the lowest common denominator." Says Stevenson: "I fear the Brandeises and Carswells alike will be screened out and a high level of mediocrity will be enshrined in the judiciary." Some desirable candidates have refused to be considered by selection committees; they did not want to go through the public-screening process and face possible rejection.

Other potential candidates see a federal judgeship less as a prestigious and challenging job than as very hard work for low pay. Senator Charles Percy has privately remarked that he has had to offer the job to ten people just to get one. Says U.S. Court of Appeals Judge Edward Allen Tamm: "Federal judges are working harder than they ever did in private practice, but they never get their heads above water." Worn down by the work load, comparing their salaries ($54,500 to $57,500) with the six-figure incomes of really successful lawyers, a discouraging number of federal district and circuit judges are going back into private practice. One of the 17 who have left since 1970, former Chief Judge Sidney O. Smith Jr., of the U.S. District Court in Atlanta, returned to his old law firm in 1974 to make enough money (twice as much) so that he could comfortably afford to pay his three children's college tuitions.

Something is seriously wrong if the federal bench cannot attract and hold the very best. So much is expected of it. The judiciary is supposed to be democracy's hedge on majority rule and executive highhandedness. "There is no character on earth more elevated and pure than that of a learned and upright judge. He exerts an influence like the dews of heaven falling without observation," said Daniel Webster, no doubt casting his eyes heavenward. Definitions of a good judge read like recommendations for sainthood: compassionate yet firm, at once patient and decisive, all wise and upstanding.

Measured against that sort of standard, the human foibles and plain ordinariness of most judges are inevitably disappointing. Yet even unlikely characters can be good, if unorthodox, judges. New Orleans Municipal Court Judge Eddie Sapir wears jeans and turtleneck sweaters under his robes and compares himself to Joe Namath ("Both of us drive Cadillac convertibles, both were born in Pennsylvania, both have brothers named Frank, both like women . . ."). His chambers have pictures of racehorses and celebrities, and his campaign motto is "I gotta be me." But Sapir is considered an efficient and capable judge by the lawyers who come before him; he is particularly well known for making slumlords obey housing laws.

Expecting a great deal from judges can have a self-fulfilling effect. "The robes and all the trappings of the courtroom can make a judge rise above himself," says Columbia Law School's Richard Uviller. It can give an otherwise unremarkable man a zeal for simple justice. Judge John Sirica was regarded as a man of mediocre intellect who browbeat counsel and was frequently overturned on appeal. Yet he had the guts to push Watergate from the break-in to the White House. He remained stubborn and unyielding. Criticized for taking a too active role questioning witnesses, he growled, "I couldn't care less what happens on appeal." His single-mindedness produced the truth.

Sirica's example is proof that the robe can elevate the man, and a reminder of the need to preserve judicial independence. But it is also an exception. The real work of the judiciary is the day-to-day, case-by-case job of striking what Judge Rothwax calls "the balance between fairness and efficiency." When courts provide neither, there can be no justice, nor the appearance of justice. When people stop believing in the law, lawlessness follows. A society of laws is sustained partly by pure faith; courts that work well are the visible, basic affirmation of public trust. They are, as well, the final judgment on the judges.

Scaring Off Witnesses

Testifying can be time consuming, costly—and risky

Last December a man wearing a ski mask and carrying a shotgun broke into Richard Morgan's San Francisco Bay-area home. Morgan, a burly Teamster, managed to chase him away and get his license number. But after the suspect was arrested and released on bail, police say, he threatened Morgan over the phone, assaulted him in the courthouse hallway and stole one of his dogs. Finally, the suspect tried to blow Morgan up. Returning to Morgan's house late one night in mid-August bearing 75 sticks of dynamite, the suspect was scared off by barking dogs and fled, leaving the bomb to explode in the driveway. The blast rocked the neighborhood, shattering windows in nearby houses, but Morgan escaped unharmed. Now in hiding, Morgan says he will still testify.

Not everyone is so determined. "People are afraid," says Robert Kaye, chief of the Florida State Attorney's Office Strike Force. "They ask themselves, 'Is the defendant going to get me when he gets out of jail?'" When the Institute for Law and Social Research asked witnesses in Washington, D.C., what they needed most, the largest single response was "better protection." Intimidation is not just limited to witnesses who squeal on the mob or run afoul of mad bombers. In suburbia, parents wonder what retribution is in store for them—or more worrisome, for their small children—if they turn teen-agers in for petty vandalism. Intimidation is a major problem, not just in felony cases, but in misdemeanor courts as well.

The criminal justice system, of course, depends on civilian witnesses, as well as the police. In many instances, say prosecutors around the country, the loss of one key witness means no case. Though statistics of witness no-shows are spotty and hard to come by, a recent study in high-crime Brooklyn, N.Y., by the Vera Institute of Justice found that as many as half the witnesses required to come to court for trial just did not show up.

Fear is not the only reason. Not wanting to "get involved" makes potential witnesses behave like the three monkeys who hear no evil, see no evil and speak no evil. "With a shooting in a bar," says one Detroit law officer, "you'll have 30 people tell you they were in the john at the same time." However un-Samaritan it may seem, the unwillingness of witnesses to go to court is understandable. Witness waiting rooms are grim, if they exist, and court procedures can be exasperating. Getting cross-examined by a zealous defense lawyer is often a fearful experience in itself, especially for rape victims. The typical experience of a witness, says a former head of the Law Enforcement Assistance Administration, is to be "abused, ignored, attacked. At the end of a day in court, he is likely to feel that he himself is the accused."

In Brooklyn, Mark Feinstein, executive director of Vera Institute's Victim/Witness Assistance Project, admits that intimidation accounts for some no-shows. But more are due to misunderstanding of the criminal-justice system. Lots of people call for a cop to protect them, but, says Feinstein bluntly: "The large majority have no intention of going to court when they make their complaint." To combat disaffection, the Vera program provides a special reception center for witnesses in the courthouse, free transportation to court, day care for witnesses' children, a "victim's hot line" so prospective witnesses can get instant advice and reassurance. There is even a repair service to board up victim's broken windows and fix damaged locks. Since 1974, the National District Attorneys Association has sponsored victim-witness assistance programs through 68 offices all over the U.S. Other groups, including the Junior League in Chicago, have pitched in, providing encouragement to witnesses. With some success apparently: in one Chicago courtroom the Junior League ladies have cut the number of no-show witnesses in half. But progress is slow where the problem is deep-seated; Vera's Brooklyn project, for instance, has made what Feinstein calls "minor improvements," whittling down the nonappearance rate from 55% to 35% to 40%.

To protect high-risk witnesses, like the ones testifying against organized crime, the Justice Department in 1970 embarked on a Witness Security Program that has cost $62 million so far. What the Government is up against is shown by a March 1978 report on the fate of witnesses and informers not protected by the program in 50 narcotics-related cases: 45 murders, nine attempted murders, nine death threats and assorted physical assaults.

Many states lack the resources to protect witnesses. John Kaplan, a Stanford Law School professor, suggests another alternative: speedier trials and stiffer bail. "The longer the delay, the more likely the witness will be intimidated. Our lenient bail practices have not helped," says Kaplan, noting that they put the accused back on the street, where he can seek out his accusers. Some district attorneys have proposed a starkly realistic solution: compulsory pretrial depositions, which roughly means getting a witness's testimony quickly on the record. That way, Boston Special Assistant D.A. Thomas Dwyer explains, "if the witness is murdered before the trial, you can use the deposition."

Speedier trials would also help witnesses less patient than Patricia Finck, a Philadelphia A & P cashier who went back to court 46 times to get two stickup men convicted. "After three or four continuances of a case," says Patrick Healy, the executive director of the National District Attorneys Association, "unless you're really a devoted witness, you'll kiss it off. After all, what's in it for you? This business of civic pride goes only so far. And the smart defendant and the smart defense lawyer will delay a case to death."

Criminal Justice

Some community groups work to improve local agencies—police, courts, and corrections.

A Louisville, Kentucky, group has trained volunteers as "court-watchers"— people who monitor trials and proceedings. The purpose: to assure that courts are effective and fair, especially where crime victims and witnesses are concerned.

"We want to make sure the victim is treated properly," declares George Baker, who heads the community group that conducts court-watching and other anti-crime projects. "There was too little concern for the victim in the past."

Acting as "the eyes and ears of the community," court-watchers rate everything from a judge's propriety to whether prosecutors were prepared and court facilities clean.

They are instructed to note anything unusual about a case, for example, whether fines seem discriminatory. They pay close attention to such things as attempts by defense attorneys to intimidate witnesses or victims and whether a victim's and witness's safety may be jeopardized.

Their data and observations are recorded on checklists. They answer questions such as:

• "Did the judge use language that most defendants appeared to understand? Did you usually understand the judge?"

• "Did the judge explain the instructions to the jury clearly?"

• "Did the clerk appear to accord special treatment to certain individuals? If 'yes,' explain."

Mr. Baker expects to sign up 200 court-watchers for the program and to make public a wealth of data on the county's circuit and district courts.

A Detroit group helped form citizen-police patrols that help to reduce crime while incidentally improving residents' understanding of police work. Some 30 people help patrol six neighborhoods involving a population of 6,000. Says a group spokesperson, "People are much more aware now of probems."

A Runnells, Iowa, community group helped correct a critical police-fire problem in a rural area. The problem: no address signs to guide police officers or firefighters in emergencies.

Firefighters and other volunteers installed metal reflector signs, obtained by the group. They show a resident's address as well as the township, section, and fire district.

Why Suppress Valid Evidence?

Malcolm Richard Wilkey

Mr. Wilkey is a United States Circuit Judge on the U.S. Court of Appeals for the District of Columbia Circuit.

Among nations of the civilized world we are unique in two respects: 1) We suffer the most extraordinary crime rate with firearms, 2) in criminal prosecutions, by a rule of evidence which exists in no other country, we exclude the most trustworthy and convincing evidence.

These two aberrations are not unconnected. In fact, the "exclusionary rule" has made unenforceable the gun control laws we have and will make ineffective any stricter controls which may be devised. Its fetters particularly paralyze police efforts to prevent, detect and punish street crimes involving not only weapons but narcotics.

What is this "exclusionary rule" that permits a professional criminal to swagger down the street with a handgun bulging in his hip pocket, immune to police search and seizure? It is not required by the Constitution. The Fourth Amendment only forbids "unreasonable searches and seizures." The exclusionary rule is a judge-made rule of evidence which bars "the use of evidence secured through an illegal search and seizure."

When it was adopted in 1914 it was applied only to evidence seized by federal agents and offered in federal courts. In 1960 it was broadened to bar in federal courts evidence originally seized by state police, over which the federal government had no control. Finally, the ban was extended in 1961 to evidence seized by state officials and offered in state courts.

Four out of literally tens of thousands of cases illustrate its application. In *United States v. Robinson (1973),* Robinson was arrested for driving with a forged driver's license. He was searched and a packet containing heroin was found.

The court of appeals held Robinson's search illegal, and, applying the exclusionary rule, suppressed the heroin evidence illegally seized. The Supreme Court reversed, holding the evidence was obtained by a legal search and therefore the exclusionary rule did not apply.

In *United States v. Montgomery (1977),* two police officers patrolling a residential neighborhood observed Montgomery driving as if he were "sizing up" the area. A stop for identification revealed Montgomery had an arrest warrant outstanding. A protective search turned up a .38 caliber bullet, a magnum revolver loaded with six rounds and a sawed-off shotgun with shells.

Writing a Dissent

The court of appeals reversed the conviction, holding that no probable cause existed for stopping Montgomery, hence all evidence was the product of an illegal search. The exclusionary rule mandated suppression of evidence about the loaded revolver and sawed-off shotgun, which was essential to conviction.

(It is well to cite here my own involvement: I wrote the dissent in our court of appeals 5-4 decsision in *Robinson* and our dissenting position was upheld in the Supreme court. I dissented in the 2-1 decision of our court in *Montgomery* in which time for seeking *certiorari* has now expired.)

In *Brewer v. Williams (1977),* a prisoner charged with murder of a 10-year-old girl was subtly induced to take police officers to the site of the body. The Supreme Court held 5-4 that: The prisoner's Sixth Amendment right to counsel was violated (*Robinson* and *Montgomery* involved Fourth Amendment illegal searches and seizures), the confession was thus illegally obtained, the evidence of location of the victim's body was thus tainted because it was derived from the illegal confession, therefore, the exclusionary rule barred evidence of the prisoner's statements and the location of the body.

Also in 1977, the conviction of a New York doctor who pled guilty to sexual abuse was reversed and eyewitness testimony suppressed. After complaints of sexual misconduct against the doctor during gynecological examinations of patients under anesthetic gas, a police-woman posing as a patient visited the doctor's offices. At the same time a male investigator was outside to protect her. He peered through the heavily curtained windows and saw the doctor commit sex acts on another patient.

The court of appeals held the search (observation) illegal, suppressing the investigator's eyewitness testimony under the exclusionary rule, thus eliminating any possibility of conviction.

The legal argument in these cases is whether the police had a valid basis, *i.e.,* "probable cause," for their action. Where to draw the line between "reasonable" and "unreasonable" under the Fourth Amendment is one issue. Whether evidence should automatically be excluded as a result of an illegal search is quite another, and is the issue addressed here. At present no court but the Supreme Court has any choice on the latter.

The impact of the exclusionary rule is that the most valid, conclusive and factual evidence is excluded from the jury. This rule produces a distortion of the truth. Irrefutable facts of decisive importance are forever barred.

In exclusionary rules cases involving material evidence there is never any question of reliability. Reliability is in question, for example, with a coerced confession or a faulty lineup for identification. Exclusion of evidence is then proper, because the evidence is inherently unreliable. But when a pistol or narcotics is found on a person the legality of the search cannot impair the truth of the physical evidence.

Then why the exclusionary rule? The justification is purely theoretical: Excluding evidence will punish the officers committing the illegal act and thus deter policemen from repetition. As Justice Cardozo predicted in 1926, in describing the complete irrationality of the exclusionary rule, "The criminal is to go free because the constable has blundered. . . . A room is searched against the law, and the body of a murdered man is found. . . . The privacy of the home has been infringed, and the murderer goes free."

Shunned by Other Countries

If the exclusionary rule had merit, surely at least one other country since 1914 would have followed our example. All have shunned it. The rule in all other countries—in England, Canada, Germany, Israel, for example—is that relevant evidence is admitted, whether obtained legally or illegally.

The exclusionary rule has been devastating to gun control laws. Unless a police officer has "probable cause" to make a reasonable search, nothing found during the search—no sawed-off shotgun, automatic pistol or submachine gun—can be introduced as evidence. Therefore, since it is virtually impossible to be convicted in the U.S. of carrying a weapon illegally, American criminals do carry guns and use them. Since police know they carry and use them, they engage in far more searches and seizures than in the countries mentioned above, and some of those searches and seizures are blatantly illegal.

Thus under the exclusionary rule, Americans have the worst of it both ways: The public is harassed more by both criminals and police than are citizens of many other countries.

The only excuse offered for this irrational rule is that there is "no effective alternative" to make the police obey the law. But other civilized countries control their police by disciplinary measures against errant policemen, not by freeing the criminal. Judging by the results in England and Canada, among others, disciplinary measures work very well.

But there are other alternatives to disciplinary measures. Every prosecution in which an illegal search is claimed might be followed by a minitrial of the accused officer, at the conclusion of which the same judge who heard the evidence at the principal trial would mete out deserved punishment for any proven infraction.

Unlike the exclusionary rule, this would not free the convicted criminal, but it would provide a deterrent against officers violating constitutional rights. And in instances not resulting in prosecution, offended citizens could be given a right to sue the governmental entity by which the individual officer is employed.

Handguns—crimes by handguns—are one of our gravest problems. No laws on gun control will work if the laws cannot be effectively enforced. No gun control law can be enforced with the unique American exclusionary rule keeping out the most reliable evidence necessary for conviction.

There are proven workable alternatives to the exclusionary rule. Either the Supreme Court (which created it) or Congress can abolish it, and surely one or the other will do so.

It's legal gambling

Science peers into the jury box

Gioia Diliberto

In January, Princeton researchers telephoned 478 Bergen County residents and asked them questions about murder and medicine, marriage and magazines, and children and death.

In March, another 150 Bergen residents were asked similar questions by County Judge William J. Arnold at the Hackensack courthouse, where they had been called for jury duty.

For four days, defense attorney Raymond A. Brown scrutinized the jurors and compared their answers against the telephone survey, designed to determine what kind of person would be sympathetic to Brown's client, Dr. Mario Jascalevich.

Brown paid $10,000 for the survey. In a few weeks, a verdict should be in on whether it was money well-spent.

Even crusty, old-fashioned defense attorneys like Brown, who for years relied exclusively on intuition and luck, are now embracing some unorthodox and expensive techniques for jury selection.

An increasing number of criminal lawyers are employing social scientists, pollsters, and even psychics to help them pick favorable juries.

Some attorneys dismiss it as worthless, and others attack it as jury tampering, because yesterday's survey respondent could be tomorrow's prospective juror. But "scientific jury selection" has been used in many recent celebrated cases, including the political corruption trials of John Mitchell, Maurice Stans, and former congressman Henry Helstoski; the weapons possession trial of Wendy Yoshimura, Patrica Hearst's fugitive companion, and the murder trials of Joan Little, Rubin "Hurricane" Carter, Roxanne Gaye, and Richard Herrin.

Michael Rappeport, director of the Princeton research firm that did the Jascalevich survey, estimates that each year jury surveys are conducted for 40 criminal trials across the country.

The legal purpose of voir dire, the questioning of prospective jurors, is to pick people who are fair and impartial. In reality, most attorneys are trying to choose jurors who are biased in their client's favor.

Selection has always been guesswork. So trial lawyers, like gamblers, are always searching for a better system.

Some of the most successful criminal lawyers, such as Ramsey Clark and William Kunstler, have turned to social science.

Phone book sample

Typical is the Jascalevich survey, which Judge Theodore Trautwein admitted into evidence, but refused to reveal to the public.

Rappeport's researchers chose Bergen County residents at random from the telephone book. They were asked their age, education, reading habits, religion, politics, names of their doctors, and opinions about medicine. Dr. Jascalevich is accused of murdering three patients at Riverdell Hospital in Oradell 12 years ago.

The answers were fed into a computer. A profile emerged of the ideal juror: an educated, white-collar or skilled blue-collar worker, with some higher education.

Results were a surprise.

"Brown thought he'd want a lower-class, uneducated juror, because that's what he's had the most success with in the past," said Jay Schulman, who devised the first jury survey for the federal conspiracy trial of the Harrisburg 7 in 1971.

It's common wisdom among defense attorneys that uneducated people make good jurors in most murder cases because they are believed to respond emotionally to the defendant and acquit on mitigating circumstances.

"But in an ambiguous, complicated case like the Jascalevich trial, you want analytical, educated people who can accept reasonable doubt and the presumption of innocence," said Schulman, who has worked on 150 criminal trials.

Prosecutor's view

"That's why two accountants were picked for the jury," said Rappeport. Usually, accountants, like carpenters, mathematicians, and architects would be dismissed immediately by defense lawyers "because they require things to fit too neatly."

On the other hand, Assistant Prosecutor Sybil Moses was looking for people who showed strong respect for government. She ruled out young people, professionals, and anyone who showed any sign of eccentricity.

She also dismissed a great many young, married women. Schulman said he thinks "she was concerned

"It's Legal Gambling: Science Peers into the Jury Box," Gioia Diliberto, *The Record*, October 11, 1978. Reprinted by permission from *The Record*, of Hackensack, N.J.

about their possible identification with the doctor and their possible alienation from her as a career woman."

Schulman, who bears a striking resemblance to pictures of Santa Claus, found himself in the jury selection business in 1971, when his friend Daniel Berrigan asked him to assist Berrigan's defense on federal charges of plotting to kill Henry Kissinger and blow up heating tunnels in Washington, D.C.

Schulman conducted a community survey, and the defense team used the results during jury selection. The Harrisburg 7 case ended in a mistrial, and Schulman founded the National Jury Project.

The nonprofit organization went on to pick juries in the political conspiracy trials of the Camden 28, the Gainesville 8, the Wounded Knee trial of Indian leaders Russell Means and Dennis Banks, and four trials related to the Attica prison riot.

None of the defendants was convicted, although Means was later sent to prison on riot charges.

Evidence important

Schulman concedes that trial evidence is always more important than jury selection, and that jury selection is not important in every case.

If the evidence is very strong or very weak, the composition of the jury isn't going to make much difference, said Schulman. But if it's close, jury selection could be the key.

In a trial such as Dr. Jascalevich's, where the case has boiled down to an argument between experts, jury selection is crucial, Schulman said.

Brown has a good jury, in Schulman's view. Originally composed of 11 men and seven women, only 13 jurors are left after seven months. Among them are a plant manager, one of the accountants, a salesman, an advertising copywriter, an electrical engineer, a nurse, and a bank teller.

The jurors are mostly middle-aged. None has advanced training in biology or chemistry, two subjects that figure heavily in the testimony.

Schulman said the trial of Maryland Gov. Marvin Mandel is an example of how haphazard jury selection can be fatal.

"The attorneys realized jury selection was important, but they saw no difference between any of the people in the jury pool—they thought they were all bad," Schulman said.

"Consequently, they only spent about 10 minutes on jury selection. But their big mistake was in selecting a 21-year-old male social worker. It's obvious that in a political corruption trial you don't take young people in the social service fields. The jury was out eight days—without the social worker, they might have had a hung jury."

Mandel is now appealing a four-year sentence.

'Mind-boggling'

Although most attorneys think they know how to pick juries, they don't, Schulman said. "The judgments attorneys have to make in jury selection are so complex it's mind-boggling. Unless you're an Edward Bennet Williams and you can think about nine things at once, you need some help."

Jack Litman, with the help of the National Jury Project, was able to pick "the right jury" for his client, Richard Herrin, said Schulman. In June, the 24-year-old Yale graduate was found guilty of manslaughter rather than murder in the hammer slaying of Bonnie Garland, his girlfriend of more than two years.

Herrin admitted he killed Miss Garland as she slept in her parents' Scarsdale home. The issue was whether Herrin was insane at the time.

A survey of the residents of White Plains, where the trial was held, showed that the ideal jurors would be working-class women who resented the Garlands and their upper-class life style.

"Litman also wanted jurors who wouldn't be so closed-minded about the horror of the crime that they wouldn't listen to the psychiatric testimony," Schulman said.

Too successful?

"The trouble with the new [jury selection] methods is they're too successful," said Columbia University sociologist Amitai Etzioni. "This wouldn't matter so much if they were available to everyone, but they're not. You have to be either very rich or very radical."

The National Jury Project and the few firms across the country that do this kind of work charge $1,000 to $40,000. Some cases that Schulman considers important he handles for free.

Schulman said hiring social scientists is no different from spending a lot of money to get a good lawyer.

"This is not jury loading," said Rappeport, "because in 99 percent of the cases, the odds are against the defense. The average juror automatically assumes the defendant is guilty."

However, some attorneys object that the new methods slow and complicate things so much that trials by jury become juries by trial.

"I think the use of social science methods complicates an already overburdened system. Once you get involved in trying to psychoanalyze jurors, you waste too much time," said Irwin Kimmelman, who is defending Nelson Gross's appeal of a 1974 campaign fraud conviction. Gross charges that a deputy marshal was romantically involved with a woman juror.

For the North Carolina trial of Joan Little, accused of killing a jailer by stabbing him 11 times with an ice pick, 150 prospective jurors were scrutinized by the seven-member defense team for 10 days. A psychologist studied the jurors' behavior, and a body language expert watched their gestures.

As each prospective juror gave his age, an astrologer and psychic sitting with Miss Little determined whether the person's horoscope was in conflict with her "freedom planet." Miss Little was acquitted.

The Wounded Knee trial of Indian leaders Means and Banks was even more unorthodox.

Two medicine men ruled on the defense's choice of jurors.

"William Kunstler and the volunteers from the National Jury Project would decide on a juror in the afternoon, and the medicine men would go home that night to perform their ceremonies. They'd come to court the next day and make us knock the person off the jury because 'the sticks didn't fall right,' " Schulman recalled.

"And no one, not Kunstler or anyone else, argued that our magic was better than theirs."

Victims/Witnesses

"The buck stops here," is the motto of the Metropolitan Atlanta Crime Commission's victim/witness assistance program. The project serves Cobb County, Georgia.

Staff members worked so hard that a wing of the courthouse was given to them to house four of their representatives. Victims and witnesses go there when they are due in court to testify.

"It's beautiful," said project director Anne Rager. "It's a place where victims and witnesses can wait and not feel alone."

Because part of the county is not served by public transportation, project staffers also provide transportation for victims and witnesses to and from court, or perhaps the doctor's office or the hospital.

Project staff use volunteers to do the paperwork, often an enormous amount, Ms. Rager said. Volunteers also provide escort and daycare services when needed.

"A lot of people don't know how to retrieve their property when it's been used as evidence," she said, "so we help them to do that, too."

Police officers give cards to crime victims. The cards refer the citizens to Ms. Rager's program—where the buck stops.

Most community anti-crime programs offer services to victims and witnesses because there is growing awareness by the public and criminal justice practitioners to be responsive to the victim—so long forgotten.

Senator Edward M. Kennedy (D-Mass.) wrote in a recent editorial, "These programs have come into being because the human needs they address are stark and tragic. The new programs serve another important purpose—to earn greater public confidence in our agencies of justice, whose effectiveness is often crippled for lack of trust by the very citizens they seek to protect."

Some other local services provided by community groups include:

- emergency shelters
- legal services
- hotlines
- counseling
- restitution

THE MURDEROUS MIND:
Insanity vs. the Law

Richard Gambino

Richard Gambino is a professor of educational philosophy at Queens College and the author of Vendetta: The Largest Lynching in American History *(Doubleday, 1977).*

THE CELEBRATED "Son of Sam" murder case has exposed yet again an appalling weakness in our criminal legal system: its inability to deal sensibly with the problem of insanity. Son of Sam is, of course, the man who terrorized New York City by killing a long string of victims with his .44-caliber pistol. David Berkowitz, the man arrested and charged with the crime, has been declared mentally incompetent by two psychiatrists, but he will probably stand trial anyway.

Whatever disposition is made of Berkowitz's case, the point is that any treatment of him possible under our legal system will be egregious, for our laws simply cannot cope with the kind of individual he represents. The law of criminal insanity is such a Pandora's box that its defenders seem perfect examples of "conservatives" who love existing evils. At the same time, the law's critics appear as "liberals" who would replace existing evils with others.

The conservative dinosaur in question is something known as the M'Naghten rule. It is the standard by which insanity is determined, and it is written into virtually every legal jurisdiction in the United States. New York State's version of this standard is typical. It says that in order for an accused person to be found "not guilty by reason of insanity," one of two conditions had to exist "at the time of the alleged criminal act": Either the accused "did not know the nature and quality of the act he was doing" or he "did not know that the act was wrong." The concept of "knowing" has been interpreted so narrowly in legal precedent that only drooling idiots and raving madmen could be said to be legally insane. Under the law, a countless number of pathetic mentally disordered individuals have been found guilty and put into prison with hardened criminals. Frequently, the law has also resulted in society's broiling the brains of psychotic people in the electric chair. At times this form of execution has satisfied our desire for vengeance, but the record hardly gives us pride in being human. For example, there is the case of Frederick Charles Wood, the last person executed in New York State. Wood went to Sing Sing's electric chair on March 22, 1963. His "sanity" was evident in his enjoyment of the experience. He walked into the grim execution room smiling. "I got a little speech to make," he announced to the witnesses. "Gents," he went on

good-naturedly, "this is an educational project. You are about to witness the damaging effect electricity has on Wood. Enjoy yourselves." Then he turned to the electric chair, pulled out a handkerchief, dusted the chair off, and sat down. He continued to joke until the switch was thrown.

Wood, age fifty-two, confessed to murdering five people in his lifetime. The first murder occurred when he was fifteen, a crime that went unsolved at the time. He had a crush on a young girl and because he "couldn't have her," he explained some 35 years later, he sent her a box of cream puffs—laced with arsenic. At age twenty-one, he bludgeoned and stabbed 140 times a woman who was a total stranger because, he said, he had gotten venereal disease from another woman. This case too went unsolved. Seventeen years later, Wood fed liquor to a friend in a drinking spree, then stuffed the drunken man's head into a gas oven and bashed in his skull for good measure. The man, Wood explained, had made a disparaging remark about Wood's girl friend. Wood was sentenced to 20-years-to-life imprisonment for second-degree murder (and later boasted that it was really first-degree). He was paroled after 17 years of good behavior. Less than a month after leaving prison, he killed two men in Queens: one, whom he had just met, because the man had made a pass at him, and the other, a stranger, simply because he was sleeping in the house where the murder took place. Ghoulishly, Wood mutilated the two bodies and left two notes at the scene. One read: "And God bless the Parole Board. They're real intelligent people." The other said: "Now, aren't these two murders a dirty shame. I'm so-o sorry."

Wood was a conspicuous example of the failure of both our legal and our psychiatric systems to deal with mentally disordered criminals. He had been arrested 22 times and had spent a total of 32 years in New York's prisons and mental hospitals—having first heard "the voice of God" when he was four. During and after his last trial, he was in a cheerful mood, expressing relief that his life would end. He said on the stand that he was sane and that he wanted to die. One week before his execution, he wrote, "I really want to ride the lightning." Throughout his life, psychiatrists repeatedly disagreed on whether he was insane under the M'Naghten rule; and Wood boasted that he was so used to their testing routines that he had been "fooling the psychiatrists all along" and "could do it anytime"—a claim that was endorsed by a Kings County psychiatrist in 1961. At his last trial, the jury rejected Wood's lawyer's plea of insanity, despite the fact that the many diagnoses made of him in state hospitals since 1927 consistently found him "psychotic" and "psychopathic."

Wood was a figure who provoked anger and hatred among the public and presumably among jury members as well. An example of the opposite reaction of a jury is found in a case tried during the years of the Great Depression. On a beautiful summer day in August 1935, a woman took her two-year-old son for a walk down a secluded lane, came to a brook, and held the child's head underwater for a half hour. Then she dressed the body in a clean suit and carried it to a police station in Newburgh, New York. "Here he is," she said to the startled desk cop. "You killed him?" "Yes, I drowned him." "What did you do that for?" "I couldn't take care of him any longer, and I thought he would be better off dead." Investigation revealed that the woman's husband had died of tuberculosis some months before, that she could not find work, that she was broke, and that she and her two children had just been evicted from their apartment. At her first-degree murder trial, an earnest jury agonized over its verdict, returning to the court during its deliberations to question the judge about finding some way out of its dilemma. Her plea was "not guilty by reason of insanity," yet her own words showed the jury she "knew" what she was doing when she drowned the boy and "knew" it was wrong. Finally the jury came in with a verdict of guilty and a recommendation of mercy. The recommendation, incidentally, was pointless: New York State law at the time *mandated* the death penalty for first-degree murder. In a parallel case in the state of Maine, a grand jury refused to indict a woman with a record of attempted suicides in 1954 when a team of psychiatrists opined that the woman was insane under the M'Naghten rule. The charge against her was the drowning of three of her children in a bathtub. She was committed to a state mental hospital and released in 1959. In 1966, the woman drowned three more of her children and attempted suicide, leaving a note saying: "God told me to do it. They are in heaven safe from evil."

If the M'Naghten rule is a procrustean bed, attempts to replace it seem no better, or worse. The "New Hampshire rule," one of the oldest and the most radical of the reforms, has been law in that state for over a hundred years. In essence, the rule is a rejection of all standards used to determine sanity and leaves it up to a jury to find "as a question of fact" whether a defendant is sane or insane. The problem is that juries are given no guidance at all, leaving different jurors free to vote guilty or not on different notions of sanity. Of course, it also leaves a jury free to condemn any defendant on the basis not of sanity but of outrage, as with a Frederick Wood, or to condemn with a recommendation of pity, as with someone like the woman in Newburgh. The rule of law is replaced by the personal feelings of jurors or by the bias of judges, who are free to guide jurors in whatever way they choose.

SHOULD WE, then, scrap the M'Naghten rule and replace it with some other standard of sanity? For a while there was great hope among reformers when a federal court in Washington, D.C., came up with another sanity test in 1954. This test forms the basis of the Durham rule, so named after a defendant, which states that "an accused is not criminally responsible if his unlawful act was the product of mental disease or mental defect"—a definition so broad that virtually everyone coming to trial could be considered legally insane, since no one is totally free from at least some form of neurosis. (On September 15, 1977, the President's Commission on Mental Health issued a report estimating that 20 million to 40 million Americans have diagnosable mental disturbances and that 25 percent of the nation's population suffer from severe emotional stress.) In addition, psychiatrists have disagreed about specific defendants, just as they have under the M'Naghten test. And the vagueness of the Durham rule has led to more practical problems than that of M'Naghten. Terms like "mental disease" and "mental defect" are impossible to define meaningfully. In 1961, the American Law Institute recommended a new test, which was a merger of the M'Naghten and Durham rules. Unfortunately, it has served little purpose except to compound the difficulties of both standards.

Psychiatry is a healing art. Its function is to understand and cure, not to define moral or legal responsibility or to accomplish justice. In fact, the profession of psychiatry does not use or recognize the terms "sanity" and "insanity." They are strictly legal terms. On the other hand, the law does not recognize psychiatric terms or comments as tests of criminal insanity. As a result, confrontations between opposing lawyers and psychiatrists at criminal trials have the quality of a conversation between Alice and the Mad Hatter in Wonderland. And psychiatry is a good deal less than a precise discipline, least of all in its diagnostic methods, which have often proved embarrassing to members of the profession, who like to pretend it is an exact science. For example, a study conducted at Stanford University in 1972 caused much blushing among shrinks. Eight researchers feigned hearing "voices" and gained admission to 12 different psychiatric hospitals. None of the eight falsified their real life history, except for the voices, nor did any of them have a history of pathological behavior. Yet in 11 of the 12 instances, the researchers were diagnosed as "schizophrenic," while in the twelfth, the diagnosis was "manic depressive." Although other patients regarded the researchers as normal, no member of the hospitals' staffs did. Then, in a follow-up experiment, the staff of a psychiatric hospital were told that one or more fake patients would be sent to them. Although none were actually sent, 41 of 193 patients admitted for treatment in the following period of time were thought to be fakes, in each case by at least one member of the hospital's staff.

One of the open scandals of psychiatry is the standard courtroom "battle of psychiatrists." In virtually every court case in which insanity is the defense plea, different psychiatrists examining the same defendant arrive at opposite conclusions regarding his "sanity" as defined by the M'Naghten rule and often his mental condition as categorized by psychiatric concepts as well.

The M'Naghten rule is 135 years old. In 1843, a man named Daniel M'Naghten, who suffered from unfounded delusions of persecution, sought to end his pain by taking a shot at a man he thought was the prime minister of England. In fact, the victim was the prime minister's male secretary, and M'Naghten's bullet killed him. Englishmen were outraged, not least of all Queen Victoria. She sent her husband, Prince Albert, to M'Naghten's trial as an observer. The queen was angry because M'Naghten's crime was but the latest in a series of four attempted assassinations of government people. The previous assault had occurred three years before, when a man named Oxford took a shot at the queen herself. He and the two earlier assailants had been found by the courts to be legally insane. When, despite the prince's dour presence, M'Naghten also was found not guilty by reason of insanity, Victoria showed her royal pique by sending a letter to the House of Lords, deploring the verdicts on Oxford and M'Naghten, who were, she wrote, "perfectly conscious and aware of what they did." She insisted that "judges be bound to interpret the law in this and no other sense." The Lords summoned England's top 15 judges (that country has no Supreme Court), who under pressure came up with the M'Naghten rule. It is based on pre-Freudian psychology. The human mind at the time was thought to be divided into the "faculties" of reason, emotion, and will. Moreover, and this was the critical point, it was believed a person's reason could control his emotions and behavior if only he exercised enough willpower. The M'Naghten rule, therefore, seeks only to know whether an accused person's reason was functioning when he committed a crime. If yes, then he is judged sane and is guilty, for he could have and should have willed himself not to commit the crime. The M'Naghten rule was an advance over previous legal practice in which young children, madmen, and even animals were executed. (The most recent recorded example of the last was the execution of a dog in Switzerland in 1906 for the animal's "participation" in a robbery and a murder.) The M'Naghten rule was hailed in 1843 as enlightened—and it was, when compared with the tests that fixed other reforms of "strict liability." For example, there was an eighteenth-century test that held a person insane only if he had no more reason than an animal or sane if he could count to 20, or beget a child, or had the reason of a child of fourteen. (These last three stipulations had their beginnings in the sixteenth century.)

Yet today, the "enlightened" M'Naghten rule is hopelessly out of step with in-depth concepts of the integrated human psyche. Psychopathic and even most psychotic defendants know what they are doing in the narrow cognitive sense of "reason." But, unable to function by society's rules for reasons we don't understand, psychopaths invent often highly rationalized systems of their own and frequently attribute them to something or someone higher—"the voice of God" or reportedly in David Berkowitz's case, a godlike "Sam." The Kings County Hospital report said that Berkowitz was incompetent to stand trial because he was "emotionally dead" and therefore met the legal test of incompetence—a variation on the M'Naghten rule, which holds that a person who cannot understand the nature of the charges against him or aid in his own defense is incompetent. The report was successfully refuted by psychiatrists brought in by the prosecutors.

"Shopping around" for psychiatrists whose opinion favors one side or the other in a criminal insanity claim is standard practice among DAs and defense lawyers. Once the psychiatrists have canceled each other out, the judge then has to decide for himself whether or not the defendant is competent to stand trial. If Berkowitz had been ruled incompetent, he would have been committed to a hospital for the criminally insane, as is required by law. (Such was the fate of the accused "Boston strangler" a few years back—he never stood trial.) Berkowitz may be found guilty, not guilty, or not guilty by reason of insanity. Most likely he will remain in limbo without justice being served, as often happens. Indefinite confinement to a hospital for the criminally insane awaits him if he is found not guilty by reason of insanity at his trial. He could then be released as a free man any time a panel of psychiatrists certified him as sane. On the other hand, the state hospitals for the criminally insane, in reality prisons with euphemistic names, are not required to review the status of their "patients." The case of Stephen Dennison says a lot about this mode of putting justice on the shelf. At the age of sixteen, Dennison was arrested for stealing five dollars' worth

of candy. He was ruled incompetent to stand trial and sent to a hospital for the criminally insane, *where he remained for 34 years*. Finally when his brother got him released on a writ of habeas corpus, Dennison sued the state of New York, in 1966. He was awarded $250,000 by a judge who commented, "No sum of money would be adequate to compensate the claimant for the injuries he suffered and the scars which he obviously bears."

But Berkowitz has been found competent, and his trial will no doubt be the usual sensational battle between defense and prosecution psychiatrists, each group mocked and badgered by the opposing lawyer. The most likely result in the jurors' minds, whether an upstate jury, as the defense has in effect requested, or a New York City jury, will be disgust both with the law and with psychiatric medicine. The jurors will then feel free to vote their own passions about the defendant or, rather, feel that they have no choice but to do so.

Fact is, neither our moral and legal wisdom nor our psychiatric knowledge is adequate to the dilemmas presented by a mentally disordered violent criminal. Despite our vanity as "problem solvers," in this area, as in many others, there truly are more things in heaven and earth than are dreamt of in our philosophies. But the reality of violent crimes forces us to deal with numerous sons of Sam despite our being ill-equipped to do so. The result is usually frustrating and tragic. It is an old maxim that justice without understanding and mercy is cruelty, while understanding and mercy without justice corrode respect for the law. Because of the limitations on our attempts to cope with mentally disordered offenders, we inevitably get neither justice nor understanding but end up with cruelty or with cynicism about the law—and often with both. It is as certain as it is sad that this too will be the case with Son of Sam.

Just as predictably, most newspaper coverage and public discussion of the case will remain merely sensationalistic, while the best of the press will confine itself to "just the facts" à la TV's Detective Friday. After the disposition of Berkowitz, either as a normal man serving a specified sentence in a regular prison (he would be a "feeb"—prison jargon for a hated inmate—among ordinary prisoners, with a spectacularly short life expectancy) or as an insane man indefinitely confined to a so-called hospital or, least likely, as a man set free as sane but not guilty, interest in the case will sputter out. The entire question of criminal sanity will be shelved again, until the next Son of Sam scares people and enriches the tabloids. It happened after Wood's case and after every other case that has aroused public passions in the past several generations. (In New York State, the sensational insanity cases have occurred on an average of every 15 years or so and have served as peaks completely overshadowing innumerable less theatrical cases between them.)

After 135 years, even a Queen Victoria might agree that the insanity question should be opened to careful deliberation. A golden opportunity for reassessment was missed in 1973. President Nixon recommended that the insanity defense in federal law be narrowed only to the criterion of whether a defendant acted with criminal intent. (It is one of the longest standing axioms of criminal law that there is no crime where there is no criminal intent.) Nixon also proposed a post-trial judicial hearing after an acquittal on the ground of insanity to determine whether the defendant should be sent to a hospital. Nixon's own avowed intent was to make it more difficult for accused people to successfully plead not guilty by reason of insanity and to keep them locked up should they succeed. As such, his proposal was perceived as an outright "abolition" of the insanity defense, a proposed reversal of one of the basic foundations of criminal law itself. It was regarded as an affront by conservatives as well as by liberals and was quickly buried. In a generally liberal report, the National Commission on Reform of Federal Criminal Laws, headed by California's former governor Edmund G. Brown, recommended the American Law Institute's 1961 amalgam of the M'Naghten and Durham rules. Paradoxically, the Senate Subcommittee on Criminal Laws and Procedures, chaired by the late archconservative senator John L. McClellan, also opted for the institute's standard in a tough new law and order federal criminal code. Result: status quo.

If anything good could be born of the horrible Son of Sam case, it might be an urge to reexamine a state of affairs so clearly inadequate that it demeans law, psychiatry, and morality.

LAW ENFORCEMENT OFFICERS KILLED
1969-1978

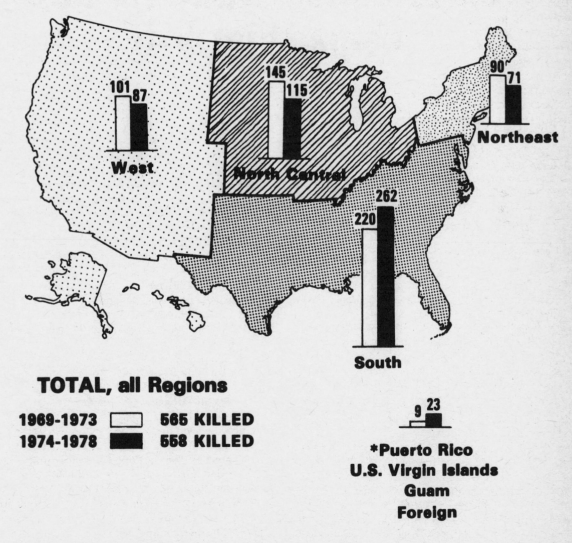

West 101 87

North Central 145 115

Northeast 90 71

South 262 220

9 23

*Puerto Rico
U.S. Virgin Islands
Guam
Foreign

TOTAL, all Regions

| 1969-1973 | ☐ | 565 KILLED |
| 1974-1978 | ■ | 558 KILLED |

*Data not available for years prior to 1971.

HOW DAN WHITE GOT AWAY WITH MURDER

And how American psychiatry helped him do it.

Thomas Szasz

THOMAS SZASZ is a contributing editor of INQUIRY and the author of numerous books, including The Myth of Mental Illness *and* Law, Liberty and Psychiatry. *This article is adapted from a speech delivered in San Francisco on June 19, 1979.*

THERE IS NO QUESTION THAT A TRAVESTY of justice occurred in the trial of Dan White. How could the killer of San Francisco Mayor George Moscone and Supervisor Harvey Milk—who fired nine bullets into his victims and shot each one twice in the back of the head, execution-style—not be found guilty of murder?

The answer is: Easily.

Anything is possible in human affairs if one has the power to redefine basic concepts—to say that day is night, that two plus two make five—and get away with it. In the trial of Dan White, the defense, aided and abetted by the prosecution, had the power to hand the case over to the psychiatrists, and the psychiatrists had the power to redefine a political crime as an ordinary crime, and an ordinary crime as a psychiatric problem. How did psychiatry gain such power? By having seized it, long ago; and by society not resisting—indeed welcoming—that seizure of power.

To understand the White affair, we must understand some things about the recent history of American psychiatry. During World War II American psychiatry became very useful to the military authorities by offering an ostensibly medical mechanism for disposing of useless or unwanted military personnel. That mechanism was the so-called NP (for neuropsychiatric) discharge. Approximately half of those separated by "medical" discharges from the military services received NP discharges. At the time, this was considered to be a great medical-humanitarian achievement. It is still so considered. The psychiatrist most responsible for it, William Menninger, was hailed as a great physician and a benefactor of the nation. Why? Because he, and the countless psychiatrists who participated in that gigantic con game, offered to obscure, and thus to deethicize and depoliticize, one of the most obvious and painful moral problems that then faced the nation—namely, the obligation to serve in the armed forces, with the grave risks to life and limb attendant on that obligation. That wartime psychiatrization of fear, self-protection, cowardice, pacifism, wisdom—call it what you may—laid the foundation on which American psychiatrists and the other enemies of freedom and dignity have been building their castles ever since.

At the end of the war, American psychiatry lost no time demonstrating its usefulness to the country at peace. Ezra Pound, one of the greatest poets of his time, was indicted for treason—a charge he vehemently denied. Whether he was innocent or guilty of that crime, psychiatry spared the nation the need to undergo the political soul-searching that his trial would have generated. Prosecution and "defense" conspired to declare Pound mentally unfit to stand trial, condemning him instead, without trial, to serve a thirteen-year sentence in St. Elizabeth's Hospital, the nation's model psychiatric dungeon in Washington, D.C. Pound's jailer was hailed as a great psychiatrist, the benefactor of Pound as well as the nation.

Neither the mass stigmatization of American servicemen as mad, nor the psychiatric diversion of the Pound case

 "How Dan White Got Away With Murder," by Thomas Szasz, *Inquiry,* August 6 & 20, 1979. Reprinted by permission.

from the criminal to the mental-health system, was considered to be an abuse of psychiatry. The American public has been led to believe that only in Russia do psychiatrists abuse psychiatry; that in the West, psychiatrists use psychiatry only to do good. But what is the nature of that good? With its service to the nation richly rewarded, postwar psychiatry proudly declared its lofty aims. "The belated objectives of practically all effective psychotherapy," declared Brock Chisholm in 1946, "are the reinterpretation and eventual eradication of the concept of right and wrong. If the race is to be freed from its crippling burden of good and evil, it must be psychiatrists who take the original responsibility." The physician who uttered this much-neglected self-revelation of the moral and political mandate of psychiatry was the former director general of medical services in the Canadian army, the head of the World Federation of Mental Health, and the director of the World Health Organization. Thirty-three years later, the men and women who sat on the jury in San Francisco in the case of Dan White proved themselves to be apt pupils of the psychiatric perverters of our system of justice.

In the postwar years, psychiatrists continued their crusade against homosexuals, whom they called, among other things, "inverts" and "perverts," and whose incarceration as "sex offenders" they enthusiastically supported. "If it is considered the will of the majority," declared one of the then leading American psychiatrists, "that large numbers of sex offenders . . . be indefinitely deprived of their liberty and supported at the expense of the state, I readily yield to that judgment." That opinion was uttered in 1951 by Manfred Guttmacher, in whose honor the American Psychiatric Association offers an annual award "for outstanding contribution to the literature of forensic psychiatry"—in other words, for the most valuable contribution to the psychiatric subversion of the rule of law.

In 1974, the American Psychiatric Association (under pressure from gay liberationists) dropped homosexuality from the official roster of mental diseases, while still maintaining that the conversion of homosexuals to heterosexuality is a bona fide treatment. Thus it would be a serious mistake to believe that these long-standing enemies of homosexuals have really changed their minds about one of their most dearly hated scapegoats. For example, Karl Menninger, the undisputed dean of postwar American psychiatry, has never retracted the following views, which he set forth in 1963. After denigrating homosexuals by classifying their "condition" as a species of "Second Order of Dyscontrol and Dysorganization," Menninger asserts: "We do not, like some, condone it [homosexuality]. We regard it as a symptom with all the functions of other symptoms—aggression, indulgence, self-punishment, and the effort to forestall something worse." While Menninger thus stigmatizes and slanders homosexuals, he tries, in every way possible, to relieve real criminals of responsibility. His crowning achievement in this enterprise is epitomized in the title of one of his most celebrated books: *The Crime of Punishment*. According to Menninger, the punishment even of persons guilty of the most heinous crimes, is, quite literally, a crime —whereas their crime is not a crime. Lest anyone think that Menninger is championing liberty for lawbreakers, let me hasten to add that he is not championing liberty for anyone; instead, he seeks to lump the "criminal" together with the rest of humanity—everyone being a fit subject for

indefinite psychiatric incarceration at the whim of the psychiatrist. In his magnum opus, *The Vital Balance*, Menninger declares "that all people have mental illness of different degrees at different times, and that sometimes some are much worse, or better."

THIS BRINGS US, HISTORICALLY AS WELL as logically, to the present psychiatric-legal situation in California: in particular, to the concept of "diminished mental capacity" as a defense in criminal law.

Modern medicine has revealed that the capacities of various organs to perform their functions may be impaired or abolished by disease. The liver, for example, may have a diminished capacity to metabolize certain nutrients and to secrete bile—the result of which may be jaundice and death. Similarly, the kidneys may have a diminished capacity to secrete metabolites and excrete urine—the result of which may be uremia and death. And so on, with the capacities of the lung, the heart, and other organs.

Psychiatry has always been living off a succession of medical metaphors. Its whole idea of mental illness, as I have shown elsewhere, is one colossal metaphor. In postwar America, psychiatry was hungry for fresh concepts to live off. Thus, the psychiatrists borrowed from medicine the idea of the "diminished capacity" of an organ and applied it, literally, to "criminal responsibility." The authority widely acknowledged to be most responsible for popularizing the doctrine of "diminished capacity" is Bernard Diamond, a professor of psychiatry and law at the University of California at Berkeley. With this mendacity through metaphor, Diamond helped to lay the ground for decisions such as the jury reached in the White case. Let us keep in mind, however, that Diamond's opinions are hardly novel, following, as they do, upon decades of psychiatric attacks on criminal responsibility as a moral concept.

Diamond writes: "[S]cientific evidence proves that there is no such thing as free will. . . . Each [criminal] case should be judged on its own clinical merits." Diamond thus takes it for granted that every defendant is a "patient" whose "case" has "clinical merits."

All human behavior—each "act of will"—is, moreover, nothing but a physiological process: "Each act of will, each choice, presumably made on a random basis, turns out to be as rigidly determined as any other physiological process of the human body."

Diamond writes as if the metaphor of diminished responsibility were an established "fact": "We thus arrive at a legal spectrum of an infinitely graduated scale of responsibility which corresponds, or could be made to correspond closely, to the psychological reality of human beings as understood by twentieth century medical psychology."

Of course, no one can see, smell, taste, or measure "criminal responsibility," normal or diminished. This makes it different from the diminished capacities of the liver, the lungs, the kidneys, and other organs, all of which are readily measurable. Nor is this a matter of technological sophistication. Criminal responsibility will *never* be measurable— because it just isn't that sort of thing. That it is not is something psychiatrists know perfectly well, which supports the impression that they are not fond of telling the truth. In the very article in which he touts the concept of diminished capacity, in the *Stanford Law Review* of December 1961,

3. THE JUDICIAL SYSTEM

Diamond writes: "I concede that this whole business of lack of mental capacity to premeditate, to have malice or to entertain intent, is a kind of sophistry [that is, a kind of lie] which must not be allowed to remain an end in itself. Right now we must utilize these legal technicalities to permit psychiatrists to gain entrance into the trial court."

Why didn't the prosecutor read these lines to the White jury? And why didn't he read Diamond's further psychiatric-imperialistic declarations published in the same article? "The next step after *Gorshen* [a 1957 trial at which Diamond testified] is to expand the principle of limited or diminished responsibility of the mentally ill offender to include all definitions of crime. . . . The ultimate step will be the extension of the treatment principle to all prisoners —sane, insane, fully responsible, and partially responsible."

Here it is, in black and white. Diamond is not in the least interested in justice—and like Menninger he says so. What he is interested in is treatment—that is, in medicalizing law, crime, and punishment.

AGAINST THIS BACKDROP WE CAN BETTER reconsider the killing of George Moscone and Harvey Milk and the psychiatric exoneration of the man who killed them. Most of the facts of this case have been well publicized and are familiar, especially to those who have paid attention to this astonishing judicial-psychiatric spectacle. It is a spectacle for which we do not have a proper vocabulary. We have a rich lexicon to describe unjust punishments meted out to innocent victims—judicial lynching by a kangaroo court being a succinct and picturesque way of describing that sort of legal crime. Revealingly, we have no comparable words to describe the inverse aberration of justice, such as occurred in the White affair. "Getting away with murder" is the closest we can come to it. This is not inaccurate, but is inadequate since it neglects to suggest how the judicial crime in question was perpetrated.

Keep in mind that according to the experts—one more of whom I shall quote in a moment—there is no such thing as a political assassination in America. In America, only "mental patients" kill political figures.

■ The mayor of one of America's great cities is killed by five shots, two of them fired into his head at close range after he is gunned down with three previous shots. The mayor is a "liberal" protector of the rights of sexual minorities. The assassin is a "conservative" foe of "social deviants." The killing is not a political crime, asserts prosecutor Thomas Norman.

■ The most prominent self-declared homosexual politician in America is killed by four shots, two of them fired into his head as he lies fatally wounded. The killer is the mayor's assassin, who reloaded his gun after the first killing. That's not a political crime either, says Norman.

What else do you expect? In an America poisoned by psychiatry, any political embarrassment or crime can be psychiatrized. James Forrestal, former secretary of the navy and the first U.S. secretary of defense, begins to act erratically and is imprisoned by psychiatrists in a suite on the top floor of the National Naval Medical Center, from which he allegedly jumps to his death. Ezra Pound is, as I have noted, incarcerated in a madhouse for thirteen years. Major General Edwin Walker, implicated in an integration riot, is imprisoned in a federal insane asylum in an effort to deprive him of his right to stand trial.

John Kennedy is assassinated. The explanation? A lone psychotic named Lee Harvey Oswald shot him. Oswald, in turn, was shot by another lone psychotic, called Jack Ruby. If you don't believe that, you are paranoid.

Robert Kennedy is assassinated. The explanation? Another lone psychotic, this time a Palestinian-American called Sirhan Sirhan, shot him. Sirhan did it, the psychiatrists claimed, because he fell off a horse when he was a child. If you don't believe that, you are paranoid.

You are paranoid because American psychiatry has established that in our "sick society" what seem to be political assassinations are, in reality, not political acts at all. As Edwin Weinstein, a professor at Mount Sinai Medical School, wrote in 1976 in one of the most prestigious American psychiatric journals: "Assassinations of heads of state of foreign countries have usually been carried out by organized political groups seeking to overthrow the government or change its policies. In the United States, on the other hand, Presidential assassinations have been the work of mentally deranged individuals."

How many more cases or authorities must one cite to prove that not only Russian psychiatry, but American psychiatry also, is a political weapon?

To return to the most recent case of a psychiatrically depoliticized political assassination—that of the assassination of George Moscone and Harvey Milk—consider the following:

■ The killer of Moscone and Milk had been informed that his political hopes had been destroyed by Moscone's refusal to reappoint him supervisor, a refusal in which Milk was thought to have had a hand. The next morning the killer came to City Hall with a well-hidden gun and ten extra bullets; gained entrance to the building through a window, thus avoiding the metal-detectors at the door; shot Moscone five times; reloaded his gun; then shot Milk four times. To the psychiatrists all this proved diminished capacity to premeditate.

■ One psychiatrist insisted that the killer was a "good man"; this also proved that he had diminished capacity.

■ White sat at home consuming Cokes, Twinkies, and other "junk food" before the killings, said another psychiatrist—additional evidence that he had diminished capacity.

■ The defense and the prosecution collaborated in deliberately depoliticizing the assassinations. After the trial, defense attorney Stephen Scherr told the *San Francisco Examiner* that "the defense was wary of having gays serve on the jury. He said the attorneys feared that a gay might believe that the slaying of Milk, San Francisco's first openly homosexual supervisor, was a political assassination committed to block gay power. Scherr said such a belief would be contrary to the facts in the case. . . ." This is like excluding black jurors from the trial of the accused assassin of Martin Luther King (the alleged assassin was, of course, never tried)—on the grounds that they might mistakenly believe that the killing had something to do with the fact that King was black.

WHEN PATIENTS DO NOT WANT TO face unpleasant facts, psychiatrists love to tell them that they are practicing "denial" and "repression." That may be true—although we must remember that patients have a right to deny or repress any fact they please. But witnesses in criminal trials are sworn to tell the truth. Journalists saw the truth—and they saw it withheld, evaded, and obscured by the psychiatrists (and the prosecution).

Charles McCabe, *San Francisco Chronicle* columnist, wrote:

[Quoting free-lance writer Mike Weiss:] "The San Francisco image-mongers—the politicians and the flacks—don't talk out loud about the seething frustrations and angers aroused by this confrontation [between straights and gays]. But, out in the neighborhoods, everybody knows San Francisco has a sexual integration crisis." . . . [Dan] White [McCabe continues] had all the old-fashioned prejudices and bigotries. He hated blacks and "queers" and made no secret of it. . . . The man [Moscone] who double-crossed him had offended his manhood. Moreover, the mayor was the most powerful friend the homosexuals had in this city. . . .

Herb Caen, another *Chronicle* columnist, was equally candid:

"What's wrong with San Francisco?" was being asked again yesterday . . . one can kill, twice, complete with coup de grace, and get away with it. The grateful defendant was a staunch defender of law and order . . . a religious man who went straight to church after he killed. . . . This is a city of undercurrents, not all of them well hidden. Many police made an open secret of their support for Dan White and their dislike (understatement) of homosexuals. . . .

If these journalists are telling the truth, what did the psychiatrists tell us and the jury? A "higher" version of the truth—or strategic untruths? Since "psychiatric expert testimony" is, legally speaking, *opinion*, it can never be perjured. This fact points to the role of the single prosecution psychiatrist in the White case. This physician was foolish enough actually to examine Dan White on the day of the killings. He testified that he found White to be sane, competent, and responsible for his actions. The jury, no doubt, concluded that he was an inept doctor who couldn't find the "diminished capacity" so easily detected by four other doctors and a clinical psychologist.

The very act of examining White was stupid and totally inconsistent with mounting a strong case for the prosecution. The fact that the DA had White examined must have proved to the jury—and rightly so—that there was something a psychiatrist *could* discover by examining him that would be relevant for establishing White's "capacity" to commit first degree murder. Therein, precisely, lies the utter hoax of "diminished capacity." In my opinion, the prosecution should have led the jury to infer malice and premeditation from the facts of the case—just as a jury is supposed to infer malpractice when a surgeon leaves a sponge in the patient's stomach.

White's defense thus rested on two separate pillars: psychiatry and the plea of "diminished capacity" was one; a subtle but persistent appeal to the jury's antihomosexual prejudices was another. This latter aspect of the defense strategy has seemingly been overlooked by most previous commentators on the trial.

"Good people—fine people with fine backgrounds—simply don't kill people in cold blood," was Schmidt's premise in interpreting, to jury and press alike, what "really" happened to Dan White. "Seeing Mrs. White," wrote a reporter for the *San Francisco Chronicle*, "it was impossible for the jury not to believe that White came from a decent, hard-working background that they, the jury

members, shared and admired. Repeatedly, Schmidt used the word 'background'. . . ."

"Background" was, indeed, the code word. For what? Primarily for "straight" (as against gay)—and secondarily, for white, Christian, policeman (as against black, Jewish, "deviant"). But if Schmidt's bigoted premise—which the prosecution never challenged and hence the jury readily accepted—is allowed to stand, then no heterosexual, married, policeman jogger will ever be convicted of first degree murder in America again.

Thus with great skill Schmidt successfully replaced the reality of Dan White, the moral actor on the stage of life, with the abstractions of White's "diminished capacity" and his "background"—and then instructed the jury to focus on those fictions and ignore the facts.

As soon as the trial was over, one of the defense psychiatrists gave an interview in which he flatly contradicted his own testimony. As a witness for the defense, Martin Blinder, a San Francisco psychiatrist, "told the jury [according to *Newsweek*, June 4] that White's compulsive diet of candy bars, cupcakes and Cokes was evidence of a deep depression—and a source of excessive sugar that had aggravated a chemical imbalance in his brain." Two weeks later, Blinder—who says he has been "involved in thousands of cases"—told a *San Francisco Chronicle* reporter: "Judges and juries should determine issues of guilt and innocence, sanity and insanity . . . psychiatrists are often pushed into making that decision for them. . . . There is a tendency for psychiatrists to find mental illness in every instance of emotional stress. I personally resist this."

But who is "pushing" Blinder or any other psychiatrist to testify in a criminal trial? No one! In each and every case, a psychiatrist who testifies in court is a hired gun. He does what he does for money or fame or because he believes in it, or, as Bernard Diamond implied, to gain eventual control of the entire judicial system. Assuredly, he does not do it because anyone forces him to—just as no one forces him to go to court to commit innocent people to mental hospitals, which hired psychiatric guns also love to do.

AFTER THE WAR, THE GERMAN PEOPLE could not claim that they did not realize what the Nazis were planning for the Jews. Hitler had warned them of his intentions clearly enough—in *Mein Kampf* and the voluminous anti-Semitic literature that accompanied the National Socialists' rise to power. After they awaken from their psychiatric stupor, the American people will not be able to claim that they did not realize what the psychiatrists were planning for all of us. The psychiatrists have warned them of their intentions clearly enough—in books with such telling titles as *The Crime of Punishment* and the voluminous antiresponsibility and procommitment literature that accompanied these pseudomedical prevaricators' rise to power.

When psychiatric testimony is used as it has been in the White trial, where are the so-called critics of psychiatry—those who timidly chastise the sensational foreign or marginal domestic abuses of the profession, and thus make headlines for themselves as humanitarians? Do they speak out against gross psychiatric abuses, such as have occurred in the White case and in other cases of political assassination? The fact is they never do.

3. THE JUDICIAL SYSTEM

Mrs. Rosalynn Carter is so tireless a promoter of this fake religion that she seems to be veritably thrice-born: as a human being, a Baptist, and a votary of psychiatry. One could reasonably expect that a person so lavish in her praise of the "good" that psychiatry has done would feel duty-bound to speak out when psychiatrists make a mockery of justice. But she has not.

Where were our conservative and neoconservative journalists and thinkers, who so lament the decline of the sense of personal responsibility in our "permissive" society? Where, when all is said and done, were the ever-ready crusaders for human rights and justice throughout the world? Did they protest the injustice of the White verdict? No, they did not.

In the struggle against the psychiatric perversion of responsibility and justice, I propose that we make Voltaire's famous battle cry—"Écrasez l'infâme!" ("crush the infamous thing!")—our own. The infamous thing that Voltaire sought to crush was the political power of the Roman Catholic church. The infamous thing that we ought to crush is the political power of the Church of Psychiatry.

Or, to take another famous example from French history, of another crusade for justice—at the end of the last century, French society was wracked by the trial and conviction of Captain Albert Dreyfus. What the Dreyfus affair was for the French at that time, the Dan White affair ought to become for us now. In the Dreyfus case, the judicial system was used to convict a demonstrably innocent man. In the White case, the judicial system was used to exonerate a demonstrably guilty one.

Dreyfus, the Jew, was the victim. White, the policeman, is the victimizer. Dreyfus became the symbol of what happens to an innocent individual when anti-Semitic hatred in the community, unacknowledged but powerful, is allowed to masquerade as justice. White should become a symbol of what happens to a guilty individual when anti-

homosexual hatred, unacknowledged but powerful, is allowed to masquerade as justice.

Who allowed—who, indeed, engineered—these carefully orchestrated miscarriages of justice? In the Dreyfus case, it was the French military and the power it then wielded in the French courts. In the White case, it is American psychiatry and the power it now wields in the American courts. As Émile Zola then accused the French generals of having perverted the legal order in "l'affaire Dreyfus," so I accuse organized American psychiatry of perverting the legal order in the White affair.

I maintain that American psychiatry is White's accomplice in crime. While White pulled the trigger of the gun that killed Moscone and Milk, American psychiatry pulled the wool over the eyes of lawmakers and journalists and the public—leading to the courtroom scenario of psychiatrists fabricating fantasies and having their fantasies legitimized by the courts as "expert medical testimony."

On Mondays, Wednesdays, and Fridays, the psychiatric prevaricators thus go to court to exonerate the guilty: That is called "psychiatric defense." On Tuesdays, Thursdays, and Saturdays, the same prevaricators go to court to incriminate the innocent: That is called "civil commitment." The lawmakers, the judges, and the attorneys (for both sides) all shamelessly use these fakes—which is why each of them is as reluctant to expose and demolish the psychiatric defense of the guilty as he is to expose and demolish the psychiatric incrimination of the innocent.

Long before Dreyfus's days, the homosexual was already one of psychiatry's favorite scapegoats. American psychiatry's true feeling about homosexuals showed in all its ugliness once more in the trial of Dan White. Let us hope that the White affair will arouse the sense of justice in the gay community in America and in the hearts of all who sympathize with such victimization; and that the result will be the long-overdue expulsion of the psychiatric liars from the courtroom—whether they come to pervert justice by imprisoning the innocent or by exculpating the guilty.

Where the System Breaks Down

Bottleneck Number One

Michael Fooner

Author of five recent books on criminal justice and police science, and numerous national magazine articles.

It is 2:15 in Arraignment Court.

The cop says, "If I'm lucky, I'll be out of here by 4, 4:30. There's only about 30 cases ahead of mine."

Thirty — in two hours? That figures handling an average of a case every four minutes.

"This judge is OK," the cop says, "he can do 'em in 3, if the lawyers don't screw up."

Arraignment is a peculiar court, a surprise to many, a mystery to some. For New York cops it's a "melting pot," where their annual 90,000 felony arrests melt down to about 30,000 felony cases, making for statistical confusion as to just how many serious crimes are there in New York. There are two viewpoints. One holds arraignment court is the mechanism that keeps the city's entire criminal justice system from grinding down to a convulsive halt. The other says it shows where the system is coming unglued.

It's a court that even looks peculiar, inside and out. On the inside, you see many cops dressed in blue jeans, plaid shirt, no tie, leather jacket. You see many of the prisoners wearing blue jeans, tieless open shirts, leather jackets. You can tell cops from prisoners because the cops sit for long periods of time in the first row of seats where there is a sign: "Reserved For Police Officers." Prisoners are the ones brought in from the bull pen for a few minutes each to stand in front of the judge's bench.

On the outside it's strange, too. In the heart of downtown Manhattan, federal, state and city courthouses are spotted close by one another. There's the United States Court House, with its classicistic row of granite columns, fulfilling the public image of a temple of justice. The State Supreme Court looks like an economy model of the same.

But the city's Criminal Court Building looks like a factory, somewhat antiquated, run down, grimy. "Factory" is not entirely a metaphor; people employed in Arraignment often speak of their work as "processing," as if they are engaged in a service industry. Their commodity happens to be criminal cases. Volume, rather than neatness, counts.

Brooklyn, Queens, Bronx and Staten Island have their own criminal courts and receive shares of the city's 200,000 plus yearly arrests for felonies, misdemeanors and violations, but Manhattan gets the big bite of the Big Apple's criminal accusations, 85,000 to 90,000 a year, and these funnel into four courtrooms at 100 Centre Street.

Pushing The Revolving Door

Room 129 is Arraignment Part 1, — a scribbled "A R 1" on a piece of paper is scotch-taped to the door — and handles most of the felony cases. Up front now, a short stocky prisoner stands facing the judge, a Legal Aid defense counsel to the left of him, an assistant district attorney to his right, arresting officer behind.

In this court, you can easily tell the lawyers from the prisoners and cops because the lawyers wear jackets, and neckties, sometimes vests. Women lawyers wear varied costumes.

The court-wise cop who has estimated he'll be out by 4:30 is watching the action for a moment but doesn't mind a bit of conversation.

"What's your case, Officer —?"

"Hollis, Arthur Hollis. Burglary, three guys, Took them from a residential building on East 98th Street. Booked them on felonies. I started my shift 10 o'clock last night."

"What do you think will happen when your case is called?"

He shrugs. "Probably my felony arrests get knocked down to misdemeanors; and they walk." He smiles. "They'll be out of here before I am."

But newspaper editorials have taught people to be as cynical about cops as cops are about courts.

"Meanwhile, you draw overtime pay."

"Maybe."

"Who's been patrolling your territory while you are down here waiting?"

"Depends what my sergeant was able to do with the precinct work schedule, vacations, sick leaves, whatever."

3. THE JUDICIAL SYSTEM

Where Is Solomon?

About 30 percent of the cases coming into the Arraignment Parts on an average day are felonies. There are also likely to be three to four dozen prostitution cases, and practically all of them will be disposed of with guilty pleas.

"About half will be sentenced to 'time served' in the lock-up while waiting for their cases to be processed, the others will be fined, $25, $50, $100, and told to bring in the money in ten days. Everybody knows where they'll get that money.

"What does this make the judge?" asks a courthouse buff named Charlie.

In New York as in America all over, burglary is the No. 1 serious crime in frequency, with robbery, assault and grand larceny right behind. Together these four types of felonies comprise about 25 percent of what comes into the court system year after year —

and two out of every five of them, in New York, end up as dismissals.

"That doesn't mean 22,000-plus people accused of serious crimes every year are innocent," says Charlie. "It could mean our fancy, billion-dollar criminal justice system has some screws loose. Why bring them to court in the first place, spend time, money and legal talent, then end up with a dismissal? — Should these people be jailed or shouldn't they? If not, why clutter up the courthouse with them? If the courts had fewer cases, couldn't everybody do a better job on the really serious cases?"

In a single year nearly six thousand persons arrested for burglary in Manhattan have their cases dismissed. Also: more than 6,000 assault cases, nearly 5,000 grand larcenies, nearly 5,000 robberies, all dismissed.

"All went through arraignment," says Charlie. "Why? Anybody could have predicted what would happen to them."

Clogging Is Not an Irish Jig

Police Officer Hollis was right: The judge is doing cases at an average of 3 minutes each.

It's after 3:00 P.M., and the court room is becoming more crowded instead of emptying out. Although Judge Alberg can move cases every three minutes, there are intervals when, for some reason, the flow stops and the waiting people accumulate. By 4:00 P.M., the scene justifies his remark, "It's like Grand Central Station."

Criminal Court Justice Harold Alberg, 44, in his eighth year on this bench, has a nice oval face, brown shell-rim eye-glasses, and a head of dark brown hair which is in full view a great deal of the time while his head is down as he reads papers put before him one after another by court attendants. He speaks his orders in a quiet voice as he scribbles on each paper and stamps it.

Arraignment operates seven days a week, 52 weeks a year.

"If we could keep an even flow of cases, there would be absolutely no problem," he says. "When the flow stops, there's clogging, and we don't know why. We can only wait for it to unclog."

The noise level of the court room has suddenly diminished as a voice up front is heard — a defense lawyer making an impassioned plea, arguing vigorously against the prosecutor's recommendation of $7,500 bail in a homicide with knife. Animation in the crowded room is suspended.

Judge Alberg listens, attentive but poker faced, then says, "$5,000 bail."

The defense lawyer resumes his passionate speech, throws his hands up high in a gesture of despair, says a few words to his client, slams angrily out of the court room, while the accused homicide is led back to the cells.

At the back of the room, Charlie murmurs confidentially to strangers nearby, "Private lawyer, earning his fee, putting on an act for the relatives."

The noise level is back up to where it was. Every ten or twenty minutes a court officer calls out for quiet, please.

At 5, Judge Alberg has one more hour to go, and he is pushing to finish his calendar. Prosecutor and Legal Aids are trying, too, but for some cases, papers, defendants and lawyers somehow aren't coordinating. Alberg directs these cases be held for Night Court.

It is past 5:30. The big doors of the public entrance swing open and Supervising Justice of the New York County Criminal Court comes in for a look around. For him the day started a little after 8:00 A.M., with routine anxiety.

A Day in Court

About 8:30 he received the routine phone call from Phil Necci, Court Clerk in Charge of the Arraignment Parts: "We got 432."

In Arraignment, no one addresses a judge as "Your Honor."

"If there's 432 cases, today must be Thursday," the judge quips.

Thursday is usually the heaviest day of the week, Sunday and Monday the lightest. Such statistics show either that criminals commit more crimes midweek, or more frequently escape undetected on weekends.

The Supervising Justice and three other judges would be working. That figures to a mathematical average of 108½ cases a judge. Working seven hours each with a one-hour lunch break, if all average 15 or 16 cases an hour, they've got the day made.

But like the first day of Genesis, most days in this court begin "without form, and void, and the Spirit of God hovering . . ."

Above the unoccupied judge's bench there appears in large letters, "In God We Trust."

The bench remains empty.

A R 1, for adult felonies, opens at 10; A R 2 across the hall for misdemeanors, opens at 9. Upstairs on the second floor, A R 2A, for juvenile and selected minor cases, also opens at 9.

There's no telling how long each bench will remain empty; 30 minutes? Could be an hour, could be more.

When Judge Alberg is sitting in A R 1, he gets to the courthouse shortly after 9:00. Ten o'clock finds him in the "robing room," a small bare high-ceiling box of a room behind an unmarked door in the rear of the courtroom, sitting in his black gown with his glasses on, reading the New York Law Journal.

There's nothing else he can do. At maybe 10:45 or 11:15, or whenever, there's a knock on the robing room door. It has happened: Three case folders are "on the table" — ready. He quick steps to the bench and signals for the first case to be called. He disposes of it and two others in short order, hoping that meanwhile additional cases are being made ready. Case folders are beginning to pile up on the assistant district attorney's end of the table, but what really counts are the case folders laid in a row on the center of the table — cases ready to be called. That's the barometer, and if that space has two or more folders on it at all times, the day is going well. If it is empty for a period of time, it means "clogging" has set in. A judge can sit there, or he can retire to the robing room, but he cannot do anything to help.

In principle, a judge runs his own courtroom. In practice a criminal court judge sitting in arraignment is run by the "ready" cases on the table, that and the tyranny of the clock.

Cases a day court judge doesn't finish are held over for night court; cases not finished in night court are hold-overs for the following day, whose case load of fresh arrests has been accumulating from the previous afternoon onward.

On an average good day, a judge will move 20 to 35 cases during the morning, recess for lunch about 1:15 or so, and hope the pace picks up by the time he gets back.

No Rush to Judgment

With all this concern for moving cases, the system has a strange domination over people rather than the opposite. The army of arrests must be kept marching, and there are people in cell blocks to consider. Delays and paper "clogging" in the system can mean people spending extra nights locked up without regard to the merit or the seriousness of their cases.

"It's like running a railroad without timetables," says the Supervising Justice. "It's as if we have to tell a passenger your train will start when it's ready, or it will arrive when it gets there."

What actually happens when a prisoner's family or lawyer asks the status of a case is that a clerk is likely to say, "Just keep watching the wall where we post the dockets."

Police Officer Arthur Hollis was, according to official record, "in court" all day, but there was nothing for him to do in the court room. He went for coffee several times, carrying it in a paper cup to the Police Officers Waiting Room which, like the arraignment court room itself, could benefit from a fresh coat of wall paint.

Cops are scattered about, sitting, talking, reading *The Daily News,* sipping coffee, sleeping, chewing gum — and waiting, waiting for their names on the public address horn or some other signal that it's time to get your case ready.

Hollis was out at midnight patrolling with his partner when a citizen's call, relayed over their radio, sent them to the scene of a burglary and resulted in their making arrests of three young men who called themselves Chris, Donnie and Jocko. The cops reported to their sergeant and after that drove their prisoners down to Police Headquarters, near Brooklyn Bridge. Hollis remained with the suspects to see to the booking, which consists of filling out report forms in multiple copies, fingerprinting each suspect, and checking them into the holding cells. Hollis and his prisoners became part of a stream of cops and suspects coming into Central Booking from all over the Island of Manhattan, their arrests part of a stream of report forms and fingerprint cards. Facsimiles of the fingerprint cards are sent by wire to Albany for a search through central police records and a report on each suspect's criminal background if any.

"How long does all this take?"

"Depends on how many others are being booked, how many are working in central booking and in Albany's central records, and if the facs machine doesn't break down."

"How often does that happen?"

"Not as often as they say, more often than you expect."

After booking, Hollis has to file his complaint, as arresting officer, and get his witness to be present if there is a witness — but that cannot be done until sometime after 8:00 A.M. when the Complaint Room opens; and it ordinarily cannot be done after 2:00 P.M. when the Complaint Room puts the 'lid' on, having all the cases on hand they can handle that day. The cop must come back the following day. The suspect stays locked up in the meantime.

In any event, a case cannot move until the arrested person's record is found in Albany, or not found, and wired back to New York, to be clipped to the cop's arrest report forms and sent to the Complaint Room.

Some time after that, the cop is called on the public address horn to go sit down with an assistant district attorney and tell his story. The ADA fills in forms and sends what is now a "package" to the typing pool — which is simultaneously receiving such packages from nine other ADAs. Eventually the multiple-typed case is sent to the Docket Room for docketing, to the Clerk's Room for notations and listing, and then delivered to the courtroom — copy for prosecutor, copy for Legal Aid defense attorney, copy for the court clerk.

No one has yet calculated how many pairs of hands have to handle paper before a case can get into the courtroom where a judge is ultimately going to consider it for 3 to 5 minutes, average time.

But everyone is acutely aware of the number of points along the way at which cases can be stalled, pile up, "clog the system."

Each of the 200,000 yearly arrests has to basically go through the same process, whether the accusation is murder or rape or stealing a truckload of something or beating the subway out of a 50-cent fare.

"Anyway, your case is now typed and foldered and in the courtroom, and you are pretty close to the end of the line."

3. THE JUDICIAL SYSTEM

"Maybe, maybe not," Officer Hollis says. "I can go down to the holding pens in the basement and bring my prisoners up to the cells behind the courtroom —

"But now we wait until a Legal Aid lawyer gets around to picking my case out of the basket, and until he or she goes out to interview my prisoners, and until they decide how they are going to handle the case."

"That takes how long?"

"Could be minutes, could be longer; depends on the individual case, depends how Legal Aid feels about the judge, or the prosecutor. My case doesn't move until Legal Aid is ready."

Hollis, age 31, with nine years on the force, has learned patience, but he still has strong opinions. "They're always pushing for leniency, you know, and if they get it, from the ADA and the judge, they move cases fast. If they think the ADA is rough or the judge is tough ——" He shrugs to convey his message that he's helpless, the system's hopeless.

"Nonsense," declare Joe Silverman and Patricia Ferguson in unison. Though youthful-looking, each has had many years of solid work as a Legal Aid criminal defense lawyer. Ask them what's wrong with the system, and they can tick off the failings of the prosecution faster than a supermarket checkout cashier runs up your grocery bill.

"Cases come in with overblown charges, based on cops' hyped-up arrest reports; the cop looks to score heavy in felony arrests to fatten his personnel folder. The average ADA working the Arraignment Part is assigned to it because he is low man on the DA's staff, hasn't too much experience, but wants to make a record as a sharp prosecutor, get the criminal off the streets, protect the public, impress his boss, the DA. They need more seasoning and experience to evaluate cases realistically, how the evidence will stand up if the case does go to trial. They play safe by asking for more bail or incarceration than necessary — all we do is redress the balance for fairness."

Police Officer Hollis is right again. His case is called just before 4:40, and he fetches his three prisoners from the cell block behind the courtroom.

He stands behind them as they arrange themselves in a row at the table before the judge's bench. A court officer holding their case papers in his left hand, raises his right hand: "You swear ——?"

"Yes" says Hollis, raising and lowering his right hand.

Looking in the direction of the prisoners, the court officer says: "Waive reading of rights?"

"Yes," answers the Legal Aid lawyer for them.

The ADA, talking fast, reads items from the case folders and recommends bail of $500 each. The Legal Aid lawyer reads other items from the duplicate folders and urges "ROR" — release on own recognizance, no bail.

The judge, also reading duplicate folders, calls both lawyers to the bench for a few moments of low-voiced talk, then says: "ROR — to return eighth of next month." He scribbles and stamps papers, and tosses them to the clerk at a desk to his right.

The next case is being called as Hollis' former prisoners march out of the courtroom, Officer Hollis half a dozen steps behind them.

"What's happened?"

"They're lucky."

"To get out, without bail?"

"Lucky I arrested them near midnight, and their papers got processed the same day. If they'd been arrested later, or if their papers weren't finished with processing until afternoon, the case would probably have to be held over until tomorrow and they'd have had to spend a night in jail."

"But they are still charged, and they have to come back to a hearing. They might even have to go to trial and be convicted."

"If they go to trial, it's better than 50-50 they'll be acquitted. The lawyers will get together, they'll plead to misdemeanors and end up with a couple of months' sentence, suspended."

It is 6:00 P.M. Judge Alberg's court, A R 1, is finished. Across the hall, A R 2 finished at 5:00. Upstairs, A R 2A also closed at 5:00. Night court, A R 3, is in session.

By 2:00 A.M., the four parts of Arraignment for New York County will have handled 432 cases — one day's work in one of five courthouses dealing with crime in the city. Some days a question gets asked: Why?

There's an easy answer, and a hard answer. The easy answer is, "Because they are there — with 200,000 people getting arrested each year, we have to do *something* with them." Today, for instance:

There were guilty pleas from 135 persons; 75 had charges dismissed or cases adjourned in contemplation of dismissal, ACDs; 41 warrants were issued against defendants who failed to show up for arraignment; in 7 cases earlier sentences were vacated; in 10 others, sentences previously suspended were ordered into effect. In 120 cases, the accused were ordered to appear in the All Purpose Part of the Criminal Court for a hearing, and some of those will go on to further stages. A small handful will be set for trial.

Of the most frequent and most worrisome felony cases — burglaries, robberies, assaults and grand larcenies — fewer than two hundred a year will end in convictions after trial. About 18 or 19 thousand will plead guilty.

But meanwhile, a more than equal number of those felonies will gain dismissal.

Getting the answer to "Why?" is to enter a part of the world where the law and the nature of human beings respond to each other like oil and water.

Husbands and wives fight, neighbors fight, bosses and employees fight, lovers fight, customers and merchants fight, landlords and tenants fight. A certain number injure each other, take property from each other, by stealth or by force, and inevitably some will seek redress by calling in "the law," charging assault, robbery, burglary or larceny — legal code words. There are complaints to the police, arrests, and "the law" takes over. Processing of a case begins, paperwork snowballs, the human side gets submerged in the procedures. The victim is suddenly transmuted into a witness, into an actor in a drama.

TABLE 3
How Felony Arrests are Disposed of in Criminal Court
(The following figures are from an analysis of dispositions of arrests in the Criminal Court for the first half of 1977 prepared by the Office of Court Administration. Numbers have been doubled to show annual rates. "Number Dismissed" omits cases where the defendant pleaded guilty to another docket number, was committed for treatment, or died during the pendency of the charges.)

	Total Felony Arrests Processed by Criminal Court	Number of Arrests Held for Felony Prosecution in Supreme Court	Number of Arrests Dismissed in Criminal Court	Number of Arrests Plea-Bargained in Criminal Court
Murder	860	746 (86.7%)	100 (11.6%)	10 (1.2%)
Rape	1432	598 (41.8%)	550 (38.4%)	218 (15.2%)
Robbery	12862	5016 (39.0%)	4102 (31.9%)	3294 (25.6%)
Assault	12532	974 (7.8%)	5582 (44.5%)	4548 (36.3%)
Burglary	16162	1606 (9.9%)	4480 (27.7%)	9242 (57.2%)
Grand Larceny	15390	866 (5.6%)	4388 (28.5%)	9516 (61.8%)

Miscasting is rife. The victim-turned-witness turns out to be forgiving, compassionate, frightened, vengeful, poor in memory, overly imaginitive, partly culpable, or even to have a criminal record of his or her own. Poor health, impatience, personal or business concerns may interfere with court appearances.

"Give the kid a chance." "His buddies will come and get you." Restitution, kiss and make up. Who will watch the store while you are in court? Who will support the family if he goes to jail? Why get involved —

"O.K.," says Charlie, the courtroom philosopher, "believe all you want in 'let the punishment fit the crime,' but there is a dilemma which can louse up the neat disposition of cases, and it is now inherent in our urban environment."

"Maybe somebody should face up to this dilemma."

Unfelonious Felons

The dilemma is not new. Exactly one hundred years ago a noted Briton, member of the bar in London, was acclaimed in New York for some thoughts on the subject. He was Sir William S. Gilbert, and together with Sir Arthur Sullivan, the composer, he suggested:

When a felon's not engaged in his employment
Or maturing his felonious little plans,

His capacity for innocent enjoyment
Is just as great as any honest man's.

The "Pirates of Penzance" opened in New York in 1879. Confronting felons, a policeman's lot was not a happy one then; now the same might be said for judges, ADAs, defense attorneys, and court clerks and officers.

But perhaps it is time for all of them to put their experience together, to anticipate, to identify cases that have no effect except in paperwork, time and frustration. A recent Vera Institute study of felony arrests has already tagged six factors — other than criminal facts — that determine the fate of a felonious offender brought to justice, including such considerations as "feelings," "quality," "acumen," and "discretion."

Evidently criminal cases give off signals to let the world know which of them will die of dismissal.

Instead of sending them to cruise the sea of paper, it could be more socially useful to get the dead-end cases out of the system earlier, maybe to try for some sort of reconciliation or restitution outside the criminal judicial process which, it appears, simply cannot properly handle those cases in the first place. Then maybe ARI, and the rest of the court, might operate more like it should.

Juvenile Justice

4

The establishment of a special criminal justice system for the handling of juvenile offenders was hailed in the 1920s by humanitarians, reformers, and social scientists and accepted, somewhat reluctantly, by the legal profession and the police. Several generations of American college students have been convinced of its necessity and its merits in courses and texts on sociology, social work, criminology, and juvenile delinquency. Only recently has the cry of dissent been heard.

A century ago children found guilty of committing crimes were punished as if they were adults. They were hanged, cast into prisons, transported to overseas penal colonies, flogged, and sold into slavery. Very young children in America were tried in adult criminal courts, often with neither an attorney nor other adult advocate, and sentenced to very harsh penalties, sometimes for quite minor crimes. Since there were few specialized juvenile detention institutions, children were thrown into jails and prisons with murderers, thieves, drunks, tramps, and prostitutes with no protection and no program for rehabilitation.

Judge Ben Lindsay and others who pioneered the juvenile court movement believed that juveniles sinned out of ignorance, as part of the growing pains of adolescence, or because they were corrupted by adults. They believed that the juvenile court should have concerned itself with finding out why the juvenile was in trouble and what society could do to help him or her. They saw the juvenile judge as parental, concerned, and sympathetic, rather than judgmental. They viewed the process as diagnostic and therapeutic, rather than prosecutive and punitive.

The proponents of this system were of course thinking of the delinquents of their time—the runaway, the truant, the petty thief, the beggar, the sexually experimental, and the insubordinate at home or in school.

The reality of the 1970s is very different. Juvenile courts are everywhere, as are juvenile police, juvenile probation officers, and juvenile prisons. Literally hundreds of thousands of American juveniles encounter this system annually. Now, however, the juvenile in court is more likely to be on trial for murder, gang-rape, arson or mugging, perhaps for the third, fifth, even tenth time. S/he usually has a defense counsel, and plea-bargaining is common as the huge volume of cases demands accelerated handling. Even when declared delinquent for the third or fourth time, the juvenile is not likely to be institutionalized. Judges have learned that the institutions do not rehabilitate but are in fact prep schools for prisons. The advocates of community correction press for probation, an assignment to a group residence, an out-patient treatment program, or foster care.

The community sees itself, and with good reason, as not being properly protected from the depredations of young criminals. The cry is raised not to correct the inadequacies of the juvenile justice system but to return to the inhumane but equally ineffective processes of the past. Thus legislation has been introduced in many states to lower the age for special juvenile protection, to try in adult criminal courts those juveniles charged with serious felonies (in New York State boys and girls as young as thirteen may now be tried as adults for designated felonies), to make mandatory confinement in juvenile prisons of those juveniles adjudged guilty of serious offenses, to provide professional prosecutors in juvenile courts, and to restore corporal punishment.

Change is needed, but a retrogression to the discredited, harsh, and rigorous measures of past generations is a pathetic admission that we have not only failed as a democratic society but that we have lost our will and our capacity to create, innovate, and experiment.

JUVENILE JUSTICE: A PLEA FOR REFORM

The nation's juvenile courts, says the author,
should focus their attention on the gravest
problems that are confronting them: the twin
evils of violence by and against the young.

Irving R. Kaufman

*Irving R. Kaufman, chief judge of the U.S. Court of
Appeals for the Second Circuit, is chairman of the Joint
Commission on Juvenile Justice of the American Bar
Association and the Institute of Judicial Administration.*

On July 27, 14-year-old Luis Bonilla sat impassively
in the starkly modern courtroom of the Bronx Supreme
Court, waiting for the jury to return. He was accused of
shooting and killing a teen-ager who had resisted Luis's
attempt to steal his portable radio; at the time of his
crime Luis was 13 years old. If the jury convicted him on
charges of second-degree murder, his sentence would
be mandatory life imprisonment, with no chance of
parole for at least five years.

That Luis had been tried in an adult criminal court at
all was extraordinary, for criminal suspects below the
age of 16 had long been under the exclusive jurisdiction
of the family court. Even for the most serious offenses,
that court could impose at most five years of "restrictive
placement," only the first 18 months of which would be
spent behind bars. But two months before the fatal
Bonilla shooting last October, New York's new juvenile-
offender law took effect. It requires that 13-year-olds
accused of second-degree murder (as well as 14- and 15-
year-olds indicted for a variety of offenses, including
burglary and assault) be treated as adults in the eyes of
the law and tried in the adult court systems. (To protect
young convicts from premature contact with adult
offenders, however, the new law still requires that a
convicted youth be confined in juvenile facilities until
he or she is old enough for transfer to adult prison.)

Spurred by a series of brutal and highly publicized
killings in the New York City subways, the State
Legislature, in an extraordinary session in July 1978,
enacted this far-reaching transformation of New York's

criminal law within a few hours after the bill's submission. Luis Bonilla was the first 13-year-old tried under
the new law, but though convicted, he was not sentenced as an adult. When the jury finally did return,
after 15 hours of deliberations, it found him guilty of
manslaughter—an offense not within the ambit of the
new law for 13-year-olds. Accordingly, he was returned
to family court for sentencing. The process had come
full circle. The New York Family Court does not place
manslaughter in the highest severity category, so the
maximum sentence available—which Luis received—
was three years, of which only the first will be in secure
detention.

The case of Luis Bonilla illustrates only one of the
problems facing those who have attempted to reform
laws dealing with juveniles. Eighty percent of the 328
youths arrested under the new law during its first seven
months were charged with theft, rather than with the
more vicious crimes that were the principal target of the
lawmakers. Over 60 percent of the youths initially
charged as adults were returned to the family court—
but not before some had undergone such experiences as
pretrial detentions in the filthy, windowless holding
pens used by the Kings County Criminal Court in
Brooklyn to house adult defendants.

All this, critics assert, demonstrates that the new law
was drafted too broadly, sweeping within its purview
many youths who should not be exposed to the adult
criminal-justice system. Most states have long provided
for the transfer to adult courts of juveniles who have
committed particularly serious crimes. But in virtually
all these states the family court determines whether
transfer is necessary, thus minimizing potentially harmful pretrial contact with adult criminals.

The new law's defenders, however, point out that
cases of neglected, abused, runaway or disobedient
children, as well as child-support controversies, make

up the bulk of the family court's docket. This court, they contend, was established to deal with youthful criminal mischief and petty thefts, not the brutal, heinous crimes that the public fears today. They also emphasize that many dangerous offenders are treated too leniently, simply because the few available secure juvenile detention facilities are already overcrowded by runaways and other nondangerous offenders. Removing youths accused of serious crimes from the family-court system, these policy makers concluded, would result in stiffer penalities, and thus serve as a more powerful deterrent of juvenile crime. But perhaps because juries are unwilling, except in compelling cases, to condemn youthful criminals to adult prisons, the "tough" new law has produced fewer and shorter detentions than the juvenile-offender law that preceded it.

New York's unsatisfactory experience with its new juvenile-offender law is illustrative of the age-old dilemma in this field. It is a fact of life that juveniles, no less than adults, are capable of killing and destruction, and must be punished for such deeds. Yet society is unwilling to abandon young delinquents to the often hopeless fate that awaits adult criminals.

On one issue, however, both sides in this often bitter debate are in agreement: the present system of juvenile justice is plagued by serious problems, problems that run too deep to be rectified by last-minute legislative fiat. Recognizing this fact, the American Bar Association, in cooperation with the Institute of Judicial Administration, has sponsored a comprehensive nine-year study, now nearing completion, of our entire juvenile-justice system. This project's goal has been to re-evaluate and produce a detailed set of guidelines, or "standards," that may serve as the basis for reform of every aspect of the child's manifold interactions with the law.

For each of 22 distinct topics, an expert, termed "reporter," was appointed to draft proposed standards and commentary. The work of the reporters was then reviewed by drafting committees drawn from the full spectrum of professionals in the field. Many were lawyers; the roster included three past presidents of the American Bar Association. The project also consulted judges, scholars, psychiatrists, psychologists, social workers, educators and experts in corrections and police work. This process insured that the standards would be well-integrated and internally consistent. In addition, they would reflect the varying perceptions of those involved in different aspects of the juvenile-justice system.

The standards, now being considered by those concerned with juvenile-justice reform, are not an exercise in theoretical armchair sociology. Rather, they draw on the best of existing, testing statutory reforms. Covering such areas as police handling of juvenile problems, youth service agencies, pretrial proceedings, juvenile records and information systems, and rights of minors, the first 17 volumes of the standards were approved by

the American Bar Association this February. Five more volumes will be submitted to the A.B.A. at a later date.

The standards represent the latest chapter in the history of troubled children in America, a history that reflects some of the meanest and the most noble aspects of the American character.

Seventeenth-century London was beset by every type of problem child now encountered by our family courts. Young criminals terrorized the middle classes, and were tried and punished in the same manner as adults. "Rogues and vagabonds," as well as "idle and needy" children who had run away from their parents and masters, were brought to the courts for punishment; orphans and neglected or abandoned children were bound out or cared for at public expense. But the Londoners had a "dispositional alternative" (in the jargon of the day's juvenile justice) that is unavailable now: they shipped many of these children to the Virginia colonies as indentured servants. The Dutch, for their part, pursued a similar policy in New Amsterdam.

The colonial policy toward children and their families was marked by a stern Puritanical view of the responsibilities of the child to his parents and of the parents to the state. The dead hand of this view continues to mold today's policy. The colonial government lent its force to the absolute rule of the parents, permitting up to 10 stripes at the public whipping post for incorrigible children who displayed a "rebellious carriage" toward their elders.

The colonies also expected much of parents. Virginia provided in 1748 that unfit parents who were either too poor to raise children properly, or who failed to bring them up "in honest courses," could lose custody of them forever.

The New England colonies (and later New York as well) provided for dependent persons, including young abandoned children, by a reverse auction known as vendue. The state offered subsidies of ever-decreasing amounts to prospective caretakers, with the lowest bidder winning. Apart from a cursory check to ascertain whether the child was being grossly abused, the child's best interests were not even considered.

By the 1820's, this reality gained broad recognition as the nation's increasing prosperity alleviated the financial pressures that had made the vendue acceptable. The search for a more humanitarian approach was galvanized by a dilemma in governmental policy toward juvenile delinquency, which was already beginning to emerge as a heated issue with the massive influx of European immigrants. In the eyes of the criminal law, youths reached maturity at age 14, and suspects as young as 6 were legally considered as adults if the state could show that they knew right from wrong. Thus, several cases are recorded of 12- and 13-year-olds tried for murder, and of 7- and 8-year-olds locked up in adult prisons. The sympathy of judges and jurors toward the

4. JUVENILE JUSTICE

young mitigated the harshness of this common-law rule; even in 1820 all were aware that brutality and instruction in "the most artful methods of perpetrating crime" awaited the youth incarcerated with adults. But if acquitted, as the New York Society for the Reform of Juvenile Delinquents noted in an 1826 report, "they were returned destitute, to the same haunts of vice from which they had been taken, more emboldened to the commission of crime, by their escape from present punishment."

The New York reform society therefore recommended the establishment of specialized institutions for children. These homes would provide a refuge not only for young criminals but also for those who had been dealt with by the vendue—the homeless, the neglected and the vagrant—and children beyond their parents' control or whose parents were considered "unfit."

The institutional movement spread rapidly, at first under private auspices and later supported by public funds. These early "child savers" deemed several years of stern, regimented discipline essential to reform. They therefore thought it necessary that institutions and the state be given extensive authority over these children, even over parental protests. In 1838, the seminal case of *In re Crouse* established this power.

Mary Ann Crouse was consigned to the Philadelphia House of Refuge on her mother's assertion that she was "incorrigible." The Pennsylvania Supreme Court rejected her father's petition to recover custody, defending its usurpation of the rights of "unworthy" parents by stating, "She in fact has been snatched from a course which must have ended in confirmed depravity, and, not only is the restraint of her person not lawful, but it would be an act of extreme cruelty to release her from it."

With these noble-sounding words, the court planted in American jurisprudence a dangerous and alien seed that flourished most fully in the juvenile-court system founded 60 years later. A central principle in Anglo-American law is that crimes must be charged and proved precisely. One is convicted not of "being a robber" but of robbing John Jones at 2 P.M. on the corner of Fifth and Main. A law that confines a child in an institution because a parent is "unworthy" or because the child is destined for "depravity" presupposes that a court can divine the most salutary remedy for an individual by peering through some magic window into the soul. A homogenous community like Puritan New England may tolerate such official moral judgments, but in the diverse society dedicated to free thought that the United States has become, such institutional presumptuousness appears pernicious.

These considerations did not impress those active in the institutional movement, nor reformers who attempted other means of grappling with the problems of youth. The Children's Benevolent Society, for example, like its predecessors in London 150 years before, sought to "drain the city" of its delinquent children and ship them westward to "the best of all asylums, the farmer's home." And as the frontier began to close after the Civil War, yet another new phenomenon—the reform-school movement—swept the North and the West.

Two principles were central to the reform school ideal. First, youths could be properly treated as criminals for offenses peculiar to their status as minors; for example, truancy, running away, incorrigibility. Second, because the mission of the reform school was a benign, rehabilitative one, the normal procedural protections of the adversary criminal trial—the rights of confronting witnesses, prior disclosure of specific charges, of counsel and of trial by jury—could be abrogated with no constitutional qualms.

Initially, these principles suffered a major setback. In *People v. Turner,* the Illinois Supreme Court rejected a statute that mandated the confinement of children under 16 "growing up in mendicancy, ignorance, idleness or vice." "Vice is a very comprehensive term," wrote the court. "Acts, wholly innocent in the estimation of many good men, would, according to the code of ethics of others, show fearful depravity. What is the standard to be? What extent of enlightenment, what amount of industry, what degree of virtue, will save from the threatened imprisonment? The principle of the absorption of the child in, and its complete subjection to the despotism of the State, is wholly inadmissible in the modern civilized world."

The *Turner* decision represented a subtle wisdom that would not become widely evident for nearly a century. The Illinois child savers ignored its warning and lobbied to create a new institution that would further their interventionist, paternalistic goals within constitutional limitations. Finally, in 1899, at the prompting of the Chicago Women's Club, Illinois founded the nation's first juvenile court. Its jurisdiction encompassed all children in trouble, including those found living "with any vicious or disreputable person." This idea of a separate court for juveniles, able to address and cure the problems of youth with a special fatherly concern, quickly spread to every major city in the Union.

The juvenile court was the culmination of a growing belief that children were institutionalized far too frequently, both in degrading, unhealthy almshouses and in reform schools, which were already perceived as dehumanizing in their regimentation and brutal in their operation. Foster care and adoption were the practices preferred by the juvenile court for children with unsatisfactory homes, and for the first time home relief was offered on a broad basis to "worthy" mothers of dependent children. Juvenile probation officers were another innovation. These men and women—at first, unpaid volunteers—were to supply the court with investigations of the young offender's background. More importantly, they would supervise the child living at home, thus providing an alternative to punishment in an institution.

"Juvenile courts," noted Thomas D. Eliot, a critic of the system, in 1914, "were to fill every gap in the child-caring system. However, if this be granted, no line can be drawn short of a court administering all the children's charities. . . .Some courts actually state this as their ideal; they are all things to all men." The juvenile courts had, indeed, set themselves an ambitious, perhaps impossible, task. As a leading juvenile-court judge, Paul Alexander, noted in 1944, the judge must apply "not only man-made law, but the moral law and the laws of social science, psychology, psychiatry and the general laws of human nature." But the states never gave the juvenile courts the resources to carry out their mission. As late as 1967, one-third of the juvenile courts in the country did not have social workers or probation officers available to them, and 83 percent lacked psychologists or psychiatrists.

Confronted with massive waves of runaways in the 30's and the 40's, as well as a steady increase in youth crime, the system steadily broke down. Insufficiently staffed to follow its proclaimed purposes, the juvenile court—despite its origins as an alternative to institutionalization—with increasing frequency referred delinquents to an ever-growing network of misleadingly and euphemistically named "reform" and "training" schools. By 1966, 51,000 children were living in 292 institutions for delinquents.

Discipline, rather than rehabilitation or education, preoccupied these prisonlike facilities. As late as 1949, the punishment for possession of tobacco at the Indiana State School for delinquent boys was 10 strokes on the bare back with a leather paddle; for impudence and vulgarity, 15 strokes. At the Hudson School in New York State in the 1950's, rebellious girls could be locked up in solitary confinement for up to 81 days and fed only milk and bread for two of their daily meals. And reports emerged in the 1960's from one Massachusetts training school of children who were punished by "staff dunking youngsters' heads in toilets, dousing them them with pails of water, forcing them to march around with a pail over their heads, and using one 12-year-old boy as a mop and dragging him through urine in the boys' washroom."

With the heightened social consciousness of the 1960's, many of these aspects of the juvenile-justice system began to appear archaic, if not cruel. Recognizing at last the essentially punitive nature of reform schools, Justice Abe Fortas, writing for the Supreme Court in 1967, noted that "however euphemistic the title, a 'receiving home' or an 'industrial school' for juveniles is an institution of confinement." Before making a finding of delinquency, therefore, juvenile courts were required to observe the "essentials of due process and fair treatment."

The 1960's also witnessed a second, more massive deinstitutionalization movement. It took its most strik-

ing form in Massachusetts, where the entire training-school system was closed and replaced with a network of small-scale, community-based residences.

There was, therefore, little disagreement in 1967 when the President's Commission on Law Enforcement and the Administration of Justice wrote: "The great hopes originally held for the juvenile court have not been fulfilled. It has not succeeded significantly in rehabilitating delinquent youth, in reducing or even stemming the tide of juvenile criminality, or in bringing justice and compassion to the child offender."

The Juvenile Justice Standards Project of the American Bar Association and the Institute of Judicial Administration thus convened in a day of growing disenchantment with the institutions used to deal with problems of youth. At that time, it was clear that a substantial number of adult criminals had started as juvenile offenders and invariably returned to lives of crime. The depth of dissatisfaction, however, provided the project with an ideal opportunity to achieve its ambitious goal: to structure a new juvenile justice system that by heeding the lessons of the past would better serve us in the future.

After nearly a decade of research and discussion, the project members concluded that the juvenile court must abandon the "moralistic" model that had guided it since the turn of the century. Some members supported this view because they believed courts could not meaningfully pass upon the "worthiness" or "depravity" of those who came before them. Others argued that such judgements have no place at all in modern society. All agreed that the juvenile courts—like all other courts—should be tightly bound by the rule of law. Acts that would be crimes if committed by adults should be charged, proved and punished in a similar manner. Senator Edward Kennedy, chairman of the Senate Judiciary Committee, has forcefully decried the cruel ironies of the present system: "If juveniles want to get locked up, they should skip school, run away from home, or be deemed 'a problem.' If they want to avoid jail, they are better off committing a robbery or burglary." Children whose actions do not amount to adult crime—the runaways, truants and incorrigibles—should be dealt with outside the judicial system. The term "delinquency," therefore, with its attendant stigmatization and possibility of incarceration, should be reserved exclusively for juveniles who have committed crimes.

A few examples will illustrate the basic philosophy that undergirds the Juvenile Justice Standards Project:

Parental Abuse and Neglect. Under the standards, children may not be removed from their homes because of alleged parental misconduct without a finding that specific physical harm, clinically recognized psychiatric disturbance, or sexual abuse has occurred or is imminently threatened. This standard is intended to reduce sharply the widely deplored extent of state intrusion into family life that the child savers thought proper. Although state intervention is clearly called for when a child is, for example, battered by a parent, physical abuse was reported in only 10 percent of the 300,000 neglect petitions filed annually. More often, the petition for juvenile-court intervention to remove the child from the home is based on such complaints as the tendency of a single mother to bring home overnight male visitors. Separation of child from mother in such cases, which once may have appeared imperative, has become distasteful in a society that has learned respect for the dignity of all and has come to recognize the necessity of keeping hands off the parent-child relationship except in particularly dangerous situations.

Experts agree that unnecessary intervention often harms rather than helps the child, shattering parental bonds. The wiser course, the standards conclude, is for the state to leave the child with the family and supply voluntary social services to assist the family unit in the home.

Youth Crime. In cases of juvenile delinquency, the standards frankly recognize that although reform schools may have rehabilitative goals, they are dominated by their punitive aspect. Cliches about saving a child from a life of crime do not alter the stark reality— and necessity—of punishment. For the protection of society, it is necessary that legislatures increase many of the maximum prison sentences for juveniles who have committed serious crimes. And, under carefully defined circumstances, juvenile courts must be permitted to transfer the most hardened young criminals to the adult system for the severest punishments allowed by law. But in either court, juveniles accused of crime should have the right to the same adult procedural protections that guard against conviction of the innocent. Consequently, the standards accord accused juveniles, beyond the minimal due process that the Supreme Court has held is constitutionally required, the rights to counsel and to a six-person jury. The juvenile-court judge must remain free to act leniently in an appropriate case. The standards require no minimum sentences, but where the judge deems a heavier determinate sentence necessary, no parole commission should be permitted to release the offender prematurely. Under the existing system, as Senator Kennedy recently said, "certainty of punishment is a joke."

Noncriminal Misbehavior. The standards permit incarceration only for conduct forbidden by the adult criminal law. Large segments of juvenile court jurisdiction would therefore be removed, for adults cannot be convicted for disobeying their parents, truancy or running away. In recent years, some states have begun to treat youngsters who have committed such acts, but no crimes, as "Persons [or Children] in Need of Supervision" (PINS or CHINS), rather than as delinquents. The change, however, is one in name only. PINS children continue to be confined alongside young criminals, an experience destined to do more harm than good. In fact, through PINS petitions, juvenile courts have intervened in family disputes over household chores, abusive language and undesirable boyfriends. The juvenile courts, in these cases, have allowed themselves to be used as birch rods by angry parents disgusted with, but unable to control, their adolescent children's behavior.

The project concluded that all services rendered to PINS children should be provided on a strictly voluntary basis, and preferably outside the judicial system. For example, in recent years, concerned adults—many of them former runaways—have established "crash pads" and runaway houses where young people who have left home can live for a time, safe from the dangers of the street. At first, these shelters were often hostile both to parents and authorities, but today, with the help of government funding and state certification, they have evolved into an important adjunct to the social-services system. Experience has shown that after a runaway child spends a few days in such a shelter, an amicable reunion with parents usually ensues. The standards endorse this system of licensed shelters and recommend that it be augmented substantially.

For other troubled children who have not broken the law, the standards prescribe voluntary psychiatric or other medical care, and educational, vocational, and legal couseling appropriate to the needs of the particular child. Where a child chooses to avail himself of such services, the chances of success will be enhanced by the fact that he has chosen this course voluntarily. The key, then, is to make these services adequate, well-known and easily accessible.

The long history of justice and injustice in our nation's children counsels that the juvenile court focus its power, its wisdom and its compassion on the gravest problems that confront it: the twin evils of violence by and against the young. Courts must mete out fair and even-handed justice to young criminals. No longer should they try to serve as surrogate parents in attempting to control youthful mischief. As the legislatures of our states join in this effort and draw upon the standards' recommendations, the age-old promise of justice for our nation's youth may at last be fulfilled.

People v. Juvenile Justice: The Jury Is Still Out

John M. Rector

John M. Rector is the administrator of the Office of Juvenile Justice and Delinquency Prevention of the United States Department of Justice.

When young people confront our juvenile justice system, injustice is a frequent result. The system seldom provides the individualized justice promised by reformers at the turn of the century; it does not often help the many non-criminal youths who fall within its jurisdiction; and it often fails to protect communities from the violence of a few who terrorize our citizens.

Understandably, we are all horrified by examples of the brutal reality of violent juvenile crime:

Richard, 11, dead in Detroit after 13-year old Kenneth shot him in the head with a 10-gauge shotgun. Police said the two boys had argued over which of them was responsible for a broken window. Richard's body was found wrapped in a plastic garbage bag and stuffed into a remote corner of Kenneth's attic.

In Baltimore, a three year old took his father's .357 magnum pistol – which had been left within his reach – and shot a seven year old playmate at point-blank range. The children had been in a minor argument prior to the shooting. The small boy died before the ambulance arrived.

Willie, 12, Selma, 11, Michael, 11, and Freddie, 11, have all been taken into custody by the Atlanta Police Department during the past four years. All were picked up in connection with homicides. Willie was accused of killing a female playmate after she had thrown water at him; Selma told police she had killed her little brother following an argument; Michael confessed to killing his sister because they had fought over a piece of candy; and Freddy was believed to have killed his mother's common-law husband because he thought the man was hurting her.

Recently, *Time Magazine* (July 11, 1977) shocked the American people with its cover feature "The Youth Crime Plague." It opened with similar bone-chilling chronicles. Its authors argued that: "Many youngsters appear to be robbing and raping, maiming and murdering as casually as they go to a movie or join a pickup baseball game. A new, remorseless, mutant juvenile seems to have been born, and there is no more terrifying figure in America today."

It is absolutely essential that we ask several elementary questions.

What do we mean by violent crime?

The US Department of Justice, FBI Uniform Crime Reports define the offenses of murder, forcible rape, robbery, and aggravated assault as violent crime.

To what extent are youths responsible for crime?

In 1976, 7,912,348 persons were arrested. Three out of four of those arrested were adults; the remaining 1,923,254 were juveniles. In the category of serious crime, juvenile arrests accounted for 666,910 or 46.1 percent of the property crimes (burglary, larceny, theft, and motor vehicle theft) and 22 percent or 74,715 of the violent crime arrests.

Thus, 95 percent of all juvenile arrests were for non-violent crimes (74,715/1,973,254). Furthermore, violent juvenile arrests account for less than one percent of all arrests (74,715/7,912,348). These figures should help separate the reality of violent juvenile crime from myth.

What do we know about violent crime trends?

From 1967 to 1976, adult arrests for violent crime increased from 91,986 to 151,769 or 65 percent. During the same period, juvenile arrests for violent crime increased from 22,919 to 45,468 or 98 percent. However, from 1972-1976 adult arrests for violent crime increased 32.5 percent while juvenile arrests for violent crime increased 28 percent.

Lastly, a recent comparison, 1975-76, revealed that adult arrests for violent crime decreased 9 percent and juvenile arrests for violent crime decreased 12 percent.

Statistics, percentages, and trends help focus our attention on the actual magnitude of violent crime but are of little comfort to victims.

Interestingly, juveniles are most likely to be the victims of violent crimes.

The 1976 LEAA National Crime Survey, for example, found that youths are two and one-half times more likely to be robbed and more than 10 times more likely to be assaulted than are citizens over age 65. Similarly, one-fourth of juvenile victims and one-sixth of elderly victims are hospitalized.

The fear of crime can be as debilitating as the crime itself. While we work to help citizens better understand how to protect themselves and their families, it is essential that work is done to counteract misconceptions regarding juvenile violence and its victims. Hopefully, such efforts will help assure that all of our citizens are better protected and

4. JUVENILE JUSTICE

at the same time not as fearful of our 66 million young citizens.

Understanding Violent Youth Crime

Several projects, funded by the Office of Juvenile Justice and Delinquency Prevention, have made important contributions to our understanding of serious and violent delinquency and ways of dealing with these seemingly intractable problems.

A three-year study at the Institute for Juvenile Research in Chicago has involved analyzing data collected during 1972 through a statewide Illinois survey of a random sample of over 3000 youth aged 14-18. Delinquency involvement was measured through self-reports from the youths themselves and correlated with such factors as family, peer group, community, and school influences. The results have shed new light on the nature of delinquency. Among the major findings were the following:

1) Contrary to popular conceptions based on arrest data, kids reporting delinquent behavior are nearly as likely to be white as black, just about as likely to be a girl as a boy, as likely to live anywhere in Illinois as in highly urbanized Chicago, and just as likely to come from an intact as a broken home;

2) Peer group pressure is the single most important factor in determining the presence or absence of delinquent behavior;

3) The community context serves as an important mediating influence in delinquency – particularly in the case of violent conduct; and

4) Much of delinquency arises out of youths' responses to contradictions or tensions displayed by authority figures in the family, school, and juvenile justice system contexts.

Two studies have made significant contributions to our understanding of delinquent career patterns as they relate to adult careers in criminality. The first of these is a follow-up study made of the landmark Philadelphia research conducted in the early 1960s of almost all males born in that city in 1945.

The follow-up study involved gathering data up to age 30 on the offender careers of a 10 percent sample of the original group. Notable findings from this effort include the following:

1) About 15 percent of youths in the 10 percent sample were responsible for 80-85 percent of serious crimes; and

2) Chronic offenders (five or more police contacts), who made up only 6 percent of the larger group from which the 10 percent sample was drawn accounted for 51 percent of all offenses among the total sample – including over 60 percent of the personal injury and serious property offenses.

The second of the two major offender career studies is a project currently underway at the University of Iowa, which is assessing the relationship of adult criminal careers to juvenile criminal careers. This project consists of a follow-up study of 1352 juveniles born in 1942, and 2099 juveniles born in 1949, in Racine, Wisconsin. The study is designed to provided information on the nature of urban delinquent careers (including age, race, sex, and other offender characteristics, such as seriousness of offense) and their relationship to later adult careers; to determine the extent to which various alternative decisions by juvenile justice system authorities or by the juvenile have contributed to continuing careers; and to evaluate the effectiveness of the juvenile justice system and other community factors in deterring or supporting continuing delinquent and criminal behavior. The major preliminary findings to date follow:

1) About 5 percent of the white males in the 1942 and 1949 groups accounted for over 70 percent of the felony offenses (police contacts);

2) About 12 percent of the white males in these two groups accounted for all police contacts of white males for felonies; and

3) Minorities (blacks and hispanics) were disproportionately represented, among those referred to court and placed in correctional institutions.

These data make it clear that, at least in Philadelphia and Racine, Wisconsin, a very small proportion of juvenile offenders account for an extremely large volume of serious and violent crime. However the difficulty in taking the next step – that of

responding appropriately to reduce crime through focusing on chronic offenders – is in predicting who will in the future be a chronic offender. A major conclusion of the Philadelphia and Iowa research is that juveniles do not specialize in particular types of offenses nor do they necessarily progress from less serious to more serious offenses. Prediction of delinquency remains an elusive goal.

Additionally, we recently concluded a seven year evaluation of the Massachusetts experience in its statewide community-based movement. During 1969-1972 Massachusetts replaced its training schools for juveniles with community-based alternatives to traditional incarceration. This is the only state that has de-institutionalized its correctional institutions statewide, in either the juvenile or adult area. The results of the evaluation have indicated that youths do as well in the new programs as they did in the old training schools. However, youths in less secure programs did better than those in the more secure community-based programs.

In addition, the community-based programs provided a much more humane and fair way of treating youth than did the large institutions previously used. A major conclusion of the study was that the important factors affecting success or failure with individual youth lay not so much in the qualities of specific individual programs to which the youths were exposed, but in the characteristics of the total social network for each youth in the community.

The results of this research and the success of the Massachusetts experience led to two other projects that we have undertaken in the state. The first of these is a research effort focused on the problem of secure care in a community-based correctional system. This research will examine how the state, particularly police, court, and correctional agencies, is making decisions about those youths who require secure care treatment. The research will also involve an examination of how a few other states are addressing the secure care problem. In Massachusetts these youths constitute about 10 percent of the total number of youths presently committed to the Massachusetts Department of Youth Services. The significance of this project is that the key to long-run success in persuading states to adopt policies of de-institutionalization and establishment of community-based programs depends in large measure on devising means to alleviate public fears about protection in the community.

The second of the two new Massachusetts projects will be a rather large-scale training program. Through it, along with other OJJDP training, technical assistance, and action programs, we hope to persuade a few other states to de-institutionalize statewide their large juvenile correctional institutions. The content of the training program will draw mainly upon the results of the seven year Massachusetts study, the new secure care study, and the results of the OJJDP research, evaluation, and action programs activities in the de-institutionalization area.

Facts alone, however, will not provide the exclusive basis for juvenile crime policy. Our values and a commitment to justice will help us to better protect our communities while neither undermining our basic Constitutional freedoms and guarantees nor undermining the taxpayer with tithes for unsound but costly policies and programs.

The Juvenile Justice and Delinquency Prevention Act of 1974, which established my office, was the outgrowth of a four-year intensive investigation conducted by Senator Birch Bayh's United States Senate Subcommittee to Investigate Juvenile Delinquency. The Act was developed and supported by citizen groups, and criminal and juvenile justice professionals throughout the country. It was passed by overwhelming majorities in both houses of Congress in recognition that the juvenile justice system in this country is ineffective, that it does not meet the needs of youth who are brought into it, and that major reforms were required to address its inconsistencies.

The Act reflected the consensus that far too many juveniles are locked up. Many of the youth detained and incarcerated, particularly those whose conduct would not be illegal if they were adults, require at most non-secure and usually temporary placement out of their homes. In fact many would be better off if the state refrained from intervening in their lives at all, because what they really need – a stable and supportive living situation in the community – we fail to give them. Children are too often entangled in the expensive web of the child welfare/juvenile justice industry that was established ostensibly to protect them, but in practice far too often has rendered them subject to arbitrary and excessive authority exercised by parents, custodians, and the state and its agents.

On October 3, 1977, President Carter signed the Juvenile Justice Amendments of 1977. In stressing its significance, he said in part:

"In many communities of our country, two kinds of crimes – one serious and one not very serious – are treated the same and young people have been incarcerated for long periods of time, who have committed offenses that would not even be a crime at all if they were adults....This Act very wisely draws a sharp distinction between these two kinds of crimes."

The aim of the Juvenile Justice Act is to minimize the harm sometimes caused by state intervention. The aim is to help secure basic human rights for children and their families. The aim is to protect our communities while also assuring justice for our youth. The traditional solution for juvenile delinquency has been to upgrade personnel, improve services, or refurbish facilities. The Juvenile Justice Act tells us that this is not adequate. What we need is an uncompromising departure from the current practice of institutional overkill which undermines our primary influence agents – family, school, church, and community. The Juvenile Justice Act was designed to help states, localities, and public agencies working collaboratively with private agencies and citizen groups to develop and conduct effective delinquency prevention programs, to divert more juveniles from the juvenile justice process, and to provide urgently needed alternatives to detention and correctional facilities.[1]

The current overreach of the child welfare juvenile justice system in its reliance on detention and incarceration is particularly shocking as it affects non-criminal cases. These youths are actually more likely to be held in confinement than those who are charged with or convicted of actual criminal offenses. Incredibly, 70 percent of the young women in the system are in this category. This system then is clearly the cutting edge of the double standard.

Many status offenders are arrogant, defiant, and rude; some are sexually promiscuous. Detention or incarceration, however, helps neither them nor us. Some of these children cannot be helped, and others do not need help. Real help, for those who need it, might best take the form of diverting them from the vicious cycle of detention, incarceration, and crime.

Some youthful offenders must be removed from their homes. For those who committ serious, usually violent offenses, detention and incarceration should be available; preferably such facilities should be secure and community-based.

The overloaded juvenile justice system is under fire for not stemming the tide of youthful criminal violence. Many are, however, often and understandably blinded by the lurid publicity given a relatively small handful of violent juveniles and we lose sight of the fact that the net of the juvenile system is very wide. Many noncriminal acts and minor delinquencies subject youth to unwarranted and unjust detention and incarceration, grossly disproportionate to the harm, if any, done by the behavior involved. Our collective errors in this regard are compounded by the fact that these indiscriminate incarceration policies which overloaded the juvenile correctional system permit the punishment of ever fewer serious violent youthful offenders.

Violent crimes put the *parens patrie* doctrine – the basis for the juvenile

---

[1]In 1979 the office will assist communities throughout the country in establishing community-based programs aimed at hard-core juvenile delinquents fashioned after the exemplary "Project New Pride" in Denver, Colorado. The office in 1978, for example, provided $25 million in funding for restitution as an alternative to incarceration. Restitution is one way to right the wrong done to a victim, it can help the young offender regain self-esteem and increase the confidence of the community that the system is just.

justice system – to its most severe test. It is not only that the few critical cases are not dealt with seriously but that many less grave cases are treated as serious.

There are important issues in the area of sentencing. Sentences based solely on the juvenile's needs and background, in lieu of consideration of the crime add to inequity. Even when youths are convicted of the same crime and have similar criminal records, the current system imposes vastly different sentences. While some discretion is essential, sentencing guidelines would be more consistent with justice and community protection. Otherwise we will be unjustly punishing youths on the basis of family background, race, color, creed, wealth, and status rather than for their crimes. The development of model standards by the office will assist states in their struggle to modify the system to help assure justice for citizens.

When we discuss juvenile crime we should address the policies of a state and its respective communities rather than focus solely on the individual juvenile. The case-by-case emphasis on the needs of individuals often permits those intimately involved with the implementation of policy to overlook the cumulative impact of their practices.

The Juvenile Justice Act has been a catalyst for a long overdue and healthy assessment of current policy and practices. Additionally, it has stimulated the development of sound, cost-effective criteria for imposing incarceration while stressing certainty of punishment for violent offenders.

The Government Accounting Office has called the Act the most promising and cost effective federal crime prevention program. No one would claim that the Act is a panacea. There are no federal answers to the problems of juvenile crime and delinquency. Its authors did not intend to divert attention from major reforms aimed at ameliorating the poverty, unemployment, sexism, and racism so relevant to the quality of life and opportunities for our youth. Nor were they naive about the capacity for resistance to change, especially by those entrenched in and sustained by the status quo.

Still, by its enactment of the Juvenile Justice and Delinquency Prevention Act of 1974, Congress has called upon the states, localities, public and private agencies, and others to reassess the rationale which has made institutionalization the favored alternative far too often.

Inside the Juvenile-Justice System:

How Fifteen-Year-Olds Get Away With Murder

Nicholas Pileggi

"...George Adorno's journey through the juvenile-justice system provides a fascinating glimpse of failure and frustration..."

The teenagers were small, not much more than five feet tall, weighing no more than 120 pounds, and one of them carried a gun. They had young, almost guileless faces, and they punched and sassed each other in the West 111th Street tenement doorway as they waited for their friend to come back with a cabdriver they could rob.

At 1:15 A.M., a yellow Checker taxicab pulled up to the tenement. The youngster inside the cab was even smaller than his friends waiting outside. The driver, a 26-year-old Brooklyn College student, began to automatically roll up his half-closed window. The glass pane was about three inches from closing shut when a shot rang out. The driver slumped forward, lifeless, a bullet hole in his left temple.

The youngsters immediately tried opening the driver's door, but it had been locked. They ran around to the other side. Locked. One of them jumped into the rear of the cab and tried sliding open the partition separating the driver from the passengers. They tried wedging their arms through the partially opened window, but that didn't work either.

Suddenly one of the trio ran part of the way down the block and returned, half carrying a ten-year-old boy whose arm was thin enough to fit through the narrow window opening. It was the ten-year-old who unlocked the cab.

Once inside, the youngsters rifled through the dead man's clothing and took $60 from his wallet. They were about to run off when one of the three remembered the driver's radio. He ran back to the cab. The radio was covered with blood. He took it anyway.

That, according to information gathered by police, homicide detectives, and the Manhattan district attorney, was the sequence that resulted in Steven Robinson's death last February 23.

George Adorno, the diminutive eighteen-year-old gunman who is currently on trial for the homicide, had been charged once before with killing a taxicab driver. On that occasion, however, George Adorno was only fifteen years old and the charges against him were dismissed by a family-court judge because Adorno's mother had not been present when he admitted the killing. There had been additional charges pending against him at the time, including one other homicide, but they, too, had been dismissed.

The journey of George Adorno through the juvenile-justice system provides a fascinating glimpse of a multilayered, super-secret bureaucracy unable to deal with a problem that has literally altered the quality of life in New York City. Whether justified by the statistics or not, the fear of random and senseless juvenile violence on the city's streets has forced people to change apartments, sell houses, limit their movie habits, give up evening classes, forgo walks after dinner, and take taxicabs they cannot afford. It has created a generation of schoolchildren prepared to give up their bus passes and bicycles without a whimper. It has terrified their parents into carrying enough cash to placate the nightmare muggers they have come to expect. There is, in fact, probably no aspect of urban society that strikes more terror in city residents than the prospect of being confronted by George

Adorno—and yet, the multimillion-dollar juvenile-justice system, set up specifically to deal with this problem, has actually made the situation worse.

The juvenile-justice system is incapable of dealing with the crisis mostly because of the constraints of its special-interest groups. The judges, probation workers, unions, cops, religious and secular child-care agencies, mental-health officials, legal-aid societies, corporation counsel prosecutors, district attorneys, the politically connected realtors who have the multimillion-dollar sweetheart contracts for the group homes where many of the youngsters are sent, even the upstate dairy lobbyists—all have a piece of the action. According to officials at the Department of Social Services, it is the dairy lobbyists who managed to have the state and federal laws funding juvenile programs written in such a way as to demand that the youngsters consume huge quantities of milk and dairy products. In places such as Spofford, where 72 percent of the youngsters are nonwhite, this creates terrible medical problems, since many of the youngsters suffer from lactose intolerance, a physical aversion to excessive quantities of milk.

According to Dr. Karen Hein, who runs the excellent Montefiore Adolescent Medical Unit at Spofford, large numbers of youngsters detained at Spofford (the majority of whom are being held on juvenile-delinquency petitions, though some are there as PINS, youngsters in need of supervision) suffer intense stomach pains, nausea, and diarrhea from the milk. Nevertheless, the dairy lobby has made it impossible for the heavy milk diet to be reduced without the loss of federal and state funds.

Many realtors, some of whom were caught up in the recent nursing-home scandal, are reluctant to see any change in the system of farming out thousands of disturbed youngsters to poorly designed and poorly supervised group homes and group residences, because they have worked out generous rental contracts with the city for buildings in ghetto areas that add up to millions upon millions in rental fees. Realtors Sydney and Arthur Engel, for instance, receive $90,650 a year rent for an Atlantic Avenue, Brooklyn, building used by the city as a diagnostic/reception center for 24 children. Another realtor, Jerry Fessler of JAO Construction Company of Massapequa, Long Island, also has a tremendous income. Fessler, for instance, has three group centers in Brooklyn, housing 24 youngsters each, for which he receives $202,151 in rent annually. Because of his twenty-year lease arrangement with the city, Fessler will eventually receive over $4 million in rentals on those three buildings. Other realtors familiar with the area claim the city could have bought the three buildings for the price of a year's rent.

It is a system, in other words, that gets most of its direction from political and social pressures exerted upon it by the vested interests within. Neither the children, nor their survival and rehabilitation, nor the safety of their potential victims enter into any of the equations being calculated by various pressure groups. It is a system that grew without direction and without any self-evaluation. No one within the system, for instance, ever really kept tabs on George Adorno. Neither the police, DFY, the probation department, family court, social workers, nor aftercare workers ever coordinated their records on George Adorno. He went from one agency to another like the cipher he was considered. Along the way, thumb-fingered civil-servant typists misspelled his name, lost his mother, forgot his address, and even took a year off his life. They sent him to secure facilities and forgot he escaped; they gave him weekend passes home whether or not he had bothered to return from his last weekend pass; and aftercare workers let him remain on the streets despite the fact that they knew George was accumulating his elaborate wardrobe of color-coordinated sneakers through robberies. The mistakes, the goofs, the inept judicial decisions were all neatly tucked away under the shroud of family-court secrecy, but the price paid in George

Adorno's case was fatal for at least four people. (It should be noted that Judge Joseph B. Williams, the current administrator, has tried—and in many cases succeeded—to move his Kafka court out of its madness. Unfortunately, it is not his court alone.)

As a fifteen-year-old, George Adorno was literally immune from criminal prosecution. His arrests were not even called arrests; his indictments were called petitions; and his family-court trials were called fact-findings. Family court, a civil rather than criminal court, was established in 1962 "as a special agency for the care and protection of the young and the preservation of the family." At that time the juvenile courts in New York City were processing about 600 robberies a year, fewer than a thousand larcenies, and an insignificant number of homicides.

By 1975, an unexpected and dazzling increase in the amount of violent juvenile crime had swamped the court. In New York City alone, arrests of kids under sixteen had risen from 3,424 in 1950 to 26,153 in 1975. What had once been a safe, politically cozy judicial appointment became a nightmare. Chicken-soup psychologists and family counselors had no background for dealing with junkie families, eleven-year-old hookers, and twelve-year-olds capable of beating 80-year-old couples to death for a dime.

"You talk to these kids about what they've done," one family-court probation officer said, "and they fall asleep on you. That's how concerned they are, that's how scared."

Most of the pension-savvy bureaucrats stuck in the family court have pretty much given up and can be found hunkered down between the overflowing file cabinets crossing off the days remaining before their retirement.

The simple logistics involved in trying to process a grand total of 94,329 youngsters between ten and fifteen years old for everything from truancy to murder has deluged the system. (Those figures include over 2,500 youngsters ten and under who have been arrested for major crimes such as murder, manslaughter, assault, robbery, burglary, rape, and grand larceny.) Family-court record-keeping has been so overburdened that information about hundreds of cases a year is lost or misfiled. In fact, a recent Division of Criminal Justice Services study was unable to locate any information about 645 violent youngsters (10.4 percent of a 6,322 sample) in either probation reports or court records. The youngsters

and their cases, which included 14 homicides, 25 rapes, 57 assaults on police officers, 167 assaults on civilians, 16 cases of sodomy, 504 robberies, and 27 cases involving dangerous weapons, had simply disappeared.

As a result, when a youngster such as George Adorno is brought before the family court at twelve, his chances of being diagnosed as potentially dangerous and of being helped are virtually nil. In addition, and perhaps even more important, the legislative mandate of the court is rehabilitation, not punishment, so as long as George Adorno remains under sixteen, no matter what he has done and no matter how often, he will be seen in the eyes of the court as a youngster in need of help.

A sound enough principle, except that the rehabilitation efforts of the family court, the State Division for Youth (DFY), and the Department of Social Services are virtually nonexistent.

According to Adorno's sister, Iris, he received no assistance from anyone, despite any number of warning signs.

"Even after George had gotten into serious trouble," Iris said recently, referring to his two homicide arrests, "his aftercare worker didn't do anything for him. I remember George once asked, 'Why don't you do something for me?' and the worker said that he was. I remember once the aftercare worker came to the house to see George and all he did was sit around and drink coffee, smoke cigarettes, and tell George to 'be cool.'"

Most aftercare work is by telephone and mail, certainly not the kind of effort that is going to bring about much change in badly disturbed youngsters. A form letter to a child who cannot read, mailed to a tenement mailbox that is regularly ripped out and scavenged for welfare checks by junkies, is not the kind of rehabilitative effort that will help George Adorno or save the lives of his victims.

"Those aftercare workers and probation officers are just doing all that paperwork to justify their jobs," Iris Adorno continued. "That way, if we complain they can pull out their folders and show all the letters they mailed out. But that doesn't fool the people they're supposed to be trying to help. It only fools people who don't know what it's all about."

With little real confinement and almost no rehabilitation, youngsters such as George Adorno are continuously fed through a blank juvenile-justice conveyor belt toward their sixteenth birthdays and their first confrontation with the criminal court—a cruelty to the kids and a cruelty to their victims. For a while, the youngsters feel immune and statistics seem to bear out their sense of subsixteen invincibility. As incredible as it may seem, 70 percent of all the violent juvenile crime in the city is committed by fourteen- and fifteen-year-olds.

The recently enacted Juvenile Justice Reform Act of 1976 is supposed to allow judges to commit fourteen- and fifteen-year-olds for three years to five years if they are classified as having committed a "designated felony act"—which includes first-degree homicide and kidnapping. While some politicians have tried to make it appear that this law will put violent youths away for years, that is not quite true. "Designated felony acts" are just a small percentage of the violent juvenile crimes. Also, the law's small print makes it clear that these youngsters can only be held in a secure DFY facility for a maximum of twelve months, then transferred to a residential setting for another maximum of twelve months, after which they may resume the usual weekend passes for home.

Until they turned sixteen, Adorno and his pals could literally do no wrong. The family-court system and state laws not only kept their names out of the newspapers, but kept the histories of their past crimes from ever entering police-department records. In an effort to protect the reputations of the overwhelming number of youngsters who get involved with the family court once or twice and no more, the system has simply not found a mechanism by which to identify and isolate the potentially dangerous youngsters such as Adorno.

"The Department of Mental Hygiene and the psychiatrists associated with juvenile violence on a part-time basis generally think of the kids as a pain in the ass," one medical official within the system "who did not want to be identified" said.

"And don't think these kids don't see right through the doctors," the official continued. "Al Shanker may not be able to teach them how to read, but they can read us pretty good. You know what they call one of the part-time psychiatrists who interview them up here? They call him 'Neutral.' When I asked if they gave him that nickname because he was a wishy-washy guy they just laughed at me. They called him Neutral because his visits were so brief he never bothered to take his car out of gear."

The State Department of Mental Hygiene, which has the second-largest budget in the state, after education,

admits that it has no beds for these youngsters, no treatment facilities, and no research (except for a moribund Bronx state project) into what can be done about the problem. Almost all the psychiatrists and psychologists allegedly working with the youngsters are part-timers (earning up to $26,000 a year) whose main source of income comes from their private practices. One psychologist turned up on thirteen different state and city payrolls. Psychiatrists such as Dr. Michael Pawel, who has done much original work with violent youths, are the exception.

George Adorno was born in New York on December 23, 1958, shortly after most of his family moved here from Puerto Rico. Until his most recent arrest for homicide, George lived with his mother, Mercedes, and his twenty-year-old sister, Iris, on the top floor of a five-story brick tenement at 215 West 111th Street. George's father, Miguel, has lived apart from the family for many years. George's older brother, also named Miguel, has had a number of arrests for purse-snatching and auto theft but wasn't sent to a juvenile-detention center until after he had struck a court attendant in front of a judge.

The Adorno apartment is large and well maintained. Like many of the other families along West 111th Street, the Adornos are worried about crime and they have not only a stout metal front door but three heavy-duty locks to guard against break-ins. George is so concerned about crime in the street that when he's not in custody, he usually insists upon escorting his sister, home from the subway when she has finished work.

"The thought of his sister or mother getting mugged or his property taken drives George absolutely bananas," says Homicide Detective Mike Casale, who has known Adorno for several years.

"Whenever I used to ask him about how he would feel if somebody ripped off his mother, like he and his pals were ripping off other people's mothers, it just never registered. He seemed unable to transfer the anger he felt about his own family getting robbed into any empathy at all for his victims."

Before George Adorno had reached his sixteenth birthday he had admitted committing two homicides, having been in robberies involving two more killings, and having taken part in innumerable nonfatal robberies (about 40 taxicab stickups alone), some burglaries, and even an arson. Adorno was only five feet two inches tall and didn't

weigh more than 130 pounds (he is still not much larger), but he was unquestionably one of the most feared youngsters in Harlem. Even the organized street gangs with their flashy jackets, bizarre initiation rites, and taste for savage violence stayed clear of Adorno. At fifteen, he had a reputation on the street not only as a killer but as a totally unpredictable youngster who was capable of sharing a soda with a pal one minute and blowing his brains out the next. He was even capable of jumping out of the second floor of the East 119th Street police station without checking how high up he was first.

"George was just sitting there setting up two of his friends," Detective Casale said, "when it must have dawned on him we weren't buying. In a flash he's up and going out the second-floor window headfirst. I leaped over the desk and grabbed hold of one leg just as he's going out. 'George!' I'm screaming at him. 'George, for God's sake, you're going to get killed.'

"But all he's doing is dangling out the window and thrashing like mad to get his foot loose. In a few seconds I can't hold on anymore and I feel his foot begin to go and I feel my heart stop. I lose my grip and down he goes two stories to the concrete and I can't believe it. He hits the ground in a crouch and is up, over a Cyclone fence with barbed wire on top, across a vacant lot, and gone in a blink. You or me, we'd be dead or with permanently slipped disks. George? He was gone. Fastest thing I ever saw."

On another occasion, when he was still only fifteen, Adorno managed to escape from two detectives who were holding him as a material witness in a homicide in the George Washington Hotel on East 23rd Street.

Adorno escaped, it turned out, because the New York City Police Department would not allow him conjugal visits from his girl friend.

"It's weird," one of the detectives familiar with the case said. "Here you've got this material witness in a homicide who you know has done stickups and hit people, but he's only fifteen years old. I mean, he's a kid. He's only up to your chest. But he sits around all day showing you how he can pick handcuffs loose with a paper clip. Otherwise, he's watching kiddie television programs. He eats the worst kind of junk food you can imagine. And then he says he wants one of his girls to visit him. Visit? He wants one of his girls up there to spend the night. I mean he's only fifteen and God knows how old she's going to turn out to be.

"His request had to be denied," the

detective continued. "I mean we would have all gone away for aiding and abetting minors. So, what does George do? He ducks out of the door one afternoon and is flying down the stairs. Two detectives chase after him, but when they hit the street, he's gone."

Because he was under sixteen George Adorno was free to roam about the city despite the serious crimes he had committed, despite his mother's pleas that he was uncontrollable, despite the fact that he hadn't been to school since the fourth grade and did not intend to return, and despite the fact that he could neither read nor write and had no hope whatever of finding a job. Adorno was allowed to remain in his home despite the report by his aftercare worker that he was wearing expensive clothes for which he could not account and despite a Division for Youth psychiatric report that identified Adorno as a highly dangerous and aggressive youngster who belonged to a criminal subculture functioning at a borderline intellectual level.

The report went on to say that Adorno spoke about his exploits without embarrassment or remorse and concluded that he needed a "carefully designed educational program" that would probably raise his self-esteem.

There was, of course, no "carefully designed educational program." There was only George Adorno and his terrifying "Clockwork Orange" friends.

Adorno was part of a loosely organized neighborhood band of about a dozen teenage purse-snatchers, street muggers, armed holdup men, and killers. Robbing was what they did on a daily basis and, as a result, they not only terrorized the residents of their own South Harlem community, but they made larcenous and sometimes murderous excursions all over the city. They moved about in groups of three or four, usually with a gun they had rented from a local fence for between $3 and $10 a day. Police cannot even estimate the number of muggings and stickups these youngsters may have committed in the course of a year. The usual rule of thumb used by police is that for every arrest, there are at least ten or even twenty street muggings or stickups committed. An informal poll by police in the East 119th Street precinct where Adorno and his pals lived showed that between them they had accumulated well over 100 arrests before their sixteenth birthdays. Kiki, for instance, an almost angelic-looking youngster of tiny proportions, had been charged by the age of twelve with two burglaries, two robberies, a grand larceny (there also were three

family-court appearances for which no records could be found), plus nine juvenile-delinquency petitions for shoplifting, throwing rocks at automobiles and trains, disorderly conduct, and menacing other boys at a day camp. T-Boy, another member of the group, had been charged by the time he was fifteen with nine grand larcenies, five robberies, two jostlings, two illegal possessions of weapons, one riot, one auto theft, and one attempted escape.

Breakfast for the group usually began at about noon at the Indian Hole Social Club, a poolroom hangout at 114th Street and St. Nicholas Avenue, where the youngsters drank Orange Crush and gobbled down cream-filled Hostess Twinkies and pink Sno-Cone cupcakes. School no longer figured in any of their lives since their truancy was actively encouraged by their teachers, who found they were not only impossible to control but disruptive in class. According to Bronx District Attorney Mario Merola, there are 200,-000 truants wandering around in New York City every day.

"They're young, hyperactive, with nothing to do, no place to go, and nothing to lose," Merola said. "They can tear concrete apart."

By late afternoon the boys usually drifted away from the Indian Hole to begin their day by grabbing purses from women returning from work. Sometimes they clustered around local Harlem subway exits waiting for their victims and sometimes they went downtown to either the Upper West Side, the garment center, or Herald Square. The method the youngsters employed almost never varied, however. They'd wait, arms draped across the kiosk railing, until one of them, usually the biggest, ran up behind his victim and knocked her to the ground. For a second one might even think it was an accident. Another of the youngsters then darted in, grabbed the woman's pocketbook, and raced off, slipping waist high through the crowds. Two other youngsters simultaneously raced off in opposite directions, creating as much chaos as possible. It all took place in a matter of seconds and, even if one of the youngsters was caught and returned to the scene, it was almost impossible for any of the victims or onlookers to be certain whether or not the child—usually crying and protesting his innocence—had actually been involved.

After grabbing a purse, the youngsters usually met at a designated spot to split up the money. If the first pocketbook had enough money, fine. If not, the boys would repeat the proce-

dure until they had as much money as they wanted for their immediate needs. Once the purse-snatching money had been spent on junk food, kung fu films, and pinball, the youngsters often headed toward Central Park, where they quietly surrounded bike riders and strollers, showing either a gun or knife, and demanded more money.

The group's specialty, however, was sticking up taxicab drivers. Cabdrivers, they found, always had lots of money and rarely pressed complaints.

"No matter what you as a passenger might think of taxicab drivers," Detective Walter Thompson of the Sixth Homicide Zone said, "most of them are notorious noncomplainers. It's a tough job, and a day equals a day's pay. If they lose a day's pay in a stickup, it comes out of their pockets. They've got to make that money up by working more hours, not losing still another day's pay pressing a complaint in court. It's wrong, but that's the mentality. They know the kid's not going to jail anyway. They just cut their losses and go back to work. More kids identify cabdrivers they've stuck up rather than the other way around."

The preferred method for robbing cabs, according to the youngsters, is for one of them to approach the driver from the passenger's side while the cab is stopped for a light. While the first youth asks the driver about being taken to some address or other and the driver's attention is momentarily diverted, the other youngsters gather around the driver's window. One of the youngsters always has the gun and only rarely does the driver resist.

On Friday and Saturday nights, Adorno and his pals, as well as any number of other adolescents engaged in similar pursuits, usually gather at Mr. Soul Social Club, a storefront late-night hangout at 1400 Fifth Avenue, near 115th Street. According to precinct cops, it's the "21" of muggers. Police have picked up youngsters at Mr. Soul's who were still carrying the weapons fired in homicides earlier in the evening.

The music in Mr. Soul's is continuous, sensuous, and loud, and many of the youngsters keep time by blowing police whistles they wear on chains around their necks. There is a lunch counter along one side of the place and a chintz-covered morris chair and sofa near the entrance. Girls usually join their boyfriends in Mr. Soul's and it is there that they are given the $30 and $40 "allowances" they demand of their boyfriends in order for them to remain loyal. According to police, for

$30 or $40 every couple of days, twelve-, thirteen-, fourteen-, and fifteen-year-old girls will carry their boyfriends' guns; get them their endless sacks filled with fast-food hamburgers, fried chicken, and barbecue; expertly roll their long, thin, tightly packed marijuana cigarettes; and wander with them into a curtained alcove in the rear, where they have sex on a blanket-covered iron double bed.

"If some nut ever planted dynamite under this place and sent it sky-high some Friday night," one disgruntled precinct cop said, "you'd reduce the crime rate of the city by 60 percent."

Station-house exaggeration, perhaps, but the extraordinary thing about youngsters such as George Adorno and T-Boy and Kiki is how few of them there really are in the city. A recent study by the State Division of Criminal Justice Services brought out some amazing statistics that showed a surprisingly small number of juveniles commit an exceptionally high percentage of the crimes.

The study chose a scientifically selected sample of 4,857 youngsters under sixteen who had been arrested in connection with violent street crimes such as murder, assault, armed robbery, and rape. The study showed that of the 4,857 arrested in connection with 3,639 violent crimes, 624 accounted for 1,443 of the arrests all by themselves. That meant that 12.9 percent of the kids accounted for 25.5 percent of the group's violent crimes.

A further analysis of the 624 repeaters showed that 489 of them had been arrested twice before; 99 had been arrested three times; 18, four times; 14, five times; 2, six times; and 2 more, seven times. These statistics, it must be remembered, are for fifteen-year-olds and under.

Tracing what happened to these 4,857 youngsters after their arrests, however, was even more revealing. Of the 4,857 youngsters arrested, 2,165 never even got to court. Their cases were "adjusted" or thrown out at the family court's intake area by probation officers who have the power of judges and juries over the youngsters' cases. Of the rest who did go through the family-court fact-finding process, only 336 out of the original 4,857 were placed in training schools or given supervised probation. Supervised probation, which accounted for 218 of the 336, incidentally, means little more than a monthly telephone check between the youngster and an overburdened aftercare worker who may look after up to 200 kids a month.

That meant only 113 out of the 4,847 youngsters originally arrested for serious violent crimes were institutionalized in any way. Of that 113, however, only 79 were sent to secure training schools, while 26 were sent to nonrestrictive group homes or residences. Eight of the original 4,857 youngsters were adjudged psychotic and sent to a mental-health facility.

George Adorno has been through it all, he has been through so many sessions with so many intake officers, corporation counsels, judges, DFY counselors, probation officers, aftercare workers, and part-time hit-and-miss city psychiatrists that there is almost nothing about juvenile justice he does not know. He certainly knows that the city and state's secure juvenile-detention centers are not at all secure. Last year, for instance, according to unpublished DFY data, 37 youngsters out of a total population of 72 managed to escape or went AWOL from the state's secure facilities: Goshen, Brookwood, and Bronx State. Eventually, many of those youngsters wound up back in DFY facilities, but that was usually as a result of yet another arrest for yet another violent crime. At Spofford, the city's only secure facility for juveniles, executive director Ron Curylo suspects that many of the city's street-gang members have keys to the facility's 28 external and 60 internal doors, but Curylo has been unable to get the locks changed for over two years because of the budget crunch. In addition, the front gate to Spofford does not close for months at a time because of maintenance-personnel cutbacks. As a result, about 100 youngsters slip away from Spofford every year, some of them, like the push-in mugger Raymond Timmons, still have the keys to the place on them when arrested in connection with other crimes.

George Adorno even knew that he didn't have to show up in court. From the age of twelve on, George Adorno always had family-court warrants outstanding against him, but he knew that none of them had ever been served. It wasn't because Adorno was on the lam. He was not in hiding. He always lived with his mother and sister at 215 West 111th Street, top floor, metal door on the left. He always hung out on the same streets, went to the same clubs, danced at the same centers. The reason that George Adorno was never picked up on family-court warrants is simply that the Manhattan family court doesn't have any warrant officers to execute the warrants. In truth, the court does have one warrant officer, but he spends all of his time in his office trying to keep tabs on the hundreds of youngsters with outstanding warrants who get picked up daily for committing other crimes.

By piecing together Adorno's record from various sources, most of whom cannot be revealed, and from discussions with Adorno's family and friends, a textbook for failure emerges that is clearly as much an indictment of a system as it is of a young man.

After years of appearing before various probation officers and family-court judges for robberies and other crimes, on May 18, 1973, George Adorno, at fourteen, was placed in Warwick, a secure DFY facility. The petition against him on that occasion was armed robbery.

"There for the first time you had him in one place," one DFY worker said. "Did anyone try anything at all to help him? Did anyone try to teach him how to read? He wanted to learn, you know. He was embarrassed at not knowing how to read. So were most of the other kids like him. Vocational training consisted of making wooden lamps out of excess lumber. Inside, by the way, George was a perfect soldier. He was a good kid. He did very well. So, instead of working with him, and because he didn't belt anyone with the fire nozzle, after three months Adorno was given weekend passes in preparation for his early release.

"The truth is," the DFY worker continued, "if we kept everybody as long as we are supposed to, we'd need twice as many facilities, and we don't have the money."

Thus, on September 5, four months after his having been sent to Warwick for eighteen months, Adorno was arrested for a robbery in Harlem while on a one-week pass. The police did not know he was on a weekend pass, and the family court, because of its backlog, routinely postponed his appearance, so Adorno was able to go back to Warwick on September 10, no one the wiser.

The next week, September 17, Adorno was free on another pass. This time he was arrested for robbery on the same day he was supposed to have returned to Warwick. Because of the delays incurred by his arrest and arraignment, Adorno didn't get back to Warwick until he was three days late. Warwick, of course, did not know he had been arrested again, and the police still did not know he was supposed to be in Warwick on armed-robbery charges. Adorno, meanwhile, balanced the various bureaucrats and court appearances while checking in at War-

4. JUVENILE JUSTICE

wick every once in a while to pick up new passes.

On November 12, family court issued a warrant for his arrest in connection with his repeated failure to appear on his September robbery arrest, but since they do not have any warrant officers to pursue the youngsters, and family-court secrecy kept them from finding out he was in Warwick, Adorno was undeterred. At fourteen he was already manipulating the system perfectly.

On February 7, 1974, Adorno was transferred to Goshen, another DFY secure facility, and his weekends home continued right up until he was officially released, four months early. DFY never found out—in fact, they probably still don't know—that he had been arrested on two armed robberies during his stay with them and that he had two outstanding family-court warrants pending against him.

On July 19, 1974, George Adorno was released from Goshen. Within four months, according to his own statements, there were four murders in which Adorno was either a witness or a killer. Whatever else he did during the period is unknown. The murders started, in fact, on July 19, the same day he was released. Adorno later said that he was walking along Lexington Avenue near 117th Street when he ran into two friends. One, a fourteen-year-old, was carrying a silver-plated .45 automatic. The other, who was fifteen, had a hunting rifle. The pair, Adorno said, told him they were on their way to stick up a local pawnshop owner. When they got to the location, Adorno said, the other two went inside while he waited across the street. He said he was not acting as a lookout but just "wanted to see how they were going to do it." In a few minutes, Adorno heard some shots and saw the boys running out of the pawnshop with rings and gold medallion chains streaming through their fingers. The pawnshop owner was killed in the stickup.

Within a month, on August 18, 1974, there was another murder when Adorno and five of his pals wanted a car. They were wandering around midtown a little after midnight, and they went into the Hemisphere Garage at 65 West 56th Street. Willie Daniels, the 26-year-old parking attendant, confronted the tiny intruders as they raced down the ramp into the basement garage. Suddenly a shot rang out and the attendant doubled over. According to Adorno, one of his friends shot Willie Daniels.

Willie Daniels, the parking attendant, died of the gunshot wound.

Three weeks later, on September 7,

a balmy Saturday night, Adorno and two other pals were walking toward Eighth Avenue looking for a taxicab driver to stick up. On 115th Street, between Seventh and Eighth avenues, the youngsters saw a woman get out of a bright-yellow medallion cab. There are so few medallion taxis in Harlem that most of the time George and his pals send the tiniest of them down to 96th Street and Broadway with instructions to bring the cab back to a prearranged location for a robbery. This cab, however, was there on its own, and as soon as the passenger had gotten out, one of the boys went to the window opposite the driver and asked to be taken to 110th and Lenox. Meanwhile, George walked up to the driver's window and saw that the man had some folded bills in his shirt pocket.

George never hesitated. He simply put his hand in the cabdriver's shirt pocket and began to remove the money. The driver, almost instinctively, reached up to grab Adorno's hand. It was a mistake. Adorno was outraged.

"He grabbed my hand," Adorno later said, his usual monotone rising as he recalled the incident.

"He's trying to, you know, drive off. I go, 'Oh, oh,' right? So the dude is trying to grab me, trying to drive off, so I just shot him. I just went pop."

Six days later, September 13, Adorno was picked up as a material witness in the taxicab driver's death, having temporarily conned the police and courts that two of his friends had killed the cabdriver.

Adorno's story about his friends killing the cabby did not finally ring true, and Judge Nanette Dembitz ordered that everyone involved be given lie-detector tests. Adorno failed and was so angry with Nat Laurendi, the polygraph expert and a former detective in District Attorney Frank Hogan's office, that he threatened to kill him.

"Nobody ever threatened to kill me before," Laurendi later said, "except Joe Valachi, but this kid I believed."

Meanwhile, George was walking the streets and dropping into the Indian Hole and Mr. Soul's. He knew that the police and courts had not bought his story about the cabby killing. According to police, he probably heard that his pal Mushmouth was rumored to be talking to the police about the cabdriver killing. Mushmouth, the nickname for fourteen-year-old Michael Hurd, was also supposed to have cheated Adorno out of $100 in a crap game at the time. "He spoke up to my face," Adorno told friends, when Mushmouth refused to give him back the $100.

Whatever the motive, on October 24, five weeks after the cabdriver killing, George, T-boy, and Ray were shooting pigeons on a rooftop at 116th Street when they saw Mushmouth on the street below. The rifle, which belonged to Ray, had a scope. George said he took the rifle from Ray, aimed at Mushmouth's head and fired. Mushmouth died instantly.

Peter Edelman, who now heads DFY, was appointed by Governor Carey in 1975, and, therefore, cannot be blamed for the mismanagement of George Adorno's life. In fact, he was not at all pleased with the situation he found upon his appointment and has initiated any number of changes. Once again, however, a tight budget, civil-service work rules, union regulations, and a basic philosophy on the part of DFY employees that rehabilitation does not work has limited his successes. In addition, while Edelman and the governor emphasize "deinstitutionalizing" youngsters under sixteen as soon as possible before turning them into a permanent prison population, they have yet to devise a system whereby the potentially violent youngster can be distinguished from the youngster who could benefit from early release. Since it is impossible to know in advance what the best behaved and socially secure adolescent will do a month from now, DFY officials say, how then can they be expected to make such a prognosis?

On October 28, four days after the Mushmouth killing, Adorno was picked up in connection with the murder of taxicab driver Morris Rotter. Adorno was questioned by Assistant D.A. Juris Cederbaums of the Manhattan district attorney's homicide bureau.

With him during the interrogation were the homicide detectives, Mike Casale and Walter Thompson, who had talked with him in the past. Since George was still only fifteen years old (he had exactly two months to go), his parent or legal guardian had to be present during the interrogation. His sister, Iris, who was eighteen at the time, was present during the entire questioning period.

Adorno's statements were then turned over to the family court for a fact-finding and possible placing or psychiatric confinement, but Family Court Judge Shirley Wohl Kram dismissed the homicide charges, because his mother had not been present during the interrogation.

"Judges can only enforce what is the law," Judge Kram recently said when asked about the dismissal. "The legislature and the public must understand what's happening before we can be di-

174

rected toward a solution."

Juris Cederbaums, who took the Adorno confession, is no longer an ADA. He is still angry about the Adorno dismissal, however.

"I couldn't believe it," Cederbaums said. "The law simply requires that a parent or guardian be present. George had no father we could find. His mother was in Puerto Rico and, believe me, she was in no shape to act as a witness for anybody. She had her own problems. His sister, Iris, however, is one of those sociological phenomenons. Given exactly the same background as her brother, she goes to college and has a job in a midtown office to help pay her way. She was an adult and probably the most responsible person who could sit in during the interrogation. The entire questioning session was recorded and there were witnesses. George was advised of his rights. And still family court threw out his admissions because his mother wasn't there. I couldn't believe it. The family court didn't even call me to ask why I had used his sister instead of his mother as a witness during the interrogation. It made me sick."

On January 20, 1975, just a few weeks after his homicide confessions had been thrown out by one family-court judge, another signed a warrant for his arrest in connection with several armed-robbery appearances he had failed to attend. The warrant carried warning to all police officers: "This respondent is alleged to have committed three murders. May be armed and is very dangerous."

Despite the fact that Adorno was still living at home, he was not picked up until February 7, when he was arrested in a doorway on West 105th Street with a loaded .38 and seven envelopes filled with cocaine. Since this was his first arrest as an adult, his name was sent to the state crime computer in Albany. The computer, of course, had no knowledge of the recent family-court warrant which urged caution. Nor did it have any knowledge of any of George Adorno's history. The computer, from its data bank of wisdom, chattered back:

"The above response shows no available prior information for this individual."

Adorno did eventually serve part of an armed-robbery sentence, but early last February, having just turned eighteen, he was released from Elmira, eighteen months early. On February 22, 1977, Adorno, sixteen-year-old Mark Davis, and fifteen-year-old Calvin Gaddy headed toward the 110th Street IRT subway station in order to rob the token-booth attendant. The youngsters had been shooting baskets earlier and had missed the critical midnight shift change, the only time when the bulletproof, $37,000 air-conditioned subway token bunkers are vulnerable. Annoyed, George Adorno told Mark Davis to take the train down to 96th Street and Broadway and "bring back a cab."

Then, Adorno and the arrest-proof fifteen-year-old Gaddy, who carried the gun, went to the prearranged doorway at 40 West 111th Street to wait for their pal Davis and taxicab driver Steven Robinson to arrive.

Word about the Steven Robinson murder spread through the area quickly, and soon Homicide Lieutenant Herman Kluge said, "Everybody was dropping dimes on everybody else." After sorting out the dimes, detectives Mike Casale and Richard Henderson picked up Adorno, Gaddy, and Davis. They found the cabdriver's bloodstained radio in Davis's apartment. Gaddy was too young for arrest, so he went directly to family court, where he admitted he had been in on the robbery but said he had no idea the driver was going to be killed. Before making a determination about Gaddy, Family Court Judge Cesar Quinones sent him to the court's unguarded sixth-floor clinic for a psychiatric examination. When the doctors had finished talking with the youngster, Gaddy simply walked out of the building and went home. Nobody even bothered to look for him for a least a week, when the D.A.'s office realized that one of their possible witnesses was missing. Lieutenant Kluge was notified and he sent one of his detectives to find Gaddy. Calvin was dancing at a community center on the ground floor of his West 115th Street apartment project.

George Adorno has pleaded not guilty to the Robinson murder. His lawyer, Arthur Hammer, was appointed to defend him by the Appellate Division from a specially drawn list of highly experienced defense attorneys who represent defendants in capital cases. Hammer refuses to discuss the Adorno case. If convicted, of course, Adorno could receive 25 years. During his brief appearances in court so far, Adorno looks like a tiny, vulnerable child, surrounded by the four towering corrections guards who are assigned to stand around him like points of a compass. His mother and aunt and brothers and sister have been to most of his court appearances and they often smile at each other.

On the street, in the Indian Hole, and at Mr. Soul's, Adorno's status has risen, not only as a result of his case being tried in supreme court, rather than family court, but because Adorno is being represented by a big-time appellate-division lawyer.

"When I go to court, that's what I want," one twelve-year-old said. "I want a pelican lawyer, not no legal aid."

Juvenile Inmates:

The Long-Term Trend Is Down

Diversion into community programs has continued — despite public reaction to youth crime.

Rob Wilson

THE number of juvenile offenders in state institutions has been declining for more than 10 years, and has continued to decline in the last three years, despite heavy political pressure in some states to get tough with juvenile criminals.

These facts were disclosed in an exclusive national survey of population trends in state juvenile institutions recently completed by *Corrections Magazine*. The survey, conducted by questionnaire and telephone, sought to establish the population of state juvenile institutions in all 50 states, the District of Columbia, and in selected adult and county institutions on January 1 of 1965, 1970, 1975 and 1978.

It will come as no surprise to those familiar with the field of juvenile corrections that the institutional population has declined substantially since 1965, since it is well known that large numbers of juvenile offenders were diverted out of institutions and into community programs during the late sixties and early seventies. What is surprising is that the decline has continued in the last three years, despite what some observers have described as a hysterical reaction by the public against youth crime, a reaction that has been supported in many state legislatures by a wave of legislation aimed at locking up more juvenile offenders for longer terms.

The survey clearly indicates that the administrators and judges responsible for the sentencing and incarceration of juveniles have so far successfully resisted the effort to put more of them in state institutions. What also may be happening in some states is that while larger numbers of serious juvenile offenders are being sent to institutions, a greater number of "status" and other minor offenders are being diverted into community programs.

To the public at large, the actual statistics on the number of juveniles incarcerated (see chart) will seem surprisingly low. Statistics from the states on their juvenile populations in 1965 were fragmentary and, sometimes, nonexistent. But based on the figures supplied to *Corrections Magazine* and other surveys of the same period done by other organizations, the population was probably about 40,000. By 1970, the number

had declined to about 37,000; by 1975 it had dropped to 28,298; on January 1, 1978, the number was exactly 26,000. This last figure is less than one-tenth of the 294,000 people jamming adult state and federal prisons, though law enforcement officials claim that persons under the age of 18 are responsible for 40 to 50 percent of all crimes reported in the United States. Clearly there is an immense amount of diversion of juvenile offenders going on in every state.

Some juvenile corrections experts who examined the *Corrections Magazine* survey said that they thought the statistics were artificially low because state officials failed to report the population of programs that the officials consider community programs but which are actually secure institutions, and because privately operated secure institutions were not included. The number of such juveniles — some delinquents, some not — has been estimated in a federal census at about 20,000. But even if this were true, and as a result the numbers doubled, juveniles would still constitute a small proportion of the total imprisoned population.

For the purposes of the survey, juveniles were defined as those under the age of 18, which is the age cutoff that most states use. There are some exceptions to this rule, including Alabama, New York and Missouri, where the age cutoff is 16, and Georgia and North Carolina, where it is 17. All of these states therefore have substantial numbers of juveniles in their adult correctional systems. Almost every state has at least a few juveniles in its adult system because of laws permitting prosecutors and judges to transfer serious juvenile offenders to the adult courts for trial.

Another factor that complicates the statistics is that several states have substantial numbers of juveniles in county correctional institutions. The most extensive county systems are in California; Los Angeles County has more juveniles in institutions — 1,200 — than all but four of the states.

All but seven of the states have shown declines in the juvenile institution population since 1965; more than half of the states have shown declines of 30 percent or more; 11 showed declines of 50 percent or more. Of the seven states that showed increases since 1965, six had increases that were very small.

Only Georgia experienced a substantial increase over the period, from 700 to 1,400, and this was entirely due to the absorption into the state system of thousands of youths held in county institutions. In fact, few states in recent years have demonstrated more devotion to the notion of community corrections than Georgia; from 1975 to 1978 its juvenile institution population declined 40 percent, from 2,400 to 1,400.

The uniform, nationwide decline in the population of state juvenile institutions has happened despite wrenching demographic shifts and despite increases in youth crime that are measured in the hundreds of percentiles. The two most important demographic considerations are the heavy increase in the number of juveniles in the population over the last 20 years, and the heavy migration of citizens from the Northeast and Midwest to the South, Southwest and West. But these factors appear to have had no impact at all on the population trends in juvenile institutions. Arizona, for instance, almost doubled its population between 1965 and 1978; but its juvenile institution population declined by almost half, from 677 to 344. In Texas, the institution population declined by more than 1,500 inmates between 1965 and 1975, though in the last three years the population has increased more than that of any other state.

The population figures were no more reflective of national crime trends than they were of national demographic trends. A report by the Vera Institute of Justice released last summer showed that violent crime by juveniles tripled between 1960 and 1975. Police arrested more than two million youths in 1975. Although youths aged ten to 20 were less than 20 percent of the population that year, they accounted for half of the arrests.

The population decline has been greatest in those states where the concern about youth crime has been greatest. In California, the number of youths under 18 being held in California Youth Authority institutions dropped from 3,577 in 1965 to 1,389 in 1978. And those youths diverted out of the California state system were not simply spilled into the county systems. The population of Los Angeles County juvenile institutions held steady over the 13-year period of the *Corrections* survey at between 1,000 and 1,200 youngsters; in San Francisco County, the in-

Corrections Magazine Survey of Juveniles under 18 in Secure and Semi-Secure Facilities

A. STATE JUVENILE SYSTEMS

	1/1/65	1/1/70	1/1/75	% change 70-75	1/1/78	% change 75-78
ALABAMA	773*	406*	369	− 9	315	−15
ALASKA	NA	63*	97	+54	108	+11
ARIZONA	677*	468*	362*	−23	344*	− 5
ARKANSAS	516	490	476	− 3	335	−25
CALIFORNIA	3,577	2,643	1,256	−52	1,389	+10
COLORADO	586	360	297	−17	369	+24
CONNECTICUT	300*	275*	160*	−42	170*	+ 6
DELAWARE	NA	NA	249(1/31/75)	NA	176	−29
D.C.	868	935	606	−35	530	−12
FLORIDA	NA	1,012	1,070	+ 6	1,087	+ 2
GEORGIA	713	1,534††	2,453††	+60	1,468	−40
HAWAII	143	68	112	+65	77	−31
IDAHO	172	176	123	−30	109	−11
ILLINOIS	2,100*	2,030	1,172	−42	1,121	− 4
INDIANA	860	919	600	−35	674	+12
IOWA	288	343	295	−14	382	+29
KANSAS	350	358	349	− 2	380	+ 9
KENTUCKY	772*	611	362	−41	470	+30
LOUISIANA	1,382	1,321	1,191	−10	880	−26
MAINE	204	212	142	−33	208	+46
MARYLAND	NA	1,253	1,002	−20	1,052	+ 5
MASSACHUSETTS	1,118	895	49	−94	71	+45
MICHIGAN	1,200*	1,199	562	−53	669	+19
MINNESOTA	670*	763	424	−44	248	−41
MISSISSIPPI	NA	500(2/19/70)	631(12/16/74)	+26	331	−47
MISSOURI	713	553	450	−19	361	−20
MONTANA	249	181	163	−10	179	+10
NEBRASKA	369	293	218	−25	212	− 3
NEVADA	191	220	229	+ 4	169	−26
NEW HAMPSHIRE	NA	184	188	+ 2	165	−12
NEW JERSEY	1,894	1,122	659	−41	784	+19
NEW MEXICO	342	262	247	− 6	321	+30
NEW YORK	2,046**†	2,280(31/12/69)**†	567**†	−75	471(7/1/78)	−17
NORTH CAROLINA	1,653(6/30/65)	NA	939	NA	807	−14
NORTH DAKOTA	130	101	92	− 9	118(11/30/77)	+28
OHIO	NA	2,786	2,476	−11	1,709	−31
OKLAHOMA	607(6/30/65)	350(6/30/70)	377(6/30/75)	+ 8	375(6/30/77)	0
OREGON	569	507	414	−18	680	+64
PENNSYLVANIA	959	927	1,082	+17	750	−31
RHODE ISLAND	172*	120*	79*	−34	74	− 6
SOUTH CAROLINA	NA	NA	650	NA	469	−28
SOUTH DAKOTA	161	136	98	−28	110	+12
TENNESSEE	NA	1,160(3/2/72)	1,063	− 8	1,134	+ 6
TEXAS	2,310*	2,215*	756	−66	1,274	+68
UTAH	329	279	184	−34	156	−15
VERMONT	185	183	95	−48	98	+ 3
VIRGINIA	1,148	1,324	944	−29	820	−13
WASHINGTON	1,400*	1,015*	760	−25	703	− 8
WEST VIRGINIA	444	264	286	+ 8	211	−26
WISCONSIN	944	1,078	763	−29	749	− 2
WYOMING	158	133	110	−17	138	+25
TOTAL STATES	34,242 (42 jurisdictions)	36,507 (48 jurisdictions)	28,298	−28	26,000	− 8

B. SELECTED COUNTY JUVENILE SYSTEMS

	1/1/65	1/1/70	1/1/75	% change 70-75	1/1/78	% change 75-78
CALIFORNIA						
LOS ANGELES	1,202	1,099	1,059	− 4	1,260	+19
SAN DIEGO	306	408	329	−19	367	+12
SAN FRANCISCO	233	209	190	− 9	143	−25
MINNESOTA						
HENNEPIN	108*	95	83	−13	84	+ 1
RAMSEY	88	103	55	−46	56	+ 1

NA means not available   *Estimate   **Includes some volunteers
† Excl. youth in camps (325 on 7/1/78)   ††Increase largely due to takeover of county systems

4. JUVENILE JUSTICE

Corrections Magazine Survey of Juveniles under 18 in Secure and Semi -Secure Facilities

C. SELECTED STATE ADULT SYSTEMS

ALABAMA	204(10/1/64)	164(10/1/69)	170(10/1/74)	+ 4	134(10/1/77)	− 21
FLORIDA	76*	96*	164	+71	190	+ 16
GEORGIA	582(admissions)	677(admissions)	54(admissions)	−97	57(admissions)	+ 6
MISSOURI	200*	211	333	+50	318	− 5
NEW YORK	3,658†	2,131†	1,494†	−30	2,111†	+41
NORTH CAROLINA	NA	450	650	+44	680	+ 5

*estimate   † includes 18-year-olds
NA means not available

stitution population declined from 233 to 143. So there is no doubt that those youngsters who would have gone to institutions 20 years ago have been diverted into probation programs, or into the hundreds of community programs established in California in recent years, many of them by the Youth Authority itself.

New York has seen an even more drastic reduction in its juvenile population than California. The number of youngsters aged 13 to 16 held in state Division for Youth institutions declined from more than 2,000 in 1970 to only 470 today. In New York, 16- and 17-year-olds are incarcerated in the adult system, generally in "reformatories" that hold only youthful inmates. Though state officials could not break out this group, they supplied statistics showing that the prison population of offenders aged 16 through 18 dropped between 1965 and 1975 from more than 3,600 to only 1,400. New York, however, is one of the few states where there are indications that judges and other officials are taking seriously the public's demand that young criminals be locked up. The 16 to 18-year-old reformatory population there has jumped 40 percent, from 1,400 to 2,100, in the last three years.

Other urban states with serious youth crime problems that have nonetheless shown sharp drops in juvenile institution population are New Jersey (1,894 in 1965 to 784 today), Illinois (2,100 to 1,121) and Michigan (1,200 to 669).

While it is relatively easy to establish that the populations of state correctional institutions for juveniles have gone down, finding out exactly what is happening to those that are diverted is a much more difficult task. The most comprehensive attempt to answer this question was the National Assessment of Juvenile Corrections (NAJC), a ten-year, $5 million project funded by the federal Law Enforcement Assistance Administration (LEAA). According to Dr. Robert Vinter, who was co-director of the project along with Dr. Rosemary Sarri, NAJC research showed that between 1970 and 1974 there was a 49 percent drop in the numbers of juveniles committed to county camps, ranches and institutions, and a 36 percent decline in the commitments to state facilities.

A large part of that drop was clearly due to the birth of "community corrections." NAJC found that in 1974, 23 percent of the youths committed to juvenile authorities were placed in some form of group home or other non-institutional setting — a category that didn't even exist four years earlier.

That category was continuing to expand in 1975, the last year for which national figures on community programs are available. The LEAA "Children in Custody" Report for 1975 showed a 23 percent jump over 1974 in the halfway house and group home population, and that did not even include private facilities working under contract to the states.

But even as community corrections was catching on, an LEAA census also showed a slight increase in institutional populations between 1974 and 1975. Some state officials said their community-based alternative programs had already exceeded their capacity to draw off offenders from institutions by that year.

"We think the pendulum swung a little bit too far," said Vergil M. Pinckney, Michigan's Director of Juvenile Institutions. "We dropped from over 1,300 in the sixties to under 600 in 1974. Now we're climbing back up."

1975 may indeed have been a turning point for some policymakers in juvenile corrections, when the law-and-order forces began to gain on the prison reformers. But it is impossible to identify any one overriding national trend in a field clouded with imprecise accounting, vague definitions and varying statutes. The rising crime rate and the toughening public stance on criminals clearly have had an effect on the adult system in the past three years, with increased commitments and a wave of mandatory and determinate sentencing laws that have contributed to a huge adult prison population. But the same simple formula cannot be applied to the juvenile system.

The eight percent drop in institutionalization between 1975 and 1978 indicated by the *Corrections* survey is at best a rough indicator; some states admit their figures could go up or down by several hundreds if definitions of "institutions" or "community-based" facilities were slightly altered. Longtime observers who have attempted to document the population changes express

exasperation at the near impossibility of discovering precisely how and where the nation is treating its juvenile offenders.

"We have no reason to believe that they have any more sense in the states in 1978 than they did in 1975," complained Vinter of the NAJC survey. "They didn't know where the kids were, whether their figures were up, down or sideways."

It is possible, however, in that jumbled picture to pick out the effects of both the deinstitutionalization reform movement and the public "backlash" to rising crime.

Various states' efforts to reduce their dependence on institutions may have exceeded public tolerance. What is happening now may be the start of "rationalizing" of the system, suggested Dr. Lloyd E. Ohlin of the Harvard Law School.

The backlash, with its demands for more and longer prison terms for adults, has only recently begun to affect the juvenile system, according to Ohlin. Some states have begun to consider determinate sentencing for juveniles and the opening of juvenile records to adult courts. And there may also be an increasing tendency to simply turn youths over to the adult system.

"People say maybe we've overused institutions, but there's still some of this population that we don't want out there," said Ohlin. "I think it really comes down to how you handle the secure care cases that people are concerned about. I think if you have a clearly defined, visible way of handling that, you get the freedom you need to do what you want with the other kids."

The debate is over just what portion of the juvenile caseload needs secure care. Ohlin considers the experience of the Massachusetts Department of Youth Services (DYS), which reduced its institutional population from more than 1,000 in 1970 to about 50 in 1973, to be a good indicator of how far the concept can be carried.

Citing the extensive study of the Massachusetts reform that he conducted with Harvard colleagues Drs. Robert Coates and Alden Miller, Ohlin said, "One would have to say that it is clearly demonstrated that we overinstitutionalize juvenile offenders in this country. . . . There's been an overreliance on the training school model.

"If one can reverse the policies," Ohlin continued, "instead of 90 percent, we could institutionalize ten percent of the population and do a much better job, without any increase in the threat to the community."

When he was in the process of closing the Massachusetts juvenile institutions, Dr. Jerome Miller's strategy was to work "from the top down," that is, release and find community placements for the most serious juvenile offenders first.

The rest of the states, with few exceptions, have chosen the opposite strategy — to glean from the system the least serious offenders and reserve the institutions for those convicted of serious crimes. The first target of every state was the status offender, convicted only of running away from home, promiscuity, incorrigibility and other offenses that are not adult crimes.

In the last two to three years, the states have received a hard push to complete the deinstitutionalization of their status offenders from the federal government. LEAA's Office of Juvenile Justice and Delinquency Prevention (OJJDP), created by the Juvenile Justice and Delinquency Prevention Act of 1974 (the J. D. Act), has made it a condition for the receipt of federal juvenile justice funds that the states remove all status offenders from institutions.

While there have been major problems with the implementation of OJJDP's deinstitutionalization effort, it is clear that many states have followed the federal guidelines and removed many of their lesser offenders from institutions. A survey by the National Center for Juvenile Justice Research, a branch of the National Council of Juvenile Court Judges, reported last year that at least 21 states now legally prohibit the detention of status offenders, and 35 prohibit the commitment of such offenders to correctional institutions.

While passage of laws does not necessarily mean status offenders automatically disappear from institutions, the flurry of legislation was "like a revolution," according to OJJDP Director John Rector.

In its effort to monitor compliance with provisions of the J.D. Act requiring removal of status offenders from institutions, Rector expressed the same frustration as Vinter. "You can't solely rely on those figures," he said. "But it's not all a game. ... These states have made radical and major changes in their whole statutory scheme for juveniles."

"There appears to be little doubt that the will to deinstitutionalize status offenders is strong throughout the country," said Hunter Hurst, director of the National Center for Juvenile Justice Research. Speaking before the Senate Subcommittee to Investigate Juvenile Delinquency last fall, he added, "I have no doubts that the Juvenile Justice and Delinquency Prevention Act of 1974 has played a prominent role in stimulating and strengthening that will."

The movement of status offenders out of institutions in recent years is one of many hypotheses — and they are only hypotheses — that experts posit to explain the drop in the juvenile population since 1975. Two other hypotheses are that the population dropped recently because of a decline in the proportion of the national population made up of juveniles, and, second, that it is related to a decline in juvenile arrests.

FBI Crime statistics show that the peak age for property offenses is 13 to 14, and the peak age for violent crimes is 18. According to the Bureau of the Census, the numbers of young people ten to 14 declined from 20,409,000 in 1975 to 19,201,000 in 1977, or a drop of .7 percent to 8.9 percent of the total population. The older group, those from 15 to 19, held steady at about 21 million, or 9.8 percent of the population, over that period. Both groups are expected to shrink in the coming years, until by 1985 the ten to 14 year old group will comprise only seven percent of the population, and the 15- to 19-year-old group 7.7 percent.

That decline is explained by some as a result of the gradual shift of the "baby-boom bulge" through adolescence into adulthood. The number of post-war births peaked in the early fifties, and started to decline in 1958. Those children are now passing out of the juvenile range into their twenties and out of those peak "at risk" categories, a shift that appears directly related to a drop in juvenile arrests.

The FBI reported that arrests for violent crimes of people under 18 decreased 12.1 percent from 1975 to 1976, and property crime arrests of juveniles dropped 7.9 percent. This was the first time in six years that arrests had declined, and preliminary figures for 1977 indicate that the curve is continuing downward. The FBI reported that all crime in the U.S. declined four percent last year.

But it is clear that the population shifts cannot be the whole explanation for the drop in crime. One inconsistency is that much serious crime is concentrated among minority inner-city youth, a group that has *not* been declining in proportion to the rest of the population. Yet, FBI statistics for last year show that in cities with more than a million residents, crime dropped six percent — even more than the national decline.

In any case, a discussion of crime rates may be irrelevant to a discussion of juvenile institution populations, since no one has ever established that there is a relationship between one and the other.

Whatever the cause of both the historical and recent institution population decline, most observers agree that several factors now working in combination will continue to exert downward pressure on offenders inside secure institutions. "If you have a policy of locking up the dangerous kids," said Lloyd Ohlin, "and you also have a policy of pulling out the status offenders and lesser delinquents [who are more numerous] and the

combined effect of the population change, diversion and declining arrest rates . . . you have to predict that not only will you have a decline but that it will continue."

Along with that decline, observers say that institutions are having to adapt to handling only the tougher, older offenders, with more serious criminal records.

"I think what is happening is that much of the fat has been squeezed out of juvenile correctional facilities over the period [of the *Corrections* survey]," said Franklin E. Zimring, director of the Center for Studies in Criminal Justice at the University of Chicago Law School.

"The big question is what's left and who's left," Zimring said. "My guess is you're looking at an older, more male, more minority and more offense-oriented population than has been the case in this century."

But narrowing the harsh institutional sanction to only the toughest offenders has brought other problems. An important part of the society's system of sanctions has been the ability of a parent, police officer, or judge to threaten an errant youngster with the prospect of being sent to "reform school" if he didn't behave. The institution loomed at the end of the line — like the father's belt, or the strap on the wall — swollen with lurid tales of what punishments awaited there.

Increasingly now, that threat is being removed from juvenile justice for the majority of offenders. Many officials complain that without it, we are weakening our ability to alter young people's behavior before they reach that ten percent class of truly dangerous criminals.

"What they mean is they want a very visible and credible threat for the kid," said Ohlin. "They want to be able to say, 'If you don't shape up, you're going to X place.' The name keeps changing. But it's the end of the line, it's lock-up, it's heavy, it's tough, and it's a mean place to do time. This is really the fundamental question you get down to, and it touches something very deep in people's notions of child rearing: Can you handle kids — tough, aggressive, acting out kids, very hostile to authority — can you handle them without some viable threat of that sort? . . . It seems to me that is a very serious argument, and it has to be taken seriously."

In the view of some observers, that "viable threat" is not being given up. The decline in the population of state training schools reported in the *Corrections* survey, according to these observers, projects a false image of deinstitutionalization. Far more significant, the critics say, is what the figures *don't* show.

Removal of status offenders or minor delinquents from state-run institutions may simply mask transfers to private facilities that are equally or more restrictive, it is charged. At the same time, local law enforcement officials and juvenile court judges — more aware of the reduced likelihood that an offender will be incarcerated when he leaves the courtroom — may be making greater use of local pre-trial detention as punishment. And it is widely suspected that more and more juveniles are being turned over to the adult system as juvenile corrections becomes less punitive, or are being sent to private institutions. But there is virtually no reliable data on the extent of these practices.

In the 1974 NAJC study, for example, Vinter said that it was impossible to identify what types of private institutions existed, let alone the numbers of juveniles committed to them. "The states couldn't track them all," he said. "They'd lose kids . . . and many privates were conglomerates of mental health, boarding schools, juvenile delinquents, all mixed together. So we gave up." Consequently, private facilities are excluded from the NAJC survey.

The LEAA "Children in Custody" report, however, listed 21,033 juveniles being held in 1,261 private correctional training schools, ranches, camps and farms in 1974, in addition to 30,629 youths in public facilities. The 1975 figure was 16,754 juveniles in 1,211 private facilities, and 32,133 in public.

Because private facilities are not run by state authorities, they tend not to be included in official population reports (and they are not reflected in the figures reported by the states in the *Corrections* survey). That posed a particular problem for the federal OJJDP in its attempt to monitor compliance with the 1974 JD Act, which required removal of status offenders from institutions. Only five of 45 states included private institutions in their first compliance reports.

"When the law was passed, a lot of states assumed it just meant *state* institutions," said David West, a grant administrator for OJJDP. "But we were talking about all institutions, state and private. Almost half of the juveniles placed end up in private facilities. If we had said only to deinstitutionalize the state-run facilities, they would just have transferred the kids out to the privates."

According to some critics, that is precisely what is happening. "Everyone wants to look good," said Jerome Miller. "With the Justice Department getting into deinstitutionalization, everyone wants to look like they're getting kids out, when in fact they're doing lateral transfers ."

Miller cited examples of private facilities officially listed as vocational schools, farms, camps or homes where punitive practices were as bad or worse as those associated with traditional institutions.

"I'm not saying people make up statistics," he continued. "They don't. But a lot of games are played with labels — open, locked private, public. There are all sorts of ways a basically locked facility can be made to appear to be a benevolent group home."

Miller and Vinter agree that if private facilities were included in assessments of juvenile corrections, the institutionalized population would be about double the public figure. "And if you include the child welfare in-

stitutions, where the label [dependent or neglected] is misapplied," said Miller, "it would probably triple or quadruple it."

Another area where critics fear large numbers of juveniles may be "hidden" from official statistics is in detention.

It is estimated that each year 400,000 young people are incarcerated in local and state juvenile detention centers, and perhaps as many as 600,000 youths in adult jails. Many of those young inmates have not yet been adjudged "offenders," and many are being held on status offense charges.

Several experts share the impression — again unsupported by hard data — that use of detention as punishment is increasing.

"There is no way to determine how many of the hundreds of thousands of detentions that occur annually are motivated by the desire to punish or 'teach the young offender a lesson,' " writes Zimring, "but the practice is probably common."

The charge that judges are delaying hearings while youths sit in detention, and then letting the detention serve as the punishment, is "easy to say, but difficult to prove," said Louis McHardy, executive director of the National Council of Juvenile Court Judges. "I think you might find isolated examples of that, but I don't think it's a universal practice."

Most states have statutes requiring early detention hearings, limiting the time juveniles may be held before trial, requiring that they be separated from adults, or that they not be jailed at all. Several court cases have branded unconstitutional the jailing of juveniles before trial. Nevertheless, researchers who have investigated the use of detention claim the practice is widely abused and vastly underreported.

Of particular concern is the confinement of juveniles in adult jails, a practice that has been largely ignored in most studies of institutionalization. Rosemary Sarri, in the 1974 NAJC report *Under Lock and Key,* estimated that half a million young people pass through adult jails each year. The 1970 National Jail Census done by LEAA found 7,800 juveniles in 4,037 adult jails in March of 1970. Two-thirds of those young inmates were awaiting court hearings; the rest were serving sentences or awaiting transfer.

A team from the Children's Defense Fund (CDF) in Washington, visited 449 jails in nine states in 1974 - 1975, and found 350 youths confined. Almost 200 of those jails had not been included in the 1970 census, leading the CDF to conclude that "the number of children we found in jails grossly understates the true extent of the problem."

In addition, CDF said its 1976 report, "Children in Adult Jails," that "the overwhelming majority of children we found in adult jails were not detained for violent crimes and could not be considered a threat to themselves or the community."

"Few of the children found in adult jails had even been charged, let alone convicted, of violent or serious offenses against a person,"

wrote Justine Wise Polier, director of the CDF juvenile justice program. "Jails are used to hold children in haphazard fashion, sometimes for the convenience of the arresting officer or a judge, sometimes to frighten a child, and, at times, because there is 'no other place for shelter.' "

"I have seen where a kid was in jail for two months for a status offense," said David Smiley of the National Center for Social Responsibility, which reviews state monitoring reports for OJJDP. "The judge was not going to be able to do anything with the kid, so in order to punish him for the status offense, he did not bring it up for a hearing."

Though the numbers of juveniles in adult prisons is currently small, there is a clear tendency across the country to try to solve the problem of violent juvenile crime by remanding more and more youths to the adult courts.

Virtually every state allows for the transfer of juvenile offenders to adult courts for serious crimes. One statute permits offenders as young as ten years old (for murder in Indiana) to be certified as adults and sentenced to the state penitentiary.

Some observers say the juvenile courts have "given up" on growing numbers of serious offenders, turning them over to adult criminal courts. There is a trend across the country to lower the legal age at which such a transfer can occur.

Such a movement signals the erosion of the boundaries between the adult and juvenile systems, and the abandonment of the century-old, protective, paternalistic juvenile justice model.

According to Jeanette Ganousis, an attorney with the National Center for Youth Law in St. Louis, "increased use of the transfer process may account for the decline in juvenile institutional populations."

Louis McHardy of the National Council of Juvenile Court Judges said that, although he had seen no data showing an increase in transfers, "subjectively, I'm afraid it's so, and that's one of my very deep concerns. In almost every workshop or seminar I've attended lately on violent juvenile crime, one of the number one proposals is certifying kids for trial as adults. I have a great fear that that has increased."

Many lawyers defending juveniles are increasingly having to fight motions for adult certification, Ganousis said. "I've found it's becoming increasingly difficult to argue against the transfer of a juvenile to the adult system, and that's what's giving us the impression that it's increasing," she said. "It's nearly impossible to win one of those. They'll transfer anybody."

But, while juvenile court judges may be making greater use of the "safety valve" of transferring tough cases to adult courts, and that may indeed be causing a drop in the population of juvenile institutions, it is not certain that those juveniles are ending up in adult prisons. In fact, what seemed too serious a crime for a juvenile court to handle may end up seeming too trivial a crime for an adult court judge to reward with imprisonment.

McHardy says he opposes transfer of juveniles to adult court primarily because he feels it does not achieve the intended goal. "I think people would find most of these kids never get a trial, many are not convicted, and of those who are convicted, very few of them see the inside of a prison," he said. "Insofar as protecting the community, I'm not sure it's a valid practice."

In some states, there is no need for transfer to adult courts, since juveniles are already treated as adults. In New York, all offenders who are 16 are considered adults, and more than 2,000 16 to 18-year-olds are in adult facilities.

"I think the 16- and 17-year-old property offender is getting a bad deal in this state," said Peter Edelman, director of the state's Division for Youth, "because he goes to county jail or even state prison, and that's an area I think ought to be covered by the juvenile system."

There has been steady pressure for years in the New York legislature to drop even further the age at which a juvenile could be transferred into the adult courts. Finally, the pressures of the current campaign for New York governor forced the politicians to succumb to what they perceived as the public will. A bill was passed by the legislature allowing the adult courts to try children as young as 13 years old and sentence them to terms as long as life, though they would be incarcerated in juvenile institutions until they reached the age of 21. Governor Hugh Carey, who was trying to bolster his image of being tough on crime after he vetoed a death penalty law, signed the bill into law.

Such pressures are not uncommon across the country. Many state juvenile authority administrators, wary of toughening public attitudes, have taken steps to assure legislators that they can handle the serious offenders inside their own systems.

In New York, Edelman is spending most of his time trying to find new secure facilities for the increased numbers of serious offenders being committed by the juvenile courts. "We don't have enough secure beds," he said, "And we never did."

A law that went into effect last year allows juvenile judges to require "restrictive placement" of 14- and 15-year-old youths who commit very serious crimes such as murder, rape, kidnapping or aggravated assault.

Edelman acknowledged that New York has in the past incarcerated "very few delinquents, disproportionate to the amount of juvenile crime going on." But he said that in the last few years, particularly in New York City, "there's been a phenomenal tightening of the system."

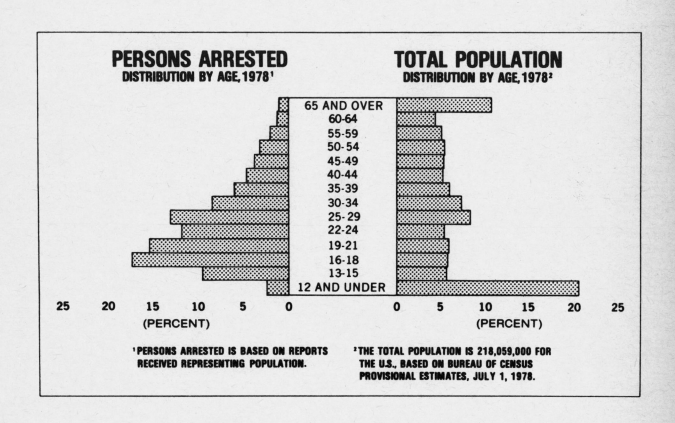

Are Our Juvenile Courts Working?

No!
Senator
Edward M.
Kennedy

Senator Edward M. Kennedy is Chairman of the Senate Committee on the Judiciary. This article is adapted from a speech he gave last October to the International Association of Chiefs of Police.

As I travel around the country I find that the problem of crime ranks right alongside unemployment and inflation as the chief concerns of the American people. Crime is not confined to our urban ghettos; it stalks everyone, everywhere. The inner-city resident refuses to open the door to anyone after nightfall. The suburban family's neighborhood stroll is a thing of the past. The farmer in the wide open plains locks his door to secure his family and property. The elderly couple waits for police escorts before venturing out to the local supermarket.

Crime has become an integral part of our existence. We read about it, think about, talk about it—and experience it.

And what is Congress doing about the problem? We have committee after committee dealing with the issues of the economy and energy, but there isn't much discussion about crime. There are plenty of hearings about what to do about inflation and unemployment, but when it comes to crime there is a strange silence.

The Cancer of Juvenile Violence

When we speak about violent crime

(continued on page 183)

Yes!
Judge
William S.
White

The Honorable William Sylvester White is Presiding Judge, Juvenile Division, Circuit Court of Cook County, and President, National Council of Juvenile and Family Court Judges.

Senator Kennedy, in response to what he refers to as "the growing wave of violent juvenile crime," has called for some drastic changes in the way society handles juveniles charged with violent offenses. To mention a few, he would eliminate juvenile court jurisdiction over minors charged with violent offenses and proposes that they be tried and sentenced by adult criminal courts. Implicit in this recommendation is the notion that the criminal justice system is effective in protecting the public from such behavior and that the juvenile justice system is not.

I submit that the deficits of juvenile courts in this regard pale in comparison to the deficits in the assumptions the Senator makes about juvenile crime and the ability of criminal court processing to protect society from its depredations.

Kennedy Assumption #1

There is a new plague of violent juvenile crime. One of the examples used by the senator is Chicago, where the rate at which black youths committed homicide nearly tripled from 1966 to 1970.

Fact: The worst is over. In Chicago,

(continued on page 184)

(continued from page 182)

one problem stands out above the rest— the plague of juvenile violence. Juvenile crime is more than a fact of life today; it is a fact of death. A gang of girls aged 14 to 17 is formed for the sole purpose of terrorizing the elderly; a 16-year-old youth mugs an 86-year-old woman and steals her purse; two young boys murder a minister in the course of a petty robbery.

Juveniles themselves are often the victims of such violence; in one recent study, over one-half of all black ghetto youths stated that they were afraid to walk streets more than one block from home.

The statistics are foreboding and all too familiar: although juveniles under the age of 18 constitute only about one-fifth of the population, they account for nearly one-half of all those arrested for serious crime. And juvenile violence has been increasing faster then crime generally. Practical steps must be taken to check this growing cancer of violent juvenile crime.

We must start with our juvenile justice system. Although juveniles commit a disproportionate amount of violent crime, their chances of being arrested, convicted, and punished are *lower* than for an adult! Indeed, recent research by James Q. Wilson and others confirms that the chances of punishment are especially low for the chronic, repeat offender, who manages to commit numerous crimes without being caught. Yet it is this repeat offender who commits the bulk of serious juvenile crime.

Juvenile Court Shortcomings

What has led us to this terrible state of affairs? The obvious inefficiency of juvenile courts—highlighted by delays of a year or more, even for the most violent crimes—contributes to the high dismissal rate. Delay undercuts any effort to make certainty of punishment a reality.

The juvenile courts often lack the evidence needed to sustain the charges. Legal constraints—which prevent the police from fingerprinting or photographing a juvenile or placing him in a lineup—often make arrests and convictions impossible.

Even when a conviction is obtained the judge may be hampered by incomplete information about a juvenile's prior record. Without fingerprints and mug shots, the police often cannot link an arrested juvenile to other previously unsolved crimes. Concerns over privacy may prevent even the sentencing court itself from examining the sealed record of the defendant. If the offender's prior record is

unknown or unavailable, the result is likely to be an arbitrary sentence; one juvenile may be sentenced too severely, another too leniently.

But the major problem confronting the juvenile justice system is much more fundamental, and can be traced to an unrealistic myth: that juvenile courts are somehow equipped to rehabilitate and treat *all* juveniles, whether they be status offenders, juvenile delinquents, or violent criminals.

The special juvenile court was created in the name of benevolence, in the name of doing good. The original purpose of the court was to promote rehabilitation by establishing special procedures which would prevent juveniles from drifting into a life of crime. Forget the nature of the crime, forget the prior record of the offender; if you are a juvenile, you receive a special pass, entitling you to bypass the regular criminal justice system and receive "treatment" in a court bent on helping you.

But good intentions are not enough. We now know that the ability of such courts to rehabilitate the violent juvenile or predict future criminal behavior must be viewed with increasing suspicion. The idea of independent juvenile courts—established as an alternative to the stark world of the adult criminal justice system —has backfired. There has been a notorious lack of rehabilitation and an equally notorious increase in arbitrariness and injustice.

Status Offenders Hardest Hit

And, while the violent juvenile is often let off with a slap on the wrist, these very same courts are not so lenient when it comes to the great bulk of youngsters who appear before them every day. I am talking about the status offender—the truant, the runaway, the so-called "stubborn child." According to LEAA, at least three-quarters of a million juveniles were jailed in 1974; of these, less than 12% were arrested for violent crimes! Most of the punishment was directed against juvenile delinquents who had committed petty crimes, status offenses, or no offense at all!

Astoundingly, almost 5% of those jailed had not committed any offense, but were there because the authorities "didn't know what to do with them." One boy was jailed because his mother had been hospitalized and there was no other adult at home. One child was in jail to protect her from her own father, who had been accused of beating her.

Other children were held in custody because they were deemed mentally ill or retarded.

The message is clear—if juveniles want to get locked up they should skip school, run away from home, or be deemed "a problem." If they want to avoid jail, they are better off committing a robbery or burglary. The two-track system of separate adult and juvenile courts often makes a mockery of our criminal justice system and undermines respect for law. The chronic violent juvenile, in particular, reaps the benefits of a sentencing system that reserves the heaviest punishment for adult offenders nearing the end of their criminal careers.

The impact of such sentencing arbitrariness is clear. The violent juvenile knows that if he is occasionally arrested not much will happen. Crime pays handsomely. His prior record is unknown; the juvenile court makes a half-hearted effort to rehabilitate; certainty of punishment is a joke.

The juvenile does not feel unjustly treated; rather, he is contemptuous of our criminal justice system. He scoffs at the threat of punishment and boasts about beating the odds. He is a hero among his pals.

Some Remedies for the Future

What should be done? First, some significant punishment should be imposed on the young offender who commits a violent crime. This should translate into jail in a special juvenile facility for the most serious violent offenders; victim restitution, community service, periodic detention, or intensive supervision are all promising alternatives for less violent offenders.

Second, we must eliminate the two-track criminal justice system for serious violent juvenile offenders. Dual tracks should be defined by the nature of the criminal career rather than by the age of the offender. Age cannot justify treating the 17-year-old rapist or murderer differently from his adult counterpart. The poor, the black, the elderly—those most often victimized by crime—do not make such distinctions. Nor should the courts.

Third, the rules of the game should be changed concerning efforts to identify violent juveniles—especially the chronic offender. The law should permit the photographing and fingerprinting of offenders; lineup identifications should be permitted. Most importantly, an up-to-date criminal history of the offender should be readily available to judges at the time of sentencing.

Fourth, we must make every effort to take the juvenile courts out of the business of punishing status offenders or jailing the "problem child." Imprisonment should be prohibited and penalties vastly scaled down. In my own state of Massachusetts, for example, all status offenders are referred to the Office of Social Services rather than the state juvenile correctional department. No status offender is locked up. Instead, social workers attempt to solve the family and school problems which have brought these juveniles to the attention of the courts.

Finally, we must address the underlying social causes of crime. We cannot surrender in our continuing battle to demolish ghetto slums, eliminate poverty and discrimination, and provide decent education and health care to all our citizens. We must reaffirm our commitment to social justice. Such a commitment is an integral part of any long-range crime-fighting program.

(continued from page 182)

the absolute number of juveniles referred to juvenile court for homicide declined from 133 in 1973 to 102 in 1978. Further, according to the FBI's *Uniform Crime Reports*, between 1974 and 1977 the proportion of juveniles arrested for violent crimes declined by 7%.

Ironically, Paul Strasburg's *Violent Delinquents* (Simon & Schuster, 1978), which Mr. Kennedy cites, concludes that the concept of juvenile violence is not useful for program purposes for two primary reasons: (1) there are too few of these youngsters; and (2) their violent behavior usually appears to be a random subset of other predominant actions. This finding was echoed by a more recent study by D. M. Hamperian and others, *The Violent Few: A Study of Dangerous Juvenile Offenders* (Lexington Books, 1978): "If there is a substantial number of youth who are repetitively committing violent acts, their delinquencies have not come to the attention of the police." Consequently, researchers have turned their focus to the "chronic offender." (M. G. Neithercutt, *Effectiveness of Intervention Impacting Violent Juvenile Offenders,* Bay Area Research Design Associates, San Francisco, California, page 3.)

How appropriate, then, is this recent intense interest in juvenile justice? It is welcomed, but much can be filed under "a day late and a dollar short." Since 1974, under the rubric of "diversion," the U.S. Senate has directed most of its attention and the bulk of federal dollars away from the serious offender, away from juvenile justice, to the status offender and voluntary agencies.

Kennedy Assumption #2

The courts and corrections have a significant impact on crime statistics.

Fact: Neither the cause nor the cure for crime, juvenile or adult, can be found in the justice system. Even a casual look at the juvenile court will tell you that, like criminal court, it is a poor people's court and that violent crime is principally a problem associated with the inner-city poor. Until the millenium, which will provide a good economic base and the good social environment needed by every person, we must use our most effective methods to control the offender who assaults, robs, rapes, and kills.

Kennedy Assumption #3

The juvenile justice system has been less effective in coping with the serious violent offender than the adult system.

Fact: Juvenile courts are more likely to act in cases of violent crime, and, when they do, they are more effective than adult criminal courts. In a recent study comparing processing of 16- and 17-year-old offenders in the criminal versus the juvenile system, it was found that the criminal court was much more likely to do nothing than was the juvenile court. (R.J. Gable, *The Pittsburgh-Buffalo Project: An Investigation of the Outcome of Judicial Proceedings Involving 16- and 17-Year-Old Youth,* National Center for Juvenile Justice, Pittsburgh, Pennsylvania, 1979, pages 26, 28-29, 39.)

In a matched sample of 100 offenders appearing before criminal court in Buffalo, New York, and the juvenile court in Pittsburgh, Pennsylvania, the study found that the criminal court dismissed 74% and juvenile court dismissed only 48%. The juvenile court was just as likely to impose the sanction of commitment to a facility: 15% (juvenile court) versus 16% (adult court). But perhaps more important when addressing the matter of violent crime, the juvenile court was twice as likely (20% versus 10%) to commit an offender to a facility for offenses involving injury of persons.

Quite coincidentally, the crime rate for juveniles aged 14 through 17 appears to be lower in Pittsburgh, where 16- and 17-year-olds go through the juvenile system, than in Buffalo, where they are tried as adults. This difference exists even though the two communities are demographically identical on all critical social indicators, *i.e.,* sex, race, age, density, etc.

In another recent study of over 800 juveniles found delinquent in Cook County in 1974 for committing violent offenses (rape, robbery, homicide, assault and battery), some 200 of these were committed to the Youth Division of the Department of Corrections. The remaining 606 constituted the base group of a recidivism study. They were traced from their base findings of delinquency in 1974 through March, 1977, for finding on new offenses. The study reveals that, of the 606 juveniles in the base group, only 84 had findings for new offenses—violent or nonviolent. In other words, the proportion with any overall recidivism was 1 in 7, or 14%. (Michael Brennan, *Recidivism Study of Violent Offenders,* Juvenile Division, Circuit Court, Cook County, Illinois, September 22, 1977.)

Other studies also indicate that the juvenile system is succeeding. In Cook County we have had a federally funded program called UDIS, an acronym for Unified Delinquency Intervention Services. This agency receives from the juvenile court referrals of youths who have been adjudicated delinquent so often, or for an offense so severe, that they would otherwise have been committed to the Illinois Department of Corrections (DOC). UDIS deals with these juveniles without institutionalization.

Recently, a report of UDIS operations has been filed with the Illinois Law Enforcement Commission. The report contains three findings of great significance:

1) Significant reductions in the incidence of offenses, as high as 2/3 of the pre-intervention rate, can be achieved even with the most chronic, serious delinquents in Cook County through the use of energetic correctional intervention;
2) Whether the program was UDIS or DOC, correctional intervention in the life of the chronic juvenile offender in this study had a powerful and apparently long-term inhibiting effect on subsequent delinquent activity;
3) The recidivism analysis did not make a case for the overall superiority of either UDIS or DOC. It concludes, however, that reports of the futility of juvenile corrections have been greatly exaggerated. (Charles A. Murray, Doug Thomson, and Cindy B. Israel, *UDIS: Deinstitutionalizing the Chronic Juvenile Offender,* prepared for the Illinois Law Enforcement Commission, American Institute for Research, January 1, 1978.)

Kennedy Assumption #4

The juvenile court has the following defects which require elimination of jurisdiction over serious and "career offenders":

1) Delays in trying cases;
2) High dismissal rates;
3) Uncertainty of punishment;
4) Restrictions on fingerprinting of juveniles;
5) Lack of necessary evidence due to privacy restraints;
6) Lack of capacity to rehabilitate "all offenders."

Fact (1): Delays are no more characteristic of the juvenile court than other courts. A survey of 13 states, representing 40% of the nation's population, shows that 75% of all juvenile court cases were disposed of in 90 days or less. Less than 3% of all cases took a year or more. (D.D. Smith, *Preliminary Report: National Uniform Juvenile Justice Reporting System,* National Center for Juvenile Justice, Pittsburgh, Pennsylvania, 1979, page 35, Table 12.) Unfortunately, I doubt if this prompt disposal can be found in the criminal system.

Fact (2): The Pittsburgh-Buffalo study previously mentioned does not support the Kennedy charge of high dismissal rates.

Fact (3): The same can be said of his charge of uncertain punishment. (Strasburg, *Violent Delinquents,* page 107.)

Facts (4) and (5): I was completely puzzled by the Kennedy claim that police were hampered by restrictions on juvenile fingerprinting and photographing, and by juvenile court privacy restraints. An analysis of the statutes of the 50 states indicates that most permit fingerprinting and photographing of juveniles. (T.S. Vereb and C. Sheaffer, *Juvenile and Family Court Records: Statutes Analysis,* Preliminary Draft, National Center for Juvenile Justice, Pittsburgh, Pennsylvania, 1978.)

Fact (6): The Senator is correct. The juvenile courts cannot rehabilitate all offenders. However, this rebuke is especially painful when it comes from a member of the U.S. Senate, an appropriating body that has withheld funds from juvenile courts for rehabilitation of the violent juvenile offender. Recognition of the courts' inability to rehabilitate all violent juvenile offenders is reflected in the statutes of all 50 states, which permit certain juveniles who commit serious offenses to be prosecuted as adults. (H. Hurst, *Juveniles as Criminals—A Profile of the Statutes on Waiver of Children to Criminal Court,* Address to American Academy of Child Psychiatry Annual Conference, St. Louis, Missouri, October, 1975.)

Senator Kennedy calls for elimination of juvenile court jurisdiction over violent juvenile offenders. In this regard, I observe that neither the LEAA Task Force (National Advisory Committee on Criminal Justice Standards and Goals) nor the Institute of Judicial Administration and American Bar Association Joint Commission on Juvenile Justice Standards (two of the most severe critics of juvenile court methods for dealing with delinquent youths) has advocated criminal court processing of all, or even most, juveniles charged with serious crime. Both groups have opted for a separate system of justice for most minors accused of serious crime. They have done this because they know, as I know, that criminal court processing would not provide greater public protection but would instead shunt more young people into an overloaded system with a record of proven failure.

PUTTING JOHNNY IN JAIL

"Get 'em off the streets!" is the new cry in the juvenile justice system. Politicians, judges, and DAs have found an anxious public receptive to calls for a crackdown. But with reform neglected in favor of severity, juveniles are cycled through deteriorating institutions, emerging as hardened adults.

Lucy Komisar

The cover showed three menacing youths clad in washed-out denims. The blade of a knife flashed in one boy's hand. "Across the U.S. a pattern of crime has emerged," declared the story inside. "A new remorseless, mutant juvenile seems to have been born...the deck is stacked in favor of the defendant...."

Time magazine had the answer to "the youth crime plague" it described: a tougher policy toward violent delinquents. It was the summer of 1977, and some analysts disputed that youth crime had indeed exploded, but no one had any doubts about the explosion of interest by the media and politicians.

Real or not, the "youth crime wave" has provoked stormy reaction among state legislators. In the past two years, at least 18 states have amended their juvenile justice codes to require minimum sentencing or waiver to adult courts for certain crimes. Half a dozen states expect to adopt similar amendments soon. And an American Civil Liberties Union study done last year by Alan Sussman found that "in virtually every state, bills have been proposed which would increase penalties for young people convicted of serious offenses."

At the forefront of this get-tough movement is the New York legislature. In 1976, it passed bills which required that juveniles charged with certain felonies be fingerprinted and photographed and their records opened to law enforcement agencies. It turned down a proposal that youths charged with homicide, rape, robbery, and serious assault be waived to adult courts at the age of 13, but it passed another bill that set minimum sentences for certain designated felonies.

Under the legislation, five-year sentences could be imposed for the Class A felonies of murder, kidnapping, and arson. Youthful offenders could be sent to a secure facility for the first year, a residential setting for the second, and could be placed in a nonresidential program for the rest of the time. The family court could discharge an offender after three years or extend the sentence another year until his 21st birthday. Class B felonies (assault, robbery, attempted murder or kidnapping) required three-year sentences similarly structured.

Then in the fall of 1976, the Timmons case exploded. When police arrested 19-year-old Ronald Timmons for beating and robbing an 82-year-old woman, he was released on $500 bail. Senator Ralph Marino, chairman of the Crime and Corrections Committee, violated the rules on youth record confidentiality to tell the press that Timmons had a long history of delinquency—67 court appearances, suspected of murdering a 92-year-old-man, in and out of state training schools since he was eight, and "known to the police and juvenile authorities as a cruel predator of old people." If the criminal court judge had had access to that sealed juvenile record, Marino charged, he would not have released Timmons back to the streets. The senator quickly won approval of a bill that established mandatory sentencing for assault against the elderly and increased maximum restrictive time from a year to a year-and-a-half.

In the 13 months from February 1977 to March 1978, 56 juveniles in New York State were sentenced to restrictive placement under the law. That was apparently not enough, and Governor Hugh Carey recommended changes to expand the list of offenses and include 13-year-olds twice found guilty of certain felonies.

"If the kids are not going to go out and commit the kinds of crimes they're supposed to commit to be restrictively placed,

the state will have to go out and increase the crimes and kids covered," says the deputy director of the Vera Institute of Justice Family Court Disposition Study, Sheridan Faber.

Faber was being sarcastic, of course, but the "get-tough" forces seriously complain that some judges are counteracting the stern intent of the law. "Judges are signing off on adjustments to reduce them out of class," says Paul Macielak, counsel to Marino's committee. Because even some youths found guilty of felonies are not being sent away under that category, Marino has introduced a new bill to reduce plea bargaining in family court and make restrictive placements mandatory.

Legislators who do not trust family court judges to treat youths firmly would like to remove their jurisdiction altogether. A bill in New York's hopper this year would send certain felony offenders to adult court and place them in adult jails for up to 15 years.

Such waiver laws are a key part of the "get-tough" strategy. By lowering the age at which juveniles can be sent to adult courts, many states have made it easier for juvenile courts to impose what David Howard, director of the National Juvenile Law Center in St. Louis, calls the most serious sanction a juvenile can receive. "Waiver can amount to a death penalty," he says. "The danger is not just the adult sanction they can receive, but what can happen to a young person in an adult penitentiary."

Most states allow some juveniles to be transferred to adult courts for serious offenses, several states have lowered the age for waiver, and a few have made transfers or transfer hearings mandatory in certain situations. In Arkansas, for instance, the law now allows waiver of any child charged with a misdemeanor or felony. Before, the child had to be 15 and accused of a felony. Likewise, Connecticut now permits transfer for 14-year-olds who are charged with

Originally, the juvenile court system was set up to resemble a social agency, providing a good talking to, professional counseling, or "institution for their own good." But the general trend now is to view these youthful offenders less as children to be helped and more as criminals to be punished.

A or B felonies and have convictions of the same magnitude on their records. Previously, waiver was allowed only for accused murderers. Maine courts must transfer youths if violence is involved, if there is probable cause the juvenile committed the crime, and if the protection of the community requires his detention in some place more secure than a juvenile facility.

The toughness trend is not uniform, though, since some states have been careful to temper their new waiver laws with restrictions. Idaho reduced the age for waiver from 16 to 15 but stipulated that the youth must be charged with a felony instead of, as before, any criminal offense. West Virginia, which formerly allowed transfers of all 16-year-olds, now limits them to youths accused of committing violent felonies or felonies endangering the public. Similarly, Alabama, which used to allow waiver of any accused 14-year-old, now says they must be charged with felonies. And Kentucky, California, and Oregon now require judges to consider the minor's previous history, the seriousness of the offense, and his prospects for rehabilitation.

Mandatory minimum sentencing is the other chief tool that "get-tough" advocates favor to deal with serious offenders. Historically, juvenile courts have operated on the theory that they are to treat a child's "need" rather than his "deed." Whether a minor committed vandalism, burglary, car theft, arson, rape, or murder, he or she was sent away with an indeterminate sentence for "rehabilitation." As a child, he was not considered responsible for his actions; he was to be "treated," not "punished."

It followed that children should be released when they appeared to be cured. In practice, however, institutional officials sometimes got rid of difficult children and kept those who were more docile or whose parents did not want them. A Rand Corporation study published two years ago found treatment programs to be sporadic and to have limited success when they worked at all. Most of them, it said, excluded serious offenders altogether. In any event, there was no way to tell when a child had been "rehabilitated," and he could not be kept forever. Most were back home in less than a year.

Some states have been changing that practice by setting minimum sentences for serious crimes, thus limiting the discretion of juvenile judges and social agencies. In

California, 16-year-olds found guilty of certain felonies can be held until 23 (two years longer than before), although they cannot be held longer than adults convicted of the same crimes. And in Colorado violent and repeat offenders must get minimum one-year sentences and cannot be released without court approval.

Other states, however, have moved to limit restrictive placements. West Virginia law says courts must give preference to the least restrictive placement and terms cannot exceed adult sentences. Pennsylvania also calls for the "minimum confinement" necessary. And youths in Oklahoma institutions must be released at 18 instead of 21.

It is true that most states have tried to design their new laws to separate the serious delinquent from the minor offender, but the legislators' patience with all juvenile delinquency is clearly running out. The general trend now is to view offenders less as children to be helped and more as criminals to be punished. "In every state I know of except Iowa, the legislative trend is regressive," says David Howard. "There's a move afoot in many states to lower the juvenile court jurisdiction age limit to 16. And there's also a move to expose juveniles to the public eye by ending the confidentiality safeguards that have existed." For instance, in Pennsylvania, information about a child charged with a second serious crime can now be released to the newspapers.

While the legislatures are passing laws designed to put juveniles away for longer terms, the courts have been moving toward granting them more due process rights. Like the move to get tough, the trend toward due process rejects the traditional way of treating youthful offenders.

Originally, the juvenile court system was set up to resemble a social agency. Juvenile offenders might need a good talking to, professional counseling, or a stay at a group home or institution "for their own good." The idea that the court was out to help the child became an excuse for ignoring due process. The judge conducted the proceedings without benefit of rules of evidence or procedure. The public was not permitted to attend or see records. Without sentencing standards, judges could be arbitrary. As an Institute for Judicial Administration/American Bar Association study found, racial and class bias intruded into decisions. Serious offenders who knew how to finesse the system could get short

terms, and other youths charged with serious crimes could get longer confinements than if they had been tried before adult courts.

Beginning in the late sixties, the Supreme Court issued several decisions that gave juveniles some minimum due process rights. One of the first such cases involved 15-year-old Gerald Gault, who had been sentenced to six years in the state reformatory for making an obscene phone call. Noting that an adult would have gotten a maximum of two months, the Court held in In re Gault that accused juvenile delinquents are entitled to notice of charges, the right to counsel, the right to remain silent, and the right to confront and cross-examine adverse witnesses.

Later, the Court went even further. In the 1970 case of In re Winship it held that the standard of proof in a juvenile trial must be beyond a reasonable doubt, and in a 1975 decision, Breed v. Jones, it said that juveniles are protected by the double jeopardy clause.

Legal analysts think the rulings have been significant. "The system is being judicialized in a way that never seemed imaginable before," says Fred Cohen, professor of law and criminal justice at the State University of New York at Albany. "It's taking on the trappings of a mini-adult system."

Still, civil libertarians charge that the juvenile courts fall far short of granting due process rights—or justice—to youthful offenders. Rena Uviller, who heads the ACLU Children's Rights Project, says, "No matter what judges say about children's welfare, when a child is sent to a training school or a residential treatment center, he or she is being punished, often with terms longer than an adult would get for the same crime."

Without a jury trial based on the evidence rather than adjudication on a child's "best needs," claim the civil libertarians, the results of a recent Tennessee case will continue to be unexceptional. Two youths there were accused of murdering a nurse. The 16-year-old was transferred to criminal court, tried, and acquitted. But the 14-year-old, who was charged with equal culpability, was tried in juvenile court. Lacking the same right to defend himself and be judged on the evidence, he was sent to a juvenile institution, where he remains.

The ACLU calls for the same due process rights adults enjoy and for set sentences for all offenses—both serious and

In a recent case in Tennessee, two youths were accused of murdering a nurse. The 16-year-old was acquitted in criminal court; but the 14-year-old, comparably charged in a juvenile court where he lacked rights of evidence and self-defense, was sent to an institution, where he remains.

minor—based on the seriousness of the crime. The problem now, it says, is that some states are setting minimum sentences for the hard-core offenders without setting maximums for minor offenders.

The civil libertarian position received a substantial boost last year when the conclusions of a mammoth seven-year, 23-volume study were published by the Juvenile Justice Standards Project of the Institute of Judicial Administration and the American Bar Association. They call for a total overhaul of the system because of its demonstrated failure to either protect society or help children.

"The confusion and overreach implicit in the expectation that a court is capable of devising disposition 'in the best interest' of the child in the absence of guidelines, of reliable predictive measures of future criminal behavior, or of models for effective rehabilitation or treatment programs, punctured the myth of the medical model of juvenile justice," the study said. It recommended that the following basic principles guide any new standards:

1. Proportionality in sanctions based on the seriousness of the offense rather than the court's view of the youth's needs. 2. Determinate sentences. 3. Choice of the least restrictive alternative; restrictive sentences explained by the judge in writing. 4. Status offenses and victimless crimes (except narcotics possession) removed from the juvenile court's jurisdiction. 5. Visibility and accountability of decision-making instead of closed proceedings and unrestrained official discretion. 6. Right to counsel at all stages. 7. Juveniles' right to decide on actions affecting their lives and freedom unless they are found incapable of making reasoned decisions. 8. A redefined parents' role with attention paid to conflicts between their interests and the child's. 9. Limitations on detention, treatment, or other intervention before adjudication and disposition. 10. Strict criteria for waiver to adult courts.

Under the IJA/ABA standards, waiver to adult court would be permitted only for 16- or 17-year-olds who are accused of "class one" juvenile offenses (crimes for which adults would be subject to death or imprisonment for 20 years to life), who have records involving acts or threats of serious personal injury, and who cannot, according to the determination of the judge, be dealt with in juvenile facilities.

The study also advocates that youths have the right to a public jury trial and

that the rules of evidence of criminal trials be used in juvenile proceedings. Proof, it says, should be beyond a reasonable doubt, and the judge should not receive social history about the defendant.

As to sentencing, the standards stipulate that juveniles be sent to secure facilities only for the most serious or repetitive offenses and only if such detention is needed to prevent them from causing bodily harm or substantial property injury. In any case, the standards say, juvenile detention centers should hold no more than 20 youths and should be co-educational or at least provide frequent social contact between boys and girls. The standards also establish set sentences for different classes of crimes. Up to 5 percent time off would be allowed for good behavior, but youth agencies would no longer be able to cut sentences dramatically because of rehabilitation or other reasons.

If the proposals are accepted by the ABA House of Delegates at its winter 1979 meeting, they will be sent to the state bar associations and likely become the basis for legislative changes. But nobody thinks that adoption by lawmakers will be easy. Already family court judges, youth service officials, district attorneys, academics, and legislators are engaged in a national debate over the standards.

The judges favor due process procedures, but they disagree strongly with the ABA proposals on disposition and treatment of status offenders. They do not want to give up their traditional jurisdiction or social work role. Judge Eugene Arthur Moore of Detroit, head of the committee on juvenile justice standards for the National Council of Juvenile Court Judges, says, "The judge should look at the offense, but in addition you have to look at the social service factor—the home, I.Q., ability to relate to others, self-control, and other factors."

The family court judges propose a compromise on sentencing as well. "The court ought to be able to set minimum periods of time," Moore explains, "but indeterminate sentences should be maintained depending on the needs of the child and subject to judicial review." The maximum penalties in the ABA standards are too short in his view. "I think two years for murder is wrong," he says. "I would suggest four or five years. If the judge wanted to reduce it, that would be the prerogative of the court."

Many judges would agree that both de-

linquents and the public have been ill-served by the juvenile justice system, but they believe it has never been given the resources to do the job. Justine Wise Polier, for many years a New York City family court judge, says, "I'm not defending the courts. They've been starved, inadequately manned, and never had the services they should."

Her reservation about the ABA standards is that they emphasize the offense rather than the child. "In the long run, that's not the way to put to work whatever knowledge we have on the problems of children," she says. By giving juveniles determinate sentences in institutions that don't help them, "we're just temporarily getting them out of sight when they look bad."

Juvenile agency officials agree with the judges that rehabilitation has not yet been given a fair chance. "At present there is almost no care," says Jerome Miller, a former Massachusetts and Pennsylvania juvenile corrections chief. "It's either total punitiveness or neglect masquerading as permissiveness." The danger of the civil libertarian approach, Miller claims, is that its reforms stop at proportional sentencing. He thinks people ought to also worry about what is done with offenders after they are sent away. "Dangerous kids shouldn't be out on the streets running loose," he says, "but that doesn't mean they should be in these crimenogenic institutions. For what it costs to institutionalize a kid, you can assign someone to him full time."

Agency officials and judges part company, though, when Judge Moore says that "judges should have the power to remove youngsters from the streets without state agencies being able to release them." New York State Commissioner of Youth Administration Peter Edelman replies, "Judges assume they know more than they really know in fixing the type of institution and length of time a youngster needs to spend there." In New York, Edelman's agency now makes those decisions, and he does not want it to lose that power.

Though he favors the ABA standards of determinance and fitting the sentence to the crime, Edelman wants agencies to have some discretion within those bounds, and he worries that "in getting rid of gross indeterminacy, virtually all states will be tougher than the ABA contemplates." The result, he fears, may be that kids will spend longer stretches in facilities than they should.

The district attorneys, for their part, think the courts should get tougher with serious offenders and stop picking up youths who do not belong in the system at all. They favor due process procedures but insist that some special protections for juveniles must be maintained. "The juvenile court has been run for too long as a social agency," says Robert Leonard, president of the National District Attorneys Association. "But I still believe in certain protections—the confidentiality of the juvenile court proceedings, for instance. I don't think we gain anything by opening juvenile courts up to public view. I think we can accomplish the protection we need for the public by having the advocacy procedure strictly adhered to."

Rather than waive more cases to adult court, Leonard would prefer that adversary proceedings be used in juvenile courts. "In most cases those people who would come in to the adult court would be given probation anyway. Even if they were sent to prison, that's not going to improve

the situation. They would be better helped in juvenile court where there are more facilities—social workers and psychologists."

While the ABA standards continue to be debated by those within the juvenile justice system, the Twentieth Century Fund has issued its own report calling for proportionality in sentencing with maximums fixed by legislatures, actual periods of confinement set by judges, and earlier release dates at the discretion of state juvenile authorities. The report also urged that the top sentence for the most serious crimes should be two-and-a-half years, with two years the limit for property offenses. Waiver, it says, should be allowed only where there is probable cause that a serious violent crime has been committed and where the juvenile court cannot impose the punishment deemed necessary. Similarly, the report advocates lower sentences for 18- to 21-year-olds tried in adult courts.

Amidst all the debates and proposals, about the only thing no one disputes is that the current juvenile system is not working. The media and state legislatures say get

tougher, stop "mollycoddling" serious offenders and start treating them more like adults. Civil libertarians say give juveniles the due process rights of adults and stop foisting time on them in the guise of rehabilitation. The juvenile agency people agree with the need for due process, but remind critics that social workers can help kids and that offenders shouldn't simply be sent to serve time.

Aside from the philosophical differences among experts, there is the issue of institutional turf. "Everyone wants to know how changes in the law will affect them," says David Gilman, director of the ABA project. "Will they lose or gain money or power?"

In the long run, the opinions of the experts and the interest groups involved in the debate are likely to have less effect than the headlines in newspapers and the pronouncements of politicians. "The ABA input is more likely to be theoretical than real," predicts Sheridan Faber. "The politicians are running the show, and they see getting tough on crime as a way to get votes."

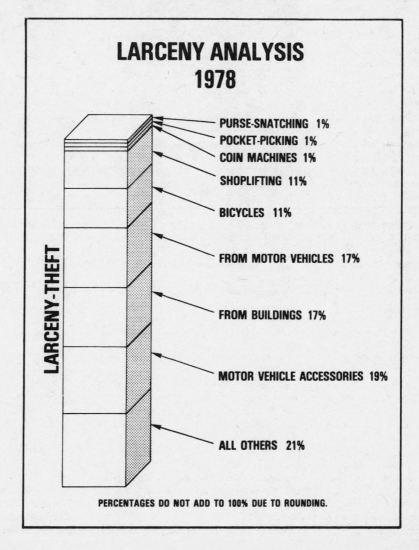

LARCENY ANALYSIS
1978

LARCENY-THEFT

PURSE-SNATCHING 1%
POCKET-PICKING 1%
COIN MACHINES 1%
SHOPLIFTING 11%
BICYCLES 11%
FROM MOTOR VEHICLES 17%
FROM BUILDINGS 17%
MOTOR VEHICLE ACCESSORIES 19%
ALL OTHERS 21%

PERCENTAGES DO NOT ADD TO 100% DUE TO ROUNDING.

Punishment and Corrections

5

The correctional process begins with the sentencing of the convicted offender. Although there has recently been great pressure for a return to mandatory, definite sentences, the predominant sentencing pattern in the United States encourages maximum judicial discretion and a range of alternatives from probation—supervised conditional freedom within the community—through imprisonment for indeterminate terms, to the death penalty, although only three men have been executed in the United States since 1967.

Increasingly, first offenders and those convicted of nonviolent crimes have been placed on probation while only repeated offenders and those convicted of serious crimes—murder, rape, aggravated assault, and armed robbery—are being sent to penal institutions. The theory has been that prisons are brutal and brutalizing, increase the level of hostility to society, teach the offender new criminal skills, introduce him to new criminal associates, are sexually perverse and disgorge into society a product much more dangerous than the raw material they received—all at enormous expense to the taxpayer. Conversely it is held that keeping as many convicted offenders as possible in the community under supervision and guidance is not only much cheaper but is actually more effective in deterring them from continuing with crime.

Most offenders, even those sentenced to long terms for multiple, serious crimes, do not serve their maximum terms in confinement due to parole. Parole, like probation, is a system of supervised freedom in the community under certain limitations and conditions. Probation, however, is imposed at the time of sentencing by the court, while parole requires serving a portion of the sentence in prison and a positive finding by a parole board that the prisoner is no longer dangerous to the community. Thus, the average sentence served by felons is somewhat less than two-and-one-half years, and by lifers somewhat less than eight years.

A considerable number of prisoners enjoy limited freedom in the community even while supposedly confined in prisons. For example, under work release and school release programs, thousands of prisoners leave the institutions each morning, work or attend school during the day, and return to the prison in the evening, all without supervision by custodial personnel. A somewhat lesser number enjoy short, unsupervised furloughs from prison either for compassionate reasons (to attend a family funeral or to get medical attention not available in the institution) or as a reward for good institutional behavior. Most of the prisoners who have benefited from these progressive programs have proven themselves trustworthy, but there have been a sufficient number of escapes and, more seriously, a well-publicized number of murders, rapes, robberies, and narcotics offenses committed by such favored inmates to raise questions about the operations of these programs if not to their basic rationale.

A major controversy among corrections professionals is the issue surrounding the introduction of behavior modification techniques into prisoner rehabilitation regiments. Behavior modification involves rewarding desired behavior and punishing unacceptable behavior. Experience has demonstrated the potential for abuse in such treatment interventions, and criminologists and civil libertarians have alerted us to the danger of punishing under the rationalization of treating.

On the other hand, the almost total failure of most permitted rehabilitative efforts has led some to advocate more frequent use of the death penalty, castration of sex offenders, heavy dosages of tranquilizing and sedating drugs, and even recourse once again to the prefrontal lobotomy. As in many controversies, emotion conquers scientific objectivity. Proponents and opponents exaggerate both potential benefits and dangers of abuse as they polarize their positions.

The next decade will probably see substantial changes: diminished use of probation, constraints on judicial discretion in sentencing, tougher parole criteria, and increasingly larger prison populations.

CHANGING CRIMINAL SENTENCES

James Q. Wilson

James Q. Wilson is the Shattuck Professor of Government at Harvard and the author of Thinking About Crime *and* Varieties of Police Behavior.

THE CHANGES NOW under way in the laws governing the sentencing of criminals are perhaps the most important development in American criminal justice in the past half century. For, whatever the mode of punishment of criminals, the problems of defining and managing judicial discretion, of deciding on an appropriate scale of penalties, and of trying to discover the relationship between the penalty imposed and the crime rate that exists remain exactly the same. At present we accord to prosecutors and judges more discretionary authority, more unchecked freedom to punish and reward, than we allow to virtually any other part of government. And unless the problem of discretion is satisfactorily resolved, *any* penalty (or "treatment") for crime will be subject to the criticism that it is arbitrarily or capriciously imposed, that it fails to accord with prevailing community standards of justice, or that it insufficiently deters or incapacitates criminals.

New laws, which in various forms have been adopted in Maine and California and which are under active consideration by Congress and the legislatures of several states, have in common the objective of undoing an earlier "reform." The discretion now under attack was originally proposed, early in this century, as a device that would enable the criminal-justice system to achieve the rehabilitation of the offender. If the system was to "correct" the miscreant, then the amount of time he would spend under the supervision of that system should depend on his corrigibility, rather than on the nature of his offense. This, in turn, required that judges forswear setting a definite sentence, and instead either pick a min-

imum term of supervision (with the maximum decided by a correctional or parole board) or set a maximum sentence (with actual time served decided by the board). It is these central principles of the correctional philosophy—the "indeterminate sentence" and the "individualized sentence"—that are now being reexamined.

What is surprising, perhaps, is that criticisms of this philosophy have been slow in acquiring official support. When the criminal laws of many states, and of the federal government as well, permit persons convicted of, say, robbery, to be sentenced to prison for "zero to twenty years," or "for some period of time not to exceed twenty-five years," or "for no less than one year," they invite judges and parole boards to give expression to their own conceptions of what the protection of society, the rehabilitation of the offender, and the precepts of justice require. Liberal critics of this system point with outrage at examples of persons convicted of trivial offenses (the favorite example is possession of a small amount of marijuana) kept in prison for many years. Conservative critics point with equal outrage at examples of armed robbers and wife-murderers released from prison after absurdly short sentences, if in fact they were sent to prison at all. Those persons, liberal or conservative, who are concerned about fairness and equity object to offenders receiving utterly different sentences though they have committed similar, if not identical, offenses. Many believe, moreover, that these differences in treatment are affected by the race, income, or privilege of the offender.

These criticisms, to the extent they are true, would be telling ones even if the system of indeterminate, individualized sentences helped to rehabilitate the convict. But a large body of evidence suggests that, though some programs may work under some circumstances for some offenders, by and

large we do not know how to change the recidivism rate for large numbers of persons and for long periods of time. If rehabilitation is not achieved, the major argument for indeterminacy collapses, and the ethical objections to it become overpowering. These objections have of late been forcefully argued by an imposing number of legal scholars and philosophers.

THE PROPOSED solution has been to devise ways of making sentencing more determinate, or known at the time of sentencing. One way is simply to restore power over sentences to the judge, reducing or eliminating the role of parole boards. This was done in Maine, where a new criminal law requires the judge to pick a fixed sentence from within a broad range allowed by law. With a few exceptions, there are no required minimum sentences, and probation can always be granted. Parole supervision and the parole board were abolished. The Maine plan made the punishment determinate, but it remains individualized, and thus disparities will no doubt persist.

A second solution is the so-called flat-time law proposed by a former correctional official, David Fogel, in Illinois and under consideration in several states. Like the Maine law, this requires the judge to pick the sentence, but unlike it the range of possible sentences from which the judge can select is sharply narrowed. A judge would be free to place an offender on probation or to send him to prison; if he goes to prison, however, it must be for a period falling within a narrow, legislatively determined range. The present Illinois law, for example, allows a person convicted of a class-two felony such as robbery or burglary to serve one to twenty years in prison. Under Fogel's flat-time law, an offender would have to be sentenced to three to seven years, unless he were adjudged a career criminal, in which case the term would be between seven and eleven years. The actual time served would be the judge-imposed sentence, less "good time" (one day off his sentence for every day of good behavior while in prison).

A variant of this plan, sometimes called a "presumptive-sentencing" law, was enacted in California in 1976 and took effect on July 1 of this year. For each common felony, the law specifies three possible prison sentences, with the judge instructed to impose the middle sentence unless aggravating or mitigating circumstances lead him to conclude that the higher or lower term is appropriate. (He could still put an offender on probation.) Furthermore, the judge can "enhance" the basic sentence with additional terms of imprisonment if the crime was committed with a firearm, or in a way that caused great bodily injury or a large property loss, or by a person with a prior prison record. For example, a person convicted of robbery in the first degree could, under the old indeterminate-sentencing law, be imprisoned for five years to life. Under the presumptive- or determinate-sentencing law, the judge could imprison him for two, three, or four years, the assumption being that he would select three years unless the nature of the crime suggested that mitigating or aggravating the penalty was appropriate. To the basic three-year term the judge could add one year if the person was armed and two years if he used the firearm, three years if he caused great bodily injury, and three years if he had been in prison for a violent crime within the preceding ten years. The judge cannot add on enhancements to his heart's content, however—the maximum fully enhanced term may not exceed twice the base term unless the crime was violent. Obviously, the law and the arithmetic it requires are complex in the extreme.

Another way to limit judicial or parole discretion is by developing sentencing guidelines of the sort proposed in the new federal criminal code developed by Senators Edward M. Kennedy and John McClellan. This bill, S. 1437 of the Ninety-fifth Congress, is chiefly a much-revised substitute for the heavily criticized S. 1 of a year ago, which offered both a codification of the federal criminal laws and a set of new provisions dealing with such matters as leaking government documents. The new bill strips away most of the features criticized by civil libertarians, leaving the codification plus some new features more to the liking of liberals (such as decriminalizing the private possession of small amounts of marijuana), and—perhaps most important of all—creates a Sentencing Commission of nine members that will establish sentencing policies and guidelines for the federal system.

These guidelines will, among other things, create for each federal crime a suggested range of sentences that will take into account the nature of the offense and its circumstances, the community's view as to its gravity, and the deterrent effect of the sentence. Once promulgated, the guidelines take effect provided that neither house of Congress has, within 180 days, voted to disapprove them. The courts are obliged to take these guidelines into account in fixing a sentence but need not obey them. If, however, the court-imposed sentence is less than the minimum recommended by the Sentencing Commission, the prosecution may appeal, while if it is more than the recommended maximum, the defense may appeal. In any event, the guidelines cannot call for sentences in excess of those allowed by statute. For example, a class C felony under the new federal code (which would cover rape, arson, robbery, burglary, manslaughter, aggravated assault, counterfeiting, and large thefts) carries a maximum prison term of twelve years.

The guideline approach suggested by Kennedy and McClellan recognizes the intellectual difficulty of prescribing by statute precise penalties for scores of crimes and many kinds of offenders and defers to the political objections, raised most strongly by judges, to any sentencing system that denies them discretionary power. The check on that power in S. 1437 is the moral suasion and practical utility of the Sentencing Commission's opinions combined with the risk of appeal if its guidelines are violated.

The law gives little guidance to the commission itself except to say that a "substantial sentence of imprisonment" shall be recommended "in most cases" in which the defendant has a long record of prior convictions, is part of an organized criminal racket, or reveals himself to be participating in a pattern of criminal conduct from which he derives a "substantial portion of his income."

In addition to the voluntary nature of the sentencing guidelines, the Kennedy–McClellan plan differs from flat-time and presumptive-sentencing laws in retaining the authority of a parole board that could release the offender after a small portion (roughly one-fourth) of his sentence has been served, unless the judge specifically extends the period during which a convict is ineligible for parole. Indeed, if there is any criticism to be made of S. 1437, it is that its sponsors promise greater benefits from its enactment than the law seems capable of producing.

No one can know what effect any of these changes in sentencing policy will have on offenders or on society or its institutions. One can, however, compare the principles of these laws with what we now know about crime and criminal justice.

THAT JUDGES DIFFER in sentences imposed on cases presenting similar facts is beyond dispute. Federal Judge Marvin Frankel presided over a test in which fifty of his colleagues in the Second Circuit recommended sentences for a group of imaginary offenders described in thirty presentence reports which gave full details on the nature of the offense and the characteristics of the offender—not only the prior record, if any, but race, age, sex, occupation, drug use, and so forth. The disparities were vast—for drug trafficking, they ranged from one year to ten years in prison, and for bank robbery, from five years to twenty years in prison.

The results of this experiment, reported by Frankel in his book, *Criminal Sentences*, are amply confirmed by the actual behavior of judges. James Eisenstein and Herbert Jacob find, in their detailed study of judges in Baltimore, Chicago, and Detroit, that the average sentence for robbery, adjusted to take into account when a person would become eligible for parole, ranged from a low of twenty-four months awarded by Detroit judges to a high of fifty-seven months given by Baltimore judges. Peter W. Greenwood and his colleagues at Rand found in a study of Superior Court dispositions in Los Angeles County that the chances of a convicted burglar with a prior prison record going to prison ranged from only one in eight in the city of Los Angeles to one in three in Long Beach. Within a single court, such as that in Long Beach, the chances of that burglar going to prison ranged from one in five for one judge to one in seventeen for another.

But, contrary to what one might suppose, there is not much systematic evidence to show that disparities in treatment conform to racial or class differences among offenders. Eisenstein and Jacob found that black defendants in the three cities fared no worse than white ones and that poor defendants were treated about the same as others. Greenwood and the Rand group found a complex and somewhat surprising pattern: blacks who pleaded not guilty to a felony were slightly more likely to be convicted than whites, but if convicted got lighter sentences than whites. In another study of California sentencing practices, Carl E. Pope found that there were some racial differences in prison sentences given by judges in rural areas but scarcely any such differences among urban courts.

John Hagan reviewed twenty studies of sentencing done between 1928 and 1973 and found that blacks were more likely to be executed than whites, especially in the South, but that for noncapital sentences involving defendants with no prior record, there were no significant racial differences. Stevens Clarke and Gary Koch looked closely at sentences awarded in one Southern community (Mecklenburg County, North Carolina) and found that race had no effect on the chances of going to prison once one held constant offense and prior record. Nor did income seem to affect the chances of being convicted, though it did affect the chances of going to prison—largely, it would seem, because poorer defendants could not afford bail or private attorneys.

Theodore G. Chiricos and Gordon P. Waldo, in a large-scale study of prison sentences received by more than 10,000 persons in three Southern states for seventeen offenses, found no relationship between the social status of the defendant (measured by income, education, and occupation) and the

length of the sentence received.

In juvenile courts, where judges are charged with acting *in loco parentis,* one can easily imagine even a well-meaning judge sending black youths to an institution more frequently than white ones, if for no other reason than that the judge recognizes the higher frequency of broken (and thus, he might think, unsuitable) homes among blacks. But of the many studies done of juvenile courts, most find no relationship between race or social status and court outcome.

One can think of all sorts of possible objections to these studies. Perhaps poor, black defendants were wrongly convicted and better-off white ones wrongly acquitted. (Given the vast number of persons screened out of the criminal-justice system before sentence is imposed, and based on interviews with many defense counsels, I would have to say that this explanation is unlikely.) Or perhaps the proportion of blacks going to prison is an average value reflecting, especially in the South, a tendency to *over*penalize blacks for crimes against whites and *under*penalize them for offenses against blacks. We know this to be the case with rape and murder, but no studies have yet been done to find out if it is true for less serious but more common property crimes.

Whatever the arguments, one thing is clear—there is not as yet much systematic statistical support, despite many efforts to find it, for the widespread view that poor persons and blacks are obviously and automatically the victims of the discriminatory use of judicial discretion, except in the case of capital punishment.

Does this mean that the case against unfettered judicial discretion is wrong? Not unless you believe that the only injustice is racial discrimination. The evidence from the Frankel experiment and from other studies shows that persons committing like offenses are receiving unlike penalties. That this disparity is on the whole being administered without regard to race or income is no defense. It simply means that judges are for the most part men and women who try to avoid allowing race or status to affect their judgment as to the gravity of a given offense, but who differ fundamentally as to how they might define that gravity.

This suggests that the problem of minimizing the harmful consequences of judicial discretion is much more difficult than was once supposed. Were it simply a matter of ending racial discrimination, sentencing guidelines and sentence review by appellate courts would probably eliminate most abuses, and such wrongs as remained would be easily detected by simple statistical measures. But when judges sentence differently because they have different philosophic beliefs as to what crime means and what justice requires, guidelines may well be either so complex or so loose as to permit disparities to persist. Appellate review may simply shift the disagreement to a different panel of judges.

This does not mean that sentencing guidelines are undesirable. Quite the contrary: they will probably do some substantial good, if only by getting serious people to work seriously on the problem. Reasonable guidelines will probably eliminate the worst abuses. But a Sentencing Commission will face a formidable task, for it will be obliged not merely to devise constraints against clear abuses, but to define what justice requires.

To MANY, PERHAPS MOST, citizens, sentencing laws should be revised more to reduce crime than to eliminate disparities, and the changes under way in California and elsewhere will probably be judged by the criterion of public safety rather than by sentence equity. This may not be what the lawmakers intended, but it is what people expect.

No one can be sure how many people will be sentenced under the California law and the laws proposed for Illinois and the federal government. A judge can always place a convicted person on probation. All the new laws say is that *if* a person goes to prison, it must be for a more determinate, or at least less variable, sentence. In short, these are not "mandatory prison" laws.

The scholarly studies that suggest that crime rates will be lower, other things being equal, where the probability of apprehension and punishment is higher continue to accumulate. There are now perhaps two dozen studies done with United States data and several using data from England and Canada. But there remain some methodological difficulties that prevent one from saying that these studies *prove* that sanctions deter crime. The major problem arises out of the possibility that crimes "deter" sanctions. For example, if crime rates rise rapidly, the criminal-justice system, especially the courts and prisons, may become so overloaded with cases that, in order to keep up with the deluge, judges start letting more and more persons off with no penalty. To an outside observer, it would appear that crime rates are going up because sentences are becoming less common when, in fact, the reverse is true.

I am reasonably confident that, other things being equal (such as economic conditions, especially the employment rates of young males), more certain penalties and a higher risk of apprehension will in fact reduce somewhat rates of property crime. My own research on police effects on crime rates, together with studies by Daniel Nagin on the effect of penalties on draft evasion during the Vietnam war, by Kenneth Wolpin on the consequences for English crime rates of changing the risks of punishment, and by other scholars studying different aspects of the problem, are all consistent with that belief. A special panel (on which I served) of the National Academy of Sciences has wrestled with this issue and is producing an appropriately cautious report, suggesting ways in which the deterrence hypothesis can be put to better tests.

But suppose, as I think quite likely, that more certain penalties will deter crime. Is it possible, as a practical matter, to produce greater certainty? The best answer seems to be a guarded yes, though so far that can only be said for certain crimes under certain circumstances. For example, the so-called Rockefeller drug law in New York State resulted in an increase in the proportion of persons going to prison for selling an ounce or more of heroin from 46 percent before the law to 94 percent after it was implemented. Whether this change affected the amount of drug dealing on the streets is far less clear.

EVEN IF NEW sentencing laws do not deter would-be criminals, they may affect crime rates by taking known repeaters off the streets for extended periods of time, thus sparing society the crimes that might have been committed by them. Criminologists call this the "incapacitation effect" to distinguish it from deterrence.

To calculate what incapacitative effect on crime rates new sentencing laws will have, one must know, among other things, how many persons will be in prison and for how long, and how many crimes those persons would have committed if they had been left on the streets. The determinate- and the mandatory-sentencing laws tell us how long convicts will be in prison, but we have only a crude idea of how many people will be serving those sentences and only a vague notion of the number of crimes such persons commit each year while free.

Based on studies of a large group of young men by Marvin Wolfgang at the University of Pennsylvania, we are fairly confident that a small proportion of offenders commits a large proportion of the more serious crimes. But, because of our maddeningly inadequate statistics, we don't really know how long and how frequently these chronic offenders are in prison. And we shall never know for certain how many crimes they commit while free; at best, we can only know how many times they are arrested.

Still, some informed guesses are possible. The first serious study of the incapacitative effect of prison was published two years ago. That study suggested that the average offender committed ten crimes per year. More recent studies suggest that the number may be closer to two. If the true figure is ten, then doubling the *average* number of years served by a convicted offender would cut the crime rate by 27 percent; if the true value is two, however, then doubling time served would reduce crime by only 10 percent. (This calculation ignores whatever additional crime reduction might occur because of the deterrent effects of longer sentences on would-be criminals.)

Ideally, we might prefer to give long sentences to repeat offenders (who, if left free, would commit many crimes each year) and short or no sentences to one-time or casual offenders. This would make for the most efficient use of expensive prison space and, in addition, would reduce the chances of casual criminals being mingled with hardened ones. To a great extent, this is what most judges now attempt to do. Almost every study of sentencing indicates that persons with long criminal records get longer sentences than persons with shorter records who commit the same offense. Whether we can do a better job by applying more systematic information to the task of identifying repeaters is not clear, however. For one thing, we do not have good information on how many crimes persons have actually committed, only information on how many times they have been arrested. For another, many of the most serious offenders are juveniles, who by law may not be kept in custody beyond a certain age (often twenty-one) no matter what they have done.

EVEN THOUGH most of the major proposals for new sentencing laws have yet to be enacted, the prison population is already rising rapidly. The great decline that occurred during the 1960s, although the crime rate was going up, has now been reversed. From a postwar high of 213,000 adults in state and federal prison in 1960, the numbers fell more or less steadily to 196,000 in 1972. The following year they started up and increased by 10 percent or more in each of the following years until now the prison population (as of the end of 1976) is officially counted at 265,674.

Prison populations went down while crime rates were going up rapidly; now that the rate of increase in crime has begun to slow, and without any fundamental change in sentencing laws, prison populations have shot up. Why? Frankly, no one knows for certain. One possibility is that judges, out of their own beliefs or in reaction to public criticism, have become tougher. No doubt that is true in some cases, but since we have almost no good information on sentencing practices, we cannot say whether this accounts for most or only some of the change.

Another possibility is that the vast crop of new young offenders who came of age in the 1960s (as a result of the baby boom after World War II) began to accumulate longer and longer arrest records so that judges who initially gave them probation or suspended sentences when they first appeared in court are now giving them prison terms as a reward for their felonious diligence. In short, the judges may not have changed, but the offenders have: the baby boom produced more juvenile one-time losers in the 1960s but more adult three-time losers in the 1970s. (Whether the one-time losers would have become three-time losers if they had been treated more severely in the first place is hard to say.)

If we cannot explain precisely why the prison population is larger, we can say with some confidence that it has changed in composition. Increasingly, prison has been reserved for only the most serious offenders. Persons convicted of homicide, robbery, and assault accounted for one-third of the prison population in 1960 but nearly one-half by 1974. The percentage of prisoners who are nonviolent felons—burglars, auto thieves, and larcenists—has declined, as has the percentage who are "white-collar" criminals (embezzlers, forgers, and defrauders). Only a small fraction of all prisoners—about 6 percent—are there for dealing in marijuana or for merely possessing a drug.

The question of what kind of offender ought to be in prison is a complex one. It will not do to parrot the phrase, uttered by some prison reformers, that only 10 or 15 percent of all inmates "need" to be in prison. To decide on who "needs" to be in prison, one must first decide on the purpose of prison. If it is only to restrain the uncontrollably violent offender, then it is true that most inmates could be safely released. But one would also have to release John Mitchell, H. R. Haldeman, and John Ehrlichman (they are scarcely violent), and one would never have imprisoned Jimmy Hoffa or any one of several dozen corrupt state legislators, mayors, and businessmen.

If prison exists only to incapacitate persons who, if left free, would continue to commit crimes, then white, middle-aged, middle-class wife-murderers should be released instantly and black, young, drug-addicted auto thieves should be kept locked up indefinitely. It is virtually a statistical certainty that the former will not kill again but that the latter will steal again. But the result is obviously ludicrous: we are, by such a policy, in effect saying that a human life is worth nothing, and a stolen car is worth everything.

If prison exists only to deter would-be criminals, then one would confine convicted offenders only if one believed that would-be offenders notice this and take it into account in deciding whether to commit crimes themselves. If one were fairly certain that no one knew whether anyone went to prison for a crime, there would be no point in sentencing anyone. If people began to doubt the reality of the prison sanc-tion, it would be far cheaper simply to mount a public-relations campaign in which you claimed that people go to prison for committing crimes even if scarcely anyone does.

Even more perversely, a purely deterrent theory of punishment would justify penalties that in many cases bore no relationship to the gravity of the offense. In Boston, the shame of being caught is enough to deter most residents from stealing a bottle of cognac from the corner liquor store, but probably only a jail sentence would keep them from double-parking in front of the store. Should we, on grounds of deterrence, scold the thieves but jail the double-parkers?

If prison has any *single* purpose, it is to punish, which is to say, to do justice. It is not deterrence or incapacitation that justifies people being imprisoned; it is being convicted of a crime that justifies it. Having decided to punish lawbreakers, we are then entitled to ask what deterrent or incapacitative effects that decision will have and to adjust, at the margin, the swiftness, certainty, and perhaps severity of that punishment to maximize deterrent or incapacitative objectives while remaining faithful to the fundamental premise that, as Andrew von Hirsch has put it in the title of his book, the choice of punishments should be based on "doing justice." If we do justice to all, we shall, I suspect, also cut crime.

Making Prisons Pay

A new idea spreading through America's penal system—real work, for real employers, at real wages— promises real inmate rehabilitation for the first time. And substantial savings for taxpayers

Roul Tunley

IN MANY WAYS, Dick Quillen appears to have it made. Still in his 30s, he heads his own data-processing company, housed in an attractive five-room suite with wall-to-wall carpeting and modern equipment, including a $500,000 computer. When I talked with him recently across a gleaming directors' table in his book-lined conference room, he exuded confidence, know-how and success.

What is not enviable about Quillen is his legal status. He is a convicted murderer, serving a life sentence. And his offices are in the state prison at Framingham, Mass.

Quillen's company highlights a significant trend: the arrival of free enterprise in our correctional system. Most taxpayers would say it's about time. During the past decade, prison populations and costs have exploded. It now takes up to $30,000 to keep a man or woman locked up for a year— not including substantial welfare costs for the prisoner's dependents.

A century ago, all prisoners worked, and their sweatshop or road-gang labor made prisons self-supporting, even profitable. But business and labor leaders began complaining about unfair competition, and laws were passed forbidding the selling of prison products and services on the open market. By the 1960s, almost no prisoners had prison-industry jobs.

Work was replaced by activities that were supposed to "rehabilitate": education, group therapy, behavior modification, even transcendental meditation. None of it helped. The percentage of released inmates who subsequently return to prison has remained depressingly high—for federal prisons, estimates range from 60 to 80 percent.

It's hard to pinpoint exactly where the back-to-work movement began. It could have been in a Walpole, Mass., prison in 1967, when a prisoner noticed that the want ads in the newspaper were full of offers for data processors. Knowing that he would need a job when released, he asked his chaplain if one of the computer firms near Boston would train prisoners. The chaplain approached Malcolm Smith, a group manager of Honeywell, Inc., and Smith took up the challenge. A program was set up, with Honeywell providing unpaid volunteer teachers and even loaning the prisoners a computer.

Since then, more than 1000 inmates have passed through the program at Walpole and three other Massachusetts prisons. Of these, at least 350 have subsequently been released, and only four percent of them have been returned to the state's prisons.

Mike Callahan is one of the men whose lives were turned around by this program. By age 19, Mike had been arrested 16 times and seemed a good bet to spend the rest of his life in jail. Then he was sent to prison again, learned about the computer program and applied. Five years after his release in 1971, he was earning $18,000 a year as a systems analyst for a New Hampshire firm. Last year, at age 28, he started his own firm. "Without that course," he says, "I never would have made it."

Meanwhile, people in other states have been chipping away at the prison problem in different ways. In 1975, Bill Benzick and Cecil Turner, who had just launched a food-service-management firm in St. Paul, saw an ad for a food-service director at Stillwater, the state's maximum-security prison.

Investigating, they decided that what the 900-man prison really needed was a dose of private enterprise. Stillwater's food was terrible, the waste appalling, morale rock-bottom. Mindful that many prison riots are over food, the two men offered to take over the operation. They guaranteed to save the state money, serve better meals and employ inmates at a working wage.

Benzick and Turner's small company thus became the first private food operation in prison annals. They served hot food hot, and cold food cold, put real salt and pepper shakers on the tables, installed a salad bar and an on-premises bakery, and offered a varied menu that included Rock Cornish hens at Thanksgiving and prime ribs of beef at Christmas.

The cost of all this was $1.59 a day per man compared with the previous $1.87, saving the state close to $100,000 a year. Instead of the 12 civilians and 163 inmates it had taken to operate the dining room before, it now took only ten civilians and 12 inmates. And those prisoners were paid $2 an hour instead of the previous $1.65 a day.

Taking note of such programs, the federal government's Law Enforcement Assistance Administration (LEAA) 2½ years ago launched a $2-million "free venture" program at prisons in Illinois, Connecticut and Minnesota. The program called for a seven- or eight-hour workday, wages based on productivity, and payment by participating prisoners of taxes, as well as board, room and aid to dependents where required.

How has it worked? I recently visited the three states to find out. In Connecticut and Illinois, where laws still prohibit the sale of prison products and services on the private market, results have been modest but promising. In Sheridan, Ill., for example, a medium-security prison has established a successful furniture-and-upholstery shop that employs almost ten percent of the prison population. Two years ago, 23-year-old Israel Pequeno was earning less than a dollar a day doing general kitchen work at Sheridan; now he makes over $200 a month as an inventory and materials clerk, and is sending a good part of it to his family. He has learned a skill and has been promised a job outside when he comes up for parole in 1980. "It gives you something to look forward to," he says.

In Connecticut, 400 inmates—20 percent of the state's prison population—are in the free-venture program. They work at least seven hours a day pursuing such crafts as printing, furniture making, upholstering and eyeglass manufacturing. The pay is still low, a maximum of $4 a day plus bonuses, but Commissioner John Manson is working to get legislation that will permit prison products to be sold not just to state governmental institutions, but also to non-profit organizations and other organizations funded by the state and federal governments. This could be the first step toward reaching productivity levels that would make wage increases feasible.

But Minnesota is the real success story. In 1976, a Control Data Corp. study of the state's prisons proposed setting up shops patterned on those outside, with modern equipment, regular work schedules and managers who could hire and fire. With the help of LEAA and a revised state law allowing prisoners to work for private companies, the proposal

was put into operation 2½ years ago.

To date, two industries have set up shop within prison walls, and another 18 or 20 operate on a sub-contract basis. At Lino Lakes, a medium-security prison, approximately 60 percent of all inmates are employed in printing, metal-deburring, furniture-making and telephone-refurbishing shops. Although wages are not yet on a par with those outside, prisoners make anywhere from 70 cents to $3.10 an hour.

At maximum-security Stillwater, about 12 percent of the inmates are in free-venture programs, including a data-processing company that pays perhaps the highest prison wages in the country: $5.64 an hour. Former prisoner Jim Willman entered data processing because "it was clean." By 1977, he was doing so well that he paid state and federal income taxes of some $4000 that year (more than his guard paid) and saved $7000 in "gate money." After his release, he went to work for General Mills at almost twice his prison salary. But he still serves on the board of directors of Stillwater Data Processing Systems, Inc. "I can't tell you how much satisfaction that work gives me," he says.

Although free venture has operated in Minnesota for less than three years, inmates working in it have paid $65,000 in taxes and returned $150,000 to the state in board and room. Moreover, from January to June 1978, only 9.5 percent of free-venture graduates (8 of 84) returned to prison, compared with the usual rate of 25 percent. Indeed, the LEAA program has been so successful that last fall it was extended to four other states: Washington, Colorado, Iowa and South Carolina.

How do labor unions react to the program?

"I don't see it as a threat to the union movement at all," says Leonard LaShomb, executive vice president of Minnesota's AFL-CIO. Pointing out that there are only 2100 prisoners in Minnesota against more than 1.9 million men and women with jobs, he says, "We support the program because it's in the interest

of all of us to solve the problem of recidivism."

Another prolificating program demonstrating the resurgence of the work ethic is "work release," under which prisoners work for private companies and return to minimum-security facilities after work. They earn prevailing wages, but pay board, room, taxes and transportation. Although not new (it was first tried in 1913), work release has come into its own only in the last few years. More than 40 states have adopted it.

I recently visited a center housing 62 work-release prisoners in Hollywood, Fla. It was a one-story modern building, with a dining room, library and recreational area, on the grounds of a state mental institution. Though no doors were locked, only two prisoners have escaped in the last two years. All the men had regular jobs, paying from $3 to $10 an hour.

One 52-year-old inmate who had been twice imprisoned was working as a freight handler at $4 an hour during the last few months of his sentence. He has hopes of becoming an X-ray technician after his release. "It's reality therapy," he explained of work release. "And it has changed my thinking."

In the last decade, Florida's work-release prisoners have earned more than $43 million, paid $13 million in board, room and transportation, another $6 million in taxes and other payroll deductions, and sent over $3 million home to dependents.

Of all the advantages of the back-to-work movement, perhaps the most important is the increased self-respect gained by employed prisoners.

"How do you think I felt after going back to prison time and again?" Mike Callahan asked me. "The thing I needed most was self-respect, and the confidence that I could make it in some other sort of life. Employment gave me that, just as it can for thousands of others. Employment is what made me go straight, and employment is why I'll never go back."

Scared Straight!

Frightening crime out of delinquents isn't pretty, but it may work!

Andrew Hagen

KER-SLAMM!! The heavy, booming sound of metal prison door clanging shut with grim finality, echoing down the long corridors of steel and concrete—this is one of the most depressing and frightening sounds that falls on human ears. For increasing numbers of teenage lawbreakers, it is the last sound they'll ever hear as normal human beings.

Once that door closes behind them, the young criminals are helplessly trapped in a man-made jungle which convicted killer Frank Bindhammer calls "schools of hatred, humiliation, and homosexuality." They come out, some of them decades later, bitter and broken men and women. They return to a world which has no use for an "ex-con," usually with no marketable skills to offer even should they find someone willing to give them a decent job. Filled with hatred for the society which robbed them of their youth, it is all too easy to return to crime, as revenge and simply as a way to survive.

Some aren't even this lucky. They leave the prison quietly, by a back door, as still forms under sheets, with identification tags on their toes. These are the ones not smart or vicious enough to survive—the ones who are stabbed to death over petty quarrels or who hang themselves in their cells—victims of a living hell from which there is no escape but death.

These hard facts have long been known—at least in a detached, intellectual way—by every person in every nation with a prison system. Far less obvious, however, is what—if anything—can be done to improve the situation. Since imprisonment largely replaced execution, corporal punishment, and banishment in the mid-18th century, it has often done almost as much harm as good. However, few would deny that some persons must be kept locked up for the good of society, and most cultures have hoped that imprisonment could also serve as a means of rehabilitation.

Regretfully, this has largely been a forlorn hope. Sixteen recent studies of U.S. rehabilitation programs show a recidivism rate (convicted criminals who are known to have returned to crime) of from 24 to 68 percent, with the overall rate of 44 percent. Dr. Robert Martinson, professor of sociology at the U.S. City University of New York, summed up the results of an exhaustive five-year study by saying: "With a few and isolated exceptions, the rehabilitative efforts that have been reported so far have had no appreciable effect on recidivism." This statement put Martinson in the center of a heated controversy, but he has continued his work, and his current research leads to both more hopeful and more depressing conclusions. Early results now show some programs *do* have a positive effect, but some also work the other way, actually driving the convicts deeper into a life of crime.

With juveniles, the picture is even bleaker. Up to 90 percent of U.S. young people in trouble with the law are chronic offenders; many are arrested weekly. Juvenile court measures have no impact on these "incorrigibles," so it is generally accepted that nothing can be done except to sentence them to an adult prison—from which they eventually emerge bitter and hardened criminals.

Now, one dramatic and controversial program is demonstrating that imprisoned robbers, rapists, and killers—once juvenile delinquents themselves—may have the best chance of reaching tough street kids.

In the process, the convicts find hope and self-respect they never had before. Since childhood, these men had accepted society's evaluation of themselves and their kind: worthless, beyond helping, the scum of the earth. But now that they are working to turn young people away from the sure path of prison's living hell, all that has changed. As one convict put it, "Doing something for somebody else gives you the feeling that the time you spend in here isn't completely wasted."

These men are members of the "Lifers Group" at Rahway (New Jersey, U.S.A.) State Prison. All are serving sentences of 25 years or more for violent major crimes. Four years ago, they formed an organization to help rehabilitate each other through self-taught educational programs and "rap" sessions.

Then, about a year after their program began, Richard Rowe, one of the Lifers, became frantic when he heard that his own teen-aged son was getting in trouble for petty crimes. He was starting down the same lawless road his father had taken—straight to a prison cell. Pacing the floor night after night, Rowe racked his brain for a way to help his son, thinking over and over again: "If only there were a way to show him what it's *really* like in here!"

Three other Lifers responded to that idea, and, after winning the initially reluctant cooperation of prison and juvenile authorities, the Juvenile Awareness Program was born. At first the convicts approached the young offenders as "big brothers," but they quickly found this just convinced the kids they would find "nice guys" who'd be their friends if they ever went to prison.

So the convicts—most of whom are *not* the world's nicest guys anyway—changed their tune, and now do just about anything to frighten the crime right out of the trembling teens. Their goal: to scare juveniles straight!

"I'm in for murder, kidnapping, robbery, armed robbery, conspiracy, breaking a dude's jaw, and breaking both his woman's arms," yells one scar-faced convict. "I'm in here for life. From now on! *Forever!* Till the day I die! That means I'm never gonna see the streets no more."

The mechanics of the program are simple. Twice a day, Monday through Friday, groups of from 12 to 20 youngsters, both boys and girls, from the surrounding area are driven to the prison. All have been in trouble repeatedly with the juvenile authorities, and for many this is the last stop before an actual prison sentence.

They walk into the prison strutting and cocky. "They *don't* scare me!" says one, referring to the convicts the group is about to meet. Grinning, another brags, "In my future, I think I'll be a professional thief. I'm gonna take everything you have, if you give me the chance."

But as the heavy steel doors slammed behind them and they are confronted with the harsh realities of the prison jungle, their smiles fade. They're jammed four in a cell, the filthy, stinking toilet a nauseating statement of conditions in today's overcrowded prisons. They are marched past solitary confinement cells where troublemaking prisoners shout homosexual taunts and insults through the bars.

Finally, the youngsters are led into a small auditorium, and are ordered to sit on hard wooden benches. The guards withdraw, the double doors slam shut, and the teens are locked in with a dozen of the toughest robbers, rapists, and killers any prison could offer.

In raw, brutal street language that pulls no punches, the kids are told exactly what is waiting for them inside those cold grey walls. If they doubt that prison is where they're headed, the cons have something to say about that, too. "I been in this stinkin' cesspool 10 years," says a man serving a double life sentence for murder. "I seen thousands of guys go through this joint, and I ain't never met anybody yet that *planned* to come to prison."

Another convict, serving 27 years for armed robbery, adds: "Every time one of your so-called friends tells you, 'Come on, let's go steal something, let's go mug somebody,' all he's really doing is saying, 'Let's go to jail'." Long before the convicts finish the three-hour session, the kids' cocky smiles are gone, and every last one is convinced that jail is a place he never wants to go again.

"When you look at us, what do you see?" asks a man serving 37 years for armed robbery. *"What do you see?* Convicts! You know what we see when we look at you? We see ourselves. So when you look at us, you try to see yourselves, 'cause this is the future for you.

"The men in here don't know what it's like to hear a dog bark, or hear a bird chirp. But if you ask us what it's like to hear a man getting stabbed to death, we'll tell you about that. If you ask us what it's like to hear a man screaming because four guys are raping him in his cell, we'll tell you about that, too. We hear it every day!"

Yet another convict, serving 25 years for murder, drives home even further the inevitability of prison in the future lives of the young boys and girls: "The police can make a thousand mistakes," he tells them as he paces back and forth like a caged animal. "But *you* can make only one mistake and you're done." Then, out of the corner of his eye, he sees a surly smile flit across one young face. In an instant, he's bending close to the youth, speaking in a soft but threatening snarl.

"Get that smile off your face. Let me tell you something—I'll break your nose off your face, and if you think someone's gonna stop me from doing it, you're wrong. By the time they get here it will be too late—it'll be all over with. I got so much time they can't give me no more. You understand what I'm telling you?"

The terrified kid swallows and whispers, "Yes."

The big convict nods and leans even closer. "Fine. Please don't make me hurt you."

The implied—and sometimes stated—threat of physical violence is always present in the crude auditorium. The delinquents are kept very much aware of the fact that they're alone in a locked room full of killers—men who are meaner and more violent on their mildest days than the kids ever dreamt of being themselves.

Suddenly they're facing raw reality, and it's a brutal shock. Instead of Burt Reynolds swaggering through a prison, never losing his cool, or Charles Bronson casually masterminding a break-out, they're face to face with a real-life convict who shows them an empty eye socket and tells them, "I was like you when I came to prison. I was wild; I was one of those tough throw-down guys. Nobody could tell me a goddamn thing I didn't wanta hear. But you know how they showed me? By taking my eye right out of my head! *Look!*" Some of the kids do look. Some of them look away.

Very few, however, seem able to emerge from the session unshaken. One girl is led away from the group when she becomes hysterical; one boy will become sick on the ride away from the prison and the juvenile officer will stop the car so he can vomit by the side of the road.

This brutal destruction of the delinquents' former arrogance and "cool" posture is exactly what the program is designed to accomplish, stresses Frank Bindhammer, one of the four founders and the first of the Lifers to be paroled. He was released in September 1978 after serving 16 1/2 years for first-degree murder. He now travels the U.S.A., helping set up similar programs at other prisons.

"We pick out the leaders of each group and verbally attack them," Bindhammer explains. "Actually, they're only so-called leaders, because their leadership is superficial. It's based on their illusions of themselves as 'tough guys,' as romantic outlaws—images they pick up from all the crap they see on TV and in the movies.

"We destroy these illusions. When they leave the session, we've torn them apart as much as we possibly can. Then they're vulnerable, because they've got no self-image to replace what we've taken away from them."

This is the crucial point, say the convicts involved in the program. With their defenses destroyed, these young boys and girls are ready, perhaps for the first time in their lives, to listen to someone who can show them the way to a more rewarding lifestyle.

At present, such follow-up guidance is provided by youth-help agencies already in operation. Eventually, Bindhammer and the other convicts would like to establish their own organization, made up largely of ex-cons dedicated to helping young people avoid the mistakes they made, to provide counseling specifically designed to complement Juvenile Awareness-type programs.

Whatever form it takes, some post-session work with the young people is crucial. Otherwise even the worst scare will quickly fade, to be replaced by the same swaggering bravado, the same wild lawlessness; and the kids will return to the streets which were the breeding-places for their antisocial behavior in the first place. "What we do inside the prison is only the first step," Bindhammer emphasizes. "It's a vital part of the program, but it can't stand alone."

Even with such follow-up support, expert opinion on the effectiveness of the program is sharply divided. The positive viewpoint is most strongly represented in a television documentary filmed in May 1978. Entitled "Scared Straight," this 50-minute film pulls no punches in showing a session in Rahway Prison just as it happens. All the raw street language and graphic descriptions of violence and brutal homosexual sex are left intact, which makes the program very strong viewing indeed.

Nevertheless, it has been shown across the U.S.A. on commercial television and, despite the initial fears of its makers, received few serious protests. In Chicago, for example, of 550 letter writers, only two attacked the film; of more than 400 phone calls received by the station, only about 10 were negative. In all parts of the

country, nearly all the protesting calls came during the first 15 minutes of the film. Once viewers realize exactly what the convicts are attempting to accomplish, they seem to be able to accept the action and the brutal language.

"Scared Straight" has received much critical acclaim as well. Reviews have been favorable, and, best of all, the film won the "Best Feature-Length Documentary" Oscar at the 1979 Academy Awards last April.

The filmscript claims that, over the three-year period the Juvenile Awareness program has been in existence, between 80 and 90 percent of the 11,000 delinquents who have taken part in sessions have indeed been "scared straight," as measured by their not having again run afoul of the law. Many now have jobs or are back in school, and juvenile and law enforcement officials from the Rahway area are unanimous in their praise of the program.

George J. Nicola, presiding judge at the Middlesex County (New Jersey) Juvenile and Domestic Relations Court, a respected jurist deeply concerned with preventing delinquency and one of the earliest advocates of the program, states: "When you view the program and review the statistics that have been collected, there's no doubt in my mind that the Juvenile Awareness project is perhaps the most effective, inexpensive deterrent in the entire American correctional process today."

Others in the field are considerably more cautious. Leonard Tropin, a spokesman for the National Council on Crime and Delinquency, admits the program "sounds dramatic," but he has "some reservations. One cannot assume this is the answer to curing delinquency." Mr. Tropin also stresses the necessity for proper follow-up if the scare is to be lasting in its benefits.

For Dr. Sol Chaneles, associate professor of criminal justice at Rutgers University, New Brunswick, New Jersey, the question of whether any one factor is effective in turning young people away from delinquency is "ultimately not knowable." He feels that the many variables involved prevent meaningful statistics and says that "the program of striking fear into delinquents through their speaking with adult offenders in the hopes of 'scaring them straight' is just wishful thinking."

However, Dr. James Finckenauer, also an associate professor of criminal justice at Rutgers, has just released the results of a study which he feels contains some valid—if disappointing—data on the project's effects on the teens experiencing it.

Earlier, Dr. Finckenauer gave the kids nine before-and-after tests of attitude change. He found no significant change in eight tests, but a positive change in the ninth, which was a test of the young subjects' attitude toward the concept of "crime" before and after Rahway.

In the second, most recent, section of his study, Dr. Finckenauer found that 41 percent (19 young people) of an experimental group of 46 who had experienced Rahway had become involved in serious crimes within six months. By contrast only 11 percent (four of 35) of the teens in a control group which did not visit the prison were known to have committed crimes.

According to these figures, he says, "The Juvenile Awareness Project does not deter crime, and one cannot dismiss the possibility that it could even contribute to it."

Naturally, such a statement ignited immediate controversy. The press widely reported that Dr. Finckenauer had claimed the project "caused" crime, which was a critical misinterpretation of his actual words. And many legislators and agencies across the nation, who had enthusiastically embraced the program's concept in the wake of "Scared Straight," did a rapid reverse and became highly critical.

Frank Bindhammer angrily stressed that the study dealt with only 81 juveniles out of more than 11,000 and predicted that a new study, now underway with a larger sample, would yield more positive results.

Dr. Finckenauer maintains that his random sampling methods enabled him to pick a sample representative of all the teens sent through the program, even though he himself would have preferred to study a larger number. "Actually," he says, "any statistical difference in that small a sample would only be likely to increase as the sample size increased."

Other defenders of the program do not argue with the data, but claim that figures tell only part of the story. Ms. Janet Storti, who collected data for the attitude tests, says "the project is a truthful look at a tragic side of our culture," and feels its negative aspects are a result of inadequate follow-up guidance.

Judge Nicola strongly agrees, saying, "The appro-priate position of the program is just to motivate the kids to be more willing participants in suppositive services. The convicts can only do so much." He cites probation officers' figures in "hundreds of letters" which report up to 90 percent success and adds, "even 59 percent success (the study's figure) in a program which costs nothing is not what I'd call a failure."

Where does this confusion of conflicting expert opinion leave a Rotary club or individual Rotarian who wishes to make some sort of juvenile delinquency prevention effort? Perhaps, as Dr. Chaneles maintains, a precise evaluation of these programs' effectiveness is simply not possible. But this is no excuse for not gathering all the data which may be available or for failing to work in support of whatever program seems best suited to any given community.

The Juvenile Awareness Program, controversial though it may be, has positive aspects which cannot be denied, and, although it is no panacea, it does have a place in the fight against delinquency.

With juvenile crime skyrocketing, no community can afford to ignore any program which offers hope of success. The savage barbarians are not only at the gates; they roam our every street, for they are our own children.

We owe it to these children, and to all children of the future, to take a stand against juvenile crime. Today's young punks are tomorrow's "Lifers." We cannot reform them all, but programs like this one at Rahway, can deter many from the waste and depravity of a life of crime.

"Y'all have the best opportunity in the world to go straight," a weary 26-year-old convicted murderer at Rahway told the youngsters scared speechless by his lecture. "You gotta be a damn fool not to take it!"

The case against capital punishment

Abe Fortas

Abe Fortas was an Associate Justice of the United States Supreme Court from 1965 to 1969. He now practices law in Washington, D.C.

I believe that most Americans, even those who feel it necessary, are repelled by capital punishment; the attitude is deeply rooted in our moral reverence for life, the Judeo-Christian belief that man is created in the image of God. Many Americans were pleased when on June 29, 1972, the Supreme Court of the United States set aside death sentences for the first time in its history. On that day the Court handed down its decision in *Furman v. Georgia*, holding that the capital-punishment statutes of three states were unconstitutional because they gave the jury complete discretion to decide whether to impose the death penalty or a lesser punishment in capital cases. For this reason, a bare majority of five Justices agreed that the statutes violated the "cruel and unusual punishment" clause of the Eighth Amendment.

The result of this decision was paradoxical. Thirty-six states proceeded to adopt new death-penalty statutes designed to meet the Supreme Court's objection, and beginning in 1974, the number of persons sentenced to death soared. In 1975 alone, 285 defendants were condemned—more than double the number sentenced to death in any previously reported year. Of those condemned in 1975, 93 percent had been convicted of murder; the balance had been convicted of rape or kidnapping.

The constitutionality of these death sentences and of the new statutes, however, was quickly challenged, and on July 2, 1976, the Supreme Court announced its rulings in five test cases. It rejected "mandatory" statutes that automatically imposed death sentences for defined capital offenses, but it approved statutes that set out "standards" to guide the jury in deciding whether to impose the death penalty. These laws, the court ruled, struck a reasonable balance between giving the jury some guidance and allowing it to take into account the background and character of the defendant and the circumstances of the crime.

The decisions may settle the basic constitutional issue until there is a change in the composition of the Court, but many questions remain. Some of these are questions of considerable constitutional importance, such as those relating to appellate review. Others have to do with the sensational issues that accompany capital punishment in our society. Gary Gilmore generated an

enormous national debate by insisting on an inalienable right to force the people of Utah to kill him. So did a district judge who ruled that television may present to the American people the spectacle of a man being electrocuted by the state of Texas.

The recent turns of the legislative and judicial process have done nothing to dispose of the matter of conscience and judgment for the individual citizen. The debate over it will not go away; indeed, it has gone on for centuries.

Through the years, the number of offenses for which the state can kill the offender has declined. Once, hundreds of capital crimes, including stealing more than a shilling from a person and such religious misdeeds as blasphemy and witchcraft, were punishable by death. But in the United States today, only two principal categories remain—major assaults upon persons, such as murder, kidnapping, rape, bombing and arson, and the major political crimes of espionage and treason. In addition, there are more than 20 special capital crimes in some of our jurisdictions, including train robbery and aircraft piracy. In fact, however, in recent years murder has accounted for about 90 percent of the death sentences and rape for most of the others, and the number of states prescribing the death penalty for rape is declining.

5. PUNISHMENT AND CORRECTIONS

At least 45 nations, including most of the Western democracies, have abolished or abandoned capital punishment. Ten U.S. states have no provision for the death penalty. In four, the statutes authorizing it have recently been declared unconstitutional under state law. The Federal Criminal Code authorizes capital punishment for various offenses, but there have been no executions under Federal civil law (excluding military jurisdiction) since the early 1960's.

Public-opinion polls in our nation have seesawed, with some indication that they are affected by the relative stability or unrest in our society at the time of polling. In 1966, a public-opinion poll reported that 42 percent of the American public favored capital punishment, 47 percent opposed it and 11 percent were undecided. In 1972-1973, both the Gallup and Harris polls showed that 57 percent to 59 percent of the people favored capital punishment, and a recent Gallup poll asserts that 65 percent favor it.

Practically all scholars and experts agree that capital punishment cannot be justified as a significantly useful instrument of law enforcement or of penology. There is no evidence that it reduces the serious crimes to which it is addressed. Professor William Bowers, for example, concludes in his excellent study, "Executions in America" that statutory or judicial developments that change the risk of execution are not paralleled by variations in homicide rates. He points out that over the last 30 years, homicide rates have remained relatively constant while the number of executions has steadily declined. He concludes that the "death penalty, as we use it, exerts no influence on the extent or rate of capital offenses."

I doubt that fear of the possible penalty affects potential capital offenders. The vast majority of capital offenses are murders committed in the course of armed robbery that result from fear, tension or anger of the moment, and murders that are the result of passion or mental disorder. The only deterrence derived from the criminal process probably results from the fear of apprehension and arrest, and possibly from the fear of significant punishment. There is little, if any, difference between the possible deterrent effect of life imprisonment and that of the death penalty.

In fact, the statistical possibility of execution for a capital offense is extremely slight. We have not exceeded 100 executions a year since 1951, although the number of homicides in death-sentence jurisdictions alone has ranged from 7,500 to 10,000. In 1960, there were only 56 executions in the United States, and the number declined each year thereafter. There have been no executions since 1967. In the peak year of 1933, there were only 199 executions in the United States, while the average number of homicides in all of the states authorizing capital punishment for 1932-33 was 11,579.

A potential murderer who rationally weighed the possibility of punishment by death (if there is such a person), would figure that he has considerably better than a 98 percent chance of avoiding execution in the average capital-punishment state. In the years from 1960 to 1067, his chances of escaping execution were better than 99.5 percent. The professional or calculating murderer is not apt to be deterred by such odds.

An examination of the reason for the infrequency of execution is illuminating:

(1) Juries are reluctant to condemn a human being to death. The evidence is that they are often prone to bring in a verdict of a lesser offense, or even to acquit, if the alternative is to impose the death penalty. The reluctance is, of course, diminished when powerful emotions come into play—as in the case of a black defendant charged with the rape of a white woman.

(2) Prosecutors do not ask for the death penalty in the case of many, perhaps a majority, of those who are arrested for participation in murder or other capital offenses. In part, this is due to the difficulty of persuading juries to impose death sentences; in part, it is due to plea bargaining. In capital cases involving more than one participant, the prosecutor seldom asks for the death penalty for more than one of them. Frequently, in order to obtain the powerful evidence necessary to win a death sentence, he will make a deal with all participants except one. The defendants who successfully "plea bargain" testify against the defendant chosen for the gallows and in return receive sentences of imprisonment.

This system may be defensible in noncapital cases because of practical exigencies, but it is exceedingly disturbing where the result is to save the witness's life at the hazard of the life of another person. The possibility is obvious that the defendant chosen for death will be selected on a basis that has nothing to do with comparative guilt, and the danger is inescapable that the beneficiary of the plea-bargain, in order to save his life, will lie or give distorted testimony. To borrow a phrase from Justice Byron R. White: "This is a grisly trade . . . ." A civilized nation should not kill A on the basis of testimony obtained from B in exchange for B's life.

(3) As a result of our doubts about capital punishment, and our basic aversion to it, we have provided many escape hatches. Every latitude is allowed the defendant and his counsel in the trial; most lawyers representing a capital offender quite properly feel that they must exhaust every possible defense, however technical or unlikely; appeals are generally a matter of right; slight legal errors, which would be disregarded in other types of cases, are grounds for reversal; governors have, and liberally exercise, the power to commute death sentences. Only the rare, unlucky defendant is likely to be executed when the process is all over.

In 1975, 65 prisoners on death row had their death-penalty status changed as a result of appeals, court actions, commutation, resentencing, etc. This was more than 20 percent of the new death-row prisoners admitted during that peak year.

It is clear that American prosecutors, judges and juries are not likely to cause the execution of enough capital offenders to increase the claimed deterrent effect of capital-punishment laws or to reduce the "lottery" effect of freakish selection. People generally may favor capital punishment in the abstract, but pronouncing that a living person shall be killed is quite another matter. Experience shows that juries are reluctant to order that a person be killed. Where juries have been commanded by law to impose the death penalty, they have often chosen to acquit or, in modern times, to convict of a lesser offense rather than to return a verdict that would result in execution.

□

The law is a human instrument administered by a vast number of different people in different circumstances, and we are inured to its many inequalities. Tweedledee may be imprisoned for five years for a given offense, while Tweedledum, convicted of a similar crime, may be back on the streets in a few months. We accept the inevitability of such discriminations, although we don't approve of them, and we constantly seek to reduce their frequency and severity. But the taking of a life is different from any other punishment. It is final; it is ultimate; if it is erroneous, it is irreversible and beyond correction. It is an act in which the state is presuming to function, so to speak, as the Lord's surrogate.

We have gone a long way toward recognition of the unique character of capital punishment. We insist that it be imposed for relatively few crimes of the most serious nature and that it be imposed only after elaborate precautions to reduce the possibility of error. We also inflict it in a fashion that avoids the extreme cruelty of such methods as drawing and quartering, though it still involves the barbaric rituals attendant upon electrocution, the gallows or the firing squad.

But fortunately, the death penalty is and will continue to be sought in only a handful of cases and rarely carried out. So long as the death penalty is a highly exceptional punishment, it will serve no deterrent or penological function; it will fulfill no pragmatic purpose of the state; and inevitably, its selective imposition will continue to be influenced by racial and class prejudice.

All of the standards that can be written, all of the word magic and the procedural safeguards that can be devised to compel juries to impose the death penalty on capital offenders without exception or discrimination will be of no avail. In a 1971 capital-punishment case, Justice John Harlan wrote on the subject of standards. "They do no more," he said, "than suggest some subjects for the jury to consider during its deliberations,

and [the criteria] bear witness to the intractable nature of the problem of 'standards' which the history of capital punishment has from the beginning reflected."

Form and substance are important to the life of the law, but when the law deals with a fundamental moral and constitutional issue—the disposition of human life—the use of such formulas is not an acceptable substitute for a correct decision on the substance of the matter.

The discrimination that is inescapable in the selection of the few to be killed under our capital-punishment laws is unfortunately of the most invidious and unacceptable sort. Most of those who are chosen for extinction are black (53.5 percent in the years 1930 to 1975). The wheels of chance and prejudice begin to spin in the police station; they continue through the prosecutor's choice of defendants for whom he will ask the death penalty and those he will choose to spare; they continue through the trial and in the jury room, and finally they appear in the Governor's office. Solemn "presumptions of law" that the selection will be made rationally and uniformly violate human experience and the evidence of the facts. Efforts to bring about equality of sentence by writing "standards" or verbal formulas may comfort the heart of the legislator or jurist, but they can hardly satisfy his intelligence.

If deterrence is not a sufficient reason to justify capital-punishment laws and if their selective application raises such disturbing questions, what possible reason is there for their retention? One other substantive reason, advanced by eminent authorities, is that the execution of criminals is justifiable as "retribution." This is the argument that society should have the right to vent its anger or abhorrence against the offender, that it may justifiably impose a punishment people believe the criminal "deserves." Albert Camus, in a famous essay, says of capital punishment:

"Let us call it by the name which, for lack of any other nobility, will at least give the nobility of truth, and let us recognize it for what it is essentially: a revenge."

We may realize that deepseated emotions underlie our capital-punishment laws, but there is a difference between our understanding of the motivation for capital punishment and our acceptance of it as an instrument of our society. We may appreciate that the *lex talionis*, the law of revenge, has its roots in the deep recesses of the human spirit, but that awareness is not a permissible reason for retaining capital punishment.

It is also argued that capital punishment is an ancient sanction that has been adopted by most of our legislatures after prolonged consideration and reconsideration, and that we should not override this history.

But the argument is not persuasive. If we were to restrict the implementation of our Bill of Rights, by either constitutional decisions or legislative judgments, to those practices that its provisions contemplated in 1791, we would indeed be a retarded society. In 1816,

5. PUNISHMENT AND CORRECTIONS

Thomas Jefferson wrote a letter in which he spoke of the need for constitutions as well as other laws and institutions to move forward "hand in hand with the progress of the human mind." He said, "We might as well require a man to wear still the coat which fitted him when a boy, as civilized society to remain ever under the regimen of their barbarous ancestors."

As early as 1910, the Supreme Court, in the case of *Weems v. United States,* applied this principle to a case in which the defendant had been sentenced to 15 years in prison for the crime of falsifying a public document as part of an embezzlement scheme. The court held that the sentence was excessive and constituted "cruel and unusual punishment" in violation of the Eighth Amendment. In a remarkable opinion, Justice Joseph McKenna eloquently rejected the idea that prohibitions of the Bill of Rights, including the Eighth Amendment, must be limited to the practices to which they were addressed in 1791, when the great amendments were ratified. He said, "Time works changes, brings into existence new conditions and purposes. Therefore a principle, to be vital, must be capable of wider application than the mischief which gave it birth. This is peculiarly true of constitutions. They are not ephemeral enactments, designed to meet passing occasions." As to the "cruel and unusual punishment" clause of the Constitution, he said that it "is not fastened to the obsolete, but may acquire meaning as public opinion becomes enlightened by a humane justice."

We have also long recognized that the progressive implementation of the Bill of Rights does not depend upon first obtaining a majority vote or a favorable Gallup or Harris poll. As the Supreme Court stated in the famous 1943 flag-salute case, "The very purpose of a Bill of Rights was to place [certain subjects] beyond the reach of majorities and officials. . . ."

Indeed, despite our polls, public opinion is unfathomable; in the words of Judge Jerome Frank, it is a "slithery shadow"; and if known, no one can predict how profound or shallow it is as of the moment, and how long is will persist. Basically, however, the obligation of legislators and judges who question whether a law or practice is or is not consonant with our Constitution is inescapable; it cannot be delegated to the Gallup poll, or to the ephemeral evidence of public opinion.

We will not eliminate the objections to capital punishment by legal legerdemain, by "standards," by procedures or by word formulas. The issue is fundamental. It is wrong for the state to kill offenders; it is a wrong far exceeding the numbers involved. In exchange for the pointless exercise of killing a few people each year, we expose our society to brutalization; we lower the essential value that is the basis of our civilization: a pervasive, unqualified respect for life. And we subject ourselves and our legal institutions to the gross spectacle of a pageant in which death provides degrading, distorting excitement. Justice Felix Frankfurter once pointed out: "I am strongly against capital punishment. . . .When life is at hazard in a trial, it sensationalizes the whole thing almost unwittingly; the effect on juries, the bar, the public, the judiciary, I regard as very bad. I think scientifically the claim of deterrence is not worth much. Whatever proof there may be in my judgment does not outweigh the social loss due to the inherent sensationalism of a trial for life."

Beyond all of these factors is the fundamental consideration: In the name of all that we believe in and hope for, why must we reserve to ourselves the right to kill 100 or 200 people? Why, when we can point to no tangible benefit; why, when in all honesty we must admit that we are not certain that we are accomplishing anything except serving the cause of "revenge" or retribution? Why, when we have bravely and nobly progressed so far in the recent past to create a decent, humane society, must we perpetuate the senseless barbarism of offical murder?

In 1971, speaking of the death penalty, Justice William O. Douglas wrote: "We need not read procedural due process as designed to satisfy man's deep-seated sadistic instincts. We need not in deference to those sadistic instincts say we are bound by history from defining procedural due process so as to deny men fair trials."

I hope and believe we will conclude that the time has come for us to join the company of those nations that have repudiated killing as an instrument of criminal law enforcement.

Medical Model in Corrections Requiescat in Pace

Donal E.J. MacNamara

John Jay College of Criminal Justice
City University of New York

The medical model for corrections, confidently espoused by several generations of behavioral scientists although never empirically validated, is now reeling under attacks from an interdisciplinary (though unorganized) army of critics. Attacking its basic premise (that the offender is "sick" and can be "cured"), the new penologists advocate a justice model based on individual responsibility with uniform penalties consistently imposed for like crimes. Out would go the indeterminate sentence, virtually unlimited judicial discretion, parole, and coerced participation in rehabilitation programs. Deterrence, retribution, and incapacitation would be restored as respectable rationalizations for imprisonment; but in general long prison terms would be reserved only for the habitually violent.

Of all the many correctional shibboleths religiously communicated to their students by professors of sociology, social work, criminology, and corrections, the "medical model" has proved most durable, and strangely so since there has been little, if any, empirical demonstration of its validity. The concept is at once so humane, so modern, so professional, and seemingly so scientific as to commend it to men of good will; and the process of follow-up evaluation so neglected and so fraught with methodological pitfalls as to permit widely disseminated claims of rehabilitative success based on little more than an overly optimistic belief in the ultimate perfectibility of even the most dangerous and recidivistic offenders coupled with a statistical innocence more appropriate to an adolescent interest in batting and fielding averages. Its enduring quality, too, owes not a little to the neanderthal opposition: those who, however valid their overall negative evaluations of the model in practice, couch their countervailing arguments in such discriminatory, punitive, retributive, and unscientific language as to offend the sensibilities and reinforce the basic premises of the reformers and rehabilitators.

In its simplest (perhaps oversimplified) terms, the medical model as applied to corrections assumed the offender to be "sick" (physically, mentally, and/or socially); his offense to be a manifestation or symptom of his illness, a cry for help. Obviously, then, early and accurate diagnosis, followed by prompt and effective therapeutic intervention, assured an affirmative prognosis—rehabilitation. Diagnosis was the function of the presentence investigation (confirmed, expanded, or perhaps corrected during institutional classification); therapeutic intervention was decreed in the sentence and made more specific in the treatment plan devised by the classification committee; and the parole board decided (within certain legal constraints) when the patient was to be discharged back into the community as "cured." Basic to the medical model, although rather surprisingly denied by many of its proponents, is that the criminogenic factors are indigenous to the individual offender and that it is by doing "something" for, to, or with him that rehabilitation can be effected.

There are, to be sure, many illustrative cases to which this model applies: the offender with a glandular imbalance correctable by chemotherapy; the cosmetic elimination of a disfiguring blemish with a consequent minimizing of social discrimination and reactive hostility; even the surgical removal of the testes of an habitual rapist. Somewhat more questionable are the claimed successes for psychiatric interventions; and it is difficult, indeed, since the more credulously religious days of past centuries, to find acceptable examples of moral regeneration. But the medical model school depended less on an affirmative showing that success crowned their programs than on aggressive excuses for failure: rehabilitation was underfunded; treatment was sabotaged by custodial staff; judges and parole boards responded to political and public pressures rather than to treatment imperatives; society had a lust for punishment; even rehabilitated offenders suffered socioeconomic discrimination which drove them back to criminal activity; the brutal, coercive, institutional atmosphere negated therapeutic interventions; "prisonization" (the resocialization of newly incarcerated offenders into the mores and folkways of the inmate community) was contra-rehabilitative; and, among those labelled "radical" criminologists, a retreat position inconsistent with the medical model that denounces the society which defines criminality rather than the offenders who violate society's laws.

The medical model has further implications for criminal justice. It entails wide discretion for the criminal court judiciary, permitting diversion of cases from the criminal justice system; sentencing alternatives ranging from probation to indeterminate sentences of polar dimensions (e.g., one day to life); paroling authorities with in many cases equally liberal alternatives; and to some lesser degree an expanded use of the commutation and pardoning powers of the executive branch. Implicit in the model was the availability of a wide range of treatment alternatives, institutional and community; and anticipated too was an army of professional probation and parole officers, with a department store of social services awaiting referrals, who would not only supervise but service and support manageable caseloads, consisting of clients specially selected by judges and parole boards as being of minimal danger to the community and good prospects for societal readjustment. That judicial discretion has been abused and incompetently administered, that the arsenal of treatment alternatives has seldom been provided, that paroling authorities have proved incapable of either resisting pressures or distinguishing dangerous from nondangerous offenders, that probation and parole officers have for a variety of reasons failed either to supervise adequately or provide services and support, that the retributive forces in correction and in the public have inhibited certain rehabilitative approaches, and even that some humane and libertarian proponents of the medical model have, perhaps inconsistently, opposed the more draconian treatment interventions (e.g., behavior modification) may all be accepted as possible explanations for the failure of the rehabilitative ideal. But it is perhaps more likely than not that, even if these negatives could be corrected, the custodial-deterrent-retributive school would be vindicated. For the basic flaw of the medical model is its basic premise: that the offender is "sick" when in fact he is far more likely to be as "normal" as most nonoffenders but inadequately, negatively, or contraculturally socialized, at war with a world he never made, a world in which he has been subjected to abuse, brutalization, discrimination, and exploitation. No program of education, vocational training, medical or psychiatric therapy is relevant to his "cure" and none is likely to reverse his twenty or thirty years of antisocial conditioning. What alternative remains? Incapacitation by custodial control with perhaps some rather speculative deterrent impact on either the offender or on prospective offenders, or both.

5. PUNISHMENT AND CORRECTIONS

Now these views would have earned an academic criminologist naught but contumely less than a decade ago, but correctional fads, fallacies, and fashions change. A proliferating literature, bearing the names of such respectable academicians as Norval Morris, James Q. Wilson, Andrew von Hirsch, Robert Martinson, David Fogel, and Ernst van den Haag, now rejects equally the "tear down the walls" war cry of those who would abolish prisons (in favor of a just society which would eliminate criminogenic factors) and the prison reform movement which campaigns and litigates for smaller, treatment-oriented institutions, court-mandated inmate rights, expansion of community corrections, decriminalization of victimless offenses, and diversion from the criminal justice system for many now subject to its sanctions. The new penologists, if one can so label a quite disparate group, accept prisons as a societal necessity, advocate a narrowing or elimination of judicial discretion in sentencing (flat or definite sentences imposed uniformly and consistently on those convicted of identical crimes), an end to coerced institutional treatment (although they favor voluntary participation by inmates in a variety of educational, vocational, and therapeutic programs), abolition or severe constraints on parole, and acceptance of a deterrent-retributive-punitive rationalization for dealing with offenders. Some implicitly, others more explicitly, justify imprisonment in terms of societal protection by incapacitating for at least the definite period of their confinement those dangerous and habitual offenders who are responsible for the almost paranoid fear of criminals widespread among certain segments of our population and reflected in the increasingly punitive orientation of courts and legislatures.

My colleague, Robert Martinson (and his co-authors Douglas Lipton and Judith Wilks) has perhaps received a less cordial reception for the highly significant monograph, *The Effectiveness of Correctional Treatment* (1975), than has been accorded Morris, Wilson et al.; yet he has furnished us with a more massive and convincing documentation of the irrelevancy and ineffectiveness of therapeutic interventions than have the authors of the more readable polemics. Certainly his book, articles, and lectures have stimulated much of the new and highly controversial correctional dialogue; yet he is actually anti-prison and to a limited extent pro-probation and parole (advocating a transfer of funding which would permit highly intensified, almost one-for-one, supervision or surveillance in the community), thus eliminating the negative impact of imprisonment and at the same time enhancing societal protection against recidivistic crimes by convicted offenders. Martinson advocates the removal of the criminal justice system from the "treatment business," abolishing the indeterminate sentence and parole boards, developing three categories of offenders (suspendees, restrainees, and isolates). *Suspendees* are first offenders to be returned to the community under neither supervision nor coerced treatment, but who are eligible for voluntary services arranged through broker-advocates (not too different from an idealized version of a probation officer) and under the sole injunction that they not be convicted again of a criminal offense. *Restrainees,* either suspendees who recidivate or offenders classified as nondeterrable by mere threat of punishment, would be placed under intensive surveillance within the community ("each *restrainee* will be assigned his own private policeman") by an agent who is unknown to him, with whom he is not to have interpersonal contact, and whose sole function would be to report to the police whenever he observes the restrainee committing a criminal offense. *Isolates,* either suspendees or restrainees who commit new and serious offenses or a small class of first offenders who are convicted of heinous, violent crimes and are too dangerous to be supervised in the community, would be imprisoned in one of a greatly reduced number of existing prisons, with neither treatment, reform, nor rehabilitation as the aim.

Norval Morris, prestigious dean of the University of Chicago Law School, in *The Future of Imprisonment* (1974), argues that prisons are necessary; that they can be made less brutal, corrupt, and dehuman-

izing; that all rehabilitative and treatment programs be entirely voluntary; that the range of judicial discretion in sentencing be severely constrained; that mandated programs of graduated community release precede parole; that terms of imprisonment be uniform and related to the seriousness of the offense rather than to speculative evaluation of "dangerousness" or potential for recidivism; and that model prisons, not unlike the Danish institution at Herstedvester, be provided for the custody and treatment of such habitually aggressive offenders as recidivistic rapists and murderers.

Ernst van den Haag, prolific polemicist on the faculty of the New School, advocates in *Punishing Criminals: Concerning a Very Old and Painful Question* (1975) a return to the pleasure-pain calculus, balancing temptation with swift and certain punishments, albeit somewhat less harsh than those advocated by many, e.g., day fines (related to the offender's income) for minor crimes; one- or two-year sentences for more serious offenders; longer, indeterminate imprisonment for incorrigibles; and perhaps "exile" for some (i.e., banishment with their families either to special penal communities or to small, isolated villages in which they might be more intensively supervised). This is in fact a feature of Italian penal law, used rather inconsistently as a means of controlling members of the Mafia, and was for centuries a basic penalty in China with the banishment distance in miles correlated to the offense but with the rigors of the climate and type of work available also inputs into the calculus. Van den Haag, probably the essential pragmatist of the new penologists, subordinates even charity and justice to the preservation of social order.

Andrew von Hirsch, of the Rutgers University School of Criminal Justice, in *Doing Justice: The Choice of Punishments* (1976), rejects the medical-rehabilitative model, advocates elimination of both the indeterminate sentence and parole, accepts punishment as the basic rationalization of society's response to criminality, opts for somewhat harsher sentences than does van den Haag (a five-year maximum, for all crimes except murder, which—although von Hirsch does not mention it—has been established by psychological research as the outer parameter of the human ability to project into the future), and emphasizes that offenders "deserve" to be punished in proportion to the gravity of their crime(s) against society.

James Q. Wilson, Harvard political scientist, has unlike the great majority of his disciplinary colleagues devoted much of his attention to the criminal justice system, forcefully dissenting from *The Challenge of Crime in a Free Society* (Ruth et al., 1971) and publishing an insightful study, *Varieties of Police Behavior* (1968). In a collection of essays, *Thinking About Crime* (1975), Wilson comes down hard on the side of prisons and punishments as mechanisms to reduce crime incidence substantially. Seeing the habitual, career criminal as responsible for a high proportion of serious criminality, he call for incarceration, and holds out hope that imprisonment might additionally have some deterrent impact on others not yet committed to a life of crime. He, too, feels that swift and certain short terms of imprisonment (up to two years) can be effective, perhaps more effective than the much harsher maximum penalties provided for in the statutes but rarely imposed and even more rarely served. Wilson strongly implies that the failure of the prison population to increase proportionately to the significantly higher crime incidence after World War II was itself a cause of the increased criminality. And finally, he has short shrift for rehabilitation ("whatever it means") which he avers has no role in the prison sanction.

David Fogel's name has become synonymous with the rehabilitation of the "flat" or definite sentence and the "justice model" for corrections. While commissioner of corrections in Minnesota and later as director of the Illinois Law Enforcement Commission, he expressed very clearly his belief that rehabilitation and therapists have nothing to do with justice and safety, that rehabilitation should have nothing to do with whether an offender is sentenced to prison or when an offender should be released, and that the justice model must include justice for the victim (which led to his establishing the Minnesota restitution program). Fogel's sentencing recommendations divided crimes into categories based on degree of seriousness and provided limited judicial discretion (sentences could vary by as much as 20% if there were mitigating or aggravating factors); and, importantly, only offenders who were clearly dangerous to society would go to prison (e.g., he believes that all or most property offenders, many of whom now get committed to penal institutions, can be safely supervised within the community). Fogel's ineptly titled *We Are the Living Proof: The Justice Model for Corrections* (1975) is a clear and forceful presentation of his views and an especially convincing argument in favor of limiting the sentencing discretion of America's criminal court judges.

Finally, mention must be made of *Prison Without Walls* (1975), the report on parole in New York State by the Citizens' Inquiry on Parole and Criminal Justice (of which the author was a member and a consultant). Ramsey Clark and Herman Schwartz, both of whom might well be classified as prison abolitionists, headed the inquiry, and Jack Himmelstein, David Rothman, Richard Cloward, David Fogel, Michael Meltsner, Tom Wicker, Edward Bennet Williams, and William vanden Heuvel were among the better known students and practitioners of criminal justice lending their expertise. *Prison Without Walls* recommends that parole be abolished (as has Attorney General Edward Levi) because it is an adjunct of a sentencing process that attempts to reconcile elements of law, justice, and societal protection with considerations of rehabilitation and treatment. The result is an uneasy amalgam, as unfair to the offender as it is ineffective in the achievement of society's goals. Prisons do not "treat" offenders; they do not rehabilitate. Parole boards have little demonstrated competence in distinguishing dangerous from nondangerous inmates. Predictions of postinstitutional behavior, based largely on adjustment to the abnormal routines of institutional life, have proved disastrously inaccurate (in a California study, almost 90% so). The parole decision-making process is itself inequitable, if not unconstitutional (arbitrary and without empirically derived guidelines, subject to whim and pressure). In addition to concluding that the parole board be abolished, the report made both long-term and transitional recommendations, including elimination of compulsory community supervision, shorter sentences within a much narrower range of judicial discretion, development of rational criteria for early release, development of new alternatives to incarceration, public scrutiny of correctional decision-making, a wide range of voluntary programs to be offered to offenders before, during, and after incarceration, a specific code of inmate rights in parole board proceedings, shifting the burden of proof to parole boards in denying parole, open hearings, one year maximum on parole supervision in the community, simplification of the parole contract, abolition of the law enforcement function of parole agents (revocation to be based only on a new crime), financial assistance for parolees, extensive social services, and crediting of time on conditional release toward maximum sentence. *Prison Without Walls*, though somewhat different in its genesis and orientation, fits comfortably into the matrix of justice model studies; and better than many documents its far-reaching and quite controversial conclusions are fortified with persuasive data from the official archives but, even more importantly, from the client population.

The new penologists posit a basic conflict between a medical model maintaining that crime is the product of individual defects and disorders that can be corrected in a program of medical, psychiatric, and social rehabilitation and a readjusted or reformed offender returned to his rightful place in society *versus* a justice model based on the more classic doctrine of the free moral agent and of individual responsibility for one's criminal behavior. The controversy is somewhat complicated by reform and pragmatic considerations—reformers who want not to abolish prisons but rather to make them more humane and their rehabilitation programs more effective, and realists who insist that society has a right to protect itself from predatory elements by confining them in prisons, whether or not this leads to their rehabilitation and in fact irrespective of whether it contributes to their further criminality after release. The battle lines involve power dynamics as well as ideological conflicts. Judges wish to retain the tremendous discretion with which the medical model has invested them over the past half-century, and parole board members fight valiantly to retain their posts of power and prestige; both probation and parole officers are defending their jobs and their careers; program staff members in institutions (educators, vocational training specialists, therapists) see themselves threatened by making inmate participation voluntary; custodial elements scent victory over the hated head-shrinkers; law and order politicians and some punitive-retributive legislators and pressure groups misread Morris, Wilson, Martinson, Fogel, von Hirsch and van den Haag as "lock 'em up and throw the key away" neanderthals; and the general public, ill-served by the communications media, is confused and unhappy. Perhaps least perturbed is the target population, offenders in or out of prisons. To a man they see this conflict as a charade . . . they *know* from past experience that nothing good ever happens to them. They have every expectation that no matter how things change, justice for them will remain very much the same.

REFERENCES

Citizens' Inquiry on Parole and Criminal Justice (1975) Prison Without Walls. New York: Praeger.

FOGEL, D. (1975) We Are the Living Proof: The Justice Model for Corrections. Cincinnati: W. H. Anderson.

LIPTON, D., R. MARTINSON, and J. WILKS (1975) The Effectiveness of Correctional Treatment. New York: Praeger.

MORRIS, N. (1974) The Future of Imprisonment. Chicago: Univ. of Chicago Press.

RUTH, H. et al. (1971) The Challenge of Crime in a Free Society. New York: Da Capo.

van den HAAG, E. (1975) Punishing Criminals: Concerning a Very Old and Painful Question. New York: Basic Books.

von HIRSCH, A. (1976) Doing Justice: The Choice of Punishments. New York: Hill & Wang.

WILSON, J. Q. (1975) Thinking About Crime. New York: Basic Books.

——— (1968) Varieties of Police Behavior: The Management of Law and Order in Eight Communities. Cambridge: Harvard Univ. Press.

ON PAROLE SUCCESS
A Reply to MacNamara

George Torodash

George Torodash has an M.A. in Criminal Justice. He is past president of the New York State Parole Officers Association, has been a parole officer for sixteen years, and has published numerous articles on parole and related subjects.

The article by MacNamara (1977), "The Medical Model in Corrections,"*unfairly and incorrectly criticizes parole. MacNamara scorns the medical model, but offers no viable alternatives. He claims that the parole system is failing in its rehabilitative concept, an allegation that is short-sighted and ill-defined. Terms such as rehabilitation, or for that matter reintegration and reformation, are created by social science lexicographers: these concepts have no demonstrable utility in evaluating parole supervision.

Parole success is based on a totally different concept. Throughout their lives, the majority of convicts have had an absence of restraint, supervision, and order. The parole officer imposes these elements upon an erratic lifestyle, and to this he adds an additional essential element, namely guidance. In this way, the parole officer assists the criminal in abandoning his antisocial attitudes and patterns.

Critics of parole find fault with the officers' function of imposing order and restraint on the activity of parolees, as well as the use of sanctions against the failure to comply. It is naive to imagine that without these tools, only the art of conversation will reverse the criminogenic pattern of a lifetime.

A parole system that does not accentuate law enforcement as its primary purpose cannot function at its maximum capability. For this reason, the federal system, which requires little "street work," is ineffective and vulnerable, unlike the New York state system, which emphasizes surveillance and police work and leads the country in efficiency of its operation.

MacNamara writes that "parole officers have for a variety of reasons failed either to supervise adequately or provide services and support," but he does not detail the "variety of reasons," making reference only to *Prison Without Walls,* the report on parole in New York State by the Citizens' Inquiry on Parole and Criminal Justice. That report, however, has been assailed by psychiatrists, psychologists, social workers, statisticians, law enforcement personnel, ethnic and racial groups, and district attorneys. In fact, the former director of

the Citizens' Inquiry and chief architect of the report referred to it as an "unfortunate publication" (Rodenstine, 1976).

MacNamara also states, without citing pertinent studies or offering statistical proof, that "paroling authorities have proved incapable of distinguishing dangerous from non-dangerous offenders." As against this, I should like to cite the following.

1. A study in New York State, examining released prisoners for one year, that concluded: "It may readily be seen that parolees do substantially better than mandatory releasees with more favorable outcomes and fewer new arrests for every group comparison and fewer technical or absconding violations in every comparison but one. Parolees average 74% favorable outcomes compared to 52% for mandatory releasees; 12% technical and absconding violations compared to 19%; and 14% new arrests compared to 28%" (Hoffman, 1974: 547).

2. A five-year examination of the comparative criminal experience of inmates released to parole supervision and those directly discharged from prison without such supervision revealed that 23.1% of those directly discharged were subsequently recommitted to prison with new sentences, as opposed to 2.3% committed to prison while under parole supervision. In addition, 29.7% directly discharged were convicted of misdemeanors as opposed to 10.4% of those convictions for parole supervision cases (Hoad, 1970).

3. A survey of parolees discharged after five years of supervision under the provision of Chapter 126 of the Correction Law indicates that from 1960 through 1973 a total of 2,917 parolees were granted discharges. Follow-up information is available on 1,889 discharged between 1960 and 1967 which indicates that only six were reported to have been recommitted to New York State correctional institutions (NYS Department of Correctional Services, 1973). Further, the majority of parolees receiving five-year discharges were initially considered serious offenders; this includes many who had been sentenced to life imprisonment and who obviously benefited from the supervision and guidance of parole officers.

4. A study by Bailey (1975) compared short-term treatment effects (one year or less) with long-term prognosis (10 years or more) for the same group of experimentally treated adult male opiate addicts. During the experimental period cases were categorized into individual counseling, field examination, and routine parole supervision. In comparing the results during the postexperimental period, Bailey found that the individual counseling group had the highest rate of criminal involvement, while the routine parole supervision group had the lowest.

5. An ongoing study by Martinson and Wilks (1976) has

Editor's note: See A/E article 47, page 207.

The original version of this article appeared under the title "On Parole Success: A Reply to MacNamara," by George Torodash, published in CRIMINOLOGY Vol. 16, No. 1 (May 1978) pp. 109-114 and is reprinted herewith by permission of the publisher, Sage Publications, Inc.

been examining recidivism rates on a nationwide basis. It has revealed that for those who were released from prison without parole supervision, the recidivism rate was 32%. For those released with parole supervision, the recidivism rate was 24%. The difference is not outstanding, but significant. However, these are national figures. In New York State, the rate of recidivism for those released with parole supervision is 11%. Broken down still further, 7.8% were reincarcerated for technical violations, while only 3.2% were returned for new convictions. Obviously, most of the 7.8% would have been arrested for renewed felonious activity if it were nor for the timely intervention of alert parole officers who initiated preventive measures.

6. A study of the New York State parole system by Lerner (1977) indicated that parole supervision substantially reduced the criminal activity of parolees, as compared to a control group of persons released from the same local institutions (New York City, Westchester, and Dutchess counties) but not to parole supervision. On a one-year follow-up on each inmate, it was noted that over twice as many discharges were arrested within the year than were parolees. Even when factors accounting for parole board selection of inmates for parole were controlled, parolees demonstrated a better adjustment in every category of risk and offense severity, offering evidence that parole supervision is effective in the reduction of criminal behavior.

There are several additional statistical and empirical studies attesting to the efficacy of parole (Gottfredson, 1975; Waller, 1974; Adams et al., 1969; Adams et al., 1971; Wisconsin Division of Corrections, 1974). However, it is insufficient to render judgment on parole solely on the basis of statistical evidence. It is impossible to measure accurately the positive effects and the value to the community when a parolee's personal situation is aided through the judicious counseling and direction of a parole officer, or when a potentially explosive situation is neutralized by the direction of parole personnel. Thousands of incipient criminal acts are aborted each year by parole officers who are acquainted with the behavioral tendencies of former inmates and obtain personal information resulting in the seizure and confiscation of weapons, narcotics, and other illegal paraphernalia before they could be utilized in further assaults upon society. Parole officers, due to their unique position and attendant powers of arrest and search, usually confiscate the aforementioned tools of torment before they can be utilized in nefarious activity.

Note, further, the cost effectiveness of parole supervision. To institutionalize a convicted felon in New York State costs five to ten times as much as the maintenance of an individual under parole supervision. On parole, an employed individual pays taxes; as an inmate, he is maintained by the taxes of others. Actually, parole is one of the few governmental agencies paying for itself and contributing to the economy (Richmond, 1972).

The cities of America are currently in the grip of a paralysis generated by the fear of violent crime. The American dream has been transformed into a nightmare of explosive violence. A mitigating influence that contributes to the prevention of further deterioration of this situation is the dedication of personnel engaged in the protection of the community, and among the principal participants in this endeavor are parole officers.

REFERENCES

ADAMS, S., W. S. HEATON, and J. D. SPEVACEK (1969) "Post-release performance of 432 reformatory releasees." Washington, DC: District of Columbia Department of Corrections.
ADAMS, S., W. CALDWELL, B. ALLEN, and C. BARROS (1971) "Twelve-month performance of correctional complex releases by category by release." Washington, DC: District of Columbia Department of Corrections.
BAILEY, W. C. (1975) "Addicts on parole: short-term and long-term prognosis." Int. J. of Addictions 10: 423-437.
GOTTFREDSON, D. M. (1975) "Some positive changes in the parole process." Paper presented at American Society of Criminology meeting, Toronto.
HOAD, D. (1970) "Five year release study." Office of Program, Planning, Evaluation and Research, New York State Department of Correctional Services.
HOFFMAN, P. (1974) "Mandatory release: a measure of type II error." Criminology 11: 541-554.
LERNER, M. J. (1977) "The effectiveness of definite sentence parole program." Criminology 15: 211-224.
MacNAMARA, D.E.J. (1977) "The medical model in corrections: requiescat in pace." Criminology 14: 439-448.
MARTINSON, R. and J. WILKS (1976) "Knowledge in criminal justice planning: a preliminary report." Report submitted to National Institute of Law Enforcement and Criminal Justice.
New York State Department of Correctional Services (1975) Annual Statistical Report.
——— (1973) Bureau of Research and Evaluation. Report.
RICHMOND, M. S. (1972) "Measuring the cost of correctional services." Crime and Delinquency 18: 243-252.
RODENSTINE, D. (1976) Speech delivered before Bar Association of City of New York, December 1.
WALLER, I. (1974) Men Released from Prison. Toronto: Univ. of Toronto Press.
Wisconsin Division of Corrections (1974) "Outcomes for one-year followup of 1972 adult insitution release cohort, by sex, type of release, and type of outcome." (mimeo)

Ex-Offenders

"These people need more than $25 gate money. They need jobs," says Fredric Penman, discussing ex-offenders.

Last year 238 former prisoners got jobs, entered training programs, or returned to school in the Salt Lake City area because of efforts by Mr. Penman's group—a coalition of local organizations engaged in various anti-crime activities.

EXPRES (Ex-Offender Program for Resources and Employment Services) actually begins in prison when

EXPRES workers assess a prisoner's skills, interests, and the things he or she will need to live in the community.

"We see that they have a place to live—find an apartment if necessary—and arrange for food stamps if they're eligible," says Mr. Penman.

EXPRES seeks out jobs from business and industry, particularly jobs with upward mobility.

Special cases are treated with special care. One man burned in a prison accident was self-conscious about his injuries and was ill at ease in job

interviews. Nobody would hire him. Finally, EXPRES helped him obtain cosmetic surgery on an injured, disfigured hand. Next time around, he was hired.

A Nevada parolee was worried about her sick daughter in Salt Lake City. EXPRES arranged for her parole to be transferred to the Utah capital.

A Houston, Texas, program works through a network of jail chaplains and area church congregations to provide emergency services and job referrals to county prison releasees.

In Search of Equity: The Oregon Parole Matrix

ELIZABETH L. TAYLOR

Member, Oregon Board of Parole

D URING the past several years, criminal justice agencies in general and parole boards in particular have increasingly become the subject of criticism. Popular scapegoats, parole boards have been disparaged by the public media, district attorneys, judges, politicians, citizens,·and prisoners. The Oregon Board of Parole is no exception.

In Oregon, criticism concentrated around what was perceived as arbitrary, capricious, and disparate decisionmaking by the parole board. The lack of published standards to guide decisionmaking, combined with the lack of written reasons for decisions, contributed to this perception. Additionally, the durational uncertainty of prison terms caused much unrest for both prisoners and prison administration alike. Prisoners often did not know until well into their terms how long they would actually have to serve. Prison administrators could not effectively manage bed space and transitional programs without the knowledge of whether prisoners were near release or not. These problems became increasingly critical as the institution population continued to grow.

These criticisms led to a movement for more durational certainty in prison terms with a variety of bills to attain this objective surfacing during the 1977 session of the Oregon Legislature. The final result, after months of consideration, was the passage of House Bill 2013. This bill, itself supported by the Board of Parole, was an aggressive response to the criticisms of Oregon's parole system. The purpose of this article is to analyze the movement for greater determinacy in Oregon and its impact upon parole practice. This experience may provide useful insights for other states facing similar concerns.

Historical Sketch of the Oregon Parole Board

The Oregon parole system dates back to 1905 when paroling authority was first given to the governor. As one might expect, Oregon governors had little time to thoroughly consider individual cases and paroles were seldom granted. In 1915, Oregon's first parole officer was appointed. Nevertheless, few changes occurred in the ensuing years. Not many paroles were granted and the supervision of parolees was practically nil.

In 1937 Governor Martin appointed a special commission on the Improvement of Oregon's Parole, Probation and Sentencing System. This commission was composed of three associate justices of the Oregon Supreme Court, two circuit judges, one district attorney, the chairman of the State Probation Commission, one member of the Board of Governors of the Oregon State Bar, and the chairman of the House and Senate Judiciary Committees of the 1937 State Legislature. Wayne Morse, then serving as administrative director of the United States Attorney General's Survey of Release Procedures and formerly dean of the University of Oregon Law School, chaired the commission. In December of 1938, the commission submitted its findings and recommendations to the governor. Two bills, drafted by the commission, were subsequently passed by the state legislature creating Oregon's first parole board, with three part-time members. Although the Board became full time in 1969 and its membership was expanded to five in 1975, its basic operations and procedures remained the same until 1977.

Traditionally, Oregon parole boards believed that the primary purpose of incarceration was rehabilitation, but that the rehabilitative process could not be completed while in prison. The Board's basic function, therefore, was to determine who was "ready" for release into the community on parole without unreasonable risk to the public at large. To accomplish this, officials believed that broad, unchecked discretion was necessary. This philosophy governed the Board's decisionmaking until 1975.

Political Environment

About 1975, vocal dissatisfaction on the part of Oregon's citizenry toward what it perceived as an overly lenient and unresponsive criminal justice system became apparent. Violence seemed to appear everywhere, especially on the front page of the daily newspapers. Disagreements between various components of the criminal justice system frequently were aired through the mass media. Elected officials, in particular, chose newspapers as their battleground.

At the same time, prison administrators found their populations growing substantially[1] and, as a result, began to experience serious management problems. Not only had the size of the population at criminal risk increased,[2] but expanded police efforts and more vocal public demands for stringent prosecution and punishment contributed to a rising rate of prison commitments. Furthermore, the median length of stay in state institutions had increased significantly.[3]

Consequently, the Board of Parole found itself in a dilemma. Overcrowding created prisoner unrest and an increase in incidents of misconduct. But the Board's practice at that time of routinely deferring release for prisoners reported by the prisons to have violated institutional rules resulted in still more overcrowding.

Additionally, prison officials were frustrated by the unpredictability of release decisions. Lack of firm release dates created a barrier to rational planning for programming and for population management. Prisoners, moreover, found uncertain release dates and the absence of articulated reasons for parole decisions to be anxiety-inducing and seemingly irrational.

Oregon judges were also expressing concern and discomfort with the parole process. Functionally, the parole board was, in many respects, the sentencing agency for all felons committed to prison, because it had control (within the judicially imposed maximum sentence, less good time) over the duration of the prisoner's term and of the period of parole supervision. Many of the judges were frustrated by the lack of explicit criteria in parole decisionmaking, and there seemed no way for them to participate or intervene in the process. As a result, the judiciary

began exerting pressure on the legislature to amend the statutes to permit greater judicial intervention. Some supported mandatory minimum sentences with the total elimination of parole. Most, however, favored retaining the parole board with some additional judicial control and participation in the setting of prison terms.

Moreover, the parole board's visibility made it a target for general frustration with the criminal justice system. Since prosecutors, courts, and legislators had no control over the release of inmates, anything that went wrong was obviously the fault of the parole board, which had been either too harsh or too lenient. Civil libertarians saw the Board's practices as arbitrary, capricious, biased, and too punitive, while law enforcement personnel felt the Board lacked accountability to the public and was too lenient. The media was always quick to cover a sensational story regarding a parolee who had committed a new crime or the plight of an inmate whom the Board had not released. As the attacks on its use of discretion mounted, the Board became more cautious and often deferred release because the inmate was "not ready." Criticism, however, continued to increase.

The public was incensed by incidents resulting from the release of two inmates. Both were convicted murderers: one had been released by the institution administration on a social pass; the other had been paroled by the Board. Shortly after release, both men murdered again. Stiffer penalties were demanded; petitions to reinstate the death penalty were circulated; and proposals for mandatory sentences began to surface.

A number of groups, including the Governor's Task Force on Corrections (appointed by Governor Bob Straub to design a 15-year master plan for corrections in Oregon), a research team from the *Oregon Law Review* (an American Bar Association funded project), and the Interim Joint Judiciary Committee of the Oregon legislature initiated studies of the correctional system. Interestingly, the findings of these groups differed significantly from those embraced by the public. These groups concluded that building a large, new prison would be an expensive, short-lived and unacceptable solution. Instead, they looked to community corrections programs and to reform of policies and practices of the institutions and the parole board. Basically, they suggested that inmates committed for less serious crimes be incarcerated for shorter, more certain terms. Recommendations aimed at the parole board included proposed requirements that the basis for parole decisionmaking be explicit; that the board develop

---

[1] In 1973, the average daily population in Oregon prisons was 1781. In 1975 this figure was 2254. Personal communication with Neil Chambers, Executive Assistant to Administrator of Corrections Division, November 6, 1978.

[2] I.e., population between the ages of 15 and 29. See Governor's Task Force on Corrections, *Oregon Corrections Master Plan*, (December, 1976), p. 9.

[3] In 1973, the median time served prior to release was 16.8 months. By 1975, it had increased to 25.2 months.

guidelines articulating the weight given to specific factors considered and that these guidelines be made available to prisoners and to the public; and that the uncertainty of terms be reduced.

During this period, the Board itself was undergoing structural and philosophical changes. Between 1974 and 1975 two members left the Board and, consequently, with the statutory increase from a three to five-member board, four members were appointed. The change in membership stimulated an atmosphere for innovation. New members felt uncomfortable having unguided discretion and far-reaching responsibility without rules and guidelines for decisionmaking. Consequently, the Board began to examine its decisionmaking process. Members scrutinized the actions of previous Oregon boards, studied the policies and practices of other paroling jurisdictions, and reviewed recent texts by academicians involved in the study of criminal justice. From this, the Board developed and began to use a "guideline" model for decisionmaking. This model was the prototype of the rules and guidelines adopted by the Board under the State Administrative Procedures Act in January 1977.

House Bill 2013

During the 1977 legislative session, the Oregon legislature was deluged by proposals for mandatory sentences. The public was continuing to demand stiffer penalties with less emphasis on rehabilitative programming. At the same time, Oregon judges were exerting substantial pressure on the legislature to strengthen their role in the prison term decision.

Rather than eliminate the parole release authority, as some had suggested, the legislature chose to adopt a model supported by the parole board itself. Through its development and adoption of explicit rules based on a "just deserts" principle, the Oregon Board had already structured its own discretion. The House Judiciary Committee, upon consideration of testimony and proposals by, among others, Peter Hoffman of the U.S. Parole Commission, Andrew von Hirsch of Rutgers University, and Ira Blalock, chairperson of the Oregon Board of Parole, endorsed House Bill 2013. The bill was passed by the 1977 legislature and was enacted into law.[4]

As enacted, HB 2013 required the Oregon Board of Parole to operate under what is primarily a "just deserts" model. In doing this, the bill required the parole board to structure and limit its discretionary powers through promulgation of published rules. Increased due process was also mandated.

Specifically, the new law required the parole board to establish a matrix of ranges for terms of imprisonment to be served for felony offenses prior to release on parole based on offense and offender characteristics.[5] These ranges must be designed to achieve the primary objective of punishment commensurate with the perceived seriousness of the prisoner's criminal conduct. That is, ranges are to give primary weight to the seriousness of the present offense[6] and the criminal history of the prisoner. To the extent not inconsistent with this primary goal, the deterrence of criminal conduct and the protection of the public from further crimes by the prisoner were additional objectives.

Thus, the Oregon legislation calls for a "modified just deserts" rationale, which provides that the Board consider not only the seriousness of the offense but also the secondary objectives of deterrence and incapacitation. This allows the Board some leeway to consider the risk of recidivism. Nonetheless, "just deserts" is the limiting principle—prediction, incapacitation, and deterrence may only be considered to the extent that punishment imposed is justly deserved given the seriousness of the criminal conduct. The Board was also required to adopt rules regulating variations from the ranges to be applied when aggravating or mitigating circumstances exist.

In addition, the Board was required to conduct its hearings to determine the duration of imprisonment within the first 6 months of the prisoner's incarceration. Thus, each prisoner, as well as the administration, would know near the beginning of his or her imprisonment the probable duration of confinement prior to release on parole or, in rare cases, release upon expiration of sentence.

Almost all prisoners in Oregon now are released via parole. Under exceptional circumstances, however, the parole board may deny parole, in which case the prisoner is released by expiration of sentence.[7]

Once a parole release date has been set, release can be postponed beyond the scheduled date only if: (1) the Board, after a hearing, determines that the prisoner has engaged in serious miscon-

[4] Oregon Revised Statutes, Chapter 144, as amended 1977.
[5] The ranges, of course, may not exceed the maximum sentence prescribed by Oregon statute.
[6] The harm done or risked by the commission of the offense, as well as the culpability of the offender, defines its seriousness.
[7] These exceptional circumstances are limited to: (a) a prisoner sentenced for a particularly violent or otherwise dangerous offense; (b) whose present offense was preceded by two or more Class A or B felonies (the most serious felonies under Oregon law); or (c) whose record includes a psychiatric or psychological diagnosis of severe emotional disturbance. The Board is required to develop specific rules governing such cases.

duct during his confinement (rules must define serious misconduct and specify allowable periods of postponement), (2) psychiatric or psychological diagnosis of present severe emotional disturbance has been made, or (3) the prisoner's parole plan is inadequate under the Board rules specifying the elements of an adequate parole plan. The Board may postpone release for up to 90 days for an unacceptable parole plan. Findings and written reasons must be provided when release is deferred.

Through HB 2013, the Oregon legislature has specifically structured the parole board's discretion in determining the duration of imprisonment and the granting of parole release through its requirement for explicit guidelines. In addition to reducing the disparities through the use of explicit criteria, the legislation also increases due process protections afforded prisoners by providing for written notice of hearings, access to information relied upon, and the requirement of written reasons for parole decisions.

The legislation has also enhanced cooperation among the various components of the criminal justice system. Criteria for parole decisionmaking is now available to law enforcement agencies, corrections agencies, and the judiciary. Of great significance is the Advisory Commission on Prison Terms and Parole Standards established by the legislation. This Commission is composed of the five parole board members, five circuit court judges appointed by the Chief Justice of the Oregon Supreme Court, and the legal counsel to the governor, who serves as an ex-officio member voting only to break ties. The Administrator of the Corrections Division acts as an advisor to the Commission. All judicial commission members serve staggered 4-year terms. The purpose of the Advisory Commission is to propose to the Board rules to be adopted in the establishment of the ranges for prison terms, as well as the rules regulating variations from the ranges when aggravating or mitigating circumstances exist.[8] Although advisory in nature, the Commission wields great strength due to the communication and cooperation it creates between the judiciary and the parole board. The Commission combines the sentencing expertise and sensitivity to the public of the judiciary with the experience of the parole board in the development and application of explicit guidelines to all individual cases under the jurisdiction of state institutions. The involvement of the Administrator of Corrections has made the

Commission aware of problems and needs of the institutions and correctional programs and how they may be affected. The judiciary's involvement in the policy and rule making of the parole board has increased confidence in those guidelines systemwide.

In addition to their involvement in the Advisory Commission, the judiciary has been given further opportunities for input into the parole release decision by HB 2013. The judiciary, at the time of sentencing, is provided a presentence report that includes the same information which will be used by the parole board in establishing a release date. The judge's sentence and reasons for its imposition then become the framework within which the prison term will be defined. The legislation also allows the judge to impose a minimum term of up to one-half of the executed sentence which must be served prior to parole release. The parole board, however, may override such a sentence upon affirmative vote of at least four members of the Board. In addition, when a judge imposes two or more consecutive sentences, the Board must sum the ranges established for the offense when determining the prison terms for those prisoners, subject to rules governing aggravation or mitigation.

Administrative Rules and Guidelines

By January 1977 the parole board had already, on its own initiative, filed its rules under the State Administrative Procedures Act. During the year after the legislation became effective, the Advisory Commission on Prison Terms and Parole Standards met three times to review the Board's existing rules and guidelines and to propose revisions to the Board. The Board accepted the recommended changes and filed them for public comment with the Secretary of State in March 1978. During the next two months, public hearings were held to take testimony from interested persons in a variety of locations around the state, including within the prisons.

The Board's administrative rules cover 110 pages, including six exhibits. The heart of those rules is the "matrix" (Exhibit 1), which indicates the ranges of time to be served in light of the seriousness of the crime and the prisoner's criminal history and perceived risk of repetition. All felonies are categorized within seven severity ratings (Exhibit 2). The harm done or risked by the commission of the offense was considered in determining the "severity rating" of each crime. Twenty-one crimes have been further "subcategorized" based upon the specific circumstances surrounding the particular episode.

---

[8] The Commission is advisory and cannot set standards due to the separation-of-powers provision of the Oregon Constitution.

5. PUNISHMENT AND CORRECTIONS

The prisoner's prior criminal history is assessed through the use of a "criminal history/risk assessment" scale (Exhibit 3). The instrument weighs prior convictions; prior incarcerations; age at the time of first incarceration; prior escapes and failures on probation and parole; alcohol or heroin abuse problems; and a 5-year conviction-free period in the community.

The rules governing parole board decisionmaking and actions require the Board to specifically record how it has assessed the guidelines in each prisoner's case and the specific reasons for any departure therefrom. If a prisoner is dissatisfied with a decision of the Board, internal administrative review by the chairperson and state judicial review can be sought.[9]

The structuring of the parole board's discretion through explicit rules and guidelines has prompted the Corrections Division to do likewise. The Division has developed rules for determining custody status of prisoners and classifications for types of supervision of parole and probation cases using the parole board guidelines as a base. In addition, the parole board and Corrections Division have developed joint rules governing sanctions for serious misconduct by prisoners and defining specific procedures. There is a general movement within the entire corrections system in Oregon to structure broad discretion by explicit rules and guidelines, stimulated by the Board's efforts in this area. The development of these rules has increased cooperation and coordination between the various parts of the system. In addition, several Oregon judges have begun to utilize a sentencing matrix based primarily on the Board's matrix to assist in the determination of appropriate sentence length.

Policy in Practice

Given the present state of corrections, HB 2013 seems to be the best available option if justice and fairness are to be sought. The decision to make such a major policy change concerning rehabilitation was not an easy one. The Board sympathizes with the views of Willard Gaylin and Dave Pathman in their introduction to *Doing Justice:*

> It is not easy to abandon the rehabilitative model, for it was a scheme born to optimism and faith, and humanism. It viewed the evils in man as essentially correctable, and only partially the responsibility of the individual . . . The simple fact is that the experiment

has not worked out. Despite every effort and every attempt, correctional treatment programs have failed. The supporters of rehabilitation will say, and perhaps rightly so, that it was never really given a complete chance, that it was only accepted in theory, while in practice the system insisted on maintaining punitive practices. On the other hand, the question remains whether one can reasonably continue to expect anything different given the extended trial that rehabilitation has had.[10]

But for all of its altruistic intentions, the rehabilitative model has in many ways been a very punitive one. Indeterminacy and unfettered discretion were frequent byproducts of that system. Injustices can be easily cloaked beneath the helpful hand of rehabilitation. As McMurphy fatally discovered in Ken Kesey's *One Flew Over the Cuckoo's Nest,* where a prisoner traded a determinate jail sentence for an indeterminate mental hospital sentence, it is possible literally to be "treated" (rehabilitated) to death.[11]

By adopting the "just deserts" model, Oregon has announced that the commission of certain acts is wrong and demands punishment. Furthermore, the state has admitted that prisons actually punish. More importantly, though, the state has limited the degree of punishment depending upon the seriousness of particular crimes and has emphasized fairness. At the very least, an attempt is being made to prevent further injustices and inequities in the system.

Nevertheless, the new legislation and administrative rules of the parole board, although innovative, are not welcomed by all. A significant number of inmates and prison reform groups are extremely disturbed by the use of the word "punishment" and the minimization of rehabilitative considerations under the new system of "just deserts." Some say it is in violation of the Oregon State Constitution, which calls for "reformation," not "vindictive justice." In particular, inmates serving long prison terms feel all hope of release has been taken away. Under the present rules, inmates feel there is no way they can earn early release even if treatment programs are successfully completed. Prison reform and prisoner advocate groups feel it is cruel to remove all hope and incentive for rehabilitation and treatment. Prison officials have expressed concern that they will be unable to coerce prisoners into behaving appropriately absent traditional rewards and that this may cause management problems in the future. The parole board has recently attempted to respond to these concerns by establishing rules provided for periodic reviews to consider certain

---

[9] Although the extent of judicial review by the State Court of Appeals has not yet been determined, a case is presently pending which is expected to resolve this question. *Harris v. Board of Parole,* Oregon Court of Appeals No. 11130. Other judicial recourse (for example, habeas corpus or mandamus) is also available.

[10] *Doing Justice,* A. von Hirsch, New York: Hill and Wang, 1976, pp. xxxvii-xxxviii.

[11] Ironically, the Oregon Board of Parole now occupies one of the buildings, formerly part of Oregon State Hospital, in which the movie version of "Cuckoo's Nest" was filmed.

exceptional circumstances which may warrant modification of the originally established parole date.

By publishing explicit rules, the parole board has made it possible for its critics to be specific. Criticism can now be focused and therefore constructive. The rules have tremendously improved the internal operations of the Board. They offer a reference point for settling disagreements among Board members. This has significantly increased equity in decisions. Additionally, the plea bargaining process is made more fair due to the knowledge on the part of the defendant of the probable duration of his or her prospective incarceration.

Standards for parole decisionmaking have improved the Board's relationship with the Corrections Division and its institutions. Program and custody planning can now take place early in an inmate's term. Prison officials can more effectively manage bed space and program utilization, being assured that they know when release will occur. Rules governing their own decisionmaking process can now be developed and implemented. Inmate anxiety caused by uncertainty has been reduced. Inmates now know early in their terms when they will be released if no serious misconduct occurs.

Establishment of the Advisory Commission on Prison Terms and Parole Standards has proven a highly successful endeavor. It taps the input and output expertise of the Oregon criminal justice system, while preserving the independence of both the judiciary and the parole board. It strengthens the system by its very existence through communication, coordination, compromise and understanding.

The durational prison term decision in Oregon is delegated to a small specialized body: the parole board. This specialization allows for ongoing consultation and sharing of views, as well as a view of the full spectrum of cases committed to prison. This, combined with use of the guidelines matrix, reduces unwarranted disparity in prison terms, as well as uncertainty on the part of both the prisoner and the system. Nevertheless, the ability to respond to significant changes in circumstances is retained.

Oregon, by embracing the "just deserts" model, has admitted that for a variety of reasons—lack of resources, lack of sufficient knowledge, and so on—the "coercive rehabilitation model" in prisons has failed.[12] And, although HB 2013 by no means presumes to provide the total solution, its supporters believe the new system is a step in the right direction. Through further research and study, the Oregon Board of Parole hopes to gain new insights in the development of a truly just and humanistic model for parole decisionmaking in Oregon.

[12] This does not mean that rehabilitative programs in prison are to be diminished. It does mean that program participation will be made more voluntary by being substantially detached from the parole release process.

EXHIBIT 1.—*Total Time to be Served**
CRIMINAL HISTORY/RISK ASSESSMENT SCORE

	11-9 Excellent	8-6 Good	5-3 Fair	2-0 Poor
OFFENSE SEVERITY RATING				
		(All ranges in Categories 1-6 shown in months)		
Category 1	≦ 6	≦ 6	6-12 (4-8)[1]	12-22 (8-18)
Category 2	≦ 6	6-10 (4-8)	10-18 (8-14)	18-28 (14-24)
Category 3	6-10 (4-8)	10-16 (8-12)	16-24 (12-20)	24-36 (20-32)
Category 4	10-16 (8-12)	16-22 (12-18)	22-30 (16-24)	30-48 (24-42)
Category 5	18-24 (12-20)	24-30 (20-26)	30-48 (26-40)	48-72 (40-62)
Category 6	36-48	48-60	60-86	86-144
Category 7				
Subcategory 2	8-10 yrs	10-13 yrs	13-16 yrs	16-20 yrs[2]
Subcategory 1	10-14 yrs	14-19 yrs	19-24 yrs	24-Life

1. Months in parentheses represent ranges for youthful offenders (21 or younger at time of conviction).
2. See Exhibit 2 for subcategory explanation.
* From Oregon Administrative Rules, 254-30-032.

EXHIBIT 2.—*Offense Severity Scale**

OFFENSE	RATING
MURDER	
Subcategory 1 (stranger to stranger, extreme cruelty, prior conviction for murder or manslaughter, significant planning/preparation)	7
Subcategory 2 (all other cases)	7
TREASON	7
MANSLAUGHTER I	6
KIDNAPPING I	6
RAPE I	
Subcategory 1 (stranger to stranger, aggravated custodial interference, breaking/entering, weapon, serious physical/emotional harm, female victim under 12 years old)	6
Subcategory 2 (all other cases)	5
SODOMY I	
Subcategory 1 (same as Subcategory 1—Rape 1)	6
Subcategory 2 (same as Subcategory 2—Rape 1)	5
ROBBERY I	
Subcategory 1 (discharge of firearm/actual use of weapon; explicit threats by word or gesture, of death or serious bodily harm; serious injury)	6
Subcategory 2 (all cases except those described in Subcategory 1)	5

5. PUNISHMENT AND CORRECTIONS

ASSAULT I
Subcategory 1 (all cases except those described in Subcategory 2) 6
Subcategory 2 (cases in which victim(s) provoked the crime to substantial degree, or evidence that misconduct of victim contributed substantially to criminal episode) 5

ARSON I
Subcategory 1 (knowing premises were occupied at time of act, actual serious injury) 6
Subcategory 2 (all other cases) 5

ESCAPE I 5

BURGLARY I
Subcategory 1 (involves actually or regularly occupied building where used or threatened to use dangerous weapon and caused or threatened physical injury) 5
Subcategory 2 (involves a non-dwelling/value of goods taken is over $5,000 or involves a residence or temporary residence except cases described in Subcategory 3) 4
Subcategory 3 (all other cases involving a non-dwelling or a residence or temporary residence where defendant is not armed, no extensive property damage and value of goods taken was below $1,000) 3

ASSAULT II 4
KIDNAPPING II 4
RAPE II (non-forcible intercourse involving incapacitated female or female under 14)
Subcategory 1 (all cases except those fitting Subcategory 2) 4
Subcategory 2 (not both under 16 and incapacitated; no coercion or undue influence; and no position of trust (e.g., counselor, doctor) 3

SODOMY II 4
COMPELLING PROSTITUTION 4
ROBBERY II 4
CRIMINAL ACTIVITY IN DRUGS (involving minors)
Subcategory 1 (furnishing heroin or other opiates; or sale for profit of any drug) 4
Subcategory 2 (furnishing any drug other than heroin, opiates or less than one ounce of marihuana) 3
Subcategory 3 (furnishing less than one ounce of marihuana) 2

CRIMINAL ACTIVITY IN DRUGS (other)
Subcategory 1 (manufacture, cultivation or sale for profit, or possession with intent to sell for profit of any heroin or opiate derivative) 3
Subcategory 2 ([same as above] of any other drug) 2
Subcategory 3 (manufacture for own use or possession for own use) 1

NOTE: Possession of less than one ounce of marihuana is not a crime

COERCION; THEFT BY EXTORTION
Subcategory 1 (threat of serious bodily harm or death) 4
Subcategory 2 (all others) 3

MANSLAUGHTER II 3
BRIBE GIVING 3
BRIBE RECEIVING 3
SEXUAL ABUSE I 3
RIOT 3
BURGLARY II
Subcategory 1 (over $5,000 loss) 3
Subcategory 2 ($1,000 to $5,000 loss) 2
Subcategory 3 (less than $1,000 loss) 1

THEFT I, Theft of Services; Theft by Deception; Forgery I
Subcategory 1 (theft or receiving of over $5,000) 3
Subcategory 2 (theft or receiving of $1,000 to $5,000; of a firearm or explosive; of a livestock animal; or theft during a riot or catastrophe) 2
Subcategory 3 (theft under $1,000 except those included in Subcategory 2) 1

PERJURY 2

ESCAPE II
Subcategory 1 (all cases of escape except those fitting Subcategory 2) 2
Subcategory 2 (escape from minimum custody for no more than 30 days) 1

FAILURE TO APPEAR I 2
BRIBING A WITNESS 2
WITNESS RECEIVING BRIBE 2
CRIMINALLY NEGLIGENT HOMICIDE 2
CRIMINAL MISTREATMENT 2
CUSTODIAL INTERFERENCE 2
RAPE III 2
SODOMY III 2
ABANDON CHILD 2
THEFT BY RECEIVING 2
UNATHORIZED USE OF A MOTOR VEHICLE
Subcategory 1 (injury to others or loss, destruction or severe damage to vehicle or property) 2
Subcategory 2 (other) 1

ARSON II 2
ROBBERY III 2
ASSAULT III 2
SPORTS BRIBERY 2
SPORTS BRIBERY RECEIVING 2
EX-CONVICT IN POSSESSION 2
SALE RELATED (firearms) 2
CARRYING A WEAPON WITH INTENT TO USE 2
PROMOTING PROSTITUTION 2
OBTAINING DRUGS UNLAWFULLY 2
POACHING
Subcategory 1 (poaching of game valued over $3,000 or commercial operation) 2
Subcategory 2 (other) 1

SUPPLYING CONTRABAND 1
HINDERING PROSECUTION 1
BIGAMY 1
INCEST 1
CRIMINAL NONSUPPORT 1
THEFT: Lost, Mislaid 1
CRIMINAL MISCHIEF I 1
FORGED INSTRUMENT 1
FORGERY DEVICE 1
FRAUDULENT USE OF A CREDIT CARD 1

FRAUDULENT COMMUNICATION DEVICE 1
PROMOTING GAMBLING 1
POSSESSION OF GAMBLING RECORDS I 1
TAMPERING WITH DRUG RECORDS 1
WELFARE FRAUD 1
FELONY TRAFFIC 1
INTERCEPTION OF COMMUNICATION 1

* From Oregon Administrative Rules, 254-30-030

218

EXHIBIT 3.—*Criminal History/Risk Assessment Score**

ITEM	SCORE

(A) No prior felony or misdemeanor convictions as an adult or juvenile=3
One prior conviction=2
Two or three prior convictions=1
Four or more prior convictions=0   ____

(B) No prior incarcerations (i.e., executed sentences of 90 days or more) as an adult or juvenile=2
One or two prior incarcerations=1
Three or more prior incarcerations=0   ____

(C) Age at first commitment of 90 days or more
26 or older=2
19 thru 25=1
18 or younger=0   ____

(D) Never escaped, failed parole or probation=2
One incident of the above=1
Any two or more incidents of the above=0

(E) Has no admitted or documented heroin or opiate derivative abuse problem, or has no admitted or documented alcohol problem=1
One or more of the above=0   ____

(F) Verified period of 5 years conviction free in the community prior to present offense=1
Otherwise=0   ____

TOTAL HISTORY/RISK ASSESSMENT SCORE: ____

(1) Do not count convictions over 20 years old, convictions that have been pardoned, or juvenile or adult "status offenses" (runaway, truancy, incorrigibility, drunk in public).

(2) If no prior commitment, use age at present conviction.

(3) Count probation failure only if it resulted from new crime, count any parole failure.

* From Oregon Administrative Rules 30-031

Co Corrections

The idea of putting men and women together

in the same prison has been considered a potent prescription for trouble— but in a few places, it has begun to work.

David C. Anderson

SUE and Buster are about as compatible as oil and water. She is well schooled, born to affluence — a woman with class. He is a small-time hoodlum who survived to his mid-thirties on street smarts and a sixth-grade education. Most of her adult life has been spent involved with marriage, children and reputable jobs in an insurance agency and a political campaign. His has been spent in crime.

But Sue and Buster are deeply in love. "We have a very acute sensitivity to each other," says Sue. "She's one of the better things that ever happened to me," says Buster. They plan to get married as soon as their circumstances permit.

●

"I'm 37," says Webster, "and I haven't ever met a better woman" than Claudine. They're friends, he says — and a little more than friends. "We do help each other." As far as Claudine is concerned, that's a powerful understatement. She would like to marry Webster. But he is wary. His divorce a few years ago was too painful. He's not about to risk that again. "But we will always be friends," he declares, as if that could end the matter.

●

At first it was more like father and daughter with Stan and Shirley. She was in her early 20's, coming off a heavy drug habit. He was on the verge of middle age, coping with a heart condition. But Stan took an interest in the confused young woman who seemed to need him so much. He helped her confront her problems, sort out her values, find some direction. "I straightened her out," Stan says. "I'm proud of that." And Shirley was passionately grateful. She tagged around after Stan. She did little favors for him — washing his clothes, clipping his nails. Now, Stan admits, their friendship "has become romantic." But he knows the involvement doesn't have a future. For Stan is married.

There are enough stories to keep Ann Landers in business for years, and no two are ever alike. But the characters do have something in common: All are doing time together in federal prisons that house both male and female inmates. As such, all are participants in a bold and relatively unpublicized experiment known as "co-corrections." Since the federal Bureau of Prisons began housing men and women together in 1971, a dozen states have followed suit. Some have cancelled the experiment after a short time; but the program has worked well enough in the federal and state prisons where it still operates that co-corrections promises to become a permanent part of the American corrections scene.

In the United States, the assumption has always been that the absence of the opposite sex is one of the punitive aspects of a term in prison. While conjugal visiting programs have been started in three states, they are by no means a standard feature of American prison life, and the idea of putting men and women together in the same facility has been regarded as a potent prescription for trouble. In the past few years, however, a combination of practical need and theoretical innovation has led some prison officials to change their minds.

The first modern effort to open an adult prison to house men and women together began with the decision of the federal Bureau of Prisons to convert a public health service hospital in Fort Worth, Texas, to a minimum security facility. One of the bureau's aims was to use the old "narcotics farm," with its Spanish colonial buildings, campus-like atmosphere and elaborate medical facilities, as a place to deal with prisoners with special needs: alcoholics and drug abusers, older prisoners with chronic health problems — and perhaps women, who were then over-populating the federal women's facilities at Alderson, West Virginia, and Terminal Island, California.

In the planning stage, the notion of women at Fort Worth remained something of an after-thought. There was some feeling that female inmates would have to be chosen carefully to inaugurate the program. But "none of us had much idea of what we were talking about when we talked about co-corrections," recalls Bud Grossman, now warden at Terminal Island, who served as assistant warden at Fort Worth when the bureau converted it to a prison.

But events forced co-corrections upon the bureau before the planners could catch up with it. In September, 1971, in the aftermath of the nationally publicized riot at New York's Attica Correctional Facility, inmates rioted at Alderson, and the bureau decided to transfer 45 of the ringleaders and disciplinary cases to preserve peace at the West Virginia women's facility. But where could they go? For a few weeks they stayed at the Federal Correctional Institution at Seagoville, Texas. But then the bureau decided to make them the first women inmates at Fort Worth, which was due to open as a prison that November. It all began, remarks bureau Director of Research Howard Kitchener, because "we needed a place to put this busload of tough ladies from Alderson."

There were some who believed that the decision was a horrible mistake. "The anger of the women as they left the buses transporting them from Seagoville to Fort Worth startled both the staff and the male inmates," according to a report on co-corrections by Koba Associates and funded by the federal Law Enforcement Assistance Administration, and "for a brief period the administration questioned the feasibility of integration."

The staff at Fort Worth, however, did not consist of tough bureaucrats and hardened guards interested primarily in discipline and security. Most in those early days were the same people who had been running the old narcotics hospital, and they were naturally inclined to view the new inmates as patients as well as prisoners. They were led by Charles Campbell, remembered as a "charismatic" administrator with deep commitment to the idea of "mutuality" — inmates and staff working together in a spirit of mutual concern and support. These attitudes, and, perhaps, as time went on, the awareness of the inmates themselves that the bureau had handed them a rare opportunity, led to an era that some recall as "times of peace and love." The inmates were forbidden to have sex, but they were permitted to walk together in the yard, eat meals together, go to class together and participate in various recreational events.

The effects were dramatic. Instead of increasing violence, co-corrections seemed to diminish it. Inmates began to take more pride in their appearance. Permitted to wear their own clothes rather than uniforms, Fort Worth inmates strolling the yard in the evening became some of the best turned-out prisoners anywhere. Predatory homosexuality did not arise among inmates, and levels of less aggressive homosexuality remained much lower than at single-sex institutions. And predictions of rampant sex between men and women simply did not materialize.

As word of the events at Fort Worth spread, other corrections officials began to consider co-corrections as a realistic possibility, especially when inmate population pressures offered the opportunity. In March, 1973, for example, the Massachusetts Correctional Institution at Framingham became a coed prison, one of the first state facilities to do so. The hundred-year-old women's facility was below half its capacity, while the state's male institutions were filled to overflowing. So corrections officials decided to fill up the empty beds at Framingham with men. There were no disasters there, either, and before

---

At Fort Worth, co-corrections began because 'We needed a place to put this busload of tough ladies from Alderson."

---

long, prison officials in Illinois, New Jersey, Delaware, Minnesota, Wisconsin, Connecticut, Missouri, Vermont, Maine, Idaho, Tennessee and Indiana were planning or implementing co-correctional programs.

Meanwhile, the Bureau of Prisons proceeded in 1974 to convert another public health service hospital to a coed prison in Lexington, Kentucky, to open a new coed prison at Pleasanton, California, and in 1975 to turn the complex of male and female facilities at Terminal Island into a single, integrated co-correctional unit. At one point last year, according to the Koba report, 997 females and 2,077 males were incarcerated in

coed federal prisons. They constituted 58.1 percent of the female and 7.5 percent of the male federal prisoners. The study also calculated that 1,232 females and 1,277 males were in state coed prisons, constituting 9.7 percent of female and .53 percent of male state prisoners.

Not all of the experiments in co-corrections have been successful or permanent. In April of last year, for example, co-corrections began at the Memphis Correctional Center in Tennessee, but it was cancelled after six months. "We started it as a voluntary thing," explains Warden Mark Luttrell, "with places for about 40 women in our men's facility. But only about 25 women wanted to come." The women were incarcerated at the Tennessee Prison for Women in Nashville; only those whose homes were in the western part of the state were interested in making the transfer to Memphis.

That left Warden Luttrell with a space problem. "I've got six units with room for about 65 in each. Here was one unit with 25 women and about 40 empty beds. Meanwhile, the men's sections began to get overcrowded. I had men sleeping on the floor in some units. It was hard to justify the program." There were other problems, too, the warden said. The prison's male population was about 325 during the experiment; the lopsided ratio of men to women made it hard to organize social activities. And the Memphis staff had never worked in a female institution. "They didn't do the job they should have done," the warden admits.

The Correctional Institution for Women in Clinton, New Jersey, began co-corrections in 1974 with a policy of admitting men aged 55 or older. That year, 39 men were admitted and the total population stood at about 325. But by 1977, the age restriction had been abandoned for all practical purposes, and the population of 305 included 70 men of all ages. By that time, however, co-corrections had led to problems — "mainly problems with sex" among the inmates, according to S. Phil Dwyer, the current superintendent. "Co-corrections really put a lot of pressure on the men. The women would flirt with them. We had a few pregnancies." Now, says Dwyer, Clinton has gone back to admitting only older men. "I believe men 50 or older are better able to handle co-corrections," Dwyer says. "I'm not saying that they don't have the same urges as the younger fellows, but they'll tend to stop and think before they do something irrational." The prison's current population stands at about 235, including 40 men.

Late last year, Fort Worth and Lexington came alive with rumors that the federal co-corrections program was in deep trouble after the Bureau of Prisons terminated co-corrections at its two California facilities. Bureau officials now explain that that decision had mainly to do with population shifts. Co-corrections was working well at Pleasanton, explains Bud Grossman, but it never really caught on at Terminal Island, largely because the staff had been so used to keeping the

men and women apart over the years that many were simply unable to adjust to the new policy. So when the problem of overcrowding became severe on the West Coast, the bureau decided to make maximum use of its space at Terminal Island by turning it into an all-male institution and putting two men in each room that had been occupied by a single woman. That forced the abandonment of co-corrections at Pleasanton because there was nowhere else to put the women who had been at Terminal Island.

Last spring, the Bureau of Prisons convened a conference of its officials at Lexington to consider the problems of the female offender, and co-corrections became a major topic of discussion. Wardens of co-correctional institutions spoke in favor of the practice, as did a random selection of Lexington inmates. In the end, according to a summary of the conference distributed by the bureau, federal prison Director Norman Carlson said that he had "no intention to phase out co-corrections."

In an interview more recently, Carlson reiterated his qualified support for the concept. "It's not a panacea; it's not for all inmates in all institutions, but I believe there is a place for co-corrections in the federal system." A bureau task force is currently at work to plan for the future expansion of co-corrections in federal prisons.

With that kind of endorsement from the boss, few bureau officials are today willing to go on the record with critical comments about co-corrections, but there is no question that the policy remains the subject of some controversy within the bureau. "I'm not sure co-corrections is harmful," says one dubious middle level official, "but I have a hard time saying it's all that good. I don't know if there really is therapeutic value to having men and women together. When I went down to Fort Worth, I was disturbed by what I saw. I thought there were problems of control, problems of sanitation, problems of attitude with inmates and staff. The whole thing just didn't seem to gear up right. I like a prison that runs well — where everybody knows what they should do, everybody knows where it's at."

Whatever the misgivings, the bureau's decisions about co-corrections in the future will be governed by practicalities as much as by theory. "Co-corrections really comes down to the problem of small numbers," bureau executive John Minor explained. The bureau believes that the optimum prison population is 500 — small enough to manage on a relatively personal basis, but large enough to support substantial programming. But the bureau also believes that inmates should be incarcerated as close to their home communities as possible.

"Now we have about 1,500 female offenders," Minor went on. "That's enough for only three single sex institutions. But if we did that with them, many would have to be far from home. So co-corrections is a solution." Furthermore, the bureau projects an increase in the female population in the next few

Photos by Tony O'Brien

Inmates, male and female, lounge on the yard at
Fort Worth (top) and go to classes (bottom).

years, according to Ray Gerard, the bureau's assistant director for correctional programs. "We've got a women's facility in the East [Alderson] and one in the West [Pleasanton], but in the Midwest, our major expansion to accommodate females will be in the area of co-corrections."

Whatever the bureau's goals in terms of population, it is not possible to say that they are precisely realized at Fort Worth and Lexington. Fort Worth's population now stands at about 630, divided nearly equally between men and women. That represents rapid growth for women, since in the prison's first year of operation, total population was between 300 and 400, including only 45 women. As recently as three years ago, the female population was only 40, though total population had risen to 550. At Lexington, current population is about 1,100, divided about 60-40, men to women. In its first year of operation, from 1974 to 1975, Lexington had a population of 566, divided 75-25, men to women.

An inmate used to conditions at single-sex, maximum-security prisons may be profoundly disconcerted by his first glimpse of the yards at Fort Worth or Lexington, especially if he arrives during lunch or late in the afternoon. The inmates appear relaxed and even cheerful strolling hand in hand, arm in arm, bantering with each other or with the few visible guards, who carry only walkie-talkies. On hot, sunny days, couples converse quietly on benches in the shade of leafy trees or spread blankets on the grass and lie down together with soft drinks and portable radios. Eye-catching female inmates wander about in brief cut-off shorts; at Fort Worth, some even don scanty bathing suits and stretch out on the lawn in front of a women's unit building to deepen their rich suntans.

"When I got out of the [U.S.] marshall's van and saw all the males and females on the compound, I was shocked," recalled a Fort Worth inmate named Jim, who had been transferred from a tougher federal prison to serve out the last part of a sentence for armed bank robbery. "It took me 30 days just to adjust to the presence of women and another 30 to figure out how to deal with it."

But bureau officials like to emphasize that the presence of women is only one element in a larger picture. The populations of the two co-correctional facilities are diversified in many ways in addition to sex. They house drug addicts, alcoholics, the chronically ill and the aging. They take in a wide spectrum of white-collar criminals — the welfare cheat does his time alongside the millionaire stock manipulator or embezzler.

Furthermore, most of the inmates are in prison for relatively short periods — the average stay is about 15 months — and roughly half have transferred in from single-sex institutions, rather than being referred directly from the courts. The prisons emphasize preparation for release, and invest heavily in therapy and education programs. The bureau wants the prisons to seem more "normal" than others, and their administrators consider co-corrections a key part of the atmosphere. "This place has more of a ballpark similarity to the outside world than any other I'm aware of," declares John Koechel, chief psychologist at Fort Worth.

"If it was a shocking experience coming in here [from his previous prison], what would it have been like going right to the streets?" asks Jim. "Now that I've been here, it won't be that big an adjustment. It's made a big difference."

In general, the prisons try to be "facilitative rather than coercive," explains Ken Neagle, associate warden at Lexington.* "We're able to establish expectations here in a normal institutional environment; we expect you to act like a normal adult. We insist on responsibility and accountability." An inmate is encouraged to participate in the process of working out his own program of therapy, education or work assignments in collaboration with his unit team of counselors, caseworkers and other staff. An inmate who doesn't like his job assignment is encouraged to canvass the various inmate-staffed operations in the prison and talk his way into a better job. Inmates are responsible for washing their own clothes, and, at Lexington, they are even permitted to carry small amounts of cash to spend in the commissary. An inmate who doesn't wish to participate may simply do his time on the yard or in his room, but the staff will not look favorably on his requests for furloughs or other benefits.

"The overall message in this institution is, 'If we start to hassle you, it's because you're not living up to expectations,'" explains a

Lexington inmate named Ruth. "Everything is here if you want to get yourself together; all the tools are here."

As much as the staff emphasizes the total concept, however, relations between the sexes remains a pervasive preoccupation of everyone at the co-correctional prisons. Both Fort Worth and Lexington have carefully spelled out their "contact policy." At Lexington, a couple may only hold hands; at Fort Worth they may hold hands or put their arms around each other so long as they are standing or seated; if they lie down next to each other they may not touch each other at all. Serious or repeated violation of the contact policy is grounds for the ultimate sanction — summary transfer to a single-sex institution. "If we go down into the kitchen and discover a couple screwing in the icebox," deadpans a Fort Worth administrator, "then we have to conclude that they aren't able to handle a co-correctional environment." The staff is constantly on the lookout for lesser violations as well. In fact, the merest breach of the contact policy — a stolen kiss, the brush of a hand across breast or buttock — is possible grounds for disciplinary action.

Both institutions are set up to deny the inmates access to privacy in areas where men and women are allowed to be together. "It appears that there are a lot of nooks and crannies in this place," says Lexington's Neagle, "but there aren't many that we haven't taken care of in terms of supervision. You'll probably see more glass in this place than in other institutions." In addition, the staff keeps informal tabs on "walk partners" — the inmates' term for couples who keep steady company — to make sure they do not go on furlough at the same time or have other opportunities to see each other out of sight of the prison staff.

The inmates at both institutions are keenly aware of all the supervision. At Fort Worth, some even protest with great conviction that the yard is watched at all times by guards hidden in surrounding buildings and equipped with high-powered telescopes. Fort Worth administrators burst into laughter at the suggestion, though they do acknowledge that there is a single tripod-mounted telescope gathering dust in a corner of the head corrections officer's office. "But listen, don't tell them there's only one," pleads an official. "Let them keep thinking we have them everywhere."

There is no question that walk partners still try to do more than walk together, and some are successful. Inmates at Fort Worth recall a memorable incident in which a male inmate sought to conceal his girlfriend in painter's drop cloths in order to spirit her into his room (they were apprehended by staff). And when a group of nine female inmates agreed to a conversation with an outside visitor in the absence of prison staff, two admitted to having sex on the premises.

Last year at Lexington, according to a report prepared by John Burkhead, regional administrator of research in the bureau's

Southeast Region, there were 95 incident reports written for violations of the contact policy by heterosexual couples. Thirty women and 29 men were written up for being found "in a compromising situation" and 29 women and seven men were written up for having engaged in sexual intercourse. (The discrepancy between men and women, Burkhead explains, occurred because some of the women written up weren't actually caught in the act; they simply turned up pregnant without having left the institution. In other cases, the women were caught in the act, but their partners fled without being identified. "The men seem to be faster at making a getaway when that happens," Burkhead explains, "and the women will never identify them.") All 36 of those who engaged in intercourse were transferred.

The 95 incident reports in 1977 represented 7.4 percent of the prison's population that year, an increase over the previous year level of 5.6 percent and a big jump from the 1.2 percent level in 1974, the year Lexington opened as a coed prison. Burkhead attributes the increase to the fact that the inmate population increased in those three years while the size of the staff remained constant. "The inmates' perception of what they could get away with changed," he explains, "and that led to more violations and more getting caught." At Fort Worth, administrators say, about 12 inmates per year are shipped out for violations of the contact policy.

Even if one assumes that each act of sexual intercourse written up represents a few more that went undetected, the image of institutions given over to licentiousness and debauchery simply doesn't hold up. Many of the inmates seem proud of and a bit defensive about their behavior. "This place isn't just one big continuous party," said one. "We don't have an orgy every five minutes," said another. Some say they have sworn off sex because they wouldn't be able to enjoy it under the circumstances. "I wasn't interested," explained one Fort Worth inmate who said her walk partner had pressured her for sex. "I didn't want to do it down in some stairwell or off in a corner, always worried about getting caught." Others who have done time in less comfortable prisons are too appreciative of the other amenities at Fort Worth and Lexington to risk losing them over sex. "Physical contact is the one thing they'll ship you out for," says Webster, a Lexington inmate. "I just want to do my time here and go home. I'm going to be a good boy."

The more important aspects of co-corrections have to do with its broader implications for the inmate experience and the nature of the relationships men and women manage to carry on without sex. Administrators of the prison point out that many beneficial effects seem to derive directly from the simple fact that men and women are together in the same place. At both Lexington and Fort Worth, everyone seems to agree, incidents of violence or even overt conflict among inmates occur less frequently than once a month, and few are really serious. The prisons are considered so safe that the bureau uses them to house inmates who might be subject to attack at other places — former police officers and federal law enforcement agents, former judges, politicians and blatant homosexuals. Inmates agree with bureau officials that co-corrections has something to do with the low levels of violence. "People always are on their best behavior in mixed company," comments Ruth. And Jim observes: "I have known of people who have been killed over homosexual relationships in other prisons. When I first came here and they explained the walkie thing to me, I said, O.K., how many people are getting killed here? But I've never even heard of anybody getting hit over a woman."

In addition, the staff contends, co-corrections has a salutary effect on programming, since inmates will decide to go to classes or therapy groups in order to spend more time in the company of their walk partners.

Administrators also claim that levels of homosexuality are lower in the co-correctional institutions than they are elsewhere. Peter Nacci, research analyst for the bureau, who is conducting a major study of sexual behavior in the entire federal prison system, reports an early finding: "Co-corrections is connected to lower levels of consensual homosexuality among male offenders, and the link has something to do with the environment rather than with the nature of the inmate population." He refuses to elaborate, however, since the research has not been completed in all the federal institutions. The Fort Worth inmate named Sue, who spent time at Alderson before coming to Fort Worth, claims that "homosexuality is rampant at Alderson," but that there is "a lot less" at Fort Worth. She repeats the common observation that, especially among women, homosexuality at an all-female institution tends to be situational, arising from the women's needs for close relationships rather than from a truly homosexual orientation, and that it does not develop when there are men around.

"I knew one girl who was at Alderson for five or six years. She wasn't homosexual on the street, but the need for physical closeness becomes necessary, and she had a girlfriend at Alderson. When she came here, there was no question of whether it would be a man or a woman. It was a man."

Perhaps the most important benefit of co-corrections, in the view of the staff, has to do with its effects on the inmates' feelings about themselves. One benefit derives from the basic situation. "If you put a man in an all male institution," says William Rauch, warden at Lexington, "one of the things you're saying to him is, 'We don't trust you around women.' That has to do something to his self-image."

But the benefits go further than that, in the opinion of the prison staff. They believe that many of the inmates have never been able to deal with the opposite sex in other than

exploitive or manipulative ways. Many of the women, staff members believe, have fallen into destructive patterns of dependency. "Most of the women here wouldn't be here if it weren't for a man," declares Bob Garcia, manager of the women's general unit at Fort Worth.

By establishing relationships that do not involve physical sex, the administrators contend, the inmates learn to deal with each other in more wholesome, more constructive ways.

"I've had people say to me, 'This is the first man I've had a relationship with when I didn't have the feeling that all he wants is my body,'" says Mary Alice Conroy, psychologist for the women's drug abuse program at Fort Worth. "That can do a lot for a woman's self-image."

Jim confirms her observation: "In an all-male institution, you watch TV, and the main topic of conversation is the women you see. The women are treated like objects — just another object to have. But here, the women are actually here. They're real. You see them, you have to deal with them. You accept them as friends, as people, rather than as sex objects."

In 1975, Esther Heffernan and Elizabeth Krippel completed a lengthy study of Fort Worth in which they analyzed walk-partner relationships in some detail. They concluded that the relationships play an integral role in the lives of 68 percent of the men and women at Forth Worth and that most of the relationships fall into three major categories:

• Companionship — genuinely platonic friendships. These relationships were carried on by married inmates who wished to "enjoy the supportive company of the opposite sex while mutual respect and understanding protect their marital status. Other participants include men and women who previously had been involved in pimping or prostitution and who find the relationship provides a "comfortable means of exploring nonexploitive ways of relating to the other sex."

• Counselor relationships, which may follow the "protective uncle" or "mothering aunt" models, depending on the people involved.

• Dating, in which the walk partners develop genuine romantic interest in each other.

For purposes of their study, Heffernan and Krippel divided the inmates at Fort Worth into four types: "squares" — white collar convicts who did not perceive themselves as criminals; "operators" — criminals who previously had managed to avoid incarceration; "street people," who have had a large number of arrests and whose offenses involve drug-related crimes; "old cons" who have spent long stretches of their adulthood "in the life" in prison, and who consider prison a major focus of their lives.

Perhaps the most interesting conclusion of their study has to do with the relationship of these sub-groupings to sexual behavior in the

co-correctional prison: "Single-sex relationships . . . are almost exclusively within the various subsystems; squares associate with squares, those in the life with those of similar orientation, operators with operators and street people with street people. Heterosexual relationships, however, are more likely to cross the boundaries of the subsystems. This is a crucial point because, while much has been made of the fact that the coed setting allows for the development of wholesome relationships between men and women, it becomes equally clear that the coed setting is also responsible for the degree to which the resident population is truly heterogeneous, not simply a 'peaceful coexistence' of subsystems."

The walk partners themselves look upon their relationships with varying degrees of seriousness. Some, like Sue and Buster, feel deeply committed to each other and talk of marriage after their release. They agree that there are benefits to romance without sex.

"Here you have to be able to deal with your feelings — whether sexual or violent — in words," Buster explains. "That's new for me. I'd always done it through temperament. You don't have the options here that you do on the outside. You have to be able to communicate or you don't survive."

"Because we are denied physical intimacy, we learn to communicate by talking and feeling," Sue adds. "We probably communicate as if we had been together for many years. Merely by the way Buster touches my hand or arm, I can tell if he's upset about something." Both readily admit that they are frustrated about sex. But they insist on the benefits of their forced celibacy. "We can't release tension physically," Sue says, "so we learn to do it verbally. That's what co-corrections can do."

Others take a more philosophical if not cynical view. Marie, an attractive blond woman in her thirties, has had a walk partner for several months, but as do many other inmates, she views the relationship as just one more way to pass her time. "I would never be emotionally involved with somebody here," she declares. But what does she get out of her relationship? "I like to look pretty for him; I like to hold his hand. I like his company, and to be able to feel like a woman. We realize that one day he'll leave, or I'll leave, and that will be it."

For still others, the idea of getting involved in any way presents too many problems. "I have a wife in Washington," explains one inmate lounging in the yard at Lexington. "It's frustrating for me to be here away from her and my two kids. If I begin to make friends with a woman here, spend time with her, that leads to feelings; they build up. But then I'll have to leave her when I'm released, and that's frustrating, too. It's just a circle of frustration."

The bureau has yet to document the genuine therapeutic value of these relationships in any definitive way, and there is some reason to ask if for some inmates they might not do as much harm as good. ("There are a lot of very *bad* relationships here," Sue observes matter-of-factly.) Prison officials claim they are trying to make the prisons more "normal," yet they permit men and women access to each other while denying them sex. How normal is that?

Not very, the officials agree. But Fort Worth Associate Warden George Diffenbaucher points out that forced celibacy is closer to "normal" than predatory homosexuality. In moments of greatest honesty, officials say that the real reason for prohibiting sex is that the public would not stand for it. "[The environment] is artificial," says Lexington's Neagle, "because that's the only way it can be. American society just won't accept [full sexual relationships in prison] at this time."

Bureau officials agree that co-corrections puts special strains on a prison staff. Enforcing the contact policy is a lot of work, and may require a special combination of firmness and tact on the part of guards. At the same time, male-female relationships create special anxieties for inmates. The potential is great for confusion and demoralization on all sides — not enough to cause a riot, perhaps, but certainly enough to generate problems of control and attitude, the sense that an institution "doesn't seem to gear up right" detected by some in the bureau.

That is why a visitor to Lexington and Fort Worth comes away with misgivings about the repeated complaints of inmates — more at Fort Worth than at Lexington — that they feel psychologically abused by their circumstances and by the staff. Fort Worth inmates point out that the staff there has been changing from the older, more benevolent, public health service people to the younger, more ambitious and aggressive Bureau of Prisons employees. The younger staff, inmates complain, tend to be petty and arbitrary, overly eager to write up incident reports for minor infractions, obsessively zealous in enforcing the contact policy and too subjective in interpreting the loosely defined rules.

Such complaints might be heard in any institution, but inmates at Fort Worth and Lexington contend that co-corrections aggravates their dealings with the staff. "They figure, since we're so lucky to have women here, they don't have to do much else for us," grumbles one. "The unit manager will say, 'You're a grown man; you can stay up all night if you want to,'" says another. "But then an officer comes up and says, '10:30, lights out.' And you say, 'But they said I could stay up,' and he'll say, 'Well, I'm running things right now — you turn it out.' Then the next night, it'll be somebody else; they won't care 'n the least whether your light's on or not."

"Inconsistency is going to occur in any large system where you've got a lot of different people," responds Fort Worth Associate Warden Bert Ricks. "Besides, this is a flexible institution."

He and Diffenbaucher agree that there has been a lot of turnover in the staff recently, with a lot of newcomers replacing the older PHS people. Others in the bureau suggest that, in a larger sense, the inmates' sense of confusion and frustration may arise from the efforts of the prison's current warden, Louis Gengler, who took over from Warden Campbell in 1975, to impose a more structured routine on an institution that had grown used to Campbell's more personal style and commitment to "mutuality."

The pattern of a looser administration during the implementation of co-corrections, followed by an effort to tighten up — with all the confusion it may generate — may be a common feature of many coed prisons, according to the Koba study of state and federal facilities. "Not only has there been a general increase in the level of control," the study states, "but also a shift away from control based on a spirit of respect and cooperation between staff and inmates, "and toward control through the fear of disciplinary action and its effects on parole dates, as well as possible transfer."

The study quotes inmates in coed prisons as complaining that prison administration is "haphazard, has no direction"; "I don't know what's happening"; "It's sick the way they change the rules all the time," and, "It's coed in name only."

In their defense, Fort Worth officials point out that when federal prisons at Fort Worth, Alderson, Seagoville and Lexington were evaluated according to the Correctional Institutions Environment Scale (CIES), a measure of an institution's social climate as perceived by staff and inmates, inmates at Fort Worth scored above other inmates in involvement, support, autonomy, practical orientation, personal-problem orientation and clarity.

But to a visitor, it is still curious to find inmates dealing with their frustrations by falling into open debate about the concept of the "therapeutic no."

"They try to frustrate you to see how you'll react, how well you cope," declares an inmate sitting with friends on the yard at Fort Worth. "The policy says you're eligible for a furlough if you do this, this and this; so you meet the requirements, you ask for a furlough. They have you fill out everything, call your family, make all the arrangements. Your counselor will encourage you, tell you he thinks you should have a furlough. But then you go before your unit team to get the final approval, and that same counselor will sit there and tell you, 'I don't think you need a furlough.' Then they write down your reactions. They write down everything."

"I think it would be better if they didn't play the games," comments another inmate sullenly. "If you meet the requirements to be eligible for a furlough, they should give you a furlough."

"No, no," objects the first, proud of his theory, "games are a part of life. It happens on the outside too. They throw obstacles at you to teach you how to attain your goals. It's therapeutic. I believe it."

Psychologist Koechel scoffs at the idea of a contrived "therapeutic no" situation. "We have 230 staff to deal with 630 people here," he says. "How could we possibly have the time to set up situations like that?" On the other hand, he acknowledges, "we do have different opinions about people, and we do have a right to argue about them. Often we disagree, and people get jacked around. Life isn't fair."

Building A Small Prison With Modern Concepts

ROGER W. CRIST

Warden
Montana State Prison
Deer Lodge, Mont.

For 20 years, attempts had been made to replace the State of Montana's 100-year-old territorial prison with a new facility, and at a cost of $300,000, no less than five major studies had resulted, without exception, in recommendations that a new prison be built. Finally, $5.5 million was appropriated for the project.

Considering the relatively limited amount of money allocated, prison administrators recognized from the outset that the architects responsible for designing the new prison were faced with an extremely difficult task. And actually, the project would have been impossible had authorities been unable to remodel and add on to three existing buildings on prison-owned land. Basic roads, existing utilities, and support buildings, such as warehouses, a slaughterhouse, and a dairy and motor vehicle center, were ultimately to be incorporated into the new facility. Still, a great deal of innovative thinking and planning were required.

"It was necessary that the new Montana State Prison be all things to all people."

It was necessary that the new Montana State Prison be all things to all people. With the small State population, low tax base, and comparatively small inmate population, there would be no way that a number of institutions could be built economically to house prisoners categorically. The new prison had to be designed to include maximum, close, medium, and minimum security inmates. The concept of creating separate housing units, each with a staff complement and regulatory strictures predicated upon the degree of security required, came into effect. This idea, the responsible living concept as it is called, utilizes the housing unit design in such a way that the more responsibility an inmate is able to accept, the more freedom he will have.

One problem that had plagued the old Montana State Prison was the inability to logically segregate inmates—the old from the young, the aggressive from the nonaggressive, the sex offenders from the nonsex offenders, and the criminally sophisticated from the nonsophisticated. The new Montana State Prison, therefore, was designed to include a maximum security, close security, medium security, and minimum security building. The maximum security building, which is architecturally traditional, is comprised of five separate units ranging in size from a 4-man unit to a 14-man unit. The close security, medium security, and minimum security buildings are identical in terms of physical construction. Each has three stories, with four eight-man units per floor. Each three-story building is connected to its own one-story commons building by a cement wall, a geographical divider which surrounds the security unit and its commons building. The ornamental wall creates a separate yard for each housing unit, separating them from the main yard. This yard gives the inmate a choice. Should he not want to involve himself with the entire inmate population at the big recreation yard which is located outside of the ornamental wall

and away from the security units, he may remain in his own unit area out-of-doors in the unit yard. As previously mentioned, each floor of the three-story housing unit is broken down into four eight-man units. A unit consists of eight single rooms that come out on a common dayroom. The unit has common sanitary and shower facilities, as well as a common counseling room. Using the institution's classification system and this type of design, a maximum amount of separation, based on each inmate's ability to assume responsibility for his actions, has been effected.

Officials wanted to provide a comfortable, free-style visiting environment for responsible inmates, but saw a need also to insure tight security during visiting periods for those who could not accept the responsibility. This was accomplished by building a large open visiting room where inmates classified as close, medium, and minimum security could visit quite freely. Maximum security inmates now visit in the maximum security building under strict security procedures, and the building is constructed in such a way as to deny them access beyond the visiting room. Close, medium, or minimum security inmates, after checking with an officer, are allowed to go to an outside visiting area adjacent to the visiting room. Inmates in the general population who have attempted to smuggle contraband into the institution, the sexually aggressive, or those prone toward violence receive their visits in the special security area adjacent to the free visiting room. In effect, inmates are being shown that they can enjoy a great deal of flexibility in visiting, if they conduct themselves in a respon-

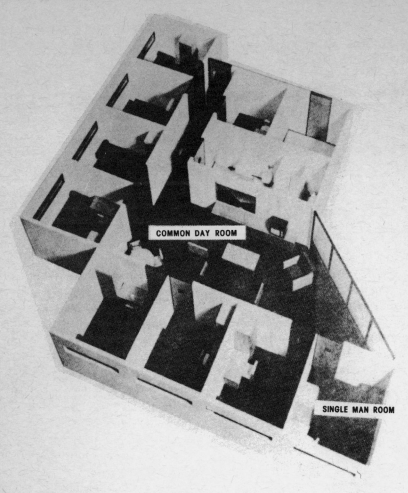

COMMON DAY ROOM

SINGLE MAN ROOM

been arranged in such a way that they would serve as multiple use rooms. In other words, no single academic teacher occupies a classroom exclusively. Instead, the classroom is used variously by academic teachers, vocational education teachers, self-help group leaders, and college program personnel. Likewise, the principle has been carried over to the housing unit with each housing unit enjoying a large multipurpose room located in the commons building adjacent to a specific living area.

Officials wanted to encourage increased contact between key staff, line staff, and inmates, and as a consequence, the institution was designed so that no interviews would be held in the offices of the warden, deputy warden, associate warden of security, director of classification and treatment, or business manager, which are all located outside of the security perimeter. When key people conduct interviews, they must enter the security perimeter and hold these interviews in all-purpose rooms within the prison proper. These rooms have been set up in the commons buildings which are attached to each security unit. Through this arrangement, key staff members come in contact with line staff and inmates, as well as the interviewees.

"Adequate perimeter security was a major consideration."

Adequate perimeter security was a major consideration. In the old institution, seven towers were in operation. But by strategically locating a single tower on a high hill overlooking the new institution, it was possible to reduce the number of towers from seven to one. Since it takes five men to man one tower, 24 hours a day, 7 days a week, this design freed 30 staff members to work on the grounds in direct relationship with the inmates. Incorporated within the plans are two cyclone fences which are equipped with an intrusion device and separated by a medial bramble wire barrier. A

sible manner. If they can't, their visits will be held in the security area.

Prison officials wanted to enable treatment staff to be involved with the security staff in a unit treatment-management approach. The four separate housing units based on the security classification enabled treatment personnel to retain the traditional administration building and enter the commons building with its easy access to the housing units. The treatment staff, working in conjunction with the security staff, could then become part of the treatment-management team that would in effect run the unit. A unit classification team made up of both treatment and security staff would administer all matters pertaining to the unit. Where their recommendations crossed unit lines, the recommendations would have to be approved by the institution classifica-

tion committee. It was felt that a certain degree of autonomy should be given to the staff actually working the unit, but precautions have been taken to preclude the development of four small separate institutions in a haphazard manner.

"[A] certain degree of autonomy [is] given to the staff actually working the unit, but precautions have been taken to preclude the development of four small separate institutions in a haphazard manner."

Facilities for treatment, individual therapy, group therapy, and religious, vocational, academic, and recreational programs were needed. Toward meeting this need, almost all of the treatment rooms in the institution have

5. PUNISHMENT AND CORRECTIONS

motorized patrol maintains radio contact with the institution as it safeguards the prison perimeter. Additional security is provided by a staff accoutered with walkie-talkie radios, open intercoms in five control centers as well as the tower, and red signal lights on the roof of each building that will alert staff to emergencies in that building. Contributing also to security of the facility is a telephone communications system. If, for instance, any phone is left off or knocked off the hook, the control center will be alerted immediately. By dialing two numbers in an emergency situation, 21 phones will ring in the homes of key staff, even though one or more phones may be in use.

The geographic location of the institution, which is in the middle of a 40,000-acre ranch, provides an inherent security feature.

Adequate space where staff could get together in a comfortable environment away from work and away from inmate contact was totally lacking in the old facility, and this had led to

"[T]he responsible living concept . . . utilizes the housing unit design in such a way that the more responsibility an inmate is able to accept, the more freedom he will have."

Inmates' visiting room.

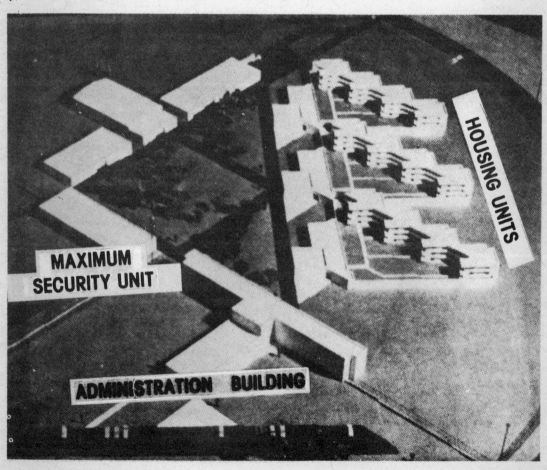

Dining area in food services building.

a situation in which social workers tended to take their coffeebreak in the social service department with other social workers. Teachers similarly tended to take their breaks in the school with other teachers. Consequently, the staff had not been communicating adequately among the disciplines. Naturally, officials wanted to allocate space enabling the staff to meet before going to work and provide an informal environment in which psychologists, security staff, chaplains, maintenance staff, social workers, teachers, and accountants would meet and exchange ideas. This was arranged by constructing coffeebreak areas in the staff dining room and in a staff room located in the new administration building.

It was necessary that the institution be accommodated to its environs. The outstanding feature of the environment was a mountainous region rising to 10,000 feet just west of the institution. Planners wanted a colorful institution but realized that if all of the buildings were painted different colors, the result could be a circuslike appearance. On the other hand, if all buildings were painted the same color, regardless of the particular color selected, it could become a monotonous "institution color." The problem was solved by painting the buildings a variety of colors on a continuum from light cream through beige and sand colors to a dark brown color used exclusively for trim. This approach offered the desired continuity, and no single color became either offensively conspicuous or superfluous.

The Law Enforcement Assistance Administration (LEAA) and the Montana Board of Crime Control, the agency in Montana responsible for administering LEAA funds, had an important role in establishing the

new Montana State Prison. Through these agencies, officials obtained assistance from both the LEAA Regional Office in Denver and the National Clearinghouse on Correctional Architecture. The well-equipped library and education complex at the new institution which cost over $200,000 was supplied through Crime Control Commission funds. The advice and financial assistance these agencies provided is very much appreciated, and their interest and support throughout the entire project was outstanding.

Montana, like all States, has experienced an extreme population increase. When the planning of the new institution began, there had been a steady

5-year downward trend in terms of prison population and an actual count of 249 inmates. Since that time, the population has more than doubled to a current population of 533. In 1975, there was a 10-percent population increase, and in 1976, a 29-percent population increase. The new prison was designed and built to house 334 inmates. This means that while the new institution is occupied by 333 men, 200 men have had to be retained in the old territorial prison that officials had hoped to abandon. To alleviate crowding, the Montana State Legislature appropriated $3.8 million from the general fund in 1977 to add a celled, close security housing unit for 200 more inmates.

Ninety-six-man housing unit. This type of building is used for close security, medium security, and minimum security inmates.

A Criminal Rehabilitation Program that Works

Bernard F. Hillenbrand

The author is executive director of the National Association of Counties and of its Research Foundation. He is also founder and editor of County News, a weekly newspaper about county government.

The philosophy embraced in our early history was that criminals should be punished. But during a 19th-Century wave of penal reform, the notion of rehabilitating criminals began to replace the earlier emphasis on retribution.

In recent years, however, the pendulum of opinion has swung back again. Many corrections specialists are turning a skeptical eye at what can and cannot be done to reform criminal behavior.

In a study released in 1975, Robert Martinson of the City University of New York examined 231 rehabilitation programs conducted around the country between 1945 and 1967. He concluded that "with few and isolated exceptions, the rehabilitation efforts that have been supported so far have had no appreciable effect on recidivism."

Indeed, despite the range of vocational, group therapy, and individual counseling programs, most violent crimes continue to be committed by "revolving door" offenders. According to the FBI, the chance of a person repeating the same crime within four years after release from prison is 64 percent for murder, 81 percent for burglary, 77 percent for robbery and 73 percent for rape.

Before corrections specialists declare rehabilitation dead, however, they should examine a maverick program in the heart of Georgia that seems to be defying all the statistics.

For the past eight years, rehabilitation efforts in Dougherty County have centered around a technique called Emotional Maturity Instruction (EMI). This 15-week course features a curious blend of wisdom from an ancient Aramaic Bible, the Socratic method of teaching, and the firm belief that people can change their attitudes and behavior by improving their mind controls.

But the most singular aspect of the course is that it appears to be working. EMI was first tested in 1968 on 22 "hardened" criminals in Georgia's maximum security prison at Reidsville. Typical of these inmates was the first man to be taught EMI. He had committed every crime on an FBI checklist except rape and child molesting and had been in and out of jail all his life.

But when he left Reidsville, it was the last time he went through a prison door. A followup this year of the "original 22" shows that not one is in trouble with the law today.

Asa Kelly, the director of the Department of Correction during the Reidsville experiment, was so impressed with EMI that he brought it with him when he was appointed chief judge of the Dougherty Judicial Circuit in 1970.

Kelly helped set up a nonprofit corporation, the Judicial Services Agency, which conducts about 25 EMI classes a week and buttresses the technique with remedial reading, nutritional education, and a volunteers-in-probation (VIP) program.

For adult offenders, Kelly uses EMI "as an alternative to state prison." When a person is found guilty, Kelly requests a full social and psychological history. Individuals are either placed on probation or in a county jail while undergoing EMI instruction two hours a week. Standard psychological tests are given periodically during the course to determine an individual's progress.

"Ordinarily it takes 12 to 16 weeks to find out whether or not a person has changed attitudes to the extent that he can live in free society," says Kelly.

Of the 880 adult offenders who have participated in the program since 1971, 706 have never been re-arrested. That is a recidivism rate of 20 percent at a time when the national average ranges between 60 and 90 percent.

And Wilbur McCarty, director of the Judicial Services Agency, points out that the program's 80 percent success rate represents substantial cost savings. "The county spends about $100 to put a person through the EMI course whereas it would cost the state $20,000 per year to keep them in prison."

EMI has also proved so successful with youthful offenders that Juvenile Court Judge Gene Black Sr. said "I wouldn't know how to operate without it." Black sends 80 to 90 percent of the juveniles that come through his court to EMI classes. "Whenever possible, I also require the parents to attend," Black added.

Recently, Dougherty County was able to eliminate two jobs from its prosecutorial staff because, according to Black, the juvenile caseload "has gone down steadily every year."

The man who developed EMI is Dr. Dan Mac-Dougald, director of Social Research Laboratories in Atlanta. EMI is based on the assumption that a person's behavior is determined by his perceptions of himself and others—his unconscious goals and attitudes. In turn, his attitudes are influenced by his comprehension of key words—what MacDougald calls the "regulatory speech system."

"Nobody goes criminal before the age of 10 to 13. That's because the regulatory speech system of the human mind controls social behavior. And it is not fully operational until about the age 13. If the content of that speech system is criminal, the social behavior will be criminal," MacDougald explains.

MacDougald dipped into translations of an Aramaic New Testament to find practical definitions of words like "love," "authority," "hostility," "honor," and "forgiveness." EMI uses discussions of such words to help an individual crystallize his goals and attitudes.

MacDougald also borrowed from the Greeks. Instead of indoctrination, EMI relies on the Socratic method of teaching. "You ask questions. Improper answers set up stresses. And the human mind is genetically programmed to work to reduce its stresses," he says.

Here's the way the dialogue might go during the first class. The instructor would begin by asking, "Do you manage your own mind?" Normally students will reply "yes." Then the instructor inquires, "Do people sometimes make you angry?" Once again, the response is "yes."

The instructor follows up by inquiring, "Who's managing your mind when someone makes you angry?" "The other guy," say the students. "But you just said you manage your own mind," replies the instructor.

According to MacDougald, the class will eventually arrive at the proper answer which is "you make yourself angry." And once students learn to accept responsibility for their own actions, he says, they can begin to learn "intelligent use of the mind controls" to reduce inner tension that produces hostile behavior.

"If the way a person sees something is not the way he wants it [his goals], he will be dissatisfied," explains MacDougald. EMI teaches that a person can always be satisfied by rearranging his goals.

"For example, he says, "you want your mother-in-law to show more respect. Well, she's not going to do it. So the mother-in-law ends up with bodily harm.

We suggest the individual cancel the goal that his mother-in-law show respect. Then the conflict between the way you see it and the way you want it ended. The internal stress disappears."

He adds that, unlike the modern English definition, the word "forgiveness" in ancient Aramaic means "to cancel."

These examples are only the tip of the iceberg. The sessions continue for 15 weeks as students explore concepts such as perceptual love (how to think positively), judgmental love (positive behavior), patience, truth, how to react to criticism, etc.

Students are given "homework"—simple excercises to carry out in their daily lives that reinforce EMI's premise that certain sets of behavior will produce more favorable reactions than others and lead to a more successful life.

"It can be as simple as a student trying to be extra nice one day. That may sound elementary to most people, but you'd be surprised at the number of criminals who have never tried it," says MacDougald.

He admits that the course is designed to "build character"—the kind of education most people received at mother's knee but many criminals have missed.

The EMI technique is considered unorthodox in some circles, particularly among those who believe it is unscientific to teach that one set of values is better than another.

But for those who have been intimately involved with the program—from the judges in Dougherty County to the prisoners who have taken the course—EMI has produced overwhelming enthusiasm and diehard loyalists.

The latest convert is Carl Schmidt, a police detective who came to Albany in 1972 after spending four years with the FBI. After hearing about EMI from other police officers, Schmidt was skeptical. "When a cop spends six months trying to break a burglary case, it's frustrating to see the offender end up in class rather than prison," he says.

A Ph.D. candidate in psychology, Schmidt decided to analyze EMI for his dissertation. "Basically, I set out to prove it didn't work," he says.

For several months, Schmidt poured over court records and data in the probation and police departments on every person that had taken the course in Dougherty County since 1971. He ran checks through the National Crime Information Center (NCIC) to see if these individuals had been arrested again anywhere in the country.

It was Schmidt who discovered that the recidivism rate for adult offenders who had undergone EMI instruction was 20 percent. Today he says: "There's no doubt about it. It's the only rehabilitation program I've seen that's a success. Being a police officer and knowing the people I've personally sent to jail and then talking to them after they finish the EMI course is like black and white. It's unreal."

It probably is too soon to determine whether EMI is as effective as its supporters claim. Nor is it likely that this approach could be applied everywhere. But Dougherty County's experience does raise Socratic-type questions for those who are dubious about rehabilitation in general.

Is it that rehabilitation itself doesn't work? Or is it simply that many of the rehabilitation methods we have been using thus far don't work?

Article 53

ON THE WOMEN'S SIDE OF THE PEN

Excerpted from a forthcoming book by Sandee Bonham, as told to Gina Allen

Gina Allen

Gina Allen, chairwoman of the AHA Women's Caucus, is co-author with Dr. Clement Martin, M.D. of Intimacy: Sensitivity, Sex and the Art of Love.

As an island, Terminal Island is no great shakes, but the grounds of the prison are a trip. Nothing like plenty of unpaid, live-in labor to make a bunch of old navy barracks and some shapeless concrete replacements look like a country estate.

You can take a tour—lots of people do—and see the busy prisoners at work. See the well-treated prisoners at play. They go to classes, learn skills. Soon they will be returned to the outside world, ready to take their places as responsible citizens. Half of them will be back within the year, but never mind. Is it society's fault if prisoners don't take advantage of their advantages?

Better to be on a tour of Terminal Island than to be a resident, I'll clue you. I checked in on January 5, 1972. That was for ninety days psychiatric observation, which actually took four and one-half months. That time didn't count against the time I would have to do once the judge made up his mind about my sentence. Neither did the year I had spent in more than half a dozen jails on my way from Canada, where I got busted, to southern California.

I spent the time waiting. Waiting to be charged. Waiting to be tried. Waiting to be convicted. Waiting to be sentenced. Waiting to be transported. I spent the time in overcrowded jails with a lot of other women who were also waiting. At first I was scared and cried a lot and broke out in a nervous rash. I'd never been in a jail before and nobody was at all interested in making me feel at home. They questioned and they threatened and they moved me around a lot from one jail to another; and they never

gave me a reason. Even after the judge found me guilty and ordered me to Terminal Island for psychiatric observation, they kept me hanging around in the Portland jail waiting to be transported south.

Women prisoners spend a lot of time waiting to be transported. In order to transport a woman, the male driver needs a female chaperone. So, he waits for a long weekend or a holiday, loads up his wife or girl friend, and has a mini-vacation, all expenses paid and overtime besides. If he doesn't want to spend his holiday at your destination, then you get dumped somewhere en route and wait some more.

I knew why I was in jail, even though I didn't know why I was being shuffled around from one jail to another. At least I *had* robbed a bank and been found guilty. A lot of prisoners going through the same thing to this day are merely under suspicion of breaking the law. From 80 percent to 90 percent are never convicted of a crime. We would need fewer prisons if innocent people weren't put behind bars and if everybody was processed in a reasonable period of time. But, or course, this would do nothing for the builders and administrators, the manufacturers of steel bars and alarm systems, the guards, instructors, and parole officers who make their livings—and sometimes their fortunes—from our fifteen-billion-dollar-a-year prison industry.

Arrest rates were soaring in the 1970s when I got busted—particularly for women. In the first three years of this decade arrests were up 28 percent for men and 95 percent for women. The prison planners just weren't prepared for almost double the usual number of women occupants. They started building Pleasanton (where Patty Hearst is now in residence) as a facility for men only. When it opened in 1974, it was coed. Now it's for women only. There were one hundred forty women at Terminal Island when I got there in 1972. Within a year there were one hundred ninety. Now it's well over two hundred—the number is increasing daily.

I got unloaded at Terminal Island at night, handcuffs, leg

irons, the works. At A & O (Admittance and Orientation) they not only relieved me of those, but of everything else I had—my clothes, valuables, everything. They gave me receipts. I even got a receipt for my body. And they gave me a number—2306-171. Try being a number some time. It's not exactly guaranteed to make you feel like somebody you'd like to know a bunch.

They also invaded my most private sexual parts. "Hey, I'm in for bank robbery, not prostitution!" I protested. A lot of good that did. They explore a woman's sexual parts whenever she comes in, no matter where she has been. Maybe some of the C.O.'s (Correctional Officers) get their jollies from this. I don't know. I don't think they harassed the men on the men's side of the prison that way. They said they had to be sure we women weren't packing dope or disease in our hidden orifices.

As for my thinking I could play the big shot because I was a bank robber instead of a whore, it didn't come down that way. I had only robbed one bank. One woman, already there, had robbed six. Women weren't just committing more crimes in the seventies, they were also committing bigger ones.

Life at Terminal Island is a bore. It never changes. At least not for the better. Residents are counted at five every morning. Sick or well, tired, hung over, grieving, depressed, suicidal—it doesn't matter. At five you're sitting on the end of your bed or in your chair—visible to the C.O. coming down the hall, counting: "1—2—3—4—." And then the other side. And if the count doesn't come out right she does it all over again. The problem is that some of those bitches can't count. Sometimes it takes them half an hour to count sixty people. A first-grader could do it in half the time. And then you can sit and wait another half-hour because some other building hasn't checked out. You spend a lot of your time sitting, visible, waiting for the PA system to announce: "Count's clear! Count's clear!" Then, in the morning, you can go back to sleep or line up for breakfast.

Report for work at 8:00 A.M. This is your rehabilitation. Where you learn skills. Who's kidding who? You don't do the jobs you want to do, or might be able to continue on the outside. You do what needs doing. You peel potatoes in the kitchen or haul out garbage or scrub floors or water flowers or sew uniforms. There's a beauty shop, but nobody to teach you how to be a beautician—which is probably just as well. Mostly, having been in the joint, you couldn't get a beautician's license on the outside anyway.

After I got my sentence—five years—I got assigned to key punch. Women did key punch, and men did programming and other important parts of the IBM operation that took smarts and made money for the prison. In this way the prison system perpetuates injustice against women in the workplace.

If you're looking for a reason more and more women are giving up prostitution, shoplifting, and writing bad checks in favor of better-paying crimes like robbery, grand larceny, and embezzlement, don't blame it on the women's movement—as is popular with a lot of the criminologists and sociologists I've been reading lately. Blame it on the fact that the changes the women's movement are trying to bring about haven't happened yet. Like equal opportunity and equal pay, for instance. If a female college graduate earns on the average what a male high school dropout earns, then where does that leave the female high school dropout? Down and out—that's where—without money for bread or dope or milk for her kids.

Well, learning key punch at Terminal Island as a way to make a living on the outside was a laugh riot—in any case, that's what I found out when I got paroled. Machines like the ones we used in prison hadn't been seen in the rest of the world in years.

Anyone who hired you would have to retrain you on modern equipment—which didn't make you the hottest thing on the job market. And everyone knew where you had got your training on the outmoded machines, so if an employer wasn't into hiring ex-cons he didn't have to say so—he just turned you down because your skills were out of date.

At Terminal Island we stopped work at 4:00 P.M., had dinner, and then "free" time until the 9:00 count. After which you could have guests in your room until 11:00. You had to be in bed —alone—by 11:30. On Thursdays you got to buy soap and toothpaste and other necessaries from the commissary. Saturday nights there was a movie. On Sundays you washed your sheets and towel and sometimes there was a softball game.

Most prisoners are young, at the height of their sexuality. But sexual needs and desires are supposed to be checked at A & O when you walk into the joint. This has changed. Today Terminal Island is coed and there is some intermingling of the sexes. Which is healthy. When I was there the men stared out their windows at the women crossing the compound and some of the women tossed notes wrapped around radio batteries into the men's side. But never the twain did meet. As a result, homosexuality was the only sexual outlet on both sides of the prison. Men used it as part of their power trip. In the pecking order some men were "stuff" and some controlled "stuff." Having lots of "stuff" at your command was one way of exerting power.

Women lived differently in prison, as they live differently in the world. Most of them came out of family situations or had been searching for that ideal, loving family. More than half had kids on the outside, whose fate and whereabouts were a constant worry. Most of the mothers were in custody battles— which most of them lost, since just being in the joint is proof positive that you're an unfit mother.

We had "families" on the women's side of the joint, some large, some small. Ours, upstairs in Palms, was one of the larger families—from fifteen to twenty-five, depending on who got released and who "got violated back in." We called ourselves "hippies, hypes, whores, and homosexuals."

We took care of each other. There were homosexual couples in our family and straights, and, at first, blacks and whites and browns. We kept the C.O.'s from coming down too hard on the gays, and we helped gay couples find a place and time to get together. That took vigilance. Just touching another woman could get you a D.R. (Disciplinary Report). If you were caught getting down with a woman you could land in the Hole. And one of you might be shipped to another prison. We kept gays from pestering the straights in our family for sexual favors. Lots of straight women turn gay inside the joint, but we wanted that to be their decision.

One of the first women I went with at Terminal Island was a smart little black chick named Tilly, who got sent out on educational furlough and then was sent back again, pregnant. But she didn't come back to me. She joined a family headed by a big, black stud broad named Jacky. Jacky had once gone with Peg and had been a member of our family. I didn't trust her. I warned Peg that Jacky was just using her for her beautiful clothes and outside dope connections. Eventually Peg and Jacky split and Jacky started her own family, which was all black. And our family was suddenly lily-white.

We had never been divided according to color before, but I didn't think much about it. I had other things to think about. I had been chosen the father of our family and elected dorm representative to the Inmates Council. Then I was elected vice-president of the council.

5. PUNISHMENT AND CORRECTIONS

The council on the women's side was fairly new then. The men had had a council for years. But for some reason the administration—the White House, we called it—didn't want the women to have one. They didn't think prisoners had rights—just privileges. And they didn't want a council informing them otherwise, I guess.

Then there was the matter of education. Despite the increase in women inmates, women still make up only 5 percent of the prison population, so they get only 5 percent of the funds. Most of that goes for security, with nothing left over for the kind of education and recreation the men get. I thought we should be allowed to go to the men's side for some of their classes. That was a shocking idea to the White House at first, but we finally won out. The other big victory the women's Inmates Council had scored (before I was a member) was our right to wear our own clothes instead of impossible prison-issue rags.

That was important to the women. Because if you've lost your identity and your freedom, and you're just a number and being treated like nobody, then it helps to be able to look in the mirror with a little pride in what you see. Then, at least in your own head, you're still a person.

Of course, it took money and time and outside contacts to get a wardrobe together. One of the worst things you could do to another convict was tear her clothes off her. Some women did that when they were mad at somebody. Or they'd just get mad at their condition and tear the clothes off whoever was handy.

Peg had about the neatest wardrobe on the compound. On the outside she was a high-priced whore and a check runner besides. She was used to having money and spending it on clothes. When she and Jacky were going together, Jacky, the dyke, owned Peg, the femme, and everything she possessed. We were really on a sexist trip in Terminal Island in those days. So Jacky wore Peg's clothes and looked like somebody. Since she and Peg had broken up Jacky was looking pretty seedy.

She didn't expect to remain that way, apparently. One Saturday afternoon, as we were sitting waiting for a softball game with an outside team to begin, Jacky came over and told Peg: "I'm coming to your room to get my clothes when this game is over. Have them ready."

"Your clothes!" I cried. "You've got your nerve!"

"Butt out, you blue-eyed devil, " she told me, and walked away.

We thought it was a hoot. We had managed to sneak some dope on our way to the field and were feeling as mellow as the autumn afternoon. To add good vibes was the fact that we won the game and were planning to celebrate in upstairs Palms with a spot of tea for the family. Nothing fancy, mind you. Everybody had to bring her own Tang jar to drink from.

Who wasn't invited was Jacky, but she arrived with the pregnant Tilly, demanding Peg's clothes and swinging at Peg when Peg didn't hand them over. We stopped preparations for the tea party to pull the two of them apart, whereupon Tilly raced from the building toward her own building, Cedars, screaming: "The blue-eyed devil and her gang are trying to kill Jacky!"

The next thing we knew there was a pitched battle in the hallway, with lamps as weapons. By the time the pigs got there to break it up Peg and some of the others were pretty battered. The pigs started handing out D.R.s and the P.A. system began bellowing: "Count time! Count time! Back to your rooms for count!"

That was all that happened. Nobody got tossed in the hole and we in upstairs Palms stayed right in our territory, bandaging our wounded, wondering if we were going to be attacked again. Peg didn't have any permanent damage. No broken nose or anything like that. Still, when I went in to call for her for breakfast the next morning she wasn't dressed. She said, "We can't go out after what happened last night. They'll get us for sure."

I should have listened to the voice of experience. Peg had been in more jails than I had and knew how things came down. But I said we couldn't let Jacky and her bunch of bullies keep us from eating and doing the things we wanted to do. We'd go in a group, I told her. They wouldn't dare attack all of us.

So we did. Except that I ran back for Abbie's cigarettes, which she had left behind. As a result I was trailing after the group as we crossed the compound. Rounding the medical building, there was Jacky and a dozen others charging toward us. Our group closed tight around Peg. But it was me Jacky charged, with the help of a woman I didn't know who was as big as Goliath.

This giant, weighing in at two hundred fifty pounds, grabbed hold of me—all one hundred ten pounds—and swung me around so I was facing Jacky. I thought she was going to hold me so Jacky could beat on me and I was worried about my glasses, Jacky pulled off her bandana, so that I wouldn't pull it over her eyes, I supposed, and then struck me on the cheek.

I felt the impact, but it didn't hurt too much. I was worried that she'd break my glasses with another blow. But there wasn't one. Jacky turned and ran, throwing a shiv to one of her women as she fled. She had had it in her hair. The woman ducked into A & O with the shiv and probably flushed it down a john. End of evidence.

I still didn't understand that the shiv had anything to do with me. The pigs came and broke up the fight. I reached up to my glasses, brushing my cheek. It was wet and sticky. My hand was bloody. So was my blouse and fatigue jacket. Radcliffe, a C.O. I liked, put an arm around me, gently. My whole family was staring at my face. My face! That bitch Jacky had slashed my face!

"Let's get her! I'll kill her!" I cried. But nobody was into revenge. They took me back to my room and got ice and towels for my cheek. I got a look at myself in the mirror. It made me sick to my stomach. My face was purple and puffy, with this great, gaping, ragged hole in it, pouring out blood like Niagara Falls. I couldn't stand up. It was like all the blood was coming from my knees. My legs were spaghetti.

By this time all the C.O.'s were screeching through the P.A. system and running around to telephones trying to locate someone resembling a doctor. That's hard enough to do at any time. Most of the medics who take care of prisoners are parameds and they weren't even around. It was Sunday. Bad time to get cut. You could bleed to death.

Finally they located the officer of the day who also happened to be the administrator in charge of the medical department. He was more interested in trying to get me to snitch on whoever had done the dastardly deed than in fixing up my wound. But he finally got the hole in my face more or less fastened together with butterfly tape. Then they threw me in the hole for having been part of the riot. They threw Jacky in the hole, too, and later shipped her out to another institution. They couldn't ship me out because while I was in the hole the Inmates Council voted me president. What did come down on me was fourteen months added to my sentence by the Parole Board.

I was cut on September tenth. All winter the damned hole in my face kept hurting and oozing and festering and breaking open. Finally, in May, two specialists came out to Terminal Island from the University of California Medical School and decided to operate. The whole healing process had to be lived through all over again.

One thing kept me going. I was determined to sue the government for the scar on my face. They had given me a receipt for my body when I came to Terminal Island. That should have been a contract to return it in the same condition that they got it. They weren't keeping their part of the bargain.

Yet, even looking at my scarred face I knew that the worst scars I would be taking with me out of that joint—that every convict takes—would be invisible. They would be battered psyches and souls—whatever your terminology. Those scars were horrendous. They were so bad that nobody wanted to look at them or acknowledge them—particularly not those responsible for inflicting them. Besides, you can't prove those scars. You can't sue. They're disabling, not disfiguring. In most instances they last a lifetime, which is a major reason that convicts keep returning to the joint. Damaged merchandise. Where else can you unload it?

Afterword

If you think this is a grim tale you've just read, I agree. It was grimmer living it. If you're interested in knowing whether or not there was a happy ending for me, yes. I sued the government for the scar on my face and got compensation. The scar is still with me. I fought for, and won, the right for a license to sell cars, which was my bag before my seven-week crime spree. The license can be, and usually is, denied to ex-cons. I've helped, and housed, a lot of women convicts coming out of prison. I've worked with NOW and other organizations trying to humanize the criminal injustice system. I've organized NOW chapters behind prison walls.

My parole was over at midnight, May 29, 1976. My flat was filled with friends celebrating the occasion with me. They were of all colors, ages, and persuasions. There were ex-cons, women's liberationists, male chauvinists, gays, straights, and musicians making music. We danced and sang and watched the clock. A silversmith had made me a miniature ball and chain. At the stroke of midnight I broke the chain. Everybody cheered. They hugged and kissed me and wished me well. It was a great night. I was free again.

Now I live in San Francisco with a terrific woman, a musician, who is into adding culture to my life. I dig it because I dig her. I sell cars for a living. It beats robbing banks and I'm good at it. But I don't go to bed at night without remembering my sisters behind bars. Warehoused humans, caught up in an inhumane system. They haunt my life. They will forever.

Bibliography

Abraham, H., *The Judicial Process*, Oxford University Press, 1968.

Adler, F., *Sisters in Crime*, McGraw-Hill, 1975.

Allen, H. and C. Simonsen, *Corrections in America*, Glencoe Press, 1978.

Amos, W., *Delinquent Children in Juvenile Correctional Institutions*, C.C. Thomas, 1966.

Atkins, B. and M. Pogrebin, *The Invisible Justice System*, W.H. Anderson, 1978.

Balton, M., *European Policing*, John Jay Press, 1978.

Bartollas, C., S. Miller, and S. Dinitz, *Juvenile Victimization*, Sage Publications, Inc., 1976.

Bartollas, C. and S.J. Miller, *Correctional Administration: Theory and Practice*, McGraw-Hill, 1978.

Bartollas, C. and S.J. Miller, *The Juvenile Offender: Control, Correction and Treatment*, Allyn & Bacon, Inc., 1978.

Bayley, D., *Police and Society*, Sage Publications, Inc., 1978.

Beigel, H., *Beneath the Badge*, Harper and Row Publishers, Inc., 1977.

Bell, J.B., *Time of Terror: How Democratic Societies Respond to Revolutionary Violence*, Basic Books Inc., 1978.

Bequai, A., *Organized Crime*, Lexington Books, 1979.

Bequai, A., *White Collar Crime*, Lexington Books, 1979.

Berkeley, G., *The Democratic Policeman*, Beacon Press, 1969.

Berns, W., *For Capital Punishment: Crime and the Morality of the Death Penalty*, Basic Books, Inc., 1979.

Best, A., *The Politics of Law Enforcement*, Lexington Books, 1974.

Bittner, E., *The Functions of Police in Modern Society*, U.S. Government Printing Office, 1970.

Bittner, E., and S. Krantz, *Standards Relating to Police Handling of Juvenile Problems*, Ballinger Publishing Co., 1978.

Blumberg, A., *The Scales of Justice*, Aldine Publishing Co., 1970.

Blumberg, A.S., *Criminal Justice: Issues and Ironies*, New Viewpoints, 1979.

Bond, J., *Plea-Bargaining and Guilty Pleas*, Clark Boardman Co., 1975.

Bouza, A., *Police Administration*, Pergamon Press, Inc., 1979.

Bowker, L., *Women, Crime, and the Criminal Justice System*, Lexington Books, 1978.

Bracey, D.H., *"Baby-Pros"—Preliminary Profiles of Juvenile Prostitutes*, John Jay Press, 1978.

Butler, A., *The Law Enforcement Process*, Alfred Publishing Co., Inc., 1976.

Carlson, D.L., *Criminal Justice Procedure*, W.H. Anderson, 1979.

Carrington, F., *The Victims*, Arlington House, Inc., 1975.

Carte, G., *Police Reform in the United States*, University of California Press, 1975.

Carter, R. and L. Wilkins, *Probation, Parole and Community Corrections*, Wiley, 1976.

Carter R., et al., *Correctional Institutions*, Lippincott, 1972.

Challenge of Crime in a Free Society, The, Presidential Commission on Law Enforcement and Administration of Justice, 1967.

Chambliss, W., *Law, Order, and Power*, Addison-Wesley Publishing Co., 1971.

Chevigny, P., *Cops and Rebels: A Study of Provocation*, Random House, Inc., 1972.

Clinard, M.B., *Cities with Little Crime*, Cambridge University Press, 1978.

Collins, M.C., *The Child-Abuser*, Publishing Sciences Group, 1978.

Conklin, J., *"Illegal But Not Criminal": Business Crime in America*, Prentice-Hall, Inc., 1977.

Conley, J.A., *Theory and Research in Criminal Justice*, W.H. Anderson, 1979.

Conrad, J., *Crime and Its Correction*, University of California Press, 1965.

Conrad, J., *The Dangerous and the Endangered*, Lexington Books, 1978.

Conrad, J. and S. Dinitz, *In Fear of Each Other: Studies of Dangerousness in America*, Lexington Books, 1978.

Cook, J.G., *Constitutional Rights of the Accused, The*, Lawyers Co-Operative Publishing Co., 1972.

Cotte, T.J., *Children in Jail*, Beacon Press, 1978.

Creamer, J., *The Law of Arrest, Search and Seizure*, W.B. Saunders Co., 1975.

Cressey, D., *Criminal Organization*, Harper & Row Publishers, Inc., 1972.

Davis, K., *Discretionary Justice*, University of Illinois Press, 1971.

Delin, B., *The Sex Offender*, Beacon Press, 1978.

Devine, P.E., *The Ethics of Homicide*, Cornell University Press, 1979.

Douglas, J.D., *Crime and Justice in American Society*, Bobbs-Merrill Co., Inc., 1971.

Dowling, J., *Criminal Procedure*, West, 1976.

Drapkin, I. and E. Viano, *Victimology*, Lexington Books, 1974.

Empey, L.T., *American Delinquency: Its Meaning and Construction*, Dorsey, 1978.

Falkin, G.R., *Reducing Delinquency*, Lexington Books, 1978.

Felkenes, G., *Constitutional Law for Criminal Justice*, Prentice-Hall, Inc., 1977.

Felkenes, G., *The Criminal Justice System*, Prentice-Hall, Inc., 1973.

Felkenes, G., *Criminal Law and Procedure*, Prentice-Hall, Inc., 1976.

Felt, M., *The FBI Pyramid*, G.P. Putnam's Sons, 1979.

Field, H.S. and N.J. Barnett, *Jurors and Rape*, Lexington Books, 1978.

Folley, V.L., *American Law Enforcement*, Allyn & Bacon, Inc., 1980.

Fogel, D., *The Justice Model for Corrections*, W.H. Anderson, 1979.

Foucault, M., *Discipline and Punish*, Pantheon Books, Inc., 1978.

Fox, J.A., *Forecasting Crime Data*, Lexington Books, 1979.

Fox, J.G., *Women in Cages*, Ballinger Publishing Co., 1979.

Fox, V., *Introduction to Corrections*, Prentice-Hall, Inc., 1973.

Frank, B., *Contemporary Corrections*, Reston Publishing Co., 1973.

Frankel, M., *Criminal Sentences*, Hill & Wang, 1972.

Freeman, J.C., *Prisons Past and Future*, Heinemann, 1979.

Gardiner, J. and M. Mulkey, *Crime and Criminal Justice*, Heath, 1975.

Gaylin, W., *Partial Justice*, Knopf, Inc., 1974.

Geis, G., *Not the Law's Business*, NIMH, 1972.

Geis, G. and R. Meier, *White Collar Crime*, Free Press, 1977.

Gerber, R., *Contemporary Punishment*, University of Notre Dame Press, 1972.

Germann, A., et al., *Introduction to Law Enforcement*, C.C. Thomas, 1973.

Gibbs, J., *Crime, Punishment, and Deterrence*, Elsevier North-Holland, Inc., 1975.

Gifis, S.H., *Law Dictionary*, Barron's, 1975.

Glaser, D., *Adult Crime and Social Policy*, Prentice-Hall, Inc., 1972.

Glaser, D., *Crime in Our Changing Society*, Holt, Rinehart & Winston, Inc., 1978.

Goldsmith, J. and S.S. Goldsmith, *Crime and the Elderly*, D.C. Heath, 1976.

Goldstein, A., et al., *Police Crisis Intervention*, Pergamon Press, Inc., 1979.

Goldstein, H., *Policing a Free Society*, Ballinger Publishing Co., 1977.

Gottfredson, M.R. and D.M. Gottfredson, *Decision-Making in Criminal Justice*, Ballinger Publishing Co., 1979.

Greenberg, D., *Corrections and Punishment*, Sage, 1977.

Greenwood, P., *The Criminal Investigation Process*, Rand McNally Co., 1975.

Gross, Hyman, *A Theory of Criminal Justice*, Oxford University Press, 1978.

Guide to Criminal Justice Information Sources, National Council on Crime and Delinquency, 1977.

Hahn, P.H., *Crimes Against the Elderly*, Davis, 1976.

Hahn, P.H., *The Juvenile Offender and the Law*, W.H. Anderson, 1978.

Harris, R., *The Crisis of Law, Order and Freedom in America*, E.P. Dutton & Co., 1970.

Haskell, M.R. and L. Yablonsky, *Crime and Delinquency*, Rand-McNally Co., 1978.

Hemphill, C.F., *Criminal Procedure: The Administration of Justice*, Goodyear Publishing Co., Inc., 1978.

Heumann, M., *Plea-Bargaining*, University of Chicago Press, 1978.

Hills, S., *Crime, Power and Morality*, Chandler, 1971.

Jacob, H., *The Potential for Reform of the Criminal Justice System*, Sage Publications, Inc., 1974.

Jahnige, T., *The Federal Judicial System*, Holt, Rinehart and Winston, Inc., 1968.

James, H., *Crisis in the Courts*, McKay, 1971.

Johnson, N., *The Human Cage: A Brief History of Prison Architecture*, Walker, 1973.

Johnson, R.E., *Juvenile Delinquency and Its Origins*, Cambridge University Press, 1979.

Jones, D.A., *Crime and Criminal Responsibility*, Nelson-Hall Publishers, 1978.

Jones, D.A., *Crime Without Punishment*, Lexington Books, 1979.

Kalven, H. and H. Zeisel, *The American Jury*, Little, Brown and Co., 1966.

Kamisar, Y., et al., *Criminal Law and Procedure*, West, 1974.

Kassebaum, G., *Prison Treatment and Parole Survival*, Wiley, 1972.

Katz, L.R., L. Litwin, and R. Bamberger, *Justice Is the Crime-Pretrial Delay in Felony Cases*, Case-Western Reserve University, 1972.

Killinger, G. and P. Cromwell, *Penology*, West, 1973.

Killinger, G.G. and P.F. Cromwell, *Corrections in the Community*, West, 1978.

236

Klein, F.J., *Administration of Justice in the Courts*, (Annotated Bibliography), Oceana Publications, 1976.

Klein, I., *Law of Evidence for Police*, West, 1973.

Klein, M., *The Juvenile Justice System*, Sage Publications, Inc., 1976.

Klotter, J. and J. Kanovitz, *Constitutional Law for Police*, Anderson, 1977.

Kratcoski, P. and D. Walker, *Criminal Justice in America*, Scott, Foresman and Co., 1978.

Kratcoski, P.C. and L.D. Kratcoski, *Juvenile Delinquency*, Prentice-Hall, Inc., 1979.

Kukla, R., *Gun Control*, Stackpole Books, 1973.

LaFave, W.R., *Principles of Criminal Law*, West, 1979.

LaPatra, J.W., *Analyzing the Criminal Justice System*, Lexington Books, 1978.

Levin, M., *Urban Politics and the Criminal Courts*, University of Chicago Press, 1977.

Lewis, P.W. and K.D. Peoples, *The Supreme Court and the Criminal Process*, W.B. Saunders Co., 1978.

Lieberman, J., *How the Government Breaks the Law*, Stein and Day Publishers, 1972.

Lipton, D., R. Martinson, and J. Wilks, *The Effectiveness of Correctional Treatment*, Praeger Publishers, Inc., 1975.

Loeb, R.H., *Crime and Capital Punishment*, Franklin-Watts, 1978.

MacNamara, D. and F. Montanino, *Incarceration*, Sage Publications, 1978.

MacNamara, D. and E. Sagarin, *Perspectives on Correction*, Thomas Y. Crowell Co., 1971.

MacNamara, D. and E. Sagarin, *Sex, Crime, and the Law*, Macmillan-Free Press, 1977.

MacNamara, D. and M. Riedel, *Police: Problems and Prospects*, Praeger Publishers, Inc., 1974.

Marmor, J., *Homosexual Behavior: A Modern Reappraisal*, Basic Books, 1979.

McDonald, W., *Criminal Justice and the Victim*, Sage Publications, 1976.

Menninger, K., *The Crime of Punishment*, Viking Press, 1968.

Miller, F., *The Correctional Process*, The Foundation Press, 1971.

Miller, F., *Prosecution*, Little, Brown and Co., 1970.

Mitford, J., *Kind and Usual Punishment*, Knopf, Inc., 1973.

More, H., *Effective Police Administration*, West, 1979.

Morris, N., *The Honest Politician's Guide to Crime Control*, The University of Chicago Press, 1970.

Morris, N., *The Future of Imprisonment*, The University of Chicago Press, 1974.

Munro, J., *Administrative Behavior and Police Organization*, W.H. Anderson, 1974.

Nagel, S., *Modeling the Criminal Justice System*, Sage Publications, 1977.

Nagel, S., *The Rights of the Accused*, Sage Publications, 1972.

Nagel, S. and H.G. Neef, *Decision Theory and the Legal Process*, Lexington Books, 1979.

Navasky, V. and D. Paster, *Law Enforcement: The Federal Role*, McGraw-Hill Book Co., 1976.

Neary, M., *Corruption and Its Management*, American Academy for Professional Law Enforcement, 1977.

Netter, G., *Explaining Crime*, McGraw-Hill Book Co., 1978.

Neubauer, D., *Criminal Justice in Middle America*, General Learning Press, 1974.

Newman, C., *Probation, Parole and Pardons*, C.C. Thomas, 1970.

Newman, G., *The Punishment Response*, J.P. Lippincott Co., 1978.

Niederhoffer, A., *The Ambivalent Force*, Ginn and Co., 1970.

Niederhoffer, A., *The Police Family*, Lexington Books, 1978.

O'Brien, J.T. and M. Marcus, *Crime and Justice in America*, Pergamon Press Inc., 1979.

Ohlin, L.E., *et al.*, *Reforming Juvenile Corrections*, Ballinger Publishing Co., 1979.

Oswald, R., *Attica: My Story*, Doubleday Publishing Co., 1972.

Packer, H., *The Limits of the Criminal Sanction*, Stanford University Press, 1968.

Platt, A., *The Child Savers: The Invention of Delinquency*, The University of Chicago Press, 1977.

Price, B., *Police Professionalism*, Lexington Books, 1977.

Quinney, R., *Critique of the Legal Order*, Little, Brown and Co., 1974.

Rawls, J., *A Theory of Justice*, Harvard University Press, 1971.

Reid, S.T., *Crime and Criminology*, Holt, Rinehart, & Winston, Inc., 1979.

Reiss, A., *The Police and the Public*, Yale University Press, 1971.

Reppetto, T., *Residential Crime*, Ballinger Publishing Co., 1974.

Reppetto, T., *The Blue Parade*, The Free Press, 1978.

Revelle, G., *Sentencing and Probation*, National Gallery of the State Judiciary, 1973.

Rich, V., *Law and the Administration of Justice*, Wiley, 1979.

Rieber, R.W. and H.J. Vetter, *The Psychological Foundations of Criminal Justice*, John Jay Press, 1979.

Rifai, M.A., *Justice and Older Americans*, D.C. Heath and Co., 1977.

Rossett, A. and D. Cressey, *Justice by Consent*, J.P. Lippincott Co., 1976.

Rothman, D., *The Discovery of Asylum*, Little, Brown and Co., 1971.

Rubin, S., *Law of Criminal Correction*, West, 1973.

Rush, G.E., *Dictionary of Criminal Justice*, Holbrook Press Inc., 1977.

Sagarin, E., *Deviants and Deviance*, Praeger Publishers, Inc., 1976.

Saks, M.J., *Jury Verdicts*, D.C. Heath and Co., 1977.

Sanders, W., *Detective Work*, The Free Press, 1977.

Saunders, C., *Upgrading the American Police*, The Brookings Institution, 1970.

Schultz, D.D., *Modern Police Administration*, Gulf Publishing Co., 1979.

Schur, E., *Crimes Without Victims*, Prentice-Hall, Inc., 1965.

Senna, J. and L. Siegel, *Introduction to Criminal Justice*, West, 1978.

Shanahan, D.T. and Whisenand, P.M., *Dimensions of Criminal Justice Planning*, Allyn & Bacon, Inc., 1980.

Sheehan, S., *A Prison and a Prisoner*, Houghton Mifflin Co., 1978.

Sherman, L.W., *The Quality of Police Education*, Jossey-Bass, Inc., 1978.

Sherman, L.W., *Scandal and Reform: Controlling Police Corruption*, University of California Press, 1978.

Silberman, C., *Criminal Violence—Criminal Justice*, Random House, Inc., 1978.

Simon, R., *Women and Crime*, Lexington Books, 1975.

Simon, R., *The Jury System in America*, Lexington Books, 1979.

Simonsen, C.E. and M.S. Gordon, *Juvenile Justice in America*, Glencoe Press, 1979.

Snortum, J. and I. Hadar, *Criminal Justice*, Palisades Publishers, 1978.

Stanley, D., *Prisoners Among Us: The Problem of Parole*, The Brookings Institution, 1975.

Stead, P.J., *Pioneers in Policing*, Patterson Smith, 1977.

Strasburg, P., *Violent Delinquents*, Monarch Books, 1978.

Strickland, K.G., *Correctional Institutions for Women in the United States*, Lexington Books, 1978.

Stuckey, G.B., *Evidence for the Law Enforcement Officer*, McGraw-Hill Book Co., 1979.

Szasz, T., *Psychiatric Justice*, Macmillan, 1965.

Toch, H., *Living in Prison*, The Free Press, 1977.

Turk, A., *Legal Sanctions and Social Control*, NIMH, 1972.

Ungar, S., *F.B.I.*, Little-Brown and Co., 1976.

Ulviller, H., *Adjudication*, West, 1975.

Van Dyke, J.M., *Jury Selection*, Ballinger Publishing Co., 1977.

Vetter, H. and C. Simonsen, *Criminal Justice in America*, W.B. Saunders Co., 1976.

Viano, E.C., *Victims and Society*, Visage Press, 1976.

Von Grimme, T.L., *Your Career in Law Enforcement*, ARCO, 1979.

Von Hirsch, A., *Doing Justice: The Choice of Punishments*, Hill and Wang, 1976.

Walker, S., *A Critical History of Police Reform*, Lexington Books, 1977.

Warren, E., *The Memoirs of Chief Justice Warren*, Doubleday, 1977.

Weaver, S., *Decisions to Prosecute*, M.I.T. Press, 1977.

Weinreb, L., *Leading Constitutional Cases on Criminal Justice*, Foundation Press, 1978.

Wheeler, R. and H. Whitcomb, *Judicial Administration*, Prentice-Hall, 1977.

Whisenand, P., *Crime Prevention*, Holbrook Press, 1977.

Weiss, J.A., *Law of the Elderly*, Practicing Law Institute, 1977.

Wice, R., *Bail and Its Reform*, National Institute of Law Enforcement and Criminal Law, 1974.

Wilkins, L., *Evaluation of Penal Measures*, Random House, 1969.

Wilson, J., *Varieties of Police Behavior*, Harvard University Press, 1968.

Wilson, J., *Thinking About Crime*, Basic Books, 1975.

Wilson, J.Q., *The Investigators: Managing the FBI and Narcotics Agents*, Basic Books, 1978.

Witt, J.W., *The Police, the Courts and the Minority Community*, Lexington Books, 1978.

Wolf, J.B., *The Police Intelligence System*, John Jay Press, 1978.

Wolfgang, M.E., *Prisons: Success and Failure*, Lexington Books, 1978.

Wolfgang, M.E. and F. Ferracuti, *Diagnosis in Criminal Justice Systems*, Lexington Books, 1978.

Wootton, B., *Crime and Penal Policy*, Allen & Unwin, 1978.

Wright, E., *The Politics of Punishment*, Harper & Row, 1973.

Zimring, F. and G. Hawkins, *Deterrence*, University of Chicago Press, 1973.

Glossary

—A—

Abet—To encourage another to commit a crime. This encouragement may be by advice, inducement, command, etc. The abettor of a crime is equally guilty with the one who actually commits the crime.

Accessory after the Fact—One who harbors, assists, or protects another person, although he knows that person has committed a crime.

Accessory before the Fact—One who helps another to commit a crime, even though he is absent when the crime is committed.

Accomplice—One who is involved in the commission of a crime with others, whether he actually commits the crime or abets others. The term *principal* means the same thing, except that one may be a principal if he commits a crime without the aid of others.

Acquit—To free a person from an accusation of criminal guilt; to find "not guilty."

Affidavit—A written declaration or statement sworn to and affirmed by an officer having authority to administer an oath.

Affirmation—To swear on one's conscience that what he says is true. An *oath* means that one calls upon God to witness the truth of what he says.

Alias—Any name by which one is known other than his true name. *Alias dictus* is the more technically correct term but it is rarely used.

Alibi—A claim that one was in a place different from that charged. If the person proves his alibi, he proves that he could not have committed the crime charged.

Allegation—The declaration of a party to a lawsuit made in a pleading, that states what he expects to prove.

Appeal—A case carried to a higher court to ask that the decision of the lower court, in which the case originated, be altered or overruled completely.

Appellate Court—A court that has jurisdiction to hear cases on appeal; not a trial court.

Arraignment—The appearance before the court of a person charged with a crime. He or she is advised of the charges, bail is set, and a plea of "guilty" or "not guilty" is entered.

Arrest—To take a person into custody so that he may be held to answer for a crime.

Autopsy—A post-mortem examination of a human body to determine the cause of death.

—B—

Bail—Property (usually money) deposited with a court in exchange for the release of a person in custody to assure later appearance.

Bail Bond—An obligation signed by the accused and his sureties, that insures his presence in court.

Bailiff—A court attendant whose duties are to keep order in the courtroom and to have custody of the jury.

Bench warrant—An order by the court for the apprehension and arrest of a defendant or other person who has failed to appear when so ordered.

Bill of Rights—The first ten amendments to the Constitution of the United States which define such rights as: due process of law, immunity from illegal search and seizure, the ban on cruel and unusual punishment, unreasonably high bail, indictment by a grand jury, and speedy trial.

Bind Over—To hold for trial.

"Blue" Laws—Laws in some jurisdictions prohibiting sales of merchandise, athletic contests, and the sale of alcoholic beverages on Sundays.

Booking—The procedure at a police station of entering the name and identifying particulars relating to an arrested person, the charges filed against him, and the name of the arresting officer.

Burden of Proof—The duty of affirmatively proving the guilt of the defendant "beyond a reasonable doubt."

—C—

Calendar—A list of cases to be heard in a trial court, on a specific day, and containing the title of the case, the lawyers involved, and the index number.

Capital Crime—Any crime that may be punishable by death or imprisonment for life.

Caseload—The number of cases actively being investigated by a police detective or being supervised by a probation or parole officer.

Change of Venue—The removal of a trial from one jurisdiction to another in order to avoid local prejudice.

Charge—In criminal law, the accusation made against a person. It also refers to the judge's instruction to the jury on legal points.

Circumstantial Evidence—Indirect evidence; evidence from which the principal fact can be proved or disproved by inference. Example: a finger-print found at the crime scene.

Citizen's arrest—A taking into custody of an alleged offender by a person not a law enforcement officer. Such an arrest is lawful if the crime was attempted or committed in his presence.

Code—A compilation, compendium, or revision of laws, arranged into chapters, having a table of contents and index, and promulgated by legislative authority. Criminal code; penal code.

Coercion—The compelling of a person to do that which he is not obliged to do, or to omit doing what he may legally do, by some illegal threat, force, or intimidation. For example: a forced confession.

Commit—To place a person in custody in a prison or other institution by lawful order.

Common Law—Law that derives its authority from usage and custom or court decisions.

Commutation—To change the punishment meted out to a criminal to one less severe. Executive clemency.

Complainant—The victim of a crime who brings the facts to the attention of the authorities.

Complaint—A sworn written allegation stating that a specified person committed a crime. Sometimes called an *information*. When issued from a *Grand Jury*, it is called an *indictment*.

Compulsion—An irresistible impulse to commit some act, such as stealing, setting a fire, or an illegal sexual act.

Confession—An admission by the accused of his guilt; a partial admission (e.g., that he was at the crime scene; that he had a motive) is referred to as "an admission against interest."

Confinement—Deprivation of liberty in a jail or prison either as punishment for a crime or as detention while guilt or innocence is being determined.

Consensual Crime—A crime without a victim; one in which both parties voluntarily participate (e.g., adultery, sodomy, etc.).

Conspiracy—A secret combination of two or more persons who plan for the purpose of committing a crime or any unlawful act or a lawful act by unlawful or criminal means.

Contempt of Court—Behavior that impugns the authority of a court or obstructs the execution of court orders.

Continuance—A delay in trial granted by the judge on request of either the prosecutor or defense counsel; an adjournment.

Conviction—A finding by the jury (or by the trial judge in cases tried without a jury) that the accused is guilty of a crime.

Corporal—Corporal punishment is pain inflicted on the body of another. Flogging.

Corpus Delicti—The objective proof that a crime has been committed as distinguished from an accidental death, injury or loss.

Corrections—Area of criminal justice dealing with convicted offenders in jails, prisons; on probation or parole.

Corroborating Evidence—Supplementary evidence that tends to strengthen or confirm other evidence given previously.

Crime—An act or omission prohibited and punishable by law. Crimes are divided into *felonies* and *misdemeanors;* and recorded as "crimes against the person" (murder, rape, assault, robbery) and "crimes against property" (burglary, larceny, auto theft). There are also crimes against public morality and against public order.

Criminal Insanity—Lack of mental capacity to do or refrain from doing a criminal act; inability to distinguish right from wrong.

Criminology—The scientific study of crime and criminals.

Cross-Examination—The questioning of a witness by the party who did not produce the witness.

Culpability—Guilt; *see also mens rea*.

—D—

Defendant—The person who is being prosecuted.

Delinquency—Criminality by a boy or girl who has not as yet reached the age set by the state for trial as an adult (the age varies from jurisdiction to jurisdiction and from crime to crime).

Demurrer—In court procedure, a statement that the charge that a crime has been committed has no sufficient basis in law, despite the truth of the facts alleged.

Deposition—The testimony of a witness not taken in open court but taken in pursuance of authority to take such testimony elsewhere.

Detention—To hold a person in confinement while awaiting trial or sentence, or as a material witness.

Deterrence—To prevent criminality by fear of the consequences; one of the rationalizations for punishing offenders.

Directed Verdict—An instruction by the judge to the jury to return a specific verdict. A judge may not direct a guilty verdict.

Direct Evidence—Proof of facts by witnesses who actually saw acts or heard words, as distinguished from *Circumstantial Evidence*.

Direct Examination—The first questioning of a witness by the party who produced him.

Discretion—The decision-making powers of officers of the criminal justice system (e.g., to arrest or not, to prosecute or not, to plea-bargain, to grant probation, or to sentence to a penal institution).

District Attorney—Prosecutor; sometimes County Attorney, (U.S. Attorney in Federal practice).

Docket—The formal record maintained by the court clerk, listing all cases heard. It contains the defendant's name, index number, date of arrest, and the outcome of the case.

Double Jeopardy—To be prosecuted twice for the same offense.

Due Process—Law in its regular course of administration through the courts of justice. Guaranteed by the 5th and 14th Amendments.

—E—

Embracery—An attempt to influence a jury, or a member thereof, in their verdict by any improper means.

Entrapment—The instigation of a crime by officers or agents of a government who induce a person to commit a crime that he did not originally contemplate in order to institute a criminal prosecution against him.

Evidence—All the means used to prove or disprove the fact at issue.

Examination—An investigation of a witness by counsel in the form of questions for the purpose of bringing before the court knowledge possessed by the witness.

Exception—A formal objection to the action of the court during a trial. The indication is that the excepting party will seek to reverse the court's action at some future proceeding. *Objection.*

Exclusionary Rule—Rule of evidence which makes illegally acquired evidence inadmissible; *see* Mapp vs. Ohio.

Expert Evidence—Testimony by one qualified to speak authoritatively on technical matter because of his special training or skill.

Ex Post Facto—After the fact. An ex post facto law is a criminal law that makes an act unlawful although it was committed prior to the passage of that law.

Extradition—The surrender by one state to another of an individual accused of a crime.

—F—

False Arrest—Any unlawful physical restraint of another's freedom of movement. Unlawful arrest.

Felonious—Evil, malicious, or criminal. A felonious act is not necessarily a felony, but is criminal in some degree.

Felony—Generally, an offense punishable by death or imprisonment in a penitentiary. More serious than *Misdemeanors*.

Forensic—Relating to the court. Thus, forensic medicine would refer to medicine in relation to court proceedings and the law in general.

—G—

Grand Jury—A group of 16 to 23 citizens of a county who examine evidence against the person suspected of a crime, and hand down an indictment if there is sufficient evidence to warrant one.

—H—

Habeas Corpus (writ of)—An order that requires a jailor, warden, police chief, or other public official to produce a person being held in custody before a court in order to show that they have a legal right to hold him in custody.

Hearsay—Evidence not originating from the witness' personal knowledge.

Homicide—The killing of a human being; may be murder, negligent or non-negligent manslaughter, or excusable or justifiable homicide.

—I—

Impeach—To discredit. To question the truthfulness of a witness. Also: to charge a president or governor with criminal misconduct.

Imprisonment—The act of confining a convicted felon in a federal or state prison.

In Camera—In the judge's private chambers; in secrecy; the general public and press are excluded.

Indictment—The document prepared by a prosecutor and approved by the grand jury which charges a certain person with a specific crime or crimes for which that person is later to be tried in court. Truebill.

Inference—A conclusion one draws about something based on proof of certain other facts.

Injunction—An order by a court prohibiting a defendant from committing an act.

Intent—A design or determination of the mind to do or not do a certain thing. Intent may be determined from the nature of one's acts. Mens Rea.

Interpol—International Criminal Police Commission.

—J—

Jail—A short-term confinement institution for the detention of persons awaiting trial and the serving of sentences by those convicted of misdemeanors and offenses.

Jeopardy—The danger of conviction and punishment that a defendant faces in a criminal trial. *Double Jeopardy.*

Judicial Notice—The rule that a court will accept certain things as common knowledge without proof.

Jurisdiction—The power of a court to hear and determine a criminal case.

Jury—A certain number of persons who are sworn to examine the evidence and determine the truth on the basis of that evidence. Grand jury; trial jury.

Juvenile delinquent—A boy or girl who has not reached the age of criminal liability (varies from state to state) and who commits an act which would be a misdemeanor or felony if he were an adult. Delinquents are tried in *Juvenile Court* and confined in separate facilities.

—L—

L.E.A.A.—Law Enforcement Assistance Administration, U.S. Dept. of Justice.

Leniency—An unusually mild sentence imposed on a convicted offender; clemency granted by the President or a state governor; early release by a parole board.

Lie Detector—An instrument which measures certain physiological reactions of the human body from which a trained operator may determine whether the subject is telling the truth or lies; polygraph; psychological stress evaluator.

—M—

Mala In Se—Evil in itself. Acts that are made crimes because they are, by their nature, evil and morally wrong.

Mala Prohibita—Evil because they are prohibited. Acts that are not wrong in themselves but which, to protect the general welfare, are made crimes by statute.

Malfeasance—The act of a public officer in committing a crime relating to his official duties or powers. Accepting or demanding a bribe.

Malice—An evil intent to vex, annoy, or injure another; intentional evil.

Malicious Prosecution—An action instituted in bad faith with the intention of injuring the defendant.

Mandamus—A writ that issues from a superior court, directed to any person, corporation, or inferior court, requiring it to do some particular thing.

Mens Rea—A guilty intent.

Miranda warning—A police officer when taking a suspect into custody must warn him of his right to remain silent and of his right to an attorney.

Misdemeanor—Any crime not a *Felony*. Usually, a crime punishable by a fine or imprisonment in the county or other local jail.

Misprision—Failing to reveal a crime.

Mistrial—A trial discontinued before reaching a verdict because of some procedural defect or impediment.

Modus Operandi—Method of operation by criminals.

Motions—Procedural moves made by either defense attorney or prosecutor and submitted to the court, helping to define and set the ground rules for the proceedings of a particular case. For example: to suppress illegally seized evidence or to seek a change of venue.

Motive—The reason for committing a crime.

—N—

N.C.C.D.—National Council on Crime and Delinquency.

No Bill—A phrase used by a *Grand Jury* when they fail to indict.

Nolle Prosequi—A declaration to a court, by the prosecutor that he does not wish to further prosecute the case.

Nolo Contendere—A pleading, usually used by a defendant in a criminal case, that literally means "I will not contest."

—O—

Objection—The act of taking exception to some statement or procedure in a trial. Used to call the court's attention to some improper evidence or procedure.

Opinion Evidence—A witness' belief or opinion about a fact in dispute, as distinguished from personal knowledge of the fact. Expert testimony.

Ordinance—A statute enacted by the city or municipal government.

Organized crime—The crime syndicate; cosa nostra; Mafia; an organized, continuing criminal conspiracy which engages in crime as a business (e.g., loan sharking, illegal gambling, prostitution, extortion, etc.).

Original jurisdiction—Trial jurisdiction.

Overt Act—An open or physical act, as opposed to a thought or mere intention.

—P—

Pardon—Executive clemency setting aside a conviction and penalty.

Parole—A conditional release from prison, under supervision.

Penal Code—The criminal law of a jurisdiction, (sometimes the criminal procedure law is included but in other states it is codified separately).

Peremptory Challenge—The act of objecting to a certain number of jurors without assigning a cause for their dismissal. Used during the *voir dire* examination.

Perjury—The legal offense of deliberately testifying falsely under oath about a material fact.

Petit Jury—The ordinary jury composed of 12 persons who hear criminal cases. Determines guilt or innocence of the accused.

Plea-bargaining—A negotiation between the defense attorney and the prosecutor in which defendant receives a reduced penalty in return for a plea of "guilty."

Police Power—The authority of the legislature to make laws in the interest of the general public, even at the risk of placing some hardship on individuals.

Post Mortem—After death. Commonly applied to examination of a dead body. An autopsy is a post mortem examination to determine the cause of death.

Preliminary Hearing—A proceeding in front of a lower court to determine if there is sufficient evidence for submitting a felony case to the grand jury.

Presumption of Fact—An inference as to the truth or falsity of any proposition or fact, made in the absence of actual certainty of its truth or falsity or until such certainty can be attained.

Presumption of Law—A rule of law that courts and judges must draw a particular inference from a particular fact or evidence, unless the inference can be disproved.

Prima Facie—So far as can be judged from the first appearance or at first sight.

Prison—Federal or state penal institution for the confinement of convicted felons. Penitentiary.

Probation—A type of penalty whereby a convicted person is put under the jurisdiction and supervision of a probation officer for a stated time, instead of being confined.

Prosecutor—One who initiates a criminal prosecution against an accused. One who acts as a trial attorney for the government as the representative of the people.

Provost Marshal—Military police officer in charge of discipline, crime control and traffic law enforcement at a military post.

Public Defender—An appointed or elected public official charged with providing legal representation for indigent persons accused of crimes.

—R—

Reasonable Doubt—That state of mind of jurors when they do not feel a moral certainty about the truth of the charge and when the evidence does not exclude every other reasonable hypothesis except that the defendant is guilty as charged.

Rebuttal—The introduction of contradicting testimony; the showing that statements made by a witness are not true; the point in the trial at which such evidence may be introduced.

Recidivist—A repeater in crime; a habitual offender.

Recognizance—When a person binds himself to do a certain act or else suffer a penalty, as, for example, with a recognizance bond. Release on recognizance is release without posting bail or bond.

Relevant—Applying to the issue in question; related to the issue; useful in determining the truth or falsity of an alleged fact.

Remand—To send back. To remand a case for new trial or sentencing.

Reprieve—A stay of execution of sentence.

—S—

Search Warrant—A written order, issued by judicial authority in the name of the state, directing a law enforcement officer to search for personal property and, if found, to bring it before the court.

Sentence—The punishment (harsh or lenient) imposed by the trial judge on a convicted offender; major options include: fines, probation, indeterminate sentencing (e.g., three to ten years), indefinite sentencing (e.g., not more than three years), and capital punishment (death).

Stare Decisis—To abide by decided cases. The doctrine that once a court has laid down a principle of law as applicable to certain facts, it will apply it to all future cases when the facts are substantially the same.

State's Evidence—Testimony given by an accomplice or participant in a crime, tending to convict others.

Status Offense—An act which is punishable only because the offender has not as yet reached a statutorily prescribed age (e.g., truancy, running away, drinking alcoholic beverages by a minor, etc.).

Statute—A written law passed by the legislature.

Stay—A stopping of a judicial proceeding by a court order.

Subpoena—A court order requiring a witness to attend and testify in a court proceeding.

Subpoena Duces Tecum—A court order requiring a witness to testify and to bring all books, documents, and papers that might affect the outcome of the proceedings.

Summons—An order to appear in court on a particular date, which is issued by a police officer after or instead of arrest. It may also be a notification to a witness or a juror to appear in court.

Suspect—One whom the police have determined as very likely to be the guilty perpetrator of an offense. Once the police identify a person as a suspect, they must warn him of his rights (Miranda warning) to remain silent and to have legal advice.

—T—

Testimony—Evidence given by a competent witness, under oath, as distinguished from evidence from writings and other sources.

Tort—A legal wrong committed against a person or property for which compensation may be obtained by a civil action.

—U—

Uniform Crime Reports(U.C.R.)—Annual statistical tabulation of "crimes known to the police" and "crimes cleared by arrest" published by the Federal Bureau of Investigation.

—V—

Venue—The geographical area in which a court with jurisdiction sits. The power of a court to compel the presence of the parties to a litigation. See also *Change of Venue.*

Verdict—The decision of a court.

Victimology—Sub-discipline of criminology which emphasizes the study of victims; includes *victim compensation.*

Voir Dire—The examination or questioning of prospective jurors.

—W—

Waive—To give up a personal right. For example: to testify before the grand jury.

Warrant—A court order directing a police officer to arrest a named person or search a specific premise.

Witness—One who has seen, heard, acquired knowledge about some element in a crime. An *expert witness* is one who, though he has no direct knowledge of the crime for which the defendant is being tried, may testify as to the defendant's sanity, the amount of alcohol in the deceased's blood, whether a signature is genuine, that a fingerprint is or is not that of the accused, etc.

WHO'S WRITING AND WRITTEN ABOUT

INDEX

Credits/Acknowledgments

Cover design by Charles Vitelli

1. Crime and Justice in America
Facing overview—David Attie
41—Jeff Albertson/Stock Boston.

2. Police
Facing overview—Freelance Photographers Guild/Douglas Wetzstein. 50—New York Police. 51—Norman Sklarewitz. 52-53—U.S. News & World Report. 54—Gene Daniels/Black Star.

3. The Judicial System
Facing overview—Freelance Photographers Guild/Kerwin B. Roche. 114-116—U.S. News & World Report.

4. Juvenile Justice
Facing overview—Freelance Photographers Guild/Newsworld

5. Punishment and Corrections
Facing overview—Freelance Photographers Guild/Peter Karas 222—Photos by Tony O'Brien.

WE WANT YOUR ADVICE

ANNUAL EDITIONS: CRIMINAL JUSTICE 80/81

Article Rating Form

Here is an opportunity for you to have direct input into the next revision of this reader. We would like you to rate each of the 53 articles listed below, using the following scale:

1. **Excellent: should definitely be retained**
2. **Above average: should probably be retained**
3. **Below average: should probably be deleted**
4. **Poor: should definitely be deleted**

Your ratings will play a vital part in the next revision. So please mail this prepaid form to us just as soon as you complete it.
Thanks for your help!

Rating	Article	Rating	Article
	1. A General View of the Criminal Justice System		27. Justice for Whom?
	2. The Criminal Ethos		28. Preventive Detention
	3. Two Hundred Years of Social Economic Change Have Shaped Our Crime Problem		29. Verdicts on Judges
	4. UN Leader Gives Views on Worldwide Crime		30. Judging the Judges
	5. Crime in the Suites		31. Scaring Off Witnesses
	6. Why the Cops Can't Catch the Mob		32. Why Suppress Valid Evidence?
	7. Let's Take the Profit out of Organized Crime		33. It's Legal Gambling: Science Peers into the Jury Box
	8. A Mutual Concern: Older Americans and the Criminal Justice System		34. The Murderous Mind: Insanity vs. the Law
	9. The Crime-Unemployment Cycle		35. How Dan White Got Away with Murder
	10. World of the Career Criminal		36. Where the System Breaks Down
	11. A Cold New Look at the Criminal Mind		37. Juvenile Justice: A Plea for Reform
	12. Police Under Fire, Fighting Back		38. People v. Juvenile Justice: The Jury Is Still Out
	13. Integrated Professionalism: A Model for Controlling Police		39. How Fifteen-Year-Olds Get Away with Murder
	14. Police for Hire		40. Juvenile Inmates: The Long-Term Trend Is Down
	15. The Nun Who Became a Cop		41. Are Our Juvenile Courts Working?
	16. Burned-Out Cops and Their Families		42. Putting Johnny in Jail
	17. Protecting Thy Father and Thy Mother		43. Changing Criminal Sentences
	18. The New Truth Machines		44. Making Prisons Pay
	19. Probes, Trials and Tribulations Shake the LAPD		45. Scared Straight
	20. Police Leaders Find FBI Mandate Is a Flawed Gem		46. The Case Against Capital Punishment
	21. Citizen Cops		47. Medical Model in Corrections: Requiescat in Pace
	22. The Future of Local Law Enforcement in the United States: The Federal Role		48. On Parole Success: A Reply to MacNamara
	23. Discipline in American Policing		49. In Search of Equity: The Oregon Parole Matrix
	24. A Decade of Constitutional Revision		50. Co-Corrections
	25. Are Grand Juries Getting Out of Line?		51. Building a Small Prison with Modern Concepts
	26. Advocacy and the Criminal Trial Judge		52. A Criminal Rehabilitation Program That Works
			53. On the Women's Side of the Pen

(continued on back)

About you

Name _____ Date _____

Address _____

City _____ State _____ Zip _____

Telephone _____

---

1. What do you think of the Annual Editions concept?

2. Have you read any articles lately that you think should be included in the next edition?

3. Which articles do you feel should be replaced in the next edition? Why?

4. In what other areas would you like to see an Annual Edition? Why?

CRIMINAL JUSTICE 80/81